MANCHESTER UNITED
Player by Player

IVAN PONTING

MANCHESTER UNITED

UNITED
Player by Player

IVAN
PONTING

DEDICATION

To David Sadler, a European Cup winner the first time around and one of the classiest defenders of his generation, with appreciation for two decades of patience, generosity and unfailing good humour.

ACKNOWLEDGMENTS

The author would like to thank the following: Pat, Rosie and Joe Ponting; Trevor Hartley, whose stylish design adds so much to this book's appeal; Steve Small; Bob Bickerton; Cliff Butler; Wilf McGuinness; the late John Doherty; David Sadler; Bill Foulkes; Jack and Sheila Crompton; Albert Scanlon; David Herd; Paddy Crerand; Arthur Albiston; Stuart Pearson; Jimmy Greenhoff; Paddy Roche; Chris and Jo Forster; Les Gold; Barry Hugman; John Peters; Simon Lowe and Tony Lyons at Know The Score; and finally photographer Andy Cowie of Colorsport, for whom nothing ever seems to be too much trouble.

ILLUSTRATIONS

Almost all pictures have been supplied by Colorsport, with other contributions from Getty Images, John Peters and Cliff Butler. Every effort has been made to trace the copyright holders of all photographs used in this book. We apologise for any omissions, which are unintentional, and would be pleased to include appropriate acknowledgement in any subsequent edition.

PREVIOUS EDITIONS

First published by The Crowood Press in 1989.
Second edition published by Tony Williams Publications in 1994.
Third, fourth, fifth and sixth editions published by Hamlyn in 1997, 1998, 1999 and 2000 (the last two as The Red Army).
Seventh edition published by Polar in 2002.

Published in 2008 by Know The Score Books

Design by Trevor Hartley
Printed & Bound In Poland
www.polskabook.co.uk

COPYRIGHT

ISBN 978-1-84818-300-1

INTRODUCTION

Back in the late 1980s, when I set out to write *Manchester United Player By Player*, I could never have imagined that some 20 years on I would be working on an eighth edition. But such is the enduring fascination with this unique club, and the never-ending procession of footballers who continue to fire the passions of the Old Trafford faithful, that there are always fresh deeds to chronicle, more characters whose essence I can attempt to capture in words and pictures.

This time, as well as bringing the volume up to date to include the gilded modern era of Rooney, Ronaldo and company, I have turned my attention backwards to offer a profile and an illustration of every man to represent United in senior competition since the Second World War, from the revered Johnny Carey, Matt Busby's first regular captain, all the way through to Ben Foster, the most recent new boy to make his breakthrough. Of course, football never stands still, so many of the previous pieces have been comprehensively revised and updated.

In addition there are detailed assessments of some of the pre-war giants – the likes of Billy Meredith, Charlie Roberts, Sandy Turnbull and Joe Spence – as well as a concise entry on every man who has ever kicked a ball for United, and indeed for their predecessors, the Newton Heath Lancashire and Yorkshire Railway Football and Cricket Club, stretching all the way back to the first FA Cup tie in 1886/87.

Since *Player By Player* first saw the light of day in 1989, United have experienced almost non-stop excitement under the inspirational guidance of Sir Alex Ferguson, encompassing three European trophies, no fewer than ten Championships, five FA Cup victories and two successes in the League Cup. These glories have been attained through the efforts of a glittering cavalcade of world-famous performers, yet through it all there has been a gratifying involvement of precociously gifted youngsters, so that an uplifting parallel can be drawn with the Busby Babes.

Writing about them all, stars and rookies alike, has been pure pleasure for a country boy whose first idol was Davy Crockett, the king of the wild frontier, but whose second and more enduring hero was Bobby Charlton. I began supporting the Red Devils as a wide-eyed youngster in the mid-1950s, a time before motorways criss-crossed the country and when excursions to Old Trafford from deepest Somerset were rare treats. But even though the majority of my early football-watching days were spent on the terraces of Eastville and Ashton Gate, historic homes of Bristol Rovers and City, there was never the slightest doubt where my heart resided. Accordingly, as I grew up I became a regular visitor to Manchester and began to form the impressions that I have set down here. In that process I have been aided immeasurably in my task by many interviews with plenty of shrewd and unfailingly kind former footballers who plied their trade at Old Trafford. To them I am eternally grateful, in particular to the wisest and wittiest of them all, namely the former Busby Babe John Doherty, who died in 2007 and is sorely missed by his massive circle of friends as well as his lovely family.

The final ingredient in the *Player By Player* mix is statistical, and I have stuck mainly to the basics – games played and goals scored. The United figures refer to all senior matches for the club (a breakdown for each competition begins on page 360) but under the heading of 'Other Clubs' the appearances and goals are for League matches only. The dates in large type refer to the seasons in which the player appeared in the first team, not when he joined or left the club. Under 'Honours' I have included only those gained at United, except in the case of individual awards and international caps, the entries for which cover each man's complete career to date. Transfer fees are unofficial, being those favoured in the press. All statistics are complete to 21 May 2008.

To be putting the final touches to *Manchester United Player By Player* at the conclusion of a campaign in which Sir Alex Ferguson has guided his exhilarating team to both European Cup and Premier League success, and in which exciting newcomers such as Carlos Tevez and Anderson have settled in so seamlessly alongside old favourites like Paul Scholes and Ryan Giggs, has been a joy. Of course, the story goes ever on and I hope this will not be the final edition of the book. Here's to the next time!

Ivan Ponting,
Chewton Mendip,
August 2008

CONTENTS

· · · · · · · · · · · · · · · · · ·

PLAYER BY PLAYER

The Early Years 16
Busby And Beyond 36

THE MANAGERS
Ron Atkinson 13
Matt Busby 10
Tommy Docherty 13
Alex Ferguson 14
Wilf McGuinness 12
Jimmy Murphy 12
Frank O'Farrell 13
Dave Sexton 13

THE PLAYERS
Arthur Albiston 200
Reg Allen 62
Anderson 354
Johnny Anderson 58
Trevor Anderson 152
Viv Anderson 215
Willie Anderson 114
Michael Appleton 245
John Aston Snr 50
John Aston Jnr 134

Gary Bailey 184
Bill Bainbridge 60
Tommy Baldwin 180
Johnny Ball 64
Phil Bardsley 323
Michael Barnes 339
Peter Barnes 205
Frank Barson 34
Fabien Barthez 304
Peter Beardsley 195
Russell Beardsmore 223
David Beckham 288
Alex Bell 30
David Bellion 324
Geoff Bent 79
Henning Berg 271
George Best 138
Johnny Berry 68
Paul Bielby 151
Brian Birch 64
Cliff Birkett 65
Garry Birtles 194

Clayton Blackmore 221
Laurent Blanc 316
Jackie Blanchflower 76
Jesper Blomqvist 294
Tommy Bogan 64
Ernie Bond 65
Mark Bosnich 303
Warren Bradley 106
Harold Bratt 98
Alan Brazil 204
Derek Brazil 226
Shay Brennan 120
Ronnie Briggs 98
Berry Brown 61
Wes Brown 296
Steve Bruce 236
George Buchan 151
Martin Buchan 174
Ted Buckle 61
Ronnie Burke 60
Francis Burns 145
Nicky Butt 272
Roger Byrne 66

Fraizer Campbell 339
Eric Cantona 258
Noel Cantwell 108
Johnny Carey 38
Joe Carolan 101
Michael Carrick 346

Roy Carroll 307
Chris Casper 257
Laurie Cassidy 64
Luke Chadwick 306
Bobby Charlton 118
Allenby Chilton 44
Phil Chisnall 113
Gordon Clayton 98
Jonathan Clark 180
Michael Clegg 261
Frank Clempson 64
Henry Cockburn 48
Andy Cole 278
Cliff Collinson 60
Eddie Colman 80
John Connaughton 151
Tom Connell 180
John Connelly 116
Terry Cooke 260
Ronnie Cope 101
Peter Coyne 180
Steve Coppell 170
Paddy Crerand 126
Jack Crompton 54
Garth Crooks 226
Stan Crowther 93
Jordi Cruyff 262
Nick Culkin 310
Laurie Cunningham 226
John Curtis 261

Joe Dale 61
Gerry Daly 165
Peter Davenport 216
Alan Davies 204
Ron Davies 180
Simon Davies 257
Wyn Davies 149
Jimmy Davis 311
Alex Dawson 95
Jimmy Delaney 42
Mark Dempsey 226
Eric Djemba-Djemba .. 321
Bojan Djordjic 311
John Doherty 78
Mal Donaghy 228
Ian Donald 151
Dong Fangzhuo 339
John Downie 62
Dion Dublin 244
Dick Duckworth 30
Pat Dunne 128
Tony Dunne 142
Mike Duxbury 203

Chris Eagles 324
Sylvan Ebanks-Blake ... 338
Adam Eckersley 339
Duncan Edwards 72
Paul Edwards 144
Jonny Evans 358
Patrice Evra 342
Sonny Feehan 64

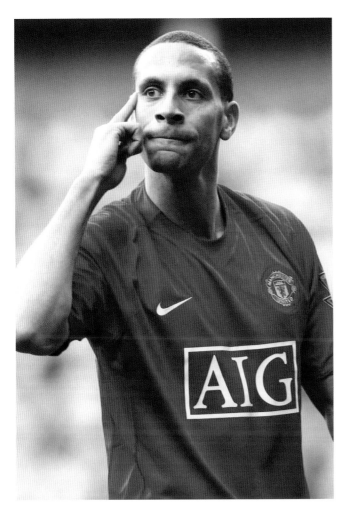

Ian Greaves 92
Brian Greenhoff 164
Jimmy Greenhoff 176
Jonathan Greening 298
Harry Gregg 96
Clive Griffiths 151
Ashley Grimes 191
Tony Grimshaw 181

Harold Halse 31
Johnny Hanlon 59
Owen Hargreaves 350
Bobby Harrop 99
Tony Hawksworth 98
Frank Haydock 114
David Healy 310
Gabriel Heinze 330
David Herd 110
Tommy Heron 98
Danny Higginbotham . 295
Mark Higgins 227
Lal Hilditch 35
Gordon Hill 172
Graeme Hogg 205
Jim Holton 158
Stewart Houston 161
Tim Howard 320
Mark Hughes 238
Reg Hunter 98

Paul Ince 246
Denis Irwin 284

Tommy Jackson 168
Steve James 146
Ronny Johnsen 268
Eddie Johnson 338
David Jones 323
Mark Jones 74
Peter Jones 98
Ritchie Jones 338
Joe Jordan 186
Nikola Jovanovic 179

Andrei Kanchelskis 248
Roy Keane 286
Jimmy Kelly 181
Paddy Kennedy 65
Brian Kidd 136
Albert Kinsey 114
Jose Kleberson 321
Frank Kopel 151
Tomasz Kuszczak 349

Rio Ferdinand 318
Darren Ferguson 243
Bill Fielding 61
John Fitzpatrick 129
Darren Fletcher 336
Peter Fletcher 151
Alan Foggon 181
Diego Forlan 317
Alex Forsyth 160
Quinton Fortune 299
Ben Foster 358
Bill Foulkes 102

Billy Garton 214
David Gaskell 115
Colin Gibson 216
Darron Gibson 338
Don Gibson 65
Terry Gibson 214
John Gidman 202
Ryan Giggs 264
Johnny Giles 104
Tony Gill 222
Keith Gillespie 244
Don Givens 151
Freddie Goodwin 92

Andy Goram 311
Alan Gowling 148
Arthur Graham 206
Deiniol Graham 226
George Graham 153
David Gray 339

Joe Lancaster 64
Henrik Larsson 348
Denis Law 124
Nobby Lawton 106
Kieran Lee 339
Jim Leighton 219
Eddie Lewis 99
Tommy Lowrie 61
Mark Lynch 338
Sammy Lynn 61

Lou Macari 162
Neil McBain 35
Jim McCalliog 152
Brian McClair 234
David McCreery 169
Ted MacDougall 149
Noel McFarlane 65
Scott McGarvey 195
Pat McGibbon 245
Billy McGlen 60
Chris McGrath 168
Paul McGrath 212
Wilf McGuinness 94
Sammy McIlroy 182
Eddie McIlvenny 65
Colin McKee 245
Sammy McMillan 112
Tommy McNulty 64
Gordon McQueen 188
Harry McShane 63
Giuliano Maiorana 222
Phil Marsh 339
Lee A Martin 224
Lee R Martin 339
Mick Martin 157
David May 270
Billy Meredith 24

Liam Miller 325
Ralph Milne 218
Charlie Mitten 52
Harry Moger 31
Ian Moir 113
Charlie Moore 35
Graham Moore 112
Kevin Moran 207
Willie Morgan 154
Kenny Morgans 79
Johnny Morris 56
Remi Moses 199
Arnold Muhren 198
Philip Mulryne 260

Nani 359
Daniel Nardiello 311
Gary Neville 266
Phil Neville 276
Erik Nevland 310
Jimmy Nicholl 178
Jimmy Nicholson 107
Bobby Noble 130
Alex Notman 310

Liam O'Brien 218
John O'Kane 245
Les Olive 63
Jesper Olsen 211
Tommy O'Neil 150
John O'Shea 308

Gary Pallister 252
Ji-Sung Park 352
Paul Parker 240
Steve Paterson 181
Steve Pears 227
Mark Pearson 100
Stan Pearson 40
Stuart Pearson 166
David Pegg 70
Ken Pegg 61
Micky Phelan 229
Kevin Pilkington 256
Mike Pinner 98
Gerard Pique 349
Karel Poborsky 263
William Prunier 245
Danny Pugh 338

Albert Quixall 105

Paul Rachubka 310
Billy Redman 65
Ricardo 338
Kieran Richardson 322
Jimmy Rimmer 146
Andy Ritchie 191
Jack Roach 60
Charlie Roberts 26
Mark Robins 225
Bryan Robson 230
Lee Roche 311
Paddy Roche 179
Martyn Rogers 181
Cristiano Ronaldo 326
Wayne Rooney 340
Giuseppe Rossi 348
Jack Rowley 46
Jim Ryan 129

Massimo Taibi 298
Ernie Taylor 93
Tommy Taylor 84
Carlos Tevez 356
Mickey Thomas 190
Ben Thornley 256
Paul Tierney 338
Mads Timm 338
Graeme Tomlinson 245
Wilf Tranter 114
Sandy Turnbull 28
Chris Turner 217
Michael Twiss 310

Ian Ure 147

Raimond van der Gouw 302
Edwin van der Sar 334
Ruud van Nistelrooy ... 312
Juan Sebastian Veron ... 314
Nemanja Vidic 344
Dennis Viollet 90

Dennis Walker 114
George Wall 31
Danny Wallace 220
Ronnie Wallwork 295
Gary Walsh 217

Jack Warner 59
Enoch West 31
Colin Waldron 181
Joe Walton 60
John Walton 65
Willie Watson 151
Jeff Wealands 227
Neil Webb 232
Danny Webber 311
Colin Webster 100
Richard Wellens 310
Bert Whalley 59
Anto Whelan 181
Billy Whelan 86
Jeff Whitefoot 78
Walter Whitehurst 98

Norman Whiteside 208
Neil Whitworth 227
Ray Wilkins 192
Ian Wilkinson 227
David Wilson 227
Mark Wilson 298
Nicky Wood 227
Ray Wood 82
Harry Worrall 61
Paul Wratten 227
Billy Wrigglesworth 60

Dwight Yorke 292
Tony Young 150

STATISTICS
Players' Records 360

David Sadler 132
Louis Saha 332
Carlo Sartori 144
Albert Scanlon 88
Peter Schmeichel 254
Paul Scholes 274
Johnny Scott 98
Les Sealey 242
Maurice Setters 109
Lee Sharpe 250
Ryan Shawcross 339
Teddy Sheringham 282
Arnold Sidebottom 157
Jack Silcock 35
Mikael Silvestre 300
Danny Simpson 358
John Sivebaek 214
Tom Sloan 181
Alan Smith 328
Jack Smith 60
Ole Gunnar Solskjaer .. 280
Jonathan Spector 325
Joe Spence 32
Jaap Stam 290
Frank Stapleton 196
Alex Stepney 140
Michael Stewart 299
Nobby Stiles 122
Ian Storey-Moore 156
Gordon Strachan 210

SIR MATT BUSBY

TEAM MANAGER: 1945 → 1969
GENERAL MANAGER: 1969 → 1971
DIRECTOR: 1971 → 1982
PRESIDENT: 1980 → 1994

Football managers provoke a variety of emotions among players and supporters. Few, though, inspire reverence. But that's really the only word to describe the feeling for Sir Matt Busby among the people who were close to him – and many more who never met him – during his 48 years at Old Trafford.

Matt made Manchester United. It's as simple as that. True, when the former Manchester City, Liverpool and Scotland wing-half took over, the Red Devils could already look back on 60 years of history. But the United the world knows today, the club with an indefinable aura of magic which transcends its periodic traumas, is essentially a creation of the miner's son from Lanarkshire. After the war he inherited a bankrupt outfit with a bombed-out ground, and almost immediately he breathed life into the place. Donning a tracksuit to work alongside his new charges, he built a dashing side and soon he was lifting English football's major honours: the FA Cup in 1948, the League title four years later, to say nothing of finishing as runners-up in four seasons out of five.

Matt's creed was to entertain. He had a clear vision of how the game should be played and the ability to communicate it to his players. But there was more to the man than his flair and charisma. By demolishing his first Championship side to bring together the Busby Babes – a label of which he was never enamoured – he demonstrated a rare combination of steel and judgement.

His young side shook the soccer world. After winning two League titles with a squad which could weather the most ruinous injury crisis, a decade of dominance beckoned. The Munich air disaster of February 1958 put paid to that, but Matt was not done. He fought back from the brink of death to build a third wonderful team, taking two more Championships and the FA Cup in the 1960s.

Ultimately there was that most glittering prize,

the European Cup, something of a holy grail to the United boss, who had blazed the British trail in Europe after refusing to bow his knee before the Football League's stern opposition to participation. How he wanted that trophy for the lads who had died. The triumph, when it came in 1968 and following which he was knighted, was glorious and deserved, and with that last great battle won, soon he handed over to Wilf McGuinness.

The new man was not a success and many have criticised Matt for letting the side grow old together. He was even called soft. But, as anyone who played under Busby will testify, he was a ruthlessly hard man. He proved this in breaking up one exceptional side to build a better one in the 1950s, by dealing summarily with a wage revolt by Denis Law in the 1960s and by quietly dispensing iron discipline throughout his reign.

Perhaps he felt it fair to let his successor do his own weeding and plant his own seeds for the future. Unfortunately it didn't work, and Matt resumed control briefly until the appointment of Frank O'Farrell.

It was a pity that such a monumental tenure should end in anti-climax, but Matt's reputation was unassailable. The man who set the trend for modern management, then went on to become first a director and then president of his great club, would never cease to be held in respect, even awe, throughout the football world. Importantly, he was a gentleman first and a soccer boss second, reflecting the absolute truth of Law's declaration that he was the greatest ambassador the game had ever known.

Almost until the end of his life, he graced Old Trafford with his presence, revelling in the exhilarating fare served up by the new Red Devils. When he died, aged 84 in January 1994, millions of people around the world mourned his passing. Sir Matt Busby was one of a kind, and Manchester United owe him everything.

JIMMY MURPHY

COACH: 1945 → 1955
ASSISTANT MANAGER: 1955 → 1971
ACTING MANAGER: February → August 1958

Some of the greatest players ever to come out of British football owed a huge debt to Jimmy Murphy. The forthright, often fiery little Welshman joined Matt Busby at Old Trafford in 1945 with special responsibility for nurturing young talent, and started a production line which turned out the likes of Duncan Edwards, Bobby Charlton and George Best.

Working in harness with the loyal Bert Whalley, a former United player who was to die at Munich, Jimmy loomed large in the life of the club's juniors. He was sergeant major, father confessor and psychologist rolled into one, driving when necessary, cajoling when it was called for, always passionate in his love for the game.

Perhaps Jimmy's most memorable achievement was in leading the Reds to Wembley in the aftermath of the Munich air crash while Matt Busby fought for his life. They lost to Bolton Wanderers but United's acting boss, who had been promoted from coach to assistant manager in 1955 and who would go on to guide Wales to the World Cup quarter-finals in 1958, had truly performed a soccer miracle. Like Matt, Jimmy turned down lucrative offers to take control of leading club and international sides, the likes of Brazil, Juventus and Arsenal among them. But the tireless, fiercely loyal lieutenant preferred to stay at Old Trafford, marching shoulder to shoulder into history alongside the man who gave him a job after the war.

Jimmy Murphy was Matt's first signing for United – and unquestionably his most important. He remained a much-loved figure at the ground until shortly before his death, at the age of 81, in 1989.

WILF McGUINNESS

CHIEF COACH: April 1969 → June 1970
MANAGER: June 1970 → December 1970

When Wilf McGuinness was plucked from the relative obscurity of the Old Trafford coaching staff and entrusted with United's future, he was seen by many as the luckiest man in football. However, with the benefit of hindsight there is a strong case for believing that, far from fortunate, he was on a hiding to nothing. Some of the team's best players were on the brink of decline and many of the youngsters were not good enough. A series of forays into the transfer market for quality replacements either proved abortive or were not backed by the board. With such a catalogue of disadvantages, and with a legend to live up to, he needed to command the respect and support of all his players from the outset. In failing to do so he lost his first and most vital battle.

Confrontations with senior first-teamers did nothing to build confidence and performances slumped. He chose the same match to drop both Denis Law and Bobby Charlton but results did not improve. Finally Matt Busby, who had recommended Wilf for the job, resumed at the helm and the man who had been with United for 17 years as player and backroom boy left to coach in Greece. The effervescent Mancunian, who had earned plaudits for his work on the international scene as a part-timer in Sir Alf Ramsey's World Cup-winning set-up, need not be ashamed of his record in charge of the Red Devils: three semi-finals (two League Cup, one FA Cup) and two eighth places in the First Division would have been hailed as success by other employers. But not United, a club for whom – as he said on the day he was deposed – he would willingly bleed. Matt's desire for continuity, for a successor from within the United 'family', perhaps led him to make a rare error of judgement. Poor Wilf McGuinness, talented but unready for such a vast burden, was simply the innocent victim.

FRANK O'FARRELL

MANAGER: June 1971 → December 1972

He came a stranger and he left a stranger: that was Denis Law's succinct epitaph to the frustrating reign of Frank O'Farrell. Law was voicing a popular view that the immaculate Irishman, destined for the sack after 18 months, was too remote and used his office as a retreat. Like Ron Atkinson later, Frank was not the board's first choice, but they were impressed by his steady climb up the managerial ladder, reaching Leicester via Weymouth and Torquay. Ironically in view of this proven stability, his United team was to catapult from one end of the First Division to the other within a year.

Many aspects of the O'Farrell tenure were difficult. He was unfortunate to be in control as George Best's discontent came to a head; he was attacked for shelling out £200,000 for Third Division striker Ted MacDougall (though he could point to the astute capture of Martin Buchan); and his relationship with the board sometimes appeared strained. The Best saga – would he leave or wouldn't he? – was like a running sore and must have been both distracting and debilitating.

Yet Frank could not have hoped for a better start. By Christmas in his first season United were five points clear of the pack and had entertained royally at times. But pundits predicted a fall and, sure enough, a woeful run of defeats deposited the team in mid-table. The next campaign proved worse. Points were haemorrhaged, injuries piled up and gloom settled over Old Trafford. By December talk was turning to – say it softly – relegation. Frank was curtly dismissed and left claiming that he could have done the job given time. It was a sad exit.

TOMMY DOCHERTY

MANAGER: December 1972 → July 1977

Three years of struggle and confusion had squeezed the magic out of Manchester United. Tommy Docherty put it back, though the transformation was not without trauma.

Traditionalists were appalled when the volatile troubleshooter breezed in, determined to blow away the cobwebs together with many of the playing staff. In his first few months he was like a man possessed. He averted relegation and lived up to a lurid reputation gained in charge of five clubs and his native Scotland. The air crackled with one-liners and players came and went with bewildering rapidity.

But the next term brought catastrophe as a very poor United went down. The Doc expected the sack; instead he got a crate of champagne from the board. Clearly he enjoyed backing that his predecessors would have envied.

Critics predicted a lengthy stay in the lower flight but Tommy's team confounded them, leading the table for the whole campaign. And what a breath of fresh air the new United proved back in Division One. They played stirring, adventurous football and just missed the League and FA Cup double. The next season brought FA Cup triumph and more honours seemed certain, but then news broke of the Doc's love for the club physio's wife, and he was sacked.

During his reign he had changed a demoralised outfit into a major force and moved the club's bank balance from red to black. But his was not a serene tenure. There were well-publicised rows with Law, Crerand, Buchan, Stepney, Macari and Morgan and he made powerful enemies. Many fans, though, agreed with Steve Coppell, who said of Tommy's exit: 'Managers are not made in heaven. In the end United were the losers.'

DAVE SEXTON

MANAGER: July 1977 → April 1981

'I've got to be honest and say the image of Manchester United overawed me, but this job is the peak of ambition for any manager.' That remark by softly-spoken Dave Sexton shortly after taking control at Old Trafford perhaps furnishes a clue to subsequent events.

There is no denying that he was a top-class coach and an original thinker, a modest character of integrity and dedication. Ask anyone in football about Dave and they will talk with respect and affection about a lovely man. As a manager he knew success with Chelsea and QPR; but was he the right personality for the huge stage of Old Trafford, constantly under the media microscope, continually pressured by the fervour of the fans?

His supporters can rightly claim that he took United higher in the League than anyone since Matt Busby (second place in 1979/80), that he nearly lifted the FA Cup in 1979 and that his team recorded seven straight wins prior to his sacking. Also they can point to his strength of purpose shown, in differing circumstances, by his contentious sales of terrace favourites Gordon Hill and Andy Ritchie. Against all that can be ranged three mid-table finishes in four seasons, never mind the over-expensive purchase and questionable use of Garry Birtles.

A huge problem was surmounting the fans' regard for the Doc. With a team which played measured (some said dull) rather than flamboyant football, and a cool manner which alienated many pressmen, he never stood a chance in that vital department. 'Whispering Dave' attempted a quiet revolution at Old Trafford. He didn't realise he was tilting at an impossible windmill.

RON ATKINSON

MANAGER: July 1981 → November 1986

For a few heady months Ron Atkinson looked more likely than any of his four ill-fated predecessors to do the job for which they had all been hired – to bring home that elusive League Championship.

In the autumn of 1985 United made their best-ever start. Ron's men won their first ten games and remained undefeated until November, playing a potent brand of exuberant, attacking football. Bryan Robson and company were irresistible; the title was there for the taking.

Then bleak reality took over, first in the form of a crushing injury list, then in the inevitable shape of Liverpool. This time, though, it really was hard to deny that, with just an even break in the matter of injuries, Ron might have pinned that pennant to the Reds' flagpole. Instead the general air of disillusionment hung over into the following season, the team slumped and Atkinson was gone.

He had arrived five and a half years earlier, apparently as fourth choice. An engaging extrovert who had achieved much with little at Cambridge and West Bromwich, Ron was seen by the board, perhaps, as an acceptable blend of Docherty's brash flair and Sexton's stability – and duly his United selections entertained richly, usually with the hint of a swagger.

Ron never lacked courage and plunged into the transfer market to land some of the League's best players. In that he didn't win the title, it didn't pay off, but his side never finished out of the top four and there was the little matter of two FA Cups.

The Champagne Charlie image, beloved of the tabloids, was irrelevant; Ron Atkinson knew his business right enough. He just failed to meet his ultimate challenge.

SIR ALEX FERGUSON

MANAGER: November 1986 →

Surely now, the debate is over. As the new millennium dawned Sir Alex Ferguson was voted the greatest manager of all time and yet perversely, in the face of an overwhelmingly persuasive body of evidence compiled both before and after his arrival at Old Trafford, there were dissenting voices. Indeed, less than half a decade into the 21st century, with Chelsea seemingly impregnable thanks to the bottomless pockets of a Russian oilman, and Arsenal also on the rise, the Manchester United boss was written off in some quarters as an old warhorse clopping wearily towards his dotage. But it didn't happen quite like that. Instead his eyes flashed fire, he unsheathed yet again the razor-like edge of his competitive rage, then he rampaged his way back to the loftiest summits of the game to which he has dedicated his life. Come 2008, with 20 major trophies in United's cabinet during his 22-season reign to date – and we are talking real prizes here, not the fluff of artificial baubles trotted out by certain rivals desperate to massage their own inferior tallies – he was unassailably top of the pile.

What makes this driven Scot awesomely unique is the burning intensity of his desire for ever more success, the unshakeable belief that he will attain it no matter what the odds against him and, most telling of all, his priceless ability to inspire those same qualities in his players. Any hint of complacency is crushed; the self-satisfied are culled; the next game, the next challenge, are all that matters.

And yet, walking hand in hand with that almost frightening fervour, there is a quality to Ferguson that nudges naivety, even innocence; the one which prompts him to hop gleefully from the dugout at moments of excitement, then to launch himself into an ungainly arm-flapping jig along the touchline, like some overjoyed schoolboy trapped in the body of a pensioner.

But whatever the take on this complex personality, as the man who ended 26 years of League Championship failure by leading the Red Devils to ten titles in 16 seasons, and who marched on to capture the European Cup twice, plus a once-in-a-lifetime treble, he has written his own ticket to Old Trafford immortality. Sir Alex has built a glittering succession of United teams which have combined style with steel, glamour with character, in the process serving up the sweetest, fastest, most fluently productive passing football the English game has ever seen.

Yet there was a time when the man Bobby Charlton championed from the boardroom to take over from Ron Atkinson in November 1986 seemed in danger of leaving the club as a flop. The former toolmaking union official had arrived as the first United boss to have proved himself conclusively elsewhere, his Aberdeen side having loosened the iron grip of Celtic and Rangers on the Scottish scene. Ferguson's first job was to lift the Reds away from the foot of the table and this he accomplished, but many problems remained. United's reputation as a social club, rather than a football club, was not altogether without foundation and Alex tackled the situation head-on. In addition, he revamped the youth system and paid minute attention to every detail of club life. Fresh players arrived for 1987/88 and the new combination finished as League runners-up, but 1988/89 brought dour anti-climax. The side was hard-working, methodical, disciplined – and dull.

More expensive team surgery followed but by January 1990 United were struggling horribly and chants of 'Fergie Out' became commonplace. Though the chairman at the time, Martin Edwards, has denied it, the manager's job must have been under dire threat had there been an early exit from the FA Cup. But they won that trophy, then the European Cup Winners' Cup and, in 1991/92, the League Cup, though that was overshadowed by allowing a title that had seemed in their grasp to slip away to Elland Road. Ferguson was criticised for being too tense, for communicating pressure to his players, and many believed that recovery from such a setback would prove beyond him.

However, season 1992/93 was to bring the perfect riposte in the shape of the League Championship. Adopting an approach that, outwardly at least, was more relaxed, he finally secured the prize for which United had pined so painfully. In retrospect, the turning point was the unplanned acquisition of Eric Cantona, whom he signed after a chance inquiry made when the Leeds chairman telephoned on other business. But the way the Scot capitalised on that good fortune, realising that the brilliant French maverick must be the hub of his team, was inspired.

Come 1993/94 and his classy machine was purring along more smoothly, more joyously than ever and by late autumn there was talk of an unprecedented domestic treble. Then came trouble. Prickly reactions to public criticism, which rained on his head as sendings-off and bookings threatened to scupper the entire campaign, mushroomed into full-scale paranoia. Results declined alarmingly, the League Cup Final was lost and Blackburn reduced a 16-point chasm to goal difference. But Alex regained his poise and United their equilibrium to lift the League and FA Cup double.

Inevitably perhaps, 1994/95 was anti-climactic, though only just. The title was conceded by one point and the FA Cup Final by a single goal, though the main event of the season was the debilitating Cantona affair. The way Ferguson handled the storm which broke after the Frenchman attacked a 'fan' at Selhurst Park, and his subtle coaxing of Eric to remain in the Old Trafford fold – displaying a diplomatic touch which was to be echoed in his treatment of Cristiano Ronaldo when the brilliant young Portuguese appeared on the verge of defecting in the summer of 2006 – represented management at its best. After that trauma, the outcry surrounding the sales of Hughes, Ince and Kanchelskis in 1995 would have brought lesser men to their knees. Typically cussedly, but a good deal more imperturbably than in the past, Alex dug in to attain arguably his most remarkable triumph. He replaced the departing stars with boys from his youth team and, after being advised by TV pundit Alan Hansen that 'you win nothing with kids', his new team completed the club's second League and FA Cup double.

Season 1996/97 brought another tilt at his European Cup windmill and a fourth Championship in five seasons, then came a rare trophyless term. And so to 1998/99, which began with the much-criticised Manchester United plc coughing up some £28 million to reinforce the squad and ended in the soccer equivalent of the Promised Land. Despite the distraction of the abortive BSkyB takeover bid and the loss of right-hand man Brian Kidd, Ferguson rotated his massive squad cleverly, harnessing extravagant flair to unquenchable spirit and compiling a prodigious 33-match unbeaten run that secured the title, the FA Cup and, at long last, the European Cup.

In the two campaigns which followed he annihilated his rivals to claim two more Premiership crowns by crushing margins, becoming the first manager to complete a hat-trick of consecutive Championships and the first with seven English titles to his name. Now he had garnered even more silverware than Liverpool's Bob Paisley, whose record of 13 prizes had stood since 1983.

But strife was on the horizon. Against a background of periodic disagreement with his employers over his own financial worth – and that was despite his establishment of United as the world's richest sporting franchise – as well as the need for expensive new recruits, there was frenzied speculation that Sir Alex Ferguson would sever his links with the Red Devils in the summer of 2001, rather than retire in 2002 as previously announced. Eventually peace was declared and clearly the manager had got his way, as United splashed out nearly £50 million for the close-season purchase of Ruud van Nistelrooy and Juan Sebastian Veron for what was expected to be his last campaign.

By early winter, however, his plans were in apparently terminal disarray. Having been slammed for the controversial sale of Jaap Stam and his equally contentious replacement by Laurent Blanc, Ferguson was pilloried anew as the team's fortunes dipped disastrously after a promising start.

It did seem that he had made a calamitous mistake in declaring his retirement date so far ahead of his actual departure. As a result, it appeared, his authority was diminished and uncertainty had been introduced among the players. But even as the theory of a lame-duck boss was taking hold, and as many who had envied him for so long began to drool over the prospect of a painfully drawn-out demise, Sir Alex demonstrated his phenomenal mettle yet again.

Angrily refusing to allow a life's work to be devalued, he shook his team by the scruff of its collective neck, questioning the players' desire even as he restated his own. For several weeks England captain David Beckham was dropped, sending out an eloquent message to the rest that no one was indispensable, and duly the corner was turned.

Come February, with the wins piling up once more, Ferguson delivered the news which the majority of United fans had craved, that he was ready to stay on after all, apparently persuaded by his family, though the mere suggestion of passing the limitless potential of van Nistelrooy and company into the care of another must have been unthinkable. The U-turn stoked the fires of a renewed surge for trophies and in 2002/03 he drove his team like the hounds of hell in a successful pursuit of Arsenal to claim his eighth League crown.

That might have been a convenient juncture for many

a battle-scarred 61-year-old to step down with honour, but the eternally voracious Ferguson was far from ready for that. Instead that summer he resolved his irreconcilable differences with Beckham over his glitzy lifestyle by selling the planet's most high-profile footballer to Real Madrid, then embarked on a period of restructuring during which his fiercest critics dubbed him a dinosaur whose end was nigh.

Along the way he acquired Messrs Rooney and Ronaldo, divested himself remorselessly of crowd favourites van Nistelrooy and Roy Keane, took one or two hits with transfers that didn't pan out and lifted a couple more domestic cups, all against the tumultuously disruptive background of the Glazer takeover.

In 2005/06, following early Champions League disqualification and oppressed by the continued progress of Chelsea and Arsenal, he was subjected to abuse from the Old Trafford stands. By season's end he seemed tired and tetchy; now predictions of an imminent exit proliferated, but yet again he re-invented the best of himself and the institution of which he had been the steward for so long. He felt the building blocks of an exceptional team were in place once more, he kept his nerve and his belief, and he was vindicated spectacularly with back-to-back titles and his second European crown.

At the time of writing, this fearsome, honest, passionate, ruthlessly single-minded soccer chieftain, whose public persona can shift from charming warmth to frighteningly raw aggression and whose psychological mind games can reduce rivals to apoplexy, is scheduled to carry on for the foreseeable future, never mind that he will enter his 68th year on the last day of 2008. Whatever happens now, Sir Alex Ferguson has earned for himself the lasting devotion of all who, like him, love Manchester United. He deserves nothing less.

THE EARLY YEARS

Manchester United have not always been the most glamorous club in English football. Indeed, after their foundation as Newton Heath in 1878, early financial struggles drove them to the edge of extinction and no major honours were garnered until the first decade of the 20th century.

The breakthrough came with the League title in 1907/08, the FA Cup the following season and another Championship in 1910/11. Between the wars there followed a yo-yo period during which United suffered three relegations to the Second Division, and although they made a rapid return to the top flight after each demotion, there was no real hint of the glory to follow.

Career details in this section are for all players who represented Newton Heath and Manchester United at senior level between 1886, when the Heathens entered the FA Cup for the first time, and 1939, when competitions were suspended following the outbreak of the Second World War. The three First Division games played in the autumn of 1939, before Hitler invaded Poland and the season was aborted, are included because those fixtures were completed in good faith, the players adopting a fully competitive approach. The author of this book believes that the Football League's decision to strike them from their own official record was illogical and misguided, therefore he is disregarding it.

The statistics that follow refer to appearances and goals in the Football League (including Test Matches, which some historians choose bizarrely to ignore, despite the fact that they were the most important games of their respective seasons), the FA Cup and the FA Charity Shield. Profiles of players who appeared on both sides of the Second World War are to be found in Busby And Beyond, which begins on page 36.

ALF AINSWORTH 1933/34
Inside-forward: 2 games, 0 goals

JOHN AITKEN 1895/96
Winger: 2 games, 1 goal

GEORGE ALBINSON 1920/21
Wing-half: 1 game, 0 goals

JACK ALLAN 1904/05 → 1905/06
Forward: 36 games, 22 goals

ARTHUR ALLMAN 1914/15
Full-back: 12 games, 0 goals

ALFRED AMBLER 1899/1900 → 1900/01
Half-back: 10 games, 1 goal

GEORGE ANDERSON 1911/12 → 1914/15
Centre-forward: 86 games, 39 goals

TOMMY ARKESDEN 1902/03 → 1905/06
Forward: 79 games, 33 goals

BEAU ASQUITH 1939/40
Centre-forward: 1 game, 0 goals

JOE ASTLEY 1925/26 → 1926/27
Full-back: 2 games, 0 goals

DAVID BAIN 1922/23 → 1923/24
Forward: 23 games, 9 goals

JAMES BAIN 1899/1900
Centre-forward: 2 games, 1 goal

JIMMY BAIN 1924/25 → 1927/28
Half-back: 4 games, 0 goals

HARRY BAIRD 1936/37 → 1937/38
Forward: 53 games, 18 goals

BILLY BALL 1902/03
Half-back: 4 games, 0 goals

JACK BALL 1929/30 and 1933/34 → 1934/35
Centre-forward: 50 games, 18 goals

TOMMY BAMFORD 1934/35 → 1937/38
Centre-forward: 109 games, 57 goals

JACK BANKS 1901/02 → 1902/03
Half-back: 44 games, 1 goal

JIMMY BANNISTER 1906/07 → 1909/10
Inside-forward: 63 games, 8 goals

JACK BARBER 1922/23 → 1923/24
Inside-forward: 4 games, 2 goals

CYRIL BARLOW 1919/20 → 1921/22
Full-back: 30 games, 0 goals

FRANK BARRETT 1896/97 → 1899/1900
Goalkeeper: 136 games, 0 goals

FRANK BARSON 1922/23 → 1927/28
Centre-half: 152 games, 4 goals
See profile on page 34

ARTHUR BEADSWORTH 1902/03
Forward: 12 games, 2 goals

ROBERT BEALE 1912/13 → 1914/15
Goalkeeper: 112 games, 0 goals

R BECKETT 1886/87
Goalkeeper: 1 game, 0 goals

CLEM BEDDOW 1904/05 → 1906/07
Forward: 34 games, 15 goals

BILLY BEHAN 1933/34
Goalkeeper: 1 game, 0 goals

ALEX BELL 1902/03 → 1912/13
Half-back: 309 games, 10 goals
See profile on page 30

RAY BENNION 1921/22 → 1931/32
Wing-half: 301 games, 3 goals

BILL BERRY 1906/07 → 1908/09
Forward: 14 games, 1 goal

HERBERT BIRCHENOUGH 1902/03
Goalkeeper: 30 games, 0 goals

GEORGE BISSETT 1919/20 → 1921/22
Forward: 42 games, 10 goals

DICK BLACK 1931/32 → 1933/34
Forward: 8 games, 3 goals

PETER BLACKMORE 1899/1900
Centre-forward: 2 games, 0 goals

TOMMY BLACKSTOCK 1903/04 → 1906/07
Full-back: 38 games, 0 goals

HORACE BLEW 1905/06
Full-back: 1 game, 0 goals

SAM BLOTT 1909/10 → 1912/13
Forward: 19 games, 2 goals

BOB BONTHRON 1903/04 → 1906/07
Full-back: 134 games, 3 goals

WILLIAM BOOTH 1900/01
Winger: 2 games, 0 goals

BILLY BOYD 1934/35
Centre-forward: 6 games, 4 goals

HENRY BOYD 1896/97 → 1898/99
Centre-forward: 62 games, 35 goals

TOMMY BOYLE 1928/29 → 1929/30
Inside-forward: 17 games, 6 goals

LEN BRADBURY 1938/39
Inside-forward: 2 games, 1 goal

JACK BREEDON 1935/36 → 1939/40
Goalkeeper: 38 games, 0 goals

TOMMY BREEN 1936/37 → 1938/39
Goalkeeper: 71 games, 0 goals

FRANK BRETT 1921/22
Full-back: 10 games, 0 goals

FA Cup Winners 1909. Left to right, standing: Ernest Mangnall (secretary-manager), F Bacon (trainer), Jack Picken, Hugh Edmonds, Mr Murray (director), Harry Moger, John Henry Davies (chairman), Tom Homer, Mr Lawton (director), Alex Bell, Mr Deakin (director). Seated: Billy Meredith, Dick Duckworth, Charlie Roberts, Sandy Turnbull, Enoch West, George Stacey. On ground: Arthur Whalley, Leslie Hofton, Harold Halse, George Wall.

WILLIAM BROOKS 1898/99
Forward: 3 games, 3 goals

ALBERT BROOME 1922/23
Inside-forward: 1 game, 0 goals

HERBERT BROOMFIELD 1907/08
Goalkeeper: 9 games, 0 goals

JAMES BROWN 1892/93
Full-back: 7 games, 0 goals

JAMES BROWN 1932/33 → 1933/34
Winger: 41 games, 17 goals

JAMES BROWN 1935/36 → 1938/39
Wing-half: 110 games, 1 goal

RIMMER BROWN 1896/97
Centre-forward: 7 games, 2 goals

WILLIAM BRYANT
1896/97 → 1899/1900
Winger: 127 games, 33 goals

WILLIAM BRYANT 1934/35 → 1939/40
Winger: 160 games, 44 goals

FRANK BUCKLEY 1906/07
Half-back: 3 games, 0 goals

JIMMY BULLOCK 1930/31
Centre-forward: 10 games, 3 goals

WILLIAM BUNCE 1902/03
Full-back: 2 games, 0 goals

HERBERT BURGESS
1906/07 → 1909/1910
Full-back: 54 games, 0 goals

TOM BURKE 1886/87
Wing-half: 1 game, 0 goals

DAVID BYRNE 1933/34
Forward: 4 games, 3 goals

JAMES CAIRNS 1894/95
Full-back: 1 game, 0 goals

JAMES CAIRNS 1898/99
Inside-forward: 1 game, 0 goals

WILLIAM CAMPBELL 1893/94
Inside-forward: 5 games, 1 goal

JACK CAPE 1933/34 → 1936/37
Forward: 60 games, 18 goals

FREDDY CAPPER 1911/12
Winger: 1 game, 0 goals

JAMES CARMAN 1897/98
Inside-forward: 3 games, 1 goal

ADAM CARSON 1892/93
Forward: 13 games, 3 goals

BERT CARTMAN 1922/23
Winger: 3 games, 0 goals

WALTER CARTWRIGHT
1895/96 → 1903/04
Utility: 257 games, 8 goals

ARTHUR CASHMORE 1913/14
Forward: 3 games, 0 goals

JOE CASSIDY 1892/93 → 1899/1900
Forward: 174 games, 100 goals

STEWART CHALMERS
1932/33 → 1933/34
Inside-forward: 35 games, 1 goal

BILLY CHAPMAN 1926/27 → 1927/28
Winger: 26 games, 0 goals

REG CHESTER 1935/36
Winger: 13 games, 1 goal

ARTHUR CHESTERS
1929/30 → 1931/32
Goalkeeper: 9 games, 0 goals

TOM CHORLTON 1913/14
Full-back: 4 games, 0 goals

DAVID CHRISTIE 1908/09
Inside-forward: 2 games, 0 goals

JOHN CHRISTIE 1902/03
Full-back: 1 game, 0 goals

JOE CLARK 1899/1900
Forward: 9 games, 0 goals

JOHN CLARKIN 1893/94 → 1895/96
Winger: 74 games, 23 goals

HARRY CLEAVER 1902/03
Centre-forward: 1 game, 0 goals

JOHN CLEMENTS 1892/93 → 1893/94
Full-back: 42 games, 0 goals

JIMMY COLLINSON
1895/96 → 1900/01
Utility: 71 games, 17 goals

JAMES COLVILLE 1892/93
Forward: 10 games, 1 goal

JAMES CONNACHAN 1898/99
Forward: 4 games, 0 goals

TED CONNOR 1909/10 → 1910/11
Winger: 15 games, 2 goals

SAM COOKSON 1914/15
Half-back: 13 games, 0 goals

JIMMY COUPAR
1892/93 and 1901/02
Forward: 34 games, 10 goals

T CRAIG 1889/90 → 1890/91
Forward: 2 games, 1 goal

CHARLIE CRAVEN 1938/39
Inside-forward: 11 games, 2 goals

JOHN CUNNINGHAM 1898/99
Forward: 17 games, 2 goals

JOE CURRY 1908/09 → 1910/11
Half-back: 14 games, 0 goals

BILLY DALE 1928/29 → 1931/32
Full-back: 68 games, 0 goals

HERBERT DALE 1890/91
Inside-forward: 1 game, 0 goals

TED DALTON 1907/08
Full-back: 1 game, 0 goals

WILL DAVIDSON 1893/94
Wing-half: 44 games, 2 goals

JOE DAVIES 1886/87
Centre-half: 2 games, 0 goals

JOHN DAVIES 1892/93
Goalkeeper: 10 games, 0 goals

L DAVIES 1886/87
Winger: 1 game, 0 goals

HAROLD DEAN 1931/32
Centre-forward: 2 games, 0 goals

J DENMAN 1891/92
Full-back: 1 game, 0 goals

BILLY DENNIS 1923/24
Full-back: 3 games, 0 goals

NEIL DEWAR 1932/33 → 1933/34
Centre-forward: 36 games, 14 goals

BERNARD DONAGHY 1905/06
Inside-forward: 3 games, 0 goals

BOB DONALDSON 1892/93 → 1897/98
Forward: 155 games, 66 goals

DONNELLY 1890/91
Winger: 1 game, 0 goals

TONY DONNELLY 1908/09 → 1912/13
Full-back: 37 games, 0 goals

TOMMY DOUGAN 1938/39
Winger: 4 games, 0 goals

JACK DOUGHTY 1886/87 → 1891/92
Forward: 3 games, 3 goals

ROGER DOUGHTY 1889/90 → 1896/97
Utility: 8 games, 1 goal

WILLIAM DOUGLAS
1893/94 → 1895/96
Goalkeeper: 57 games, 0 goals

JOHN DOW 1893/94 → 1895/96
Full-back: 50 games, 6 goals

ALEX DOWNIE 1902/03 → 1909/10
Half-back: 191 games, 14 goals

BILLY DRAYCOTT 1896/97 → 1898/99
Wing-half: 95 games, 6 goals

DICK DUCKWORTH
1903/04 → 1913/14
Half-back: 254 games, 11 goals
See profile on page 30

WILLIAM DUNN 1897/98
Forward: 12 games, 0 goals

JIMMY DYER 1905/06
Centre-forward: 1 game, 0 goals

JOHN EARP 1886/87
Winger: 1 game, 0 goals

ALF EDGE 1891/92
Forward: 3 games, 3 goals

HUGH EDMONDS 1910/11 → 1911/12
Goalkeeper: 51 games, 0 goals

DAVID ELLIS 1923/24
Winger: 11 games, 0 goals

FRED ERENTZ 1892/93 → 1901/02
Full-back: 310 games, 9 goals

HARRY ERENTZ 1897/98
Full-back: 9 games, 0 goals

GEORGE EVANS 1890/91
Centre-forward: 1 game, 1 goal

SIDNEY EVANS 1923/24
Winger: 6 games, 2 goals

JOE FALL 1893/94
Goalkeeper: 27 games, 0 goals

ALF FARMAN 1892/93 → 1894/95
Forward: 61 games, 28 goals

G FELTON 1890/91
Centre-half: 1 game, 0 goals

DANNY FERGUSON 1927/28
Inside-forward: 4 games, 0 goals

JOHN FERGUSON 1931/32
Winger: 8 games, 1 goal

RON FERRIER 1935/36 → 1937/38
Inside-forward: 19 games, 4 goals

JAMES FISHER 1900/01 → 1901/02
Forward: 46 games, 3 goals

JOHN FITCHETT 1902/03 and 1904/05
Defender: 18 games, 1 goal

ARTHUR FITTON 1931/32 → 1932/33
Winger: 12 games, 2 goals

DAVID FITZSIMMONS
1895/96 and 1899/1900
Half-back: 31 games, 0 goals

TOMMY FITZSIMMONS
1892/93 → 1893/94
Forward: 30 games, 6 goals

G FOLEY 1899/1900
Winger: 7 games, 1 goal

JOE FORD 1908/09 → 1909/10
Winger: 5 games, 0 goals

TOMMY FORSTER 1919/20 → 1921/22
Wing-half: 36 games, 0 goals

FOX 1914/15
Inside-forward: 1 game, 0 goals

TOMMY FRAME 1932/33 → 1933/34
Centre-half: 52 games, 4 goals

STAN GALLIMORE 1930/31 → 1933/34
Inside-forward: 76 games, 20 goals

DICK GARDNER 1935/36 → 1936/37
Forward: 18 games, 1 goal

JAMES GARVEY 1900/01
Goalkeeper: 6 games, 0 goals

RALPH GAUDIE 1903/04
Forward: 8 games, 0 goals

RICHARD GIBSON 1921/22
Winger: 12 games, 0 goals

MATTHEW GILLESPIE
1896/97 → 1899/1900
Forward: 89 games, 21 goals

TOMMY GIPPS 1912/13 → 1914/15
Half-back: 23 games, 0 goals

GEORGE GLADWIN 1936/37
Wing-half: 28 games, 1 goal

GILBERT GODSMARK 1899/1900
Forward: 9 games, 4 goals

ERNIE GOLDTHORPE
1922/23 → 1924/25
Forward: 30 games, 16 goals

BILLY GOODWIN 1920/21 → 1921/22
Centre-forward: 7 games, 1 goal

J GOTHERIDGE 1886/87
Inside-forward: 1 game, 0 goals

JOHN GOURLAY 1898/99
Centre-half: 1 game, 0 goals

JOHN GRAHAM 1893/94
Centre-forward: 4 games, 0 goals

BILLY GRASSAM 1903/04 → 1904/05
Forward: 37 games, 14 goals

EDDIE GREEN 1933/34
Inside-forward: 9 games, 4 goals

WILSON GREENWOOD 1900/01
Forward: 3 games, 0 goals

BILLY GRIFFITHS 1898/99 → 1904/05
Centre-half: 175 games, 30 goals

JACK GRIFFITHS 1933/34 → 1939/40
Full-back: 176 games, 1 goal

JOHN GRIMWOOD
1919/20 → 1926/27
Half-back: 205 games, 8 goals

JOHN GRUNDY 1899/1900 → 1900/01
Winger: 11 games, 3 goals

WILLIAM GYVES 1890/91
Goalkeeper: 1 game, 0 goals

JACK HACKING 1933/34 → 1934/35
Goalkeeper: 34 games, 0 goals

JACK HALL 1925/26
Winger: 3 games, 0 goals

JACK HALL 1933/34 → 1935/36
Goalkeeper: 73 games, 0 goals

PROCTOR HALL 1903/04
Inside-forward: 8 games, 2 goals

HAROLD HARDMAN 1908/09
Forward: 4 games, 0 goals

A feisty little England winger who won Olympic gold for Great Britain in 1908, the year he left Everton for Old Trafford. Harold went on to serve United as a director for more than half a century, being chairman from 1951 to 1965.

HAROLD HALSE 1907/08 → 1911/12
Forward: 125 games, 56 goals
See profile on page 31

REG HALTON 1936/37
Winger: 4 games, 1 goal

MICKEY HAMILL 1911/12 → 1913/14
Wing-half: 60 games, 2 goals

CHARLIE HANNAFORD
1925/26 → 1926/27
Winger: 12 games, 0 goals

JIMMY HANSON 1924/25 → 1929/30
Forward: 147 games, 52 goals

FRANK HARRIS 1919/20 → 1921/22
Half-back: 49 games, 2 goals

TOM HARRIS 1926/27
Inside-forward: 4 games, 1 goal

CHARLIE HARRISON 1889/90
Full-back: 1 game, 0 goals

WILLIAM HARRISON
1920/21 → 1921/22
Winger: 46 games, 5 goals

WILLIAM HARTWELL
1903/04 → 1904/05
Winger: 4 games, 0 goals

GEORGE HASLAM 1921/22 → 1927/28
Centre-half: 27 games, 0 goals

RON HAWORTH 1926/27
Inside-forward: 2 games, 0 goals

TOM HAY 1889/90
Goalkeeper: 1 game, 0 goals

VINCE HAYES 1900/01 → 1910/11
Full-back: 128 games, 2 goals

JOE HAYWOOD 1913/14 → 1914/15
Wing-half: 26 games, 0 goals

JOE HEATHCOTE
1899/1900 → 1901/02
Inside-forward: 8 games, 0 goals

WILLIAM HENDERSON
1921/22 → 1924/25
Centre-forward: 36 games, 17 goals

JAMES HENDRY 1892/93
Winger: 2 games, 1 goal

ARTHUR HENRYS 1891/92 and
1892/93
Half-back: 6 games, 0 goals

HERBERT HEYWOOD
1932/33 → 1933/34
Winger: 4 games, 2 goals

SANDY HIGGINS 1901/02
Half-back: 10 games, 0 goals

JAMES HIGSON 1901/02
Inside-forward: 5 games, 1 goal

CLARRIE 'LAL' HILDITCH
1919/20 → 1931/32
Half-back: 322 games, 7 goals
See profile on page 35

CHARLIE HILLAM 1933/34
Goalkeeper: 8 games, 0 goals

ERNIE HINE 1932/33 → 1934/35
Inside-forward: 53 games, 12 goals

JAMES HODGE 1910/11 → 1919/20
Utility: 86 games, 2 goals

JOHN HODGE 1913/14 → 1914/15
Defender: 30 games, 0 goals

FRANK HODGES 1919/20 → 1920/21
Inside-forward: 20 games, 4 goals

LESLIE HOFTON 1910/11 → 1920/21
Full-back: 19 games, 0 goals

DICK HOLDEN 1904/05 → 1912/13
Full-back: 117 games, 0 goals

EDWARD HOLT 1899/1900
Winger: 1 game, 1 goal

TOM HOMER 1909/10 → 1911/12
Forward: 25 games, 14 goals

BILLY HOOD 1892/93 → 1893/94
Forward: 38 games, 6 goals

ARTHUR HOOPER 1909/10 → 1913/14
Forward: 7 games, 1 goal

FRED HOPKIN 1919/20 → 1920/21
Winger: 74 games, 8 goals

JAMES HOPKINS 1898/99
Inside-forward: 1 game, 0 goals

SAM HOPKINSON 1930/31 → 1933/34
Forward: 57 games, 12 goals

JOHN HOWARTH 1921/22
Full-back: 4 games, 0 goals

E HOWELLS 1886/87
Wing-half: 1 game, 0 goals

EDWARD HUDSON
1913/14 → 1914/15
Full-back: 11 games, 0 goals

AARON HULME 1907/08 → 1908/09
Full-back: 4 games, 0 goals

GEORGE HUNTER 1913/14 → 1914/15
Half-back: 23 games, 2 goals

WILLIAM HUNTER 1912/13
Centre-forward: 3 games, 2 goals

DANIEL HURST 1902/03
Winger: 21 games, 4 goals

RICHARD IDDON 1925/26 → 1926/27
Forward: 2 games, 0 goals

BILL INGLIS 1925/26 → 1928/29
Full-back: 14 games, 1 goal

Already a veteran when he arrived
from Sheffield Wednesday, Bill was
essentially a stand-in for the more
mobile Charlie Moore. He was best
known as a tough trainer, whose bark
was worse than his bite, between
1934 and 1961.

WILLIAM JACKSON
1899/1900 → 1900/01
Inside-forward: 64 games, 14 goals

CAESAR JENKYNS 1896/97 → 1897/98
Centre-half: 47 games, 6 goals

ROY JOHN 1936/37
Goalkeeper: 15 games, 0 goals

SAM JOHNSON 1900/01
Inside-forward: 1 game, 0 goals

BILLY JOHNSTON
1927/28 → 1928/29 and 1931/32
Inside-forward: 77 games, 27 goals

DAVID JONES 1937/38
Centre-half: 1 game, 0 goals

JOHN JONES 1898/99
Forward: 2 games, 0 goals

TOM JONES 1924/25 → 1936/37
Full-back: 200 games, 0 goals

TOMMY JONES 1934/35
Forward: 22 games, 4 goals

FRED KENNEDY 1923/24 → 1924/25
Inside-forward: 18 games, 4 goals

WILLIAM KENNEDY
1895/96 → 1896/97
Inside-forward: 33 games, 12 goals

HUGH KERR 1903/04
Centre-forward: 2 games, 0 goals

JOE KINLOCH 1892/93
Centre-forward: 1 game, 0 goals

FRANK KNOWLES 1911/12 → 1914/15
Half-back: 47 games, 1 goal

TOMMY LANG 1935/36
Winger: 13 games, 1 goal

LEN LANGFORD 1934/35 → 1935/36
Goalkeeper: 15 games, 0 goals

HARRY LAPPIN 1900/01 → 1902/03
Forward: 27 games, 4 goals

REG LAWSON 1900/01
Inside-forward: 3 games, 0 goals

NEDDY LEE 1898/99 → 1899/1900
Forward: 11 games, 5 goals

TOM LEIGH 1899/1900 → 1900/1901
Centre-forward: 46 games, 15 goals

HARRY LEONARD 1920/21
Centre-forward: 10 games, 5 goals

LESLIE LIEVESLEY 1931/32
Wing-half: 2 games, 0 goals

WILFRED LIEVESLEY 1922/23
Forward: 3 games, 0 goals

OSCAR LINKSON 1908/09 → 1912/13
Full-back: 59 games, 0 goals

GEORGE LIVINGSTONE
1908/09 → 1913/14
Utility: 46 games, 4 goals

ARTHUR LOCHHEAD
1921/22 → 1925/26
Forward: 153 games, 50 goals

WILLIAM LONGAIR 1894/95
Centre-half: 1 game, 0 goals

LONGTON 1886/87
Inside-forward: 1 game, 0 goals

GEORGE LYDON 1930/31 → 1931/32
Wing-half: 3 games, 0 goals

DAVID LYNER 1922/23
Winger: 3 games, 0 goals

GEORGE LYONS 1903/04 → 1905/06
Forward: 5 games, 0 goals

NEIL McBAIN 1921/22 → 1922/23
Half-back: 43 games, 2 goals
See profile on page 35

PAT McCARTHY 1911/12
Centre-forward: 1 game, 0 goals

JOHN McCARTNEY 1894/95
Full-back: 20 games, 1 goal

WILLIAM McCARTNEY 1903/04
Forward: 13 games, 1 goal

JIMMY McCLELLAND 1936/37
Inside-forward: 5 games, 1 goal

JAMES McCRAE 1925/26
Wing-half: 13 games, 0 goals

KEN MacDONALD 1922/23 → 1923/24
Centre-forward: 9 game, 2 goals

WILLIE McDONALD
1931/32 → 1933/34
Inside-forward: 27 games, 4 goals

BOB McFARLANE 1891/92
Full-back: 3 games, 0 goals

DAVID McFETTERIDGE 1894/95
Inside-forward: 1 game, 0 goals

CHARLIE McGILLIVRAY 1933/34
Forward: 9 games, 0 goals

JOHN McGILLIVRAY
1907/08 → 1908/09
Half-back: 4 games, 0 goals

BILL McKAY 1933/34 → 1939/40
Wing-half or inside-forward: 184 games,
15 goals

CHARLIE MACKIE 1904/05
Centre-forward: 7 games, 4 goals

GEORGE McLACHLAN
1929/30 → 1932/33
Winger: 116 games, 4 goals

HUGH McLENAHAN
1927/28 → 1936/37
Utility: 116 games, 12 goals

WALTER McMILLEN
1933/34 → 1934/35
Half-back: 29 games, 2 goals

JAMES McNAUGHT
1893/94 → 1897/98
Utility: 162 games, 12 goals

FRANK McPHERSON
1923/24 → 1927/28
Winger or centre-forward: 175 games,
52 goals

TOM MANLEY 1931/32 → 1938/39
Wing-half or winger: 195 games,
41 goals

FRANK MANN 1922/23 → 1929/30
Half-back: 197 games, 5 goals

HERBERT MANN 1931/32
Winger: 13 games, 2 goals

TOM MANNS 1933/34
Wing-half: 2 games, 0 goals

ARTHUR MARSHALL 1902/03
Full-back: 6 games, 0 goals

WILLIAM MATHIESON
1892/93 → 1893/94
Winger: 10 games, 2 goals

TOMMY MEEHAN 1919/20 → 1920/21
Wing-half: 53 games, 6 goals

JACK MELLOR 1930/31 → 1936/37
Full-back: 122 games, 0 goals

ALEX MENZIES 1906/07 → 1907/08
Centre-forward: 25 games, 4 goals

BILLY MEREDITH 1906/07 → 1920/21
Winger: 335 games, 36 goals
See profile on page 24

JACK MEW 1912/13 → 1925/26
Goalkeeper: 199 games, 0 goals

BOB MILARVIE 1890/91
Inside-forward: 1 game, 0 goals

GEORGE MILLAR 1894/95
Centre-forward: 7 games, 5 goals

JOCK MILLER 1923/24
Inside-forward: 4 games, 1 goal

TOM MILLER 1920/21
Forward: 27 games, 8 goals

ANDREW MITCHELL
1892/93 → 1893/94
Full-back: 61 games, 0 goals

ANDREW MITCHELL 1932/33
Winger: 1 game, 0 goals

J MITCHELL 1886/87 and 1890/91
Full-back: 3 games, 0 goals

HARRY MOGER 1903/04 → 1911/12
Goalkeeper: 266 games, 0 goals
See profile on page 31

ARCHIE MONTGOMERY 1905/06
Goalkeeper: 3 games, 0 goals

JAMES MONTGOMERY
1914/15 → 1920/21
Half-back: 27 games, 1 goal

JOHN MOODY 1931/32 → 1932/33
Goalkeeper: 51 games, 0 goals

CHARLIE MOORE 1919/20 → 1929/30
Full-back: 328 games, 0 goals
See profile on page 35

BILLY MORGAN 1896/97 → 1902/03
Half-back: 152 games, 7 goals

HUGH MORGAN 1900/01
Inside-forward: 23 games, 4 goals

TOMMY MORRISON
1902/03 → 1903/04
Forward: 36 games, 8 goals

BEN MORTON 1935/36
Centre-forward: 1 game, 0 goals

ROBERT MURRAY 1937/38
Inside-forward: 4 games, 0 goals

GEORGE MUTCH 1934/35 → 1937/38
Forward: 120 games, 49 goals

JOE MYERSCOUGH
1920/21 → 1922/23
Inside-forward: 34 games, 8 goals

GEORGE NEVIN 1933/34
Full-back: 4 games, 0 goals

PERCY NEWTON 1933/34
Centre-half: 2 games, 0 goals

GEORGE NICOL 1927/28 → 1928/29
Centre-forward: 7 games, 2 goals

JOE NORTON 1913/14 → 1914/15
Winger: 37 games, 3 goals

TOM NUTTALL 1911/12 → 1912/13
Inside-forward: 16 games, 4 goals

GEORGE O'BRIEN 1901/02
Winger: 1 game, 0 goals

PAT O'CONNELL 1914/15
Centre-half: 35 games, 2 goals

T O'SHAUGHNESSEY 1890/91
Winger: 1 game, 0 goals

BILLY OWEN 1934/35 → 1935/36
Winger: 17 games, 1 goal

GEORGE OWEN 1889/90
Inside-forward: 1 game, 0 goals

JOHN OWEN 1889/90 → 1991/92
Half-back: 6 games, 0 goals

W OWEN 1898/99
Winger: 1 game, 0 goals

LOUIS PAGE 1931/32 → 1932/33
Forward: 12 games, 0 goals

ALBERT PAPE 1924/25 → 1925/26
Centre-forward: 18 games, 5 goals

SAM PARKER 1893/94
Inside-forward: 11 games, 0 goals

THOMAS PARKER 1930/31 → 1931/32
Centre-half: 17 games, 0 goals

ROBERT PARKINSON 1899/1900
Centre-forward: 15 games, 7 goals

TEDDY PARTRIDGE
1920/21 → 1928/29
Winger or inside-forward: 160 games,
18 goals

ERNEST PAYNE 1908/09
Winger: 2 games, 1 goal

JACK PEDDIE 1902/03 → 1906/07
Forward: 121 games, 58 goals

JACK PEDEN 1893/94
Winger: 32 games, 8 goals

DICK PEGG 1902/03 → 1903/04
Forward: 51 games, 20 goals

FRANK PEPPER 1898/99
Centre-half: 8 games, 0 goals

GEORGE PERRINS 1892/93 → 1895/96
Half-back: 102 games, 0 goals

JAMES PETERS 1894/95 → 1895/96
Winger: 51 games, 14 goals

JACK PICKEN 1905/06 → 1910/11
Inside-forward: 122 games, 46 goals

BILLY PORTER 1934/35 → 1937/38
Full-back: 65 games, 0 goals

ARTHUR POTTS 1913/14 → 1919/20
Inside-forward: 29 games, 5 goals

Second Division Champions 1935/36. Left to right, standing: James Gibson (chairman), Ron Ferrier, Jack Griffiths, Jack Breedon, Tom Curry (trainer), Jack Hall, Billy Porter, Tom Manley, Scott Duncan (manager). Seated: Jack Cape, George Mutch, Tommy Bamford, James Brown, Harry Rowley, Bill McKay, George Vose. On ground: Billy Bryant, Bill Robertson, Billy Owen, Hubert Redwood.

JACK POWELL 1886/87 → 1890/91
Full-back: 4 games, 0 goals

JOHN PRENTICE 1919/20
Winger: 1 game, 0 goals

STEVE PRESTON 1901/02 → 1902/03
Forward: 34 games, 14 goals

ALBERT PRINCE 1914/15
Inside-forward: 1 game, 0 goals

D PRINCE 1893/94
Winger: 2 games, 0 goals

JAMES PUGH 1921/22 → 1922/23
Full-back: 2 games, 0 goals

JACK QUIN 1908/09 → 1909/10
Forward: 2 games, 0 goals

GEORGE RADCLIFFE 1898/99
Winger: 1 game, 0 goals

CHARLIE RADFORD
1920/21 → 1923/24
Full-back: 96 games, 1 goal

ROBERT RAMSAY 1890/91
Centre-half: 1 game, 0 goals

CHARLIE RAMSDEN
1927/28 → 1930/31
Winger: 16 games, 3 goals

RATTIGAN 1890/91
Wing-half: 1 game, 0 goals

BILL RAWLINGS 1927/28 → 1929/30
Centre-forward: 36 games, 19 goals

BERT READ 1902/03 → 1903/04
Full-back: 42 games, 0 goals

HUBERT REDWOOD
1935/36 → 1939/40
Full-back: 96 games, 4 goals

TOMMY REID 1928/29 → 1932/33
Centre-forward: 101 games, 67 goals

CHARLIE RENNOX 1924/25 → 1926/27
Inside-forward: 68 games, 25 goals

BILLY RICHARDS 1901/02
Centre-forward: 9 games, 1 goal

CHARLIE RICHARDS 1902/03
Inside-forward: 11 games, 2 goals

LANCE RICHARDSON
1924/25 → 1928/29
Goalkeeper: 42 games, 0 goals

BILL RIDDING 1931/32 → 1933/34
Forward: 44 games, 14 goals

JOE RIDGWAY 1895/96 → 1897/98
Goalkeeper: 17 games, 0 goals

DAVID ROBBIE 1935/36
Winger: 1 game, 0 goals

BOB ROBERTS 1913/14
Full-back: 2 games, 0 goals

BOGIE ROBERTS 1898/99 → 1899/1900
Winger: 10 games, 2 goals

CHARLIE ROBERTS
1903/04 → 1912/13
Centre-half: 302 games, 23 goals
See profile on page 26

ALEXANDER ROBERTSON
1903/04 → 1905/06
Half-back: 35 games, 1 goal

SANDY ROBERTSON
1903/04 → 1904/05
Forward: 34 games, 10 goals

TOM ROBERTSON 1903/04
Forward: 3 games, 0 goals

WILLIAM ROBERTSON
1933/34 → 1935/36
Wing-half: 50 games, 1 goal

JAMES ROBINSON 1919/20 → 1921/22
Winger: 21 games, 3 goals

MATT ROBINSON 1931/32
Winger: 10 games, 0 goals

CHARLES ROTHWELL
1893/94 → 1896/97
Forward: 3 games, 3 goals

HERBERT ROTHWELL 1902/03
Full-back: 28 games, 0 goals

GEORGE ROUGHTON
1936/37 → 1938/39
Full-back: 92 games, 0 goals

ELIJAH ROUND 1909/10
Goalkeeper: 2 games, 0 goals

JOSH ROWE 1913/14
Full-back: 1 game, 0 goals

HARRY ROWLEY 1928/29 → 1931/2
and 1934/35 → 1936/37
Inside-forward: 180 games, 55 goals

EZRA ROYALS 1911/12 → 1913/14
Goalkeeper: 7 games, 0 goals

CHARLIE SAGAR 1905/06 → 1906/07
Forward: 33 games, 24 goals

GEORGE SAPSFORD 1919/20 →
Inside-forward: 53 games, 17 goals

WILLIAM SARVIS 1922/23
Inside-forward: 1 game, 0 goals

JAMES SAUNDERS 1901/02 → 1902/03
Goalkeeper: 13 games, 0 goals

TED SAVAGE 1937/38
Wing-half: 5 games, 0 goals

F SAWYER 1899/1900
Winger: 6 games, 0 goals

ALF SCHOFIELD 1900/01 → 1906/07
Winger: 179 games, 35 goals

GEORGE SCHOFIELD 1920/21
Winger: 1 game, 0 goals

JOE SCHOFIELD 1903/04
Forward: 2 games, 0 goals

PERCY SCHOFIELD 1921/22
Inside-forward: 1 game, 0 goals

JOHN SCOTT 1921/22
Wing-half: 24 games, 0 goals

WILLIAM SHARPE 1890/91 → 1891/92
Forward: 2 games, 0 goals

JOHN SHELDON 1910/11 → 1912/13
Winger: 26 games, 1 goal

JACK SILCOCK 1919/20 → 1933/34
Full-back: 449 games, 2 goals
See profile on page 35

J SLATER 1890/91 → 1891/92
Goalkeeper: 4 games, 0 goals

ALBERT SMITH 1926/27
Centre-forward: 5 games, 1 goal

DICK SMITH 1894/95 → 1897/98 and
1899/1900 → 1900/1901
Forward: 101 games, 37 goals

LAWRENCE SMITH 1902/03
Forward: 10 games, 1 goal

TOM SMITH 1923/24 → 1926/27
Inside-forward: 90 games, 16 goals

WILLIAM SMITH 1901/02
Forward: 17 games, 0 goals

JOHN SNEDDON 1891/92
Forward: 3 games, 1 goal

JOE SPENCE 1919/20 → 1932/33
Centre-forward or winger: 510 games,
168 goals
See profile on page 32

CHARLIE SPENCER
1928/29 → 1929/30
Centre-half: 48 games, 0 goals

WALTER SPRATT 1914/15 → 1919/20
Full-back: 13 games, 0 goals

GEORGE STACEY 1907/08 → 1914/15
Full-back: 270 games, 9 goals

HARRY STAFFORD
1895/96 → 1902/03
Full-back: 200 games, 1 goal
A steady defender and the first
captain of the newly-titled
Manchester United, Harry is best
remembered for his lost dog, Major,
which attracted the attention of
benefactor John Henry Davies,
the man who saved the club from
financial ruin.

R STEPHENSON 1895/96
Inside-forward: 1 game, 1 goal

ALF STEWARD 1920/21 → 1931/32
Goalkeeper: 326 games, 0 goals

WILLIAM STEWART
1890/91 → 1894/95
Half-back: 87 games, 5 goals

WILLIAM STEWART
1932/33 → 1933/34
Winger: 49 games, 7 goals

HERBERT STONE 1893/94 → 1894/95
Half-back: 7 games, 0 goals

ERNIE STREET 1902/03
Forward: 3 games, 0 goals

JOHN SUTCLIFFE 1903/04
Goalkeeper: 28 games, 0 goals

ERIC SWEENEY 1925/26 → 1929/30
Inside-forward: 32 games, 7 goals

NORMAN TAPKEN 1938/39
Goalkeeper: 16 games, 0 goals

CHRIS TAYLOR 1924/25 → 1929/30
Inside-forward or half-back: 30 games,
7 goals

WALTER TAYLOR 1921/22
Winger: 1 game, 0 goals

HARRY THOMAS 1921/22 → 1929/30
Winger: 135 games, 13 goals

ERNIE THOMPSON
1936/37 → 1937/38
Forward: 3 games, 1 goal

WILLIAM THOMPSON 1893/94
Inside-forward: 3 games, 0 goals

ARTHUR THOMSON
1928/29 → 1930/31
Forward: 5 games, 1 goal

ERNEST THOMSON
1907/08 → 1908/09
Wing-half: 4 games, 0 goals

JAMES THOMSON 1913/14
Winger: 6 games, 1 goal

BILLY TOMS 1919/20 → 1920/21
Forward: 14 games, 4 goals

HENRY TOPPING 1932/33 → 1934/35
Full-back: 12 games, 1 goal

GEORGE TRAVERS 1913/14 → 1914/15
Inside-forward: 21 games, 4 goals

JIMMY TURNBULL 1907/08 → 1909/10
Centre-forward: 78 games, 45 goals

SANDY TURNBULL
1906/07 → 1914/15
Inside-forward: 247 games, 101 goals
See profile on page 28

TURNER 1890/91
Centre-forward: 1 game, 0 goals

JOHN TURNER 1898/99
Half-back: 3 games, 0 goals

BOB TURNER 1898/99
Defender: 2 games, 0 goals

SIDNEY TYLER 1923/24
Full-back: 1 game, 0 goals

BOB VALENTINE 1904/05 → 1905/06
Goalkeeper: 10 games, 0 goals

JAMES VANCE 1895/96 → 1896/97
Inside-forward: 11 games, 1 goal

ERNIE VINCENT 1931/32 → 1933/34
Half-back: 65 games, 1 goal

GEORGE VOSE (right)
1933/34 → 1939/40
Centre-half: 211 games, 1 goal
The blond Lancastrian was a nimble,
intelligent, ball-playing centre-
half who would surely have won
international recognition had he
not been disadvantaged by playing
for United's inconsistent side of the
1930s.

ROBERT WALKER 1898/99
Centre-half: 2 games, 0 goals

GEORGE WALL 1905/06 → 1914/15
Winger: 319 games, 100 goals
See profile on page 31

ARTHUR WARBURTON
1929/30 → 1933/34
Forward: 39 games, 10 goals

JAMES WARNER 1892/93
Goalkeeper: 22 games, 0 goals

JACKIE WASSALL 1935/36 → 1939/40
Inside-forward: 48 games, 6 goals

FRANK WEDGE 1897/98
Inside-forward: 2 games, 2 goals

ENOCH 'Knocker' WEST
1910/11 → 1914/15
Centre-forward: 181 games, 80 goals
See profile on page 31

JOE WETHERELL 1896/97
Goalkeeper: 2 games, 0 goals

ARTHUR WHALLEY
1909/10 → 1919/20
Half-back: 106 games, 6 goals

JIMMY WHITEHOUSE
1900/01 → 1902/03
Goalkeeper: 64 games, 0 goals

KERR WHITESIDE 1907/08
Wing-half: 1 game, 0 goals

JOHN WHITNEY 1895/96 and 1900/01
Wing-half: 3 games, 0 goals

WALTER WHITTAKER 1895/96
Goalkeeper: 3 games, 0 goals

JOHN WHITTLE 1931/32
Winger: 1 game, 0 goals

TOM WILCOX 1908/09
Goalkeeper: 2 games, 0 goals

HARRY WILKINSON 1903/04
Winger: 9 games, 0 goals

BILL WILLIAMS 1901/02
Forward: 4 games, 0 goals

FRANK WILLIAMS 1930/31
Wing-half: 3 games, 0 goals

FRED WILLIAMS 1902/03
Inside-forward: 10 games, 4 goals

HARRY WILLIAMS 1922/23
Inside-forward: 5 games, 2 goals

HENRY WILLIAMS 1904/05 → 1905/06
Forward: 36 games, 8 goals

JOE WILLIAMS 1906/07
Inside-forward: 3 games, 1 goal

REES WILLIAMS 1927/28 → 1928/29
Winger: 35 games, 2 goals

JOHN WILLIAMSON 1919/20
Wing-half: 2 games, 0 goals

E WILSON 1889/90
Winger: 1 game, 0 goals

JACK WILSON 1926/27 → 1931/32
Wing-half: 140 games, 3 goals

TOMMY WILSON 1907/08
Winger: 1 game, 0 goals

WALTER WINTERBOTTOM
1936/37 → 1937/38
Half-back: 27 games, 0 goals

Best known for his marathon tenure
as England's first manager between
1946 and 1962, Walter was once
a strong and intelligent centre-
half whose career was scuppered
prematurely by back problems before
it could gain momentum.

DICK WOMBWELL 1904/05 → 1906/07
Forward: 51 games, 3 goals

JOHN WOOD 1922/23
Winger: 16 games, 1 goal

WILF WOODCOCK 1913/14 → 1919/20
Forward: 61 games, 21 goals

WILLIAM YATES 1906/07
Inside-forward: 3 games, 0 goals

ARTHUR YOUNG 1906/07
Winger: 2 games, 0 goals

BILLY MEREDITH

1906/07 → 1920/21

Billy Meredith stands out as the most enduringly potent symbol of Manchester United's first era of greatness, yet even that momentous billing does scant justice to the turbulent Welsh maestro's overall significance in the history of English football.

A massive star when the professional game was in its infancy during the twilight of the 19th century, and still a top performer when it reached its adolescence some three decades later, Billy exercised a decisive influence on the first League and Cup successes enjoyed by both Manchester clubs, and his national side has never boasted a more charismatic talisman.

For all that, the colourful outside-right was not only a sublime entertainer with the ball at his feet. Also he was a controversial, often courageous campaigner for players' rights in an era when the men who pulled in the crowds tended to be treated as second-class citizens, often little better than slaves, by their club paymasters.

At times he suffered for his beliefs, occasionally humiliatingly so, but he held on to them fiercely throughout his long life and did much to pave the way for the Professional Footballers Association.

Billy Meredith was a cartoonist's dream. Crouching bandy-legged over the ball of which he was the undisputed master, with jutting elbows, gaunt cheekbones and heavy dark moustache, he cut a highly individual figure which was rounded off by his trademark toothpick. Even in action this aid to dental hygiene was frequently apparent, being rolled from one side of his mouth to the other, and how he never swallowed it was something of a mystery.

Of course, such details were fascinating only because they were related to dazzling ability, which Billy had in abundance. He was quick and strong but his forte was fabulous control, which allowed him to embark on swerving dribbles which usually culminated in deliciously accurate crosses.

Having been a miner at the age of 12, Meredith soared to soccer prominence with Manchester City, inspiring the Blues to lift two Second Division titles, then captaining them to FA Cup triumph and scoring the only goal of the 1904 final.

Meanwhile, though, Billy was heartily dissatisfied with his lot. A headstrong character, he railed passionately against the condescension and hypocrisy with which footballers were treated by employers, but still fans were shocked when he was caught up in allegations involving bribery and illegal payments.

The case against Billy and many of his team-mates was complex and confused, and while they claimed the moral high ground, the full rights of it never came to light. But the upshot was that in 1905 the Welshman was suspended until 1907, when he signed for Manchester United, along with colleagues Sandy Turnbull, Jimmy Bannister and Herbert Burgess.

This sudden infusion of talent transformed an average side into a magnificent one. Now Billy became more a maker than a taker of goals and was an ever-present as an initial League Championship was won in 1907/08. One year on he was a key performer as Bristol City were defeated in the FA Cup Final and, despite having reached the grand old age of 37, he was excelling still as a second title was claimed in 1910/11.

Indeed, his technique appeared to improve with age, but now that splendid team began to fragment, and World War One brought an end to official competition. Astonishingly, though, the veteran remained a potent force after the conflict and, following a contretemps with United over wages, he rejoined City in 1921.

When he retired, a few months short of his fiftieth birthday in 1924, he had completed a career which stretched over nearly 30 years and encompassed 48 caps for Wales – he was selected 71 times but often was not released from club commitments – at a time when the only opponents were England, Scotland and Ireland.

Beyond all that, Billy stood out as a rebel with a just cause, a man who had campaigned tirelessly for the fledgling players' union and refused to tug his forelock to authorities which, at best, were mealy-mouthed and, at worst, were downright corrupt. He wasn't perfect – clearly he looked after his own interests as any working man should be able to do – but, in essence, he was emphatically on the side of the angels.

WILLIAM HENRY MEREDITH
BORN: Chirk, North Wales, 30 July 1874.
HONOURS: League Championship 07/08, 10/11. FA Cup 08/09. 48 Wales caps (1895-1920).
OTHER CLUBS: Northwich Victoria 1893/94 (11, 5); Manchester City 1894/95-1904/05 and 21/2-23/4 (370, 146).
DIED: Manchester, 19 April 1958.

GAMES	335
GOALS	36

CHARLIE ROBERTS

1903/04 → 1912/13

Charlie Roberts was Manchester United's first Captain Marvel, one of the most courageous, articulate and skilful leaders of men in the club's history. Just as Johnny Carey and then Roger Byrne would later represent Matt Busby's beliefs on the field, so it was with the charismatic, highly principled Roberts and the Reds' first managerial father figure, Ernest Mangnall, in the years leading up to World War One.

Charlie skippered United through their first glorious era, encompassing League Championships in 1908 and 1911 and the FA Cup in 1909, all achieved against a background of bitter unrest among professional players, who were being heavily exploited by their employers and the game's authorities. Both as an irresistible force with the ball at his feet, and as an indomitable pioneer of the sorely-needed players' union, the tallish, slim north-easterner – dubbed 'The Ghost In Boots' for his unnaturally pallid complexion – was an inspiration.

Roberts was recognised by his peers as the finest centre-half of the Edwardian era, yet he won only three England caps and none after the age of 21. It was true that Billy Wedlock of Bristol City, the man who kept him on the international sidelines, was a splendid performer in his own right, but Charlie's dearth of honours was interpreted widely – and certainly everywhere north of Watford – as an unwarranted reprisal for his tireless labour in pursuit of improved pay and conditions for footballers.

He arrived in Manchester in April 1904 after United had beaten off competition from Derby County, Nottingham Forest and Manchester City to sign the multi-talented 20-year-old from Grimsby Town for £600.

Rapidly he emerged as the natural captain of the promising side Mangnall was assembling, and which would earn promotion to the top flight in 1905/06 after narrowly missing out in the previous campaign.

In that era, before the full evolution of a stopper at the heart of every defence, the wearer of the number-five shirt was expected to play an integral part in attack, and Charlie was admirably equipped for the task.

Though not short of brawn, being an implacable tackler and aerially dominant, it was for the use of brain that he was most celebrated. Blessed with an instinctive positional sense, he was a shrewd interceptor and, having gained possession, he rarely wasted it. Indeed, his distribution was invariably constructive, often penetrative, and his measured service to star forwards such as Billy Meredith and Sandy Turnbull contributed hugely to the hat-trick of trophies which established United as one of the England's top clubs.

Another crucial factor was his remarkable energy, which enabled him to pound repeatedly from box to box and earned him the tag of the Reds' sixth forward and third defender (the two full-backs being seen as the only two fully-fledged defenders in those days). He was, in effect, their seat of power, lifting them when they were down and eternally urging them forward, a similar function to Roy Keane's in the modern era.

In matters political, Charlie was no less formidable, his strength of character reflected in his passionate conviction that he and his fellow players were being grievously wronged and in his determination to do something about it. To that end he was a major figure in the reformation of the defunct union, and came perilously close to leading a strike in 1909.

The feelings of resentment had been simmering for years but they came to a head in the summer months after United had lifted the FA Cup. The Football Association attempted to ban membership of the union but some United men, led by the intrepid Roberts, refused to sign contracts to that effect. He threatened to set up a breakaway club and even coined a name, 'The Outcasts', and a team picture appeared controversially in the press.

However, the strike was called off just hours before the new season was due to kick off, when the FA agreed to recognise the union, which he would go on to chair. Of course, the clubs still held the whip hand through the iniquitous rules which allowed them to retain individuals' registrations indefinitely, a degrading system which would pertain for another half-century.

Still, Charlie and company had struck a significant blow. He returned to work with a will, never complaining about his apparent victimisation by the England selectors, and his performances became ever more imperious as United went on to their second title.

In August 1913, aged 30, he was transferred to Oldham Athletic for a club record £1,750 and enjoyed a stirring Indian summer with the Latics, whom he skippered to runners-up spot in the First Division in 1914/15. Indeed, they finished only one point behind the champions, Everton, and 15 ahead of an extremely poor United side. Charlie Roberts was a man of substance to the end.

CHARLES ROBERTS

BORN:	Darlington, County Durham, 6 April 1883.
HONOURS:	League Championship 07/08, 10/11. FA Cup 08/09. 3 England caps (05).
OTHER CLUBS:	Grimsby Town 03/04 (31, 4); Oldham Athletic 13/14-14/15 (72, 2).
MANAGER:	Oldham Athletic (21-22).
DIED:	Manchester, 7 August 1939.

GAMES	302
GOALS	23

SANDY TURNBULL

· ·

1906/07 → 1914/15

Brave and brilliant, independent and irreverent, ultimately tragic . . . Sandy Turnbull was one of the earliest in the long line of Manchester United heroes it was impossible to ignore. His free-scoring contribution as the Reds' first outstanding team collected two League crowns and the FA Cup in the wee small years of the 20th century was enough to earn a gilded niche in any meaningful hall of fame dedicated to the club.

But there was another, equally colourful, but distinctly darker dimension to 'Blithesome Sandy', as the chunky little Scot was dubbed by doting supporters in a rousing contemporary terrace anthem. That he was a born rebel, refusing so contemptuously to doff his cap to United directors that he was fined on several occasions for 'insubordination', wasn't the half of it. Even his prominent part in the initially outlawed players' union, and his enthusiastic embracing of the industrial action which speeded its overdue recognition, did not complete the picture.

No, the vein of Turnbull's notoriety ran far deeper. Always sure of his own worth, and unshakeably convinced that his wages as a footballer didn't reflect it, he ended his days at his first club, Manchester City, by being banned for his role in an illegal payments scandal.

Then, after nearly a decade of glory as a Red, in 1915 he was accused of central involvement in rigging a game with Liverpool as part of a betting scam and suspended for life from playing the game he had illuminated so vividly.

The son of a miner and a pit worker himself in his early teens, Turnbull established himself rapidly after joining City as a 17-year-old in 1902, starring as the Blues won the Second Division Championship and the FA Cup in his first two seasons. But then the storm over cash irregularities broke over Hyde Road and he was sidelined until his sentence was commuted in December 1906.

Then, the canny United boss Ernest Mangnall stole a march over his rivals by signing Sandy and three key team-mates, and a brave new era in Manchester football was under way.

Described by a newspaperman as being wide of shoulder, quick of feet and active of brain, inside-forward Turnbull lost no time in making an impact, nodding the only goal of the game on debut against Aston Villa on New Year's Day. The ammunition had been supplied by former City comrade and new United colleague Billy Meredith, the sensationally gifted Welsh winger, and the crowd at the Reds' Bank Street headquarters went wild.

In the seasons that followed, the high-class duo continued to hone what appeared to be an instinctive understanding, and the combative Ayrshireman also meshed productively with his namesake Jimmy 'Trunky' Turnbull, who excelled as leader of the forward line.

Solidly-built Sandy was a constant menace to opposing defenders. Though he could appear to be drifting aimlessly, suddenly he would explode into action and was a lethal opportunist, a finisher by turns deft and savage. For a small fellow he was a titan in the air and he was intelligent, too, being adept at decoy runs which created space for his fellow attackers.

In 1907/08 Turnbull netted 25 times in 30 League outings as United rampaged to their first title, then he defied injury to contribute the winner – a tap-in after a shot from Harold Halse had rattled Bristol City's crossbar – in the 1909 FA Cup Final.

When Old Trafford replaced the odious swamp that was Bank Street in February 1910, the Reds' marksman-in-chief struck the first goal in the new stadium, albeit in a 4-3 defeat by Liverpool, and he registered 18 times during the following campaign, when a second Championship was secured.

Always, though, there was a hint of strife in the air wherever Turnbull was involved, so it wasn't surprising that he was the first man to be sent off in a Manchester derby, in 1907, or that he was suspended for arguing with the caretaker manager, J J Bentley, in 1914.

The match-fixing, however, was to prove a tumult too far, and when he went off to war in 1916, initially as a member of the so-called footballers' battalion of the Middlesex Regiment, there was little expectation that the disgraced veteran – surely one of the finest of all uncapped Scots – would play at the top club level again.

In the event, he never got the chance. Though his body was never found, it is virtually certain that Lance-Sergeant Alexander Turnbull, a 33-year-old father of four, died in a skirmish outside the village of Cherisy, near Arras in northern France.

There is evidence to suggest that he battled courageously to the end, and testimony from men who fought at his side has him as 'a father to us all and the most popular man in the regiment.' Clearly his comrades held him in immense affection, just as he was revered by the Old Trafford faithful and by team-mates to whom he was unswervingly loyal.

'Blithesome Sandy' was no angel, but even if he bent the rules from time to time – and it must be remembered that he played in an era when footballers were both scantly rewarded and ruthlessly exploited – it does not seem fanciful to conclude that his heart was in the right place.

ALEXANDER TURNBULL
BORN: Hurlford, Ayrshire, 1884.
HONOURS: League Championship 07/08, 10/11. FA Cup 08/09.
OTHER CLUBS: Manchester City 02/03-05/06 (110, 53).
DIED: Cherisy, France, 3 May 1917.

GAMES 247
GOALS 101

ALEX BELL

1902/03 → 1912/13

There wasn't the faintest suggestion of showmanship about Alex Bell. Unlike some of his more famous colleagues, his footsteps were never dogged by cartoonists and supporters didn't gasp in anticipation whenever the ball was at his feet. But when the chips were down, no member of Manchester United's first great side fulfilled his purpose more meticulously than the South-African born Scottish international left-half.

Signed as a centre-forward from Scottish non-Leaguers Ayr Parkhouse for £700 in January 1903, Bell made scant early impact, but when he was converted to what was essentially a defensive midfield role he was a revelation.

If his hallmarks were quiet consistency and formidable steeliness, still he was skilful enough to carry the ball out from the back when his characteristic good sense dictated that it was safe, and occasionally he would surprise the crowd with a deliciously delicate flourish.

After replacing Sandy Robertson as the Reds' regular number-six in 1904/05, Bell became a regular for nearly a decade, until joining Blackburn for £1,000 in the summer of 1913. Having picked up his third title medal in his first term at Ewood Park, he became the only player from Ernest Mangnall's successful team to remain in football after laying aside his boots, enlisting as a trainer with Coventry, then Manchester City.

ALEXANDER BELL
BORN: Cape Town, South Africa, 1882.
HONOURS: League Championship 07/08, 10/11. FA Cup 08/09. Second Division promotion 05/06.
1 Scotland cap (12).
OTHER CLUBS: Blackburn Rovers 13/14-14/15 (11, 0).
DIED: Chorlton-cum-Hardy, Manchester, 30 November 1934.

GAMES 309
GOALS 10

DICK DUCKWORTH

1903/04 → 1913/14

Mancunian Dick Duckworth was a wing-half both quick and clever, a comprehensively talented all-round footballer whose cocktail of fire and flair, poise and industry, effectively made him a sixth forward in Ernest Mangnall's free-flowing combination.

If Billy Meredith was unchallenged for star billing, and Sandy Turnbull supplied the lion's share of the goals, then unquestionably the redoubtable half-back line of Duckworth, Roberts and Bell were both the heartbeat and backbone of the side. And although he was the only non-international of the trio – the nearest he came to a full cap were appearances for the Football League and a Commonwealth X1 – dynamic Dick was no poor relation.

When he was recruited from non-League Newton Heath Athletic in October 1903 he was, like Bell, a rookie centre-forward, and initially he became something of a utility man. A potent dribbler with an eye for goal, he struck six times in five games during the spring of 1905, when United missed out narrowly on promotion to the top flight.

But it was at right-half, having ousted Alex Downie, that Duckworth was to thrive throughout the Reds' first golden age, proving particularly effective in tandem with Meredith on the right flank. He remained a top performer until falling prey to serious knee trouble in the autumn of 1913.

Later his son, also Dick, played and managed in the League's lower divisions.

RICHARD HARGREAVES DUCKWORTH
BORN: Collyhurst, Manchester, 14 September 1882.
HONOURS: League Championship 07/08, 10/11. FA Cup 08/09. Second Division promotion 05/06.
DIED: Not known.

GAMES 254
GOALS 11

GEORGE WALL

1905/06 → 1914/15

What a gem was wee Georgie Wall. An explosive, dashing, feisty flankman who contributed a century of goals from the left wing, he presented his markers with an unenviable dilemma.

If they attempted to usher the hard-sprinting north-easterner down the touchline the chances were that he would outpace them and deliver a trademark searching cross towards the head of the elusive Sandy Turnbull; but if they showed him inside, he had a disconcerting habit of peppering the goal with his own high-velocity missiles.

United boss Ernest Mangnall signed Wall from Barnsley for £175 in April 1906, then watched him score the winner at Clapton Orient on his debut. His presence helped to clinch promotion to the top flight that term and soon his combination of direct running and often spectacular finishing had earned him international status. Serial glory followed, and he retained enough zest in his mid thirties to join Oldham for £200 after the war.

GEORGE WALL
BORN: Boldon Colliery, County Durham, 20 February 1885.
HONOURS: League Championship 07/08, 10/11. FA Cup 08/09.
7 England caps (07-13).
OTHER CLUBS: Barnsley 03/04-05/06 (75, 24); Oldham Athletic 19/20-20/1 (74, 12); Hamilton Academical 21/2; Rochdale 22/3 (30, 1).
DIED: Manchester, 1962.

GAMES **319**
GOALS **100**

ENOCH WEST

1910/11 → 1914/15

Enoch 'Knocker' West was destined for a murky end to his football career, but however history judges his involvement in the betting scandal which earned him a ban which was not lifted for 30 years – and it should never be forgotten that he plied his trade at a time when players were exploited ruthlessly by their employers – there was no gainsaying the former miner's ability to supply goals in copious quantities.

Having been acquired from Nottingham Forest in June 1910 to replace Jimmy Turnbull as namesake Sandy's strike partner, 'Knocker' obliged by becoming the club's top scorer in his first three seasons at Old Trafford.

Most memorably he struck 19 times in 1910/11, including an adroit back-header from a Meredith corner which enabled United to clinch the title in their last game, at home to Sunderland.

Equipped with a fearsome shot, West was also a robust charger of 'keepers who relished a physical contest, though as the Reds toiled towards the wrong end of the table shortly before the war, his scoring touch declined. Then came that sorry exit.

ENOCH JAMES WEST
BORN: Hucknall Torkard, Nottinghamshire, 31 March 1886.
HONOURS: League Championship 10/11.
OTHER CLUBS: Nottingham Forest 05/06-09/10 (168, 93).
DIED: Salford, Lancashire, September 1965.

GAMES **181**
GOALS **80**

HAROLD HALSE

1907/08 → 1911/12

Harold Halse was a snapper-up of unconsidered trifles, a man who placed footballs into nets regularly and with the minimum of fuss. Not for him the extravagant flourish or the bombshell strike from long distance; he was more likely to virtually pass the ball between the posts, often from close range, occasionally from an acute angle.

The dapper little Londoner, who had scored with prodigious freedom for non-League Southend United before becoming a Red in March 1908, gave notice of this invaluable knack in the first minute of his top-flight debut, when he slipped a shot past the Sheffield Wednesday goalkeeper.

Thereafter he continued to demonstrate it for nearly half a decade, forging a lethally productive link with Sandy Turnbull before joining Aston Villa in July 1912.

Harold's predatory gift was never illustrated to more devastating effect than in the 1911 Charity Shield, when he struck six times against Swindon Town, and it was entirely predictable that he scored twice on his sole appearance for England.

HAROLD JAMES HALSE
BORN: Stratford, London, 1 January 1886.
HONOURS: League Championship 10/11.
FA Cup 08/09. 1 England cap (09).
OTHER CLUBS: Clapton Orient 05/06 (3, 2); Aston Villa 12/13 (31,21); Chelsea 13/14-20/21 (96, 23); Charlton Athletic 21/2-22/3 (21, 5).
DIED: Colchester, Essex, 25 March 1949.

GAMES **125**
GOALS **56**

HARRY MOGER

1903/04 → 1911/12

Giant goalkeepers are par for the course in the modern era. Manchester United fans became used to Peter Schmeichel practically obscuring the net from the view of opposition attackers, and Edwin van der Sar, though rather more slender, is even taller.

But in Edwardian times, when many people were not so well nourished, a 6ft 3in custodian was the exception rather than the rule, and such was Harry Moger.

However, big Harry was no hulking brute, being distinctly willowy of build, but he was strong in body and mind, more than capable of meeting the bullish physical challenges that were part of the game when he was in his prime.

After arriving from Southern League Southampton in 1903, Moger made a distinctly nervy start, but soon he settled and throughout a period of unprecedented success for the Reds, he radiated an assurance which spread throughout his defence.

With his huge stretch, he was particularly adept at fielding crosses, yet he was agile enough, too, to deal efficiently with ground assaults and United fans were outraged that he was never capped.

HENRY HERBERT MOGER
BORN: Southampton, September 1879.
HONOURS: League Championship 07/08, 10/11. FA Cup 08/09.
DIED: Manchester, June 1927.

GAMES **266**
GOALS **0**

JOE SPENCE

1919/20 → 1932/33

In footballing terms, certainly in Manchester United circles, Joe Spence deserves be a household name. After all, only four men have scored more League goals for the Red Devils – and Bobby Charlton, Jack Rowley, Denis Law and Dennis Viollet all occupy revered niches in Old Trafford folklore.

It may be contended that the dashing north-easterner touched his zenith some three-quarters of a century ago, and that therefore the supporters who witnessed him in all his prolific glory are, inevitably, shrinking drastically in number as each year passes. However, such cherished figures as Billy Meredith and Charlie Roberts plied their trade even before Spence, yet their places among the club's legends are secure.

Presumably then, the only explanation for Joe's comparative obscurity must be that he peaked at a time when the Old Trafford trophy cabinet was not exactly groaning under the weight of accumulated silverware. In fact, ironically enough in view of the current stature of the two clubs, it took a move to Chesterfield (via Bradford City) before the free-scoring centre-forward cum outside-right pocketed his first medal. By then he had played more games and scored more goals for the Reds than anyone in their history to that point, his appearance record surviving until Bill Foulkes exceeded his tally in the mid-1960s.

Joe Spence was born in Throckley, slightly to the west of Newcastle and just up the road from Blaydon, shortly before the end of the 19th century, and before long he was showing signs of exceptional footballing prowess, netting 42 of his school team's 49 goals in one season.

However, such were the economic necessities of the times that Joe was a coal miner at the age of 13, joining the Army four years later and serving in the Machine Gun Corps towards the end of the First World War. Still, football had its place and he helped his battalion to win the Army Cup, while his long-term potential was hinted at by a handful of guest appearances for Liverpool.

Happily for United, when Joe was demobbed he did not head for Merseyside, instead returning to Tyneside where he featured for local side Scotswood, from which he was recruited to the Old Trafford cause as an amateur in March 1919.

Joe's instant impact was dramatic, as he scored four goals on his debut at home to Bury in the Lancashire Section – a wartime competition which was on the point of winding up as peace had resumed – and he turned professional without further ado.

For the next 14 campaigns the story of Joe Spence was one of consistent personal excellence in a distinctly erratic side which yo-yoed between the First and Second Divisions, and seven times he was either top or joint-top scorer. He was versatile enough to play at centre-forward, inside-right or outside-right, but in broad terms, the first few years of his Old Trafford tenure were spent as the central spearhead, then he switched to the flank to fill the void created by the return of Meredith to Manchester City.

Joe was a thrilling entertainer, skilful and industrious, quick and eager, and a spectacular finisher; his lion-hearted combativeness was balanced by a natural chivalry, and he was utterly loyal to the United cause. The supporters warmed unreservedly to the vibrant Spence style and the cry of 'Give it to Joe' became a familiar refrain.

Too often, though, it seemed he was ploughing a lone furrow, and after two seasons of relative mid-table security, the Reds were relegated from the top flight as bottom club in 1921/22. However, even during that dismal campaign, Joe gave the fans something to shout about with a hat-trick in a 3-1 home victory over Manchester City.

It took three years before United regained their place among the elite, by which time Spence was in his pomp and he was rewarded in 1926 with what would prove to be his only two full England caps and an outing for the Football League.

Back at club level, he enjoyed his most bountiful season in 1927/28 when he netted 22 times in 38 First Division matches, though it was not enough to prevent a term of travail near the bottom of the table. The downward trend culminated in demotion in 1930/31, when poor results coincided with a financial crisis which threatened the club's future. Still Joe soldiered on willingly, giving two more years of sterling service before being released, at the age of 34 in June 1933, to join Bradford City, then fellow members of Division Two. It was a low-key exit for a man who must surely have attained loftier heights had he played for a more successful club. Even in the twilight of his career, he offered further evidence for such a theory by sparkling in his first term at Valley Parade, where he topped the goal charts with 23 strikes as the Bantams went close to promotion.

Come 1935 the sprightly veteran switched to Chesterfield, where he collected that long-awaited gong as the Spireites lifted the Third Division (North) Championship. When Joe retired in 1938 he was in his 40th year and his total of 613 League appearances was a record. In addition, he played in 19 out of the 20 League campaigns between the wars, a unique achievement.

The memory of Joe Spence should be honoured. He never played for a great team but, as the record books demonstrate beyond doubt, he was a tremendous footballer.

JOSEPH WATERS SPENCE	
BORN:	Throckley, Northumberland, 15 December 1898.
HONOURS:	Second Division promotion 24/5. 2 England caps (26).
OTHER CLUBS:	Bradford City 33/4-34/5 (75, 27); Chesterfield 35/6-37/8 (58, 10).
DIED:	31 December 1966.

GAMES **510**

GOALS **168**

FRANK BARSON

· ·

1922/23 → 1927/28

Truly Frank Barson was a Red devil. A buccaneering, fearsomely forceful centre-half whose prodigious muscles had been honed in his previous existence as a blacksmith in his native Yorkshire, he must surely have won more than his solitary England cap but for a woeful disciplinary record and a penchant for straight talking that made him influential enemies in the corridors of football power.

Barson was lionised by Old Trafford fans for his voracious appetite for the game and his all-consuming passion for the United cause, and by his team-mates for his inspirational captaincy and infectious bonhomie during troubled financial times for the club.

A big man with jutting chest and mangled nose, Frank threw himself into his work, and his play, with boundless enthusiasm and woe betide anything that got in his way. His detractors saw him as a thug, and portrayed him as some sort of bogeyman, but his countless supporters swore that he was the kindest, best-hearted of fellows, often victimised by referees swayed by his dark reputation.

His problem, they admitted, was that he tended to be impetuous, and when he felt wronged he sought retribution instantly and openly, with no hint of artifice or, indeed, of lasting malice. Thus he was ordered to leave the field on numerous occasions – some accounts suggest there were a dozen dismissals during his tempestuous career – which scuppered all hope of international advancement.

Barson made his name with Barnsley, emerged as a towering talent with Aston Villa, then joined newly relegated Manchester United for £5,000 in August 1922, the Old Trafford board evidently undeterred by a lurid, and probably apocryphal, tale that he had pulled a gun on the Villa boss.

Rapidly he became a much-needed leader with the Reds, training like a demon and getting the best out of his new comrades. Duly he led United back to the First Division in 1925, and furnished a clue to the genuine nature of his character after being given the much-coveted landlordship of a pub as a reward for his efforts in the promotion push. When he opened his doors for the first time he was engulfed by back-slappers and so quickly became sick of their sycophancy that he tossed the keys of the place to a waiter, then strode out and never came back.

After helping United to consolidate their place at the higher level, no easy task in that lean era, he was freed to join Watford as a 37-year-old in 1928. Inevitably Frank Barson is remembered for the colour and controversy which so often surrounded him, but he was a majestic footballer, too, and that should never be forgotten.

FRANK BARSON

BORN:	Grimethorpe, Yorkshire, 10 April 1891.
HONOURS:	Second Division promotion 24/5. 1 England cap (20).
OTHER CLUBS:	Barnsley 11/12-19/20 (91, 0); Aston Villa 19/20-21/2 (92, 10); Watford 28/9 (10, 1); Hartlepools United 29/30 (9, 2); Wigan Borough 30/1 (19, 0).
DIED:	Birmingham, 13 September 1968.

GAMES **152**

GOALS **4**

LAL HILDITCH

1919/20 → 1931/32

Lal Hilditch was an elegant, beautifully balanced half-back who served Manchester United for more than a decade with unswerving loyalty but precious little luck or international recognition.

In some accounts, the wholesome Lal sounds almost too good to be true. As well as being scrupulously fair, he was selfless, dedicated and kind, commendably Corinthian attributes which complemented his versatility, intelligence and a highly developed positional sense which might have been his most valuable asset as a footballer.

Admittedly, he was never the quickest or the most creative, and though his physical courage was never in question, his stamina and strength were limited and his overall health was less than robust. He suffered more than his fair share of injuries, too, which cost him a place in the side which won promotion in 1924/25.

Only six weeks into his United career he represented England in an unofficial Victory international, but never gained a full cap, possibly because he was perceived to lack ruthlessness.

Lal's service to his one club extended to a spell as caretaker manager when John Chapman was sacked in 1926/27.

CLARENCE GEORGE HILDITCH
BORN: Hartford, Cheshire, 2 June 1894.
DIED: Not known.

GAMES	322
GOALS	7

JACK SILCOCK

1919/20 → 1933/34

Many perceptive observers of the Georgian era of English football ranked Jack Silcock as the finest left-back in the land. The superbly athletic Lancastrian was memorably bold and stylish in the heat of the action, delightfully unassuming away from it – an appealing combination in any age.

Silcock was working as a miner when he joined United as a teenage amateur in 1916, having been spotted by John Robson while the Old Trafford boss was scouting one of the rookie defender's team-mates at local club Atherton.

Soon there was no doubt about the wisdom of Robson's snap judgement. As he bedded in at United, long-striding Jack revealed courage, composure and impressive all-round ability. He challenged effectively both in the air and on the deck, he was composed and invariably constructive, and quickly he won renown for his accurate volleyed clearances, which became a Silcock trademark. He was brave, too, once insisting on playing in a match despite having his head stitched following a pit accident earlier that day.

An archetypal one-club man, Jack later ran a pub in the United heartland of Stretford.

JOHN SILCOCK
BORN: New Springs, Lancashire, 15 January 1898.
HONOURS: Second Division promotion 24/5.
3 England caps (21-23).
DIED: Ashton-under-Lyne, Lancashire, 28 June 1966.

GAMES	449
GOALS	2

CHARLIE MOORE

1919/20 → 1929/30

On the field Charlie Moore was an unshowy, consistently excellent right-back for a decade; off it he was Manchester United's entertainer-in-chief. Together with his close chum Joe Spence, the endlessly congenial Midlander once sang a duet on a street corner in Portsmouth to see how much cash they could raise, and while estimates of the proceeds vary in different accounts, clearly an uproarious time was had by all.

Moore went straight into United's first team after arriving from non-League Hednesford Town in 1919, but his progress was interrupted by a severe ankle injury which caused him to miss the whole of the 1921/22 campaign.

At that point Charlie was written off in some quarters – even his insurance deal was calculated – but he proved the doubters comprehensively wrong. He had always displayed plenty of heart, but on his return he added a certain poise which transformed an adequate performer into an outstanding one, and he enjoyed another eight terms in the limelight.

Probably only the fact that he spent so long in an average side cost him England recognition.

CHARLES WILLIAM MOORE
BORN: Cheslyn Hay, Staffordshire, 3 June 1898.
HONOURS: Second Division promotion 24/5.
DIED: 9 March 1966.

GAMES	328
GOALS	0

NEIL McBAIN

1921/22 → 1922/23

Neil McBain was a footballing sophisticate, but an apparently provocative refusal to consort socially with some of his team-mates outside working hours – notably the gregarious Yorkshireman Frank Barson – might well have cost him his future with Manchester United.

The Scot, a £4,600 acquisition from Ayr United in November 1921, was a half-back of exquisite style, an imaginative passer blessed with smooth control and majestic aerial ability.

He demonstrated his quality plainly during his 14-month sojourn in Manchester, collecting the first of his three full caps. But it's believed he resented being played out of position, at inside-left, to accommodate the newly-arrived Barson during his second term, and that he fell out with various players. Whatever the exact truth, certainly there was friction, and in January 1923 McBain was sold to Everton for £4,000.

In 1947 the Scot became the Football League's oldest player when he turned out as an an emergency goalkeeper for New Brighton, aged 51 years and four months.

NEIL McBAIN
BORN: Campbeltown, Argyllshire, 15 November 1895.
HONOURS: 3 Scotland caps (22-24).
OTHER CLUBS: Hamilton Academical; Ayr United 14/15;
Kilmarnock; Third Lanark; Everton 22/3-25/6 (97, 1);
St Johnstone 26/7-27/8; Liverpool 27/8-28/9 (12, 0);
Watford 28/9-30/1 (85, 5); New Brighton 46/7 (1, 0).
DIED: 13 May 1974.

GAMES	43
GOALS	2

BUSBY
AND
BEYOND

It was the autumn of 1945 and Manchester United were in an unholy mess. That they were strapped for cash was nothing new – twice in their history they had hovered perilously close to extinction before being rescued providently by local benefactors, first the wealthy brewer John Henry Davies and then James Gibson, a clothing magnate – but this time there was a demoralising extra dimension to their distress.

Though Old Trafford had never been a specific target for German bombs, its location just along the road from the sprawling Trafford Park industrial estate, the strategically important Manchester Ship Canal and the busy docks made the ground horribly vulnerable should the aim of the Luftwaffe err even the tiniest bit.

Sure enough, the Reds' headquarters were devastated by two raids in the terror-ridden winter and spring of 1940/41. Most of the main stand was reduced to rubble, the dressing rooms and offices were wrecked and the pitch was disfigured by craters and scorchmarks.

That was the grimly desolate scene which met the gaze of an immaculately dressed stranger as he strode across the pock-marked terraces from which weeds were beginning to sprout.

Though there was an air of maturity, a certain gravitas about him as he coolly appraised his surroundings, it was difficult to judge his age – he turned out to be 34 – but there was something else, too. The expression was gently benevolent as he puffed on his pipe, but there was steel aplenty in that steady gaze, the innate authority of a man born to command.

Faced with such destruction, many people would have despaired. But Matt Busby, Manchester United's newly appointed manager, was able to look beyond the sorry ruins of the stricken stadium. He had a vision . . .

The first of Matt Busby's three magnificent teams, the breathtakingly entertaining combination which won the FA Cup in 1948.
Left to right, back row: Matt Busby (manager), John Anderson, Jack Warner, Allenby Chilton, Jack Crompton, Henry Cockburn, John Aston, Tom Curry (trainer).
Front row: Jimmy Delaney, Johnny Morris, Johnny Carey (captain), Jack Rowley, Stan Pearson, Charlie Mitten.

NOTE: The following pages contain profiles of every Manchester United player since the war. Appended to them are statistics covering the Football League and Premiership; the FA Cup; The Football League Cup in all its guises; the European Cup and UEFA Champions League; the European Cup Winners' Cup; the European Super Cup; the World Club Championship; the FIFA Club World Championship; and the FA Charity/Community Shield.

JOHNNY CAREY

1937/38 → 1952/53

Johnny Carey was a thoroughbred footballer who exuded style and composure as Manchester United's first post-war captain and one of the most accomplished full-backs the British game has produced.

A soft-brogued Dubliner who earned the epithet 'Gentleman John' for his scrupulous fairness and unruffled demeanour no matter how dire the provocation, he reflected perfectly the Corinthian ideal of his manager and thus was the ideal character to represent Matt Busby on the field.

Carey won every domestic prize available to him, his collection of honours including the Footballer of the Year award in 1949, an accolade underlined by the identity of the only previous holder, Stanley Matthews.

He had crossed the Irish Sea to Old Trafford in 1936, a journey to find fortune which owed plenty to chance. The Red Devils' chief scout, Louis Rocca, had been in Dublin to evaluate another rookie, but found his eye riveted to the young Carey, whose skill and elegance were readily apparent.

The shrewd talent-spotter wasted no time in agreeing a £200 fee with St James' Gate, the boy's club, yet after the elation of signing for the Reds came a temporary deflation for Johnny, over which he chuckled later. On arrival in Manchester, the impressionable 17-year-old spied a newspaper hoarding which proclaimed 'United sign star,' and he jumped to the uncharacteristically immodest conclusion that he must be the subject of the story. But on buying a paper he found that the 'star' in question was Blackburn Rovers' Ernie Thompson, and a mere two lines at the bottom of the page were devoted to the acquisition of one J Carey. What happened to Thompson? He disappeared into obscurity after three games.

For Johnny, then an inside-forward, the 1937/38 season proved momentous. Still only 18, he broke into the United side, helping to secure promotion from the Second Division, and also won his first full cap. But just as his career was gathering momentum, the Second World War intervened and he was faced with an agonising decision. Hailing from neutral Ireland, he had the right to go home if he wished, but the highly principled youngster reckoned that 'a country that gives me my living is worth fighting for' and he joined the British Army.

By 1945, when something like normal football service was resumed, United had acquired a new and visionary manager, Matt Busby, who recognised in Carey's quiet authority and integrity the makings of a natural leader, and duly made him club captain. He was impressed, too, by the Irishman's versatility – over the years he played in every position for United except outside-left, even excelling as stopgap goalkeeper – and, being well blessed for forwards, converted him to right-back.

It was an inspired decision. John's immaculate ball control and imaginative distribution melded with his clever positional play, aerial excellence and crisp tackling – despite his virtuous reputation, he was not averse to the discreet application of physical force when necessary – to create what was something of a novelty at the time, a constructive defender. He found himself in charge of an exhilarating side whose League record between the 1946/47 and 1950/51 seasons was the impressive but frustrating one of second, second, second, fourth and second. The title arrived at last in 1951/52, with John now employed as a polished wing-half, proving enormously influential in his more advanced role.

Meanwhile consolation for the Championship near-misses was found in 1948 when Carey lifted the FA Cup after Blackpool had been beaten 4-2 in a glorious exhibition of fluent football. The skipper could take much of the credit: as well as his customarily smooth display on the pitch, he had contributed a quietly stirring half-time pep-talk when the Reds were 2-1 in arrears.

On the international front, too, Carey prospered. Thanks to his Army service, he was eligible until 1949 to play for Northern Ireland as well as the country of his birth, and he did so with distinction. His most memorable achievement with the Republic was leading them to a 2-0 victory over England in 1949, a further personal highlight being his captaincy of the Rest of Europe against Great Britain two years earlier.

Carey retired as a player in 1953, turning down a coaching post at Old Trafford to enter management, bringing flair and dignity to enterprising stints with four clubs over nearly two decades and remaining 'Gentleman John' to the last.

JOHN JOSEPH CAREY

BORN:	Dublin, 23 February 1919.
HONOURS:	League Championship 51/2. FA Cup 47/8. 29 Republic of Ireland caps (37-53), 7 Northern Ireland caps (46-49). FWA Footballer of the Year 49.
MANAGER:	Blackburn Rovers (53-58), Everton (58-61), Leyton Orient (61-63), Nottingham Forest (63-68), Blackburn Rovers (69-71).
DIED:	Macclesfield, Cheshire, 22 August 1995.

GAMES **346**
GOALS 18

STAN PEARSON

1937/38 → 1953/54

Stan Pearson was a lovely footballer, a beguiling mixture of subtle visionary and unflashy technician; and he was one of the most satisfyingly complete inside-forwards of his day.

He provided the attacking brains, and a lot of the goals, for Matt Busby's first swashbucklingly attractive United side, and but for the fact that he numbered Wilf Mannion and the incomparable Raich Carter among his contemporaries, it is reasonable to suppose that the unassuming Lancastrian would have added significantly to his inappropriately meagre total of eight England caps.

A supporter of his local club since the age of seven, Salford-born Stan rose irresistibly through the ranks of junior football before achieving his boyhood ambition by joining the Red Devils, signing amateur forms as a 16-year-old in 1935 and turning professional 18 months later. There followed a sensational senior debut in November 1937, when he set up four goals in a 7-1 victory at Chesterfield, and by season's end he was a powerfully emerging force in the team that secured promotion to the old First Division.

With the gifted rookie on the threshold of what promised to be a majestic career, the war intervened, but he played on in the forces and when the conflict ended the unscathed 26-year-old was approaching his prime. Then, slotting stylishly into one of the most exhilarating of all forward lines – Jimmy Delaney, Johnny Morris, Jack Rowley, Pearson himself and Charlie Mitten – he became a key factor as Busby's buccaneering side enchanted the massive post-war crowds, so hungry for entertainment after six years of being denied top-level soccer.

Pearson scored heavily enough, but arguably his greatest worth was in creating opportunities for team-mates through an instinctive awareness of where they would run and a priceless knack of reaching them with adroit first-time distribution. His hallmark was accuracy, whether delivering raking crossfield passes or delightful close-range flicks and glides, and though there was nothing flamboyant about either the man or his method, the supporters loved him for his craftsmanship.

He was never the fastest fellow afield and his shot was not the most powerful – the majority of his strikes coming from inside the box – but he made up for that in ample measure through his sharp intelligence, masterful ball control and remarkable stamina which enabled him to forage ceaselessly for possession.

Yet even though Stan and his attacking partners could take the breath away, the United side they graced so thrillingly was to endure a nightmarish succession of Championship near-misses and they did not claim the coveted crown until 1952. However, there was rich compensation in 1948 when they beat Blackpool to win the FA Cup in what was recognised as the most captivating final to that date. The Seasiders, who included Stanley Matthews in their ranks, led 2-1 at half-time but United fought back to win 4-2, with Stan supplying the crucial third goal ten minutes from the end.

That year, at the age of 29, the Old Trafford stalwart was rewarded for his sparkling form with an overdue international call-up, and he continued to represent his country on an occasional basis for the next four years, his most memorable contribution being the two goals which beat Scotland at Hampden Park in 1952.

Back on the club front, Pearson's consistency became a byword in Manchester and he missed only a handful of games through injury before a combination of age, and the new wave of precocious youngsters known as the Busby Babes, overtook him in 1953/54.

That February he was sold to Second Division Bury for £4,500 and he served the Shakers royally for three years before moving on to Chester of the Third Division (North) as player-boss in 1957. Still in splendid physical fettle as he approached his 40th birthday, Stan helped his new club to reach the Welsh Cup Final in 1958 before retiring as a player in 1959.

But it is at Old Trafford that Stan Pearson will be remembered most vividly, for his sumptuous ability and unswerving loyalty during an uplifting period in the club's history. Manchester United might have known greater players . . . but not many.

STANLEY CLARE PEARSON

BORN: Salford, Lancashire, 11 January 1919.
HONOURS: League Championship 51/2. FA Cup 47/8. 8 England caps (48-52).
OTHER CLUBS: Bury 53/4-57/8 (122, 56); Chester 57/8-58/9 (57, 16).
MANAGER: Chester (57-61).
DIED: Alderley Edge, Cheshire, 17 February 1997

GAMES	346
GOALS	149

41

42

JIMMY DELANEY

1946/47 → 1950/51

Jimmy Delaney became renowned among his contemporaries as the finest bargain Matt Busby ever struck, yet when the rookie Manchester United manager paid Celtic £4,000 for the 31-year-old right winger in February 1946, the snipers had a field day.

The balding newcomer, a previous victim of chronic arm and shoulder injuries, was dismissed as 'Old Brittle Bones'. According to the critics he was past his peak, a waste of money, a whimsical acquisition, at the very best a luxury which the club, poverty-stricken after Old Trafford had been bombed by Hitler, simply could not afford.

Indeed, even the future Sir Matt saw Jimmy as a short-term signing, good for perhaps a couple of seasons while the Reds reviewed their resources and constructed sound foundations for the future.

In the event, the maestro who had played a compelling part in bringing the Scottish title to Parkhead in 1936 and 1938, and lifting the Scottish Cup in 1937, confounded the doubters by completing four and a half campaigns with United, bringing balance and priceless experience to one of the greatest forward lines that ever lived, as well as regaining his Scottish international berth.

With Jimmy in the number-seven shirt, United finished as Championship runners-up in the first three terms after the war and won the FA Cup in glorious style in 1948, but surely in retrospect the Delaney success story does not come as such a surprise. After all, during his Celtic sojourn, when he operated at centre-forward as well as outside-right and netted 79 times in 178 outings, Jimmy was dubbed by shrewd judges as one of the finest footballers in the world. As one former Parkhead team-mate put it: 'You didn't play with Jimmy Delaney, you played to him!'

Thus he became a folk hero, but his career suffered a severe blow in April 1939 when his arm was stamped on, being shattered so comprehensively that surgeons considered amputation. He was unable to play for two years and even after recovering he suffered a serious shoulder injury, giving rise to the fallacy that his fitness could never be relied upon.

Matt Busby, though, who had played behind Jimmy as the Scotland right-half, saw him in 1946 as 'still the greatest match-winner in the game'. Meanwhile the gloom merchants reckoned that the Old Trafford boss would live to regret his first major purchase.

Soon, gleefully, the new Red Devil was proving his lasting worth. Belying his aged appearance, he demonstrated searing acceleration, deft ball control and a powerful shot, a devastating combination when he indulged in his favourite manoeuvre of cutting in from the right flank.

Jimmy was a canny crosser, too, both accurate and perceptive, and his knack of 'hanging up' corners was tailor-made for dreadnought centre-forward Jack Rowley. His vast experience had taught him plenty about positioning and frequently he would interchange roles with Jack, thus bewildering opponents who were more used to him lurking menacingly on the shoulder of his full-back, eager for the opportunity to spring on to penetrating passes from inside-forwards Johnny Morris and Stan Pearson.

Eventually, though, even Jimmy had to acknowledge the passing of years and in November 1950 Matt Busby sold the irrepressibly enthusiastic 36-year-old to Aberdeen for £3,500, taking a mere £500 loss on a player who had served him inspirationally for half a decade.

Still 'Old Brittle Bones' was not done, and after his spell at Pittodrie was followed by a stint with Falkirk, he joined Derry City for a then-record Irish fee of £1,500. In 1954 he helped to win the Irish FA Cup, thus becoming the first man to pocket winners' medals from the major knockout competitions in Scotland, England and Northern Ireland, and amazingly he almost improved on that record two years later, finishing as a loser with Cork Athletic in the League of Ireland FA Cup Final. Jimmy had always wanted to finish in his homeland and duly he served Highland League Elgin City until his retirement in 1957.

JAMES DELANEY
BORN: Cleland, Lanarkshire, 3 September 1914.
HONOURS: FA Cup 47/8. 13 Scotland caps (36-48).
OTHER CLUBS: Celtic 34/5-45/6 (143, 68); Aberdeen 50/1-51/2 (31, 8); Falkirk 51/2-52/3 (27, 16);
Derry City, Northern Ireland, 53/4-54/5; Cork Athletic, Republic of Ireland, 55/6.
DIED: Cleland, Lanarkshire, 26 September 1989.

GAMES	184
GOALS	28

ALLENBY CHILTON

1939/40 → 1954/55

There were hard men, there were very hard men . . . and then there was Allenby Chilton. The flinty, raw-boned north-easterner was the unyielding colossus at the heart of the Manchester United rearguard when Matt Busby set about building his first great team immediately after the Second World War.

It was a side packed with inspirational attackers and which boasted intelligent, skilful operators in every position, but no one was more influential, both on and off the pitch, than the mighty Chilton.

Indeed, although much is rightly made of the half-time lift imparted to the Red Devils by the future Sir Matt and his eloquent captain, Johnny Carey, when they were trailing 2-1 to Blackpool in the 1948 FA Cup Final, it was perhaps the earthily abrasive exhortations of the outspoken centre-half which struck the most productive chord.

After Allenby had outlined his requirements, his team-mates hardly dared to fall short, and they didn't, recovering to beat Stanley Matthews and company by four goals to two in one of the most breathtakingly entertaining of all Wembley showpieces.

No one understood the importance of the big man's contribution to the Old Trafford cause better than Busby who, when asked in 1980 to select his all-time United side, opted for Chilton in the number-five shirt.

Yet the trusty stopper might never have kicked a ball for the Red Devils. Indeed, had his earliest sporting dream been realised, he wouldn't have kicked a ball for anyone, because he trained for six months to become a professional boxer. His aspirations of glory in the ring faltered, however, and while he was playing local football he was spotted by Liverpool and enlisted at Anfield.

Allenby progressed encouragingly on Merseyside but did not feature at senior level and in November 1938 he moved along the East Lancs Road to Manchester, making his first-team debut in September 1939 at Charlton. Though United lost 2-0 at the Valley, the 20-year-old performed impressively enough, but the next day war broke out and thoughts of career advancement were placed on ice.

Instead Allenby joined the Durham Light Infantry, and there was a gap of nearly seven years before his second League outing in August 1946, when he was two weeks short of his 28th birthday. Happily the depredations of the conflict had done nothing to diminish Chilton's prowess or ambition, and so began a magnificent nine-season tenure as United's bulwark.

Commanding in the air and fearsomely competitive at ground level, Allenby presented a dauntingly formidable barrier to opponents and took it as a personal insult whenever a centre-forward found the net.

He was a natural organiser, too – nothing happened at the back without his say-so – and while he was by no means a delicate ball-player, he took his passing seriously, practising meticulously and thinking deeply about the game.

On the debit side? His critics would have it that he conceded too many penalties and free-kicks in dangerous positions, he lost pace in later years, and there was a period when barracking from the stands and terraces irritated him so much that he asked for a transfer, a request which was instantly denied and rendered irrelevant by his continued effectiveness.

On the international front, Allenby earned a niggardly two caps and didn't represent his country at all until 1950, when he was 32. Then, after being praised lavishly for his display in his victorious debut against Northern Ireland, he was left on the sidelines for another year.

Back at club level, when finally he was supplanted by young Mark Jones in February 1955, Allenby had just completed a sequence of 166 consecutive League appearances, a club record until it was broken by Steve Coppell some quarter of a century later.

One of the last of the class of '48 to give way, he proved an able and generous tutor to the Busby Babes and looked to be a natural manager in the making. Duly he became player-boss of Grimsby Town, but after transforming a poor side to become champions of Division Three (North), his fortunes declined and he left the game.

His lasting legacy, though, was at Old Trafford, where his prodigious dynamism in nearly 400 games made Allenby Chilton one of the most authoritative players in the Reds' history.

ALLENBY C CHILTON

BORN:	South Hylton, County Durham, 16 September 1918.
HONOURS:	League Championship 51/2. FA Cup 47/8. 2 England caps (50-51).
OTHER CLUBS:	Grimsby Town 54/5-56/7 (63, 0).
MANAGER:	Grimsby Town (55-59); Hartlepools United (62-63).
DIED:	16 June 1996.

GAMES	392
GOALS	3

JACK ROWLEY

1937/38 → 1954/55

Jack Rowley was the jaggedly rumbustious warhead at the sharp end of Matt Busby's first great Manchester United team, and he was not a man with whom to trifle.

Though at 5ft 9ins he wasn't tall for a centre-forward, the bluntly spoken Black Countryman was all muscular aggression and he packed a brutally explosive shot in either foot, with his left being especially destructive. Scorchingly quick, devastatingly single-minded and almost terrifyingly combative in the air, not for nothing was he known as 'The Gunner'.

Yet there was another, less trumpeted, but immensely valuable aspect to Jack's footballing make-up. In addition to his warrior-like virtues, he was an intelligent operator possessed of formidable all-round technique, thus bringing an extra dimension to the Red Devils' all-star forward line which entertained so royally in the post-war years.

Some quarter of a century before Matt Busby assembled that 'Famous Five' of Delaney, Morris, Rowley, Pearson and Mitten, Jack was born into a footballing family in Wolverhampton. His father had been a goalkeeper on the books of Walsall, and his younger brother, Arthur, was destined to become the most prolific scorer the English League has ever known, mainly through his efforts for Leicester City and Shrewsbury Town.

The senior sibling showed such massive early promise that, on leaving school, he was enlisted by Wolves. However, competition at Molineux was fierce and Jack failed to break through, instead signing for lowly Bournemouth. At this juncture, some players might have slipped into obscurity, but Rowley was a monumentally determined character and so outstanding was his form for the Cherries that within eight months he had been transferred to United for £3,000.

Yet for all his zest and ambition, Jack – an outside-left in those days – made a tentative start as a Red Devil, requesting to be rested after his senior debut and spending time in the reserves before stepping up to help United rise to the First Division in 1938.

He flourished among the elite only for his momentum to be interrupted by war, during which he scored prolifically in emergency competitions. So impressed was Matt Busby that, when the hostilities ended, he switched Jack to centre-forward; the result was an avalanche of goals from the dynamic Midlander as the Reds repeatedly rode high in the table before taking the title in 1951/52.

That term Rowley shattered the club's scoring record with 30 goals, yet his most feted personal triumph had arrived four years earlier at Wembley when he netted a brace in the 4-2 FA Cup Final triumph over Blackpool. In a breathtakingly open contest, Jack equalised twice after Stanley Matthews and company had seized the upper hand. That day he linked superbly with the deliciously skilful Pearson, and many observers reckoned the pair should have been regular partners for England.

Indeed it was in 1948, too, that Rowley won his first full cap, hitting the target on debut against Switzerland and grabbing four goals against Northern Ireland the following year. However, though his tally of six strikes in as many international outings was impressive enough, his lack of an extended run can be attributed to the undeniable prowess of such illustrious rivals as Tommy Lawton, Stan Mortensen and Jackie Milburn.

Conceivably, too, there was another factor contributing to Jack's relatively short England career. Particularly in the south, there was no shortage of critics who disapproved of his unremittingly combative, eye-for-an-eye style, and who could not warm to a personality that was either refreshingly down-to-earth or abrasively confrontational, depending on personal interpretation. Whatever, Jack didn't allow any personal disappointment to distract from club commitments and he continued to serve United nobly, becoming something of an *eminence grise* to many of the Busby Babes who emerged in the early 1950s.

Come 1955, after a stint in his former left-wing role, Rowley's Old Trafford sojourn ended and he became player-boss of Plymouth Argyle, with whom he passed the milestone of 200 League goals on the same day that his brother achieved the same feat. Jack continued playing until 1957, after which he enjoyed a varied management career before leaving the game in 1969.

JOHN FREDERICK ROWLEY

BORN:	Wolverhampton, Staffordshire, 7 October 1920.
HONOURS:	League Championship 51/2. FA Cup 47/8. 6 England caps (48-52).
OTHER CLUBS:	Bournemouth 36/7-37/8 (22, 12); Plymouth Argyle 54/5-56/7 (56, 14).
MANAGER:	Plymouth Argyle (55-60), Oldham Athletic (60-63), Ajax of Amsterdam (63-64), Wrexham (66-67), Bradford Park Avenue (67-68), Oldham Athletic (68-69).
DIED:	Shaw, near Oldham, Lancashire, 27 June 1998.

GAMES	424
GOALS	211

HENRY COCKBURN

1945/46 → 1954/55

Henry Cockburn was Manchester United's 'Mighty Mouse' . . . and how that little fellow roared! The 5ft 5ins Lancastrian operated at wing-half in Matt Busby's lovely post-war side, and in many ways he was an early version of Nobby Stiles, the pocket battleship who patrolled Old Trafford during the triumphant 1960s.

True, tactics were different in the Cockburn heyday, so usually he occupied a more advanced position than Stiles, who was most effective in a withdrawn role alongside doughty stopper Bill Foulkes.

But Henry and Nobby had so much in common. Eager, bright-eyed bundles of energy, they were both combative and constructive, their boundless spirit, honesty and endeavour making up for lack of inches. Both were quick, doggedly tenacious and endlessly courageous in the tackle, but also they were instinctive readers of the game who were endowed with more pure skill than many critics believed.

Cockburn joined United from Goslings, a local feeder club, as an amateur in September 1943 while continuing with his work as a mill-fitter, then turning professional a year later. A nippy, elusive forward at the time, he made his debut for the Reds in wartime competition, but had been converted into a right-footed left-half by 1945, when he made his senior entrance in an FA Cup encounter with Accrington Stanley.

Now Henry made such prodigious progress that he was chosen along with eight other debutants to play for England against Northern Ireland in September 1946 after only seven First Division appearances. That day in Belfast he contributed hugely to a 7-2 victory, and after excelling in the next two games he seemed set for a bountiful international future. However, he was ousted by Blackpool's Harry Johnston and although he extended his total of caps to 13 over the next five years, he never cemented the regular berth which most United supporters believed passionately to be his just deserts.

Happily, back on the club scene, the Cockburn career flourished apace. He was integral to the side which finished as Championship runners-up in each of the first three post-war campaigns, lifted the FA Cup by beating Blackpool at Wembley in 1948, then finally claimed the League crown in 1951/52.

He was particularly effective in harness with John Aston, being swift to cover when the adventurous left-back surged forward, and with left winger Charlie Mitten, who benefited constantly from Henry's crisp and clever distribution. The manager often praised Cockburn's one-touch passing technique and lauded the little man for responding to a cherished Busby maxim with which he drilled his players religiously: the ball is round, so keep it rolling!

Unusually for one of such diminutive stature, Henry was brilliant in the air, too, being capable of springing above hulking opponents from a standing start, thanks to a combination of superb athleticism and well-nigh perfect timing.

Such was his fitness and consistency that the advent of his thirties seemed unlikely to signal the end of the wing-half's Old Trafford tenure, but a broken jaw sustained in a friendly against Kilmarnock in October 1953 paved the way for the rookie Duncan Edwards, and the number-six shirt was never Cockburn's automatic property thereafter.

Still hardly a veteran at 30 , he was not content with life in the reserves and it came as no great surprise in October 1954 when he moved to Bury. At Gigg Lane Henry thrived briefly, then switched to Peterborough United, members of the Midland League at that time, in July 1956.

He loved playing football so much that he was willing to continue at lower levels, later serving Corby Town and Sankeys of Wellington before returning to the Football League as a trainer and coach with Oldham Athletic and Huddersfield Town.

He was well suited to such roles, being especially adept at working with youngsters as he had demonstrated in the twilight of his United career, when his assistance to the emerging Busby Babes had been as valuable as it had been selfless.

Indeed, Henry played an important part in the development of the Babes, and it was tragically ironic that when he was working part-time on a Peterborough newspaper in 1958, part of his job was to write the posters which told of the Munich disaster.

HENRY COCKBURN
BORN: Ashton-under-Lyne, Lancashire, 14 September 1923.
HONOURS: League Championship 51/2. FA Cup 47/8. 13 England caps (46-51).
OTHER CLUBS: Bury 54/5-55/6 (35, 0).
DIED: Mossley, Lancashire, 2 February 2004.

GAMES 275
GOALS 4

JOHN ASTON SENIOR

1946/47 → 1953/54

John Aston was not the most eye-catching member of the marvellous Manchester United team which graced the football grounds of England in the years immediately following the Second World War, but not one of his star comrades was a more versatile or accomplished all-round performer.

A specialist full-back whose game featured a remarkable fusion of culture and grit, the selfless, down-to-earth Mancunian could also double as a mightily effective centre-forward, a role in which he helped the Reds out of a major crisis to the detriment of his own international ambitions.

Beyond that, John occupies a unique position in United history as the only man alive at the turn of the century who played on all four of the grounds which the club has called home since its launch as Newton Heath Lancashire and Yorkshire Railway FC in 1878.

When he was 11 in 1932, he ran out at North Road, the pitch on which the pioneer players had strained every sinew at the end of a hard day's graft on the railways. Then, four years later, he gave his all for Clayton Methodists at Bank Street, the club's headquarters from 1893 to 1910.

The third ground, of course, was Old Trafford, John's base throughout his illustrious career, while the fourth was Manchester City's Maine Road, which United used after the Second World War because of bomb damage to their own stadium.

An archetypal one-club man, John once declared: 'After my family, Manchester United have been the number-one love of my life,' and certainly that devotion was vividly apparent during 35 years of accomplished and loyal service as a footballer of international pedigree, a respected coach and a canny chief scout.

As if that were not enough, John introduced his son, John junior, to the club and experienced the joy of seeing him light up Wembley when the Reds lifted the European Cup for the first time in 1968.

He was 15 when he enlisted as an amateur in 1937, but the war decreed that it would be September 1946 before the adaptable Aston made his League debut as an inside-forward. For his next appearance, ten days later, he was switched to wing-half and then completed his transformation from attacker to defender by settling as skipper Johnny Carey's regular full-back partner during the second half of the season.

The conversion was a typically inspirational touch by Matt Busby, who was seeking a left-back endowed with strength, speed and skill. There was no shortage of candidates who boasted the first two attributes but the third, which Aston possessed in abundance, made him an exceptional addition to the rearguard.

As team-mate Johnny Morris put it: 'John was so good with the ball that it was like having an inside-forward at full-back. A lot of our opponents simply didn't know what to make of it.'

Undoubtedly it worked as United prospered, mitigating the disappointment of being serial runners-up in the League by the scintillating Wembley triumph against Blackpool in 1948, a contest in which Aston's incisive tackling and perceptive interceptions largely nullified the great Stanley Matthews.

A consistent sequence of such composed performances earned John an England call-up and soon he had cemented his international slot for the next two years, occasionally on his favoured right side but more frequently on the left.

However, that prized adaptability was to cost him dearly. When the Reds' spearhead, Jack Rowley, was injured midway through 1950/51, Aston was switched to centre-forward and so devastating was his form – he plundered 15 goals in 22 games – that he retained the job, with Rowley moving to the left flank when he regained fitness. Unfortunately the upshot was the loss of his England place because national boss Walter Winterbottom insisted that a current left-back be selected.

The uncomplaining Aston never played for his country again, even after resuming full-back duties and helping the Red Devils to lift the League Championship in 1951/52. Though he was in his thirties by then, his form remained impressive and it came as a hammer blow when his career was ended prematurely by tuberculosis in 1954.

Happily, John's Old Trafford involvement was far from over. He took up coaching and played a part in the development of the Busby Babes before knee problems presaged a switch to become chief scout, a role he relished until he lost it following a management change in 1972.

JOHN ASTON
BORN: Prestwich, Manchester, 3 September 1921.
HONOURS: League Championship 51/2. FA Cup 47/8. 17 England caps (48-50).
DIED: Manchester, 31 July 2003.

GAMES 284
GOALS 30

CHARLIE MITTEN

1946/47 → 1949/50

Charlie Mitten was a natural showman with a rebel streak. Irrepressibly exuberant, criminally uncapped, the Rangoon-born Englishman was endearingly individual, both as a footballer and a character, and his left-flank dash and daring were compelling components of Matt Busby's first great side.

The most flamboyant member of 'The Famous Five', that coruscatingly brilliant forward line which made Manchester United the supreme soccer entertainers of the immediate post-war era, 'Cheeky Charlie' was the darling of the Old Trafford faithful. They never knew what he was going to do next, but there was a fair bet that it would be exciting, and frequently it would climax in a goal.

Mitten loved to run at defenders and there wasn't a full-back in the English game whom he couldn't master on his day. He could destroy them with outright pace, or he could bamboozle them with trickery and then, having created space for himself, Charlie would employ his fabulous left foot to wreak the maximum havoc.

He was a magnificent crosser and marksmen Jack Rowley and Stan Pearson feasted on his pinpoint service, while he was a sharpshooter himself, averaging better than a goal every three games. The Mitten tally was massaged significantly by his prowess from dead-ball situations, and he was always justly proud of his 17 converted spot-kicks.

Charlie struck the ball so crisply towards the stanchion that there never seemed any possibility that he would miss, even if the 'keeper guessed the right way. Indeed once, in the 7-0 drubbing of Aston Villa at Old Trafford in March 1950, he contributed a hat-trick of penalties, adding another goal from open play for good measure.

In addition to all this derring-do, Mitten was blessed with a shrewd football brain and integrated so smoothly with his team-mates that he could locate them with his unerring dispatches as if by radar, seemingly sure where each man would be in any given situation.

As the second half of the century dawned, with Charlie in his regal pomp, it must have seemed to outsiders that club and player were made for each other, but the relationship was doomed to a sudden and bitterly controversial end.

Viewing the situation objectively, and from such a distance, it would be a harsh judge who blamed Charlie Mitten for the split. Consider the circumstances: while clubs were filling their coffers during the post-war football boom, top players earned £8 per week during the season and a mere £6 in the summer. Out of the blue – and against a backdrop of constant muttering about a possible strike by unhappy professionals – Charlie was offered the staggering signing-on fee of £10,000 to join a leading Colombian club, Santa Fe of Bogota.

He had never dreamed of such a crock of gold. Indeed, he could have spent 25 years with United and never received anything like it. Not surprisingly, he accepted, but then his luck ran out. At the moment he left Old Trafford, Colombia was outside FIFA and any player based there was considered an outlaw. But then, after he and his family had spent one season in Bogota, the South Americans were re-admitted by the sport's governing body – but only on condition that the so-called rebels were sent home.

So Charlie was greeted as a criminal by the English soccer establishment, and that included Manchester United. He was suspended, fined and sold to Fulham, where he went on to spend four productive years before becoming player-boss of Manfield Town, then manager of Newcastle United.

Thus Charlie emerged from the nightmare intact, but 'The Bogota Bandit' was left to reflect on a further infuriating 'if only'. In the early 1950s Real Madrid were assembling arguably the finest club side of all time, and they wanted to sign three of the Colombian mercenaries. They acquired the majestic Alfredo di Stefano and his fellow Argentinian Hector Rial, but were frustrated in their quest for Charlie Mitten because his family was homesick for England.

Had he headed for Spain he might have become one of the world's soccer immortals. As Alfredo the great reflected: 'Ah, Charlee Meeten, numero uno. If we have heem we never need Francisco Gento. Gento he queeck, but Meeten, he more clever!' Few more telling testimonials have ever been delivered.

CHARLES MITTEN

BORN:	Rangoon, Burma, 17 January 1921.
HONOURS:	FA Cup 47/8.
OTHER CLUBS:	Santa Fe, Colombia, 50/1; Fulham 51/2-55/6 (154, 32); Mansfield Town 55/6-57/8 (100, 25).
MANAGER:	Mansfield Town (56-58), Newcastle United (58-61).
DIED:	Stockport, Cheshire, 2 January 2002.

GAMES	162
GOALS	61

JACK CROMPTON

1945/46 → 1955/56

When Matt Busby was piecing together the first of his three majestic Manchester United sides, he employed one of the safest pairs of hands in England as his last line of defence.

They belonged to Jack Crompton, who became a byword for reliability in the team which finished as Championship runners-up during the first three campaigns after the Second World War, and lifted the FA Cup with consummate style in 1948.

In that era there was no shortage of spectacular goalkeepers in the English game, with another Manchester custodian, Frank Swift of City, foremost among them. Hulme-born Jack was not like that. Where the larger-than-life Swift was an engaging extrovert, Crompton was quiet and unobtrusive, the very antithesis of flamboyance.

But even though he did not attain the fame and renown of the Maine Road star, there was no doubting Jack's pedigree. After all, Matt Busby picked him more than 200 times, and the United boss, for all his avuncular air, was a demanding taskmaster who demanded titanic standards of ability and dedication.

Certainly, when it came to commitment, Jack knew no peer. He was a fitness fanatic who thought nothing of putting in a lengthy training session with his team-mates, then cutting round to the YMCA for extra work before rounding off the day with a long-distance hike in the hills – just for recreation!

He was immensely strong, both physically and mentally, and invariably in magnificent condition, which stood him in tremendous stead at a juncture when a less fit fellow might have missed out on what proved to be the highlight of the Crompton career.

During the week before the 1948 final against Blackpool, when Jack was reeling from the death of his sister, he was suffering from an excruciatingly painful back abcess, which seemed certain to deprive him of his Wembley place.

But Matt was desperate not to face Stanley Matthews and company without his first-choice 'keeper. So, being well versed in the steeliness of the Crompton constitution, the Old Trafford boss made a last determined attempt to get his main man ready.

While the rest of the United party headed south, Matt took Jack to the Ancoats hospital, where a surgeon suggested that the case was hopeless, declaring that there was no way he would make the final. Still, the eminent medic was persuaded to operate, subsequently bandaging the patient so tightly that he had no need for a jockstrap.

As a result, Jack strolled out at Wembley, his sprightly gait offering no hint of the discomfort he must still have been feeling, and he played a key role in a pulsating victory. Not only did he pull off several brilliant saves when United were behind, but also he started the move which led to the match-turning strike by Stan Pearson. By then the score was 2-2 and, with just 11 minutes remaining, the Seasiders' centre-forward Stan Mortensen broke through and shot fiercely for what seemed a certain goal. But somehow Jack launched himself to clutch the flying leather, then leapt to his feet and hurled the ball to John Anderson. The diminutive wing-half passed to Pearson, who ran on to grab a decisive lead.

Thus 26-year-old Crompo was a hero and, when Swift retired at decade's end, there were those who reckoned that Jack deserved at least a trial in the England jersey. However, that call never came and his progress took a rude jolt in 1950 when he broke a wrist, prompting the Reds to recruit two new 'keepers, talented youngster Ray Wood and the frequently brilliant but periodically unwell Reg Allen.

Thereafter Jack was in and out of the team, not making quite enough appearances to earn a medal when the title was finally claimed in 1952, and as Wood matured the older man slipped back to the status of regular reserve.

He retired as a player at the end of the 1955/56 campaign, joining Luton as trainer with a view to returning to Manchester when he had garnered some experience. As events transpired, he rejoined United in the immediate aftermath of the Munich calamity, helping Jimmy Murphy to keep the team afloat, then going on to serve as trainer through the trophy-laden 1960s, leaving in 1971.

Next Jack managed Barrow briefly, then coached Bury and trained Preston for Bobby Charlton before making a second Old Trafford return in 1974. He went on to spend seven years in charge of the reserves and manage the club on the 1981 summer tour of the Far East before bowing out. Few men merit a more honoured niche in Red Devils folklore.

JOHN CROMPTON

BORN: Manchester, 18 December 1921.
HONOURS: FA Cup 1947/48.
MANAGER: Luton Town (acting, 62); Barrow (71-72).

GAMES 212
GOALS 0

JOHNNY MORRIS

1946/47 → 1948/49

Feisty little Lancastrian Johnny Morris was the 'baby' of Matt Busby's lovely side which finished as title runners-up in 1947, 1948 and 1949, but applied captivating balm to the understandable frustration of their fans by lifting the FA Cup in 1948 with one of the most breathtakingly beautiful exhibitions of football ever to adorn Wembley.

At the time of that triumph over Blackpool, inside-forward Johnny was 24 and displaying exquisite all-round ability, but it was possible only to guess just how masterful he would become with maturity. Imagine the chagrin of the Old Trafford faithful, therefore, when in March 1949 he was transferred to Derby County for what was then a British record fee of £24,500.

Now the supporters would never witness at first hand the full flowering of the Morris talent, and although he earned full England recognition during his three-year sojourn at the Baseball Ground, to what heights might he have aspired had he remained in the fabulous team to which he was so admirably suited?

Another question: exactly how good was Johnny? Well, shrewd contemporary observers declare that he was the complete inside-forward. His passing, both long and short, was immaculately accurate and invariably astute; he was brave, often beyond the call of duty, tackling with a flinty ferocity which made hulking opponents quail; he had a keen eye for goal; he was a workaholic, scampering hither and thither from first whistle to last, and he seemed to draw on an inexhaustible supply of high-octane energy.

Morris emerged with the MUJACs, United's former junior team, and while still in his teens he performed impressively during a wartime stint on loan with Bolton Wanderers before turning professional at Old Trafford in 1941. Soon, though, his football development was placed on hold and he headed for Europe as a member of the Royal Armoured Corps' tank regiment.

After that it was back to Manchester where United's new manager, Matt Busby, was delighted by Johnny's remarkable talent. Thus, by the autumn of 1946 the rookie boss had accommodated the young man in his enthrallingly enterprising side, handing Morris the number-eight shirt and switching the adaptable Stan Pearson to inside-left.

The effect was stimulating. Johnny forged a scintillating right-wing partnership with ageing Scottish flankman Jimmy Delaney, and also linked brilliantly with Pearson, centre-forward Jack Rowley and left-winger Charlie Mitten. Indeed, many of the Red Devils' most sumptuous attacks emanated from the diminutive, curly-haired schemer, who was equally adept at slick close-range passing interchanges or raking long-distance dispatches which freed his wide-men to rampage in the space beyond the opposing full-backs.

So, with United bossed by the visionary Busby and clearly on the rise, what caused the popular Morris to depart an Old Trafford scene in which he was happy and fulfilled at a time when his prime lay ahead of him so enticingly?

The plain truth is that Johnny and the future Sir Matt disagreed over a point of principle. It must be remembered that players of that era were paid a pittance while the big clubs filled their coffers as the turnstiles clicked merrily. In addition, there pertained the iniquitous retain-and-transfer system, which made footballers virtual slaves of their employers, unable to move elsewhere even when their contracts had ended.

Now Morris was a fiercely independent character, ever ready to stand up for his rights, but he got nowhere with several forthright requests for a benefit which he felt was owed to him. Duly he asked for a transfer, which was denied flatly; indeed, he was told by the manager: 'While I am here you will never leave the club.'

So Johnny boxed clever. Having recently demonstrated his golfing prowess by winning a tournament for players and staff, he demanded his employment cards, stating his intention of leaving football to become a professional golfer. Had he carried out his threat, United would have received nothing and so, reluctantly, they agreed the move to Derby.

The fans grieved his departure and, although the Red Devils eventually claimed that elusive Championship in 1952, most pundits believed that more honours would have been garnered had the split never occurred.

As for Johnny, he won three caps as a Ram, then helped Leicester City to lift two Second Division crowns before managing a succession of non-League clubs. What might have been? It never bothered the pragmatic Morris in the slightest.

	JOHN MORRIS		
BORN:	Radcliffe, Lancashire, 27 September 1923.		
HONOURS:	FA Cup 47/8. 3 England caps (49).	GAMES	93
OTHER CLUBS:	Derby County 48/9-52/3 (130, 44); Leicester City 52/3-57/8 (206, 33).	GOALS	35

56

JOHN ANDERSON

1947/48 → 1948/49

John Anderson is well overdue a generous measure of public acclaim. For more than half a century, when the tributes have been distributed, the stocky, industrious wing-half has tended to be the odd man out among his comrades in one of the greatest of all Manchester United teams.

Ten names from Matt Busby's first great creation, the side that lifted the FA Cup in 1948, invariably receive an honourable mention, while John's is cruelly omitted.

Fair enough, some might say. After all the rest were either long-serving stalwarts or fully-fledged stars, while the amiable Anderson made only 40 appearances in a senior Old Trafford career which lasted a mere 17 months. However, he did play a leading role, arguably a decisive one, in that most memorable of Wembley finals.

Some four months earlier in December 1947, after being on United's books for ten years, John made his First Division debut, performing with poise and assurance to extinguish the threat of the magnificent Wilf Mannion in a home victory over Middlesbrough. Thereafter, a few injury absences apart, he retained his place for the remainder of the season.

There was nothing spectacular about John's style, but he was steady, a constructive passer who controlled the ball easily and who read the game intelligently. Apart from his main task of fetching and carrying in midfield, he offered sensible cover when right-back Johnny Carey ventured forward, and he was adept at slipping passes behind opposing defenders, which suited the free-running style of right-winger Jimmy Delaney.

People never noticed him much, but twice towards the end of that classic 1948 final, the unassuming Anderson took centre stage. First, with the score at 2-2, keeper Jack Crompton hurled the ball to John, who supplied the perfect pass for Stan Pearson to put United in front. Next, three minutes later, he went past a tackle and netted with a deflected 40-yard drive which clinched the trophy. Understandably exultant, he started running and if Carey had not stepped in with a sobering 'Steady son' then Anderson reflected later that he might have sprinted down the tunnel and out of the stadium!

That goal capped the greatest day of John's footballing life, but it was not to prove the prelude to a long-term future with United. At the beginning of 1948/49 he found himself sharing wing-half duties with Billy McGlen, then he was tried unsuccessfully at inside-right.

Eventually, in October 1949, following a dispute with the Old Trafford board over benefit entitlement, and facing an increasing challenge from a new wave of youngsters, he was was sold to Nottingham Forest for £9,000. At the City Ground, John helped to capture the Third Division (South) championship in 1950/51, then joined non-League Peterborough United in 1952.

JOHN ANDERSON
BORN: Salford, Lancashire, 11 October 1921.
HONOURS: FA Cup 47/8.
OTHER CLUBS: Nottingham Forest 49/50-50/1 (40, 1).
DIED: Manchester, 6 August 2006.

GAMES 40
GOALS 2

JACK WARNER

1938/39 → 1949/50

Before the war, Jack Warner was a poised, skilful, formidably abrasive wing-half in his prime. After the conflict, the craggy Welsh international was a veteran past his best. But still he soldiered on gamely and sometimes irascibly, putting the fear of death into anyone – either team-mate or opponent – whom he deemed to be stepping out of line.

Warner was a first-team regular as United pushed Liverpool all the way in the League title race of 1946/47, but then lost his place to the younger Johnny Anderson during the following campaign, thus missing out on the classic 1948 FA Cup Final encounter with Blackpool.

Even then the grizzled warrior refused to yield, and having recovered to give a spirited account of himself with 25 appearances in 1949/50, he left Old Trafford with a record that would remain his own for half a century. It wasn't until the twilight of Dutch goalkeeper Raimond van der Gouw's career early in the new millennium that Jack was no longer the oldest Red Devil, at 38 years and seven months, to play senior football since the war.

He left Old Trafford to join Oldham Athletic in June 1951 and subsequently became player-boss of Rochdale, eventually laying aside his boots at the ripe old age of 42.

		GAMES	119
		GOALS	2

JOHN WARNER
BORN: Trealaw, Glamorgan, 21 September 1911.
HONOURS: 2 Wales caps (37-39).
OTHER CLUBS: Swansea Town 33/4-37/8 (132, 8); Oldham Athletic 51/2 (34, 2); Rochdale 52/3 (21, 0).
DIED: Tonypandy, Glamorgan, 4 October 1980.

BERT WHALLEY

1935/36 → 1946/47

Few Manchester United characters have been loved so dearly, and by so many people of disparate generations, as Bert Whalley. During the late 1930s he established a reputation as a classy wing-half or centre-half, a stylish operator whose distribution was smooth and whose refusal to panic no matter how desperate the defensive situation was a boon to any rearguard.

However, he lost what would surely have been his vintage years to the war, during which he played nearly 200 times for the Reds in emergency competitions and also found time to guest for Oldham, Bolton and Liverpool.

But it was when peace resumed that Bert began to make an indelible mark on Old Trafford history. After making only three senior appearances in 1946/47, he employed his vast experience and abiding good nature on bringing on the youngsters at the club, first as captain of the reserves and then, after being forced by an eye injury to stop playing, as an inspirational coach.

Working alongside the volcanic little Welshman Jimmy Murphy, the quietly avuncular Whalley exerted enormous influence on the generation of rookies who would burst upon the nation's sporting consciousness in the 1950s as the Busby Babes. Ironically, Bert was deputising for Jimmy, who was away managing Wales, when he was killed at Munich on the way back from a European Cup trip to Belgrade. United, and football, had lost a faithful friend.

HERBERT WHALLEY
BORN: Ashton-under-Lyne, Lancashire, 6 August 1912.
DIED: Munich, 6 February 1958.

	GAMES	39
	GOALS	0

JOHNNY HANLON

1938/39 → 1948/49

Johnny Hanlon was a small, pacy marksman who could shine in any forward role and whose deft passing skills created as many goals as he scored.

Before global conflict erupted, the Mancunian was identified as one of the Reds' most exciting prospects, a clever link man expected to flourish alongside the classy likes of Stan Pearson and Jack Rowley. Sadly the gathering impetus of his career was wrecked by the break, and afterwards he was never quite the same again.

However, after surviving a spell as a prisoner of war, he proved resilient enough to make 27 League appearances in 1946/47, and he proved a terrific help to youngsters at the club. But having entered his thirties, age was against him, and in October 1948 he joined Bury, whom he served for two seasons before retirement.

JOHN JAMES HANLON
BORN: Manchester, 12 October 1917
OTHER CLUBS: Bury 48/9-49/50 (31, 1).
DIED: Manchester, January 2002.

	GAMES	70
	GOALS	22

BILLY WRIGGLESWORTH

1936/37 → 1946/47

A tiny, jet-propelled winger who could shred a rearguard single-handed on his day, but who sometimes infuriated colleagues by hogging possession. Billy loved to put on a show, with a variety of ball tricks and a trademark somersault when he scored a goal.

WILLIAM HERBERT WRIGGLESWORTH
BORN: South Elmsall, Yorkshire, 12 November 1912.
OTHER CLUBS: Chesterfield 32/3-34/5 (34, 6); Wolverhampton Wanderers 34/5-36/7 (50, 21); Bolton Wanderers 46/7-47/8 (13, 1); Southampton 47/8 (12, 4); Reading 48/9 (5, 0).
DIED: 1980.

GAMES	37
GOALS	10

JACK SMITH

1937/38 → 1945/46

Smith's cluster of goals in the second half of 1937/38 were key to United's rise from the second tier. The Yorkshireman was a muscular bustler of whom fans used to say: 'If the ball's on Jack's head, it's as good as in the net!' A telling tribute.

JOHN SMITH
BORN: Batley, Yorkshire, 7 February 1915.
HONOURS: Division Two promotion 37/8.
OTHER CLUBS: Huddersfield Town 32/3-34/5 (45, 24); Newcastle United 34/5-37/8 (104, 69); Blackburn Rovers 46/7 (30, 12); Port Vale 46/7-47/8 (29, 10).
DIED: 1975.

GAMES	42
GOALS	15

JACK ROACH

1945/46

A sturdy left-back who helped to keep the United flag flying during the war, when he made 45 appearances in emergency competitions. However, when hostilities ceased there were only a couple of FA Cup outings before he returned to obscurity.

JOHN ROACH
BORN: Manchester.

GAMES	2
GOALS	0

BILL BAINBRIDGE

1945/46

A strapping front-runner who didn't possess quite the requisite style and polish for the top tier. Still, he scored on his only senior outing for the Reds before losing his place to Johnny Carey, who was yet to settle at full-back. Later Bill shone for Tranmere.

WILLIAM BAINBRIDGE
BORN: Gateshead, County Durham, 9 March 1922.
OTHER CLUBS: Bury 46/7 (2, 1); Tranmere Rovers 48/9-53/4 (168, 63).

GAMES	1
GOALS	1

JOE WALTON

1945/46 → 1947/48

A beautifully balanced, stylish footballing full-back, the affable Mancunian was far more skilful than the average defender of his era, but his path to Old Trafford seniority was blocked by the excellence of Messrs Carey and Aston. Preston benefited handsomely.

JOSEPH WALTON
BORN: Manchester, 5 June 1925.
OTHER CLUBS: Preston North End 47/8-60/1 (401, 4); Accrington Stanley 60/1 (18, 0).
DIED: Preston, Lancashire, 31 December 2006.

GAMES	23
GOALS	0

BILLY McGLEN

1946/47 → 1951/52

A fearsomely competitive defensive midfielder who excelled at man-to-man marking, Billy managed to negate the exquisite skills of many of the great inside-forwards of his era. The rise of the Busby Babes precipitated his departure from Old Trafford.

WILLIAM McGLEN
BORN: Bedlington, Northumberland, 27 April 1921.
OTHER CLUBS: Lincoln City 52/3 (13, 0); Oldham Athletic 52/3-55/6 (68, 3).
DIED: December 1999.

GAMES	122
GOALS	2

RONNIE BURKE

1946/47 → 1948/49

An eager and rumbustious spearhead who took plenty of stick from the press but who could point to an exceptional goals-to-games ratio. Standing between Ronnie and a regular place, though, was the formidably daunting obstacle of Jack Rowley.

RONALD STEWART BURKE
BORN: Dormanstown, Yorkshire, 13 August 1921.
OTHER CLUBS: Huddersfield Town 49/50-51/2 (27, 6); Rotherham United 52/3-54/5 (73, 56); Exeter City 55/6-56/7 (42, 14).
DIED: Watford, Hertfordshire, December 2003.

GAMES	35
GOALS	23

CLIFF COLLINSON

1946/47

The agile Teessider never managed to emerge from a clutch of competent 'keepers, all striving to snatch Jack Crompton's first-team jersey after the war. He impressed with a clean sheet on debut at Villa Park, but soon faded from the picture.

CLIFFORD COLLINSON
BORN: Middlesbrough, Yorkshire, 3 March 1920.
DIED: September 1990.

GAMES	7
GOALS	0

TED BUCKLE

1946/47 → 1949/50

In another era dashing winger Ted Buckle might have achieved more at Old Trafford, but with Jimmy Delaney and Charlie Mitten *in situ*, a breakthrough proved beyond him. Ted was quick and carried a rasping shot, which he put to fine use at Everton.

HERBERT EDWARD WILLIAM BUCKLE
BORN: Southwark, London, 28 October 1924.
OTHER CLUBS: Everton 49/50-54/5 (97, 31); Exeter City 55/6-56/7 (65, 12).
DIED: Manchester, 14 June 1990.

GAMES	24
GOALS	7

HARRY WORRALL

1946/47 – 1947/48

A neat and clever left-back whose smooth passing skills reflected his earlier experience as an inside-forward. However, though he was composed, strong and intelligent, he was never going to oust John Aston and he joined Swindon for £1,000.

HAROLD WORRALL
BORN: Northwich, Cheshire, 19 November 1918.
DIED: 1979.

GAMES	6
GOALS	0

BILL FIELDING

1946/47

A sound goalkeeper signed as experienced cover for Jack Crompton, Bill conceded six on his League entrance at Highbury, but was absolved of blame by Matt Busby. He performed solidly in his subsequent outings, but retired a year later.

WILLIAM FIELDING
BORN: Broadhurst, Cheshire, 17 June 1915.
OTHER CLUBS: Cardiff City 36/7-38/9 (50, 0).
DIED: Lytham St Annes, Lancashire, May 2006.

GAMES	7
GOALS	0

JOE DALE

1947/48

A skilful right winger recruited from non-League Witton Albion, Joe struggled to adapt to the top flight when called up to deputise for Jimmy Delaney on United's right flank. After a brief stint at Port Vale, he returned to Witton, where he thrived anew.

JOSEPH DALE
BORN: Northwich, Cheshire, 3 July 1921.
OTHER CLUBS: Port Vale 47/8-48/9 (9, 1).
DIED: 2000.

GAMES	2
GOALS	0

KEN PEGG

1947/48

A sound goalkeeper who made his senior debut only three days after turning professional at Old Trafford, Ken played twice in succession and showed promise in both drawn games, but never had another chance to rival the established Jack Crompton.

JAMES KENNETH PEGG
BORN: Salford, Lancashire, 4 January 1926.
OTHER CLUBS: Torquay United 49/50 (2, 0); York City 50/1 (1, 0).
DIED: Manchester, 25 August 1999.

GAMES	2
GOALS	0

SAMMY LYNN

1947/48 → 1949/50

A sleekly skilful centre-half who contrasted vividly with gritty first-team bulwark Allenby Chilton, Sammy lacked the ruthless edge which might have given him a chance to emerge from the north-easterner's gigantic shadow. A lovely player, though.

SAMUEL LYNN
BORN: St Helens, Lancashire, 25 December 1920.
OTHER CLUBS: Bradford Park Avenue 50/1-52/3 (73, 0).
DIED: Salford, Lancashire, January 1995.

GAMES	13
GOALS	0

BERRY BROWN

1947/48 → 1948/49

Yet another frustrated net-minder who couldn't find a way past the reliable Jack Crompton. The lanky Berry saved a penalty on his debut against Sheffield United at Bramall Lane, but couldn't capitalise on that positive start and soon departed.

ROBERT BERESFORD BROWN
BORN: West Hartlepool, County Durham, 6 September 1927.
OTHER CLUBS: Doncaster Rovers 48/9 (4, 0); Hartlepool United 51/2-55/6 (126, 0).
DIED: 2001.

GAMES	4
GOALS	0

TOMMY LOWRIE

1947/48 → 1950/51

Tommy Lowrie had plenty going for him as a wing-half. A bundle of energy and a perceptive distributor, he made a bright start as a Red, but he never quite seemed to recover from a chasing by Sunderland's provocative maestro Len Shackleton.

THOMAS LOWRIE
BORN: Glasgow, 14 January 1928.
OTHER CLUBS: Aberdeen 50/1-51/2 (29, 1); Oldham Athletic 52/3-54/5 (79, 5).

GAMES	14
GOALS	0

REG ALLEN

1950/51 → 1952/53

If Reg Allen had any flaws as a goalkeeper, they were not obvious to fans who marvelled at his mammoth contribution to Manchester United's first title triumph under Matt Busby. The tall, lithe Londoner was acrobatic at need, fielded crosses with consistent aplomb and exuded a commanding aura which communicated itself to his fellow defenders.

Though he was already 31 when United paid Queen's Park Rangers £11,000 to sign him in June 1950, and he had passed his entire war-shortened career in the lower divisions, he remained at the peak of his powers as the Reds finished as Championship runners-up in his first campaign, then lifted the crown in his second.

But all was not well. Reg, who had come to the United manager's attention when they had played in the same Army team during the conflict, fell demoralisingly ill, possibly a legacy of the three years he spent as a prisoner of the Germans after being captured in north Africa.

Early in 1952/53 it became distressingly apparent that he was no longer up to the mental rigours of top-flight football, and he left the club at season's end.

Though there was no shortage of high-quality custodians in England at the time, astute contemporary observers maintain that, but for his cruel infirmity, Reg Allen had all it took to have excelled at any level, even on the international stage.

ARTHUR REGINALD ALLEN
BORN: Marylebone, London, 3 May 1919.
HONOURS: League Championship 51/2.
OTHER CLUBS: Queen's Park Rangers 38/9-49/50 (183, 0).
DIED: Ealing, London, 1976.

GAMES 80
GOALS 0

JOHNNY DOWNIE

1948/49 → 1952/53

Easy-going Scot John Downie made a valiant stab at a well-nigh impossible assignment, that of replacing the brilliant and vastly popular local lad Johnny Morris in Matt Busby's dazzlingly attractive post-war side.

The newcomer, an exceptionally talented inside-forward in his own right, cost a club-record £18,000 when he was recruited from Bradford Park Avenue in March 1949. However, he was confronted instantly by intimidatingly vast expectations and, it's sad to report, there were occasions when unsympathetic Old Trafford regulars, dismayed by the departure of their hero, gave poor Downie a rough ride.

Still, although he never reached the rarefied heights of his predecessor, it would be grossly unfair to conclude that John was a failure. Although his confidence never matched his natural gifts – he was a deft finisher and smooth passer – Downie displayed abundant mettle as the Red Devils became League champions in 1951/52.

That term he netted 11 times, and set up plenty of goals for Jack Rowley and Stan Pearson, and he made a telling contribution, too, when United finished as runners-up in both 1948/49 and 1950/51.

However, with precocious youngsters such as John Doherty clamouring for recognition, his place became insecure, and after failing to convince Busby that he should switch to wing-half, he joined Luton Town for £10,000 in August 1953.

JOHN DENNIS DOWNIE
BORN: Lanark, 19 July 1925.
HONOURS: League Championship 51/2.
OTHER CLUBS: Bradford Park Avenue 46/7-48/9 (86, 33); Luton Town 53/4 (26, 12); Hull City 54/5 (27, 5); Mansfield Town 58/9 (18, 4); Darlington 59/60 (15, 2).

GAMES 116
GOALS 37

LES OLIVE

1 9 5 2 / 5 3

Though Les Olive was one of the most influential figures at Old Trafford for some half a century, it was not as a goalkeeper that he made his lasting mark. True, he never let the Reds down when he stood between their posts against Newcastle United and West Bromwich Albion during an injury crisis in the spring of 1953, but it was as the supremely efficient secretary of the club that the gently unobtrusive Salfordian truly shone.

As a boy, Les had been faced with an agonising dilemma. There was one opportunity to tilt at a future as a professional footballer, clearly a precarious business in the highly competitive era of the Busby Babes, and another to forge a much safer career in the club office. Les, usually a defender for United's junior sides, took the more secure option and neither he nor the club regretted his decision.

While still in his twenties, in the wake of the Munich disaster he took over as secretary from Walter Crickmer, who had died in the crash, and played a central role in restoring the stricken club to an even keel. It was a post he retained for 30 years, after which he became a director.

However, for all his brilliance at administration, Les remained a football man at heart, and loved to recall how he had helped United to a win and a draw in what must have seemed like another lifetime.

ROBERT LESLIE OLIVE
BORN: Salford, Lancashire, 27 April 1928.
DIED: Salford, Lancashire, 20 May 2006.

GAMES **2**
GOALS 0

HARRY McSHANE

1 9 5 0 / 5 1 → 1 9 5 3 / 5 4

Down the decades Harry McShane served the Red Devils in four contrasting roles. During the late 1960s and early 1970s, his was a familiar voice at Old Trafford as the public-address announcer and disc-jockey. Then he was a leading light in the formation of the Manchester United Former Players Association, and later he was a talent scout, listing Nicky Butt among his principal discoveries.

But before any of those important contributions Harry had gone agonisingly close to pocketing a Championship medal as a dashing winger.

Signed to replace the recently departed Charlie Mitten in a swap deal which took defender Johnny Ball to Bolton in September 1950, 30-year-old Harry was more a direct runner than a beguiling trickster in the manner of his flamboyant predecessor. Still, he did well, first on the left flank and then on the right, as United finished as title runners-up to Spurs in his first campaign at the club.

The following term his prospects seemed even brighter as he enjoyed a dozen early outings, only for knee trouble to leave him two appearances short of a coveted gong. Sentiment counted for nothing and he remained empty-handed.

Thereafter, his star faded as the Busby Babes began to emerge, and in 1954 Harry – father of the actor Ian 'Lovejoy' McShane – was sold to Oldham for £750.

HENRY McSHANE
BORN: Holytown, Lanarkshire, 8 April 1920.
OTHER CLUBS: Blackburn Rovers 37/8 (2, 0); Huddersfield Town 46/7 (15, 1); Bolton Wanderers 47/8-50/1 (93, 6); Oldham Athletic 53/4-54/5 (41, 5).

GAMES **57**
GOALS 8

JOHNNY BALL

1947/48 → 1949/50

It was terrific for United to have Johnny Ball as a classy deputy for right-back Johnny Carey, but the blond Lancastrian deserved better, so he moved to Bolton. Calm, intelligent and strong, he thrived as a Trotter and was picked for the Football League.

JOHN BALL
BORN: Wigan, Lancashire, 13 March 1925.
OTHER CLUBS: Bolton Wanderers 50/1-57/8 (200, 2).

| GAMES | 23 |
| GOALS | 0 |

LAURIE CASSIDY

1947/48 → 1951/52

Mancunian marksman who didn't find the net on his few senior outings as a Red, but made a profound contribution by setting an admirable example to rookies in the reserves and becoming a major force in youth football during a successful teaching career.

LAURENCE CASSIDY
BORN: Manchester, 10 March 1923.
OTHER CLUBS: Oldham Athletic 56/7 (4, 1).

| GAMES | 4 |
| GOALS | 0 |

BRIAN BIRCH

1949/50 → 1951/52

If his application and strength had matched his natural talent and vast self-belief Brian would have been a star for a decade. But after a brief brilliant stint halfway through 1950/51, the sumptuously skilful inside-forward lost form and joined Wolves for £10,000.

BRIAN BIRCH
BORN: Salford, Lancashire, 18 November 1931.
OTHER CLUBS: Wolverhampton Wanderers 51/2 (3, 1); Lincoln City 52/3-54/5 (56, 15); Barrow 56/7-58/9 (60, 27); Exeter City 58/9-59/60 (19, 1); Oldham Athletic 59/60-60/1 (35, 10); Rochdale 60/1-61/2 (11, 0). DIED: South Africa.

| GAMES | 15 |
| GOALS | 5 |

TOMMY BOGAN

1949/50 → 1950/51

Matt Busby had massive expectations of Tommy, an explosively pacy utility attacker who could run defenders ragged down the flanks or through the middle. But the ebullient Scot never truly adapted to the English game at any of his four clubs.

THOMAS BOGAN
BORN: Glasgow, 18 May 1920.
OTHER CLUBS: Celtic 45/6-48/9 (34, 5); Preston North End 48/9 (11, 0); Aberdeen 50/1-51/2 (4, 1); Southampton 51/2-52/3 (8, 2); Blackburn Rovers 53/4 (1, 0). DIED: 23 September 1993.

| GAMES | 33 |
| GOALS | 7 |

SONNY FEEHAN

1949/50

Tall, acrobatic Sonny enjoyed several fine days between United's posts, notably in an FA Cup triumph at Portsmouth, but when injury to Jack Crompton afforded him an extended opportunity to shine, he lacked the consistency to press his claim.

JOHN IGNATIUS FEEHAN
BORN: Dublin, 17 September 1926.
OTHER CLUBS: Waterford, Republic of Ireland, 44/5-48/9; Northampton Town 50/1-51/2 (39, 0); Brentford 54/5-58/9 (30, 0). DIED: 1995.

| GAMES | 14 |
| GOALS | 0 |

JOE LANCASTER

1949/50

Hardly a weak link as his four outings in goal produced two clean sheets, three wins and a draw, unlucky Joe was soon to return to the non-League obscurity from which he had been plucked. He had relished a rare adventure, though, and had let no one down.

JOSEPH GERARD LANCASTER
BORN: Stockport, Cheshire, 28 April 1926.
OTHER CLUBS: Accrington Stanley 50/1 (1, 0).

| GAMES | 4 |
| GOALS | 0 |

FRANK CLEMPSON

1949/50 → 1952/53

A gloriously gifted play-maker who seemed certain to carve out a top career, Frank somehow lost impetus after helping to secure the 1951/52 League title, then was overtaken by the rising tide of Busby Babes. Maybe he lacked a little ruthlessness.

FRANK CLEMPSON
BORN: Salford, Lancashire, 27 May 1930.
OTHER CLUBS: Stockport County 52/3-58/9 (246, 35); Chester 59/60-60/1 (67, 8). DIED: Worsley, Lancashire, 1970.

| GAMES | 15 |
| GOALS | 2 |

TOMMY McNULTY

1949/50 → 1953/54

A combative local boy who laid persuasive claim to the Red Devils' number-two shirt as the Championship was lifted in 1951/52. However, though he featured frequently during the next term, he lost consistency and he was sold to Liverpool.

THOMAS McNULTY
BORN: Salford, Lancashire, 30 December 1929.
HONOURS: League Championship 51/2.
OTHER CLUBS: Liverpool 53/4-57/8 (36, 0). DIED: Salford, Lancashire, 1979.

| GAMES | 60 |
| GOALS | 0 |

EDDIE McILVENNY

1950/51

The Scottish-born wing-half captained the USA to their stunning victory over England in the 1950 World Cup Finals, but he was out of his depth at Old Trafford when the new season began. Soon he lost his place to Don Gibson and never regained it.

EDWARD JOSEPH McILVENNY
BORN: Greenock, Renfrewshire, 21 October 1924.
HONOURS: USA caps.
OTHER CLUBS: Morton 46/7; Wrexham 46/7-47/8 (7, 1); Philadelphia Nationals, USA, 48-50; Waterford, Republic of Ireland, 53/4.
DIED: 1989.

GAMES **2**
GOALS **0**

DON GIBSON

1950/51 → 1954/55

Bright, industrious performer who helped to lift the Championship in 1951/52, but his straightforward efforts over half a decade were never quite enough to secure a long-term future at Old Trafford and he was overtaken by the emerging Busby Babes.

THOMAS RICHARD DONALD GIBSON
BORN: Manchester, 12 May 1929.
HONOURS: League Championship 51/2.
OTHER CLUBS: Sheffield Wednesday 55/6-59/60 (80, 2); Leyton Orient 60/1 (8, 0).

GAMES **115**
GOALS **0**

BILLY REDMAN

1950/51 → 1953/54

As quick and skilful as many a winger, Billy was a polished performer who richly merited the title gong he picked up in 1951/52 for a classy stint as deputy to John Aston. But the later challenge of Roger Byrne proved too much for him and he joined Bury.

WILLIAM REDMAN
BORN: Manchester, 29 January 1928.
HONOURS: League Championship 51/52.
OTHER CLUBS: Bury 54/5-55/6 (37, 1).
DIED: 1994.

GAMES **38**
GOALS **0**

CLIFF BIRKETT

1950/51

A teenage prodigy for whom stardom was widely predicted, right-winger Cliff found himself eclipsed all too soon by experienced campaigners such as Johnny Berry and Harry McShane. Though quick and skilful, he lacked cuteness for the top level.

CLIFFORD BIRKETT
BORN: Haydock, Lancashire, 17 September 1933.
OTHER CLUBS: Southport 56/7 (14, 4).
DIED: January 1997.

GAMES **13**
GOALS **2**

ERNIE BOND

1951/52 → 1952/53

Tiny Lancastrian left winger who sojourned only briefly at Old Trafford, but long enough to pocket a Championship medal in 1951/52. He is remembered most vividly for scoring in three consecutive matches in five days over Chistmas that season.

JAMES ERNEST BOND
BORN: Preston, Lancashire, 4 May 1929.
HONOURS: League Championship 51/2.
OTHER CLUBS: Carlisle United 52/3-58/9 (194, 23); Cowdenbeath 58/9.

GAMES **21**
GOALS **4**

JOHNNY WALTON

1951/52

A cultured inside-forward with bags of ability and 19 England amateur international caps, Johnny was not sufficiently hard-nosed to make his way in the professional game. He played in the 1952 Olympics, then concentrated on teaching.

JOHN ANDREW WALTON
BORN: Horwich, Lancashire, 21 March 1928.
OTHER CLUBS: Bury 49/50-50/1 (26, 4) and 52/3-53/4 (29, 2); Burnley 54/5-55/6 (18, 2); Coventry City 56/7-57/8 (13, 0); Chester 59/60 (1, 0).
DIED: Horwich, Lancashire, July 1979.

GAMES **2**
GOALS **0**

NOEL McFARLANE

1953/54

After scoring twice in an FA Youth Cup Final clash with Wolves, the slim outside-right was tipped for stardom. But for all his lovely skills, Irishman Noel lacked the physical presence to make the grade in England and soon returned to his homeland.

NOEL WILLIAM McFARLANE
BORN: Bray, Republic of Ireland, 20 December 1934.
OTHER CLUBS: Waterford, Republic of Ireland.

GAMES **1**
GOALS **0**

PADDY KENNEDY

1954/55

United converted the young Dubliner from centre-half to left-back, but he proved unable to mount a serious challenge to Roger Byrne and Geoff Bent for the number-three shirt, and drifted out of contention after his sole senior outing, against Wolves.

PATRICK ANTHONY KENNEDY
BORN: Dublin, 9 October 1934.
OTHER CLUBS: Blackburn Rovers 57/8 (3, 0); Southampton 59/60 (2, 0).
DIED: Manchester, 18 March 2007.

GAMES **1**
GOALS **0**

ROGER BYRNE

1951/52 → 1957/58

If a manager from another planet, attracted by Roger Byrne's exalted reputation, had sent a scout to watch him train there would have been one very confused alien when he perused the report. It might have read something like this: heading – poor; tackling – ordinary; right foot – good; left foot – average (very); general impression – disillusioned. But if that same scout, wary of making too hasty a decision, had decided to stay for a match he would have torn up his notes and advised his boss to beam Roger up without delay.

The truth is that Roger Byrne was a superlative performer, one of the most accomplished defenders in British soccer history, but that his game defied detailed and logical analysis. Break his attributes down and he could be made to sound a bad player; but watch him in action and he was a master.

Roger arrived at Old Trafford in 1948, having been enlisted from a local youth club team for whom he played alongside Brian Statham, a useful junior footballer who was destined to become one of cricket's great fast bowlers with Lancashire and England. Until that point, Byrne had never considered the game as a potential career, having left grammar school at 16 to become an apprentice laboratory technician with a dye manufacturer.

At first he played at wing-half before being converted to a left winger, the berth he filled when breaking through in United's junior sides. However, he was switched to left-back as an experiment during a training session and it was in the number-three shirt that he made his senior debut, against Liverpool at Anfield in November 1951.

So impressive was the newcomer in subduing the Merseysiders' elusive flankman, Brian Jackson, that he moved no less a judge than Matt Busby, usually so cautious when prognosticating on the prospects of his young charges, to declare: 'Let Roger Byrne get the feel of things for about three matches. If he gets on as well as I expect, then I am prepared to say he is a certainty to play for England.'

Over the next few weeks the increasingly imperious Mancunian settled seamlessly, but then, after a couple of defeats, the manager opted to experiment and the newly-created full-back found himself back at outside-left. He responded by scoring seven goals in six games as United romped to the title without losing again.

The following season, after hinting that he might leave if asked to continue in attack, Roger reverted to left-back. Duly he made the position his own and went on to fulfil Busby's prophecy by filling the same role for England on 33 consecutive occasions, from his debut against Scotland at Hampden Park in April 1954, through that summer's World Cup Finals in Switzerland, and thereafter until his death at Munich.

Roger, who succeeded Johnny Carey as United skipper, was a man who made a nonsense of soccer convention. To begin with he played on the left despite being right-footed. Even more significant was his propensity for attack in an era when most British full-backs thought their place was in their own half and there they must remain. Truly, here was a player ahead of his time.

His great asset was speed, both mental and physical. There were few opponents he could not outwit with his inspired anticipation and cool reading of the game, and it was a rare winger – Peter Harris of Portsmouth is the only one who comes to mind – who could make him struggle for pace.

Beyond the example he set on the field, Roger was a born leader in every other way. Like Carey, he was renowned for his unimpeachable integrity and embodied the footballing beliefs of his boss. Though only 28 when he died, he was a father figure to the youngsters in the first-team squad and could relate directly to their feelings, having been a periodically headstrong individual in his own youth. Indeed, on one occasion he had almost been dispatched home early from a summer tour of the United States after being sent off in Los Angeles. Matured by such experience, he understood his callow comrades thoroughly, and if his tongue seemed sharp to them when they transgressed, they accepted his discipline because they respected him unreservedly.

Roger Byrne exuded class and charisma. He would have stood out in any company, in any era.

ROGER WILLIAM BYRNE
BORN: Manchester, 8 February 1929.
HONOURS: League Championship 51/2, 55/6, 56/7. 33 England caps (54-57).
DIED: Munich, 6 February 1958.

| GAMES | 280 |
| GOALS | 20 |

JOHNNY BERRY

1951/52 → 1957/58

When Johnny Berry was a Birmingham City player, Matt Busby was sick of the sight of him. Every time the tiny, but tough, right-winger faced United he tortured the Reds' defence. In the end the Old Trafford boss decided the only way to put an end to the torment was to sign the tormentor.

Even that wasn't as simple as it sounded. Birmingham were understandably reluctant to part with a performer who was gifted with both feet and who, had he not played in the era of Stan Matthews and Tom Finney, would have added considerably to his handful of England caps.

United had to wait 18 months before getting their man for £25,000, and what an inspired acquisition he proved to be, helping to lift three League titles. Johnny came into the team as the first wave of Busby Babes were making their debuts, and his experience and willingness to help the youngsters played an important part in their development.

Of course, his contribution went way beyond that. He was a tremendous performer in his own right, a classical flankman whose game was to make for the byline and get the ball into the middle with as little fuss as possible.

Johnny was as brave a wingman as any the English game has known. When full-backs handed out punishment – and certainly there were some ferocious customers among First Division defenders of the 1950s – there were many forwards who would jump for their lives. That was not the Berry way; he would bite back, competing to the death, and the fans loved him for his courage.

However, it was Johnny's predatory instinct and icily dispassionate finishing they were cheering one unforgettable night in February 1957 as the Red Devils faced Athletic Bilbao in a European Cup quarter-final second leg at Maine Road.

Only six minutes remained of a tumultuous encounter, in which United had come from two behind to level the aggregate score at five-apiece, when the tireless flankman switched roles with Tommy Taylor, slipping through the middle to receive a sweet dispatch from the roaming centre-forward before clipping home a sensational winning goal. City's home, hosting the match because the Old Trafford floodlights were not yet operable, exploded in acclaim for a United hero as never before or since.

By the time of the Munich air disaster a year later, Johnny had lost his place to young Kenny Morgans, but few observers doubted the feisty 31-year-old's capability of bouncing back. In the event, he travelled to the European Cup quarter-final clash with Red Star Belgrade as a reserve, and so serious were the injuries he sustained on that slushy German runway that he was unable to resume his career.

Thereafter Berry returned to his hometown, where for many years he ran a sports outfitters until his death, aged 68, in 1994.

Because he was not obtrusive, either as a character or as a performer, it is easy to overlook Johnny Berry when the the leading players of his day are being considered. But Old Trafford insiders, who recall vividly his compelling cocktail of fearlessness, fire and wizardry, are in no doubt. If he doesn't quite qualify for a place in an imaginary greatest United team since the war, then certainly he isn't far away.

JOHN JAMES BERRY

BORN: Aldershot, Hampshire, 1 June 1926.
HONOURS: League Championship 51/2, 55/6, 56/7. 4 England caps (53-56).
OTHER CLUBS: Birmingham City 47/8-51/2 (103, 5).
DIED: Farnham, Surrey, 16 September 1994.

GAMES 276
GOALS 45

DAVID PEGG

1952/53 → 1957/58

With Tom Finney approaching the end of his illustrious career, David Pegg was seen by many as the man most likely, in the long term, to step into his international boots.

Then came Munich. Although Albert Scanlon was keeping him out of the United side at the time of the disaster, there was plainly a great deal more to come from David, who was only 22 when he died.

A one-time schoolboy prodigy who had been a target for every top club, he made his senior debut as a 17-year-old in December 1952, stepping out at Old Trafford for a First Division encounter with Middlesbrough. That day he shone as United shaded a thrilling contest by the odd goal in five, and he retained his place until he was rested in the spring.

Following that early first-team impact, the young Yorkshireman spent two seasons of consolidation, enjoying only a handful of League outings as Jack Rowley moved from centre-forward to outside-left to make way for new arrival Tommy Taylor.

Thus it was in 1955/56 when the 20-year-old Pegg came of age in a footballing sense, ousting his constant rival, Scanlon, in September and retaining the number 11 shirt for the remainder of a memorable term which climaxed with the Red Devils as League Champions.

Rapidly thereafter, David became one of the most respected left-wingers in the country before losing form and his place, surely temporarily, towards the end of 1957. Certainly his dropping raised eyebrows across Europe, where he enjoyed a formidable reputation, being held in particularly high regard by Real Madrid, who reportedly signed a new defender specifically to combat his wiles in the 1957 European Cup semi-final.

Anderlecht, too, must have been a tad puzzled by David's demotion, having been utterly demoralised by the sinuously elegant flankman when the Belgians had been annihilated 10-0 by United earlier in the same campaign. That night at Maine Road, which was used because Old Trafford's floodlights were not yet operable, Pegg laid on five goals, though he finished as the only forward not to score despite the concerted efforts of his team-mates to set him up.

David, who collected a second successive title medal in 1956/57, was more of a ball-playing winger than an out-and-out runner. Full-backs found him elusive to mark as he was in the habit of dropping a shoulder and jinking inside, where he did much of his best work. On these penetrative sorties he was such a smooth mover that he seemed to glide over the ground, yet despite this delicate grace he possessed a left-foot shot of destructive force and was a willing worker.

Pegg was a precise crosser of the ball, too, a boon to the likes of Dennis Viollet, with whom he formed a lethal partnership on the left flank, and centre-forward Tommy Taylor.

How the friendly, but intense rivalry with the more direct Scanlon might have been resolved had fate not intervened at Munich, it is impossible to say. When the pair played together in the youth team, Albert appeared on the flank while David figured at inside-left, but given United's plethora of forward talent, it is unlikely that such a solution would have been repeated at senior level. Whatever, it is unthinkable that David's lavish talent would have languished for long.

By the time of his death, David Pegg had won only one full cap, and that as a result of a late withdrawal by Stanley Matthews, but it's fair to speculate that England, as much as Manchester United, were robbed of a priceless asset on that bleak February day in 1958.

DAVID PEGG
BORN: Doncaster, Yorkshire, 20 September 1935.
HONOURS: League Championship 55/6, 56/7. 1 England cap (57).
DIED: Munich, 6 February 1958.

GAMES 150
GOALS 28

DUNCAN EDWARDS

1952/53 → 1957/58

The legend of Duncan Edwards was a short time in the building but, as long as men gather together to kick a football, it will never die. Duncan was a soccer titan, a once-in-a-lifetime phenomenon who thundered on to the First Division scene in the early 1950s and was snatched away just five years later, leaving the football world aching for what might have been. He had been in the United side at 16, the England team two years later, and there seemed no limit to what he would achieve.

Duncan was that hitherto mythical being, the complete player. There was nothing that could be done on a football field that this young giant couldn't master more totally than anyone else. His ball control, with both feet, was utterly assured; his passing was exemplary and he tackled like a runaway juggernaut; his shooting was awesome, both in power and accuracy; in the air he was a king; his reading of the game was startling in its maturity. The catalogue of his playing attributes was comprehensive.

And that's barely the half of it. Then there were his bravery, loyalty and dedication, and – perhaps the most crucial of the lot – a temperament that ensured he would never squander the gifts with which he was so bounteously endowed.

Not surprisingly, every leading manager in the country had striven to enlist the services of the schoolboy Edwards and the favourites for his signature had been Wolverhampton Wanderers, one of the Dudley-born teenager's local clubs. But Matt Busby prevailed, having fired the lad's imagination, and from the moment of Duncan's arrival at Old Trafford, there was no doubt that United had recruited a genuine prodigy.

Though not in the least conceited, he was aware that he was special; even so, he did not believe in sitting back and letting it all happen. Indeed, his devotion to the game bordered on the fanatical and often he would practise until the ball had to be dragged away from him. Duncan would have played all day for the love of it if he could and he was the embodiment of the Corinthian spirit.

Most of his games for Manchester United were at wing-half, a position from which he could lend his dominance to the defence but could also storm into the attack at every opportunity. Opponents seemed to bounce off him when he set off on one of those surging runs, an apparently unstoppable force. His last League match, the Red Devils' epic victory over Arsenal at Highbury by the odd goal in nine, saw one of his typical strikes when he arrived late on the edge of the penalty box to wallop a pass from Dennis Viollet past the Gunners' custodian, Jack Kelsey.

It's a testimony to Edwards' stature that respected judges who saw such men as Best, Law and Charlton in their prime nevertheless place Duncan above them. As Bobby Charlton himself once put it: 'Compared to him the rest of us were like pygmies. If I had to play for my life, and could take one man with me, it would be Duncan Edwards.'

Matt Busby, too, was unequivocal about the worth of the Midlander who, even among the multi-talented Babes, towered over his fellows like some celestial colossus: 'He was the most valuable member of one team I ever saw anywhere. He was worth two of most, and two good ones, at that. Even at 15 he looked like a man and played like a man.'

And lest there be accusations of Old Trafford bias, here is the view of Don Revie who, in his Manchester City days, played for England alongside Duncan. He declared: 'Few professionals talk about greatness because it is so rare, but that is what I saw in Duncan. He reached the same fabulous standard at left-half, centre-half, inside-left or centre-forward. Really, he could play anywhere. He was the sort of footballer any manager dreams about.'

As for the continent's top coaches, they held him in awe, several of them predicting confidently in 1957 that before long he would be out on his own as the world's premier all-round performer.

When Duncan died at Munich – after a courageous two-week fight for life during which he joked with Jimmy Murphy about being fit for the next game – he had won two Championship medals and had played 18 times for England. He was only 21, his vast potential barely tapped. Those who saw Duncan Edwards play will treasure the memory. He was a young leviathan, and his like will not be seen again.

DUNCAN EDWARDS
BORN: Dudley, Worcestershire, 1 October 1936.
HONOURS: League Championship 55/6, 56/7. 18 England caps (55-57).
DIED: Munich, 21 February 1958.

GAMES 177
GOALS 21

MARK JONES

1950/51 → 1957/58

'The Gentle Giant' was a nickname coined for the mighty Welshman, John Charles, but it was just as apt to describe Mark Jones, that seam of Yorkshire granite standing between marauding centre-forwards of the 1950s and the Manchester United goal.

Mark was the archetypal pivot, broad of beam, crushing in the tackle and majestic in the air. He was an uncomplicated sort of player and rarely ruined his ball-winning efforts by squandering possession with over-ambitious distribution. A simple pass to Duncan Edwards or Eddie Colman was his preferred option, thus making him the perfect foil for that expansively talented pair who flourished on either side of him.

The doughty stopper, who won two Championship medals with the Red Devils, relished the physical challenge presented by such craggy characters as Nat Lofthouse and Trevor Ford, yet off the field he was a mild-mannered family man who had more in common with Clark Kent than Superman.

Mark was a fellow without an ounce of malice and his gentleness was a byword. He liked nothing better than a natter about his beloved budgerigars, of which he was an avid collector, and he reacted amiably to being dubbed 'Dan Archer' by team-mates in reference to his pipe-smoking habit.

Not feted by press and public to the same lavish degree as many of the other Busby Babes, nevertheless he was arguably the most popular of them all with his team-mates. Indeed, one of them, John Doherty, named his first son after the amiable Yorkshireman.

Mark came of age in a football sense by finishing the title-winning campaign of 1955/56 as the Reds' only ever-present, but then he found his professional life complicated by a continual battle for the centre-half spot with Jackie Blanchflower, the best man at his wedding.

First one looked to have it sewn up, then the initiative would pass to the other. The Irishman edged selection for the 1957 FA Cup Final, but by the time of the Munich disaster, Mark had regained his place and was playing the best football of his career. Even the slightest injury to either man would mean a lengthy spell on the sidelines because of the other's excellence, though respected contemporary pundits reckoned that Mark was perhaps the best long-term bet as he was the more commanding of the pair.

The big, blond ex-bricklayer's apprentice, a former captain of the England schoolboys team, had joined United from Yorkshire junior football and turned professional in the summer of 1950. That autumn, still only 17, he tasted League action for the first time in a home victory over Sheffield Wednesday, but despite acquitting himself commendably he faced a four-year wait for a regular place.

Duly he emerged from the shadow of his boyhood hero, Allenby Chilton, who played an important and selfless part in the youngster's development, helping to iron out initial crudeness in the Jones technique and encouraging his eventual successor at every opportunity.

Thereafter Mark made steady progress, but was never to realise his lifelong ambition of playing for England at senior level. The nearest he came was a place on the reserves' bench, but with the long-serving Billy Wright approaching the end of his illustrious international career, then surely that elusive cap would have been clinched before long had he not perished at Munich.

		GAMES	121
		GOALS	1

MARK JONES
BORN: Long Valley, near Barnsley, Yorkshire, 15 June 1933.
HONOURS: League Championship 55/6, 56/7.
DIED: Munich, 6 February 1958.

JACKIE BLANCHFLOWER

1951/52 → 1957/58

Athoroughbred footballer imbued with the spirit of adventure, Jackie Blanchflower did not always get the credit he deserved. While plaudits were rained – rightly enough – on the heads of Duncan Edwards and company, often Jackie's name was absent from dispatches even when his contribution had been immense.

A utility man of style and subtle skills, and the younger brother of the similarly cool and clever but more famous Danny of Tottenham Hotspur, he made an impressive United debut as a wing-half at Anfield in 1951/52, but then suffered a knee injury which put him out of immediate contention.

By the time he had fully recovered, there had appeared a new wave of exquisitely talented youngsters with the aforementioned Edwards at its crest, and the consequently ferocious competition for places forced him temporarily to one side.

But Jackie – known as 'Twiggy' by colleagues who took grave liberties with his name, long before the emergence of a certain stick-like lady – was too sure of his own worth merely to fade away. Thus he returned to the reckoning as a creative inside-forward, contributing 24 goals over two campaigns before pocketing a title medal in 1955/56.

However, blessed as he was with a golden crop of outstanding young forwards, Matt Busby decreed that centre-half should be Jackie's premier position and thereafter, until the Munich tragedy, the Ulsterman waged war with Yorkshireman Mark Jones for the number-five shirt.

Blanchflower Jnr brought enviable qualities to that duel: he had an assured touch with both feet, was combative in the air and possessed a formidable footballing brain which often enabled him to turn defence into attack with one sudden, incisive pass. His most marked defect was a distinct lack of pace which, in his early days at Old Trafford, caused much ribbing.

A natural all-round sportsman, Jackie demonstrated his versatility when he took over in goal for the injured Ray Wood in the 1957 FA Cup Final. He gave a sound and courageous display between the posts, and blame for neither of Aston Villa's goals in their 2-1 victory, both scored by his rumbustious countryman Peter McParland, could be laid at the foor of the emergency custodian.

As the next season dawned Jackie retained his first-team berth but that November, as the manager reshuffled in a bid to correct a slight slump in the team's fortunes, he was replaced by Jones, one of his closest friends.

The two players offered a vivid contrast – Blanchflower cultured and constructive, Jones a traditionally physical stopper – but both meshed effectively with the sublime wing-half pairing of Eddie Colman and Duncan Edwards.

By the time of the air crash in February 1958, the Irishman remained on the sidelines and travelled merely as a reserve, being declared fit to do so only at the last moment, though unquestionably his long-term Old Trafford prospects remained diamond-bright.

Jackie, who received the last rites at Munich, survived the accident but had suffered such extensive injuries – a fractured pelvis, a complete set of broken arms and legs, shattered ribs and severe kidney damage – that he was unable to resume his career, thus confounding hopes which kept him registered on the club's books until June 1959, some 16 months later.

That proved a bitter loss not only to Manchester United, but also to Northern Ireland, for whom he had claimed a regular place alongside his brother, and he had been set to appear in the 1958 World Cup Finals when disaster struck.

JOHN BLANCHFLOWER
BORN: Belfast, 7 March 1933.
HONOURS: League Championship 55/6. 12 Northern ireland caps (54-58).
DIED: Manchester, 2 September 1998.

GAMES 117
GOALS 27

JEFF WHITEFOOT

1949/50 → 1955/56

More than a handful of well-informed observers of the Old Trafford scene in the 1950s were mystified by Jeff Whitefoot's failure to become a United star. The obvious answer was that this skilful, composed, beautifully balanced wing-half lost out through the emergence of Eddie Colman, but that alone is not a satisfactory solution.

Quite clearly, Eddie was a marvellous player who merited his place but the way the club was developing, particularly on the European front, meant that a large squad of quality performers was needed; and the football fates being what they are, it seemed likely that opportunity would knock again for Jeff. But, after winning a Championship medal in 1955/56, the man who had been United's youngest ever debutant at 16 years and 105 days when he had faced Portsmouth at Old Trafford in April 1950, moved to Grimsby for £11,500. After that he joined Nottingham Forest, with whom he experienced FA Cup glory in 1959 and spent a decade in the top flight.

After Munich, many thought that United would turn again to Jeff, an accomplished passer with both feet and a brisk tackler, but Stan Crowther was signed instead.

JEFFREY WHITEFOOT
BORN: Cheadle, Cheshire, 13 December 1933.
HONOURS: League Championship 55/6.
OTHER CLUBS: Grimsby Town 57/8 (27, 5);
Nottingham Forest 58/9-67/8 (255, 5).

GAMES 95
GOALS 0

JOHN DOHERTY

1952/53 → 1957/58

There was a time, when John Doherty's star was rising, that he looked the equal of any promising young inside-forward in the country. John was blessed with an astute football brain, an exquisite touch with either foot and a shot to compare with Bobby Charlton's.

An outstanding youth player, he made his debut in 1952/53 and was widely expected to illuminate the upper echelons of the English game for the foreseeable future. But competition was fierce among the Busby Babes and John had a knee injury which would never quite clear up, so he was denied a settled run in the team until 1955/56. That season he won a Championship medal on merit with 16 appearances, but that gammy knee continued to plague him and Billy Whelan, originally brought to England to fill in for an unfit John in an FA Youth Cup Final, had developed into an irresistible performer.

Thus a future that had once beckoned so invitingly no longer seemed so bright, and in October 1957 a £6,500 deal saw the unlucky Mancunian move to Leicester shortly before limping out of the game for good. John, and United, were left to ponder what might have been.

JOHN PETER DOHERTY
BORN: Manchester, 12 March 1935.
HONOURS: League Championship 55/6.
OTHER CLUBS: Leicester City 57/8 (12, 5).
DIED: Manchester, 13 November 2007.

GAMES 26
GOALS 7

GEOFF BENT

1954/55 → 1956/57

Geoff Bent was perhaps the unluckiest player to die at Munich on that ill-fated journey home from Belgrade. As a reserve full-back he had not been going to make the trip for the European Cup encounter with Red Star until Roger Byrne suffered a slight strain in the match at Highbury the previous Saturday. In the event, Roger was fit to face the Yugoslavians so Geoff was not needed, which made the events that followed all the more poignant.

In fact, if he had been with any other club in the First Division, Geoff would have been an automatic first choice. Indeed, during the mid-1950s many pundits reckoned he should have been a first-team regular at left-back, thus allowing Byrne to switch to his natural right side. Standing four-square in the way of that scenario, though, was the metronomic consistency of Bill Foulkes in the number-two shirt.

Whatever, the unfortunate Bent's game appeared to lack nothing. He was an aggressive tackler who could operate on the left or right flank of defence and who boasted speed, a cool head and accurate distribution among his assets. Life in the captain's shadow must have been frustrating, but it never affected Geoff's enthusiastic approach or his loyalty.

GEOFFREY BENT
BORN: Salford, Lancashire, 27 September 1932.
DIED: Munich, 6 February 1958.

GAMES	12
GOALS	0

KENNY MORGANS

1957/58 → 1960/61

The case of Kenny Morgans is as sad as it is perplexing. Before the Munich disaster Kenny, a quick and clever winger who could play on either flank, was in the first team on merit. He had displaced Johnny Berry on the right in the December, enjoyed a six-week purple patch and, come February, looked set for a lengthy run.

Then came the crash, which the chirpy Welshman survived. He was passed fit and returned to the side by April. Yet he never recaptured his form or the confidence that was his hallmark and was not picked for the FA Cup Final. And that was just about that. Soon he moved to Swansea and then Newport, where he saw out his playing days.

So what went wrong? With much of the competition for places so tragically removed, Kenny had been expected to prosper at Old Trafford. Perhaps he had hinted at more than he could deliver or, a lot more likely, maybe he had rushed back into action too soon without giving the mental scars left by the disaster a chance to heal. Either way, a lavishly promising career at the top level was cut short before it really got going.

KENNETH GODFREY MORGANS
BORN: Swansea, Glamorgan, 16 March 1939.
OTHER CLUBS: Swansea Town 60/1-63/4 (55, 8); Newport County 64/5-66/7 (125, 46).

GAMES	23
GOALS	0

EDDIE COLMAN

1955/56 → 1957/58

Watching Eddie Colman on a football pitch was like spying on a precocious small boy scrumping apples from his teacher's garden while playing truant from school. There was the same jaunty swagger spiced with a dash of daring which made him an irresistible figure to the denizens of the Old Trafford terraces, especially the Stretford End.

But, by the time the Munich disaster took the life of this irrepressible local lad – he hailed from Archie Street, Salford, later to earn TV immortality as *Coronation Street* – he had very much come of age as a football talent and his prospects appeared to be limitless.

A tiny bundle of creative energy, Eddie was the wing-half with the wiggle. The press dubbed him 'Snakehips' for his mesmeric body swerve – some over-imaginative scribes even compared his motion to that of Marilyn Monroe! – while goalkeeper Harry Gregg once remarked that when Eddie swayed, so beguiling was his movement that the Old Trafford stands swayed with him.

Colman had been a fixture in the team since making his debut, aged 19, in November 1955 against Bolton Wanderers, when he had made seasoned campaigners such as Nat Lofthouse goggle with his skill and confidence. Thereafter he had improved rapidly with experience, slamming shut the first-team door in the face of the estimable Jeff Whitefoot, no small achievement in itself.

Eddie's influence on the United side which won the Championship in consecutive seasons, 1955/56 and 1956/57, was enormous. So many of their most effective moves owed plenty to his wickedly incisive passing and devastating dribbling ability. His eye for an opening was unerring, and he was particularly adept at quicksilver 'give-and-go' incisions into enemy territory. Curling perfect dispatches around stranded defenders to set up his forwards was another weapon in his armoury.

Sometimes, like George Best in later years, he would madden team-mates by hanging on to the ball too long, but they knew that Eddie was a player who needed a free rein. To have shackled him to a rigid team plan would have stifled the inspiration which made him priceless.

In another set-up Eddie Colman might have struggled to express himself, but with the Busby Babes he was in his element. So much of his success was thanks to the manager's golden gift of creating the right blend. Although tough enough for his size and a plucky tackler, Eddie needed to play alongside a man of dominating physical presence – and who better than Duncan Edwards?

Man-mountain Duncan and 5ft 7in Eddie comprised one of the finest wing-half pairings imaginable, though they contrasted vividly, in character as well as in stature and style. While Edwards tended to be quiet, offering the impression of shyness at times, his little pal was a bubbly extrovert, a practical joker and everybody's friend.

One element missing from the Colman game was goals. He managed only two in his career, though one of those was a crucial effort in the 1957/58 European Cup quarter-final against Red Star Belgrade. Part of the reason for this drought was that he wasn't the strongest striker of the ball, his glorious passes owing more to deftness than power, but that hardly qualified as a criticism when he did so much to boost his team-mates' tallies.

Eddie Colman will be remembered as a crowd-pleaser supreme whose best days were yet to come. He was only 21 when he died and yet to appear for England. Thus country, as well as club, was deprived of a diamond.

EDWARD COLMAN
BORN: Salford, Lancashire, 1 November 1936.
HONOURS: League Championship 55/6, 56/7.
DIED: Munich, 6 February 1958.

GAMES	108
GOALS	2

RAY WOOD

. . . .

1949/50 → 1958/59

A freezing November night in Dortmund is not the time or the place most players would choose to enjoy their finest footballing hour, but so it was with Ray Wood. It happened in 1956, well before the days when television brought instant worldwide glory for any performer who excelled in a big match.

Ray was keeping goal in the second leg of the European Cup first-round tie against Borussia. United took only a one-goal lead with them, an advantage which looked increasingly slender as the Germans seized control. Borussia created chances galore and must have been confident that goals would come, but they were destined to be disappointed thanks to the inspired Wood, who gave the performance of a lifetime in preserving the clean sheet which saw the Red Devils through safely to the next round.

In fact, Ray was always a top-notch shot-stopper and his courage was unquestionable, but his handling of crosses was not of quite the same calibre and eventually he was replaced by the world-class Irishman, Harry Gregg.

Wood will be remembered always as the man whose injury in a sickening collision with Peter McParland in the 1957 FA Cup Final probably cost United the League and FA Cup double, but he deserves a more rounded epitaph than that and could point justifiably to two Championship medals and three England caps.

Ray set off on what was to become a footballing odyssey with Newcastle United after the war, only for the Magpies to release him without playing a senior game. His next stop was Darlington, from whence he was plucked with alacrity by Matt Busby, who paid £5,000 for the 18-year-old and then was forced by an injury crisis to hand the dumbfounded rookie an instant debut – against Newcastle.

Ray responded nobly, peering through curtains of rain to make several outstanding saves in a 1-1 draw, thus underlining his potential as a long-term investment. Thereafter he buckled down to learn more about his trade behind senior 'keepers Jack Crompton and Reg Allen, as well as demonstrating his all-round ability by playing three games at centre-forward for the 'A' team.

This fascinating interlude, during which he scored six goals, amazed most of his new team-mates, but not old chums from the north-east who recalled his productive days as a professional sprinter, dashing for cash at weekends in the pit villages.

For all that admirable versatility, though, Ray's future was to be between the sticks and in 1953/54, with Allen ill and Crompton having passed his peak, he established himself as first choice.

The next four years witnessed Ray's impressively productive prime, after which he was displaced by Gregg and survived the Munich air crash before moving to Huddersfield when it became clear he would not regain his United place.

A measure of Matt Busby's professional regard for the likeable custodian, who went on to become a globetrotting coach, was that the Old Trafford boss tried unsuccessfully to re-sign him when Harry suffered a serious shoulder injury during the early 1960s.

Half a lifetime later, Ray Wood remained the answer to one of the cuter soccer quiz questions doing the rounds: which goalkeeper started and finished an FA Cup Final between the posts and didn't let in a goal, yet went home with a loser's medal?

RAYMOND ERNEST WOOD

BORN:	Hebburn, County Durham, 11 June 1931.
HONOURS:	League Championship 55/6, 56/7. 3 England caps (54-56).
OTHER CLUBS:	Darlington 49/50 (12, 0); Huddersfield Town 58/9-64/5 (207, 0); Bradford City 65/6 (32, 0); Barnsley 66/7-67/8 (30, 0).
MANAGER:	Los Angeles Wolves, USA, (68); Cyprus national team (69-72); Apoel, Cyprus, (72-73); Trikkala, Greece, (73); Salymia, Kuwait, (73-74); Kenya club and national teams (74-78); United Arab Emirates clubs (78-82).
DIED:	Bexhill, Sussex, 7 July 2002.

GAMES 208
GOALS 0

TOMMY TAYLOR

1952/53 → 1957/58

When Tommy Taylor bulged Preston North End's net with a prodigiously powerful edge-of-the-box header in his first game for Manchester United, Reds supporters sensed they were in the presence of an extraordinary talent. The following five years, until he lost his life at Munich, were to prove them emphatically correct.

Tommy was an exuberant buccaneer of a footballer and one of the greatest centre-forwards that England, let alone United, have ever had. Certainly he was one of the most underrated and his scoring record would have been staggering in any era. For the Red Devils he managed two goals every three matches; put another way, he found the net once every two hours or so that he spent on a football pitch.

On top of that he weighed in with a further 16 in 19 games for England and there was every reason to believe that, at 26, he was still approaching his peak. Yet when the all-time greats are mentioned, his name does not always crop up – outside Old Trafford circles, I hasten to add.

Tommy's arrival from Barnsley in March 1953 represented the culmination of a lengthy quest by Matt Busby to replace his prolific but ageing marksman, Jack Rowley. The big, raw-boned Yorkshireman's heavy scoring for the Oakwell club had attracted nationwide interest and United beat off nearly 20 competitors before securing their quarry for what was then a record fee of £29,999 – Matt presented a tea lady with the odd pound rather than burden his new recruit with a £30,000 tag.

Thus Tommy found himself as a sole expensive newcomer in an emerging team consisting mainly of sumptuously talented rookies, the Busby Babes. It might have proved an awkward situation for a boy who had learned the game the hard way on rough, inhospitable pitches, then started work as a haulage hand in his local pit when he was 14 before getting serious about football two years later; but not a bit of it.

After breezing into Manchester with his boots wrapped in a brown paper parcel, he settled immediately and soon it was apparent that United had secured a rare bargain. Tommy, an infectiously ebullient but down-to-earth character who quickly became popular with fans and colleagues alike, scored twice on his debut and by the end of the 1952/53 campaign he had notched seven goals in just 11 games.

Unquestionably his greatest gift was for aerial combat, in which he knew no contemporary peer. He could smack the ball with his forehead more forcefully and accurately than many players could kick it, his timing was uncanny and his bravery knew no bounds. Indeed, so formidable was his prowess when he soared skywards that he can be mentioned meaningfully in the same breath as Tommy Lawton and John Charles who remain, by common consent, the two most potent headers of a ball to adorn the British game since the war.

A measure of the mayhem Tommy could induce among even the most accomplished defenders could be gauged vividly at corner-kicks: he would station himself at the far corner of the box, fix his eyes on the ball and then, invariably timing his run to perfection, he would charge to meet it, a near-unstoppable dreadnought. Concentration, in such vulnerable circumstances, was not easy for his markers to maintain.

This spectacular talent tended to obscure his other attributes, which were considerable. Perhaps because of his size, he could look clumsy on the ball but this belied excellent control, a pulverising shot in either foot, and a sharp line in first-time distribution which made him devastating, particularly in tandem with Dennis Viollet.

A strong, long-striding, selfless marauder, he had the stamina to spend 90 minutes at full stretch and was capable of retaining possession in the face of savage challenges. Often Tommy was at his best when drifting wide to the right, pulling defenders with him and interchanging positions with Johnny Berry. Such a ploy produced the little winger's unforgettable winner against Athletic Bilbao in the quarter-final of the 1956/57 European Cup.

Tommy's growing stature in the world game was illustrated immediately after the 1957 FA Cup Final, in which he scored United's goal, when Inter Milan made the then-astronomical offer of £65,000 for his services. The manager rejected the bid; his dashing young centre-forward was not for sale at any price. What a tragic shame that Matt was unable to enjoy the full fruits of his judgement.

THOMAS TAYLOR			
BORN:	Barnsley, Yorkshire, 29 January 1932.		
HONOURS:	League Championship 55/6, 56/7. 19 England caps (53-57).		
OTHER CLUBS:	Barnsley 50/1-52/3 (44, 26).	GAMES	191
DIED:	Munich, 6 February 1958.	GOALS	131

85

BILLY WHELAN

1954/55 → 1957/58

Billy Whelan was a soccer artist whose brain moved faster than his legs. On the ball he could look awkward, even clumsy, yet he had the knack of ghosting past opponent after opponent with the merest of shimmies. And once within shooting distance he was a man to respect, as his record of better than a goal every two games testifies. Indeed, in 1956/57 Billy netted 33 times in 53 senior outings – and he wasn't even playing as an out-and-out front man.

A vivid example of his talent came away to Athletic Bilbao in the European Cup quarter-final first leg that same season. He picked the ball up deep, shuffled half the length of the swamp-like pitch, leaving five Spanish defenders in his wake, before netting with a rising shot of near-uncanny precision in such awkward circumstances. What a crucial strike it turned out to be, too, reducing the Red Devils' deficit to 5-3, setting up a memorable revival back in Manchester.

The quietly-spoken inside-forward, whose engagingly modest personality was never altered by his success with United and the Republic of Ireland, played his football with a deceptively relaxed air. Certainly there was nothing casual about his work in the penalty area and he could be especially lethal with his back to goal. One of soccer's more persuasive dummy salesmen, he found an unwilling customer in the shape of a bemused Wrexham defender in January 1957; indeed, the subtle flick which found the Welshmen's net when no danger seemed imminent was the work of a conjuror.

If this dream of a dribbler had only possessed pace he would have ranked as one of football's all-time greats, even though his career – and his life – ended at Munich. As it was Billy didn't always get the credit he deserved and didn't appear to realise just how good he was.

United's coaching staff, however, were under no such misapprehension, right from the moment he was signed as an 18-year-old from Home Farm with the urgent initial task of replacing the injured John Doherty in the 1953 FA Youth Cup Final against Wolves. Billy – or Liam as he was known sometimes, particularly at home in Ireland – starred in a 7–1 first-leg victory and was marked down for an illustrious future. Indeed, so eye-catching were his gifts that, following a fabulous display in a youth tournament in Switzerland, the club received a discreet inquiry from Brazil about his availability. Needless to say, further interest was not encouraged.

The boy's development continued apace; soon he was a major creative and goal-scoring force at senior level and the honours began to mount. Yet such was the wealth of talent available to Matt Busby in that glorious era that, at the time of the Munich disaster, the 22-year-old Dubliner was being kept out of the side by one of his closest friends, Bobby Charlton. Of course, he had so much to give that, sooner or later, he must have reclaimed a place, even if it had not been at Bobby's expense.

Billy was a devout Roman Catholic and, to the last, his faith never wavered. As United's plane made its fateful third attempt at take-off from that slushy German runway, he was heard to murmur: 'If this is the end, then I am ready for it.' The tragedy was that the soccer world was far from ready to lose Billy Whelan.

WILLIAM AUGUSTINE WHELAN

BORN:	Dublin, 1 April 1935.
HONOURS:	League Championship 55/6, 56/7. 4 Republic of Ireland caps (56-57).
OTHER CLUBS:	Home Farm, Republic of Ireland.
DIED:	Munich, 6 February 1958.

GAMES	98
GOALS	52

ALBERT SCANLON

1954/55 → 1960/61

Albert Scanlon was something of an enigma. A dashing flankman of skill and verve who could wreak havoc with both feet, he didn't build the lengthy career at Old Trafford that his ravishing ability appeared to warrant.

He first made his mark as a diminutive 15-year-old, despite being one of no less than ten talented left wingers at the club. Little Albert was always capable of embarrassing any opponent, no matter how daunting, and after one practice match in which he was confronted by the formidably ruthless Bill Foulkes, he was informed by coach Bert Whalley: 'You're doing well, son, you had Bill in two minds – he didn't know whether to kick you over the stands or into the dressing room!'

Even after helping to secure the FA Youth Cup in the first two years of its existence, the perkily streetwise local lad remained a rather erratic teenager, but in 1954/55 he enjoyed a creditable run in the senior side, then found himself largely in the shadow of David Pegg for the next two seasons.

The two made a fascinating contrast: David blessed with more intricate skills and a more consistent player, Albert quicker and perhaps more exciting but with an unpredictable streak.

Halfway through the 1957/58 campaign the young Scanlon forced his way back in and he was still there on merit at the time of Munich.

One of his most memorable performances was in the last League game before the disaster, a stirring 5–4 triumph over Arsenal. That afternoon at Highbury he laid on goals for Bobby Charlton, Tommy Taylor and Dennis Viollet, tantalising the Gunners' defence with a bewildering succession of high-velocity dribbles. It was a truly spellbinding display of speed and flair, and it had the pundits talking freely about a scintillating international future which, alas, never came to pass.

Albert escaped from the crash with a broken leg and fractured skull, but he carried psychological scars which sidelined him for the rest of that campaign, ruling him out of the FA Cup Final against Bolton Wanderers. Even when he recovered physical fitness, initially he was not keen to play as, somehow, it didn't seem right to him to take the field without his fallen friends.

However, he stimulated new optimism for a productive long-term future by bouncing back resiliently in 1958/59, scoring 16 goals and not missing a game as, astonishingly in such traumatic circumstances, the new Red Devils finished a transitional term as runners-up to Wolves in the title race.

By now Scanlon was playing the best football of his career, and he was rewarded with appearances at England under-23 and Football League level, but there was always the nagging thought that a couple of blinders might be followed by a stinker.

An unfortunate turning point arrived towards the end of 1959/60, when Albert was injured and Matt Busby, striving to get the utmost out of the brilliant Charlton, temporarily converted his leading light into an outside-left, which curtailed the Mancunian's prospects drastically.

Accordingly when his uncle, Newcastle boss Charlie Mitten – who himself had graced United's left flank until his controversial departure a decade earlier – offered £18,000 for his services that November, Scanlon joined Newcastle. Sadly he failed to settle in the north east, or subsequently with Lincoln City, but then he flourished for two seasons with Mansfield Town before retiring in 1966.

That was fine in its way, but those who recall him in his prime know that Albert Scanlon had much more to offer. Unquestionably he had the raw talent to have flourished at the top level throughout the first half of the 1960s.

ALBERT JOSEPH SCANLON
BORN: Manchester, 10 October 1935.
OTHER CLUBS: Newcastle United 60/1-61/2 (22, 0); Lincoln City 61/2-62/3 (47, 11);
Mansfield Town 62/3-65/6 (108, 21).

GAMES 127
GOALS 35

DENNIS VIOLLET

1952/53 → 1961/62

Dennis Viollet was a steel dart of a player. Slim, pale, even frail of appearance, he was possessed of magnetic control and sudden, searing pace which could slice to the heart of the stoutest defence. Yet one of soccer's absurdities is that he played only twice for his country.

In the middle and late 1950s, at a time when the deceptively wiry inside-forward and his partner-in-goals Tommy Taylor were terrorising First Division defences, England deigned to select only half of the free-scoring United double-act. Never mind that Tommy was at his most lethal alongside his clubmate, or that Dennis himself was as gifted and resourceful a front-man as could be found in Britain. It was deemed desirable for the coveted white shirt to be placed on the backs of a series of worthy but uninspired individuals, and while there is no need to name names, their sheer ordinariness made the selectors' reasoning startlingly incomprehensible.

But if England fans were denied the chance to revel in the talents of such an exciting entertainer, United supporters faced no such deprivation in those heady, adventurous pre-Munich days when two successive Championship crowns were claimed. One of the most prolific goalscorers in Old Trafford history, Viollet luxuriated in the space created by the ever-bustling Taylor who, in turn, fed voraciously off opportunities fashioned by his elusive cohort. In terms of a striking duo they were the dream ticket, but anyone who doubted that Dennis was an outstanding performer in his own right was furnished with ample proof to the contrary after Tommy was killed.

Dennis was laid low by the after-effects of the crash until the end of 1957/58 – he recovered just in time to appear, albeit rather wanly, in the FA Cup Final against Bolton – before surging back with 21 goals the following term. But it was in 1959/60 that he demonstrated his quality to most emphatic effect, rattling in 32 goals in 36 League matches, more strikes in one campaign than any United player before or since.

Stop to consider a few of the men Dennis Viollet has outscored – take Rowley, Pearson, Taylor, Charlton, Law, Best and van Nistelrooy merely for starters – and the scale of his achievement is apparent. Yet there was more to his game than that. He possessed the passing technique and all-round ability to succeed in a deep-lying role, in which he operated at times for United and, more frequently, after his transfer to Stoke City in January 1962. His only discernible defect was a lack of aerial power, not serious when playing alongside big Tommy.

Dennis had arrived at Old Trafford in 1949, signing amateur forms for the Red Devils after skippering Manchester Schoolboys and playing regularly for England at that level. He made his First Division debut at Newcastle in April 1953, figuring at outside-right as Taylor, newly acquired from Barnsley, netted the brace which gave United victory. Before long, though, Dennis switched to a central role and his career took off with a vengeance.

Nearly nine years later, many observers were dumbfounded by his £25,000 switch to the Potteries, which was completed not long after his two belated England appearances. Following his recent free-scoring feats, he seemed integral to United's immediate future, but in came David Herd (ironically a boyhood pal), plans were laid to enlist Denis Law, and Viollet, hardly a has-been at 28, was on his way.

Happily, that was not the end of the footballing world for the popular, easy-going Mancunian, a sociable character who lived life to the full. Lining up alongside the amazing Stanley Matthews, who was old enough to be his father, he played a key role in Stoke's Second Division title triumph in his first full season and he remained productively at the Victoria Ground until 1967.

After that Dennis joined British soccer's mini-exodus to the USA before recrossing the Atlantic for a brief stint with non-League Witton Albion in 1969. Later that year he joined Linfield as player-coach and excelled in Ulster, pocketing an Irish Cup winner's medal in his 37th year in 1970. Perhaps fittingly for an individual so continuously under-valued in his own country, Dennis Viollet finished his football career as a successful coach in the States.

DENNIS SYDNEY VIOLLET
BORN: Manchester, 20 September 1933.
HONOURS: League Championship 55/6, 56/7. 2 England caps (60-61).
OTHER CLUBS: Stoke City 61/2-66/7 (182, 59); Baltimore Bays, USA, 67-68 (34, 7); Linfield, Northern Ireland, 69/70.
MANAGER: Crewe Alexandra (71).
DIED: Jacksonville, Florida, 6 March 1999.

GAMES 293
GOALS 179

FREDDIE GOODWIN

1954/55 → 1959/60

Freddie Goodwin was a lanky, cool, almost languid wing-half whose misfortune it was to be at Old Trafford at the same time as Eddie Colman and Duncan Edwards. A lovely passer, particularly adept at one-two interchanges, he might be described, and not unkindly, as a lesser 6ft 2in version of little Colman, minus the flair.

He made his debut in 1954/55 but, until Munich, never surpassed the status of reserve, though he was one of the classiest stand-ins in the First Division. In the wake of the crash he made the right-half position his own, appearing in the 1958 FA Cup Final and earning considerable distinction as an ever-present in the side which finished as runners-up during the following term.

After that Freddie's star began to fall as Matt Busby began building a new team, and in March 1960 he joined Leeds, whom he served with consistency for five seasons.

A former county cricketer with Lancashire, Goodwin went on to shine in soccer management, serving a series of clubs in Britain and the United States, with his spell at Birmingham City being the most notable.

FREDERICK GOODWIN
BORN: Heywood, Lancashire, 28 June 1933.
OTHER CLUBS: Leeds United 59/60-63/4 (107, 2); Scunthorpe United 65/6 (6, 1).
MANAGER: Scunthorpe United (64-67); New York Generals, USA, (67-68); Brighton and Hove Albion (68-70); Birmingham City (70-75); Minnesota Kicks, USA, (76-79 and 80-81).

GAMES 107
GOALS 8

IAN GREAVES

1954/55 → 1959/60

One inspired spell was enough for Ian Greaves to win a Championship medal, and he did it on merit in the pre-Munich days of white-hot competition. Admittedly Ian got his chance at right-back when the redoubtable Bill Foulkes was injured, but he performed so well that Bill could not win back his place until the following season. After the crash the versatile Greaves took over at left-back, a position in which he picked up an FA Cup finalist's medal, then kept the job during the next term, only for a knee injury to effectively end his Old Trafford sojourn.

Ian was a tall, sturdy, inelegant defender who looked all arms and legs. He linked well with his half-backs and was brave but never, except in that one purple patch, looked likely to make the very highest grade. If he was not in the top bracket as a player, however, there is ample evidence of his excellence as a manager. There was even a time, during his splendid spell at Bolton, when he was tipped to take over from Tommy Docherty at United. There are those who believe that had he done so, the wait for the title would have been considerably shorter . . .

IAN DENZIL GREAVES
BORN: Oldham, Lancashire, 26 May 1932.
HONOURS: League Championship 55/6.
OTHER CLUBS: Lincoln City 60/1 (11, 0); Oldham Athletic 61/2-62/3 (22, 0).
MANAGER: Huddersfield Town (68-74); Bolton Wanderers (74-80); Oxford United (80-82); Wolverhampton Wanderers (82); Mansfield Town (83-89).

GAMES 75
GOALS 0

STAN CROWTHER

1957/58 → 1958/59

Stan Crowther was a trier, but he never looked likely to have a long-term future with Manchester United. Bought for £18,000 as an emergency measure after Munich, when stand-in boss Jimmy Murphy was at his wits' end in the quest for senior players, he was an abrasive wing-half who lacked the all-round quality to succeed at the top level.

Stan gave a gutsily effective spoiling performance for Aston Villa against United in the 1957 FA Cup Final, displaying just the grit and vigour for which Jimmy was so desperate in the wake of the crash.

Though he was cup-tied with the Midlanders come February 1958, the FA waived the rule and the tall, wiry Crowther helped to tide the Reds over the immediate crisis, picking up a Wembley loser's medal against Bolton in the process.

At the outset of the 1958/59 campaign Stan lost his place to Wilf McGuinness and soon he moved on, first to Chelsea for £10,000 and then to Brighton, without managing to make much of a mark. During his spell at Villa Park, he won England under-23 recognition but that early promise was never fulfilled and he left League football at the age of 26.

STANLEY CROWTHER
BORN: Bilston, Staffordshire, 3 September 1935.
OTHER CLUBS: Aston Villa 56/7-57/8 (50, 4);
Chelsea 58/9-59/60 (51, 0); Brighton and Hove
Albion 60/1 (4, 0).

GAMES	20
GOALS	0

ERNIE TAYLOR

1957/58 → 1958/59

Ernie Taylor arrived at Old Trafford, did the job that was expected of him and departed – all within a matter of ten months. Acting manager Jimmy Murphy bought the vastly experienced little schemer from Blackpool for £8,000 immediately after Munich. His task: to hold together a gang of raw lads at the most emotional time imaginable.

In the first game after the crash, an FA Cup tie against Sheffield Wednesday, Ernie beavered shrewdly as United chalked up a heart-swelling 3–0 victory. This set the tone for his brief but vital stay. Sometimes cajoling, at other times driving, this voluble little general was the youngsters' inspiration on the field, as Jimmy was off it.

And he wasn't all talk; Ernie Taylor had the talent to lead by example. He was an ingenious, instinctive passer and a crowd-pleasing improviser, full of flicks and backheels. He played in the 1958 FA Cup Final defeat by Bolton – he had picked up winner's medals with Newcastle in 1951 and Blackpool in 1953 – but lost his place early in the next campaign. There was talk of a job helping the reserves but instead Ernie moved to Sunderland for £6,000, his task completed.

ERNEST TAYLOR
BORN: Sunderland, 2 September 1925.
HONOURS: 1 England cap (53).
OTHER CLUBS: Newcastle United 47/8-51/2 (107, 19);
Blackpool 51/2-57/8 (217, 53); Sunderland
58/9-60/1 (68, 11).
DIED: Birkenhead, Cheshire, 9 April 1985.

GAMES	30
GOALS	4

WILF McGUINNESS

1955/56 → 1959/60

If there were a prize for the keenest footballer ever to play for Manchester United then it would have to go to Wilf McGuinness. He was possessed by an all-consuming enthusiasm – passion is perhaps a more apt word – for football in general and the Old Trafford club in particular.

A defensive wing-half whose rather limited skills were outshone by a phenomenal work rate, Wilf was granted few senior opportunities during his early professional years, due to the omnipotent presence of his chum, one Duncan Edwards.

However, when the England star fell foul of flu in October 1955, up stepped the 17-year-old McGuinness to make his debut at home to Wolves, then a major power. Faced with the cunning wiles of schemer Peter Broadbent, the newcomer did an efficient job, signalling to Matt Busby that here was yet another confident young fellow with the nerve to rise to a big occasion.

Just over two years later, having earned a title medal in 1956/57 mainly as Duncan's deputy, Wilf had been due to be part of the ill-fated expedition to Belgrade, only to withdraw because of knee problems. With the joint continuing to trouble him, even the depredations of Munich did not guarantee him a place and the arrival of emergency signing Stan Crowther signalled new competition. But, his eagerness undiminished, Wilf ousted Stan at the start of 1958/59 and missed only three games in the whole campaign. Perhaps surprisingly, considering his inexperience, the former captain of England Schoolboys was rewarded with two full caps that same term.

Then, while seemingly poised on the brink of a glittering future, the lion-hearted 22-year-old was struck down. A shin injury had been limiting his effectiveness and he was seeking to test it in a reserve clash with Stoke City when he went into a routine tackle with Peter Bullock and emerged with a shattered leg. In retrospect, it seemed he might have been labouring with a stress fracture for some time.

An optimist by nature, he strove for two years to regain fitness but he never came back, a chronic blow to a manager in the throes of major team reconstruction. On a personal level it was a crushing setback to the self-assured McGuinness, who had been looking forward to another decade's active service in the Old Trafford cause.

Recognising Wilf's burning desire to serve the club, Matt Busby employed him as a youth coach and he built on that, eventually becoming influential in the England set-up under Alf Ramsey. In 1966/67 there was just the whiff of a playing comeback, when the fit-again 29-year-old got as far as the first-team substitute's bench but, sadly for a man still desperate to play, he progressed no further.

Still to come, of course, was a traumatic reign as manager of the club he loved so much it hurt, of which more follows later. After that, Wilf went on to boss York before becoming a physiotherapist.

WILFRED McGUINNESS
BORN: Manchester, 25 October 1937.
HONOURS: League Championship 56/7. 2 England caps (58-59).
MANAGER: Manchester United (69-70); Aris Salonika, Greece, (71-73); Panaraiki Patras, Greece, (73-74); York City (75-77); Bury (acting, 89).

GAMES	85
GOALS	2

ALEX DAWSON

. . . .

1956/57 → 1961/62

If Alex Dawson had not been allowed to leave United to become 'The Black Prince of Deepdale', might he one day have donned a yet more majestic crown at Old Trafford? It's impossible, of course, to say. But this tank of a centre-forward's striking rate makes the question well worth the asking.

There are fearsome characters in any era but it is difficult to imagine a more blood-curdling sight for a defender than the Red Devils' bull-necked battering ram. He would fix his eye on the ball and go for it; whatever, or whoever, was in his way usually bounced off him. As he has admitted since, there wasn't much he wouldn't do to put the ball in the net, though he maintained that he was fundamentally fair and never maimed anybody.

An England schoolboy international, having crossed the border from Aberdeen to Hull as a youngster, Alex joined United as a winger in the mid-1950s. Conversion to spearhead followed and, after helping to win the FA Youth Cup in two successive seasons, he netted on his senior debut at home to Burnley on Easter Monday 1957.

He registered in the next two games, too, as United clinched the title and there was talk that, with Tommy Taylor carrying an injury, young Dawson might face Aston Villa in the FA Cup Final.

The call never came that season, but Alex did find himself at Wembley a year later as the post-Munich Reds defied the odds to reach a second successive final, thanks in no small measure to the burly Aberdonian's hat-trick in the rousing 5-3 semi-final replay victory over Fulham at Highbury.

Yet despite continuing to demonstrate his endearing penchant for hitting the target – in his last two full seasons he managed 31 goals in 50 outings – he found a regular place hard to command.

Possibly his development as a rounded performer was adversely affected through being rushed into regular first-team action in the wake of the disaster, but whatever the reason, Matt Busby was not completely satisfied with Dawson's progress and recruited the formidable David Herd.

While Alex was no overall match for the Scottish international, he was stronger in the air and could point to his own fine record. However, and perhaps inevitably, Matt was proved right as David went on to contribute ever more impressively as the years went by.

Meanwhile, in October 1961 Alex was sold to Preston for £18,000, going on to earn that regal title before performing further gallant deeds for Bury and others.

ALEXANDER DOWNIE DAWSON
BORN: Aberdeen, 21 February 1940.
OTHER CLUBS: Preston North End 61/2-66/7 (197, 114); Bury 66/7-68/9 (50, 21); Brighton and Hove Albion 68/9-70/1 (57, 26); Brentford 70/1 (10, 6).

GAMES 93
GOALS 54

HARRY GREGG

1957/58 → 1966/67

Harry Gregg was arguably the best goalkeeper Manchester United ever had – yet he has no honours to show for it. The best that the big, flame-haired Irishman can point to after a decade with one of Europe's most successful club sides is an FA Cup finalist's medal.

The bane of Harry's footballing life was a series of shoulder injuries which cost him more than a century of appearances and, often, untold agony when he did turn out. There were times towards the end of his career when he could hardly lift his arm above his head, yet he soldiered on, displaying the same raw bravery which saw him through the ordeal of Munich and other personal tragedy.

When Harry arrived at Old Trafford from Doncaster Rovers in December 1957 for £23,500, then a world record fee for a 'keeper, he stunned the United defence. They were used to Ray Wood, as good a shot-stopper as could be found but a man who often left defenders to their own devices on crosses. Not so Harry. He was out to command his whole area, going for every ball with total commitment and then, whenever possible, setting an instant counter-assault in motion. If there could be such a thing as an attacking goalkeeper then, most definitely, this vociferous acrobat was it.

At first there were the inevitable collisions. Harry was no respecter of reputations or feelings. If England men Roger Byrne and Duncan Edwards got in his way then they found out about it quickly – and sometimes painfully. But as the defence grew accustomed to their dashing new custodian, understanding and confidence grew.

Then came Munich and the football world was never the same again. From being a sports hero, in the superficial parlance of the back page, Harry became a real hero, rescuing a woman and her baby from the wreckage of United's devastated plane. It should be stressed here that he is the last person to dwell on his own courageous actions, citing raw instinct as his motivation, but the fact remains that he saved lives while others panicked and confusion reigned all around him.

Within 13 days of that horrendous experience Gregg was back in goal and at the top of his form as the Red Devils somehow continued their unlikely march towards Wembley by beating Sheffield Wednesday in the FA Cup. The campaign was to end in gallant defeat and controversy at Wembley when Bolton dreadnought Nat Lofthouse thundered into Harry, knocking him unconscious and sending him and the ball into the net. A goal was given and United lost, gloriously.

A few months later Harry scaled new heights, starring for Northern Ireland as that tiny country battled its way to the quarter-finals of the World Cup in Sweden. Such was his magnificence against major powers such as Czechoslovakia, Argentina, West Germany and France that he was voted the best goalkeeper in the tournament, putting his absence of domestic silverware into vivid perspective and enshrining for all time his capability at the most rarefied of levels.

Then at the zenith of his powers, he was seen by Matt Busby as a cornerstone of the new United. But although Harry was a magnificent all-round athlete, often his shoulder let him down. As a result he was absent at crucial junctures, missing out on the FA Cup triumph of 1963 – he was fit in time for the final but the manager opted not to change a winning team – and the Championship two years later.

When Alex Stepney arrived, Harry, by then aged 34, joined Stoke City but soon went into management, serving various clubs in the lower divisions before putting in a coaching stint at Old Trafford.

Despite the Herculean achievements of Peter Schmeichel and the subsequent accomplishment of Fabien Barthez and Edwin van der Sar, there remain many veteran observers of the Old Trafford scene who continue to identify Gregg as the yardstick by which all United custodians should be judged, and they contend fiercely that it will be a momentous day when, finally, one matches him in every respect.

Harry Gregg was a superb entertainer blessed with courage, pride and character in ample measure. But when it came to the luck of the Irish, his was nearly all bad.

HENRY GREGG
BORN: Derry, Northern Ireland, 25 October 1932.
HONOURS: 25 Northern Ireland caps (54-63).
OTHER CLUBS: Linfield, Northern Ireland; Coleraine, Northern Ireland; Doncaster Rovers 52/3-57/8 (93, 0); Stoke City 66/7 (2, 0).
MANAGER: Shrewsbury Town (68-72); Swansea City (72-75); Crewe Alexandra (75-78); Carlisle United (86-87).

| GAMES | 247 |
| GOALS | 0 |

HAROLD BRATT

1960/61

A hard-working wing-half who excelled for England Schoolboys and helped the Red Devils to FA Youth Cup glory in 1957. Thereafter he was confined to the reserves, barring one snowy League Cup encounter with Bradford City.

HAROLD BRATT
BORN: Salford, Lancashire, 8 October 1939.
OTHER CLUBS: Doncaster Rovers 61/2-62/3 (54, 0).

GAMES 1
GOALS 0

GORDON CLAYTON

1956/57

Guarded the United net in 1953 during the first of their five successive FA Youth Cup Final victories. However, he did not progress and left Old Trafford in 1959, returning for a brief stint as assistant chief scout in the 1970s.

GORDON CLAYTON
BORN: Wednesbury, Staffordshire, 3 November 1936.
OTHER CLUBS: Tranmere Rovers 59/60-60/1 (4, 0).
DIED: Manchester, 29 September 1991.

GAMES 2
GOALS 0

TOMMY HERON

1957/58 → 1960/61

A versatile performer who arrived at Old Trafford as a dashing left winger, then was converted into an impressively mobile full-back. However, he was unable to assert himself as a Red Devil, but prospered subsequently with York.

THOMAS RUSSELL FERRIE HERON
BORN: Irvine, Ayrshire, 31 March 1936.
OTHER CLUBS: Queen's Park 56/7 (5, 1); Portadown, Northern Ireland; York City 61/2-65/6 (192, 6).

GAMES 3
GOALS 0

PETER JONES

1957/58

An accomplished England youth international who pocketed two FA Youth Cup winners' medals and who was equally effective at left-back or centre-half. Peter deputised once for Roger Byrne but received no further opportunities.

ERNEST PETER JONES
BORN: Manchester, 30 November 1937.
OTHER CLUBS: Wrexham 59/60-66/7 (227, 7); Stockport County 66/7-67/8 (54, 1).

GAMES 1
GOALS 0

JOHNNY SCOTT

1952/53 → 1955/56

A ball-playing winger whose progress at Old Trafford was halted by the red-hot competition. Later he thrived at Grimsby and represented his country in the 1958 World Cup Finals. Johnny lost his life in a building-site accident.

JOHN SCOTT
BORN: Belfast, 22 December 1933.
HONOURS: 2 Northern Ireland caps (58).
OTHER CLUBS: Grimsby Town 56/7-62/3 (241, 51); York City 63/4 (21, 3).
DIED: Manchester, June 1978.

GAMES 3
GOALS 0

RONNIE BRIGGS

1960/61 → 1961/62

A tall, muscular goalkeeper who made a traumatic entry to senior football, conceding 14 goals in his first three games in January 1961. Commendably, he recovered to perform soundly on further outings, but never made the First Division grade.

WILLIAM RONALD BRIGGS
BORN: Belfast, 29 March 1943.
HONOURS: 2 Northern Ireland caps (62-65).
OTHER CLUBS: Swansea Town 64/5 (27, 0); Bristol Rovers 65/6-67/8 (35, 0).

GAMES 11
GOALS 0

TONY HAWKSWORTH

1956/57

An athletic but relatively diminutive goalkeeper who garnered a hat-trick of FA Youth Cup winners' medals in the mid 1950s and surprised some Old Trafford insiders by not mounting a strenuous long-term challenge for a senior berth.

ANTHONY HAWKSWORTH
BORN: Sheffield, 15 January 1938.

GAMES 1
GOALS 0

REG HUNTER

1958/59

A goal-scoring winger who was on target in both legs of the Red Devils' 1957 FA Youth Cup Final victory over West Ham United. However, he was unable to make the transition to the First Division ranks and faded from contention.

REGINALD JOHN HUNTER
BORN: Colwyn Bay, Denbighshire, 25 October 1938.
OTHER CLUBS: Wrexham 59/60-61/2 (34, 3).

GAMES 1
GOALS 0

MIKE PINNER

1960/61

A solicitor who won more than 50 England amateur caps in his spare time, Mike let no one down after being recruited as extra goalkeeping cover during an injury crisis and following Ronnie Briggs' torrid experiences early in 1961.

MICHAEL JOHN PINNER
BORN: Boston, Lincolnshire, 16 February 1934.
OTHER CLUBS: Aston Villa 54/5-56/7 (4, 0); Sheffield Wednesday 57/8-58/9 (7, 0); Queen's Park Rangers 59/60 (19, 0); Chelsea 61/2 (1, 0); Swansea Town 61/2 (1, 0); Leyton Orient 62/3-64/5 (77, 0).

GAMES 4
GOALS 0

WALTER WHITEHURST

1955/56

A busy, constructive right-half, he enjoyed his sole senior United outing as a deputy for Jeff Whitefoot at Everton. But with Eddie Colman about to make his entrance, there was little chance of advancement and Walter bowed out.

WALTER WHITEHURST
BORN: Manchester, 7 June 1934.
OTHER CLUBS: Chesterfield 56/7-59/60 (92, 2); Crewe Alexandra 60/1 (3, 1).

GAMES 1
GOALS 0

EDDIE LEWIS

1952/53 → 1955/56

For one fleeting, enthralling interlude midway through 1952/53, it seemed possible that teenage centre-forward Eddie Lewis might be the prolific new marksman Matt Busby was seeking to fill the void soon to be created by the inevitable departure of the veteran Jack Rowley.

The muscular Mancunian netted within seven minutes of commencing his debut at West Bromwich Albion, and he added eight more goals in a ten-match post-Christmas purple patch which dripped with promise. The Manchester United manager was impressed, but not convinced that his long-term quest for a spearhead was at an end. Duly, in March, he handed over a record fee to sign Tommy Taylor from Barnsley, and thereafter Eddie's opportunities were strictly limited.

His hometown prospects thus reduced, Lewis sought a breakthrough elsewhere and, after overtures from Wolves and Sunderland had been spurned, he accepted a £10,000 move to Preston North End.

His niche was not to be in attack, however, and after a brief stint with West Ham, he excelled as a full-back with Leyton Orient, helping Johnny Carey's side rise to the top flight in 1961/62. Later Eddie emigrated to South Africa, where he coached and managed.

EDWARD LEWIS
BORN: Manchester, 3 January 1935.
OTHER CLUBS: Preston North End 55/6-56/7 (12, 2);
West Ham United 56/7-57/8 (31, 12);
Leyton Orient 58/9-63/4 (142, 4).

GAMES **24**
GOALS **11**

BOBBY HARROP

1957/58 → 1958/59

As a boy, it seemed, Bobby Harrop was destined for the top. After all, having been selected for both England and Great Britain youth, and having begun his career at a leading club with a visionary manager renowned for his nurturing of rookie talent, he had made giant strides while many of his contemporaries were still in the starting blocks.

But somehow it never came to pass for the solidly built Mancunian, who was propelled, prematurely but unavoidably, into senior action in the wake of the Munich disaster.

Bobby, who was versatile enough to fill practically any outfield position, made a high-profile debut as an understudy for injured left-half Stan Crowther in the FA Cup quarter-final replay against West Bromwich Albion on an almost hysterically emotional night at Old Trafford.

After that memorable but fraught victory, he appeared in a handful of League games, then receded from contention until he returned briefly as a stand-in for centre-half Ronnie Cope during the following term.

It became apparent that Bobby would not make the grade with United and in November 1959 he joined Tranmere Rovers, together with goalkeeper Gordon Clayton, for a combined fee of £4,000. Sadly he did not thrive at Prenton Park and soon left the game.

ROBERT HARROP
BORN: Manchester, 25 August 1936.
OTHER CLUBS: Tranmere Rovers 59/60-60/1 (41, 2).
DIED: Margate, Kent, 8 November 2007.

GAMES **11**
GOALS **0**

COLIN WEBSTER

1953/54 → 1958/59

A bout of flu may have saved Colin Webster's life. The Welsh international utility forward was due to travel with the side that was to meet catastrophe at Munich, but he was too ill to make the trip. In fact, Colin would have gone only as a reserve, his first-team opportunities being severely limited due to the strength in depth at Old Trafford. Eight players, for example, were in serious contention for the three places in the middle of the attack.

Though not in the top bracket, Webster was a respected member of the club. He played all across the front line, won a Championship medal in 1955/56 and, despite his lazy, loping action, he was deceptively quick and a spikily abrasive competitor. His goals-to-games ratio was impressive, too, his most memorable strike being the winner against West Bromwich Albion in the 1958 FA Cup fifth-round replay. After the crash Colin did get an extended run and faced Bolton Wanderers in the FA Cup Final, then played against Brazil in a World Cup quarter-final before moving to Swansea Town for £7,500 in October 1958.

COLIN WEBSTER
BORN: Cardiff, 17 July 1932.
HONOURS: League Championship 55/6. 4 Wales caps (57-58).
OTHER CLUBS: Swansea Town 58/9-62/3 (159, 65);
Newport County 62/3-63/4 (31, 3).
DIED: Swansea, 1 March 2001.

| GAMES | 79 |
| GOALS | 31 |

MARK PEARSON

1957/58 → 1962/63

As a youngster Mark Pearson looked a top footballer in the making. 'Pancho' – the nickname was a consequence of his sideburns and was bestowed on Mark at a time when its subsequent and better-known possessor, Stuart Pearson, was still wearing short trousers – was one of the best natural tacklers ever seen at Old Trafford; he was also a sharp, instinctive passer and was at his most effective as a foraging inside-forward, linking defence with attack.

But all that potential was never fulfilled and there is no shortage of theories for that sad circumstance. Some would have it that Mark was a victim of his own aggressive temperament, and certainly he got into his share of scrapes, being inanely dubbed a teddy boy by Bob Lord after one acrimonious clash with Burnley. Others pointed to the fact that he was pitched into the limelight before he was ready – his debut was in that emotional FA Cup tie with Sheffield Wednesday straight after Munich – while still more reckon that his unenviable injury record dragged him down.

Whatever the answer, he was not destined to make the grade with United and his later spells with Sheffield Wednesday and Fulham also proved disappointing.

MARK PEARSON
BORN: Sheffield, 28 October 1939.
OTHER CLUBS: Sheffield Wednesday 63/4-64/5 (39, 9); Fulham 65/6-67/8 (58, 7);
Halifax Town 68/9 (5, 0).

| GAMES | 80 |
| GOALS | 14 |

RONNIE COPE

1956/57 → 1960/61

For most of his time at Old Trafford Ronnie Cope was an uncomplaining reserve, albeit a classy one. With the likes of Allenby Chilton, Mark Jones, Jackie Blanchflower and, later, Bill Foulkes ahead of him in the centre-halves' pecking order, he needed to be an outstanding player to claim a long-term first-team spot – and he was never that.

Ronnie's opportunity came after Munich when he strode courageously into the breach and helped the savagely depleted Red Devils to ride a wave of public emotion all the way to the FA Cup Final at Wembley. On that dramatic afternoon, he gave a polished and staunch display in direct opposition to the fearsome Bolton and England spearhead Nat Lofthouse, emerging with immense credit even in defeat.

Thereafter Cope retained his place for two seasons, missing only a handful of outings as Matt Busby's transitional team finished as title runners-up in 1958/59. Eventually he stepped aside and joined Luton for £10,000 when the more dominant Foulkes was switched from full-back to pivot.

A loyal clubman, Ronnie was a footballing central defender who invariably attempted to play his way out of trouble rather than apply the big boot, but he lacked the ruthlessness and cutting edge to succeed at the top level.

RONALD COPE
BORN: Crewe, Cheshire, 5 October 1934.
OTHER CLUBS: Luton Town 61/2-62/3 (28, 0).

| GAMES | 106 |
| GOALS | 2 |

JOE CAROLAN

1958/59 → 1960/61

Joe Carolan was the quiet man of Old Trafford. Unassuming both by nature and in the way he played his football, he was United's regular left-back for a season and a half. During that time the club finished as runners-up and seventh in the First Division and the Republic of Ireland international did not let them down, performing competently and unflashily without ever suggesting that he had the necessary class to become a long-term fixture in the side.

Genial Joe, a lovely man who was written off as dead in the first edition of this book but merely chuckled at the author's clanger, turned down a trial with Liverpool as a teenager before joining United in 1956. A wing-half at the time, he progressed quickly after his conversion to full-back.

Joe, who managed quite adequately on the left despite being right-footed, lost his place initially to Shay Brennan, and his exit became inevitable following the arrival of his countryman Noel Cantwell. Gracious no matter what the circumstances, the dark-haired Dubliner was transferred to Brighton for £13,000 but fell victim to a managerial change, then spent a happy and productive decade with Tonbridge in the Southern League.

JOSEPH FRANCIS CAROLAN
BORN: Dublin, 8 September 1937.
HONOURS: 2 Republic of Ireland caps (59-60).
OTHER CLUBS: Brighton and Hove Albion 60/1-61/2 (33, 0).

| GAMES | 71 |
| GOALS | 0 |

BILL FOULKES

· ·

1952/53 → 1969/70

It wasn't often that Matt Busby selected a Manchester United side without Bill Foulkes. But on one of those rare occasions when the manager preferred another player – Ian Greaves towards the end of the 1955/56 Championship campaign, when Bill was stretched by National Service commitments – the indomitable Lancastrian's reaction summed up his personality and outlook better than any words.

Always a fitness fanatic, he trained harder than ever so that he would be ready to step in when called back to first-team duty. No moans, no transfer requests, just dedication and a fierce, almost frightening determination to put himself back on top. And, of course, he succeeded. The next season Bill, then a full-back, was first choice again, and he went on to hold down a place until the end of the following decade.

Bill made his senior debut at Anfield, coping capably with Liverpool's brilliant Billy Liddell, yet in truth he should never have been on the pitch that afternoon in December 1952. During the week before his breakthrough he was struggling with a sore ankle when he was summoned to Matt Busby's office. Bill feared the sack, believing that he was not as naturally talented as his fellow Babes, and was flabbergasted when the manager put him through an impromptu fitness test with a League call-up in mind. He passed only by disguising his agony, and his subsequent gutsy display ensured that the white lie was never discovered.

Amazingly, during his first few years at Old Trafford, Bill continued with the mineworking job he had taken straight from school. His record is even more unusual in that he was still a part-time footballer when he was selected for England just 22 months after that chancy Anfield entrance, then never made another international appearance despite completing an 18-season First Division career.

Perhaps the truth was that as a full-back he was never outstanding, and could best be described as a competent, workmanlike performer. But as a centre-half, which he became in the second season after surviving the Munich disaster, he was United's bulwark, a definitive old-fashioned stopper who might have been carved out of solid rock.

When faced with tough, bustling opponents, Bill was in his element. He relished the physical challenge and was particularly strong in the air. On the ground he kept it simple, knowing his ball-playing limitations and being careful not to expose them. His weakness was against trickier centre-forwards like Alex Young and Joe Baker, men who did not stand and battle it out but moved away from him, thus becoming difficult to dominate.

But year in, year out, Bill was a man who could be relied on, a hard, resilient, ruthlessly single-minded character who won more Championship medals – four – than any other United player of his era, held the club's appearance record until overtaken by Bobby Charlton, and earned a European Cup winner's medal at the age of 36.

Somehow it was fitting that this most loyal of retainers, who later extended his Old Trafford tenure still further by holding coaching posts in the early 1970s, should set up the Reds for that greatest triumph.

When George Best danced down the right touchline and pulled the ball across the penalty area near the end of the semi-final against Real Madrid, the hearts of United supporters leapt. Here surely was a chance. Perhaps Charlton or Kidd, maybe Sadler, could get on the end of it. But no, it was Foulkes, the man who managed only nine goals in nearly 700 games, sidefooting the ball home. A proud moment for a proud man, and no one could have deserved it more.

Still he was not finished. Though carrying a serious knee injury which finally forced him out of contention in 1969, the veteran went to war with Benfica's lanky centre-forward Jose Torres, a much younger, fitter individual, in the Wembley final, pursuing his quarry with such vigour and obduracy that the Portuguese beanpole was throwing up his hands in resignation long before the end. Somehow that moment summed up what the craggy ex-miner meant to Manchester United. No matter how stiff the task, or how overwhelming the odds, Bill Foulkes would in there fighting – and fighting to win.

WILLIAM ANTHONY FOULKES
BORN: St Helens, Lancashire, 5 January 1932.
HONOURS: European Cup 67/8. League Championship 55/6, 56/7, 64/5, 66/7. FA Cup 62/3. 1 England cap (54).
MANAGER: Chicago Sting (75-77); Tulsa Roughnecks (78-79); San Jose Earthquakes (80), all USA; Farstad, Stenjker (twice), Lillestrom, Viking Stavanger, all Norway, (80-88); Mazda, Japan, (88-91).

GAMES **685 (3)**
GOALS **9**

JOHNNY GILES

1959/60 → 1962/63

Johnny Giles was that rarest of birds, a Manchester United player of largely unrealised potential who moved on to become a world-class performer with another club.

He was always an inside-forward by choice but due to brisk competition for places at Old Trafford, at a time when he was yet to mature as a player, he was forced on to the wing to claim a place in the side.

Thus it was as an immensely promising, invariably efficient, but as yet far from consistently outstanding flankman that Johnny earned an FA Cup winner's medal in 1963, playing a prominent part in an exceptional team display against the favourites, Leicester City. Already he was demonstrating a delightful touch with both feet, piercingly accurate distribution and an abundance of sharp footballing guile, though his game lacked the abrasive physical edge it was to attain later at Leeds.

It was soon after that Wembley triumph that he decided his future did not lie with Matt Busby's team. Johnny was part of the United side drubbed by Everton in the Charity Shield and as a result he was dropped. A strong and fiercely independent character, he stood up for himself during subsequent discussions with the manager about team selection and his own best position, the upshot being his abrupt departure from Manchester.

Many at the club were saddened by the decision, being well aware of the curly-haired Dubliner's potential capabilities, but with so much talent at his disposal Matt could not promise a regular place as an inside man and Giles was not disposed to be patient.

Accordingly, a £37,500 switch to Leeds United was agreed, and at Elland Road he developed into a play-maker of sublime skill and vision, forming a majestic partnership with Scottish dynamo Billy Bremner and garnering an enviable haul of club honours. At the end of his playing career, which encompassed 20 years on the international stage, Johnny managed West Bromwich Albion (twice) and his country before he turned to journalism.

		GAMES	115

MICHAEL JOHN GILES

BORN:	Dublin, 6 November 1940.
HONOURS:	FA Cup 62/3. 60 Republic of Ireland caps (59-79).
OTHER CLUBS:	Home Farm, Republic of Ireland; Leeds United 63/4-74/5 (383, 86); West Bromwich Albion 75/6-76/7 (75, 3); Shamrock Rovers, Republic of Ireland, 77/8-82/3; Philadelphia Fury, USA, 78/9.
MANAGER:	West Bromwich Albion (75-77 and 84-85); Philadelphia Fury (78); Shamrock Rovers (77-83); Republic of Ireland (77-80); Vancouver Whitecaps, Canada, (80-83).

GAMES 115
GOALS 13

ALBERT QUIXALL

1958/59 → 1963/64

Albert Quixall was the golden boy who lost a little of his lustre at Old Trafford. The 25-year-old Yorkshireman arrived from Sheffield Wednesday in September 1958 as the lad who had everything. The pundits of the day were in no doubt: he was an England international, he was on the threshold of his prime, he could make a ball talk – surely there was nothing that Albert was not going to achieve as a Red Devil.

Like few players before him, he was food and drink to the media. On top of his undoubted credentials as a ball-playing inside-forward, he was blond, baby-faced and wore the shortest shorts ever seen on a football pitch to date. And to top it all he was changing clubs for a then-record fee of £45,000.

Matt Busby saw Albert as the man to restore a little of the class so cruelly ripped away from the club at Munich some seven months earlier. After an initial stutter – United suffered seven League games without a win following the Yorkshireman's arrival – everything began to go according to the script. Despite the deprivations of the air disaster, the side put together a run which saw only two defeats in 23 matches to become runners-up in the First Division.

But subsequently, although Albert enjoyed several more moderately successful seasons, often demonstrating glorious skills, results slumped and pressure mounted. His confidence, ever fragile, suffered visibly. On his day, when United were going well, he could look an outstanding player still, and produce a catalogue of crowd-pleasing tricks. But if the game turned into a battle, his contribution tended to diminish alarmingly.

Quixall, a dressing-room joker with a distinctly nervous side to his character, touched something like his finest form once more in the 1963 FA Cup Final defeat of Leicester City, but that was to prove one last highlight of his Old Trafford tenure. Soon he departed after being dropped following the 1963 Charity Shield debacle against Everton, joining Oldham for £7,000. Later he served Stockport before ending a career which was undeniably worthy, sometimes uplifting, yet which stopped frustratingly short of ultimate fulfilment.

In retrospect, it is clear that Albert Quixall peaked early with his first love, Sheffield Wednesday. Perhaps the plethora of games he played in his teens and early twenties, sometimes four per week including Army football, created a burnout effect, contributing to his premature farewell to the top flight.

ALBERT QUIXALL
BORN: Sheffield, 9 August 1933.
HONOURS: FA Cup 62/3. 5 England caps (53-55).
OTHER CLUBS: Sheffield Wednesday 50/1-58/9 (241, 63); Oldham Athletic 64/5-65/6 (37, 11); Stockport County 66/7 (13, 0).

| GAMES | 184 |
| GOALS | 56 |

WARREN BRADLEY

1958/59 → 1961/62

From non-League Bishop Auckland to Manchester United to the England side, all in the space of 15 months – that was the barely credible experience of Warren Bradley after he answered the Old Trafford club's SOS following the Munich tragedy. And even though this sturdy, hard-running right-winger was no greenhorn – he was already an established amateur international – his rise was nothing less than meteoric.

Perhaps Warren wasn't the classiest of performers, and his progress to full international status startled some observers, but there was no denying the success of his term at United.

A tough, determined little character who, in the manner of Johnny Berry, was always willing to tackle back, he could point also to an outstanding goal-scoring record for a flank player. In his first season, when United finished as runners-up, he managed 12 goals in 24 games. Indeed, during that campaign he and Albert Scanlon were the most prolific wingers, as a pair, in the First Division.

However, Warren was not part of Matt Busby's long-term plans and in 1962, having completed an admirable holding job during Manchester United's time of need, he joined Bury before going on to concentrate on his teaching career.

WARREN BRADLEY
BORN: Hyde, Cheshire, 20 June 1933.
HONOURS: 3 England caps (59).
OTHER CLUBS: Bury 61/2-62/3 (13, 1).
DIED: Manchester, 6 June 2007.

GAMES	67
GOALS	21

NOBBY LAWTON

1959/60 → 1962/63

The best thing that Nobby Lawton ever did for his career was to leave Manchester United. An intelligent, creative wing-half cum inside-forward, his only extended runs in the side came in the early 1960s when Matt Busby was assembling the components of his next great team. A lot of players, including expensive new arrivals, were being tried and it was a testing, unsettling time for youngsters.

Nobby acquitted himself well enough, especially in 1961/62 when he contributed a Boxing Day hat-trick against Nottingham Forest and toiled commendably in the FA Cup semi-final defeat by Tottenham Hotspur. However, he never imposed himself enough to establish a regular place and the appearance on the scene of Paddy Crerand made his departure inevitable.

Thus the slender, blond Mancunian, who as a teenager had fought back from a life-threatening illness diagnosed only days after committing his future to the Reds, took his subtle skills to Preston. There he found the space to develop his game that was not afforded him in the more competitive atmosphere of Old Trafford. Duly Nobby became a performer of considerable stature and richly deserved the honour of captaining North End in the 1964 FA Cup Final.

NORBERT LAWTON
BORN: Newton Heath, Manchester, 25 March 1940.
OTHER CLUBS: Preston North End 62/3-67/8 (143, 22);
Brighton and Hove Albion 67/8-70/1 (112, 14);
Lincoln City 70/1-71/2 (20, 0).
DIED: Manchester, 22 April 2006.

GAMES	44
GOALS	6

JIMMY NICHOLSON

1960/61 → 1962/63

Jimmy Nicholson kicked off his Manchester United career carrying a destructive and ludicrous millstone around his neck. Here, said various pundits who should have known better, was the new Duncan Edwards. Immediately, anything the young Irishman did was examined in a different, more demanding light, and he suffered accordingly. The fact that this creative, hard-working wing-half rose above such a fatuous comparison is a testimony to the ability which he had in abundance.

Jimmy made his United debut in August 1960 at the tender age of 17 and it offered eloquent proof of a level temperament that he was unfazed as the Red Devils crashed 4-0 to Everton at Goodison Park. Certainly Matt Busby had no doubt about his suitability for top-flight competition, keeping him in the side for the next six months, and before his next birthday Nicholson was a full international. Tantalisingly, though, that first complete campaign at Old Trafford, in which he played nearly 40 games in all competitions, proved to be far and away his most effective.

Like so many hugely promising youngsters, Jimmy did not make the expected progress, due at least in part to ill luck with injuries, but also he had to contend with formidable competition from the likes of Nobby Stiles, Maurice Setters, Nobby Lawton and – the final straw – Paddy Crerand. As a result, sorely frustrated by the situation, he moved on in December 1964.

With his new club, Huddersfield Town, who secured his services for a paltry £7,500, he achieved the consistency which had previously eluded him. Jimmy, who ended his Football League days at Bury, developed into an accomplished all-round footballer who combined fluent passing with sturdy tackling and he blossomed into a bastion of the Northern Ireland side for more than a decade. It's just possible that he left Old Trafford too soon.

JAMES JOSEPH NICHOLSON

BORN: Belfast, 27 February 1943.
HONOURS: 41 Northern Ireland caps (60-71).
OTHER CLUBS: Huddersfield Town 64/5-73/4 (281, 26); Bury 73/4-75/6 (83, 0).

GAMES 68
GOALS 6

NOEL CANTWELL

1960/61 → 1966/67

During his six years with Manchester United, Noel Cantwell was unique in that his mere presence at the club was at least as important as his performances on the field.

He arrived from West Ham United for £29,500 in late 1960, an experienced full-back cum centre-half cum occasional centre-forward who was already an established Republic of Ireland international. By that time Matt Busby had done with short-term measures after Munich and was looking to build a team for the next decade. The Old Trafford boss needed Noel to provide stability, character and knowledge, to inspire and cajole the younger players along what he realised could be a tortuous trail back to the top.

That's not to say that the versatile Irishman was not a splendid performer in his own right. He had fine control, was a precise passer and was dominant in the air, even though he was not always the sprightliest of movers, especially on the turn.

But above all he was a great thinker about the game and possessed the ability to pass on his wisdom. Intelligent, articulate, personable and a man of integrity, Noel was mooted at one time as a possible successor to Matt Busby, and there is no shortage of close observers, both inside and outside the club, who maintain that if Cantwell had been handed United's reins then the demoralising decline of the early 1970s might have been avoided.

So why didn't it happen? After all, the two men liked and respected each other, they shared an all-consuming love of the game and both had a compelling vision of how it should be played. However, though both espoused entertaining football, there was a fundamental chasm in their preferred methods. By and large the Busby creed was based on untramelled adventure, while Cantwell believed passionately in the benefits of coaching, which he felt was crucial to success in the modern game.

Still, though he was to take charge of Coventry City rather than Manchester United, Noel could look back on a distinguished Old Trafford record which included skippering the side to FA Cup triumph in 1963 and serving as an influential club captain – though he played only four games – during the 1966/67 title campaign.

NOEL EUCHARIA CANTWELL

BORN:	Cork, Republic of Ireland, 28 December 1932.
HONOURS:	FA Cup 62/3. 36 Republic of Ireland caps (53-67).
OTHER CLUBS:	Cork Athletic, Republic of Ireland; West Ham United 52/3-60/1 (248, 11).
MANAGER:	Coventry City (67-72); Republic of Ireland (67-68); New England Tea Men, USA, (72 and 78-82); Peterborough United (72-77 and 86-88).
DIED:	Peterborough, Huntingdonshire, 7 September 2005.

GAMES	146
GOALS	8

MAURICE SETTERS

1959/60 → 1964/65

One or two affectionate, if heartfelt, expletives may have been deleted, but what follows is the essence of a telling tribute from Jimmy Greaves, uttered after a 1964 United-Spurs clash which Maurice Setters had watched from the trainer's bench. 'I can't understand why such a fine wing-half as Maurice should be out of any first team. I'd certainly rather have him with me than against me. He is fair but I know, from painful experience, all about his power.' Although Spurs had lost heavily, still Jimmy felt a measure of relief at having avoided a confrontation with the bone-crunching West Countryman.

In truth, no one relished an on-the-field clash with Maurice Setters. He was a ruthlessly fearsome tackler to whom most of the cliches used about performers of his ilk could be justifiably applied, and for his height he was as good a header of the ball as could be found.

Maurice was bought from West Bromwich Albion for £30,000 in January 1960 to bring stability to United's defence at a crucial time, and this he achieved to a substantial degree. Primarily a destroyer and forager, he was not outstandingly skilful, and it was when he played the game simply, just winning the ball and laying it off, that he was at his most effective. Flaws began to appear only when he attempted 40-yard passes in the manner of Paddy Crerand or Bobby Charlton.

Unquestionably Maurice played a major role in the development of the mid-1960s title-winning side but, sadly for him, his only tangible reward was to be an FA Cup-winner's medal in 1963. Though he boasted sufficient overall quality to have graced a Championship team, it was his ill fortune to disappear during Matt Busby's relentless search for the right blend, Nobby Stiles proving too hard an act to eclipse. Certainly, from the moment the ultra-combative little Mancunian dropped back from midfield to partner Bill Foulkes in the heart of defence, Setters' path to an early Old Trafford exit could hardly have been signposted more clearly.

So it transpired as, in November 1964, another £30,000 fee took Maurice to Stoke City, where he became a great favourite, as he did subsequently with Coventry City. Later, after various coaching stints, he excelled as number two to Jack Charlton with the Republic of Ireland.

MAURICE EDGAR SETTERS

BORN:	Honiton, Devon, 16 December 1936.
HONOURS:	FA Cup 62/3.
OTHER CLUBS:	Exeter City 53/4-54/5 (10, 0); West Bromwich Albion 55/6-59/60 (120, 10); Stoke City 64/5-67/8 (87, 5); Coventry City 67/8-69/70 (51, 3); Charlton Athletic 69/70 (8, 1).
MANAGER:	Doncaster Rovers (71-74).

GAMES	194
GOALS	14

DAVID HERD

· ·

1961/62 → 1967/68

Let there be no doubt about it; David Herd was no ordinary performer. In 265 senior games for Manchester United he scored 145 goals, a record which might have been expected to place him on one of those lofty pedestals reserved for Old Trafford idols.

Yet often, particularly before the 1964/65 Championship campaign, he was the butt of brainless barrackers who saw him as something of an unskilled journeyman alongside the extravagant talents of Denis Law, Bobby Charlton and George Best. In fact, he was one of Matt Busby's most inspired buys, a classic case of acquiring exactly the right man for the job.

When David arrived from Arsenal for £37,000 in the 1961 close season, he was returning to his roots, having been raised in the same Moss Side street as a certain Dennis Viollet. In fact, the homecoming might have happened nine years earlier when his first club, Stockport County, had agreed that the rookie sharpshooter would join United with veteran wing-half Billy McGlen moving in the opposite direction. But the deal collapsed at the eleventh hour, and soon he headed to north London, where he spent seven productive years before fetching up in Manchester as a Scottish international and a proven goalscorer, yet somehow not a star.

Thus, at last, David assumed the leadership of the United front line, demonstrating an ability, honesty and enthusiasm that swiftly endeared him to the more discerning among the Red Devils' disciples. Clearly, though, the newcomer found it difficult to adjust to the club's policy of free and fluid attack.

At Highbury, everything had been channelled through Herd as the principal marksman, a direct approach which had suited him and kept him constantly involved; at Old Trafford, goals were expected to come from all quarters with players interchanging positions with bewildering rapidity, so at first he felt marginalised. As a result he roamed deep to search for the ball, which was alien to his game and made him appear uncomfortable. Happily the manager identified the problem, ordering David to spend more time in the box and, gradually but steadily, the situation improved.

However, it was the arrival of Law a year later which seemed to lift Herd into a different class. Instantly they struck up a deadly partnership which produced an avalanche of goals crucial to United's transformation from First Division strugglers into one of British soccer's dominant powers.

Yet there was a time when Herd might have missed out on that glory surge. After his two goals at Wembley helped to lift the FA Cup in 1963, he took part in a dreadful Charity Shield display against Everton and was axed along with Johnny Giles and Albert Quixall. But while Giles and Quixall were not slow to signal their disaffection and soon moved on, David knuckled down to win back his place, a task he accomplished to rousing effect. That season he notched 20 League goals, another 20 the next and a further 24 the one after. He was down to 16 as United took the title in 1966/67 although he was absent, after breaking his leg in the act of scoring against Leicester, for a third of the games.

David, as clean a striker of the ball as Old Trafford has seen, was at his best when charging on to long passes from Charlton or Paddy Crerand. He was a strong runner, hard to dispossess, and was equipped with a rasping shot. His accuracy, too, could be stunning and he could net from astonishing angles. Weaknesses? Well, for such a powerful man he was not outstanding in the air, and there were times when his confidence needed boosting by team-mates.

Overall though, Herd was a credit to the club and to himself, and it was a sad day when that shattered leg curtailed his United career, although probably the thrilling rise of young Brian Kidd would have written the 34-year-old out of the 1968 European Cup adventure anyway. David's professional playing days – which had begun in the same Stockport side as his father, Alec, in 1951 – continued with two seasons at Stoke City and ended with three months under his old pal, Shay Brennan, at Waterford.

DAVID GEORGE HERD

BORN: Hamilton, Lanarkshire, 15 April 1934.

HONOURS: League Championship 64/5, 66/7. FA Cup 62/3. 5 Scotland caps (58-61).

OTHER CLUBS: Stockport County 50/1-53/4 (16, 6); Arsenal 54/5-60/1 (166, 97); Stoke City 68/9-69/70 (44, 11); Waterford, Republic of Ireland, 70/1.

MANAGER: Lincoln City (71-72).

GAMES **264 (1)**

GOALS **145**

SAMMY McMILLAN

1961/62 → 1962/63

He was never more than a fringe player at Old Trafford, but Sammy McMillan can be proud of his achievements during one of the club's transitional periods. An honest, strong-running left-winger or centre-forward, he netted six times in 11 outings during 1961/62, when Matt Busby was still rebuilding in the aftermath of Munich.

The amiable Ulsterman was handed a few more senior opportunities during the following campaign, then scored the goal that won a friendly against Juventus in Turin in May 1963. But just when his star appeared to be in the ascendancy, Sammy suffered two serious groin injuries which hindered his progress and, with new players being recruited as United prepared for a title assault, he was sold to Wrexham for £8,000 on Christmas Eve 1963.

In fact, the manager was reluctant to let him go, even offering another year's contract, but Sammy was desperate for first-team football and bade what he felt later to be a premature farewell to Old Trafford. Though he never added to the two Northern Ireland caps he gained during 1962, he went on to noteworthy service in the lower divisions.

SAMUEL THOMAS McMILLAN
BORN: Belfast, 20 September 1941.
HONOURS: 2 Northern Ireland caps (62).
OTHER CLUBS Wrexham 63/4-67/8 (149, 52); Southend United 67/8-69/70 (77, 5); Chester 69/70 (18, 0); Stockport County 70/1-71/2 (74, 29).

GAMES	15
GOALS	6

GRAHAM MOORE

1963/64

After one of the most impressive entrances any United newcomer ever enjoyed, it was all downhill for Graham Moore at Old Trafford. The tall Welsh international inside-forward sparkled in the 4–1 home thrashing of Spurs in November 1963, displaying delightful touch and vision that promised much for the future. The Stretford Enders lapped up his skills, licking their lips at the prospect of future feasts. Sadly all that awaited them was a famine.

Graham, who joined United from Chelsea for £35,000, had problems with his weight – not of his own making, being of a naturally heavy build – and soon he was struggling. Far too ponderous for a place in Matt Busby's rebuilding plans, he wasn't picked once during the title-winning term of 1964/65 and he moved to Northampton Town in the following December, later performing classily for Charlton Athletic.

For all that welcome if belated improvement in Graham's fortunes at the Valley, it seemed a far cry from his early days with Cardiff City, when he had scored on his full international debut against England as an 18-year-old and been hailed as the new golden boy of Welsh football.

GRAHAM MOORE
BORN: Hengoed, Glamorgan, 7 March 1941.
HONOURS: 21 Wales caps (59-70).
OTHER CLUBS: Cardiff City 58/9-61/2 (85, 23); Chelsea 61/2-63/4 (68, 13); Northampton Town 65/6-66/7 (54, 10); Charlton Athletic 67/8-70/1 (110, 8); Doncaster Rovers 71/2-73/4 (69, 3).

GAMES	19
GOALS	5

IAN MOIR

1960/61 → 1964/65

The margin between a top player and an average one can be frustratingly narrow, a truism illustrated perfectly by the case of Ian Moir. In training this gifted little Scottish wingman could perform feats with a ball that only the likes of George Best could hope to equal, yet he never possessed the necessary application and consistency to go with that rich vein of natural talent.

Probably, too, the chirpy Aberdonian lacked the ruthless streak which every professional sportsman needs to succeed at the highest level.

Ian's longest run in the side came at the start of the 1963/64 season when Matt Busby shook up his front line after a woeful Charity Shield performance against Everton.

The 20-year-old was called up to replace Johnny Giles on the right flank, and with his pace and his skill in both feet he might have been on the threshold of a golden future as the team which was to win two Championships and the European Cup began to take shape.

But Moir's play, though captivatingly adventurous at times, continued to lack insight at crucial moments, and this proved fatal for his aspirations at Old Trafford. Happily for skill-lovers around the divisions, Ian went on to thrill intermittently elsewhere, notably with Blackpool and Wrexham.

PHIL CHISNALL

1961/62 → 1963/64

Few United players in modern history have flattered to deceive as much as Phil Chisnall. Here was a richly skilled inside-forward, a deft passer and assured finisher, who made his debut while the team was in a state of flux and a regular place was up for grabs. All he had to do, it seemed, was to make optimum use of his ample gifts.

But other crucial ingredients proved to be missing from the footballing make-up of this England schoolboy and under-23 international. In the heat of First Division battle, close observers identified a shortfall in determination and toughness – both physical and mental at times – and, at that exalted level, he proved a little short of pace. His confidence suffered and Phil was duly transferred to Liverpool, where he also failed to make his mark, before carving a worthy niche for himself at Southend.

However, despite not attaining the heights predicted for him, the good-natured former starlet can claim one unique niche in football history. He is the only man to have played under Matt Busby, Alf Ramsey (for England) and Bill Shankly, perhaps the three most revered of all managers, and he earned lavish acclaim from each of them. In addition, Phil remains the only senior player in more than half a century to make the transfer journey from Old Trafford to Anfield.

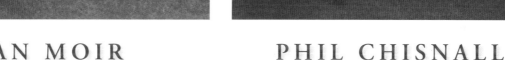

IAN MOIR
BORN: Aberdeen, 30 June 1943.
OTHER CLUBS: Blackpool 64/5-66/7 (61, 12);
Chester 67/8 (25, 3); Wrexham 67/8-71/2 (150, 20);
Shrewsbury Town 71/2-72/3 (25, 2); Wrexham
73/4-74/5 (15, 0).

GAMES	45
GOALS	5

JOHN PHILIP CHISNALL
BORN: Manchester, 27 October 1942.
OTHER CLUBS: Liverpool 64/5 (6, 1); Southend United
67/8-70/1 (142, 28); Stockport County 71/2 (30, 2).

GAMES	47
GOALS	10

WILLIE ANDERSON

1963/64 → 1966/67

A pacy, direct winger who helped to lift the FA Youth Cup in 1964, but whose opportunities were restricted by George Best and John Aston Jnr. Still, Willie reached the first team at 17 before joining Aston Villa for £20,000 in 1967.

WILLIAM JOHN ANDERSON
BORN: Liverpool, 24 January 1947.
OTHER CLUBS: Aston Villa 66/7-72/3 (231, 36); Cardiff City 72/3-76/7 (126, 12); Portland Timbers, USA, 76/7-81/2.

GAMES 10 (3)
GOALS 0

FRANK HAYDOCK

1960/61 → 1962/63

Tall, strong and combative, Frank became known as one of the trustiest stand-in stoppers in the First Division. Unable to separate Bill Foulkes from the number-five shirt, though, he was sold to Charlton for £10,000 in 1963.

FRANK HAYDOCK
BORN: Eccles, Lancashire, 29 November 1940.
OTHER CLUBS: Charlton Athletic 63/4-65/6 (84, 4); Portsmouth 65/6-68/9 (72, 1); Southend United 68/9-69/70 (33, 4).

GAMES 6
GOALS 0

ALBERT KINSEY

1964/65

An England youth international who deputised for Denis Law in an FA Cup clash with Chester and scored the first goal in a 2-1 victory. After that the burly Merseysider slipped out of the Reds reckoning and started afresh at Wrexham, where he thrived.

ALBERT JOHN KINSEY
BORN: Liverpool, 19 September 1945.
OTHER CLUBS: Wrexham 65/6-72/3 (253, 80); Crewe Alexandra 72/3-74/5 (32, 1).

GAMES 1
GOALS 1

WILF TRANTER

1963/64

An efficient centre-half who never emerged from the immense shadow cast by Bill Foulkes, Wilf did not look out of his depth when confronted with the menace of Geoff Hurst on his only first-team outing, but he wasn't tried again.

WILFRED TRANTER
BORN: Pendlebury, Lancashire, 5 March 1945.
OTHER CLUBS: Brighton and Hove Albion 65/6-67/8 (47, 1); Baltimore Bays, USA, 67/8; Fulham 68/9-71/2 (22, 0); St Louis Stars, USA, 71/2.

GAMES 1
GOALS 0

DENNIS WALKER

1962/63

When Bobby Charlton was rested in the run-up to the 1963 FA Cup Final, Dennis was selected as the star's left-wing understudy at Nottingham Forest. No more chances materialised, though, and soon he moved to Bootham Crescent.

DENNIS ALLEN WALKER
BORN: Northwich, Cheshire, 26 October 1944.
OTHER CLUBS: York City 64/5-67/8 (154, 19); Cambridge United 70/1-72/3 (56, 4).
DIED: 2003.

GAMES 1
GOALS 0

DAVID GASKELL

1957/58 → 1966/67

When 16-year-old goalkeeper David Gaskell walked on to the Maine Road pitch to represent United in the 1956 Charity Shield against Manchester City, he could have been forgiven for presuming that soccer stardom was there for the taking.

Admittedly he was coming on only as a substitute – having been called dramatically from the terraces on his night off to replace the incapacitated Ray Wood – but this was a prestigious game, his was a precocious talent and time was on his side. Certainly, after he acquitted himself impressively in the Reds' 1-0 victory, having borrowed a pair of boots from forward Colin Webster, the general view was that the club had discovered yet another youthful gem.

Yet when David played his last game for United a decade later, the Old Trafford career he looked back on had been as much frustrating as fulfilling. Despite making more than a century of senior appearances he had never made the custodian's job emphatically his own, due substantially to being a contemporary of the brilliant Harry Gregg but also in significant part to a succession of injuries, both grievous and niggling. Indeed, frequently he played in severe discomfort, his enormous courage disguising the extent of his disability.

David was a flamboyant performer, a spectacular shot-stopper whose natural athleticism enabled him to thrill the crowds with his acrobatics and his aggressive sense of adventure. He was not always as impressive when dealing with crosses, however, and there was doubt in influential quarters about the suitability of his temperament for long-term success at the top level.

He picked up an FA Cup winner's medal in 1963, being preferred rather controversially to Harry, who was just back from one of his own protracted absences. In addition, he could point to three consecutive outings in FA Cup semi-finals between 1962 and 1964, but that sequence proved to be the high-water for Gaskell as a Red.

Afterwards, his chances were limited further by the arrival of first Pat Dunne, then Alex Stepney, and he experienced a rift with the United management, going on to play rugby union for Orrell while still on the club's books before drifting into non-League football with his home-town club, Wigan Athletic.

There followed a successful comeback with Wrexham which was ended, with crushing inevitablity, by yet another injury.

JOHN DAVID GASKELL
BORN: Wigan, Lancashire, 5 October 1940.
HONOURS: FA Cup 62/3.
OTHER CLUBS: Wrexham 69/70-71/2 (95, 0).

| GAMES | 119 (1) |
| GOALS | 0 |

JOHN CONNELLY

1964/65 → 1966/67

In the pop-dominated culture of the 1960s, John Connelly always seemed an unfashionable sort of player. With his slicked-back hair and perpetual grimace he was like a refugee from the pages of the dear old *Book of Football Champions*, in which the heroes of the day were invariably pictured straining every sinew.

John was, in fact, an old-fashioned winger and none the worse for that. He was fast, equally effective on either flank, a precise crosser and a formidably deadly finisher. Indeed, as an ever-present in his first season at Old Trafford he scored 15 League goals, an outstanding tally for a wingman, and it played a mammoth part in capturing that year's Championship. As a bonus, underlining his value even more emphatically, he struck five more times in knockout competitions.

But the Connelly contribution did not end with his presence on the scoresheet. He was a sturdy customer and not averse to tackling back as he demonstrated forcibly in the crucial clash with Leeds at Elland Road near the end of that enthralling 1964/65 campaign. On a blustery April afternoon he demonstrated the steely commitment of a midfield workhorse as he harried and frustrated influential play-maker Bobby Collins, running the combative little Scot into the Yorkshire mud. Typically, too, John's goal was the sole strike in one of those grim, end-of-season encounters in which the big prizes are won and lost, sealing the match, perhaps even the destiny of the title.

Yet when Matt Busby had paid Burnley £56,000 for his services in April 1964, there had been those 'experts' who wondered why the United manager wanted a player they described, rather mysteriously, as stale and stereotyped, one who had dropped out of the international reckoning and whose best days, in their opinion, were probably behind him.

In fact, the move renewed the impetus of the Connelly career, which in reality had hardly been flagging at Turf Moor anyway. After enlisting with the Clarets in 1956 he had plundered 105 goals in 265 senior outings, picking up a title medal in 1959/60 into the bargain. Then, in his final term with Burnley – during which he had been switched from right flank to left to accommodate the luxuriant blossoming of a certain Willie Morgan – John had missed only a handful of outings, proving as penetrative as ever.

Soon after arriving at Old Trafford he was restored to England duty, fitting recognition of the smooth manner in which he had coped with the radical difference in styles between the two clubs, Burnley tending to operate methodically to a rigid plan, United adopting a more expansive, free-flowing approach.

John's ingrained, down-to-earth practicality, bolstered as it was by a comprehensive range of skills and endless determination, proved an ideal additive to a mix which was already enriched by the aristocratic talents of Charlton, Best and Law, and his transfer was duly celebrated as an unqualified success.

Then, as Alf Ramsey led his England team into the 1966 World Cup Finals, John was named as first choice at outside-right, and in the tournament opener he brought fleeting excitement to the drabbest of goalless draws by hitting the Uruguay woodwork twice. In view of his dash and enterprise in suffocatingly difficult circumstances, he was unlucky to lose his place.

Still only 28, he seemed to have plenty left to offer, certainly at the top club level, but that summer there arose a difference of opinion with his Old Trafford boss and John was sold unexpectedly to newly relegated Blackburn Rovers, United recouping £40,000 in the process.

Commendably, the experienced flankman refused to let his career merely peter out and three good years at Ewood Park were followed by a spirited Indian summer with Bury. After that came retirement and the running of a fish and chip restaurant, name of Connelly's Plaice, where he continued to give the same exceptional value for money that had characterised his 17 years as a professional footballer.

JOHN MICHAEL CONNELLY
BORN: St Helens, Lancashire, 18 July 1938.
HONOURS: League Championship 64/5. 20 England caps (59-66).
OTHER CLUBS: Burnley 56/7-63/4 (216, 85); Blackburn Rovers 66/7-69/70 (149, 36); Bury 70/1-72/3 (128, 37).

GAMES 112 (1)
GOALS 35

BOBBY CHARLTON

1956/57 → 1972/73

Football history abounds with heroes, but there has never been another like Bobby Charlton. The miner's son from Northumberland was a player with a sublime and unique talent, a soccer idol without the proverbial feet of clay, and he remains the British game's finest living international ambassador.

Those who saw him play were privileged. They will bear witness to a glorious combination of silk and dynamite which took the breath away. As Paddy Crerand, for so long his midfield partner, put it: 'You never saw a more graceful sight on a football pitch. Bobby was pure poetry.'

Paeans of praise have been sung to his most spectacular attributes – the pulverising shot, the uncannily accurate long-distance pass and the devastating body swerve – but the most precious of his gifts, and the one which made the rest so deadly, was his instinct. Charlton possessed a natural feel for his work which amounted to genius, though that isn't to say he didn't toil ceaselessly to improve his game. In the early days he could be found kicking a ball against a wall for hours at a time in an effort to hone a particular skill.

Bobby was a schoolboy prodigy. As a slender nine-year-old he dominated contests in which his opponents were five years his senior, and as a teenager his house was besieged by scouts from all the country's leading clubs.

After choosing United and while beginning to make his mark among the Busby Babes, Bobby embarked on the first of three distinct phases of his soccer development. Initially he played as an attacking inside-forward, foraging and scoring goals, and there are respected judges who cherish memories of that dazzling interlude more than any other. Undoubtedly, at that point he performed with a carefree exuberance which was to vanish forever as he took on extra responsibility after surviving the Munich crash, in which he received only superficial physical injuries but suffered deep mental scars.

Following the tragedy, there was a fundamental change of status for the 20-year-old Charlton. No longer was he merely one of a collection of exceptional players; now he was by far the brightest star in the Old Trafford firmament, and the burden of expectation was evident in the careworn expression which frequently replaced his previous habitual shy grin.

Thereafter, for four seasons in the early 1960s, he became a left-winger, and there are those who maintain that was his best position. Certainly, when he received the ball early, he was a thrilling sight as he surged along the touchline before cutting in for one of those awesome strikes, although there was a nagging feeling of waste, that he was too long on the fringe of the action instead of being at its hub.

However, most agree that Bobby was not seen in his true pomp until his third phase, when he became the deep-lying play-maker, a more demanding role which used his ability to the full. From midfield, in concert with Crerand, he orchestrated some of the most scintillating play in British soccer history. The fruits were two Championships and the European Cup. Meanwhile there was the little matter of helping England to win the World Cup, a triumph shared with his brother Jack of Leeds United in 1966, when Bobby was named as both English and European Footballer of the Year.

Was there, though, a price to pay for such excellence? Was this a player without a flaw? The answers, of course, are 'yes' to the first question, 'no' to the second. There were times when Bobby, taking his own intuitive path, strayed out of position, which could mean extra work for covering team-mates. And deep, tactical plans were not his forte, nor were desperate, neck-or-nothing tackles. But what of it? A successful team needs a blend of contrasting talents, and no one who played alongside Bobby would have had him any other way.

In his pomp, indisputably, he was one of the finest footballers in the world. But even in the twilight of his career, when the strain of striving against the odds in a declining team began to tell, still his play was infused with a certain purity, a boyish sense of wonder.

Over the years this match-winner extraordinary and gentleman supreme has grown into a national institution, and often that has made him squirm with embarrassment, although more recently he has overcome a native shyness which many mistook for aloofness, and has worn his celebrity with increasing ease. Now a director at Old Trafford, his beloved 'theatre of dreams', Bobby Charlton will be remembered as long as football itself. The knighthood which arrived in 1994 was a fitting tribute, though to his legions of long-time admirers it was barely necessary. To them, he had always been Sir Bobby.

ROBERT CHARLTON
BORN: Ashington, Northumberland, 11 October 1937.
HONOURS: European Cup 67/8. League Championship 56/7, 64/5, 66/7. FA Cup 62/3.
106 England caps (58-70). European Footballer of the Year 66.
FWA Footballer of the Year 66.
OTHER CLUBS: Preston North End 74/5 (38, 8).
MANAGER: Preston North End (73-75); Wigan Athletic (acting, 83).

GAMES	756 (2)
GOALS	249

SHAY BRENNAN

· ·

1957/58 → 1969/70

He didn't bask in the idolatry heaped on George Best or enjoy the reverence inspired by Bobby Charlton, but no member of Manchester United's European Cup-winning side of 1968 was better loved by his fellow footballers than Shay Brennan.

Despite being born in Manchester, Shay was of Republican stock and an archetypal easy-going Irishman, twinkling of eye, broad of grin, a disarming mixture of mischief and modesty. Without allowing it to interfere with his work, he was keen on a drink and relished a bet, and the manner in which he played down his own part in United's multiple triumphs defined his gentle, unassuming nature.

In fact, his role was immense and it began when the future Republic of Ireland skipper enlisted on the Old Trafford groundstaff in 1953. Though destined to mature into a high-quality right-back, Shay began as a silkily skilful inside-forward, and it was in that role that he helped the Red Devils to retain the FA Youth Cup in 1955. However, a more dramatic contribution was imminent.

United were so short of players after Munich that Brennan found himself pitchforked into his senior debut against Sheffield Wednesday in the FA Cup, the club's first game in the wake of the crash. Despite filling the unfamiliar slot of outside-left for the first time in his professional life – 'I had as little idea about playing on the wing as the man in the moon' – he emerged as the unlikely hero, scoring twice on an emotion-charged night as the Reds completed a rousing 3-0 victory.

Thereafter he was unable to hold a regular place but as Matt Busby set about the painstaking task of reconstruction, Shay's inexperience saw him slip out of contention for a season before he emerged as a wing-half during 1959/60. However, it was not until his conversion to right-back at the outset of the following campaign that he demonstrated his full worth.

Now he stood out as a poised and unflappable defender, a master of canny positional play who was more likely to jockey his opponent away from the danger area than to dive in with a wild tackle. Then, when the time was right, Brennan would steal the ball from the unsuspecting attacker's foot before releasing it into the creative custody of Crerand or Charlton.

Though out of the side for the 1963 FA Cup Final, Shay pocketed title medals in 1964/65 and 1966/67, and in May 1968 finally enjoyed his moment in the Wembley spotlight when the Red Devils won the European Cup.

In truth, whereas he had been unlucky in missing out on previous finals, this time around fortune smiled on Brennan, who had spent most of that season in the reserves while youngster Francis Burns had held sway. But come the second leg of the semi-final against Real Madrid, Busby opted for the older man's experience to counter the potent menace of the brilliant Francisco Gento. So splendidly did Shay perform that he retained his berth for the most important match in the club's history.

In parallel to his success with United, he earned international recognition, and by what was then an unconventional route. Back in 1962 Brennan had reached the fringe of the England squad but then slipped from the reckoning. But in 1965 a FIFA ruling enabled him to become the first English-born player to represent the Republic, and he went on to make 19 appearances for the land of his ancestors, five of them as captain.

Back at club level, after 1968 the slowing thirtysomething remained on the fringe of the side for two more terms before moving to Ireland, where he became player-manager of Waterford and guided his charges to two titles.

Shay Brennan died suddenly while playing golf, one of his great passions, leaving his countless friends to comfort themselves with the thought that the genial charmer couldn't have conceived of a more convivial way to go.

SEAMUS ANTHONY BRENNAN
BORN: Manchester, 6 May 1937.
HONOURS: European Cup 67/8. League Championship 64/5, 66/7. 19 Republic of Ireland caps (65-70).
MANAGER: Waterford, Republic of Ireland, (70-74).
DIED: Tramore, Waterford, 9 June 2000.

| GAMES | 358 (1) |
| GOALS | 6 |

NOBBY STILES

· ·

1960/61 → 1970/71

Everyone is familiar with the Nobby Stiles school of football, or are they? In fact, those who dismissed him as nothing more than an effective hatchet man are a long way from the mark.

It would be fatuous to assert that hardness was not a key facet of his game, witness those famous mantrap tackles. But mere physical presence was not the half of it. Nobby Stiles was one of the most tactically aware of players, his intelligent, instant assessments of dangerous situations and his capacity to act decisively combining to make him a priceless asset to Manchester United.

Nobby, who was no passing master yet had more skill than most people gave him credit for, was ideally equipped to be a sweeper. In this role he was the perfect foil for Bill Foulkes who, at least in his latter years, was most effective alongside a nippy and resourceful team-mate. The two men complemented each other perfectly, Bill dominant in aerial combat, Nobby dropping off and mopping up with a mixture of fearsome challenges and precise interception. Neither man was a showboater, instead being content to win the ball and then offer a short pass to a more creative colleague.

Certainly Bobby Charlton's game owed plenty to the little Mancunian, especially when the pair operated together in midfield for their country. Nobby's unobtrusive but astute covering allowed his more gifted clubmate the freedom to roam and gave full range to Charlton's lethal but sometimes unpredictable talents. If Bobby left a gap then it was a racing certainty that Nobby would fill it.

Evaluated in isolation, Stiles was not the most gifted of footballers, but viewed in the context of the United and England set-ups of the mid-1960s he was as close to being indispensable as an individual can be. Of course, the mechanics of his game were not the extent of his worth. Equally important was his unquenchable will to win. Nobby was an inspirational organiser and an inveterate shouter, an image so glaringly incompatible with his mild, almost meek demeanour off the pitch.

Though Stiles' fame was founded on his prowess as a ball-winner, it had been as an inside-forward that he had hoped to make his mark after enlisting at Old Trafford as the most starry-eyed of teenagers in 1957. Thus, for several campaigns after making his senior debut in 1960/61, he was deployed in an attacking role, either at wing-half or inside-forward, but although he was in the team more often than not, doubts grew about his worthiness for the top level.

The arrival of the sumptuously creative Paddy Crerand in 1963 emphasised to Nobby that a change was needed, and he set his sights on the defensive role alongside Foulkes. However, that position was filled already by the splendid Maurice Setters, who had denied him a place in the 1963 FA Cup Final, and it took an injury to the rugged West Countryman to give Stiles his chance in the spring of 1964.

Thereafter Nobby, his timing of tackles and his distribution improved vastly by the use of contact lenses, cemented a regular place and exerted huge influence throughout the Reds' subsequent successful sequence, a vivid highlight of which was his shackling of the fabulous Eusebio of Benfica in the 1968 European Cup Final. Also, two years earlier on that same Wembley turf, the widely vilified battler had endeared himself to a hitherto sceptical nation at the melodramatic climax of the triumphant World Cup campaign. Suddenly, on a sunny afternoon of pure wonder, this prancing, gap-toothed warrior was enshrined as part of England's sporting heritage, a veritable national treasure.

Towards the end of the decade Nobby was laid low by injury and, after two frustrating seasons, was allowed to join Middlesbrough for £20,000. There followed a spell at Preston North End under Bobby Charlton before he took up management, first at Deepdale, then later at West Bromwich, where he served initially under brother-in-law Johnny Giles.

Later he became involved with the youth set-up at Old Trafford before he left to hone his burgeoning reputation as an after-dinner speaker. It seemed that Nobby's entertainment value was touching new peaks, though certain retired strikers were finding his reminiscences a trifle painful . . .

NORBERT PETER STILES

BORN:	Manchester, 18 May 1942.
HONOURS:	European Cup 67/8. League Championship 64/5, 66/7. 28 England caps (65-70).
OTHER CLUBS:	Middlesbrough 71/2-72/3 (57, 2); Preston North End 73/4-74/5 (46, 1).
MANAGER:	Preston North End (77-81); Vancouver Whitecaps, Canada, (81-84);
	West Bromwich Albion (85-86).

GAMES	395
GOALS	19

DENIS LAW

1962/63 → 1972/73

When old pros get together to talk about great Manchester United footballers, one name above all gets them bubbling. They recall with reverence the wizardry of Best, the glory of Charlton and the superhuman deeds of Edwards, but it is the memory of Denis Law that really sets their pulses racing.

Denis belonged to the fans, who adored his strutting dash of devilry, that outlaw streak which almost verged on villainy, and to them he was 'The King.' But somehow, beyond that, he was the players' player. It wasn't just his phenomenal strike rate, or even those dazzling flashes of genius which could swing a game in an instant. It was something deeper, more fundamental; a quality that was indefinable and yet had a lot to do with the size of his heart.

Pale, hawk-faced and as slim as a whippet, the Lawman might have sprung from the pages of Wild West fiction, but any impression of a gunslinging desperado with murder in his heart was leavened appealingly by a puckish sense of humour which communicated itself readily through his football.

Denis' fairytale future could hardly have been predicted by Huddersfield Town supporters when a spindly, pallid teenager ran out for his debut in 1956, but he was nurtured cannily by his colourful countryman, Bill Shankly, who recognised the seeds of greatness in the gawky boy whose ferocious will to win matched his own. Soon Manchester City were impressed and took him to Maine Road for a short spell before dispatching him to the Italian club, Torino. An unhappy sojourn in the sun followed before Matt Busby stepped in with a new British record transfer fee of £115,000 in August 1962.

United made up for a poor League season by winning the FA Cup in 1963 and it was Denis who set them on the way with a typical piece of sorcery. He received the ball from Paddy Crerand, spun on the spot like a scarlet top and scored with a devastating cross-shot before the nonplussed Leicester defence could move.

This was but a taste of the feast to come from the 1964 European Footballer of the Year. A golden river of goals followed, 160 of them in just 222 games over his first five seasons. Many of them were spectacular, some seemingly impossible, and everything was done with a cocky panache the fans found irresistible.

His record owed much to sharpness of reflex and inspired control; awesome aerial ability for one of such slight stature and a downright refusal to give up any cause; toughness that would have done credit to rawhide and bravery that would have shamed a Roman gladiator.

But Denis Law's most precious gifts were awareness and anticipation. He seemed to see the action several frames ahead of everyone else and knew how to capitalise instantly on that advantage. At times it was uncanny, as though he could read the minds of defenders and colleagues alike, and when Denis moved in earnest, all opponents would see was a red flash. With such a knack he had to play up front, but what a midfield man Denis could have made! Lauded though he was, he was never given full credit for his all-round skill. His tackling and passing were exemplary and as for dribbling, how about the shoulder-dropping dash which set up Bobby Charlton's explosive strike in the 1967 Charity Shield?

But there are two abiding sadnesses about his Old Trafford years. First he was cheated by knee trouble of a role in the 1968 European Cup victory; then he endured a few seasons of anti-climax during which the club was unsettled and the knee was not improving. Eventually, and controversially, he was given a free transfer by Tommy Docherty and went on to enjoy an Indian summer with Manchester City and Scotland.

Two criticisms levelled at Denis are that he was fearfully hot-tempered and serially injury-prone. Well, the former was undeniable, but it was part of his make-up, an unchangeable aspect of the lethal Law cocktail. And the latter, apart from his final years, is a fallacy. Given the physical punishment he received, his overall appearance record was excellent.

He ranks, undeniably, with the all-time greats and his achievements will stand forever. The legend of Law will pass into posterity as an example of sport at its most blindingly brilliant.

	DENIS LAW	
BORN:	Aberdeen, 24 February 1940.	
HONOURS:	League Championship 64/5, 66/7. FA Cup 62/3. 55 Scotland caps (58-74). European Footballer of the Year 64.	
OTHER CLUBS:	Huddersfield Town 56/7-59/60 (81, 16); Manchester City 59/60-60/61 (44, 21); Torino, Italy, 61/2 (27, 10); Manchester City 73/4 (24, 9).	GAMES **398 (6)** GOALS **237**

PADDY CRERAND

1962/63 → 1970/71

If ever a man made a mockery of the traditional standards by which great footballers are judged it was Paddy Crerand. Indeed, the Scottish international wing-half – variously described as slow, ungainly, a bad header and a poor goal-scorer – veritably ridiculed the rulebook and wrote his own rich volume of Old Trafford folklore.

It's true he was not the most rapid of Red Devils; he didn't need to be. His vision, anticipation and sublime passing skills rendered lack of pace irrelevant. Paddy was able to play, and often dictate proceedings, in his own time.

It can be argued that his movement on the field was hardly reminiscent of a gazelle, but fans and team-mates could live with that, rating it, perhaps, on a par with George Best's failure to make the half-time tea. As for his ability in the air, well, it's undeniable that occasionally he dumbfounded his colleagues by heading the ball twice in one match . . .

And goals? He didn't often supply the finishing touch but, in his heyday, the majority of United's successful strikes were due in some measure to his remarkable talents. Not for nothing was it a 1960s Old Trafford truism that when Crerand was on song, then so were Manchester United. Thus, whenever possible, it was the aim of his defensive team-mates to ensure that his marking duties were as light as possible so that he could be given the ball. Then, they knew, the dismantling of the opposition could commence.

The former Celt thought deeply about his game, made it his business to know the opposition and was more aware than most about what was going on around him. An apt illustration is an incident in the 1963 FA Cup Final against Leicester City, the game which signalled the Reds' return as a major power after Munich.

Though still allegedly adjusting to English football, United's recent £53,000 signing from Celtic had done enough homework to know that Gordon Banks liked to throw the ball to Scottish schemer Davie Gibson, the springboard of so many attacks. Seeing Banks in possession and noting that Gibson was free, Paddy pounced while others idled. He beat his countryman to the ball, threaded a pass through a crowded penalty area and Denis Law did the rest.

It was a vivid cameo that captured the very essence of vintage Crerand, but sumptuous distribution was not the only weapon in his armoury. His tackles did not lack bite and his stamina was immense, as he demonstrated on a searingly humid evening at Wembley in May 1968, when he worked himself to a standstill in the European Cup Final, ferrying tirelessly from box to box while supplying a steady stream of passes which stretched the Benfica defence to breaking point.

Regular beneficiaries of Paddy's pinpoint accuracy were Messrs Best, Law and Charlton, true greats who would have shone in any company, but how they relished the subtle promptings of Crerand. Indeed, if Matt Busby's last great team could be compared to an orchestra, then the fabulous trinity were the multi-gifted soloists, but so frequently the conductor who coaxed them towards glorious crescendo was the sparky Glaswegian.

Of course, there were days when the baton slipped and inspiration deserted him, but in such games he would never hide from the ball and would always continue to probe.

An extrovert Glaswegian, raised in the Gorbals, Paddy allowed his fervour to get the better of him at times and occasionally he landed in trouble with referees. Indeed, it's been said that he never moved so fast as when headed for a melee 40 yards away! But his fiery nature was as much a part of Crerand the player as Crerand the man. It would be hard to find a United follower who would have wanted him any other way.

And if part of that huge heart will be forever at his beloved Parkhead – the home of his first club – it would be a rare Stretford Ender who wouldn't forgive him. His loyalty to Old Trafford was never in doubt, his contribution to the club's cause colossal, and it might have been more immense still had his stint as assistant manager under Tommy Docherty not ended when a severe difference of opinion between the two Scots resulted in his departure in 1975. It was a red-letter day, indeed, when Matt Busby crossed the border to claim Paddy Crerand for Manchester United.

PATRICK TIMOTHY CRERAND

BORN: Glasgow, 19 February 1939.

HONOURS: European Cup 67/8. League Championship 64/5, 66/7. FA Cup 62/3.
16 Scotland caps (61-65).

OTHER CLUBS: Celtic 58/9-62/3 (91, 5).

MANAGER: Northampton Town (76-77).

| GAMES | 397 |
| GOALS | 15 |

PAT DUNNE

· ·

1964/65 → 1965/66

No one can ever take away from Pat Dunne the fact that he won a League Championship medal in 1964/65, or that he played splendidly for much of that memorable campaign.

The £10,500 recruit from Shamrock Rovers stood between Manchester United's posts in 37 games as the title was claimed for the first time since the Munich tragedy, and clearly he possessed considerable merit or Matt Busby would not have persevered with him.

But, without wishing to understate the attributes of a respected performer who attained international status with the Republic of Ireland, it might reasonably be asserted that he will go down as one of the more fortunate goalkeepers to carry off the top domestic club prize.

Pat was a fine, occasionally brilliant shot-stopper on his line, and he was unfailingly courageous when diving at attackers' feet, but when it came to crosses and commanding his area he was not in the front rank.

One particularly costly example of his weakness in the air came near the end of a bitter FA Cup semi-final replay with Leeds United, when he flapped at a ball his defenders expected him to claim and allowed Billy Bremner to steal the winner.

With Harry Gregg absent through injury and the Reds having made a poor start to the season, Pat had been drafted in to replace David Gaskell in September 1964. His debut was away to Everton, ironically the club he had joined as a teenager before returning to Ireland after failing to break through at Goodison, and he acquitted himself ably in a 3-3 draw.

Thereafter the Reds embarked on a 15-match unbeaten sequence which formed the basis of the Championship triumph and, with Dunne now a fixture, they stormed into the semi-finals of both the Inter-Cities Fairs Cup and the FA Cup.

However, the Irishman who had sprung from obscurity so suddenly returned to the sidelines with equal alacrity early in 1965/66, rapidly falling behind Gregg and Gaskell in the pecking order. His fate was sealed by the arrival of Alex Stepney the following season and in February 1967 he joined Plymouth Argyle in a £5,000 deal.

At Home Park, perhaps, he found his true level, quickly becoming a local hero and picking up the Pilgrims' player of the year award for 1967/68, a considerable feat for a goalkeeper in a relegation season.

Subsequently Pat – no relation to namesake Tony – returned to Shamrock Rovers, later sampling management and continuing to play at various levels until the grand old age of 55.

PATRICK ANTHONY JOSEPH DUNNE
BORN: Dublin, 9 February 1943.
HONOURS: League Championship 64/5. 5 Republic of Ireland caps (65-66).
OTHER CLUBS: Shamrock Rovers, Republic of Ireland, 62/3-63/4; Plymouth Argyle 66/7-70/1 (152, 0); Shamrock Rovers 70/1.
MANAGER: Shelbourne, Turles Town, Bray Wanderers, all Republic of Ireland.

GAMES 67
GOALS 0

JOHN FITZPATRICK

1964/65 → 1972/73

Opinions differ sharply over the merits of Scottish wing-half cum full-back John Fitzpatrick. Some say the combative Aberdonian was impetuous, foolhardy even, in his tackles, that his timing was often awry and that he was not really of the class required of a Manchester United player. Others maintain that he was a canny battler with more ability than was generally realised, whose career was sabotaged by injury.

There is certainly no doubting the last-mentioned fact. John's knee problems cost him dearly, ultimately forcing him out of the game, after several operations, at the age of 26.

In his early days in first-team contention he was viewed as a stand-in for Nobby Stiles, a player whose fierce commitment he matched without having the same tactical awareness. But John's most effective spell was towards the turn of the decade when he enjoyed an extended run at right-back as Shay Brennan's distinguished service neared an end.

Despite playing nearly 150 games in a period when silverware was plentiful at Old Trafford, 'Fitz' left with no senior medals to show for his efforts, although he did help to lift the FA Youth Cup in 1964. Also he entered the record books as the Red Devils' first substitute in League football, having replaced Denis Law at Tottenham in October 1965.

JOHN HERBERT NORTON FITZPATRICK
BORN: Aberdeen, 18 August 1946.

GAMES **141 (6)**
GOALS   **10**

JIM RYAN

1965/66 → 1969/70

Jim Ryan never did himself justice the first time around at Old Trafford. Here was a player who on the training ground could give one of the best full-backs in Europe, Tony Dunne, an almighty chasing. But somehow, come match day, that confidence would have evaporated. Gone was the wizard of the dribble, to be replaced by a nervous-looking individual who never seemed likely to make a first-team berth his own. That was a shameful waste of this clever Scot, who also boasted speed and wiry strength among his attributes, and after being on the fringe of the 1968 European Cup-winning side, his prospects nosedived with the purchase of Willie Morgan.

His United path having taken a similar course to that of Ian Moir a few years earlier, the unassuming Ryan was transferred to Luton Town in 1970, one of four Red Devils who moved to Kenilworth Road in a £35,000 package. At last he became a more consistent performer, carving out a useful career with the Hatters, whom he was later to manage. In 1991 Jim returned to Old Trafford to coach the reserves, with marked success. Later he stood in as Alex Ferguson's assistant in the interregnum between Brian Kidd and Steve McClaren, before making the position his own in 2001. Subsequently he accepted a new role as a youth coach.

JAMES RYAN
BORN: Stirling, 15 May 1945.
OTHER CLUBS: Luton Town 70/1-76/7 (184, 21); Dallas Tornados, USA, 77-79; Wichita Wings, USA, 79-84.
MANAGER: Luton Town (90-91).

GAMES **24 (3)**
GOALS   **4**

BOBBY NOBLE

. . . .

1965/66 → 1966/67

If it were possible to design and build the ideal full-back then there could hardly have been a more perfect model than Bobby Noble. He was quick, his tackling was granite-hard and immaculately timed, he used the ball well and he read the game with astonishing maturity.

Indeed, in the spring of 1967 the stocky blond Mancunian was, by common consent, the most accomplished young left-back in the land and there seemed to be no clouds on his horizon. He was newly married and super-fit, excelling yet still improving in a vibrant team. But then, after playing 31 consecutive League and Cup games as United stormed towards their second title in three seasons, Bobby was snatched from football at the age of 21.

Disaster struck on the way home from a goalless draw at Sunderland, when he suffered hideous head, chest and leg injuries in a car crash near his home in Sale. For a time his life hung in the balance and the recovery, when it came, was frustratingly tortuous.

In May 1968 – ironically during the week of the Reds' European Cup triumph – Bobby underwent an operation to restore his sight for the purposes of everyday life but not, as it transpired, for top-flight football. Later he made gallant and harrowing attempts at a comeback, turning out for the club's junior teams, but it became poignantly obvious that he was not going to make it.

He trained as hard as he knew how, but always felt in his heart that he would never return to first-team action. His timing and sharpness had gone, and he could no longer anticipate the flight of the ball, a hopeless situation for a defender. When the truth sank in it dealt Bobby a devastating blow, one that left him overwhelmingly depressed.

Certainly it was a savage reversal of fortune for the feisty youngster who had captained a side including George Best, David Sadler and John Aston to FA Youth Cup success in 1964 and whose long-term prospects had appeared to be limitless.

Bobby made his senior Red Devils debut at home to Leicester City in April 1966 and acquitted himself admirably. Then, after being overlooked for the first ten games of the subsequent campaign, and with the illustrious likes of Tony Dunne, Shay Brennan and Noel Cantwell on the scene, he doubted his future with United and asked for a transfer. Matt Busby's response was unequivocal: 'Not as long as I'm here, son!'

Soon the manager demonstrated his regard for this forthright young man by shifting Dunne to the right and bringing in Bobby on the left. The boy's star rose inexorably as he grew ever more assured in his work, but then it plummeted so abruptly from the heavens and the Noble career was over almost before it had begun.

Thereafter he went on a coaching course at Lilleshall but didn't take to it. In time he was to regret his lack of patience, but by then it was too late, and he looked to a new life outside the game.

Everyone who saw Bobby Noble play was in agreement: not only was he sure to play for England, but there was nothing to stop him being a fixture at left-back for club and country for the next decade.

Beyond the ability and the hardness there was an almost unnerving certainty about his play which marked him out as something special. His accident was a personal catastrophe for a gifted young athlete and a body blow to Manchester United and England.

ROBERT NOBLE

BORN: Manchester, 18 December 1945.

HONOURS: League Championship 66/7.

GAMES 33

GOALS 0

DAVID SADLER

· ·

1963/64 → 1973/74

For a popular man, David Sadler had an unexpected knack of perplexing some of his Old Trafford team-mates. There was no doubting his ability or commitment, but a few of the more demonstrative characters to play for United during David's decade at the club never ceased to be astonished by a coolness in the face of any provocation which at times bordered on serenity – and that's a quality rarely evident in the highly competitive world of big-time football.

In fact David, certainly a model professional in deed and attitude, was also blessed with the most commendable attributes of the archetypal amateur sportsman. Hardly surprising, perhaps, as he was an England amateur international centre-forward in his pre-United days.

Sadler's rise had been both meteoric and unorhodox. While a mere 15 years old, he was cutting a dash in the number-nine shirt of a leading amateur club, Maidstone United of the Isthmian League; some 12 months later he was representing his country and riveting the attention of a host of big-time scouts. By then David was working in a Maidstone bank, but he turned professional at Old Trafford on his 17th birthday in February 1963.

His encouraging progress continued when he enjoyed his first spell in the Reds' senior side, taking over briefly from David Herd at the start of the 1963/64 season after Matt Busby made sweeping changes in the wake of an appalling display by his team in the Charity Shield against Everton. Not for the first time, the manager backed youth, replacing Herd, Johnny Giles and Albert Quixall with Sadler, Ian Moir and Phil Chisnall.

David acquitted himself pluckily, retaining his place for a dozen games, though his personal highlight that term was netting a hat-trick in the FA Youth Cup Final victory over Swindon Town.

Given subsequent outings in attack at First Division level, David performed adequately, but it seems reasonable to speculate that if he had remained a number nine then his Old Trafford career might have been a short one.

Instead the heart of defence became his domain and he played for England as a traditional centre-half. However, he was at his most effective alongside the stopper, where his fine touch, cultured passing and sharp intelligence came into their own.

David's greatest club honour was a European Cup winner's medal in 1968, a fitting addition to his Championship gong of the previous season, and his performance in the final against Benfica at Wembley highlighted the versatility which added immeasurably to his value.

That night he operated as a holding midfielder, slaving ceaselessly and dispatching the cross for Bobby Charlton's opening goal, and though he missed several scoring opportunities, he could be proud of his contribution to the Red Devils' finest hour.

It is often overlooked, too, that the tall, elegant Kentishman played a key part at the semi-final stage by netting in the second leg against Real Madrid. The goal came deep inside the second half with the Reds 3–2 down on aggregate and with hope evaporating fast; George Best nodded on a Charlton free-kick, the Spanish defenders remained leaden-footed, but David, by now committed to attack in a bid to break Real's stranglehold, read the situation to perfection, striding forward to bundle the ball over the line from close range. Not brilliant, not spectacular, but it gave the Reds new life and six minutes later the comeback was complete.

It was a typically low-key but invaluable effort from a thoroughbred footballer who, possibly, was prevented from reaching the very top class by a certain lack of ruthlessness.

Nevertheless, he went on to play more than 300 senior games for United before being allowed to join Preston North End for £25,000 in November 1973. He was only 27 at the time, and most pundits could hardly credit that Old Trafford boss Tommy Docherty had dispensed so lightly with such an experienced, accomplished and loyal retainer.

Sure enough, and ironically at a time when Manchester United were short of quality performers, it was at Deepdale that David played some of his finest, most measured football.

DAVID SADLER
BORN: Yalding, Kent, 5 February 1946.
HONOURS: European Cup 67/8. League Championship 66/7. 4 England caps (67-70).
OTHER CLUBS: Preston North End 73/4-76/7 (105, 3).

GAMES 328 (7)
GOALS 27

JOHN ASTON JUNIOR

1964/65 → 1971/72

John Aston created history as the man of the match when Manchester United defeated Benfica to become champions of Europe in 1968; yet he was never the most fortunate of footballers, his Old Trafford years being bedevilled by two problems not of his own making.

One, following in the footsteps of a famous father, he came to terms with. The other, becoming an aunt sally to sections of his home crowd, haunted him until the day he left.

John – son of John Aston Snr, a United hero of the 1940s and 1950s – was a fast, direct winger but one who boasted few frills to his game. As such he found himself an innocent victim of the spectacular success of Best, Law and Charlton. When United played badly, he was often singled out unfairly for persecution by fans who were reluctant to lash their idols. If a scapegoat was needed, usually John fitted the bill.

But he battled on philosophically, revealing ever more of the resolute spirit that had been evident from his earliest days on the Red Devils' groundstaff in 1962.

Back then, his situation had been awkward in the extreme, his father being not only a crowd favourite of days gone by, but also the club's youth coach. Thus John Snr was effectively John Jnr's boss, with all the inevitable strains such a dual relationship can cause. As a result, the youngster understood that if there were 50-50 decisions to be made, then probably they would go against him, but he refused to buckle and eventually he reaped due rewards.

The first of these was a place in the team which lifted the FA Youth Cup in 1964, shoulder to shoulder with the likes of Best, Sadler and Noble. Then came a hard-won Championship medal in 1966/67 and undreamed-of European glory a year later before a broken leg, suffered in an accidental collision with Manchester City's Francis Lee at Maine Road in August 1968, signalled the beginning of the end of his tenure at Old Trafford.

John recovered full fitness, impressing sufficiently to earn an England under-23 cap in 1969, but during a turbulent period in the club's history he never completely re-established his position.

However, drawing yet further on that seemingly bottomless well of determination, he went on to do well elsewhere, notably at Luton Town, to whom he was transferred for £30,000 by Frank O'Farrell in the summer of 1972. For five years he served the Hatters with distinction, playing an integral part in their ascent to the top flight in 1974, then served Mansfield Town and Blackburn Rovers prior to retirement.

Meanwhile, in the minds of every Manchester United supporter privileged to witness the incandescent highlight of John's career, either live or on television, the spectacle remains unwaveringly vivid.

Whatever other memories he holds of the Red Devils, both the painful and the pleasurable, the younger Aston can always cherish his performance in the most important match in the club's history – the 1968 European Cup Final.

That night at Wembley he truly walked with the gods as he lacerated the Benfica defence with pure pace. Fans may drool over the goals of Charlton and Best, the fairytale birthday celebration of Kidd and the miraculous save of Stepney; but, in truth, no one made a more mammoth contribution to that golden triumph than John Aston. What an occasion to come up with the show of a lifetime!

JOHN ASTON
BORN: Manchester, 28 June 1947.
HONOURS: European Cup 67/8. League Championship 66/7.
OTHER CLUBS: Luton Town 72/3-77/8 (174, 31); Mansfield Town 77/8 (31, 4);
Blackburn Rovers 78/9-79/80 (15, 2).

GAMES 166 (21)
GOALS 27

BRIAN KIDD

. . . .

1967/68 → 1973/74

The rise and fall of Brian Kidd as a Manchester United player remains one of the most frustrating episodes in the club's modern history. At the age of 18 he catapulted himself into the first team with spectacular performances on the 1967 Australian tour and a precocious display in the Charity Shield against Spurs. As the season progressed it was apparent that here was a potential world-beater.

In terms of ability, there was little that Brian lacked. He was a natural ball-player with sublime control, packed a thumping shot and possessed a sweet body-swerve. He was strong and gave as good as he got in his confrontations with battle-hardened First Division defenders. And he was left-sided, which brought balance to the forward line and was seen as another huge plus.

That first season was an unqualified success for the youngster, culminating with the comic-strip-hero experience of scoring in the Reds' historic European Cup triumph on his 19th birthday. The goal – United's third and the one which effectively put the trophy beyond Benfica's reach – was an unusual one, Brian's first six-yard header being parried, his second floating almost gently into the net over the heads of the stranded defenders.

To this observer, at least, it seemed to happen in slow motion; to the travelling Stretford Enders, it confirmed the callow Mancunian as a hero of the front rank. 'Kiddo' had arrived.

After such a meteoric early surge it was not surprising that his progress should slow down, but he did well enough to line up twice for England in 1970. Then, imperceptibly, the slide started. United were no longer such an impressive side, Brian did not mature tactically as fast as he did physically and, in a troubled team environment under new manager Tommy Docherty, his game suffered.

One theory is that he had grown too accustomed to playing alongside world-class stars, and that when, one by one, the likes of Paddy Crerand, Denis Law, Bobby Charlton and George Best declined in influence, he was unable to respond by raising his own level of contribution.

Certainly Docherty, whose hopes that Brian would forge a lethal striking partnership with Lou Macari were to be emphatically dashed, was unable to revive the former hero's flagging fortunes and in August 1974 a £110,000 deal took him to Arsenal.

For the Gunners, also experiencing a period of transition and struggling in the wrong half of the table, he scored regularly in difficult circumstances, before going on to creditable spells with Manchester City and Everton. Meanwhile the Stretford Enders were left to ponder on the heights to which 'Kiddo' might have aspired if he had been granted the luxury of a few more seasons in a successful side.

Later Brian, who was educated at the same Collyhurst school as Nobby Stiles, returned to Old Trafford, first as a youth coach, than as a forthright and enterprising assistant to Alex Ferguson. As all who witnessed his exuberant mini pitch invasion following Steve Bruce's late winner at home to Sheffield Wednesday in spring 1993 will have realised, Brian's enthusiasm for the cause had not waned one jot.

Clearly his talents were worthy of a top job and in 1998 he accepted the challenge offered by struggling Blackburn Rovers, only to be dismissed within a year after presiding over relegation and a poor start in the lower flight. Later he coached successfully with Leeds United, then accepted a role in the England set-up under Sven-Goran Eriksson before returning to the club scene with Bryan Robson at Sheffield United.

BRIAN KIDD

BORN: Manchester, 29 May 1949.
HONOURS: European Cup 67/8. 2 England caps (70).
OTHER CLUBS: Arsenal 74/5-75/6 (77, 30); Manchester City 76/7-78/9 (98, 44); Everton 78/9-79/80 (40, 11); Bolton Wanderers 80/1-81/2 (43, 14); Atlanta Chiefs, USA, 81; Fort Lauderdale Strikers, USA, 82-84; Minnesota Kicks, USA, 84.
MANAGER: Preston North End (86); Blackburn Rovers (98-99).

| GAMES | 257 (9) |
| GOALS | 70 |

GEORGE BEST

1963/64 → 1973/74

There are two ways to remember George Best. One will lead to anger, frustration and, unless you're blessed with a mightily strong constitution, mounting blood pressure. The other will bring joy, gratitude and, above all, a sense of wonder. So really there should be no contest, should there?

Of course, it would be a rare Manchester United fan who did not feel the odd pang of remorse that the Belfast boy, for most people's money the most naturally gifted British footballer of modern times, did not grace Old Trafford for, say, another decade.

But greed is an unsavoury sin. George spent 11 seasons with United and for perhaps seven or eight of them gave so much pleasure, created so much that was beautiful and left so many undying memories that, certainly at this distance, it is churlish to cavil about short rations.

From his first days in England it was evident that the shy, homesick wisp of a lad was special. The talent he paraded in training, teasing the likes of Harry Gregg with his trickery, assured George of rapid promotion to the first team. He remained there for that vintage side's most dazzling years, an era that effectively ended in 1968 with the European Cup triumph in which he played such an inspirational part.

Throughout the mid 1960s George, while still maturing as a player, shone as brightly as any star in Matt Busby's extravagant collection. Positioned nominally on the wing but roaming at will, he delivered one jewel of a performance after another as immortality beckoned. Two that stood out were the devilish tormenting of Chelsea full-back Ken Shellito at Stamford Bridge in 1964 and the devastating demolition of Benfica, including two goals in the first 12 minutes, at the Stadium of Light in 1966.

By 1968 Best was at his most irresistible. He was European and English Footballer of the Year and topped the First Division scoring charts with 28 goals. But also he was part of a side which, imperceptibly at first, started to slide. George remained magnificent, his individual splendour masking the general decline, and inevitably he shouldered ever more on-field responsibility, an extra burden to add to the increasing outside pressure created by his racy lifestyle. Ominously, too, he became steadily disillusioned by what he saw as lack of ambition around him,

Come 1971/72 United were facing stern criticism but temporarily silenced the snipers by topping the League in the autumn. One goal George scored during this run, involving a spellbinding dribble against Sheffield United, was made in heaven. But results fell away, his personal problems – most notably alcoholism – piled up and the rest is now distressing history. Despite various comebacks, notably with Fulham, he was lost to the game.

What made Best different from the rest? Quite simply, as a footballer, he was practically flawless. He had the assets to be outstanding in any position. Aside from his incandescent skill, perfect balance and astonishing speed, also George was deceptively tough, he could tackle like a full-back, he was naturally fit and his mental acuteness matched all that physical prowess. Sometimes he held the ball too long – this could infuriate team-mates while perhaps offering them a handy breather – but the habit was wholly paid for by the sinuous sorties on which he destroyed defences single-handedly.

As Matt Busby put it succinctly: 'George had more ways of beating a player than anyone I've ever seen. He was unique in his gifts.' Unfortunately he was singular, too, in that he was the first pop-star footballer whose every off-field action was scrutinised avidly by the media. Relevant advice was scant, there being no precedent to his situation, and eventually the ceaseless attention, in which he revelled at first but came to revile, goaded him inexorably towards self-destruction.

In the end he was unable to handle the goldfish-bowl existence which was thrust upon him. Even in retrospect, having reflected on the stark tragedy of his premature death in 2005, it is difficult to see, given his personal make-up, what could have been done to change the outcome. But let's not pine for what might have been. Let's honour George Best's memory and thank the gods who sent him to thrill us.

	GEORGE BEST	
BORN:	Belfast, 22 May 1946.	
HONOURS:	European Cup 67/8. League Championship 64/5, 66/7. 37 Northern Ireland caps (64-77).	
	European Footballer of the Year 68. FWA Footballer of the Year 68.	
OTHER CLUBS:	Stockport County 75/6 (3, 2); Cork Celtic, Republic of Ireland, 75/6 (3, 0);	
	Los Angeles Aztecs, USA, 76-78 (54, 27); Fulham 76/7-77/8 (42, 8);	
	Hibernian 79/80-80/1 (17, 3); Fort Lauderdale Strikers, USA, 79 (19, 2);	
	San Jose Earthquakes, USA, 80 (26, 8); Golden Bay, USA; Bournemouth 82/3 (5, 0).	GAMES 470
DIED:	London, 25 November 2005.	GOALS 179

ALEX STEPNEY

1966/67 → 1977/78

Alex Stepney assured himself of Old Trafford immortality in one moment of explosive action on a balmy May night at Wembley in 1968. Matt Busby's men were locked at one-apiece with Benfica in the European Cup Final. Extra time loomed as Eusebio outstripped the United defence and found only the 'keeper between himself and glory.

The brilliant Portuguese shot hard and with an extravagantly flamboyant flourish, rather than attempting to slot the ball safely into a corner of the net; Alex reacted magnificently, instinctively grabbing the ball to his midriff – or did it merely hit him? Anyway, it stuck, United were reprieved and went on to reach the end of their rainbow.

After that most Red Devils fans would have forgiven Alex anything. As it turned out they had little to pardon as, with only the odd hiccup, he built a reputation as one of the club's greatest custodians, making more appearances for United than any net-minder before or since.

He was acquired for £55,000 – then a world record fee for a 'keeper – from Chelsea soon after the start of the 1966/67 term which was to end with the Championship pennant flying at Old Trafford. With Harry Gregg's career virtually ended by injury, the manager opted for Alex after deciding that neither Pat Dunne nor the injury-prone David Gaskell was the right man for the job.

The breezy Londoner had performed marvels for Millwall and reached England under-23 status before his one-match stay at Stamford Bridge, which was terminated when the Blues changed their minds about selling Peter Bonetti. It was horribly confusing for the player but soon United were benefiting from Chelsea's vacillation as Stepney vindicated Matt's judgement instantly with a series of accomplished displays. Indeed, come the spring of '67 the Old Trafford boss was lavish in his praise, declaring that the new recruit had made the crucial difference between claiming the First Division crown and finishing as also-rans.

Thereafter Stepney remained a first-team fixture until his form dipped at the turn of the decade when, for half a season, he was replaced by Jimmy Rimmer and he asked for a transfer, which was refused. Alex reacted by winning back his place and reigning supreme – apart from a brief troubled interlude when Tommy Docherty preferred Paddy Roche – until 1977/78, his last campaign.

Spells in America and with non-League Altrincham led up to retirement as a player, after which he sampled several occupations before returning to the Manchester soccer scene as a coach with City in 1995.

Throughout most of his tenure as a Red Devil, Alex was ranked among the leading British 'keepers, though he was awarded only one England cap – against Sweden at Wembley a week before the European Cup Final – and he never attained quite the stature of his illustrious contemporaries Pat Jennings, Ray Clemence and Peter Shilton.

He was never a flashy performer and perhaps his most impressive quality was his positioning, though certainly he was agile enough when required. Alex was a good 'talker' who expected – and usually got – the final say in his penalty box, and he was a constructive user of the ball who would never hoof it upfield when he could throw to a well-placed colleague.

During his early years at Old Trafford he was subject to occasional short spells when confidence on crosses appeared to desert him, but as his game matured such aberrations became fewer and arguably he was at his most solid towards the end of his career.

Alex was the one constant figure throughout an incident-packed, often turbulent 12 years in which he played for five managers and which saw United take the game's most glittering prizes, plunge into the pit of relegation and emerge transformed to record new triumphs.

A dressing-room joker and a lethal five-a-side striker – who could forget that he headed the Reds' scoring list halfway through the traumatic relegation term of 1973/74, courtesy of two penalties? – Alex Stepney was one of the club's most influential and entertaining characters.

ALEXANDER CYRIL STEPNEY
BORN: Mitcham, Surrey, 18 September 1942.
HONOURS: European Cup 67/8. League Championship 66/7. FA Cup 76/7. Second Division Championship 74/5. 1 England cap (68).
OTHER CLUBS: Millwall 63/4-65/6 (137, 0); Chelsea 66/7 (1, 0); Dallas Tornados, USA, 79-80.

GAMES	539
GOALS	2

TONY DUNNE

1960/61 → 1972/73

Before the advent of Paul Parker and Denis Irwin, there was no vestige of doubt that Tony Dunne was Manchester United's most accomplished full-back since the Munich disaster. Indeed, even taking generous account of Alex Ferguson's marvellous modern pairing, and of the Neville brothers and Patrice Evra subsequently, there is a persuasive argument that the diminutive Irishman remains the finest to wear the red shirt on either defensive flank since the incomparable Roger Byrne.

The very fact that Tony is mentioned in tandem with the venerated ex-skipper illustrates his standing more eloquently than pages of the purplest prose. Furthermore, casting the net wider than Old Trafford, it's fair to say that at the zenith of the dapper Dunne's career – the middle 1960s – only Everton's Ray Wilson among British left-backs was a more complete footballer.

Plucked by the far-sighted Matt Busby from the virtual obscurity of the League of Ireland club, Shelbourne, for a mere £5,000, the 18-year-old who crossed the water in the spring of 1960 was a waspish whippersnapper blessed with the precious gift of extreme pace. He could make a sliding tackle, see his winger waltz away with the ball and yet recover and win it back within five or six yards.

Then, once in possession, it was rare that Tony would waste it. Instead of trying fancy tricks, invariably he would take the simple option, usually a gentle sidefoot to Paddy Crerand or Bobby Charlton. This consistency, allied to bravery and that unnerving speed, made him a bastion of United's defence for more than a decade. But could he have contributed more?

Some critics would have it that any man who could sprint like Tony should have been more prominent in attack. Well, it's true that he was hardly the bane of opposition defences – although he did, at times, overlap effectively – but in a team of such gifted creators that was not his priority. It was more important that he concentrated on defence and thus created a solid base for the makers of magic. In their mid-1960s pomp, United saw him as their ultra-reliable last man, always covering if his colleagues were wrong-footed or had ventured forward. Then later, as the glory days began to drift away, he was more than adequately occupied at the back.

Tony made his senior debut at Burnley in October 1960 just six months after arriving in Manchester, then donned the number-three shirt regularly throughout most of 1961/62 following an injury to his countryman, the club captain Noel Cantwell. Dunne's form was metronomically consistent and he could operate with equal facility on either side of the rearguard, so it came as no surprise when he was switched from left-back to right, at the expense of Shay Brennan, to accommodate Noel as the FA Cup was won in 1963. Soon, though, he was back on the left and forming a splendid partnership with the skilful, only slightly less mobile Shay for club and country, until the affable Mancunian declined at decade's end.

Often United have been accused of letting top players go on for much too long, but in the case of Tony Dunne the reverse is palpably true. When he was allowed to move to Bolton Wanderers in 1973, the hugely enthusiastic 32-year-old was still the best full-back at the club and there was no comparable replacement on the horizon.

At Burnden Park he added a further 166 League games to his tally of 414 with United and maintained an impeccable standard to the end. And ironically, finding himself in the company of less illustrious colleagues, he blossomed as an all-round performer, taking responsibility on the pitch in a way that he had never deemed necessary before.

Under the management of another former United full-back, Ian Greaves, he emerged as a moulding defensive influence on the Trotters' younger players, and sometimes even a creator of attacking opportunities with distribution more ambitious than he had attempted previously. Relishing his role as Bolton's doyen, he played on until he was 38 and picked up a Second Division title medal into the bargain.

Thus, assuredly, whatever the rights or wrongs of his departure from Old Trafford during the early days of Tommy Docherty's reign, Tony Dunne can be proud of a magnificent career.

ANTHONY PETER DUNNE

BORN:	Dublin, 24 July 1941.
HONOURS:	European Cup 67/8. League Championship 64/5, 66/7. FA Cup 62/3.
	33 Republic of Ireland caps (62-76).
OTHER CLUBS:	Shelbourne, Republic of Ireland; Bolton Wanderers 73/4-78/9 (170, 0);
	Detroit Express, USA.
MANAGER:	Stenjker, Norway, (82-83).

GAMES	534 (1)
GOALS	2

PAUL EDWARDS

1969/70 → 1972/73

Despite making almost 70 appearances for Manchester United and winning three England under-23 caps, Paul Edwards was a moderate performer. The lanky defender enjoyed two first-team runs – one at full-back and the other in the centre – without ever looking completely at home in the top flight. To be fair to him, it should be stressed that his attempts to become established were made during a turbulent period of Old Trafford history which was hardly conducive to bolstering the confidence of a tentative rookie.

Paul, a modest, amiable fellow, was blessed with an unflappable temperament but his all-round game, particularly his distribution, was not outstanding. There was one incandescent highlight to savour, however, an explosive long-range strike in a League Cup semi-final against Manchester City at Old Trafford in December 1969, his sole goal for the Reds.

Most of Paul's games were played under Wilf McGuinness, and after Frank O'Farrell took over his opportunities were strictly limited. In March 1973 he was transferred to Oldham Athletic for £15,000, going on to help the Latics lift the Third Division title in 1974.

PAUL FRANCIS EDWARDS

BORN: Crompton, Lancashire, 7 October 1947.
OTHER CLUBS: Oldham Athletic, first on loan 72/3-77/8 (112, 7); Stockport County on loan 76/7 (2, 0); Stockport County 78/9-79/80 (67, 2).

GAMES 66 (2)
GOALS 1

CARLO SARTORI

1968/69 → 1971/72

If Carlo Sartori had happened along a few years earlier – or later come to that – the chances are that he would never have got near the United first team. That is not to be unkind to the popular, red-haired midfielder; it is simply an opinion that he was not quite the top-drawer material which the Reds traditionally demand, and it always seemed unlikely that he would carve a long-term niche for himself at Old Trafford.

His chance came during a period of change, as the great side of the 1960s was being dismantled. After making his senior debut as a substitute for Francis Burns at White Hart Lane in October 1968, he worked prodigiously and cheerfully, but was short of pace, lacked ingenuity and his all-round technique was unexceptional. He contributed several important goals, though, notably a timely strike in Belgium which saw United through a tense European Cup encounter with Anderlecht in November 1968, and winners at home to Arsenal in 1969/70 and at Nottingham Forest a season later.

Carlo, who was born in Italy but moved to England when he was very young, joined Bologna in a £50,000 deal on leaving the Reds in 1972.

CARLO DOMENICO SARTORI

BORN: Calderzone, Italy, 10 February 1948.
OTHER CLUBS: Bologna, Spal, Lecce, Rimini, Trento, all Italy.

GAMES 40 (16)
GOALS 6

FRANCIS BURNS

1967/68 → 1971/72

If Denis Law thought he was unlucky to miss the 1968 European Cup Final, at least he could blame the callous fate that had put him on the injured list. Poor Francis Burns had no such scapegoat.

Francis, a polished full-back enjoying an impressive first season in the team, had played 36 League matches and seven out of the eight European encounters leading up to that historic clash with Benfica. But, come the appointment with glory, he found himself dropped.

In fact, he had been omitted for the semi-final second leg against Real Madrid at the Bernabeu Stadium because Matt Busby had felt the vastly experienced Shay Brennan would cope better with the great Francisco Gento. Shay did well and retained his place for the final, leaving Francis to rue his ill fortune, a sadly familiar situation as it turned out.

The former captain of Scotland Schoolboys was a cultured, competitive performer with an exemplary attitude who was perhaps just half a yard of pace short of being truly outstanding. He was dedicated to fitness, but it was that, or the lack of it, which was to scupper his United future. He needed three cartilage operations in 18 months and his Old Trafford career lost impetus, though he fought back to win a Scottish cap against Austria in Vienna in November 1969.

There followed a £50,000 transfer to Southampton in June 1972 but he experienced further injury problems at The Dell and went on to settle with Preston North End, for whom he played frequently in midfield, for seven successful years before emigrating to Australia.

FRANCIS BURNS

BORN: Glenboig, Lanarkshire, 17 October 1948.
HONOURS: 1 Scotland cap (69).
OTHER CLUBS: Southampton 72/3 (21, 0); Preston North End 73/4-80/1 (273, 9); Shamrock Rovers, Republic of Ireland, 81/2.

GAMES 143 (13)
GOALS 7

JIMMY RIMMER

1967/68 → 1972/73

In many ways Jimmy Rimmer was the equal of Alex Stepney, the man who denied him a lengthy career with Manchester United. Indeed in some respects, such as dealing with crosses, Jimmy was superior, at least in Alex's early days at Old Trafford.

But in one crucial department the Londoner was in a different league. When it came to confidence, so vital for any footballer but particularly a goalkeeper, Jimmy lagged well behind.

The only sustained first-team spell for the 1964 FA Youth Cup winner came in 1970/71, during the trouble-torn reign of Wilf McGuinness, and many thought he was unlucky to lose his place when Sir Matt Busby resumed control.

When it became clear there was no future with the Red Devils, Jimmy was sold to Arsenal for £40,000 in April 1974. At Highbury he excelled in a distinctly poor Gunners side before reaching his peak with Aston Villa, with whom he bagged a European Cup winners medal to go with the one he received as a United substitute in 1968. While at Villa Park he won one England cap before finishing his career with Swansea City.

JOHN JAMES RIMMER
BORN: Southport, Lancashire, 10 February 1948.
HONOURS: 1 England cap (76).
OTHER CLUBS: Swansea City on loan 73/4 (17, 0); Arsenal 73/4-76/7 (124, 0); Aston Villa 77/8-82/3 (229, 0); Swansea City 83/4-85/6 (66, 0).
MANAGER: Swansea City (caretaker, 95-96).

GAMES **45 (1)**
GOALS **0**

STEVE JAMES

1968/69 → 1974/75

A chronic lack of self-belief stood between Steve James and a real tilt at the top with Manchester United. After demonstrating huge potential in the club's junior sides, he took over Bill Foulkes' centre-half role midway through 1968/69 but failed to make the position his own and lost it to Ian Ure the following season. After another year of slipping in and out of the side, Steve was back in regular possession in 1971/72, a campaign in which United flattered to deceive and frittered away a substantial Championship lead.

Thereafter life was something of a battle for James at Old Trafford, and it became a losing battle the moment Tommy Docherty signed Jim Holton to shore up the centre of his defence. The big Scot quickly became a fixture and Steve was suddenly a perpetual reserve.

A handful of opportunities followed when Jim broke his leg, but even after the tall Midlander helped to clinch the Second Division title in the spring of 1975 there was no future for him at Old Trafford, and he moved on to York City.

A hard-working, conscientious performer, he was a competent tackler and powerful in the air, but his game lacked that competitive edge needed for survival in the First Division.

STEVEN ROBERT JAMES
BORN: Coseley, Staffordshire, 29 November 1949.
HONOURS: Second Division Championship 74/5.
OTHER CLUBS: York City 75/6-79/80 (105, 1).

GAMES **160 (1)**
GOALS **4**

IAN URE

1969/70 → 1970/71

Ian Ure was the only player bought by Manchester United during the managerial reign of Wilf McGuinness, albeit at the instigation of Sir Matt Busby rather than his harassed successor. But whoever bore ultimate responsibility for what was to prove an unsatisfactory signing, after six weeks it bore the hallmark of inspiration.

The acquisition of the rugged Scottish international centre-half from Arsenal, for £80,000 in August 1969, coincided with the end of a chronic run which had culminated in the dropping of Bobby Charlton and Denis Law on the same night; dire straits indeed.

Ian, who stood out like a beacon with his flopping mop of blond hair, played eight League games before tasting defeat and it appeared that he had stabilised a defence which had been unacceptably rickety since injury and the passing years had blunted the effectiveness of its veteran cornerstone, Bill Foulkes.

Sadly the improvement was not maintained and by the following season he was fighting a losing battle to stay in the side, unable to overcome the relatively modest opposition of first Steve James and then Paul Edwards.

To be fair to Ian, his best days were behind him when he arrived at Old Trafford. In his time at Dundee, for whom he had starred on the trail to a European Cup semi-final, and, to a lesser extent, during his Highbury sojourn, he was a far more reliable performer.

With United he retained his characteristic aggression, a by-product of which had been a sending-off along with Denis Law when the combative pair had skirmished at Old Trafford in 1967, but now he seemed to have lost his poise and composure. All too frequently he was dragged out of position, being lured into wild challenges which left the Reds' rearguard woefully exposed.

A complex character – clever and driven, sensitive yet often abrasively outspoken – Ian departed to join St Mirren in August 1972. At Love Street he replaced fleetingly a promising young man, name of Gordon McQueen, before spending a short spell as manager of East Stirlingshire.

JOHN FRANCOMBE URE
BORN: Ayr, 7 December 1939.
HONOURS: 11 Scotland caps (61-67).
OTHER CLUBS: Dundee 58/9-62/3 (106, 0); Arsenal 63/4-69/70 (168, 2); St Mirren 72/3 (3, 0).
MANAGER: East Stirlingshire (74-75).

GAMES 65
GOALS 1

ALAN GOWLING

1967/68 → 1971/72

Alan Gowling was not a pretty sight on the football field. He bounded about energetically, with all the grace of a gangling crab. But this lack of poetry in his motion belied the fact that he could be an effective, occasionally devastating performer.

For four seasons the England amateur international, a supremely fit front-runner capable of prodigious amounts of honest endeavour, hovered on the fringe of the first team, having shrugged off earlier strain imposed on his soccer development by simultaneous university studies.

The highlight of that period, achieved at home to Southampton in February 1971, was scoring four goals in a game, something no United man was to equal at senior level until Andy Cole's beanfeast against Ipswich nearly a quarter of a century later.

However, it was the 1971/72 campaign that was to prove the most eventful during the Gowling tenure at Old Trafford. New manager Frank O'Farrell converted him into a foraging wing-half and it seemed Alan had found his most productive niche. He helped United take an early lead in the title race and captained the England under-23 side.

Unhappily this new-found stature was not to last, at least not at Old Trafford. The team's fortunes tumbled and at the end of the season Alan, still only 23, was sold to Huddersfield Town for £65,000. At Leeds Road he reverted to a striking role and enjoyed a subsequent career of much merit, particularly in productive spells with Newcastle United and Bolton Wanderers.

A dedicated individual of even temperament who, in his time, has chaired both the Professional Footballers Association and the United Former Players Association, he will go down as a player who made the absolute most of rather limited natural ability.

Intelligent and articulate, Alan was blessed with richer gifts in other fields, going on to make full use of his economics degree in the world of business.

ALAN EDWIN GOWLING
BORN: Stockport, Cheshire, 16 March 1949.
OTHER CLUBS: Huddersfield Town 72/3-74/5 (128, 58); Newcastle United 75/6-77/8 (92, 30); Bolton Wanderers 77/8-81/2 (149, 28); Preston North End 82/3 (40, 5).

GAMES 77 (10)
GOALS 21

TED MacDOUGALL
· ·
1972/73

Ted MacDougall may be excused if his memories of Old Trafford are not of the charitable variety. He arrived from Bournemouth with a prodigious strike rate to live up to – he netted 103 times in 146 games for the Dean Court club – and a fee of £200,000 on his head. His task: to score the goals to haul United away from the foot of the First Division.

Whether he was good enough to do that we shall never know; for just 18 games and five goals later, Ted MacDougall was on his way to West Ham. Frank O'Farrell, the man who bought him and who surely would have given him the extended run needed to prove himself capable or otherwise, was sacked. Tommy Docherty was appointed as the new manager and from that moment Ted's fate was sealed. The Doc quickly made it obvious that his countryman played no part in his plans and Ted departed a frustrated man.

Many respected critics assert that the nippy opportunist, sometimes so devastating with his head, did not have the class to be a success for Manchester United. But the fact remains that, after briefly experiencing further lean times at Upton Park, he went on to put in prolific scoring stints with Norwich and Southampton. At Old Trafford he was simply not given the chance.

EDWARD JOHN MacDOUGALL
BORN: Inverness, 8 January 1947.
HONOURS: 7 Scotland caps (75).
OTHER CLUBS: York City 67/8-68/9 (84, 34); Bournemouth 69/70-72/3 (146, 103); West Ham United 72/3-73/4 (24, 5); Norwich City 73/4-76/7 (112, 51); Southampton 76/7-78/9 (86, 42); Bournemouth 78/9-79/80 (52, 16); Blackpool 79/80-80/1 (13, 0).

GAMES **18**
GOALS **5**

WYN DAVIES
· ·
1972/73

Just an old jumper well past his best, or a battle-hardened campaigner whose experience would have been invaluable to United had he been given the opportunity? Those who recall Wyn Davies' brief contribution to the Old Trafford cause are divided in their opinion.

But the one man whose opinion mattered, manager Tommy Docherty, was in no doubt. After taking charge of the trauma-torn Red Devils midway through 1972/73, he allowed the Welsh international centre-forward only one more senior game before packing him off to Blackpool.

A season earlier many Manchester City fans had felt that 'Wyn the Leap' – he earned the epithet through stirring deeds during his prime with Bolton Wanderers and Newcastle United – should never have been replaced by Rodney Marsh and were aghast when he was allowed to join the old enemy for £25,000.

As events turned out Wyn, whose ball skills never approached his aerial ability, was made to look more limited than ever with the Reds, probably because he was playing for a struggling team and alongside another non-established striker in Ted MacDougall. Any hope he had of an Indian summer at Old Trafford disappeared with Frank O'Farrell.

RONALD WYN DAVIES
BORN: Caernarvon, 20 March 1942.
HONOURS: 34 Wales caps (63-73).
OTHER CLUBS: Wrexham 60/1-61/2 (55, 22); Bolton Wanderers 61/2-66/7 (155, 66); Newcastle United 66/7-70/1 (180, 40); Manchester City 71/2-72/3 (45, 8); Blackpool 73/4-74/5 (36, 5); Crystal Palace on loan 74/5 (3, 0); Stockport County 75/6 (30, 7); Crewe Alexandra 76/7-77/8 (55, 13).

GAMES **16 (1)**
GOALS **4**

TONY YOUNG

1970/71 → 1975/76

Tony Young was an aggressive utility player who was not good enough to hold his own in the top flight. His first, limited chances came during the regimes of Wilf McGuinness and Frank O'Farrell but it was not until Tommy Docherty took over that he enjoyed an extended run. That was in 1972/73 when he replaced Tommy O'Neil at right-back in a highly indifferent team.

He retained a place, either at full-back or in midfield, for most of the subsequent campaign but lost out as the Doc shifted the accent from defence to offence in an unsuccessful bid to avoid relegation.

Hardly equipped to separate talented newcomer Stewart Houston from the number-three shirt and occupying a lowly place in the queue for midfield opportunities, Tony remained mainly in the Old Trafford shadows for another two seasons, winning a Second Division Championship medal mostly on substitute appearances, before joining Charlton Athletic. Soon afterwards he linked up again with McGuinness at York City before entering non-League circles.

TERENCE ANTHONY YOUNG

BORN: Urmston, Lancashire, 24 December 1952.
HONOURS: Second Division Championship 74/5.
OTHER CLUBS: Charlton Athletic 75/6-76/7 (20, 1); York City 76/7-78/9 (78, 2).

GAMES 79 (18)
GOALS 1

TOMMY O'NEIL

1970/71 → 1972/73

Most players with more than half a century of appearances for Manchester United to their credit had more elan than Tommy O'Neil. The diminutive defender had what it took for a lengthy Football League career – he proved that with spells at Southport, Tranmere Rovers and Halifax Town – but he was not cut out for the top division.

Hailing from the rugby heartland of St Helens, Tommy was a schoolboy international in both football codes, eventually opting for soccer and making an auspicious start to his senior career in a derby victory at Maine Road in May 1971.

Tommy was always a trier and he demonstrated his tenacity, as well as the lack of genuine competitors for the right-back position, by hanging on to a first-team place throughout Frank O'Farrell's only full season at Old Trafford.

Indeed, there was a time when it looked as if he might pick up a Championship medal as the Reds led the table in the autumn. Sadly that honour eluded him, as it continued to elude United for another two decades.

THOMAS PATRICK O'NEIL

BORN: St Helens, Lancashire, 25 October 1952.
OTHER CLUBS: Blackpool on loan 72/3 (7, 0); Southport 73/4-77/8 (197, 16); Tranmere Rovers 78/9-79/80 (74, 10); Halifax Town 80/1-81/2 (40, 2).
DIED: May 2006.

GAMES 68
GOALS 0

PAUL BIELBY

1973/74

A promising winger who impressed for England Youth but made little impact in the First Division. Sadly his handful of opportunities arrived when United were a lacklustre side on the threshold of relegation, hardly an ideal scenario.

PAUL ANTHONY BIELBY
BORN: Darlington, County Durham, 24 November 1956.
OTHER CLUBS: Hartlepool United 75/6-77/8 (93, 8); Huddersfield Town 78/9 (31, 5).

GAMES **2 (2)**
GOALS **0**

GEORGE BUCHAN

1973/74

Younger brother of the magnificent Martin and an extremely quick, admirably feisty utility forward. His pace might have given the side an extra dimension, but manager Tommy Docherty sold him to Bury for £11,500 in August 1974.

GEORGE BUCHAN
BORN: Aberdeen, 2 May 1950.
OTHER CLUBS: Aberdeen 68/9-72/3 (29, 2); Bury 74/5-75/6 (65, 6).

GAMES **0 (4)**
GOALS **0**

IAN DONALD

1972/73

A composed and efficient Scotland schoolboy international full-back who raised hopes of a distinguished future under manager Frank O'Farrell, only to be discarded by new boss Tommy Docherty. Later became chairman of Aberdeen.

IAN RICHARD DONALD
BORN: Aberdeen, 28 November 1951.
OTHER CLUBS: Partick Thistle 72/3 (1, 0); Arbroath 73/4-74/5 (4, 0).

GAMES **6**
GOALS **0**

JOHN CONNAUGHTON

1971/72

An England youth international goalkeeper who excelled in his first two senior games for the Red Devils, but then struggled against Manchester City in his third. With Stepney and Rimmer on the scene, John never got another chance.

JOHN PATRICK CONNAUGHTON
BORN: Wigan, Lancashire, 23 September 1949.
OTHER CLUBS: Halifax Town on loan 69/70 (3, 0); Torquay United on loan 71/2 (22, 0); Sheffield United 73/4 (12, 0); Port Vale 74/5-79/80 (191, 0).

GAMES **3**
GOALS **0**

PETER FLETCHER

1972/73 →
1973/74

An angular, long-striding, deceptively skilful marksman, Peter was unlucky enough to make his entrance in a wretchedly poor team destined for relegation. He departed to Hull City in the deal which took Stuart Pearson to Old Trafford.

PETER FLETCHER
BORN: Manchester, 2 December 1953.
OTHER CLUBS: Hull City 74/5-75/6 (36, 5); Stockport County 76/7-77/8 (51, 13); Huddersfield Town 78/9-81/2 (99, 37).

GAMES **2 (5)**
GOALS **0**

DON GIVENS

1969/70

Striker Don Givens was valued at £15,000 when he left United as part of a package deal in 1970, but the energetic Irish dasher matured into a high-quality international marksman worth many times that sum as the 1970s progressed.

DANIEL JOSEPH GIVENS
BORN: Limerick, Republic of Ireland, 9 August 1949.
HONOURS: 56 Republic of Ireland caps (69-82).
OTHER CLUBS: Luton Town 70/1-71/2 (83, 19); Queen's Park Rangers 72/3-77/8 (242, 76); Birmingham City 78/9-80/1 (59, 10); Bournemouth on loan 79/80 (5, 4); Sheffield United 80/1 (11, 3); Neuchatel Xamax, Switzerland.

GAMES **5 (4)**
GOALS **1**

CLIVE GRIFFITHS

1973/74

A Wales under-23 international central defender who was pitched into United's unsuccessful relegation dogfight and failed to emerge as the dominant figure so desperately required. Later, though, he did well under Bill Foulkes in the USA.

CLIVE LESLIE GRIFFITHS
BORN: Pontypridd, Glamorgan, 22 January 1955.
OTHER CLUBS: Plymouth Argyle on loan 74/5 (11, 1); Tranmere Rovers 75/6-76/7 (59, 0); Chicago Sting, USA, 76-79; Tulsa Roughnecks, USA, 80.

GAMES **7**
GOALS **0**

FRANK KOPEL

1967/68 →
1968/69

A polished footballing full-back who seemed certain to become an Old Trafford fixture. However, as a youngster in turbulent times at the club, the Scotland schoolboy international did not impose himself sufficiently and departed to Blackburn for £25,000.

FRANK KOPEL
BORN: Falkirk, Stirlingshire, 28 March 1949.
OTHER CLUBS: Blackburn Rovers 68/9-71/2 (25, 0); Dundee United 71/2-81/2 (284, 7); Arbroath 81/2-83/4 (62, 1).

GAMES **10 (2)**
GOALS **0**

WILLIE WATSON

1970/71 →
1972/73

A grittily competitive Scotland schoolboy international right-back who laboured enthusiastically under both Wilf McGuinness and Frank O'Farrell, but perhaps lacked the all-round quality to secure a long-term niche at Old Trafford.

WILLIAM WATSON
BORN: Motherwell, Lanarkshire, 4 December 1949.
OTHER CLUBS: Miami Toros, USA, 73. Motherwell 73/4-77/8 (127, 2).

GAMES **14**
GOALS **0**

JIM McCALLIOG

1973/74 → 1974/75

Jim McCalliog and Manchester United should have been good for each other. Sadly they parted after 11 months, the relationship seemingly stale before it had the chance to flourish.

The Scottish international midfielder – who had also played up front in a career taking in Chelsea, Sheffield Wednesday (where he was outstanding) and Wolves – arrived at Old Trafford from Molineux for £60,000 in March 1974 as Tommy Docherty made his last desperate bid to avoid relegation. The trap-door to Division Two was already half open but Jim, after sharing in two defeats, sparked hopes of salvation as United went six games without defeat. This included a 3–0 drubbing of Everton in which he scored twice. The Stretford End sensed a new messiah, but it all proved an illusion and the Reds went down.

McCalliog played a full part in the first half of the Second Division resurgence, his silky, unhurried style and cultured passing blending successfully with the whirlwind approach of the team as a whole. But he could not hold his place, joined Southampton for £40,000, and, a season later, had the last laugh on United. It was Jim who provided the pass for Bobby Stokes to snatch away the FA Cup in one of the great Wembley upsets.

JAMES McCALLIOG
BORN: Glasgow, 23 September 1946.
HONOURS: Second Division Championship 74/5. 5 Scotland caps (67-71).
OTHER CLUBS: Chelsea 64/5-65/6 (7, 2); Sheffield Wednesday 65/6-68/9 (150, 19); Wolverhampton Wanderers 69/70-73/4 (163, 34); Southampton 74/5-76/7 (72, 8); Chicago Sting, USA, 77; Lincoln City 78/9 (9, 0).
MANAGER: Halifax Town (90-91).

GAMES **37 (1)**
GOALS 7

TREVOR ANDERSON

1972/73 → 1973/74

Trevor Anderson was one of those frustrating players with all the ability needed to become a star, yet who lacked some vital, unspecified, magical something.

It was Frank O'Farrell who bought the slightly-built, Belfast-born forward from Portadown in October 1972 to prepare for a future of which he, as an about-to-be-sacked manager, was not destined to be part. Thus it was Tommy Docherty who drafted the £20,000 recruit into the relegation battle in that same season and the move paid dividends, Trevor scoring the only goal in a win at Leeds which did much to keep the Reds temporarily in the top flight.

At that stage the skilful, elegant striker looked to be headed for the top and within weeks of his United debut he was playing for Northern Ireland. But the side made a bad start to the next campaign and Trevor was one of many players discarded by the Doc. There followed three successful years at Swindon and a short spell at Peterborough before he returned to Ireland, his full potential sadly unfulfilled.

TREVOR ANDERSON
BORN: Belfast, 3 March 1951.
HONOURS: 22 Northern Ireland caps (73-78).
OTHER CLUBS: Portadown, Northern Ireland; Swindon Town 74/5-77/8 (131, 34); Peterborough United 77/8-78/9 (49, 6); Linfield, Northern Ireland, 79/80-86/7 (327, 96).
MANAGER: Linfield (92-97); Newry Town (97-99); Ards (99-02); Dundalk (02-04), all Northern Ireland.

GAMES **13 (6)**
GOALS 2

GEORGE GRAHAM

1972/73 → 1974/75

The George Graham affair was one of the more eccentric episodes during the tumultuous reign of Tommy Docherty at Old Trafford. As one of his first acts on taking over, the Doc paid Arsenal £120,000 for George in December 1972 and described him thus: 'He's a midfield player of the highest class. I rate him alongside Gunter Netzer. I like his skill and control but most of all I like the confidence he brings to everything he does.'

Quite an introduction, and 'Stroller' duly helped United beat the drop to Division Two in 1972/73. He seemed an ideal stabilising influence and it was no shock when he was made captain on Bobby Charlton's retirement at the end of that challenging campaign.

But there was strife in store. As the Red Devils slumped again in 1973/74 George could do nothing right for sections of his home crowd, who singled him out for abuse, even when he performed admirably.

In truth, the 29-year-old play-maker's best days were behind him – at Highbury, where he had helped Arsenal to win the League and FA Cup double in 1970/71 – and his relaxed style probably gave the (false) impression that he was coasting. For all that, it was appalling that the majority of the criticism he received was more hysterical than constructive, and scant appreciation was in evidence for Graham's characteristic combination of silky distribution and aerial strength.

As the spectre of forthcoming relegation took on increasingly sharp focus in January 1974, Docherty jettisoned his elegant countryman from the team and ten months later swapped him for Portsmouth's once-great but then ageing striker Ron Davies, who was never to start a game for the Reds. It seemed a somewhat bizarre deal.

Eventually George became a manager, stunning old friends by his single-mindedness and discipline at Millwall, then hitting fabulous heights with Arsenal until his record was tarnished by the 'bung' scandal. Meanwhile his Old Trafford fall from being 'another Netzer' to the wilderness remains as a perplexing slice of United history.

GEORGE GRAHAM

BORN:	Bargeddie, Lanarkshire, 30 November 1944.
HONOURS:	12 Scotland caps (71-73).
OTHER CLUBS:	Aston Villa 62/3-63/4 (8, 2); Chelsea 64/5-66/7 (72, 35); Arsenal 66/7-72/3 (227, 60); Portsmouth 74/5-76/7 (61, 5); Crystal Palace 76/7-77/8 (44, 2); California Surf, USA, 78.
MANAGER:	Millwall (82-86); Arsenal (86-95); Leeds United (96-98); Tottenham Hotspur (98-01).

GAMES **44 (2)**

GOALS **2**

WILLIE MORGAN

1968/69 → 1974/75

Willie Morgan was a tremendous footballer – and if only he could have forgotten about George Best he would have been even better. There were times when Willie, a deliciously gifted winger who later became equally effective as a disciplined midfielder, seemed obsessed with the Irish genius. He wasted no opportunity to assert that he was in the same class as George, a standpoint ludicrous to anyone who had seen them both play. But it would be wrong if this apparent blind spot was to obscure the commendable contribution Willie made to Manchester United.

The Scottish international arrived from Burnley, where he was feted like a pop star and had become the first footballer in the world with his own fan club, for £117,000 some three months after the 1968 European Cup triumph. It was an unsettling time for a young man who had fallen out with the Turf Moor regime to the extent that he had been training alone, and he seemed short of both fitness and confidence in his early outings as a Red Devil.

Before long, Willie was dropped, and he must have wondered if he had been wise to spurn overtures from Arsenal, Tottenham Hotspur, Chelsea, Leeds United and Celtic before appending his signature to a contract at Old Trafford. But he fought back, proving that his renowned artistry masked a plentiful supply of inner steel, and, as such giants as Denis Law, Bobby Charlton and Paddy Crerand began to age, his on-field influence grew, despite differences with new manager Wilf McGuinness.

A turning point in the Morgan career came when Wilf's successor, Frank O'Farrell, moved him from the flank to midfield. In both positions Willie's instant control and dazzling dribbling skills took the eye, but in the deep-lying role a huge capacity for work and a willingness to bite into tackles gave his game an extra dimension.

On the debit side were a poor goal-scoring record – he was a rather weak striker of the ball – and, on too many occasions for it to be overlooked, a disturbing tendency to make a disappointing final pass.

However, as United struggled unavailingly to avoid relegation, Willie was one of the most effective and consistent performers, succeeding George Graham as captain and forging an apparently close bond with Tommy Docherty, yet another new boss. Indeed the Doc, who as Scotland manager had recalled Morgan to his country's colours, once went so far as to dub his skipper the best right-winger in the world!

After a major eye operation during the summer of 1974, Willie began the Second Division campaign in fine fettle, but late autumn brought disagreement with Docherty, a rift that was to flare again in the spring when the 29-year-old was replaced by young Steve Coppell.

That summer, despite a petition from some of the popular Morgan's fans, he was allowed to rejoin Burnley. After a short second stay at Turf Moor he went on to a successful spell with Bolton, a sojourn in America and a final fling with Blackpool.

What a shame that acrimony had soured his latter days at Old Trafford and that it should boil over into a court confrontation in 1978, when Tommy accused his former favourite of libel. The case collapsed and Willie was cleared after the Doc admitted lying under oath.

But the courtroom is not the arena in which Willie Morgan will be remembered most vividly. Let's focus instead on the beguiling image of this extravagantly talented entertainer swaying past a posse of bewildered defenders, and ponder pleasurably on just what he might have achieved had he been fortunate enough to find himself, long-term, in a truly outstanding Manchester United side. The mind boggles.

WILLIAM MORGAN

BORN: Sauchie, Stirlingshire, 2 October 1944.

HONOURS: Second Division Championship 74/5. 21 Scotland caps (67-74).

OTHER CLUBS: Burnley 62/3-67/8 (183, 19) and 75/6 (13, 0); Bolton Wanderers 75/6-79/80 (155, 10); Chicago Sting, Minnesota Kicks, both USA; Vancouver Whitecaps, Canada; Blackpool 80/1-81/2 (42, 4).

| GAMES | 293 (3) |
| GOALS | 34 |

IAN STOREY-MOORE

1971/72 → 1973/74

Big, powerful, goal-scoring wingers who can excite crowds and win matches out of nothing are rare and valuable beings. One such was Ian Storey-Moore. Here was a man who possessed the potential for huge achievement and his premature retirement due to injury was arguably a major factor in United's subsequent slide into the Second Division.

The loss of such a performer – who finished top scorer for Nottingham Forest in five of his last six seasons at the City Ground – would be hard for any club to take. For United, struggling manfully but without much inspiration to stay in the top flight, it was a savage body blow.

Ian had been plagued by lack of fitness during his time at Forest, a sad circumstance which had limited him to only one England cap by the time he arrived at Old Trafford in March 1972. He sustained several more injuries during his all-too-brief days as a Red Devil, the final damage being an accident to his ankle in the gym.

Yet in one way United fans were lucky to have had the chance to savour his talents at all. Ian was the subject of a transfer saga in March 1972 which reached a peak of absurdity when Derby County paraded him in front of the Baseball Ground fans, believing him to be their player. In fact, Forest had not signed the transfer forms and Frank O'Farrell stepped in with a £200,000 cheque.

Ian went on to total fewer than 50 games for the Reds but he will not be forgotten by those who saw him in his pomp. He scored on each of his first three outings, the third a stunning effort against Coventry at Highfield Road which saw him pick the ball up wide, surge past several defenders and finish with a firm shot.

Eventually Ian, who is chronicled in some records as Moore rather than Storey-Moore, was fit enough for a non-League comeback and a sojourn in the United States, but that was scant consolation for a man whose career was shattered at its peak.

IAN STOREY-MOORE

BORN:	Ipswich, Suffolk, 17 January 1945.
HONOURS:	1 England cap (70).
OTHER CLUBS:	Nottingham Forest 63/4-71/2 (236, 105); Chicago Sting, USA, 75.

GAMES **43**
GOALS **12**

MICK MARTIN

1972/73 → 1974/75

Mick Martin was a willing midfield workhorse who didn't quite have the quality to make the grade at Old Trafford. A rather one-paced player, the Republic of Ireland international would trundle manfully, and that wasn't enough for the sometimes hyper-critical United crowd. Most of his games were played for a struggling side and often the £25,000 recruit from Bohemians was singled out as a convenient scapegoat.

Yet it's possible that he was never given a chance in what might have proved to be his most effective position. During his early years with the Bohs and subsequently, on odd occasions, for his country he turned out in the centre of defence and acquitted himself admirably. In one game against England at Wembley in 1976 he managed to subdue former United colleague Stuart Pearson, although 'Pancho' did snatch his side's goal in a 1–1 draw.

One man who thought highly of Mick was another ex-United player, Johnny Giles, who took him from Old Trafford to West Bromwich Albion. Indeed, there were times when Johnny, in his capacity as Eire boss, preferred the solid attributes of Mick – whose father, Con, also wore the green shirt – to the more mercurial talents of Gerry Daly.

On leaving the Hawthorns, Martin Jnr gave yeoman service to Newcastle before a period in Vancouver. A brief tour of lower division clubs preceded retirement and a return to St James' Park as a coach.

MICHAEL PAUL MARTIN
BORN: Dublin, 9 July 1951.
HONOURS: 51 Republic of Ireland caps (72-83).
OTHER CLUBS: Home Farm and Bohemians, both Republic of Ireland; West Bromwich Albion 75/6-78/9 (89, 11); Newcastle United 78/9-82/3 (147, 5); Vancouver Whitecaps, Canada, 84; Cardiff City 84/5 (7, 0); Peterborough United 84/5 (12, 0); Rotherham United 85/6 (5, 0); Preston North End 85/6 (35, 0).

GAMES 36 (7)
GOALS 2

ARNOLD SIDEBOTTOM

1972/73 → 1974/75

When Arnie Sidebottom gave up soccer to concentrate on cricket he made the wisest decision of his professional life. As a pace bowler he enjoyed a creditable career with Yorkshire and went on to play in a Test match for England against Australia in 1985.

Had he soldiered on as a centre-half in the lower reaches of the Football League – he served both Huddersfield Town and Halifax Town after leaving Old Trafford – he would not have stood the slightest chance of international recognition.

Not that long, lean Arnie was a particularly bad footballer. Although rather spindly for a central defender, he was reasonably effective in the air and, if he was a tad ponderous over the first five yards, he could move quickly enough when he got into his stride.

But he was never a dominant figure at the rearguard's core and his stint as deputy for the injured Jim Holton during the 1974/75 Second Division Championship campaign demonstrated clearly that he would never be better than an average performer.

For Arnie that must have been a mortifying circumstance, but in the long run it was a situation for which Yorkshire cricket had ample cause to be grateful. The Sidebottom love affair with the summer game continued in the new millennium, with son Ryan shining in Tests for England.

ARNOLD SIDEBOTTOM
BORN: Barnsley, Yorkshire, 1 April 1954.
HONOURS: Second Division Championship 74/5.
OTHER CLUBS: Huddersfield Town 75/6-77/8 (61, 5); Halifax Town 78/9 (21, 2).

GAMES 20
GOALS 0

JIM HOLTON

1972/73 → 1974/75

No one was more surprised than Jim Holton to find himself a folk hero within weeks of joining Manchester United from Shrewsbury Town. There he was, a mammoth, sometimes clumsy centre-half at a club where superstar forwards were the rule and defenders, in general, were out of the limelight.

But at Old Trafford in January 1973 unusual circumstances prevailed. The Red Devils were at the foot of the table with a leaky defence and the fans were not happy. Then along came Jim and immediately gave them what they wanted – dominance, commitment and a hint that First Division survival might, after all, be just around the corner.

All this was wrapped up in a rugged, warm, man-on-the-street package that supporters took to their hearts. More cultured, calculating players such as Martin Buchan they could respect; Jim Holton they could love.

Within a few months of his £80,000 recruitment United had avoided the drop and their new centre-half was playing for Scotland in the World Cup Finals, a fairytale if ever there was one. But like so many football fantasies it was not to have a happy ending. The following season, despite Jim's ever increasing effectiveness, the Red Devils were relegated. Then, after making 14 appearances in the Second Division campaign, he broke his leg in a 4–4 thriller at Sheffield Wednesday and was never again to return to first-team duty.

A comeback in the reserves ended with another break and by the time he was ready for action once more, Brian Greenhoff had made the position his own. So Jim moved on to Sunderland for £40,000, then made fresh starts with Coventry City and Sheffield Wednesday, but he was rarely fit and quit the professional game in 1981.

He will be remembered as a superb header and tackler who was rarely drawn out of position, though occasionally he could be caught for pace. Defence was his principal concern but the giant Scot was a formidable attacker, too, his muscular presence creating panic in many an opposing rearguard, witness the goals against Coventry, Newcastle and Southampton which helped to stave off demotion in 1972/73.

At times he was vilified for his rumbustious approach. In fact, there wasn't an ounce of malice in him, and it was significant that accusations of undue violence emanated invariably from outraged spectators rather than his opponents on the pitch. That said, it was not for nothing that the Stretford End sang with bloodcurdling relish: 'Six foot two, eyes of blue, Big Jim Holton's after you!'

News of his sudden death, at the age of 42 in October 1993, shocked the entire soccer community. Having overcome two major disappointments in his time – failure to make the grade as a teenager with Celtic, then injury-induced early retirement – Jim had carved out a happy niche as a pub landlord in Coventry. For a while life was good, but tragedy was lying in wait for one of the game's more engaging cult idols.

JAMES ALLAN HOLTON
BORN: Lesmahagow, Lanarkshire, 11 April 1951.
HONOURS: Second Division Championship 74/5. 15 Scotland caps (73-74).
OTHER CLUBS: Shrewsbury Town 71/2-72/3 (67, 4); Miami Toros, USA, on loan 76; Sunderland 76/7 (15, 0); Coventry City 76/7-79/80 (91, 0).
DIED: Warwick, 4 October 1993.

GAMES	69
GOALS	5

ALEX FORSYTH

1972/73 → 1977/78

When Tommy Docherty took over an ailing Manchester United towards the end of 1972 one of his first moves was to sign Alex Forsyth. It was perhaps not surprising that the new manager should tempt Partick Thistle with a £100,000 cheque for the up-and-coming full-back, as it was he who had first picked Alex for the Scottish international side.

It was not one of the Doc's most widely hailed forays into the transfer market but Forsyth, who had enlisted at Firhill in 1968 after being released by Arsenal as a homesick teenager, never let club or colleagues down. Indeed, he played his part, rousingly at times, in the glory of promotion from the Second Division, having shared the despair of the big drop the previous season.

'Bruce,' as inevitably he became known, was a strong tackler and a supremely clean striker of the ball, but he was too slow for a regular berth among the elite. Despite his determination and excellent positional play he could be shown up by the trickier speed merchants of the day and it was no surprise when, ultimately, he lost his place to the more mobile Jimmy Nicholl.

Much loved by the home crowd, particularly the Stretford End, Alex was a potent threat when rampaging forward and he possessed a thunderous shot. This was never demonstrated more spectacularly than during a First Division encounter

with Wolves at Old Trafford in December 1975, when he crashed the ball against the post from fully 30 yards and it rebounded almost to the centre circle.

The crispness and timing of his kicking were apparent also in his characteristically massive clearances, which were a delight to the likes of mobile front-runners Stuart Pearson and Sammy McIlroy.

When it became clear that he had no future at Old Trafford, Alex left for Glasgow Rangers, initially on a season's loan before committing himself to a contract. Later he served Motherwell and Hamilton Academical before quitting the game.

ALEXANDER FORSYTH

BORN: Swinton, Berwickshire, 5 February 1952.
HONOURS: Second Division Championship 74/5. 10 Scotland caps (72-75).
OTHER CLUBS: Partick Thistle 70/1-72/3 (52, 5); Glasgow Rangers 78/9-80/1 (25, 5); Motherwell 82/3 (19, 0); Hamilton Academical 83/4-84/5 (63, 9).

GAMES	116 (3)
GOALS	5

STEWART HOUSTON

1973/74 → 1979/80

When Stewart Houston arrived at Old Trafford from Brentford in December 1973 he was something of a surprise recruit. United were struggling to avoid relegation, the defence was shaky and most observers were expecting an expensive buy to help tighten it up. Instead Tommy Docherty paid just £55,000 for Stewart, who had played under him at Chelsea, failed to make the grade and moved on to Griffin Park, apparently destined for a career in the League's lower reaches.

The next five years proved the Doc's judgement, in this case, to be impeccable. Stewart matured into one of the most consistent left-backs in the country and went on to play for Scotland, albeit only once.

The absence of further caps perplexed many Reds followers, not least because the rival who kept him out during his prime was a Manchester City man, Willie Donachie, though it should be stressed that Willie was a formidably classy operator and a fine all-round footballer.

The same could be said of Houston. A magnificent athlete, he was tall for a full-back, which was invaluable in United's somewhat under-sized rearguard of that time, and he made his height count in both penalty areas, being especially useful on the opposition's far post at set pieces.

But Stewart's greatest asset was the accuracy of his left foot. His speciality was the long ball along the touchline, usually to Gordon Hill or the wide-ranging Stuart Pearson, a manoeuvre which set up countless attacks. The lack of comparable ability on his right side was offset by his mobility and reading of the game, which also made little of a slight lack of pace.

Stewart picked up a loser's medal in the 1976 FA Cup Final and was cheated of compensation the following year when he broke a leg at Bristol City shortly before the Wembley clash with Liverpool. Thereafter he was never the same again and lost his place to Arthur Albiston, his young countryman who had excelled when stepping up for the 1977 final.

In July 1980 Houston moved to Sheffield United on a free transfer, later assisting Colchester United before shining as a coach and joining Arsenal in that capacity.

STEWART MACKIE HOUSTON

BORN:	Dunoon, Argyllshire, 20 August 1949.
HONOURS:	Second Division Championship 74/5. 1 Scotland cap (75).
OTHER CLUBS:	Chelsea 67/8-69/70 (9, 0); Brentford 71/2-73/4 (77, 9); Sheffield United 80/1-82/3 (94, 1); Colchester United 83/4-85/6 (107, 5).
MANAGER:	Arsenal (caretaker, 95 and 96); Queen's Park Rangers (97).

GAMES	248 (2)
GOALS	16

LOU MACARI

1972/73 → 1983/84

'I always like to give value for money' said Lou Macari in a TV interview after poaching a typically opportunistic late equaliser on his debut for Manchester United at home to West Ham one bleak afternoon in January 1973. When he departed to become player-manager of Swindon Town some 11 years later, he had done that, and then some.

At the time of joining the Red Devils, the Edinburgh-born 23-year-old – who had incurred the scorn of Bill Shankly for spurning Anfield in favour of Old Trafford – was fresh from several seasons of success as a striker with Celtic, and it was in this role that he started his stay south of the border. But the stint up front for United turned out to be a traumatic experience for the tiny Scottish international. He failed to make an impact and looked set to be branded a £200,000 misfit.

Then Tommy Docherty shuffled his pack and gave Lou a midfield position that afforded him the freedom to roam. As a result he was transformed from a liability into one of the most effective players in the land throughout the second half of the 1970s. The new Lou Macari was an inspirational footballer, a key member of the Doc's lovely attacking side which won promotion in 1974/75 and made an exhilarating return to the top flight the next season.

Though never a heavy scorer in his Red Devil days, he chipped in with his share of strikes; however, the most priceless he had a hand in was an outrageous fluke with which he was not even credited. The goal which beat Liverpool in the 1977 FA Cup Final came when the wee fellow hit a wildly off-beam shot which rebounded from the chest of Jimmy Greenhoff, then caromed in a crazy arc beyond stranded 'keeper Ray Clemence and into the net. Of course, he claimed cheekily that it was the product of much hard work on the training ground, but listeners that gullible were hard to find!

That was a freak occurrence, but the basics of Lou's game owed nothing to fortune. A teetotaller and non-smoker, he was so fit that he didn't seem tired even after hustling his way through the most hectic of encounters. The Macari method combined frenetic energy and raw courage with subtle skills, a rare blend which got both crowds and colleagues buzzing. One of his most spectacular attributes, despite standing just 5ft 5in, was his ability in the air, where he was especially lethal at the near post.

Few players had more influence on their eras at Old Trafford than Lou Macari. He would have won more honours at Liverpool, but he couldn't have created a more indelible impression.

As a boss, too, he cut a considerable, often controversial dash – he faced the possibility of prison before his name was cleared in a scandal over illegal payments at Swindon Town – and his reigns tended not to be boring. The ultimate judgement on Macari the manager seemed likely to depend on the outcome of the massive challenge he accepted in November 1993, that of restoring the glory days to Celtic. However, eight months later he was sacked before bouncing back in typically indestructible manner to commence a second sparky spell at Stoke.

LUIGI MACARI

BORN: Edinburgh, 4 June 1949.
HONOURS: FA Cup 76/7. Second Division Championship 74/5. 24 Scotland caps (72-78).
OTHER CLUBS: Celtic 68/9-72/3 (58, 26); Swindon Town 84/5-85/6 (36, 3).
MANAGER: Swindon Town (84-89); West Ham United (89-90); Birmingham City (91); Stoke City (91-93); Celtic (93-94); Stoke City (94-97); Huddersfield Town (2000-02).

GAMES **374 (27)**
GOALS **97**

BRIAN GREENHOFF

. . . .

1973/74 → 1978/79

There has probably never been a Manchester United player who made more of relatively limited natural talent than Brian Greenhoff. But that is not to belittle the achievements of a man whose career was punctuated by serious injuries, who played a vital role in one of the most exciting club sides of the 1970s and who won 18 England caps.

Brian, who was to be joined later at Old Trafford by his elder brother Jimmy, broke into the first team as a central defensive replacement for the injured Jim Holton at Ipswich in the autumn on 1973, then flourished as an industrious midfielder for the remainder of that ill-fated season.

He was one of the few players to enhance his reputation during the unsuccessful bid to stave off relegation and his star rose further during the promotion year that followed, despite being so reliant on contact lenses that, without them, he reckoned he could recognise individual team-mates only by the way they ran!

At the start of the 1975/76 campaign, with Holton sidelined by a broken leg, Brian found himself back at the rearguard's core alongside Martin Buchan, and it was there that he enjoyed his most successful spell.

For two and a half years, until the arrival of Gordon McQueen, he did a sturdy, dependable job. Brave, determined and never flashy, he lacked dominance in the air and was not as fast as his partner, but generally he held his own against the country's top strikers.

No one at Old Trafford was more fiercely committed than Brian and his depth of feeling was strikingly evident at Wembley in 1976, when he left the pitch with tears pouring down his face following the shock FA Cup Final defeat by Southampton. Consolation arrived a week later in the form of his first full cap, and he collected his coveted winner's medal in 1977 when United defeated Liverpool.

After a run at right-back in the early part of 1978/79 Brian, who was so versatile that occasionally he was pressed into service as emergency front-man or even goalkeeper, struggled to hold his place in the senior line-up and the next summer spurned an offer from West Ham to join Leeds United for £350,000.

But injury continued to plague him and his time at Elland Road was not productive. There followed a brief stint at Rochdale under brother Jimmy's management before Greenhoff Jnr retired. He could congratulate himself on a career in which not a single shred of ability was wasted.

BRIAN GREENHOFF
BORN: Barnsley, Yorkshire, 28 April 1953.
HONOURS: FA Cup 76/7. Second Division Championship 74/5. 18 England caps (76-80).
OTHER CLUBS: Leeds United 79/80-81/2 (72, 1); Hong Kong football; Rochdale 82/3-83/4 (16, 0).

| GAMES | 268 (3) |
| GOALS | 17 |

GERRY DALY

1973/74 → 1976/77

One of Tommy Docherty's shrewdest moves was the signing of Gerry Daly – and one of his most questionable was allowing the gifted Republic of Ireland midfielder to slip away following a difference of opinion.

Gerry was bought from Bohemians for just £20,000 and dispatched to Derby County for £180,000 four years later. The profit was undeniably handsome but most Reds fans were left with the feeling that a potentially outstanding player had been lost unnecessarily.

When he arrived at Old Trafford as a pale, slender youngster he looked as though a puff of wind would blow him away; but there was more to Gerry Daly than met the eye. Light he may have been but the young Irishman was deceptively wiry and, after

he had built up his stamina with a new and strenuous training regime, he lost little time in demonstrating his abundant talent.

Gerry made his debut in the 1973 Anglo-Italian tournament and then found himself in and out of the side which slumped out of the top flight during the traumatic term that followed. But the subsequent Second Division campaign proved the making of him and he became an integral part of the promotion combination with his precise passing, tireless running and fierce shooting.

Back in the First Division, Daly became an increasingly influential member of the team, notably from the penalty spot, where he succeeded with 16 out of 17 efforts during his Old Trafford career after taking on the job from Alex Stepney. But then, in late 1976, he was dropped and replaced by converted striker Sammy McIlroy following the reshuffle precipitated by the arrival of Jimmy Greenhoff.

Easy-going Gerry clashed with the Doc and in the spring he departed for the Baseball Ground where, ironically, the two were reunited some six months later in September 1977.

Despite numerous further moves in this country and America, the deliciously gifted Dubliner never quite recaptured the early form which might, arguably, have flowered more luxuriantly in the headier atmosphere of Old Trafford to which he was best suited.

At international level he flourished, though, serving the Republic over a 13-year span, his 48 appearances yielding 13 goals. Gerry ended his footballing days as player-boss of non-League Telford United.

GERARD ANTHONY DALY

BORN: Dublin, 30 April 1954.

HONOURS: Second Division Championship 74/5. 48 Republic of Ireland caps (73-86).

OTHER CLUBS: Bohemians, Republic of Ireland; Derby County 76/7-79/80 (112, 31); New England Teamen, USA, 78-79; Coventry City 80/1-83/4 (84, 15); Leicester City on loan 82/3 (17, 1); Birmingham City 84/5-85/6 (32, 1); Shrewsbury Town 85/6-86/7 (55, 8); Stoke City 86/7-87/8 (22, 1); Doncaster Rovers 88/9 (39, 4).

| GAMES | 137 (5) |
| GOALS | 32 |

STUART PEARSON

1974/75 → 1978/79

The upraised fist, the infectious, boyish grin; they said it all. Stuart Pearson had struck again. There was no more joyful sight for Manchester United fans in the second half of the 1970s when 'Pancho' – so named after another colourful Old Trafford Pearson, Mark – was in his swashbuckling pomp.

Tommy Docherty enlisted Stuart from Hull City in a £200,000 deal, which saw Peter Fletcher move in the opposite direction, in the summer after United were relegated in 1973/74. His first task was to inject punch into a hitherto rather feeble attack and this he did to the tune of 17 goals as the Red Devils surged to the Second Division title.

Many of his strikes during that helter-skelter campaign – notably a superbly placed drive in the crucial home clash with promotion rivals Sunderland – remain vivid in the memory.

But there was much more to the Pearson game than scoring. He was primarily a target man and every team-mate, from Alex Stepney through to Gordon Hill, knew that Stuart was always available to receive a pass. When he did get the ball his first touch was usually immaculate, either a subtle first-time lay-off or a deft piece of control. Then, belying that characteristic knock-kneed gait, there was searing pace to take him past defenders, and, although his finishing could be unreliable, his fierce shot produced many a spectacular goal.

The England man's quicksilver mobility made him difficult to mark and, together with the equally elusive Jimmy Greenhoff, he presented a confusing, ever-changing set of problems which stretched most defenders.

Stuart has been called injury-prone and that has always rankled. He did miss almost all of 1978/79 after a series of knee operations made necessary by a mishap on a close-season tour, but for four years before that it was unusual for his name to be absent from the team sheet.

He regained fitness but was not satisfied with the one-year contract offered by manager Dave Sexton and in September 1979 he moved to West Ham for £220,000. Within eight months he had pocketed an FA Cup winner's medal to add to the one he had gained with United against Liverpool in 1977, when he had embellished a typically sparky personal performance with a sharply-taken opening goal, beating Ray Clemence with a fierce near-post drive after deft work by the inimitable Greenhoff.

Sadly his Upton Park sojourn was curbed prematurely by further knee problems, a monumental frustration to the eager Pearson, who reckoned he had been approaching his prime in 1978 and might have doubled his five-year tenure at Old Trafford had he remained in peak condition.

In 1986 Stuart became boss of non-League Northwich Victoria, then proved he could still muster a clean pair of heels with a spell on the wing for Sale Rugby Club. Thereafter he returned to the Football League, coaching with West Bromwich Albion before serving as Frank Stapleton's assistant manager at Bradford City. Until the pair of them were dismissed, rather surprisingly, in the spring of 1994, aspiring young strikers at the Valley Parade could hardly have asked for more eminent role models.

But it is with the Red Devils that the name of Stuart Pearson will remain most closely associated. He was a laughing cavalier of a footballer and he epitomised the Doc's brave new United. When he bade farewell to Old Trafford, 'Pancho' left behind him the lasting affection of the fans and exhilarating memories of a centre-forward who played the game with dash.

JAMES STUART PEARSON

BORN: Hull, Yorkshire, 21 June 1949.
HONOURS: FA Cup 76/7. Second Division Championship 74/5. 15 England caps (76-78).
OTHER CLUBS: Hull City 69/70-73/4 (129, 44); West Ham United 79/80-81/2 (34, 6).
MANAGER: West Bromwich Albion (caretaker, 91).

| GAMES | 179 (1) |
| GOALS | 66 |

CHRIS McGRATH

1976/77 → 1980/81

Chris McGrath represented a £30,000 gamble by Manchester United which didn't pay off. There was never any doubt about the natural ability of the Irish international winger, but after a spell with Tottenham Hotspur had begun with rich promise only to fizzle out in frustration, and a loan period with Millwall had also ended in failure, he did not look a promising bet.

However, Tommy Cavanagh, then training the Red Devils, thought otherwise and his enthusiasm convinced manager Tommy Docherty to offer Chris the chance to salvage his career.

Sadly it was not to be. Chris could look brilliant on the ball but all too often he would beat three defenders only to be robbed by the fourth when colleagues were better placed. When his Old Trafford contract was cancelled he spent two seasons in America but was never given another chance in the Football League.

ROLAND CHRISTOPHER McGRATH
BORN:	Belfast, 29 November 1954.
HONOURS:	21 Northern Ireland caps (74-79).
OTHER CLUBS:	Tottenham Hotspur 73/4-75/6 (38, 5); Millwall on loan 75/6 (15, 3); Tulsa Roughnecks, USA, 81-82.

GAMES **15 (19)**
GOALS 1

TOMMY JACKSON

1975/76 → 1976/77

When Tommy Jackson joined newly-promoted Manchester United in the summer of 1975 it was on the express understanding that his job would be to captain the reserves. But watching the experienced Irish midfielder in action during pre-season training gave manager Tommy Docherty other ideas.

The Red Devils at that time were an exciting, but also excitable, young side. Someone was needed during the initial months in the First Division to calm things down, hold the midfield, while the likes of Steve Coppell, Gerry Daly and company buzzed effervescently in all directions.

Tommy, an ex-Evertonian who had earned a title medal with the Toffees before joining United on a free transfer from Nottingham Forest, was the surprise choice and he carried out the task in a workmanlike, unspectacular fashion until the arrival of Gordon Hill changed the pattern of play. He stayed to make just two appearances the following season before getting a free transfer and leaving the League.

THOMAS JACKSON
BORN:	Belfast, 3 November 1946.
HONOURS:	35 Northern Ireland caps (68-77).
OTHER CLUBS:	Glentoran, Northern Ireland; Everton 67/8-70/1 (32, 0); Nottingham Forest 70/1-74/5 (81, 6).

GAMES **22 (1)**
GOALS 0

DAVID McCREERY

1974/75 → 1978/79

David McCreery shared a dubious distinction with David Fairclough of Liverpool: they were both dubbed 'Supersub.' Both players invariably wore the number-12 shirt for their clubs and both were frequently called to arms. And while Fairclough's contributions were usually more dramatic, little David McCreery – who was brought on to replace Gordon Hill in the 1976 and 1977 FA Cup Finals – offered at least equal value in terms of effort and consistency.

His earliest flirtations with the first team were as understudy to striker Stuart Pearson, but although he toiled like a slave and was probably the fastest man at the club – he was known as 'Roadrunner' for his rapidity – David lacked the necessary physical presence for that role. He progressed to become stand-in for all the forwards and midfielders and soon it became obvious that he was best used in the latter position.

McCreery, who was picked for Northern Ireland after starting just a dozen League games for United, was a tireless forager endowed with infectious enthusiasm but, at that stage, he lacked the polish and creativity to become a Reds regular. With so many outstanding players at Old Trafford, it was difficult to see him making that final breakthrough, and it was no surprise in August 1979 when he left to link up again with Tommy Docherty at Queen's Park Rangers, the Reds banking a £200,000 cheque.

But it wasn't until he had played in America and moved to Newcastle that he served up the most compelling football of his career, relishing the responsibility that had never been vested in him at Old Trafford.

Come 1993/94, there were few blades of Brunton Park not being covered by the 36-year-old David in his role as Carlisle United's player-manager, and no one greeted his success and longevity with more pleasure than his old United team-mates. They recall him fondly as an irrepressible trier and a smashing lad.

DAVID McCREERY
BORN: Belfast, 16 September 1957.
HONOURS: FA Cup 76/7. 67 Northern Ireland caps (76-90).
OTHER CLUBS: Queen's Park Rangers 79/80-80/1 (57, 4); Tulsa Roughnecks, USA, 81-82; Newcastle United 82/3-88/9 (243, 2); Heart of Midlothian 89/90-90/1 (29, 0); Hartlepool United 91/2 (30, 0); Carlisle United 92/3-93/4 (35, 0); Hartlepool United 94/5 (9, 0).
MANAGER: Carlisle United (92-93); Hartlepool United (94-95).

GAMES	57 (52)
GOALS	8

STEVE COPPELL

1974/75 → 1982/83

The Manchester United career of Steve Coppell divides neatly – if, to many observers, frustratingly – into two parts. First came the exciting young performer of the Docherty days, knocking the ball past full-backs, running them ragged and slinging over centres with a style and accuracy reminiscent of that glorious age before Alf Ramsey made wingers unfashionable.

Then came the Sexton reign and with it a marked change in the role of the intelligent young Liverpudlian. Those buccaneering surges, which so personified the reborn Red Devils on their emergence from their Second Division nightmare, were largely replaced by tidy, thoughtful play wide on the right of midfield.

Certainly the new Steve Coppell was a vastly valuable member of Dave Sexton's reshaped side, which came so close to League and FA Cup triumph without lifting a trophy, but he never pleased crowds like the old one.

It was always going to be difficult for Coppell to live up to his early years with United. In fact, his arrival reads like a *Boys' Own* adventure. The rookie wingman – just signed from Tranmere Rovers for £40,000 with another £20,000 to follow if he made 20 appearances! – was pulled on to replace Willie Morgan during an Old Trafford encounter with Cardiff City, 11 games from the end of the 1974/75 Division Two campaign.

The Reds had been expected to win comfortably but after an hour there was no score and the supporters were getting restless. Thirty minutes later United ran off 4–0 winners with the new boy having made two of the goals.

Steve retained his place for the rest of the season and henceforth was an automatic choice until a knee injury, caused by a futile foul when playing for England in a World Cup qualifier against Hungary at Wembley in November 1981, ultimately forced him to quit at the age of 28, after three operations and much heartache, in September 1983.

Perhaps one reason why his exhilarating football of 1975/76 and 1976/77, when he formed such a thrilling wing tandem with Gordon Hill, became more subdued was that in later years the more canny defenders worked out how to combat his direct running. They would lay off him, which made it harder to pass them, and thus they could reduce his effectiveness. In fairness to Sexton, that factor may have had a lot to do with the change in Steve's approach.

In the new role he enjoyed four seasons as an ever-present, during which his work rate, determination and overall contribution to the team effort were immense. And even if the old panache was less evident still there were moments of attacking brilliance and vital goals to savour.

Steve's international career blossomed correspondingly and, deservedly, he attained a Bobby Charlton-type image for integrity and sportsmanship. Combined with an astute brain, these qualities enabled Steve, at one time chairman of the Professional Footballers Association, to move smoothly into management and he achieved impressive early success with Crystal Palace.

Inevitably this inspired forecasts that one day he might occupy the boss's seat at Old Trafford, and even his resignation from the Selhurst Park job following relegation in 1993 did not scupper the thought altogether. However his subsequent inability to cope with the stress of running Manchester City – he walked out of Maine Road after only 33 days in charge – made the chances of Steve Coppell managing Manchester United, even in the distant future, seem exceedingly slim.

Still, he continued to ply his trade with both resilience and enterprise, deserving colossal credit for steering Reading into the Premiership in 2006, and considerable sympathy when the unfashionable Royals were relegated two years later.

STEPHEN JAMES COPPELL
BORN: Liverpool, 9 July 1955.
HONOURS: FA Cup 76/7. 42 England caps (77-83).
OTHER CLUBS: Tranmere Rovers 73/4-74/5 (38, 10).
MANAGER: Crystal Palace (84-93 and, as technical director, 95-96); Manchester City (96); Crystal Palace (97-98, 99-00); Brentford (01-02); Brighton and Hove Albion (02-03); Reading (03-).

GAMES | 393 (3)
GOALS | 70

GORDON HILL

1975/76 → 1977/78

Gordon Hill was the final piece in Tommy Docherty's jigsaw who found himself painfully surplus to Dave Sexton's requirements. And his departure from Old Trafford, to rejoin the Doc at Derby, somehow summed up the vastly different attitudes of the two managers.

Undoubtedly Gordon was blessed with sumptuous gifts, and we are not talking here about his riotous Norman Wisdom impression. At Millwall his wing sorcery earned him the nickname of 'Merlin', and he purveyed a brand of magic for which Docherty was delighted to pay £80,000 in November 1975, beating off reported competition from Arsenal and Tottenham Hotspur in the process. That boldest of bosses believed the confident Londoner could put a spell on First Division defences and bring a swaggering new dimension to the newly-promoted Red Devils; and so, to a large degree, it proved.

Gordon's left-flank flair was a major factor in United's glittering form as they played their most captivating football for nearly a decade. There were few full-backs he couldn't skin as he belted for the byline or cut in towards goal. And that finishing! There were times when it was nothing less than world-class, as in the 1976 FA Cup semi-final against Derby County when two 20-yarders – one a delicate curler, the other a fearsome drive – saw his side through to Wembley.

The Hill strike rate, too, was awesome for a winger, culminating in a record very close to a goal every two games in his final season.

But despite all that instinctive ability there was another side to Gordon, one which some colleagues could tolerate but which infuriated others. When the Reds were defending he did not seem interested. Chasing and tackling were alien to him and when he was pressurised into doing so his cocky attempts to dribble out of trouble often angered his own defence. Indeed, skipper Martin Buchan was once moved to box his ears in remonstration in the heat of a match.

A parting between Gordon and Sexton, with whom the winger got on admirably on a personal level but for whom individual skill would always come second to teamwork, was inevitable, and in April 1978 a £275,000 deal took the confused and frustrated England man to Derby and the Doc.

At the Baseball Ground, his displays alternated between the exasperating and the enchanting and soon he was off to Queen's Park Rangers, where his new boss was . . . Tommy Docherty. But Loftus Road didn't see the best of the mercurial flankman, either, and before long he had crossed the Atlantic to try his luck in the North American League.

Meanwhile the more romantic United fans continued to mourn his departure from Old Trafford. Gordon may have been a soccer eccentric, but on his day he took the breath away.

GORDON ALEC HILL
BORN: Sunbury-on-Thames, Middlesex, 1 April 1954.
HONOURS: FA Cup 76/7. 6 England caps (76-77).
OTHER CLUBS: Millwall 72/3-75/6 (86, 20); Chicago Sting, USA, 75; Derby County 77/8-79/80 (24, 5); Queen's Park Rangers 79/80-80/1 (14, 1); Montreal Manic, Chicago Sting, New York Arrows, Kansas Comets, Tacoma Stars, all USA; HJK Helsinki, Finland; Twente Enschede, Holland.

GAMES **133 (1)**
GOALS **51**

MARTIN BUCHAN

1971/72 → 1982/83

For a decade Martin Buchan stood alone as Manchester United's most influential player. There were few observers who didn't hail the Scottish international central defender as world-class, although a handful reckoned his use of the ball did not merit such a lofty accolade.

But wherever Martin is placed on the global scale, none could seriously deny the immense contribution he made to the Reds after Frank O'Farrell brought him south from Aberdeen in March 1972 as the first major step in rebuilding a defence that was beginning to creak alarmingly.

By then, though still only 23, Martin had played for his country, captained his club, won a Scottish Cup medal and been voted Scottish player of the year. For a man of this calibre and maturity United willingly parted with £125,000 – Leeds and Liverpool were also keen to acquire his services – and rarely have they struck a better bargain.

A supremely self-confident and disciplined individual, he settled quickly and began turning in the cool, classy displays which became his hallmark. By now United were a poor side, though, and after two seasons of travail they were relegated. Martin, by this time skipper and privately appalled by the indifferent standard of certain of his colleagues, led them back up at the first attempt, setting an exemplary personal example.

But it was during the next five seasons that he reached his zenith, forming two effective partnerships, first with Brian Greenhoff and then Gordon McQueen. Martin was a firm rather than ferocious tackler and could read the game well, but his prime asset was his speed. If he made a mistake, which was not common, usually he could change gear and rectify it before opponents could take advantage.

Perhaps his quality of passing didn't always equal other facets of the Buchan game, but this rarely mattered as he tended to limit his distribution to the simple variety. Occasionally, when feeling more ambitious, he might give the ball away but there was always the insurance of that scorching acceleration.

A man of unyielding principles, Martin upset some people with an uncompromising attitude which could border on the eccentric. He expected those around him to meet his own high standards and could be formidable when they didn't – ask Gordon Hill, whose ears he once boxed in public.

But above all Martin Buchan will be remembered as one of those United players the fans could not bear to see missing from the line-up, in much the same way as Bryan Robson's absence was dreaded in later years. When he looked likely to miss the 1977 FA Cup Final against Liverpool, the prophets of doom were out in force. On that occasion, though not fully fit, he played – majestically – and largely snuffed out the threat of Kevin Keegan as the Red Devils took the trophy.

As the 1980s dawned, Martin faced increasing fitness problems and in August 1983 he bowed out of Old Trafford, believing firmly that manager Ron Atkinson was dispensing with his services rather earlier than was necessary. He was linked with Manchester City, but a misguided notion among Maine Road fans that a Buchan tackle had ended the career of Colin Bell rendered such a move unwise.

Instead he embarked upon a short spell as a player at Oldham and an even shorter one, 110 days to be precise, as boss of Burnley, a task for which he had the sense to realise he was not cut out. The final word, if one is needed, on Martin's prowess at his peak can rest with the managers. They voted him First Division player of the year in 1977; and they should know.

MARTIN McLEAN BUCHAN
BORN: Aberdeen, 6 March 1949.
HONOURS: FA Cup 76/7. Second Division Championship 74/5. 34 Scotland caps (71-78). Scottish Footballer of the Year 71.
OTHER CLUBS: Aberdeen 66/7-71/2 (136, 9); Oldham Athletic 83/4-84/5 (28, 0).
MANAGER: Burnley (85).

GAMES 456
GOALS 4

JIMMY GREENHOFF

1976/77 → 1980/81

Jimmy Greenhoff was born to be a footballer, and he didn't need flashy tricks to prove it. Just a glimpse of the blond Yorkshireman doing something basic – say, taking a pass and laying off an instant return – was enough to demonstrate his sheer, unadulterated quality.

The Greenhoff game was simple and unadorned, but somehow it was beautiful, infused with a deft certainty which charmed as it entertained. He had bags of charisma, too, which was a tad surprising in such a homely, gentle fellow, and his rapport with the fans was enduringly affectionate.

Jimmy was introduced by Tommy Docherty into an essentially buoyant United side which had lost a little of its characteristic zest. A new face was needed and when financial pressure forced Stoke City to put him up for sale at a mere £120,000 in November 1976, the Doc saw him as the ideal tonic.

By turns subtle and explosive, the mobile front-man – who was joining his younger brother, Brian, at the club they had both supported as boys – soon forged a formidable link with Stuart Pearson and both marksmen scored in the 1977 FA Cup Final triumph over Liverpool. In fairness to the Merseysiders, though, it should be admitted that Jimmy's winner was an utter fluke, as he unwittingly deflected a wayward shot from Lou Macari into the goal.

Injury to 'Pancho' split the seemingly telepathic partnership which had so delighted connoisseurs of first-touch football, but Jimmy proved an equally fine foil to Joe Jordan and maintained his productive form until he himself fell prey to pelvic problems.

However, even after his career had been written off by two specialists, he resurfaced, only partially fit but relentlessly determined, to prolong the 1979/80 title race with a neatly glanced winner at home to Liverpool, a rousing effort which proved to be his United finale.

Eight months later in December 1980, half-way through his 35th year and with the expensive Garry Birtles having arrived on the scene, Greenhoff Snr accepted a move to Crewe Alexandra. There were three years remaining on his contract, but he couldn't bring himself to remain at Old Trafford when he was past his best.

Though Jimmy was a brilliant volleyer, the former Leeds United and Birmingham City favourite's finishing lacked that consistently clinical quality possessed by the most prolific of goal-scorers. But he could claim some spectacular and vital strikes.

A typical stroke of inspiration came against Liverpool in the 1979 FA Cup semi-final replay on an emotional night at Goodison Park, when he adroitly headed Mickey Thomas's awkwardly bouncing cross past Ray Clemence to book the Reds' passage to Wembley. This time the men from Anfield had fallen victim to a masterly piece of opportunism and could not blame Dame Fortune, as they could in that dramatic final two years earlier.

Perhaps the enduring sadness about Jimmy's association with Manchester United is that it didn't begin earlier. Often he is dubbed the best player never to be capped by England, and if his peak years had been spent at Old Trafford rather than in the Potteries – with all due respect to Stoke, who had to make the most of limited resources – surely he would not have been condemned to the international wilderness, apart from five appearances at under-23 level.

Nevertheless, the deeds of 'Jimmy the One', whose delicious elan was matched only by his engaging modesty, will linger long in the memories of all who relished his four years as a Red Devil.

JAMES GREENHOFF

BORN: Barnsley, Yorkshire, 19 June 1946.

HONOURS: FA Cup 76/7.

OTHER CLUBS: Leeds United 62/3-68/9 (96, 19); Birmingham City 68/9 (31, 14); Stoke City 69/70-76/7 (274, 76); Crewe Alexandra 80/1 (11, 4); Toronto Blizzard, USA, 81; Port Vale 81/2-82/3 (48, 5); Rochdale 82/3-83/4 (16, 0).

MANAGER: Rochdale (83-84).

GAMES **119 (4)**

GOALS **36**

JIMMY NICHOLL

1974/75 → 1981/82

The experience of Jimmy Nicholl illustrates vividly how a change of manager can devastate a footballer's career.

Jimmy was 25 years old, at the height of his powers, a Manchester United regular and a bastion of the Northern Ireland back four when Dave Sexton was sacked as Old Trafford boss in the spring of 1981 and Ron Atkinson was appointed in his place.

Now Ron had always admired John Gidman and it transpired that the Everton right-back was available for purchase. Not unnaturally, then, the Red Devils' new supremo made the England international one of his first signings – and that, effectively, was the end of Nicholl's days with United.

When the axe fell so unexpectedly, the flame-haired, Canadian-born defender had already amassed more than 200 appearances and seemed set for a marathon stint. One moment his prospects were unlimited, the next he was a back number.

Jimmy had been a much-lauded youth star who made his senior entrance during United's brief Second Division sojourn. Then came an impressive run during the next campaign and soon pundits were predicting that he would oust senior right-back Alex Forsyth for keeps. So it proved and, far from being overawed at replacing such a crowd favourite, Jimmy grew rapidly in confidence.

Perhaps his outstanding passing ability, natural ball control and mature reading of the game masked a lack of speed, occasional rashness in the tackle and a slight deficiency in the air, but he formed an effective and promising full-back partnership with fellow rookie Arthur Albiston.

Nicholl's detractors accused him of being too casual but his apparently relaxed approach belied a deep-seated will to win and, ironically, pace and aggression became more apparent in his game during his last full season with the Reds.

Some reckoned he would have been better employed by United at sweeper than full-back, but he never excelled in that position when given the chance for his country, and the opportunity did not arise at club level.

After being sold to Toronto Blizzard for £250,000 in April 1982, Jimmy served Sunderland, West Bromwich Albion and Glasgow Rangers among others, before making a nonsense of the evidence on his birth certificate by continuing to turn in sterling performances as player-manager of Raith Rovers into his 40th year.

JAMES MICHAEL NICHOLL
BORN: Hamilton, Canada, 28 February 1956.
HONOURS: FA Cup 76/7. 73 Northern Ireland caps (76-86).
OTHER CLUBS: Sunderland on loan 81/2 (3, 0); Toronto Blizzard, Canada, 82-83; Sunderland 82/3 (29, 0); Glasgow Rangers 83/4 (17, 0); West Bromwich Albion 84/5-85/6 (56, 0); Glasgow Rangers 86/7-88/9 (65, 0); Dunfermline Athletic 89/90-90/1 (24, 0); Raith Rovers 90/1-95/6 (128, 7).
MANAGER: Raith Rovers (90-96); Millwall (96-97); Raith Rovers (97-99).

GAMES **235 (13)**
GOALS 6

PADDY ROCHE

1974/75 → 1981/82

Paddy Roche was an accomplished goalkeeper whose only real flaw was lack of self-belief – now there's a statement to surprise many a loyal Reds fan. The frightening, some would say sinister, truth is that after one round of bad press at the time he was picked to replace Alex Stepney for four games in 1975/76, he was labelled for life as a bungler and the public was largely brainwashed into believing it. Not so his team-mates. They never doubted that Paddy was good enough.

The self-effacing, slender Irishman's unenviable reputation was founded on an incident in a top-of-the-table clash with Liverpool when he appeared to drop the ball for a soft goal. It looked bad and he was pilloried, but later Brian Greenhoff admitted colliding with the custodian, thus causing the clanger. But the damage was done and a destructive myth was born.

The problem was that the United defenders were used to playing in front of Alex, a line 'keeper. Paddy, who throughout six years as understudy to Stepney and Gary Bailey was granted only three brief runs as first choice, liked to command his area and at first his colleagues would get in his way. In fact, the agile Eire international, who later served Brentford before a marvellous spell with Halifax, possessed as safe a pair of hands as any United custodian since the war. What a shame that he didn't have the confidence to go with them.

PATRICK JOSEPH CHRISTOPHER ROCHE

BORN:	Dublin, 4 January 1951.
HONOURS:	8 Republic of Ireland caps (72-75).
OTHER CLUBS:	Shelbourne, Republic of Ireland; Brentford 82/3-83/4 (71, 0); Halifax Town 84/5-88/9 (189, 0).

GAMES	53
GOALS	0

NIKOLA JOVANOVIC

1979/80 → 1980/81

Nikola Jovanovic had all the class and talent to become a resounding success at Old Trafford. The lanky Yugoslav international central defender cum midfielder was blessed with skill and intelligence in abundance, was elegant on the ball and had an eye for goal, as he demonstrated with an impressive brace against Leicester City in the autumn of 1980.

So why did the £350,000 signing from Red Star Belgrade, who had nursed a lifelong ambition to be a Red Devil and who turned down a more lucrative offer from Bayern Munich to become Old Trafford's first foreign recruit, return so soon to his own country, his potential unfulfilled?

Probably it boiled down to a lack of instinctive communication with his colleagues on the pitch. Nikki could speak English but perhaps he could not think in English, and when split-second decisions are made in the heat of battle it is vital for players – particularly defenders – to have instant understanding of their team-mates' intentions. Also Nikki struggled to adjust to the pace of the English game, being used to the more deliberate build-up of Yugoslav soccer, and he was troubled on and off by a niggling back injury. On top of all that, it could not have been easy for an overseas recruit to settle at an under-achieving club in the throes of transition.

So the courteous Montenegran's move to Manchester United was a gamble that failed, but it was an imaginative experiment by Dave Sexton and one that deserved praise for its boldness.

NIKOLA JOVANOVIC

BORN:	Cetinje, Yugoslavia, 18 September 1952.
HONOURS:	Yugoslavia caps.
OTHER CLUBS:	Red Star Belgrade and Buducnost, both Yugoslavia.

GAMES	25 (1)
GOALS	4

TOMMY BALDWIN

1974/75

The zenith of Tommy's career as a prolific snapper-up of unconsidered trifles in front of goal was emphatically behind him when he was taken on loan from Chelsea as a stand-in for the injured Stuart Pearson. He was not a success.

THOMAS BALDWIN
BORN: Gateshead, County Durham, 10 June 1945.
OTHER CLUBS: Arsenal 64/5-66/7 (17, 7); Chelsea 66/7-74/5 (187, 74); Millwall on loan 74/5 (6, 1); Brentford 77/8 (4, 1).

GAMES 2
GOALS 0

JONATHAN CLARK

1976/77

A host of top clubs battled for the signature of the prodigiously promising young Welsh midfielder, but after signing for the Red Devils he didn't develop as expected and a £50,000 deal took the under-21 cap to Derby in 1978.

JONATHAN CLARK
BORN: Swansea, Glamorgan, 12 November 1958.
OTHER CLUBS: Derby County 78/9-80/1 (53, 3); Preston North End 81/2-86/7 (110, 10); Bury 86/7 (14, 1); Carlisle United 87/8-88/9 (49, 2).

GAMES 0 (1)
GOALS 0

TOM CONNELL

1978/79

A left-back who had just risen to full international status when he was enlisted from Coleraine in August 1978, he deputised twice for Stewart Houston but never looked capable of rivalling Arthur Albiston for a long-term berth.

THOMAS EUGENE CONNELL
BORN: Newry, Northern Ireland, 25 November 1957.
OTHER CLUBS: Coleraine and Glentoran, both Northern Ireland.

GAMES 2
GOALS 0

RON DAVIES

1974/75

What a shame it was that Matt Busby failed in his bid to sign the great Welsh centre-forward during his Southampton prime in the 1960s. As it was, the Reds acquired a shadow of that performer, who made little impact and scored no goals.

RONALD TUDOR DAVIES
BORN: Holywell, Flintshire, 25 May 1942.
HONOURS: 29 Wales caps (64-74).
OTHER CLUBS: Chester 59/60-62/3 (94, 44); Luton Town 62/3-63/4 (32, 21); Norwich City 63/4-65/6 (113, 58); Southampton 66/7-72/3 (240, 134); Portsmouth 73/4-74/5 (59, 18); Millwall 75/6 (3, 0).

GAMES 0 (10)
GOALS 0

PETER COYNE

1975/76

Scored goals for fun at junior level but didn't follow through in the top grade, though he did find the net in his only senior start for United, a 2-1 reverse at Leicester. Subsequently he was passably prolific under Lou Macari at Swindon.

PETER DAVID COYNE
BORN: Hartlepool, County Durham, 13 November 1958.
OTHER CLUBS: Crewe Alexandra 77/8-80/1 (134, 47); Swindon Town 84/5-88/9 (110, 30); Aldershot on loan 89/90 (3, 0).

GAMES 1 (1)
GOALS 1

ALAN FOGGON

1976/77

An experienced goal-scoring winger, pacy and strong with an assured touch, seemed an enticing prospect when Tommy Docherty signed him for £27,000 in 1976. But two months and three brief outings later, Alan had been shipped out.

ALAN FOGGON
BORN: Chester-le-Street, County Durham, 23 February 1950.
OTHER CLUBS: Newcastle United 67/8-70/1 (61, 14); Cardiff City 71/2-72/3 (17, 1); Middlesbrough 72/3-75/6 (115, 45); Sunderland 76/7 (8, 0); Southend United 77/8 (22, 0); Hartlepool United on loan 77/8 (18, 2).

GAMES 0 (3)
GOALS 0

JIMMY KELLY

1975/76

So impressively did the teenage midfielder perform on his senior debut, as a substitute at home to Wolves, that pundits were freely predicting an illustrious career. It never materialised in England, but later Jimmy thrived in the USA.

JAMES WILLIAM KELLY
BORN: Carlisle, Cumberland, 2 May 1957.
OTHER CLUBS: Chicago Sting 76-77, Los Angeles Aztecs 78-80, Tulsa Roughnecks 80, all USA; Toronto Blizzard, Canada, 81.

GAMES 0 (1)
GOALS 0

TONY GRIMSHAW

1975/76

A diminutive midfielder whose impetus was halted cruelly by a broken leg. Tony began 1975/76 in United's 'A' team so brightly that by the autumn he was pitchforked into senior action. Then came the injury and Old Trafford oblivion.

ANTHONY GRIMSHAW
BORN: Manchester, 8 December 1957.
OTHER CLUBS: Ballymena United, Northern Ireland, on loan 78/9.

GAMES 0 (2)
GOALS 0

STEVE PATERSON

1976/77 → 1979/80

A towering centre-half who made his senior entrance as a substitute against Ajax, and also faced Juventus, only to have his momentum halted by an ankle injury. Steve, who could double as a centre-forward, was released in 1980.

STEVEN WILLIAM PATERSON
BORN: Elgin, Morayshire, 8 April 1958.
OTHER CLUBS: Hong Kong and Japanese football.
MANAGER: Inverness Caledonian Thistle (95-03); Aberdeen (03-04).

GAMES 5 (5)
GOALS 0

MARTYN ROGERS

1977/78

An accomplished left-back who riveted the eye with England schoolboys, Martyn was only 17 when called up as a deputy for the injured Arthur Albiston. However, he never earned another chance and was freed by United in 1979.

MARTYN ROGERS
BORN: Nottingham, 26 January 1960.
OTHER CLUBS: Queen's Park Rangers 79/80 (2, 0).
DIED: Ringwood, Hampshire, March 1992.

GAMES 1
GOALS 0

TOM SLOAN

1978/79 → 1980/81

Dave Sexton entertained high hopes of the creative midfielder whom he recruited for £20,000 from Ballymena United in August 1978, but Tom's game lacked the authority necessary to carve a niche in the English top flight.

THOMAS SLOAN
BORN: Ballymena, Northern Ireland, 10 July 1959.
HONOURS: 3 Northern Ireland caps (79).
OTHER CLUBS: Ballymena United, Northern Ireland; Chester 82/3 (44, 3).

GAMES 4 (8)
GOALS 0

COLIN WALDRON

1976/77

Early in his development, Colin was touted as a future England centre-half, the pundits being seduced by his decisiveness, composure and skill. However, though only 27 when he joined the Reds, his best days proved to be behind him.

COLIN WALDRON
BORN: Bristol, 22 June 1948.
OTHER CLUBS: Bury 66/7 (20, 1); Chelsea 67/8 (9, 0); Burnley 67/8-75/6 (308, 16); Sunderland 76/7-77/8 (20, 1); Tulsa Roughnecks 78, Philadelphia Fury 78, Atlanta Chiefs 79, all USA; Rochdale 79/80 (19, 1).

GAMES 4
GOALS 0

ANTO WHELAN

1980/81

After enlisting at a cost of £30,000 from Bohemians, defender Anto rose rapidly to the status of under-21 international, but he could not force himself into senior contention and made the return journey across the Irish Sea in 1983.

ANTHONY GERARD WHELAN
BORN: Dublin, 23 November 1959.
OTHER CLUBS: Bohemians, Shamrock Rovers (twice), Cork, Bray Wanderers, Shelbourne, all Republic of Ireland.

GAMES 0 (1)
GOALS 0

SAMMY McILROY

· ·

1971/72 → 1981/82

Sammy McIlroy was Irish, he had bags of natural talent and he scored a fine goal against Manchester City on his debut as a 17-year-old for the Red Devils. So there was never any doubt with whom the media would compare him. It is to Sammy's eternal credit that he rose above the fatuous headlines about 'the new George Best' and, in commendably level-headed manner, went on to build his own immensely successful United career.

The slim Ulsterman started first-team life as a striker but the fanfares following his dramatic Maine Road entrance in a memorable 3-3 draw did not win him a regular place and for a season and a half he remained on the fringe. Then a car accident, in which Sammy suffered four broken ribs and a punctured lung, sidelined him for several months and, with United desperately blooding new men in an unavailing bid to find a winning blend, his future looked rocky. He battled back into contention but it wasn't until the Second Division campaign of 1974/75 that he hit convincing form.

Though never a prolific marksman, he formed an effective partnership with Stuart Pearson which lasted for two and a half years until Jimmy Greenhoff arrived. Then Sammy moved to midfield, at the expense of Gerry Daly, and played the best football of his life. He was given a free role, popping up frequently on the left despite being right-footed, and he prospered for four years.

Sammy, who won nearly 90 caps, had tremendous instinctive ability and his twinkling feet could take him dancing past challenges that would floor less gifted operators. This natural nimbleness was revealed to sparkling effect two minutes from the end of the 1979 FA Cup Final. With United a goal down to Arsenal, he scurried into the area, squirmed past one defender, then nutmegged another before squeezing the ball past Pat Jennings for the equaliser. Because of the Gunners' heart-stopping response a minute later, Sammy never garnered the full credit for an inspired effort and it remains a neglected gem.

On the negative side there is little to report, though the hyper-critical might point out that he was poor in the air, not a great tackler and lacked the strength and toughness that would have made him a still more formidable all-round performer.

Sammy's character, though, was never in doubt and it spoke volumes for his approach that he retained his enthusiasm after the colossal disappointment of being discarded by Ron Atkinson when he was only 27 and barely at his peak. That was in February 1982, when he was sold to Stoke City for £350,000.

Thereafter he beavered on through spells at Manchester City, Bury and Preston before managing several non-League clubs, notably Macclesfield Town, whom he led into the Third and then the Second Division, invariably winning bouquets for his passionate advocacy of sweet-passing football.

But for all that mature endeavour, which was capped by his appointment as Northern Ireland boss as the century turned, it was as a Red Devil in his youth and early prime that Sammy McIlroy knew his finest footballing hours.

SAMUEL BAXTER McILROY
BORN: Belfast, 2 August 1954.
HONOURS: FA Cup 76/7. Second Division Championship 74/5. 88 Northern Ireland caps (72-86).
OTHER CLUBS: Stoke City 81/2-84/5 (133, 14); Manchester City 85/6 (12, 1); Orgryte, Sweden, 86;
Manchester City 86/7 (1, 0); Bury 86/7-87/8 (43, 6); FC Moedling, Austria, 88;
Bury 88/9-89/90 (57, 2); Preston North End 89/90 (20, 0).
MANAGER: Macclesfield Town (93-00); Northern Ireland (00-03); Stockport County (03-04); Morecambe (06-).

GAMES **391 (28)**
GOALS **71**

GARY BAILEY

$1978/79 \rightarrow 1986/87$

ig, blond and bursting with self-belief, Gary Bailey somehow conveyed the impression that here was a man born to keep goal. But if the image was perfect, did the performance match up to it? In fact, Gary's career was something of a paradox. On the one hand he was often vilified, particularly for his handling of crosses; on the other he became a full England international and was the last line of defence for one of Britain's leading clubs for nearly a decade.

The son of former Ipswich Town custodian Roy Bailey, who earned a Championship medal under Alf Ramsey in 1961/62, Gary was sent to Old Trafford for a trial by ex-United marksman Eddie Lewis, who discovered him playing for Witts University in South Africa.

The precocious youngster made a quick impression, survived a scare when – prophetically as it was to prove – his knee locked in training, and he was offered an early first-team breakthrough when a deal for Coventry City's Scottish international Jim Blyth fell through at the 11th hour.

With characteristic confidence, Bailey made the most of his chance. He kept a clean sheet on his debut against Ipswich at Old Trafford in November 1978, despite having to peer through curtains of rain, and thereafter made the position his own. His rapid progress was confirmed when, just three months later, he was honoured by England at under-21 level.

That first season ended on a traumatic note when United were beaten by a late Arsenal goal in the FA Cup Final, and some commentators blamed the rookie 'keeper for not cutting out the cross from which Alan Sunderland netted his dramatic winner. That said, it should be noted that the build-up from an inspired Liam Brady and the delivery from Graham Rix were sheer perfection.

Come 1983 Gary repaid any real or imaginary debt by making the last-minute point-blank save from Brighton's Gordon Smith that enabled the Reds to earn a Wembley replay, then go on to lift the trophy. Two years later, he kept a clean sheet and earned a second FA Cup winner's medal as United beat the favourites, Everton.

By then Gary, who gained a physics degree during his Manchester years, had developed into a top-notch shot-stopper who faltered occasionally when he left his line, though rarely with catastrophic results. He was a good talker on the pitch and benefited hugely from the coaching of Harry Gregg.

So where does all this leave him in the historical goalkeeping pecking order? Always just behind the very front rank, certainly; but equally without doubt he had the edge on most of his First Division peers. When a knee injury halted Gary's English League career at the age of 29, it probably deprived him of his best years.

GARY RICHARD BAILEY

BORN: Ipswich, Suffolk, 9 August 1958.
HONOURS: FA Cup 82/3, 84/5. 2 England caps (85).
OTHER CLUBS: Kaiser Chiefs, South Africa, 78.

GAMES 375
GOALS 0

JOE JORDAN

. . . .

1977/78 → 1980/81

When Joe Jordan crossed the Pennines from Elland Road he carried with him a villainous reputation of the darkest hue. He was the big bad wolf, the snarling warrior who devoured defenders and cleaned those famous fangs on the corner flag.

True to form, his introductory days at Old Trafford did little to dispel the lurid image. Before Joe could pull on the red shirt in earnest he had to serve a suspension for misdeeds at Leeds, and when he did take the field as Dave Sexton's first signing in January 1978 he was booked in two of his earliest games.

United fans who revelled in the subtle delights of the Pearson-Greenhoff tandem squirmed in apprehension at the prospect of the £350,000 battering ram replacing one of their trusty rapiers.

As it turned out, Joe did not prove to be the destructive ogre they had feared and by the end of his third full campaign for the Reds, most supporters were sorry to see him leave. Indeed the Stretford Enders, who had loved to hate the glowering striker during his days as an idol of Elland Road, now took him to their hearts, revelling in his Attila-like reputation and warming to that famous gap-toothed grin, or grimace, as the fancy took him.

In fact, despite the fangs and the frequent frowns, the Scottish international was an intelligent, thoughtful player whose control, finishing and overall contribution to the team effort improved radically under Sexton, though his fearsome penalty-area presence, especially in the air, remained his forte.

Perhaps Joe, never a heavy scorer himself, would have been even more effective if the manager had persisted with the briefly prolific Andy Ritchie as his new partner after the departure of Greenhoff, instead of introducing the newcomer Garry Birtles. As it was, season 1980/81 turned out to be Jordan's best for the Reds, with 15 goals from 33 matches, a commendable return for a specialist target man.

Ironically, it turned out to be his last, too, as he fulfilled a lifelong ambition to play in Europe by joining AC Milan, who signed him in July 1981 for a mere £175,000, thanks to European transfer-fee restrictions.

From United's viewpoint Joe's departure was abominably timed, as there were genuine grounds for believing that, had he remained at Old Trafford for one more campaign, then an improving side boosted by the arrival of the inspirational Bryan Robson might have lifted the Championship at long last.

But even the renowned silver tongue of Ron Atkinson could not persuade the Red Devils' player of the year for both 1980 and 1981 to tarry, and so title talk receded to the realms of pure speculation.

The Scot's next stop was Verona before he returned to England to serve first Southampton and then Bristol City, whom he went on to manage. His stints in the hot seats at Ashton Gate and elsewhere, while not wildly successful overall, were characterised by a mixture of acumen and integrity which suggested that Joe Jordan remained a man to watch.

Although his second departure from Bristol appeared to cast doubt on his long-term future as a soccer boss, he returned to the game at international level, assisting Lawrie McMenemy with Northern Ireland before beginning a third stint with the Robins, this time as director of football. More recently he has been helping Harry Redknapp to claim silverware for Portsmouth.

JOSEPH JORDAN

BORN: Carluke, Lanarkshire, 15 December 1951.

HONOURS: 52 Scotland caps (72-82).

OTHER CLUBS: Morton 68/9-70/1 (12, 2); Leeds United 71/2-77/8 (169, 35); AC Milan 81/2-82/3 (52, 12); Verona 83/4 (12, 1), both Italy; Southampton 84/5-86/7 (48, 12); Bristol City 86/7-89/90 (57, 8).

MANAGER: Bristol City (88-90); Heart of Midlothian (90-93); Stoke City (93-94); Bristol City (94-97); Portsmouth (caretaker, 04).

GAMES **125 (1)**

GOALS **41**

GORDON McQUEEN

1977/78 → 1984/85

Gordon McQueen may not have been the greatest centre-half Manchester United ever had, but he was certainly one of the most entertaining. The blond giant provided a gloriously exciting spectacle as he soared above the opposition, whether to clear his own lines or to launch one of those murderous attacking headers that became his trademark.

Then there were those mazy, lolloping left-wing dribbles past three or four defenders, an added and very occasional delight indulged in only when his side were a few goals to the good. Such adventurous sorties, on which somehow he brought to mind a lovably clumsy, overgrown puppy, further endeared him to most Reds supporters, who had taken him to their hearts from the moment of his arguably overpriced £500,000 transfer from Leeds in February 1978.

Yet those very antics were symptomatic of the 6ft 3in Scottish international's one weakness: he was drawn out of position too easily. If the centre-forward he was marking fell back into midfield or roamed to the wing, Gordon would often chase him, sometimes leaving a yawning gap.

It was this unpredictable element in his game – Don Revie tried so hard to curb it at Leeds – which prevented him from attaining the very highest standard, although McQueen's extensive Elland Road fan club could point out, with some justification, that it did not hamper his contribution to the Yorkshiremen's Championship triumph in 1973/74.

Whatever, at Old Trafford the imperturbable Martin Buchan, an immaculate covering player, did much to limit the consequences of his countryman's penchant for roving and the two formed a formidable partnership. But when Gordon was paired with less organised individuals the alarm bells would ring.

For all that, the popular centre-half, who supplemented his aerial dominance with a deceptive turn of speed, was a consistently impressive performer for the Reds and he was much missed when injuries curtailed his appearances, allowing Kevin Moran and Paul McGrath to cement their claims to the central defensive positions.

Gordon – whose father Tommy kept goal for Hibernian and Accrington Stanley, among others – was freed at the end of 1984/85, and could look back on an eventful Old Trafford sojourn after taking the trans-Pennine trail blazed a month before him by his pal, Joe Jordan.

His most memorable form came in 1979/80, when he netted nine times and toiled mightily at the back as United finished as League runners-up to Liverpool. More tangible reward came in 1983 when he gained an FA Cup winner's medal against Brighton, making up for his Wembley disappointment of four years earlier when his late goal against Arsenal signalled a rousing fightback that ended in gallant failure. In addition, he had picked up another loser's gong at Wembley, when the Red Devils were bested by Liverpool in the 1983 League Cup Final.

Gordon ended his playing days in Japan, where he survived a serious illness, before moving into management with Airdrieonians. Later he coached with St Mirren, his first senior club, and then Middlesbrough.

GORDON McQUEEN

BORN: Kilbirnie, Ayrshire, 26 June 1952.
HONOURS: FA Cup 82/3. 30 Scotland caps (73-81).
OTHER CLUBS: St Mirren 70/1-72/3 (57, 5); Leeds United 72/3-77/8 (140, 15), Seiko, Hong Kong.
MANAGER: Airdrieonians (87-89).

GAMES 229
GOALS 26

MICKEY THOMAS

1978/79 → 1980/81

If the footballing merits of Gordon Hill personified the Tommy Docherty era – sometimes brilliant, occasionally awful, always mercurial – then those of little Mickey Thomas, the man recruited to replace Gordon on the left wing, summed up the methodical, industrious approach of new manager Dave Sexton.

In reality Mickey was more midfielder than winger and he faced a well-nigh impossible task in replacing his crowd-pleasing predecessor in the affections of the Old Trafford faithful.

The fact that he went so far towards doing so says much for the ability and application of the mop-haired Welsh international workhorse, who was bought from Wrexham for £300,000 in November 1978 to – in the words of the Old Trafford boss – bring more balance and shape to the team.

During his three seasons with the Red Devils, Mickey won himself a reputation for selfless running that was second to none, and the fans identified with him as a trier who was more skilful than many pundits reckoned.

His left-foot crosses, rather erratic on his arrival, showed a marked improvement under the coaching attentions of Sexton and, as he began to throw off an apparent inferiority complex, Thomas started to score his quota of goals. His most prolific term was 1979/80, during which he netted ten times in senior competition, including a sequence of four in five games in the spring.

Often the Anfield Reds seemed to bring the best out of Mickey. Indeed, arguably the greatest all-round performance of his lengthy career was in the drawn FA Cup semi-final at Maine Road in March 1979; then he it was who ploughed through the Goodison Park mud to deliver the pinpoint dispatch from which Jimmy Greenhoff nodded the winner in the replay.

Also, a year later, he netted in a stirring 2-1 triumph over the Merseysiders at Old Trafford, thus ensuring that the title race went full distance, with the Red Devils finishing only two points adrift of Bob Paisley's champions.

But hopes of a long-term future with United were dashed by the demise of Dave Sexton and the advent of Ron Atkinson, who wasted no time in swapping him for Everton's John Gidman in August 1981. Thus the Welshman departed with no winner's medals to show for his Manchester sojourn, though he did have a loser's gong from the 1979 FA Cup Final as a souvenir.

At times an awkward man to manage, Mickey didn't settle at Goodison and became a wanderer whose travels brought him but limited joy, while a misdemeanour off the field landed him a jail term.

MICHAEL REGINALD THOMAS
BORN: Mochdre, North Wales, 7 July 1954.
HONOURS: 51 Wales caps (77-86).
OTHER CLUBS: Wrexham 71/2-78/9 (230, 33); Everton 81/2 (10, 0); Brighton and Hove Albion 81/2 (20, 0); Stoke City 82/3-83/4 (57, 14); Chelsea 83/4-84/5 (44, 9); West Bromwich Albion 85/6 (20, 0); Derby County on loan 85/6 (9, 0); Wichita Wings, USA; Shrewsbury Town 88/9 (40, 1); Leeds United 89/90 (3, 0); Stoke City 89/90-90/1 (46, 7); Wrexham 91/2-92/3 (34, 2).

GAMES 110
GOALS 15

ANDY RITCHIE

1977/78 → 1980/81

Any teenage striker who started 26 League games and scored 13 goals for a top side might reasonably expect that club to nurture his talent with the hope that one day he might save his employers a hefty fee. But if such were the expectations of Andy Ritchie, then he was sorely disappointed by Dave Sexton and his assistant, Tommy Cavanagh.

After making his debut in 1977/78, he seemed to stake an undeniable claim during the following campaign when he netted ten times in 17 outings, including a hat-trick against Leeds – after which he was dropped! In 1979/80 he was offered just three starts and managed three goals, all in one thrilling display of opportunism against Tottenham. The fans loved it. That day the youngster and Joe Jordan looked the ideal pair. Now surely, despite talk that Andy might leave, there would be a happy outcome. The manager was using psychology to get the best out of him, wasn't he? Then the unthinkable: in October 1980 Andy joined Brighton for £500,000. What had United lost? A fine striker of the ball with both feet who was greedy for goals, strong, willing and with good control. All he lacked was true pace.

In came Garry Birtles, a £1,250,000 recruit who was to represent no more than a sadly forlorn footnote in the Reds' history. True, United received a handsome sum for a teenager and Andy, while enjoying a worthy career, never hit real heights elsewhere. But in the heady environment of Old Trafford, where he had already tasted success, who knows what he might have achieved?

ANDREW TIMOTHY RITCHIE
BORN: Manchester, 28 November 1960.
OTHER CLUBS: Brighton and Hove Albion 80/1-82/3 (89, 23); Leeds United 82/3-86/7 (136, 40); Oldham Athletic 87/8-94/5 (217, 82); Scarborough 95/6-96/7 (69, 17); Oldham Athletic 96/7-97/8 (25, 2).
MANAGER: Oldham Athletic (98-01); Barnsley (05-06); Huddersfield Town (07-08).

GAMES 32 (10)
GOALS 13

ASHLEY GRIMES

1977/78 → 1982/83

Lean, loping Republic of Ireland international Ashley Grimes was one of Old Trafford's 'nearly men.' An immensely skilful and competitive left-sided utility player, he was hit by a double dose of misfortune at a crucial time for his long-term aspirations as a Red Devil.

In 1979/80, when United missed the title by only two points, Ashley – who was equally at home in midfield or at left-back – played in more than half the matches and just might have been on the verge of that vital breakthrough to become a first-team regular. But then came two seasons when first injury, then illness, destroyed his momentum and it became clear that the man who had cost £20,000 from Bohemians was destined to be no more than a fringe player.

This was confirmed in 1982/83, first by the arrival of Arnold Muhren, then by a case of Wembley heartache. When Steve Coppell was unfit to face Brighton in the FA Cup Final, the Irishman, an eternal substitute who had performed admirably in the semi-final against Arsenal, remained on the bench while Steve's place went to the inexperienced Alan Davies.

That summed up his time at United and Ashley – who was blessed with a precise left foot and limitless stamina – decided it was time to go. For a while he served Coventry before a more productive spell at Luton Town saw him come closer, but not close enough, to realising his rich potential.

AUGUSTINE ASHLEY GRIMES
BORN: Dublin, 2 August 1957.
HONOURS: 17 Republic of Ireland caps (78-88).
OTHER CLUBS: Bohemians, Republic of Ireland; Coventry City 83/4 (32, 1); Luton Town 84/5-88/9 (87, 3); Osasuna, Spain, 90/1; Stoke City 91/2 (10, 1).

GAMES 77 (30)
GOALS 11

RAY WILKINS

· ·

1979/80 → 1983/84

When Dave Sexton paid Chelsea £825,000 for Ray Wilkins in August 1979 there was much rejoicing in the Old Trafford camp. There was a genuine feeling that England's 22-year-old midfield general would be the long-sought-after missing link, the man who held the key to United winning the title for the first time in more than a decade.

After all, Ray was a richly gifted play-maker possessed of maturity and experience unusual for one of his age. Both Liverpool and Arsenal had tried to sign him and failed. Now, the theory went, this thoroughbred footballer's time was ripe and Old Trafford would witness the flowering of a great talent.

As it turned out, he gave United five seasons of trusty service, yet somehow he failed palpably to reach the lofty pinnacles predicted for him.

What was special about Ray? His touch was inspired; his passing could reach sublime heights; his reading of the game was exemplary and his temperament was impeccable. But often his play was flawed by an apparent lack of ambition, a propensity to play safe, which led to Ron Atkinson uncharitably christening him 'The Crab' – because he was always passing sideways – and to the fans becoming frustrated by his laid-back style.

At times, presumably, Ray's cautious approach reflected team tactics, but nevertheless it created a sadly unsympathetic image of a man who had the raw materials to become a Reds immortal.

To be fair, he did turn in many magnificent performances for United, and though his scoring rate was disappointly negligible – something like one goal every 19 matches – occasionally he would come up with a classic, such as his 25-yard left-foot curler in the first instalment of the 1983 FA Cup Final against Brighton.

For a time, Ray was skipper of both club and country before he suffered a fractured cheekbone and lost both jobs to Bryan Robson. In the wake of that setback, his form dipped noticeably, but he recovered to deliver some of his most compelling displays in his farewell season before joining AC Milan for £1.5 million in the summer of 1984.

Should he have stayed? If he had it would certainly have been harder, for financial reasons, to keep Robson out of the Italians' clutches, so it could be argued that by the mere acting of leaving, Ray did Manchester United a priceless service.

Of course, such an immaculate performer and decent man deserves better than such a glib epitaph and for a moment in 1991 it seemed he might get the chance to write a new ending to his personal chapter of the Old Trafford story.

Alex Ferguson pondered deeply on the need for a top-quality schemer and was said to be on the verge of offering the job to Ray, whose game was improving with every passing year. But it never happened; the personable thirtysomething continued to pull the midfield strings for Queen's Park Rangers and Alex pursued other options. What might have transpired if Ray and the Reds had been reunited, we'll never know.

RAYMOND COLIN WILKINS

BORN:	Hillingdon, Middlesex, 14 September 1956.
HONOURS:	FA Cup 82/3. 84 England caps (76–86).
OTHER CLUBS	Chelsea 73/4–78/9 (179, 30); AC Milan, Italy, 84/5–86/7 (73, 2); Paris St Germain, France, 87/8 (10, 0); Glasgow Rangers 87/8–89/90 (70, 2); Queen's Park Rangers 89/90–93/4 (154, 7); Crystal Palace 94/5 (1, 0); Queen's Park Rangers 94/5–96/7 (21, 0); Wycombe Wanderers 96/7 (1, 0); Hibernian 96/7 (16, 0); Millwall 96/7 (3,0); Leyton Orient 96/7 (3, 0).
MANAGER:	Queen's Park Rangers (94–96); Fulham as chief coach (97–98).

GAMES **191 (3)**

GOALS **10**

GARRY BIRTLES

1980/81 → 1981/82

The name of Garry Birtles became synonymous with failure during his troubled two years at Old Trafford, yet here was a fine player who had looked one of the most effective strikers in the country with Nottingham Forest. Just promoted to the England team, he had seemed ripe for the move to United in October 1980. Glory beckoned, but it was footballing disaster which overtook him.

Reds fans, who to their credit treated Garry with patience and good humour, had to wait 30 games before the £1,250,000 signing struck his first League goal, and when it finally came – a 25-yarder against Swansea City – it was greeted with a mixture of joy, relief and irony.

But why such an interminable wait? Well, it's true that Garry didn't have the best of luck, hitting the woodwork in several early games, after which his confidence took a dive. But that wasn't the whole story.

More relevant was the fact that he was not suited to partner Joe Jordan. Garry and Joe, although players of a different type, were both left-sided and both gravitated naturally to the inside-left channel. So, through no fault of their own, they were attacking the same area and getting in each other's way, a likely consequence which presumably did not worry Dave Sexton when he bought the Forest man. As a result Garry scored just once in the 26 games in which he played alongside the Scot. Yet with Frank Stapleton the following season he managed 11 in 33 matches; not outstanding, but certainly respectable.

Despite this improvement, he was still not the Birtles of old, whose dashing runs had made such an impact. Duly, in September 1982, new boss Ron Atkinson let him return to the City Ground for a mere £275,000 and he regained his form, later shining also for Notts County. For Garry an ordeal was over, though the chance of a lifetime had passed him by.

GARRY BIRTLES		
BORN:	Nottingham, 27 July 1956.	
HONOURS:	3 England caps (80).	
OTHER CLUBS:	Nottingham Forest 76/7–80/1 (87, 32) and 82/3–86/7 (125, 38); Notts County 87/8–88/9 (63, 9); Grimsby Town 89/90–91/2 (69, 9).	

GAMES	63 (1)
GOALS	12

SCOTT McGARVEY

1980/81 → 1982/83

Scott McGarvey was the archetypal golden boy who dazzled in youth football but whose light dimmed all too soon at the top level. In his mid-teens, startling claims were made for the ability of the blond Glaswegian striker; a glittering international future was predicted and, indeed, he did turn out for Scotland under-21s.

After making his United debut in 1980/81, Scott was given a run of nine successive games towards the end of the following campaign. Admittedly there were glimmers of sumptuous promise, such as the flashing header he netted against Spurs at Old Trafford, but in general he failed to convince.

Nevertheless Scott, undeniably skilful but rather willowy and easily brushed off the ball, impressed in the subsequent pre-season friendlies. But soon he found himself overlooked in favour of another emerging youngster, name of Norman Whiteside. He drifted off for loan service with Wolves followed by moderate spells elsewhere, all that potential just a wistful recollection.

SCOTT THOMAS McGARVEY
BORN: Glasgow, 22 April 1963.
OTHER CLUBS: Wolverhampton Wanderers on loan 83/4 (13, 2); Portsmouth 84/5-85/6 (23, 6); Carlisle United, first on loan 85/6-86/7 (35, 11); Grimsby Town 86/7-87/8 (50, 7); Bristol City 88/9 (26, 9); Oldham Athletic 89/90 (4, 1); Wigan Athletic on loan 89/90 (3, 0); Mazda, Japan, 90.

GAMES 13 (12)
GOALS 3

PETER BEARDSLEY

1982/83

Peter Beardsley merits inclusion in this section purely out of curiosity value. For the question will always be asked: if Liverpool were ready to pay Newcastle £1.9 million for the England man, why didn't United snap him up for £250,000 from Vancouver Whitecaps when they had the chance?

He had been recommended by an enthusiastic Jimmy Murphy, who was sure the youngster had the makings of a star striker, and when Ron Atkinson saw him he agreed that the former Carlisle player was worth a trial. But despite demonstrating huge potential in training, Peter was only ever to get one first-team chance – in a Milk Cup tie against Bournemouth in October 1982 – before making the return trip to Canada.

In retrospect, with the Geordie looking a more complete footballer than ever in his mid thirties back at St James' Park, such judgement seemed calamitous. But at the time Ron was blessed with Frank Stapleton, an emerging Norman Whiteside and the promising Scott McGarvey; and there was a young fellow called Mark Hughes coming through the reserve sides.

Win some, lose some . . .

PETER ANDREW BEARDSLEY
BORN: Newcastle, 18 January 1961.
HONOURS: 59 England caps (86-96).
OTHER CLUBS: Carlisle United 79/80-81/2 (104, 22); Vancouver Whitecaps, Canada, 81 and 83; Newcastle United 83/4-86/7 (147, 61); Liverpool 87/8-90/1 (131, 46); Everton 91/2-92/3 (81, 25); Newcastle United 93/4-96/7 (129, 47); Bolton Wanderers 97/8 (17, 2); Manchester City on loan 97/8 (6, 0); Fulham on loan 97/8 (8, 1); Hartlepool United 98/9 (22, 2).

GAMES 1
GOALS 0

FRANK STAPLETON

· ·

1981/82 → 1986/87

When Ron Atkinson signed Frank Stapleton from Arsenal in August 1981 – after bitter negotiations which ended in the hands of a transfer tribunal – he described his £900,000 capture as the best centre-forward in Europe.

Now Frank was not short of admirable attributes but, at least in retrospect, Ron's mountain of praise does seem a little steep. After all, in six years at Old Trafford the Republic of Ireland striker never exceeded 14 League goals in a season, although admittedly there was a great deal more to his game than supplying the finishing touch.

He was a majestic leader of the line, always acutely aware of what was going on around him. This subtle talent, which involves pulling defenders out of position with selfless running and creating dangerous positions for team-mates with delicate deflections and flicks, is not a flashy one but – certainly to the degree of excellence attained by Stapleton – it is rare indeed.

His control was impeccable with both feet and he possessed a fierce shot, but it is probably his power and timing in the air for which he will be best remembered. Prolific he was not, but Frank's greatest goals – his simple yet exquisitely directed header in the away draw with Dukla Prague in 1983 is a cherished example – were to be savoured. Against all that, he lacked half a yard of pace and was not the deadliest snapper-up of the half, or sometimes even whole, chance.

A cool, self-possessed individual, never one to indulge overmuch in laddish bonhomie, Frank was utterly dedicated in his preparation and offered an impressive level of consistency.

That thoroughly professional approach had impressed United coaches as far back as the early 1970s, when the tall Dubliner had been on the club's books as a schoolboy, but he was allowed to slip away to Highbury and the Old Trafford bank balance suffered accordingly.

In 1979 there had been a price to pay on the field, too, when Frank turned in one of his finest Arsenal performances in the FA Cup Final, scoring one of the goals that beat the Red Devils. Of course, four years later he redressed the balance, contributing a close-range equaliser in the first Wembley meeting with Brighton, thus becoming the first man to score for different clubs in two FA Cup Finals.

Towards the end of his United days there was speculation that he might be converted to a central defender – in emergencies he had performed creditably in that position in two finals – but it was perhaps an unrealistic thought, and in July 1987 he was freed to join Ajax of Amsterdam.

An uncomfortable, injury-stricken period followed, then service with four English clubs and one French before Frank moved into player-managership with Bradford City, only to be sacked after failing narrowly to reach the Second Division promotion play-offs in 1994.

FRANCIS ANTHONY STAPLETON

BORN: Dublin, 10 July 1956.
HONOURS: FA Cup 82/3, 84/5. 70 Republic of Ireland caps (76-90).
OTHER CLUBS: Arsenal 74/5-80/1 (225, 75); Ajax, Holland, 87/8 (4, 0); Derby County on loan 87/8 (10, 1); Le Havre, France, 88/9; Blackburn Rovers 89/90-90/1 (81, 13); Aldershot on loan 91/2 (1, 0); Huddersfield Town 91/2 (5, 0); Bradford City 91/2-93/4 (68, 2).
MANAGER: Bradford City (91-94).

GAMES **267 (21)**
GOALS **78**

ARNOLD MUHREN

1982/83 → 1984/85

Arnold Muhren arrived from Ipswich Town in the summer of 1982 to become, at that time, the most skilful Red Devil since George Best. Though his talents were of a contrasting variety to the Irish magician's – deliberate and delicate rather than overtly breathtaking – his command of the ball was similarly complete. And just as George bowed out when he had much more to offer, so did the subtly superb Dutch schemer, albeit in utterly different circumstances.

Not that Ron Atkinson, then the United boss, could be blamed for letting such a world-class performer slip through his fingers. After all, Arnold was 34, plagued by injury and had been unable to command a regular place in the side when he was allowed home to join Ajax of Amsterdam in June 1985.

New faces such as Gordon Strachan and Jesper Olsen were arriving to increase the competition for places, which was already on the warm side, and who was to know that the slightly-built, left-sided creator still had at least four years of top football in him, including a masterly contribution to Holland's European Championship victory in 1988?

Some critics even questioned Ron's judgement in bringing Arnold to Old Trafford in the first place. When the Dutchman became a free agent at the end of four fabulous years as the artistic hub of Bobby Robson's Ipswich Town, there were those who claimed he was past his prime and, even though no fee was involved, not worth signing.

But his early form removed the doubts. He gave the Reds a new dimension with his immaculate, unhurried passing and all-round vision, so much so that Martin Buchan – not a man to give praise lightly – remarked that Arnold was the only man in English football whom he would pay to watch. Certainly in his first two United campaigns the side looked at its best only when he was playing, and in 1983/84 a hitherto confident Championship surge faltered in March when he was injured.

When Arnold left, his exit was scarcely mourned amid the euphoria of the 1985 Wembley triumph over Everton. In the light of title failures over the next few seasons, a period of wailing and gnashing of teeth might have been appropriate.

ARNOLDUS JOHANNUS HYACINTHUS MUHREN

BORN: Volendam, Holland, 2 June 1951.

HONOURS: FA Cup 82/3. 23 Holland caps (78-88).

OTHER CLUBS: Volendam 70/1 (26, 2); Ajax 71/2-73/4 (62, 16); Twente Enschede 74/5-77/8 (108, 39), all Holland; Ipswich Town 78/9-81/2 (161, 21); Ajax 85/6-88/9 (99, 14).

GAMES	93 (5)
GOALS	18

REMI MOSES

1981/82 → 1987/88

Somebody up there didn't like Remi Moses. Ever after joining United, the club he followed as a boy, Remi was doomed to see soccer's glittering prizes dangled tantalisingly in front of him, only to be whisked away as he reached out to grab them.

In fact, the abrasive yet becomingly modest little midfielder could shoulder the blame himself for his first disappointment, that of missing the 1983 FA Cup Final through suspension after being sent off in a League game at Highbury. But it was not his fault that he was injured and absent from the Reds' next FA Cup triumph in 1985. And when he did make it to Wembley, for the 1983 League Cup Final, all he picked up was a loser's medal.

There was worse to endure. In 1984/85 the under-21 international's form was so consistent that he was elevated to the full England squad. Then came the big moment: he was selected for the national team. And the inevitable letdown: injury prevented him from claiming that much-deserved cap.

But the ultimate heartache was still in store. After three seasons of sporadic appearances, Remi succumbed finally to an ankle problem and retired from the game in May 1988 while still only 27.

He had arrived at Old Trafford from West Bromwich Albion in September 1981 as a £650,000 makeweight in the £2.4 million package that also included Bryan Robson. Thus reunited with his former boss, Ron Atkinson, who perceived that he was needed to toughen up the team's soft centre, Moses briefly faced terrace jibes that he was the manager's favourite.

But his spirited ball-winning and honest approach won over most of the doubters and it's a fact that the Reds looked harder to beat when the formidably combative Mancunian was in the side.

His all-round game, especially his passing, was becoming more accomplished as his fitness deteriorated; yet another cruel irony for a man who had already suffered more than enough.

REMI MARK MOSES
BORN: Manchester, 14 November 1960.
OTHER CLUBS: West Bromwich Albion 79/80-81/2 (63, 5).

GAMES 188 (11)
GOALS 12

ARTHUR ALBISTON

1974/75 → 1987/88

Arthur Albiston was never lauded as a superstar, he never figured in a transfer saga and his name was never tainted by even the faintest whiff of controversy. But when it comes to the final reckoning, when all the media hype is cast aside for the meaningless pap it truly is, and when the player's real worth down the years is reviewed, there will be few names that stand comparison with that of the plucky little Scottish left-back.

For a start, only nine men – Messrs Charlton, Giggs, Foulkes, Scholes, Gary Neville, Stepney, Dunne, Irwin and pre-war goal-scorer Joe Spence – have played more senior matches for the Reds at the time of writing. While statistics alone can mislead, such a record speaks volumes of a consistency and loyalty beyond reproach.

Arthur was only 19, with just handful of first-team appearances behind him, when injury to Stewart Houston presented him with his big chance. The dark-haired, diminutive rookie came into the side towards the end of 1976/77 and was immediately pitched into the FA Cup Final against Liverpool. He confounded critics who predicted that he would be a weak link, that the Merseyside flyer Steve Heighway would cut him to ribbons, and he played an accomplished part in a stirring victory. As well as locking up the left flank of the Red Devils' rearguard, he found time to attack on the overlap, leaving England internationals Phil Neal and Tommy Smith staggering in his wake on one scintillating run that was marred only by a wayward cross.

After the game, amid the inevitable euphoria, Arthur remained commendably level-headed, and it was typical of the generous youngster that he offered his winner's medal to the unfortunate Houston. Though much touched by the gesture, Stewart declined with thanks.

Once in the team Arthur remained a fixture for a decade. The reason was plain: he was good at his job. He had speed, assured control with both feet, first-class distribution and a canny tackle. His only weakness was a lack of height which occasionally left him exposed against big strikers, especially when defending deep crosses to the far post.

Albiston didn't score many goals – that department was hardly his responsibility – but one remains vivid in the memory of this writer, an 89th-minute winner against Liverpool at Anfield in October 1981. United had enjoyed the better of exchanges but a first-half strike by Kevin Moran had been cancelled out by a Terry McDermott penalty and, as time ebbed away, a draw seemed inevitable. However, Arthur hadn't absorbed that particular plotline. Surging through ankle-deep mud, he played a slick one-two with Frank Stapleton, danced past Graeme Souness and slightly mishit a low shot which crept into the far corner of Bruce Grobbelaar's net. It was one of his sweetest moments on a football pitch, especially as it sealed a deserved triumph over the old enemy.

Arthur played for his country – though probably not as often as his unflashy ability merited – and pocketed three FA Cup winner's medals, a Red Devils record at the time, though it has been outstripped since by Ryan Giggs and Roy Keane.

When he was allowed to join West Bromwich Albion on a free transfer in August 1988 at the age of 31, he was as fit and mobile as ever and, arguably, he was still the best left-back at the club. Manchester United, and football in general, need more men like Arthur Albiston.

ARTHUR RICHARD ALBISTON
BORN: Edinburgh, 14 July 1957.
HONOURS: FA Cup 76/7, 82/3, 84/5. 14 Scotland caps (82-86).
OTHER CLUBS: West Bromwich Albion 88/9 (43, 2); Dundee 89/90 (10, 0); Chesterfield 90/1 (3, 1);
            Chester City 91/2-92/3 (68, 0); Molde, Norway, 93/4; Ayr United 93/4 (1, 0).

GAMES   **467 (18)**
GOALS   7

JOHN GIDMAN

1981/82 → 1985/86

The memory of John Gidman galloping joyously down Manchester United's right flank is a precious one to all those Reds supporters who love their soccer with a smile on its face.

John, so typical of the Ron Atkinson era, was a buccaneering full-back who was at his happiest, and most impressive, when surging into attack. Particularly beloved of the Stretford End, he had the flair and charisma to become something of a folk hero, but a succession of serious injuries prevented him from making the maximum impact.

Gidman was Ron's first signing, moving to Old Trafford from Goodison Park in exchange for Mickey Thomas and £50,000 – his own worth was put at £450,000 – in August 1981. With Jimmy Nicholl already at the club, right-back was not a weak position but the manager, always an admirer of the Everton man, could not turn down the chance to add him to United's roster of stars.

John, who made his name and played his sole game for England during a distinguished spell with Aston Villa, surely would have enjoyed an even more illustrious career but for two off-the-field accidents, one of which nearly cost him his sight and the other his life.

Also he was cursed with soccer maladies, being sidelined for most of his second and third campaigns at Old Trafford. John regained fitness in time for the 1985 FA Cup triumph over his former employers but was struck down again in the second match of the next term. On recovery he won back his place but soon it became obvious that he was surplus to requirements and he moved to Manchester City, then Stoke City, before becoming player-coach at Darlington and boss of non-League King's Lynn.

John had his critics, who reckoned he was not defensively sound, and at times that may have been true. But he was exciting and his presence brought an extra dimension to the team. In short, he was the stuff of which Red Devils are made and he will be remembered with pleasure.

JOHN GIDMAN

BORN: Liverpool, 10 April 1954.

HONOURS: FA Cup 84/5. 1 England cap (77).

OTHER CLUBS: Aston Villa 72/3-79/80 (197, 9); Everton 79/80-80/1 (64, 2); Manchester City 86/7-87/8 (53, 1); Stoke City 88/9 (10, 0); Darlington 88/9 (13, 1).

GAMES	116 (4)
GOALS	4

MIKE DUXBURY

1980/81 → 1989/90

What a pity that Mike Duxbury had departed the Old Trafford scene some 12 months before the infusion of a particularly precocious crop of bright young things into the United youth team. The likeable Lancastrian, who served the Reds nobly and unselfishly throughout the 1980s, would have been an impeccable role model for that multi-talented new wave.

Mike's United career may have been overshadowed to a large extent by the comings and goings of expensive star performers, but few of them contributed more to the Red Devils' cause than this loyal, adaptable – and yes, talented – local lad.

He emerged first in 1980/81, Dave Sexton's final season in charge, wearing eight different numbers on his back in the course of 33 games, operating in midfield, at full-back and as sweeper. Many thought right-back was his niche and the arrival of John Gidman seemed to dent his prospects. But Duxbury was so versatile that throughout the reign of Ron Atkinson he was usually somewhere in the starting line-up.

Then, when injury forced John to take a lengthy lay-off, Mike grabbed his chance to such effect that he won ten England caps at right-back. Indeed, on several international occasions his precise distribution, well-timed tackles and fine anticipation made him look one of the most able performers on view.

Perversely it was Mike's exploits for his country which led to a setback in his career. He made several blunders for England which rocked his confidence, and his club form suffered accordingly.

In typically resilient manner Mike battled on. He shrugged off the chance of a move to Everton and resurfaced as one of the most flexible weapons in new boss Alex Ferguson's armoury, undeterred even by the arrival in 1987 of England international right-back Viv Anderson.

Sadly, his efforts in 1988/89 and 1989/90 were marred by knee problems and in the summer of 1990, after making major contributions in the first four ties of United's victorious FA Cup campaign, Mike was freed to join Blackburn Rovers. Later he served under Frank Stapleton at Bradford City.

MICHAEL DUXBURY

BORN: Accrington, Lancashire, 1 September 1959.
HONOURS: FA Cup 82/3, 84/5. 10 England caps (83-84).
OTHER CLUBS: Blackburn Rovers 90/1-91/2 (27, 0); Bradford City 91/2-93/4 (66, 0).

GAMES 345 (33)
GOALS 7

ALAN DAVIES

1981/82 → 1983/84

For a month in 1983 Alan Davies had a tantalising taste of the big time. First the young Welshman, who had turned out in only four League games, played on United's left wing against Brighton in the FA Cup Final. A few days later he was a star turn in the Reds' 4–0 replay triumph, laying on the first goal for Bryan Robson.

Then came an international debut against Northern Ireland and, ten days on, another cap – this time against mighty Brazil. It was hard to believe that before injury had forced Steve Coppell out of the Wembley reckoning, Alan had been just another face in United's Central League line-up.

But, as quickly as the skilful flankman cum midfielder had rocketed to prominence, he disappeared from the limelight. A broken ankle cost him the chance of a first-team spot at the start of the following campaign and he never forced himself back into contention. An entertaining dribbler and fine passer who was perhaps lacking in drive, he joined Newcastle before dropping into the lower divisions.

Ahead, though, lay the kind of tragedy which reduces sporting setbacks to utter irrelevance. In February 1992 Alan Davies, a family man, was found dead in his car near his home in South Wales. He had committed suicide.

ALAN DAVIES
BORN: Manchester, 5 December 1961.
HONOURS: FA Cup 82/3. 11 Wales caps (83–90).
OTHER CLUBS: Newcastle United 85/6–86/7 (21, 1); Charlton Athletic on loan 85/6 (1, 0); Carlisle United on loan 86/7 (4, 1); Swansea City 87/8–88/9 (84, 8); Bradford City 89/90 (26, 1); Swansea City 90/1– 91/2 (43, 4).
DIED: Gower, South Wales, 4 February 1992.

GAMES 8 (2)
GOALS 1

ALAN BRAZIL

1984/85 → 1985/86

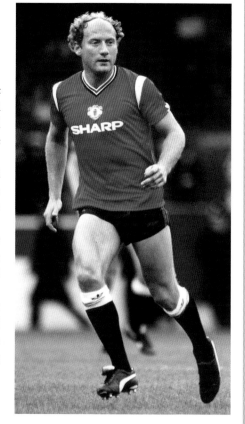

One moment in a crucial clash with Everton summed up the traumatic experience of Alan Brazil at Old Trafford. It was March 1985 and the Reds had to win to maintain their title challenge. Deep in the game the scores were level and stalemate loomed. Suddenly a chance fell to Alan. He struck it well, Neville Southall was beaten . . . and the ball hit the bar before bouncing away.

Had he scored the Championship race might have been transformed and he would have been the hero. As it was he retained the glib tag of misfit with which he had been saddled harshly not long after his £700,000 move from Spurs in June 1984.

It could all have been so different. Brazil was a skilful, strong-running striker who had oozed quality and became a Scottish international while with Ipswich Town. The transfer to Spurs should have made him, but he failed to settle and United effectively got him out of jail.

Sadly, though his strike rate for the Reds was not at all bad, he could not overcome competition from Whiteside, Hughes and Stapleton. Alan never had a real run in the side and his United career withered. Attempts to revive his fortunes elsewhere were dogged by injury and came to nothing. A distressing fall from grace was complete.

ALAN BERNARD BRAZIL
BORN: Glasgow, 15 June 1959.
HONOURS: 13 Scotland caps (80–83).
OTHER CLUBS: Ipswich Town 77/8–82/3 (154, 70); Tottenham Hotspur 82/3–83/4 (31, 9); Coventry City 85/6 (15, 2); Queen's Park Rangers 86/7 (4, 0); FC Baden, Switzerland, 88/9.

GAMES 24 (17)
GOALS 12

GRAEME HOGG

1983/84 → 1987/88

Brave, willing and dependable but not quite good enough for the top level; somehow that always seemed likely to be the verdict on the Old Trafford career of Scotland under-21 centre-half Graeme Hogg.

A burly, rather cumbersome, left-footed stopper whose aerial power was not quite matched by his all-round game, Graeme enjoyed his most successful season in 1984/85 when he played in 29 First Division matches and missed just one tie as United reached the FA Cup Final. At the time, clearly, he had the edge on Gordon McQueen and Kevin Moran in the battle to become Paul McGrath's regular partner, even though injury robbed him of a Wembley place.

Still only 20, he must have been confident that there would be other chances of glory. But after sharing in United's exhilarating start to the following campaign, his fortunes declined with those of the team. Often he was fighting for fitness and slipped out of the reckoning.

Throughout the next two seasons the muscular Aberdonian performed with admirable commitment on his intermittent first-team outings. But when the arrival of Steve Bruce confirmed that he was not part of Alex Ferguson's long-term plans, Graeme, who impressed during a brief loan spell with West Bromwich Albion, accepted that his Red Devil days were over and joined Portsmouth in August 1988.

GRAEME JAMES HOGG
BORN: Aberdeen, 17 June 1964.
OTHER CLUBS: West Bromwich Albion on loan 87/8 (7, 0);
Portsmouth 88/9-90/1 (100, 2); Hearts 91/2-94/5
(58, 3); Notts County 94/5-97/8 (66, 0);
Brentford 97/8 (17, 2).

| GAMES | 108 (2) |
| GOALS | 1 |

PETER BARNES

1985/86 → 1986/87

Whatever the knockers say about Peter Barnes they would do well to remember one thing; he played a thrilling part in the most successful start to a season ever enjoyed by Manchester United. In 1985/86 the Red Devils won their first ten League games and didn't lose until their 16th. And the mercurial winger with the dancing feet was an integral component of a breathtaking side.

Of course, the euphoria in autumn gave way to hesitation in winter and dismay in spring, and the anti-Barnes brigade will claim that summed him up – immense promise followed by failure when it mattered. And there was a cruel truth in that. No one denied his talent, most evident in early Maine Road days, but, too often, application and spirit seemed to be lacking.

Ultimately Peter justified his reputation and faded away before rejoining City – for whom his father Ken had been a brilliantly creative wing-half – in January 1987. But Ron Atkinson's £50,000 gamble in taking him from Coventry 18 months earlier was not wholly in vain. The former England flankman left behind a small but precious fund of memories to cherish.

PETER SIMON BARNES
BORN: Manchester, 10 June 1957.
HONOURS: 22 England caps (77–82).
OTHER CLUBS: Manchester City 74/5–78/9 (115, 15); West Bromwich
Albion 79/80–80/1 (77, 23); Leeds United 81/2 (31, 1); Real Betis,
Spain, 82/3; Leeds United 83/4 (27, 4); Coventry City 84/5 (18, 2);
Manchester City 86/7 (8, 0); Bolton Wanderers on loan 87/8 (2, 0);
Port Vale on loan 87/8 (3, 0); Hull City 87/8 (11, 0),
Farense, Portugal, 88/9; Bolton Wanderers 88/9 (3, 0);
Sunderland 88/9 (1, 0); Tampa Bay Rowdies, USA, 90;
Cliftonville, Northern Ireland, 92/3;
Melbourne City, Australia.

| GAMES | 24 (1) |
| GOALS | 4 |

ARTHUR GRAHAM

1983/84 → 1984/85

Chunky winger Arthur Graham was a budget-priced short-term success. Though nearing the end of his career, the diminutive but combative Scottish international was drafted in from Leeds United for around £30,000 in August 1983 after the premature retirement of Steve Coppell left the Reds without an experienced flankman.

Arthur, once a teenage prodigy with Aberdeen, made an immediate impact with an eye-catching performance in the Charity Shield defeat of Liverpool and he consolidated his position with a string of impressive displays. A strong, tricky runner and an accurate crosser of the ball, he possessed a rasping shot, could operate on either wing and was never loth to chase back and help out in defence.

Though he managed only five League goals himself – something of a disappointment in view of his three hat-tricks for Leeds – he laid on plenty for the likes of Norman Whiteside and Frank Stapleton, and it was a testimony to his outstanding form that Ron Atkinson was content to stick with him until Jesper Olsen arrived the following season.

Just three months short of his 31st birthday when he became a Red Devil, the scampering Scot was never going to be an investment for the future. But he proved such an admirable stopgap that, during one particularly heady interlude, there was even talk of an international recall.

Arthur departed for Bradford City in June 1985, his spirited spell at Old Trafford having proved a worthy sign-off from the top flight. At Valley Parade he went on to coach the youth and reserve teams, also serving a month-long stint as caretaker manager in 1989.

	ARTHUR GRAHAM		
BORN:	Glasgow, 26 October 1952.		
HONOURS:	10 Scotland caps (77-80).	GAMES	47 (5)
OTHER CLUBS:	Aberdeen 69/70-76/7 (228, 34); Leeds United 77/8-82/3 (223, 37); Bradford City 85/6-86/7 (31, 2).	GOALS	7

KEVIN MORAN

1978/79 → 1987/88

Few players have shed more of their own blood on a soccer pitch than Kevin Moran. The fearless, some might say reckless, central defender – surely the owner of the most stitched head in football – served the Red Devils with valiant distinction for an incident-packed decade before Alex Ferguson gave him a free transfer, in recognition of his splendid record, and the club doctor could take life a little more easily.

Kevin, a Republic of Ireland stalwart throughout the 1980s and well into the 1990s, arrived at Old Trafford in 1978 from top-level Gaelic football in Dublin – he had been playing soccer only at university level when he was spotted by the famous scout, Billy Behan – and took a while to adjust to what he had always considered to be his secondary game.

He battled with characteristic commitment until Dave Sexton brought him into the first team, sometimes deploying him as a midfield strongman, for example during the seven-match winning sequence which marked the end of the manager's reign in the spring of 1981.

But Kevin was more effective at the back, where gradually he became established as injuries began to take their toll of Gordon McQueen and Martin Buchan. His distribution, poor at first, improved over the years, though his forte was winning the ball, especially in the air where he made up for a comparative lack of height by his neck-or-nothing approach.

Sometimes his timing was awry, and there were occasions when he was too brave for his own good, which accounted for some of the war wounds.

Despite the tough image, Moran possessed not a vestige of malice and it is a cruel shame that he should have earned immortal notoriety as the first man to be sent off in an FA Cup Final, against Everton in 1985.

TV cameras revealed clearly that he went for the ball and not Peter Reid in the offending tackle, and later he was presented with the winner's medal which was at first withheld. Any other outcome would have unjustly besmirched the honour of an honest and accomplished professional.

On leaving Old Trafford as a 32-year-old in the summer of 1988, it seemed likely that the intelligent Dubliner would wind down to retirement from the game and then pick up the reins of a new career. But not a bit of it. After a season in the Spanish sun Kevin resurfaced at Blackburn, harder to beat than ever, to play a major part in Rovers' rousing resurgence.

KEVIN BERNARD MORAN

BORN: Dublin, 29 April 1956.
HONOURS: FA Cup 82/3, 84/5. 71 Republic of Ireland caps (80-94).
OTHER CLUBS: Bohemians and Pegasus, both Republic of Ireland; Sporting Gijon, Spain, 88/9; Blackburn Rovers 89/90-93/4 (147, 10).

GAMES	284 (5)
GOALS	24

NORMAN WHITESIDE

1981/82 → 1988/89

For four fantastic years, Norman Whiteside was Roy of the Rovers incarnate. Until 1986/87, when the script began to show signs of going wrong, the mountainously built Irish boy-man was the plaything of the headline-writers, serving up sensations seemingly to order.

He scored on his full debut for United, just a couple of months before becoming, at 17, the youngest player to appear in the World Cup Finals. Less than a year later, Norman was the youngest scorer in a Wembley final, contributing a deft strike on the turn against Liverpool in the Milk Cup. Two months on, he inscribed his name on another page of Wembley history as the youngest scorer in an FA Cup Final, thanks to a header against Brighton.

Admittedly there followed the occasional stutter as he fought for a place with the likes of Frank Stapleton, Alan Brazil and Mark Hughes but, at the next whiff of glory, Norman proved there was no one like him for the big occasion. This time it was stroking the goal, a dream of a curler, which deprived Everton of the FA Cup in 1985.

By then the young striker had moved to midfield where his lack of out-and-out pace was less of a handicap and where his consummate ball skills and formidable strength were gainfully employed. One of his greatest assets was the ability to capitalise on unexpected opportunities, perhaps by switching play with an impromptu pass, or by shaping for a piledriver before delivering the most delicate of chips – the audacious duping of Ipswich 'keeper Paul Cooper at Old Trafford in the autumn of '82 comes to mind.

Sadly, there was a less savoury side to his progress. There were incidents, far too many of them, where his natural aggression escalated into raw violence. At times, perhaps, he lost his temper; at others he appeared to be chillingly cynical. Ultimately, as he must realise, such aberrations only punished himself and his team. Running a constant risk of suspension was hardly a help to a side chasing honours.

Such strife somehow seemed linked to a downturn in his playing fortunes. In November 1986 he suffered a knee injury which cost him four matches. In his absence Alex Ferguson replaced Ron Atkinson and the young Ulsterman didn't appear the same player on his return to fitness, apparently giving undue weight to the physical side of his game.

Thereafter his contribution was never as satisfying and he became disillusioned, eventually asking for a transfer. His request was granted but, after a run of poor form and being priced at £1 million, there were no takers.

Norman was still unsettled, his career in the doldrums, when Achilles and knee damage sidelined him for most of 1988/89. There were well documented problems off the pitch, clashes with the manager took place and in July 1989 it was decided that a clean break would benefit both club and player. Accordingly – and sadly to fans who had retained faith that, somehow, there would be a miraculous reprieve for the fallen prodigy – he was sold to Everton for £600,000 down, another £150,000 payable later.

For a while at Goodison Park there were hopeful signs, but the knee trouble refused to go away and after two stop-start seasons, he was forced to retire at 25, an age when most players haven't even reached their peak.

In truth, Norman Whiteside had been descending from his zenith for some time, in a manner of which Roy of the Rovers would not have approved. Commendably, though, he did not wallow in self-pity, setting out instead to become a specialist in foot disorders in a manner that had nothing to do with comic-strip fantasy, a lot to do with real life.

NORMAN WHITESIDE
BORN: Belfast, 7 May 1965.
HONOURS: FA Cup 82/3, 84/5. 38 Northern Ireland caps (82-89).
OTHER CLUBS: Everton 89/90-90/1 (29, 9).

GAMES	256 (18)
GOALS	67

GORDON STRACHAN

1984/85 → 1988/89

Take a tiny, twisting jack-in-the-box, add a shock of red hair and an impish grin, and top it all with one of the canniest of soccer brains – and you've got Gordon Strachan.

When Ron Atkinson paid Aberdeen boss Alex Ferguson £600,000 for his much-in-demand midfielder cum winger – after a tiresome transfer saga involving FC Cologne, who claimed Gordon had signed for them – there were those who reckoned the Scottish international sprite was too small for the English game. 'He'd need to play in a team of giants to survive' was the view of one respected judge.

In his first season Strachan did rather more than survive. He positively thrived, missing only one League game and scoring 15 goals, not to mention the addition of an FA Cup winner's medal to a trophy cabinet bulging with Scottish and European silverware. He had mixed fortunes with penalties though; at first he couldn't miss them, then he couldn't score them.

United fans took Gordon to their hearts for his flair, industry and perky demeanour, glorying in his ability to pick his way daintily through seemingly inpenetrable tangles of bodies and loving his line in defence-splitting passes.

But then, in March 1989 and to the surprise of many at a time when he was enjoying one of his most effective spells, he was allowed to join Leeds United for £300,000. Ferguson reckoned that, at 32, Gordon had run out of steam in Manchester and needed a new challenge.

An Indian summer was a fair bet for such a highly motivated character, but no one could have imagined just how well he would do at Elland Road, where he went on to give six years of fabulous service, including an inspirational 1991/92 campaign in which his new club pipped his old one for the title. For that achievement, no words can convey sufficient credit.

The verdict on his days at Old Trafford? Well, at his best he was a match-winner who hinted at greatness, contributing width and variety to the Red Devils' attack. But, although he trotted out some memorable displays, he did not always live up to the promise of that rousing first term.

If that sounds curmudgeonly, it is not intended to. Gordon was one of the few talents in British soccer who could transform a game with a moment of artistry. And he didn't need giants to help him do it.

GORDON DAVID STRACHAN
BORN: Edinburgh, 9 February 1957.
HONOURS: FA Cup 84/5. 50 Scotland caps (80-92). FWA Footballer of the Year 91.
OTHER CLUBS: Dundee 74/5-76/7 (60, 13); Aberdeen 77/8-83/4 (191, 54); Leeds United 88/9-94/5 (196, 37); Coventry City 94/5-96/7 (26, 0).
MANAGER: Coventry City (96-01); Southampton (01-04); Celtic (05-).

GAMES | 195 (6)
GOALS | 38

JESPER OLSEN

1984/85 → 1988/89

In the words of one of Manchester soccer's sagest observers, the English game didn't teach much to Jesper Olsen. No one would dispute the diminutive Dane's rich talent but, equally, few could realistically describe his stay at Old Trafford as anything but frustrating.

Blind alleys seemed to hold a particular fascination for the £350,000 winger, who arrived from Ajax of Amsterdam in July 1984 with a world-class reputation. This had been fuelled by the spectacular goal he scored for Denmark against England in the European Championship in 1982, and enhanced further by his dashing part in lifting two Dutch championships and a domestic cup.

Reds fans, as ever yearning for a new idol, expected so much, especially after manager Ron Atkinson predicted that Olsen could become United's most exciting player since George Best, and to be fair, Jesper's first season did not wholly dash their hopes.

On his day he looked as though he had the ability to prise open the most clam-like of defences. Feinting, sprinting, shooting, he carried about him the aura of a top-quality entertainer and he completed a promising first campaign by helping United to win the FA Cup.

But thereafter Jesper was frequently disappointing, drifting in and out of the action, rarely leaving a memorable mark. He seemed to run in the wrong directions, possessing the close control and speed to reach the byline yet choosing instead to make wayward darts across the pitch.

His problem, perhaps, was that whereas at Ajax he had been given freedom to roam, at Old Trafford he was expected to patrol the left touchline where he did not always see too much of the ball. Thus he felt increasingly unfulfilled and when he did gain possession he would be too eager to impress, over-elaborate rather than incisive.

Though he was brave enough, Jesper exerted a markedly lightweight physical presence during the Atkinson regime. He became a more tenacious all-round performer under Alex Ferguson but he suffered injuries and it grew steadily more obvious that his style was not suited to the perpetual motion of English soccer.

It was no surprise when he returned to the Continent in November 1988, a £400,000 fee taking him to Bordeaux, where many believed he would rise to heights never scaled in this country. In fact, though he dazzled intermittently, it never came to pass; his most effective days had proved to be earlier in his career. How sad that Manchester United never saw the best of Jesper Olsen.

JESPER OLSEN		
BORN:	Fakse, Denmark, 20 March 1961.	
HONOURS:	FA Cup 84/5. 45 Denmark caps (80-90).	
OTHER CLUBS:	Naestved, Denmark, 77-81 (64,11); Ajax, Holland, 81/2-83/4 (85, 23); Bordeaux, France, 88/9-89/90 (54, 3); Caen, France, 90/1-91/2 (58, 0).	

GAMES **149 (27)**
GOALS **24**

PAUL McGRATH

1982/83 → 1988/89

In a perfect world, Paul McGrath would be recognised as one of the most accomplished British defenders in living memory. This Utopia would have no room for injuries or personal problems; a player would be free to express his talents untrammelled by life's frustrating realities. But there lies the rub in the case of the London-born Republic of Ireland centre-half.

There had never been any doubting the ability of Paul McGrath. It had been blindingly apparent to Ron Atkinson in April 1982 when he paid Dublin club St Patrick's Athletic £30,000 for the unknown youngster. The United manager was not exactly short of central defenders at the time with the likes of Gordon McQueen, Kevin Moran and Martin Buchan on his books, but he predicted that his strapping acquisition could outdo them all.

Paul was strong, fast, good in the air and skilful with both feet. It seemed that all he lacked was experience. Accordingly, he made his debut the following season and impressed both at the back, where he showed every sign of developing into a dominant force, and in midfield, where his rather ungainly gait tended to conceal his all-round competence.

For the next two years Paul's appearance record, not helped by injuries, was intermittent and it was not until the second half of 1984/85 – culminating in a classy FA Cup Final performance against Everton – that he really came into his own. His confidence grew and, despite an occasional penchant for ball-watching, Paul matured into one of the outstanding centre-halves in the First Division.

In 1987 he played for the Football League in its centenary showpiece against the Rest of the World and many observers made him man of the match. It was only a friendly but such was his poise and power when confronted by Diego Maradona and company that soon his name was being linked with some of the top clubs in Europe.

But instead of being a platform for glory with the Red Devils, the occasion proved something of a watershed in his fortunes. Knee problems plagued the Irishman with increasing regularity and off-the-pitch difficulties contributed to his woe, not all of them involving alcohol, leading to lurid newspaper headlines and an acrimonious transfer request.

This was granted but any immediate move was scuppered by a series of cartilage operations and Paul was given the chance to rebuild his Old Trafford career. For three months in the spring of 1989 he appeared to be making the most of the opportunity, and all who marched beneath the United banner were hoping against hope that he would succeed. They knew, and no one was more aware of it than Alex Ferguson, that a willing and able Paul McGrath was an asset of rare quality.

But then the Irishman was involved in another spectacular incident, which proved one too many for the patience of the Old Trafford boss, and that summer Paul was transferred to Aston Villa for a cut-price £450,000. It was a last chance and, to his eternal credit, he grasped it avidly. Often the pain in those long-suffering knees precluded training, but invariably match days found him performing at his best.

In 1992/93, when Villa pushed United so hard for the League title, Paul was voted the players' player of the year. Though there were tales, still, of the occasional scrape, and plainly all his inner demons had not been vanquished, he had salvaged plenty from a career that had been heading, rapidly and unnecessarily, off the rails.

How deeply ironic, too, that as United hunted desperately for an experienced central defender during an injury crisis nearly four seasons later, the 37-year-old McGrath, who had moved on to Derby County, continued to turn in outstanding Premiership performances. If only . . .

PAUL McGRATH
BORN: Ealing, London, 4 December 1959.
HONOURS: FA Cup 84/5. 83 Republic of Ireland caps (85-97). PFA Player of the Year 93.
OTHER CLUBS: Aston Villa 89/90-95/6 (253, 9); Derby County 96/7 (24, 0); Sheffield United 97/8 (12, 0).

GAMES 192 (7)
GOALS 16

TERRY GIBSON

1985/86 → 1986/87

There is a theory that if Terry Gibson was not good enough for Spurs, he could hardly have been up to playing for Manchester United. Although that ignores an admirable interim spell with Coventry – in which he proved that he could score goals in the top flight and without the benefit of star colleagues – there may be some truth in it. But here are some facts, not to prove a point, merely for reflection.

In the first ten League games he started for the Reds, they were undefeated. Ron Atkinson, in the 13 League matches which led to his sacking, picked Terry just once despite the team's goal drought and only three victories. When the terrier-like striker was finally given a run by Alex Ferguson, he was axed after the first defeat in eight games.

All this is not to say that Terry was the answer to United's problems – after all, he scored only one goal – but it does seem an odd way to treat a man who had cost around £400,000. Clearly he never had a realistic chance. How he deserved the change of luck that brought him FA Cup glory so soon after moving to Wimbledon.

TERENCE BRADLEY GIBSON
BORN: Walthamstow, London, 23 December 1962.
OTHER CLUBS: Tottenham Hotspur 79/80-82/3 (18, 4); Coventry City 83/4-85/6 (98, 43); Wimbledon 87/8-92/3 (86, 22); Swindon Town on loan 91/2 (9, 1); Peterborough United 93/4 (1, 0); Barnet 93/4-94/5 (32, 5).

GAMES **15 (12)**
GOALS 1

JOHNNY SIVEBAEK

1985/86 → 1986/87

Danish international Johnny Sivebaek's move to Old Trafford was ill-starred from the start. When United had agreed a £200,000 fee with his home-town club, Vejle, the skilful utility man failed the medical. Then, several weeks later in February 1986, the doctors had second thoughts and the deal went through.

Johnny was largely an unknown quantity but the fans' appetites had been whetted by his stunning goal, shown widely on television, for his country against the Republic of Ireland in a World Cup qualifier. His United debut was at Anfield where, playing in midfield, he showed neat touches but seemed disorientated and the game passed him by. He hardly played again for the rest of 1985/86, but was first choice at right-back for most of the next campaign.

Going forward, Johnny displayed running, crossing and shooting ability but there was doubt about his defensive work, and in August 1987 he joined St Etienne for £250,000, having never adjusted fully to the hectic British game.

JOHN SIVEBAEK
BORN: Vejle, Denmark, 25 October 1961.
HONOURS: 87 Denmark caps (82-92).
OTHER CLUBS: Vejle, Denmark, 80-85 (296, 41); St Etienne 87/8-90/1 (129, 1); Monaco 91/2-92/3 (23, 0), both France; Pescara, Italy, 92/3-93/4 (61, 2); Aarhus, Denmark, 95-97 (28, 0).

GAMES **32 (2)**
GOALS 1

BILLY GARTON

1984/85 → 1988/89

Billy Garton was a useful utility defender who never quite convinced, never quite demonstrated the necessary blend of ability and confidence for the top level, though illness and injury made it difficult to gauge his true prowess. Eventually, indeed, poor Billy was forced out of the game by a debilitating condition which, no doubt, had restricted his level of performance.

Garton was a local youngster who rose through the Reds' youth sides and in 1984/85 progressed into the first-team reckoning, an increasingly rare phenomenon at Old Trafford at that time.

Though a versatile performer, Billy was at his best in the centre, sometimes looking ponderous at full-back. An efficient tackler and user of the ball, his longest and best unbroken run in the senior side was one of eight games in the middle of 1986/87 when Paul McGrath was absent. He let no one down but lacked a degree of dominance, and it was no shock when he was placed on offer at the end of the next campaign.

Then a projected move to Manchester City fell through and he resumed his role as perpetual stand-in until the poignant final verdict on his health was made in May 1990.

WILLIAM FRANCIS GARTON
BORN: Salford, Lancashire, 15 March 1965.
OTHER CLUBS: Birmingham City on loan 85/6 (5, 0).

GAMES **47 (4)**
GOALS 0

VIV ANDERSON

1987/88 → 1990/91

After Manchester United's 2–0 defeat of Arsenal on a murky afternoon in January 1987, Alex Ferguson left Old Trafford a deeply impressed man. It was not so much the performance of his team that moved the Reds' new boss – though that had been encouraging enough – but the spirited showing of the visitors' right-back Viv Anderson.

That day the multi-talented defender, the first black footballer to win a full England cap, gave a display of such frenetic commitment and obvious hatred of losing that Ferguson recognised a kindred spirit. And he decided that here was a battle-hardened campaigner whom he would rather fight alongside than against.

Accordingly, the following summer, Viv signed for United amid much acrimony over the tribunal-ordained fee of £250,000, echoing previous ill-feeling with Arsenal over the purchase of Frank Stapleton.

Though 31, the former Nottingham Forest stalwart, who had played a major part in lifting two European Cups, one League title and two League Cups during his illustrious City Ground tenure, seemed to be a bargain. He was tall and strong, fast and skilful, with long, spidery legs which rendered the fascinating illusion of extending telescopically to pluck the ball away from opponents when there appeared to be no way that he could reach it. In addition, he was a top-class athlete, fitter than many players his junior.

Yet Viv's move to Old Trafford was to bring limited joy. In his first season he was competent but not outstanding, perhaps being hampered by niggling injuries which cost him ten League appearances. Then heel and back problems sidelined him for most of 1988/89, which saw the emergence of the promising Lee Martin to increase competition for full-back places. Thereafter, for the next season and a half, the livewire Midlander strove to overcome his fitness problems, showing splendid good cheer and fortitude in the face of adversity.

In January 1991, by then 34, Viv moved to Sheffield Wednesday on a free transfer and, ironically, soon he was enjoying the sort of injury-free sequence that had characterised his days at Highbury.

He became player-boss of Barnsley in 1993, then switched to Middlesbrough as Bryan Robson's assistant a year later. But the pair never attained the heights expected of them and it remained perplexing that such a determined individual as Viv Anderson, blessed with enthusiasm to burn and endless ideas, was not a long-term success in coaching or management.

VIVIAN ALEXANDER ANDERSON		
BORN:	Nottingham, 29 August 1956.	
HONOURS:	30 England caps (78-88).	
OTHER CLUBS:	Nottingham Forest 74/5-83/4 (328, 15); Arsenal 84/5-86/7 (120, 9); Sheffield Wednesday 90/1-92/3 (70, 8); Barnsley 93/4 (20, 3); Middlesbrough 94/5 (2, 0).	
MANAGER:	Barnsley (93-94).	

GAMES	64 (5)
GOALS	4

PETER DAVENPORT

1985/86 → 1988/89

Peter Davenport could be forgiven for seeing himself as a pawn in some celestial game in which Mark Hughes was very much the king. When the Welshman headed for Barcelona in 1986, United paid £570,000 for the spindly Nottingham Forest and England striker as his replacement. And when Alex Ferguson gleefully brought home the hero of the Stretford End two years later it was, ultimately, Peter who had to make way.

At first, Old Trafford must have seemed like rainbow's end to a man who had been a United supporter as a lad. But when he managed only one goal in his first dozen games, disturbing parallels were quickly drawn with the failure of another former Forest front-man, Garry Birtles. It was a difficult time for Peter to establish himself, a period of transition which saw the sacking of Ron Atkinson and the arrival of Ferguson, who made no secret of his yen for Hughes.

Davenport battled manfully for his future and there were games when his deft control, body swerve and slick turning technique were out of the top drawer, even after he was pushed on to the wing. But 'Sparky's' shadow was ominously substantial and, when it became clear that Peter's role was merely that of a classy reserve, he took himself to Middlesbrough, then Sunderland, in search of the right stage on which to excel.

COLIN GIBSON

1985/86 → 1989/90

Even before Colin Gibson's United career was plagued by mishaps to knee and hamstring, he had become a victim of his own versatility. When he moved to Old Trafford at a cost of £350,000 from Villa Park in November 1985, he seemed earmarked as an alternative for the left-back berth occupied by the excellent, underrated Arthur Albiston. But any struggle between the two for that slot was quickly shelved as an injury crisis pitchforked Colin into midfield duty.

He did a spirited, if unspectacular job, foraging tirelessly and plugging gaps wherever he was needed, but in doing so his hopes of staking a strong claim to his specialist position suffered. Such frustration was not new to Colin. At Villa he had won League Championship honours at left-back and been mentioned as an England prospect in that role, only to become an emergency utility player.

On arrival at Old Trafford his task was made harder by terrace disappointment over the disappearance of a ten-point Championship lead and, not being a 'star', he became something of a target for an unenlightened but highly vocal fringe. Colin overcame that and, without becoming fully established, he chalked up workmanlike spells at the back and in midfield before injury relegated him to the sidelines once more. In December 1990, a £100,000 deal enabled him to make a fresh start at Leicester.

PETER DAVENPORT
BORN: Birkenhead, Cheshire, 24 March 1961.
HONOURS: 1 England cap (85).
OTHER CLUBS: Nottingham Forest 81/2–85/6 (118, 54);
Middlesbrough 88/9–89/90 (59, 7); Sunderland 90/1–92/3 (99,15);
Airdrieonians 93/4 (38, 8); St Johnstone 94/5 (22, 4);
Stockport County 94/5 (6, 1); Macclesfield Town
97/8-98/9 (5, 1).
MANAGER: Macclesfield Town (00).

GAMES	83 (23)
GOALS	26

COLIN JOHN GIBSON
BORN: Bridport, Dorset, 6 April 1960.
OTHER CLUBS: Aston Villa 78/9-85/6 (185, 10);
Port Vale on loan 90/1 (6, 2); Leicester City 90/1-93/4
(59, 4); Blackpool 94/5 (2, 0); Walsall 94/5 (33, 0).

GAMES	89 (6)
GOALS	9

CHRIS TURNER

1985/86 → 1987/88

Chris Turner was a shot-stopper extraordinaire, a man who could perform wonders between the posts. But a 'keeper's jurisdiction extends beyond his white line. He must dominate his goal area, especially in the air and, quite simply, Chris did not do so for Manchester United. When he left that line for high crosses, often he looked out of his element.

Alex Ferguson made no secret of the fact that he wanted a taller custodian, even though at 6ft Chris was the equal in stature of Peter Shilton and only an inch shorter than his medium-term successor, Jim Leighton.

Ron Atkinson had paid Sunderland £250,000 for Turner in the summer of 1985 to provide competition for Gary Bailey, whose form had been variable. It seemed the newcomer had made the right move when Gary suffered serious injury. Chris did well and was even mooted for the England squad, but then came the change of management and the blooding of young Gary Walsh.

Turner asked for a transfer and, after the arrival of Leighton in the 1988 close season, his wish was granted in the form of a second spell at Hillsborough.

CHRISTOPHER ROBERT TURNER

BORN: Sheffield, 15 September 1958.
OTHER CLUBS: Sheffield Wednesday 76/7-78/9 (91, 0); Lincoln City on loan 78/9 (5, 0); Sunderland 79/80-84/5 (195, 0); Sheffield Wednesday 88/9-90/1 (75, 0); Leeds United on loan 89/90 (2, 0); Leyton Orient 91/2-94/5 (58, 0).
MANAGER: Leyton Orient (94-95); Hartlepool United (99-02); Sheffield Wednesday (02-04); Stockport County (04-05).

GAMES	79
GOALS	0

GARY WALSH

1986/87 → 1994/95

A succession of serious injuries called an alarming halt to the impressive progress of Gary Walsh, reckoned by some seasoned professionals to be potentially the finest 'keeper Old Trafford has known since the war, despite suffering six seasons in the wilderness.

The tall, blond Lancastrian displaced Chris Turner towards the end of 1986/87 and kept the job as the next campaign began. His confidence was building steadily when he was concussed at Hillsborough, but he recovered to resume first-team duty, only to take another fearful blow to his head in a friendly in Barbados. His lengthy enforced absence allowed the selflessly supportive Turner to reclaim his place, then Gary's prospects took a further dive when the Reds bought Jim Leighton in May 1988. Ill fortune continued to dog the youngster as he returned from a loan spell at Airdrie with an ankle injury which, for a time, threatened his career. Thereafter Les Sealey was signed and, more crushingly still, Peter Schmeichel arrived in 1991.

But the England under-21 international soldiered on and, after excelling as a stand-in during spring 1994, he signed a new contract. But Alex Ferguson allowed that such a brave, agile and still-youthful performer deserved better than reserve status and in August 1995 the United boss accepted a £250,000 bid from Bryan Robson to take Gary to Middlesbrough. Later he helped Bradford City to reach the top flight.

GARY WALSH

BORN: Wigan, Lancashire, 21 March 1968.
OTHER CLUBS: Airdieonians on loan 88/9 (3, 0); Oldham Athletic on loan 93/4 (6, 0); Middlesbrough 95/6-96/7 (44, 0); Bradford City 97/8-02/03 (132, 0); Middlesbrough on loan 00/01 (3, 0); Wigan Athletic 03/04 (3, 0).

GAMES	62 (1)
GOALS	0

LIAM O'BRIEN

1986/87 → 1988/89

Liam O'Brien never looked short of skill during his short sojourn at Old Trafford. Sadly, he appeared rather less well endowed with confidence. The Eire international midfielder might have benefited from a settled run in the side but, unless outstanding performances are instantly forthcoming, that is an almost extinct luxury for rookies in top-level football.

So Liam never started more than three consecutive games and left for Newcastle, price £275,000, in November 1988. How big a potential asset was allowed to slip away? Well, the tall Irishman has been described as the right-footed Muhren; rather flattering, undoubtedly, but there were games when his passes conjured up visions of the creative Dutchman.

Liam was a composed footballer who was blessed with explosive, if under-used, shooting power, but one who appeared occasionally to lack urgency. He was criticised for being one-paced but could produce a turn of speed, as he showed in one of his latter appearances for United when he came on as a substitute against Everton and almost turned the game. Come the middle and late 1990s, he was shining with Tranmere Rovers, proving that he could hold his own away from the intense pressures of the big time. Talent was never the problem for Liam, only self-belief.

WILLIAM FRANCIS O'BRIEN
BORN: Dublin, 5 September 1964.
HONOURS: 16 Republic of Ireland caps (87-96).
OTHER CLUBS: Shamrock Rovers, Republic of Ireland, 83/4-85/6; Newcastle United 88/9-93/4 (151, 19); Tranmere Rovers 93/4-98/9 (181, 11).

GAMES **17 (19)**
GOALS 2

RALPH MILNE

1988/89 → 1989/90

Ralph Milne could hardly have made a more striking contrast with the man he replaced on Manchester United's left wing. Where Jesper Olsen cut a dashing figure, Ralph was an inelegant, rather hunched mover, with a suggestion of flat feet; where the Dane possessed extravagant talent which often he failed to harness, his Scottish successor was more modestly gifted yet, arguably, a better team man; where Jesper was tricky and unpredictable, Ralph was orthodox and direct; even in appearance the blond, tousle-haired one-time Ajax hero and the neat, dark former under-21 international were worlds apart.

Was Ralph a surprise buy? Certainly he was to most Red fans, weaned on a diet of expensive stars, especially if they knew nothing of his Scottish title medal and 15 goals in European competition for Dundee United.

Refreshingly, he arrived without the now customary transfer saga, his £170,000 move from Bristol City in November 1988 being presented as a *fait accompli*. Ralph was pitched straight into the team and mixed encouraging displays, notably against Oxford in the FA Cup, with nondescript ones. Occasionally he was incisive, more often he lurked on the edges of the action. Added consistency was vital to his Old Trafford future, but he never found it and was freed in June 1991.

RALPH MILNE
BORN: Dundee, 13 May 1961.
OTHER CLUBS: Dundee United 79/80-86/7 (179, 44); Charlton Athletic 86/7-87/8 (22, 0); Bristol City 87/8-88/9 (30, 6); Sing Tao, Hong Kong, 91/2.

GAMES **26 (4)**
GOALS 3

JIM LEIGHTON

1988/89 → 1990/91

Jim Leighton could be excused for cursing the day he joined Manchester United. He arrived with a reputation as one of the world's leading goalkeepers after a decade of success under Alex Ferguson at Aberdeen, and was seen as a key figure in the rebirth of the Red Devils as a major power; he left consumed with bitterness, his football world in tatters, after undergoing a public humiliation of excruciating proportions.

The sensitive Scot's ordeal unfolded during and after United's 3–3 FA Cup Final draw with Crystal Palace in May 1990, though the nightmare scenario had been building steadily for months. Jim had appeared to lose his confidence, together with several teeth, at Wimbledon in December and since then had performed so far below his best that some United fans were turning on him.

The manager deliberated long and hard before picking him for Wembley, only to suffer the mortification of watching the grey-faced custodian sink to his lowest ebb. Jim was blamed, to a lesser or greater degree, for all three Palace goals, as he failed to deal with two high balls and was beaten surprisingly by a low shot.

Ferguson was left with an agonising selection problem for the replay, a dilemma made all the harder by the two men's close previous relationship at Pittodrie. In the end, Alex made the right decision for United: poor Jim was axed in favour of Les Sealey and the Cup went to Old Trafford.

Inevitably in such traumatic circumstances, the rangy Leighton was finished as a Red. After loan spells understudying David Seaman at Arsenal and a more active stint at Reading, he joined Dundee for £150,000 in February 1992.

Ironically, the man who had cost five times that figure in May 1988 was, and remained for the best part of another decade, a good goalkeeper. Indeed, he had started splendidly at United, impressing hugely as a shot-stopper before aerial fallibility found him out.

Some swear to this day that he was merely the victim of a temporary loss of self-belief, a theory borne out by his successful international recall in 1994 at the age of 36. Others, it must be said, still shake their heads. But either way, after all he had endured, unlucky Jim deserved to bask in a little belated glory.

JAMES LEIGHTON	
BORN:	Paisley, Renfrewshire, 24 July 1958.
HONOURS:	91 Scotland caps (82-98).
OTHER CLUBS:	Aberdeen 78/9-87/8 (300, 0); Reading on loan 91/2 (8, 0); Dundee 91/2-92/3 (21, 0); Hibernian 93/4-96/7 (151, 0); Aberdeen 97/8-99/00 (82, 0).

GAMES	94
GOALS	0

DANNY WALLACE

· ·

1989/90 → 1992/93

When Danny Wallace faced Manchester United in a Southampton shirt, invariably he was a study in effervescence, all livewire enterprise and lethal intent, the sort of performer coveted by managers and fans alike. But transposed from Saint to Red Devil, all too often the chunky flankman appeared to be consumed by inhibitions, a sad little rubber ball that had lost its bounce.

So what went wrong for the cheerful Londoner after Alex Ferguson parted with £1.1 million to sign him in September 1989? One theory is that the high-pressure Old Trafford scene was too much for him, that he was better off as a major fish in a comparatively minor pond; another is that he was undermined by a series of niggling injuries.

In retrospect, though, the most compelling explanation appears to be that Danny might have been suffering the early symptoms of the savagely debilitating illness, multiple sclerosis, with which he was diagnosed in 1997.

At the time of his United travail, some observers contended that the oldest of the three footballing Wallace brothers – Rod starred for Leeds and Rangers among others, while Ray featured most notably for Stoke – was simply unsuited to the role demanded of him.

At the Dell he had made his impact, even won an England cap, more as a left-sided striker than as an out-and-out winger. At Old Trafford, he was

usually employed to bring width to the attack by hugging the touchline, a tough task for a raider whose natural game was to cut inside at every opportunity. Occasionally Danny was used as a central striker but that proved too much to ask of such a tiny man – as Tommy Docherty had it, he had to jump for low balls! – and his contribution was minimal.

Yet the Wallace sojourn had begun promisingly enough, with a League Cup goal at Portsmouth on his debut, and in the spring of 1990 there were isolated moments of electric excitement, notably a brilliant FA Cup goal at Newcastle when he sidestepped his marker sublimely before crashing the ball home from a narrow angle.

He helped to lift the Cup that term before his 1990/91 campaign was ruined by fitness problems, though he did return from one lay-off looking sleeker and sharper than ever, and shone in the 6–2 League Cup humbling of Arsenal at Highbury.

In general, though, he seemed devoid of confidence, especially when delivering crosses, and gradually he was overhauled by the young brigade of Giggs and company. In October 1993, Danny joined Birmingham City for £250,000, leaving a tale of perplexing under-achievement behind him. Tragically, far more profound trauma was lying in wait.

DAVID LLOYD WALLACE
BORN: London, 21 January 1964.
HONOURS: FA Cup 89/90. 1 England cap (86).
OTHER CLUBS: Southampton 80/1-89/90 (255, 64); Millwall on loan 92/3 (3, 0); Birmingham City 93/4-94/5 (16, 2); Wycombe Wanderers 94/5 (1, 0).

GAMES **53 (18)**
GOALS **11**

CLAYTON BLACKMORE

....

1983/84 → 1992/93

Clayton Blackmore was both a survivor and something of a curiosity during an enigmatic Old Trafford career. Without ever being a long-term regular – only in 1990/91 could he count on his place – the personable Welshman enjoyed nearly 250 outings and watched a procession of more illustrious names come and go during a ten-year span in the top-level reckoning.

Some said his ability to switch between midfield and full-back prevented him from settling in either role and therefore limited his appearances, while others saw that very versatility as the principal key to his long service.

There was a time, during United's disappointing 1988/89 campaign, when it seemed possible that Clayton might develop into the play-maker the side was so manifestly lacking. At his best – there was one masterful display against Sheffield Wednesday at Hillsborough – he showed poise and precision, spraying passes with confidence and vision.

But the feeling persisted that, while his distribution could be immaculate, he needed a tad too much time on the ball to make it tell consistently.

Clayton's in-and-out existence continued until August 1990, when squad circumstances afforded a new opportunity at left-back. Though right-footed, he took it magnificently, proving safe in defence and exhilaratingly effective as a launcher of attacks, crossing the ball with an accuracy unmatched by many a winger.

More compelling still was the Blackmore expertise from dead-ball situations, his explosive shooting bringing eight goals in his 56 matches, none more vital than the 30-yarder that squirmed through the Montpellier 'keeper's hands to set the Reds on their way to a place in the Cup Winners' Cup semi-final. His most crucial contribution to the European triumph, though, came near the end of the final when, as Barcelona pressed for an equaliser, he cleared Michael Laudrup's goal-bound shot off the line.

Thereafter, the Welshman's fortunes faltered. Paul Parker arrived, Denis Irwin switched to the left and Clayton was back in the shadows, squeezing out just enough appearances for a title statuette in 1992/93.

A succession of injuries laid him low throughout 1993/94, after which he was freed to accept a much-needed new challenge under old chum Bryan Robson at Middlesbrough.

CLAYTON GRAHAM BLACKMORE

BORN: Neath, Glamorgan, 23 September 1964.

HONOURS: European Cup Winners' Cup 90/1. League Championship 92/3. FA Cup 89/90. 39 Wales caps (85-97).

OTHER CLUBS: Middlesbrough 94/5-97/8 (53, 4); Bristol City on loan 96/7 (5, 1); Barnsley 98/9 (7, 0); Notts County 99/00 (21, 2).

| GAMES | 201 (44) |
| GOALS | 26 |

GIULIANO MAIORANA

1988/89 → 1989/90

The football world of Giuliano Maiorana turned upside down in 1988/89, and in doing so fuelled the dreams of enthusiastic amateurs everywhere. The tall left-winger started the campaign working in his family's clothes shop and enjoying his game with Cambridgeshire part-timers Histon United; he finished it in the first-team squad at Old Trafford, with every chance of building on his fairytale foundation. There followed a season in the reserves, learning his trade, but then the script went agonisingly awry as, for no less than four years, Jools was afflicted by serious knee problems.

Events had moved swiftly after United had plucked the dashing teenager from under the noses of other interested clubs. After two brief senior appearances as substitute, he made his full debut against League leaders Arsenal and caused classy full-back Lee Dixon enough problems to suggest that a top-flight future was not out of the question. Maiorana liked to run at defenders, and though he was fearfully raw, there was something in his style that encouraged the club to bear with him. However, with the wealth of brilliant flankmen at Old Trafford in 1994, United allowed Jools to leave on a free transfer. Thus a £30,000 flutter on an unknown flyer had proved unproductive, but it had been worth a try.

GIULIANO MAIORANA
BORN: Cambridge, 18 April 1969.

GAMES	**2 (6)**
GOALS	0

TONY GILL

1986/87 → 1988/89

The footballing fates dealt savagely with Tony Gill, an exuberantly confident utility player who had every chance of fashioning a long-term future at Old Trafford until his career was sabotaged by injuries.

He made his senior debut as an 18-year-old stand-in for Bryan Robson at Southampton in January 1987 and then suffered his first reverse. Achilles tendon trouble was diagnosed and it took two operations, and nearly two years, before he returned to contention. Indeed, some observers thought that, in the way of so many promising youngsters, Tony's flame had flickered briefly before being extinguished. But then, with United gripped by an injury crisis in November 1988, he returned to fill in at full-back and in midfield, making an excellent impression.

His second arrival saw him labelled as one of Fergie's Fledglings, a ludicrous and inappropriate reference to the Busby Babes. But, unmoved by the hype, Tony established himself in the squad and made some sterling contributions, including a sweet, half-volleyed equaliser in an FA Cup replay against QPR. Then came disaster: that spring the young Yorkshireman had his leg and ankle shattered in an horrendous accidental collision with Nottingham Forest's Brian Laws and he never played again at senior level.

Typically, though, he didn't despair and made a fresh start as youth coach with Bristol Rovers before leaving the game.

ANTHONY DEAN GILL
BORN: Bradford, Yorkshire, 6 March 1968.

GAMES	**7 (7)**
GOALS	2

RUSSELL BEARDSMORE

1988/89 → 1991/92

Russell Beardsmore took the surest path into the hearts of Manchester United supporters – he put one over on Liverpool. Well, three actually.

He could hardly have chosen more glorious circumstances in which to prove his mettle: United had just gone a goal down to the old enemy in front of nearly 50,000 fans and a TV audience of millions. It was time for the chirpily waiflike crewcut kid with the scrawny frame of a pipe-cleaner to take centre stage.

First he charmed his way past three men to make a spectacular equaliser for Brian McClair, next he helped set up a goal for Mark Hughes and then, joy of joys, he volleyed the third with all the panache Old Trafford demands of its heroes.

Did this heady extravaganza on New Year's Day 1989 herald the birth of a star? Poignantly, the answer is no. Russell, a stand-in full-back before moving to a wide midfield position in an injury crisis, had abundant skill, engaging eagerness and an instinct for taking up dangerous positions. And, more than any young Red for decades, he had the crowd on his side. Perhaps satiated with costly imports, the fans warmed to the 5ft 6in local lad; indeed, when he wasn't playing, they chanted for the England under-21 international's introduction.

But in the seasons that followed, Russell failed to impose himself with any degree of consistency. The ability was always evident, but his frail body was in chronic need of more beef; quite simply, he never seemed strong enough for the physical demands of top-flight football.

The arrival of costly new players and the rapid development of other youngsters brought more competition than he could handle, and he had faded to the periphery of the squad by the time a loan stint with Blackburn offered a fresh opportunity in December 1991.

Nothing came of that, though, and Russell was freed to join Bournemouth in the summer of 1993. For half a decade and more, he thrived at Dean Court, but when chronic back trouble ended the Beardsmore career in 1999, that glorious New Year's Day seemed a long, long time ago.

RUSSELL PETER BEARDSMORE
BORN: Wigan, Lancashire, 28 September 1968.
OTHER CLUBS: Blackburn Rovers on loan 91/2 (2, 0); Bournemouth 93/4-97/8 (178, 4).

GAMES **39 (34)**
GOALS **4**

LEE MARTIN

* *

1987/88 → 1993/94

Plenty of shrewd judges reckoned Lee Martin was United's player of the year in 1989/90, and not just because the rookie full-back scored the goal that took the FA Cup to Old Trafford. He seemed to have arrived as a long-term fixture in the team and his subsequent reversal of fortune, culminating in departure to Celtic, represented a sorry anti-climax.

Locally-born Lee had broken into the senior reckoning during trying times for a United side toiling through a period of transition. Watching him perform with maturity and composure at home to Queen's Park Rangers in August 1988, it was hard to believe he was making his full debut. Clearly, here was a beacon of hope for the future.

That autumn Lee suffered an injury setback, but he was on hand to play a prominent role in revitalising the Reds' flagging fortunes at the turn of the year. The continued absence of Viv Anderson gave him the chance of a lengthy run in the team and he responded with a string of resourceful displays.

By May 1990, the Martin outlook was bright indeed; England under-21 honours had been won and Ferguson was not alone in believing the youngster had prospects at full international level.

That golden moment in the Wembley replay against Crystal Palace, when Lee galloped forward to meet Neil Webb's beautiful pass and lash the ball high into Nigel Martyn's net, should have provided inspiring extra impetus. But just as he was set to consolidate, Lee suffered a back injury and managed only a few appearances during 1990/91. When he regained fitness, even his ability to play on either defensive flank was not enough to regain lost ground, with newly arrived Denis Irwin bedding in on the right and Clayton Blackmore in prime form at number three.

Suddenly, Lee was on the margins, no fitting place for a natural full-back whose all-round efficiency needed, perhaps, only a smidgin more aggression to propel him towards the highest class. It was scant consolation that he became skipper of the reserves, in which he remained until Lou Macari paid £250,000 to rescue him in January 1994. Sadly, he was no luckier at Parkhead than he was at Old Trafford, breaking his leg in a freak accident against Falkirk. On recovery, he headed west to seek better fortune with Bristol Rovers, only for back problems to end his League career.

LEE ANDREW MARTIN

BORN: Hyde, Cheshire, 5 February 1968.
HONOURS: FA Cup 89/90.
OTHER CLUBS: Celtic 93/4-94/5 (19, 0); Bristol Rovers 96/7-97/8 (25, 0); Huddersfield Town on loan 97/8 (3, 0).

GAMES 84 (26)
GOALS 2

MARK ROBINS

1988/89 → 1991/92

Alex Ferguson dubbed Mark Robins the best finisher at Old Trafford – and then he sold him. Here was an apparent contradiction between word and deed, yet both the manager's initial statement and his subsequent course of action made sense.

Certainly, when confronted with a clear goal-scoring opportunity, the predatory little Lancastrian was likely to make the most of it with a straightforward economy missing in the work of, say, Mark Hughes. Not for Robins the dramatic flourish, the breathtaking athleticism; instead, a simple, brisk efficiency that was considerably more reliable.

Yet, the act of scoring aside, there was simply no comparison between the overall contribution of the two Marks. While the younger man was skilful enough, he offered little outside the box; in contrast, the Welshman exerted huge presence in all attacking areas, being especially adept at holding the ball, a knack crucial to United's style.

Not that Ferguson had wanted to get rid of the popular 'Mark II'. Even after the prolific 22-year-old had made it plain he was not happy to operate as a perpetual substitute – though that was his most effective niche – his boss asked him to change his mind. But, wisely perhaps, the player decided that he was likely to remain dispensable as a Red and accepted an £800,000 move to Norwich City in August 1992.

Robins had tasted senior action for the first time in 1988/89, but was goalless until the following term. Then, though granted only 13 full outings, he scored ten times, including a precisely nodded winner at Nottingham Forest in the FA Cup, a strike which, rightly or wrongly, has entered Old Trafford folklore as the goal that saved the hard-pressed Ferguson's job. Mark went on to net the semi-final replay winner against Oldham, a deliciously cool piece of work that summed up his value.

Come the autumn of 1990 he ousted Hughes on merit and did well, but at the first lapse in form he was out, destined never to be first choice again. There might have been a chance in 1992, when a goal drought cost United the title, but he was unfit and the moment was gone. So when the Canaries came calling, Mark Robins flew the United coop, making a fine start at Carrow Road before more injuries interrupted his progress. A subsequent move to Leicester brought a League Cup winner's medal in 1997, then in 2000/01 his goals helped Rotherham rise to the First Division.

MARK GORDON ROBINS

BORN:	Ashton-under-Lyne, Lancashire, 22 December 1969.
HONOURS:	FA Cup 89/90.
OTHER CLUBS:	Norwich City 92/3-94/5 (67, 20); Leicester City 94/5-96/7 (56, 12); FC Copenhagen, Denmark, on loan 96/7; Reading on loan 97/8 (4, 0); Orense, Spain, 97/8; Panionios, Greece, 98/9; Manchester City on loan 98/9 (2, 0); Walsall 99/00 (40, 6); Rotherham United 00/01-03/04 (108, 44); Bristol City on loan 02/03 (6, 4); Sheffield Wednesday 03/04 (15, 3).
MANAGER:	Rotherham United (07-).

GAMES	27 (43)
GOALS	17

DEREK BRAZIL

1988/89 → 1989/90

A Republic of Ireland 'B' international who could not force his way beyond the fringes of the Red Devils' senior squad. Derek was a strapping central defender who was sold to Cardiff for £85,000 and helped to lift the Third Division title.

DEREK MICHAEL BRAZIL
BORN: Dublin, 14 December 1968.
OTHER CLUBS: Oldham Athletic on loan 90/1 (1, 0); Swansea City on loan 91/2 (12, 1); Cardiff City 92/3–95/6 (115, 1).

GAMES	0 (2)
GOALS	0

GARTH CROOKS

1983/84

Described as 'Black Magic in the box' during his prime as a Spur, Garth was a dashing striker, imbued with endless vitality and considerable flair, who was not granted enough chances to make a significant impact on loan with the Reds from Tottenham Hotspur.

GARTH ANTHONY CROOKS
BORN: Stoke, Staffordshire, 10 March 1958.
OTHER CLUBS: Stoke City 75/6–79/80 (147, 48); Tottenham Hotspur 80/1–84/5 (125, 48); West Bromwich Albion 85/6–86/7 (40, 16); Charlton Athletic 86/7–90/1 (56, 15).

GAMES	6 (1)
GOALS	2

MARK DEMPSEY

1983/84 → 1985/86

A workmanlike midfielder who first tasted League action on loan at Swindon, he never laid claim to a long-term Old Trafford berth and was sold to Sheffield United for £20,000. Later he won a Fourth Division title medal with Rotherham.

MARK JAMES DEMPSEY
BORN: Manchester, 14 January 1964.
OTHER CLUBS: Swindon Town on loan 84/5 (5, 0); Sheffield United 86/7–87/8 (63, 8); Chesterfield on loan 88/9 (3, 0); Rotherham United 88/9–90/1 (75, 7).

GAMES	1 (1)
GOALS	0

DEINIOL GRAHAM

1987/88 → 1988/89

A goal-getter supreme for Wales schoolboy and youth sides, Deiniol never made the requisite step up to make the grade with United. He impressed early on, with a crucial FA Cup goal against QPR, but a broken arm blighted his progress.

DEINIOL WILLIAM THOMAS GRAHAM
BORN: Cannock, Staffordshire, 4 October 1969.
OTHER CLUBS: Barnsley 91/2–93/4 (38, 2); Preston North End on loan 92/3 (8, 0); Carlisle United on loan 93/4 (2, 1); Stockport County 94/5 (11, 2); Scunthorpe United 95/6 (3, 1).

GAMES	1 (2)
GOALS	1

LAURIE CUNNINGHAM

1982/83

A world-class wing talent who was feted in Spain before his lustre was dimmed by a debilitating sequence of injuries, Laurie never became established at Old Trafford and subsequently wandered Europe before his death in a car crash.

LAURENCE PAUL CUNNINGHAM
BORN: Holloway, London, 8 March 1956.
HONOURS: 6 England caps (79–80).
OTHER CLUBS: Orient 74/5–76/7 (75, 15); West Bromwich Albion 76/7–78/9 (86, 21); Real Madrid, Spain, 79/80–82/83; Sporting Gijon, Spain, 83/4; Marseille, France, 84/5–85/6; Leicester City on loan 85/6 (15, 0); Rayo Vallecano, Spain, 86/7; Real Betis, Spain, 87/8; Charleroi, Belgium, 87/8; Wimbledon 87/8 (6, 2); Rayo Vallecano 88/9.
DIED: Madrid, 15 July 1989.

GAMES	3 (2)
GOALS	1

MARK HIGGINS

1985/86

As captain of Everton and a high-quality stopper, Mark was laid low by a pelvic injury in 1984. Courageously, and against expectations, he recovered and joined United for £60,000, but he could not regain his old form and signed for Bury.

MARK NICHOLAS HIGGINS
BORN: Buxton, Derbyshire, 29 September 1958.
OTHER CLUBS: Everton 76/7–83/4 (152, 6);
Bury 86/7–87/8 (68, 0); Stoke City 88/9–89/90 (39,1).

GAMES **8**
GOALS 0

STEVE PEARS

1984/85

Gary Bailey was the obstacle between Steve and a decent first-team run as a Red Devil. Both agile on his line and assured when claiming crosses, he went on to prove his mettle at Middlesbrough and earn mention as an England possible.

STEPHEN PEARS
BORN: Brandon, County Durham, 22 January 1962.
OTHER CLUBS: Middlesbrough on loan 83/4 (12, 0);
Middlesbrough 85/6–94/5 (327, 0); Hartlepool
United 96/97 (16, 0).

GAMES **5**
GOALS 0

JEFF WEALANDS

1982/83 → 1983/84

An experienced custodian drafted in as reliable cover for Gary Bailey, loan-signing Jeff was called quickly into action when the England international was injured. He started with two clean sheets and was rewarded with a short contract.

JEFFREY ANDREW WEALANDS
BORN: Darlington, County Durham, 26 August 1951.
OTHER CLUBS: Darlington 71/2 (28, 0); Hull City 71/2–
78/9 (240, 0); Birmingham City 79/80–81/2 (102, 0);
Oldham Athletic on loan 84/5 (10, 0); Preston North End
on loan 84/5 (4, 0).

GAMES **8**
GOALS 0

NEIL WHITWORTH

1990/91

A 17-year-old centre-half who cost £45,000 when recruited from Wigan in July 1990, Neil never forced his way into permanent contention as a Red Devil, but the club pocketed £265,000 when he joined Kilmarnock some four years later.

NEIL ANTHONY WHITWORTH
BORN: Wigan, Lancashire, 12 April 1972.
OTHER CLUBS: Wigan Athletic 89/90 (2, 0); Preston North
End on loan 91/2 (6, 0); Barnsley on loan 91/2 (11, 0);
Rotherham United on loan 93/4 (8, 1); Blackpool on
loan 93/4 (3, 0); Kilmarnock 94/5-97/8 (76, 3); Wigan
Athletic 97/8 (4, 0); Hull City 98/9–99/00 (19, 2);
Exeter City 00/01-02/03 (57, 1).

GAMES **1**
GOALS 0

IAN WILKINSON

1991/92

A young goalkeeper who found it impossible to overturn the existing Old Trafford order in the daunting shapes of Peter Schmeichel, Les Sealey and Gary Walsh. Sadly, after joining Crewe, his career was ended prematurely by injury.

IAN MATTHEW WILKINSON
BORN: Warrington, Lancashire, 2 July 1973.
OTHER CLUBS: Crewe Alexandra 93/4 (3, 0).

GAMES **1**
GOALS 0

DAVID WILSON

1988/89

He never started a senior match for the Reds but showed enough potential in central midfield to suggest that he might mature into a worthy performer. The breakthrough proved elusive, however, and he was forced to lower his sights.

DAVID GRAHAM WILSON
BORN: Burnley, Lancashire, 20 March 1969.
OTHER CLUBS: Lincoln City on loan 90/1 (3, 0);
Charlton Athletic on loan 90/1 (7, 2); Bristol Rovers
91/2–92/3 (11, 0); Norwegian football.

GAMES **0 (6)**
GOALS 0

NICKY WOOD

1985/86 → 1986/87

There seemed no reason why the tall, dashing attacker, who had excelled with England Youth, should not go on to succeed at senior level. No reason, that is, until a cruel catalogue of back problems forced him to quit the game at the age of 22.

NICHOLAS ANTHONY WOOD
BORN: Oldham, Lancashire, 6 January 1966.

GAMES **2 (2)**
GOALS 0

PAUL WRATTEN

1990/91

A sparky midfielder whose Old Trafford tenure was dogged by nagging injury problems. Probably as a consequence, the England schoolboy and youth international never progressed beyond the senior bench before departing.

PAUL WRATTEN
BORN: Middlesbrough, Yorkshire, 29 November 1970.
OTHER CLUBS: Hartlepool United 92/3–93/4 (57, 1).

GAMES **0 (2)**
GOALS 0

MAL DONAGHY

1988/89 → 1991/92

Some players catch the eye, their every move on – and sometimes off – the pitch provoking reaction from supporters and media alike. Others can spend a match, a season or even a career, playing a vital role unobtrusively yet with consummate efficiency. Mal Donaghy is a perfect example of the latter category.

He joined United, the team he idolised as a boy, after ten years at Luton during which he barely missed a match. His consistency, usually at full-back or in the centre of defence but occasionally in midfield, was a byword and, with every respect to Luton, it's a wonder that a big club had not lured him away from Kenilworth Road much earlier.

When Alex Ferguson, beset by injuries, needed an all-purpose defender of proven ability, Donaghy was the natural choice.

The manager was criticised in some quarters for shelling out £650,000 for a 31-year-old but he knew that the widely experienced Northern Ireland international was fitter than many a younger man and could point to a remarkably injury-free decade.

So, in the autumn of 1988, Mal realised his childhood ambition to become a Red Devil. He lined up alongside Steve Bruce and became an unflappable bastion of the side for the remainder of that campaign, showing subtle positional sense and a sure touch on the ball. His presence helped to stabilise a season that was going downhill fast and to create a platform for the youth-inspired New Year revival.

Hamstring injuries plagued Mal for much of the following term, and when he was loaned back to Luton in midwinter it seemed that his taste of the high life was to be brief. But Ferguson knew what a gem of a standby the quiet Ulsterman was, and in 1990/91 Donaghy excelled when Bruce was sidelined. His calm reliability alongside Gary Pallister was particularly evident at home to Montpellier in the Cup Winners' Cup and in the second leg of the League Cup semi-final at Leeds.

In August 1992, a month before his 35th birthday, he joined Chelsea for £150,000, having given invaluable service to the club closest to his heart. When Mal Donaghy was in the team he played well, when he was out he didn't complain; no manager could have asked for more.

MALACHY MARTIN DONAGHY

BORN: Belfast, 13 September 1957.
HONOURS: 89 Northern Ireland caps (80-94).
OTHER CLUBS: Luton Yown 78/9-88/9 (410, 16); Luton Town on loan 89/90 (5, 0); Chelsea 92/3-93/4 (68, 3).

GAMES **98 (21)**
GOALS **0**

MICKY PHELAN

1989/90 → 1993/94

There was no trace of stardust about Micky Phelan. No hush of expectation descended on Old Trafford when he received the ball, eager interviewers didn't hang on his every word, the United souvenir shop was not festooned with posters of the down-to-earth Lancastrian. But every top club needs men like him, and if that sounds like a patronising reference to a performer who tends to be placed all too glibly in the 'bits-and-pieces' category, then this writer apologises unreservedly.

True, he was adaptable and fulfilled the popular image of the honest journeyman, labouring ceaselessly but unspectacularly, filling in ably wherever he was needed in midfield or defence. But it should not be forgotten that after his £750,000 transfer from Norwich in July 1989 – the first of Alex Ferguson's five major deals that summer and autumn – Micky completed a full set of domestic medals, adding a European Cup Winners' Cup gong for good measure. No mean achievement, no mean player.

Indeed, during his first season at Old Trafford he was United's only ever-present in the League, then missed a mere handful of outings the next term before injury curtailed his contribution in 1991/92. After that the competition for places hotted up, but still he made enough appearances to deserve his title statuette come the spring of 1993.

At first, the presence of Bryan Robson and the rest had forced the right-sided Phelan into a role on the left flank of midfield in which he looked out of place, and it was only later, when injuries to others allowed him to move into the centre, that his all-round competence was seen to full advantage.

At various junctures the former Canaries captain – he succeeded Steve Bruce in that job – also excelled at right-back and alongside the centre-half, a position which some authorities reckoned to be his best. He was an expert man-marker, too, as he proved to Roy Keane's chagrin in the 1992 League Cup Final triumph over Nottingham Forest.

Though Micky was approaching 33 by the summer of 1994, most clubs might have found continued use for his fitness, experience and general nous, but such was the pressure from a new generation of young Red Devils that he was granted a free transfer. Thereafter he served West Bromwich Albion before an interlude as Stockport's assistant manager was followed by a welcome return to Old Trafford as a coach.

MICHAEL CHRISTOPHER PHELAN

BORN: Nelson, Lancashire, 24 September 1962.
HONOURS: European Cup Winners' Cup 90/1. League Championship 92/3. FA Cup 89/90. League Cup 91/2. 1 England cap (89).
OTHER CLUBS: Burnley 80/1-84/5 (168, 9); Norwich City 85/6-88/9 (156, 9); West Bromwich Albion 94/5-95/6 (21, 0).

GAMES 127 (19)
GOALS 3

BRYAN ROBSON

1981/82 → 1993/94

When Steve Bruce placed the crown-shaped lid of the Premiership trophy on the head of Bryan Robson at the climax of one of Old Trafford's most unforgettable nights, nothing could have been more appropriate. It was May 1993, the long League wait was over and the player who had striven most ceaselessly to end it was honoured in a manner befitting his regal contribution.

That term his outings had been strictly rationed, but his great fighting heart was as inspirational as ever in lifting his team with counsel both sage and stirring. And when he did take the field, there was not the slightest doubt that, even though mobility had declined in his 37th year, the appetite for the fray was as sharp as ever.

Once or twice, it's true, the frustration at enforced inactivity boiled over into excessive vigour, but there was no condemnation from the game at large. In the context of such magnificent defiance in the face of *anno domini*, it seemed that the odd aberration from a favourite son could be excused.

Robbo had always been a lion-like competitor, as evidenced by the countless minutely documented incidents which bejewelled his glorious career. Yet 20 seconds of hectic action in a long-forgotten 1982 encounter with Notts County summed up his qualities as forcefully as any of them.

The Reds' skipper scrapped for possession on the edge of his own box, won it, bamboozled two opponents with an immaculate turn and gave the ball to Moses. Then he sprinted for County's goal as the move continued through Duxbury and Muhren and arrived in time to nod the Dutchman's cross inside the far post from eight yards. It was a typically dashing contribution by 'Captain Marvel', who had arrived at Old Trafford for a record £1.5 million fee in October 1981.

Though Bryan, already an England midfielder, was clearly an outstanding player, there were rumbles at the time that the price was exorbitant and Ron Atkinson's judgement in handing so much cash to his former club was called into question. But Ron, who had been advised by Bill Shankly, no less, to pay whatever it took to get Robson, had no doubts. As he said at the time: 'Now we have someone who can take a game by the scruff of the neck and make things happen.'

And so he did. After a solid, unflashy start, Bryan Robson became an ever more dominant force. Soon he took over the captaincy, both of club and country, from Ray Wilkins and proceeded to lead by example. A dynamo in defence, attack and all points between, he became a motivator supreme. At its peak, Bryan's game had no discernible weakness. His tackling, passing, shooting and heading were all exemplary; power and pace he possessed in abundance; and his reading of the game was mature, even looking back to his early days at the Hawthorns.

But Bryan was cursed with one bane – injury. With the Baggies he broke a leg three times in 12 months; after moving north he missed scores of games, often at crucial times for United and England. Some blamed him for being too brave – it's a testimony to his stature that critics turned what would have been a virtue in anyone else into a supposed blemish in Bryan's case – but this was patently absurd. To have asked him to hold back, even slightly, would have been to deny his nature and therefore nullify what was special about him.

His finest hour? There were so many, but the sheer strength of will which characterised his gladiatorial two-goal display at the core of the Red Devils' rousing comeback from apparent oblivion against Barcelona at Old Trafford in March 1984 summed him up to perfection and probably would win the popular vote.

Ten years later, after playing a comparatively minor, but still telling, part in claiming a second successive Championship, Bryan left to manage Middlesbrough. Now United faced a playing future without a man in whose absence they had shrivelled so often, a man who hefted the FA Cup a record three times, a man apart. Meanwhile 'Boro looked to Robbo to prove once again that he was, as Ron Atkinson put it more than once, pure gold.

There followed seven years of triumph and disappointment before he departed the Riverside, bloodied but unbowed, and it seemed certain that here was one warrior-chief of whom the battlefield that is English football had not seen the last. So it proved, and even though not all his subsequent managerial adventures ended gloriously, the Bryan Robson story was far from over as he celebrated his personal half-century in 2007.

BRYAN ROBSON	
BORN:	Chester-le-Street, County Durham, 11 January 1957.
HONOURS:	European Cup Winners' Cup 90/1. League Championship 92/3, 93/4.
	FA Cup 82/3, 84/5, 89/90. 90 England caps (80-91).
OTHER CLUBS:	West Bromwich Albion 74/5-81/2 (198, 39); Middlesbrough 94/5-96/7 (25, 1).
MANAGER:	Middlesbrough (94-01); Bradford City (03-04); West Bromwich Albion (04-06);
	Sheffield United (07-08).

GAMES	**437 (25)**
GOALS	99

NEIL WEBB

1989/90 → 1992/93

It was a day of bravado and false promise at Old Trafford, a day of flattering to deceive. First Michael Knighton, who purported to be on the verge of buying the club, did party tricks with a football in front of the Stretford End; then Neil Webb, the new midfield general, played beautifully and scored a spectacular goal in an uplifting 4–1 victory over reigning champions Arsenal. It was the perfect start to the 1989/90 campaign; the sun shone on a shirtsleeved crowd and everyone went home happy, fantasising about the Reds' latest new dawn, indulging in careless talk about the title.

The idyll didn't last: Knighton withdrew his offer, the team slumped towards the wrong end of the table and, after only four League outings, poor Neil Webb ruptured an achilles tendon while playing for England. He was never the same again.

The mild-mannered schemer had arrived from Nottingham Forest in the close season, two years after United's initial bid had been rejected by Brian Clough. Now the player was out of contract and the £1.5 million fee was determined by a transfer tribunal.

Neil's attraction was as a creator who could also score goals. Alex Ferguson wanted his vision and range of passing, his composure and control, and never mind an awkward, rather languid style that gave rise to accusations of lack of urgency. With Bryan Robson and the soon-to-be-signed Paul Ince supplying the physical edge, the manager felt the balance would be right.

The humbling of Arsenal boded well, but then came a chronic blow to Ferguson's plans, the accident in Sweden which sidelined the right-sided play-maker for seven months.

On his return in March, Neil was bulkier and slower than before but able still to exert a telling influence on a lacklustre side. He helped them stave off relegation and made a compelling contribution to their FA Cup triumph, most memorably in the final replay against Crystal Palace when his raking 50-yard crossfield pass set up Lee Martin's winner.

Yet over the next two seasons, Neil was an enigma. Sometimes he sprayed the ball around delightfully, but too often his presence was anonymous, as though he were consumed with self-doubt, his distribution lacking the degree of penetration his natural ability promised.

In 1990/91 he struggled manfully to improve his all-round fitness and was devastated when omitted from the European Cup Winners' Cup Final starting line-up. The autumn of 1991 saw him apparently brighter and hungrier than ever before, and he did so well as United led the title race that he was recalled to the international scene, captaining England 'B' in December.

But then it all went wrong. In March he was involved in a spat with Ferguson over his non-release for an England friendly, and he was dropped; indeed, some even blamed the Reds' subsequent failure to win the League on that decision.

Whatever, from that point Neil Webb's days at Old Trafford were numbered and in November 1992 he returned to Forest for £800,000. Whether he had been 'too nice' to meet United's exacting expectations, or had been treated unsympathetically, or had been plain unlucky, was all a matter for regretful conjecture.

NEIL JOHN WEBB

BORN: Reading, Berkshire, 30 July 1963.

HONOURS: FA Cup 89/90. 26 England caps (87-90).

OTHER CLUBS: Reading 79/80-81/2 (72, 22); Portsmouth 82/3-84/5 (123, 34); Nottingham Forest 85/6-88/9 (146, 47) and 92/3-93/4 (30, 3); Swindon Town on loan 94/5 (6, 0); Grimsby Town 96/7 (4, 0).

GAMES **105 (5)**

GOALS **11**

BRIAN McCLAIR

1987/88 → 1997/98

From the Red Devils' most prolific goal-scoring hero in 20 years, to selfless midfield workhorse, to faithful retainer on the fringe of the first team and the reserves' *eminence grise*: Brian McClair ran a gamut of decreasingly glamorous roles during the Alex Ferguson years. Yet there was never a murmur of public discontent from the versatile, ever-willing Scottish international, whose influential role in the renaissance of Manchester United should never be underrated.

When Brian walked into the strikers' graveyard of Old Trafford, it became clear immediately that he was not destined to be the latest in a long line of expensive stiffs. Early goals, combined with a fatalistic attitude to missed chances, furnished clues to the calibre of the man for whom Celtic had demanded £2 million before settling for £850,000 after arbitration in July 1987.

Yet on the face of it the ordeal facing the stocky marksman, who had netted 41 times and been voted Scotland's player of the year in his final campaign north of the border, was more daunting than for most United newcomers. Firstly, he had to acclimatise himself to the more rigorous demands of the English game; secondly, he was saddled publicly by his new boss with the unwelcome burden of becoming the first Red since George Best in the 1960s to score 20 League goals in a season.

The pressure from media and fans was intense, and Alex Ferguson added his two penn'orth by declaring that Brian was just the man to lay the ghost. The intelligent, level-headed 'Choccy' didn't flinch: he merely got on with the job and duly notched his 20 goals. Well, 24 in fact, not to mention another seven in the major cup competitions.

The following term he started slowly as he strove to build a partnership with returned favourite Mark Hughes. Gradually, as an understanding showed signs of blossoming, Brian began to find the net with some regularity again, never more rousingly than with a slickly executed scissor-kick at home to Liverpool on New Year's Day.

Then came a late-season lull, during which his talents were deployed occasionally in midfield, thus signalling a new phase in his career. The next three campaigns saw him giving his all, sometimes up front, at others lying deep, before settling in the engine room during 1992/93.

Brian began that term motoring up and down the right flank, later occupying a central berth as the arrival of Eric Cantona prompted a reshuffle. Some reckoned he possessed insufficient weight of tackle for his new position, but none questioned his stamina or commitment, and his nine goals were of huge significance in the final Championship analysis.

He had been Ferguson's first major signing, so it was fitting that the man whose 100th senior goal for the club settled the 1992 League Cup Final against Nottingham Forest should be instrumental in the overdue title triumph. But a cruel setback awaited: Roy Keane arrived that summer and the 29-year-old Scot found himself reduced to stand-in status.

However, the manager predicted Robsonesque longevity for his ultra-fit countryman and demonstrated good faith by offering a new contract. 'Choccy' accepted and buckled down to continue his trusty part in United's never-ending trophy quest.

He was still trucking in 1997/98, after which he was freed to complete his playing days at Motherwell before moving to Blackburn to assist his chum, Brian Kidd. Later he returned to Old Trafford as a coach, then took over as manager of the club's youth academy. With the benefit of hindsight, Celtic's original valuation of Brian McClair no longer seemed quite so extraordinary.

BRIAN JOHN McCLAIR

BORN: Airdrie, Lanarkshire, 8 December 1963.

HONOURS: European Cup Winners' Cup 90/1. League Championship 92/3, 93/4, 95/6, 96/7. FA Cup 89/90, 93/4. League Cup 91/2. 30 Scotland caps (86-93). Scottish Footballer of the Year 87.

OTHER CLUBS: Motherwell 81/2-82/3 (39, 15); Celtic 83/4-86/7 (145, 99); Motherwell 98/9 (11, 0).

GAMES	399 (72)
GOALS	127

STEVE BRUCE

1987/88 → 1995/96

You're in the trenches, up to your neck in muck and bullets and the enemy is closing in. Hope is waning fast, though maybe one final, gargantuan effort might yet turn the tide. But who will lead you over the top? In the footballing equivalent of such desperate straits, there was never any doubt that Manchester United would rally behind Steve Bruce, the sort of man any soldier would be glad to call his comrade.

They did so most famously one sunlit spring afternoon at Old Trafford, at a crucial stage of the 1992/93 campaign, when he transformed imminent defeat by Sheffield Wednesday into joyously improbable victory. After 86 minutes, United were a goal down and seemingly doomed to lose vital ground in the title race, when up charged Steve to equalise with a majestic header.

Now the Reds were rampant and, some seven heart-stopping minutes into injury time, the skipper lunged forward once more to nod a priceless winner. In that wildly exhilarating moment, as the battered Bruce features dissolved into glee, many believed for the first time that United were destined, at last, to don that elusive crown.

Of course, though Steve's attacking exploits were of inestimable value – notably his 19 strikes (including 11 penalties) in 1990/91 – it was as a courageous central defender that he earned his corn. In fact, when he arrived from Norwich City in December 1987, eyebrows were raised at the manager's choice of a solid alternative to the infinitely more gifted but less reliable Paul McGrath. Certainly it was acknowledged that the enthusiastic stopper would battle to the last drop of his blood but where, in heaven's name, was the class expected of a United player?

Yet gradually this roughest of soccer diamonds, while he remained unlikely to graduate from the Alan Hansen Academy of Smooth Operators, emerged as the classic case of an honest trier who made the absolute most of limited natural ability, getting better and better as an all-round footballer along the way.

Poise and grace would never be Steve's hallmarks, but his ball control, distribution and general composure improved out of all recognition, and while he could be discomfited by cleverly deployed pace, his experience ensured that he was rarely exposed. Add, for good measure, a fierce tackle and aerial strength, and the picture of a truly formidable centre-half was almost complete.

In fact, the final ingredient was the most important of all – the unquenchable spirit of the man. It sustained him when he was rejected by three top clubs as a boy; it ensured that, once given his chance at Old Trafford, he didn't waste it; it drove him to play on with injuries that would have brought lesser men to their knees; and it supplied the motivational powers needed to succeed Bryan Robson as captain of the Reds.

By common consent, he should have won full caps; indeed, Bobby Robson has admitted his mistake in never calling Steve to his country's colours, and Jack Charlton would have picked him for the Republic of Ireland had he not been disqualified by an England youth appearance.

That must be an eternal frustration for the affable north-easterner himself, but United fans could live with it. They were content to reflect that, of the many millions Alex Ferguson lavished on building his new team, no slice was better spent than the relatively modest £800,000 which secured the signature of Steve Bruce.

However, though his appetite for the Premiership fray remained undiminished, by the spring of 1996 the 35-year-old warhorse could no longer resist the challenge of the improving David May and, rather than hang around on the Old Trafford periphery hoping for an occasional outing, he accepted a summer move to Birmingham City. His footballing expertise, United would be able to replace. But that heroic heart? It wouldn't be easy.

There followed a spell as player-boss of Sheffield United, with whom he learned plenty, before Steve took further tickets on the managerial merry-go-round, his most memorable work to date being completed during a lengthy and eventful sojourn back at St Andrew's, before he accepted a new challenge with Wigan.

STEPHEN ROGER BRUCE

BORN: Hexham, Northumberland, 31 December 1960.
HONOURS: European Cup Winners' Cup 90/1. League Championship 92/3, 93/4, 95/6. FA Cup 89/90, 93/4. League Cup 91/2.
OTHER CLUBS: Gillingham 79/80-83/4 (205, 29); Norwich City 84/5-87/8 (141, 14); Birmingham City 96/7-97/8 (72, 2); Sheffield United 98/9 (10, 0).
MANAGER: Sheffield United (98-99); Huddersfield Town (99-00); Wigan Athletic (01); Crystal Palace (01); Birmingham City (01-07); Wigna Athletic (07-).

GAMES **411 (3)**
GOALS **51**

MARK HUGHES

• •

1983/84 → 1985/86 & 1988/89 → 1994/95

In his Red Devil days, a compelling aura of impending drama surrounded Mark Hughes. Every time he walked on to a football field, he carried with him the promise of tumultuous action. Frequently it took the form of a goal, invariably of the spellbinding variety, the type that emblazoned itself on the memory of all those privileged to witness it; occasionally his darker side was evident, when thunderclouds gathered on his brow and that celtic fire blazed. Even on less eventful days there was a stirring trial of strength with defenders, an exhibition of centre-forward play that blended power with subtlety in a manner unique in the contemporary game. Like him or not – and he did have his critics – there was no denying the star quality of 'Sparky'.

When the Welshman emerged as the cream of United's surfeit of strikers in 1984/85 – claiming his place at the expense of Brazil and Whiteside, and scoring 25 goals in senior competitions – a glow of collective contentment radiated from the Stretford End. Premature, perhaps, but the Red legions, sorely debilitated by the deeds of Dalglish, Rush and company, sensed that here they had a hero to slay the Anfield dragons.

The first months of the following campaign did nothing to disillusion them. Mark, a product of the club's youth sides, signed a five-year contract and plundered ten goals in 13 matches as United galloped to a ten-point lead in the title race. But the idyll was annihilated as results fell away and it was announced that Hughes was to join Barcelona for around £2 million.

Outraged fans accused the Old Trafford board of betrayal and there were some unsavoury exchanges, illustrating vividly the esteem in which the young marksman was held. In similar vein, when he returned for £1.6 million two years later, he was embraced once more as a favourite son. Mark was the signing the supporters wanted above all others and when they got him, by and large, he didn't disappoint them.

'Sparky' combined charisma with a rare range of talents of which arguably the most important – eclipsing even the most fearsome shot in British football – was the adhesive control and bull-like muscle which allowed him to retain possession against all-comers. This made him the physical focus of the Reds' fast-flowing attack, enabling team-mates to play the ball to him in the knowledge that he could keep it safe while they hared into new positions. He could pass with precision over long distances, too, if irking some observers with the occasional sloppy short-range lay-off.

Various detractors claimed that he was difficult to play alongside because he held the ball too long, that he spent too much time with his back to goal, that he squandered simple chances, that he was old enough to keep his temper; but all that withered before a veritable mountain of acclaim.

His peers queued up to sing his praises – he was players' player of the year in both 1989 and 1991 – and the fans positively drooled over those wondrous goals. They are too numerous to list, but this writer's favourites include the savage narrow-angled drive in the Cup Winners' Cup Final against Barcelona, the looping 25-yarder lashed home against Manchester City as if in answer to speculation about his place following the arrival of Eric Cantona in late 1992, and the last-gasp firecracker of a volley to equalise against Oldham in the 1994 FA Cup semi-final. During that campaign, in his 31st year, Mark Hughes reached new heights of all-round excellence alongside the Frenchman and was more critical than ever to United's quick-breaking style.

It couldn't go on indefinitely, of course, and in the summer of 1995 he was allowed to depart – prematurely according to some observers who doubted the suitability of Andy Cole as his replacement – to Chelsea in a £1.5 million deal.

All who wished him well were delighted by his success at Stamford Bridge and elsewhere, notably at Blackburn where he was still fighting the good fight in his 39th year, while shouldering the onerous responsibility of managing Wales. Later he returned to Ewood Park as boss, his impressive early efforts suggesting that Manchester United could do worse than select him as the long-term successor to Alex Ferguson.

Certainly back at Old Trafford, though the last thunderbolt has exploded and the final tackle has been ridden, 'Sparky' is lionised still. Few Reds have left behind them a deeper fund of pulsating memories.

LESLIE MARK HUGHES

BORN: Wrexham, Denbighshire, 1 November 1963.

HONOURS: European Cup Winners' Cup 90/1. League Championship 92/3, 93/4. FA Cup 84/5, 89/90, 93/4. League Cup 91/2. 72 Wales caps (84-99). PFA Footballer of the Year 89, 91.

OTHER CLUBS: Barcelona, Spain, 86/7 (28, 4); Bayern Munich, Germany, on loan 87/8 (18, 6); Chelsea 95/6-97/8 (95, 25); Southampton 98/9-99/00 (51, 2); Everton 99/00-00/01 (18, 1); Blackburn Rovers 00/01-01/02 (50, 6).

MANAGER: Wales (99-04); Blackburn Rovers (04-).

GAMES **453 (14)**
GOALS **163**

PAUL PARKER

· ·

1991/92 → 1995/96

Old met new in Paul Parker. The nimble little Londoner was a master of the crisp-tackling and tight-marking techniques which occupied pride of place in any self-respecting full-back's armoury before modern trends turned flank defenders into quasi-wingers, often at the expense of their traditional duties. But whereas the majority of his old-fashioned counterparts tended to rely more on power than pace, United's tenacious England international could match most Premiership speed merchants stride for stride. Quicksilver on the turn, he recovered instantly if an opponent did slip past him and usually could be relied upon to bite back with a second challenge before too much damage had been done.

But Paul was no mere greyhound. Although close (some might say pernickety) observers detected the occasional lapse in concentration, he was a perceptive reader of the game whose positional sense rarely let him down. Thus a Parker interception marked the demise of many an opposition raid, and he offered an invaluable line in cavalry-style rescues, invariably being on hand to cover if the twin centre-halves were hard-pressed.

In fact, Paul expressed a preference for operating permanently in the middle and was used there in an experimental sweeper system during part of 1991/92, his first term as a Red Devil following his close-season £1.7 million transfer from Queen's Park Rangers. On occasion, too, the dapper right-back deputised competently for Gary Pallister, and the way he shackled former team-mate Les Ferdinand at Old Trafford in October 1993 offered impressive proof of his man-marking capabilities.

But despite being a prodigious jumper, at only 5ft 7in he couldn't achieve the consistent aerial dominance demanded by a central role, and he continued to look most comfortable in the number-two shirt.

One weakness to which Paul's critics never tired of referring was his distribution and, fair enough, it was not on a par with that of his smooth-passing colleagues. However, he strove to improve his delivery, with some success, and it should be stressed that any periodic inaccuracy hardly would have attracted comment were he playing for a team containing fewer gifted individuals than United.

A less-than-serious shortfall in the Parker game was goals, Paul netting only twice in senior competition for the Reds and inevitably being ribbed by his team-mates as the lowest-scoring outfielder. His first strike was rather special, though, a perfectly angled cross-shot from close range that climaxed a sweetly executed one-two passing interchange with Brian McClair at home to Spurs in January 1993; on the other hand his second, a spectacular effort from near the right touchline during an FA Cup tie at Reading in 1996, might have owed more to a bobble on the Elm Park pitch than precision delivery.

However, to dwell on the Parker strike rate is like concentrating on Cantona's goal-line clearances, merely an aside. Overall, and despite revealing the occasional need to boost Paul's confidence, Alex Ferguson was delighted with the versatile defender who, at the time of his arrival, had just returned to action following knee problems which had threatened his career. There were to be protracted fitness worries in Manchester, too, a strained hamstring costing him much of 1991/92, then further injury sidelining him for the first three months of the subsequent title-winning campaign.

Sadly, there was worse to come. After moving into his thirties in April 1994, Paul was unavailable for long stretches of two more seasons, during which he was overhauled in the pecking order by the Neville brothers. Consequently it was no surprise when he was freed in the summer of 1996 to join Derby County, though it was a pity. A fully fit Paul Parker would have offered ideal cover when United's back-four was devastated by injuries early in 1997.

PAUL ANDREW PARKER

BORN: West Ham, London, 4 April 1964.

HONOURS: League Championship 92/3, 93/4. FA Cup 93/4. League Cup 91/2.
19 England caps (89-94).

OTHER CLUBS: Fulham 80/1-86/7 (153, 2); Queen's Park Rangers 87/8-90/1 (125, 1);
Derby County 96/7 (4, 0); Sheffield United 96/7 (10, 0); Fulham 96/7 (3, 0);
Chelsea 96/7 (3, 0).

GAMES **137 (9)**

GOALS **2**

LES SEALEY

1989/90 → 1990/91 & 1993/94

Sometimes he was United's 'Mr Angry', a ranting extrovert between the posts; mostly he was a gleeful eccentric whose madcap antics delighted the many while alienating the few. But the bottom line was that Les Sealey served the Reds royally in no fewer than four cup finals during two spells at the club – and without costing a penny in transfer fees.

Londoner Les arrived on loan from Luton Town in December 1989 after injury to Gary Walsh left United without cover for Jim Leighton. Seasoned and reliable, he was not seen as a world-beater, but Alex Ferguson had no hesitation in pitching him into the FA Cup Final replay against Crystal Palace after the Scot's traumatic experiences in the first match.

Les responded superbly, refusing to be intimidated either by the occasion or the physical force exerted by Mark Bright and company. As he picked himself up after one early, over-robust challenge, the light of battle was in his eye and soon he had shown his prowess with a crucial, if somewhat lucky save with his legs from Andy Gray's 20-yard free-kick. This was typical of a brave, unorthodox performer who was technically flawed – witness his occasionally erratic positioning – but adept at protecting his net with any part of his anatomy.

He was rewarded for his part in the victory by a one-year contract, becoming first-choice custodian for 1990/91 and keeping in two finals. First came the League Cup defeat by Sheffield Wednesday, made memorable by his, er, forthright refusal to be substituted after his knee was cut to the bone. A few hours after the game he fainted, and might have lost his leg, yet three weeks on he was between the posts to help beat Barcelona in the Cup Winners' Cup.

Now Les wanted a two-year contract, but left to join Aston Villa after being offered only 12 months' security of tenure. But in January 1993 he was back at Old Trafford as deputy to Peter Schmeichel and was called to arms when the Dane was suspended for the '94 League Cup Final.

United lost to Villa but the 36-year-old standby was blameless, and he was disappointed to be given a free transfer at the end of the season. Far from finished, he went on to banish dullness from the dressing rooms of Blackpool, West Ham and Leyton Orient, and the English football scene was immeasurably the poorer for his premature death in 2001.

LESLIE JESSE SEALEY

BORN: Bethnal Green, London, 29 September 1957.

HONOURS: European Cup Winners' Cup 90/1. FA Cup 89/90.

OTHER CLUBS: Coventry City 76/7-82/3 (158, 0); Luton Town 83/4-88/9 (207, 0); Plymouth Argyle on loan 84/5 (6, 0); Aston Villa 91/2 (18, 0); Coventry City on loan 91/2 (2, 0); Birmingham City on loan 92/3 (12, 0); Blackpool 94/5 (7, 0); West Ham United 95/6 (2, 0); Leyton Orient 96/7 (12, 0); West Ham United 96/7-97/8 (2, 0).

DIED: 19 August 2001.

GAMES	55 (1)
GOALS	0

DARREN FERGUSON

1990/91 → 1993/94

But for the identity of his father, there is a good chance that Darren Ferguson would have enjoyed a lengthy career with Manchester United. The Scotland under-21 midfielder did enough during his brief spell in the Old Trafford spotlight, especially throughout an uninterrupted sequence of 15 League games at the outset of 1992/93, to establish credentials of undeniable quality. However, being the manager's son was sure to place the youngster under intolerable pressure at some stage and, reluctantly but wisely, the Fergusons decided on a parting of their professional ways.

Darren, the subject of an inquiry from Nottingham Forest during his progress through the Red Devils' junior ranks, made his senior debut at Bramall Lane in February 1991, coming on as substitute for Neil Webb and impressing with his efficient distribution in the face of vigorous challenges. Bright pre-season form won him a place on the left of midfield that August, but then knee problems which demanded three operations put him temporarily out of contention.

Fit again a year later, Darren began another new term in the first team and now revealed his true potential. Though he wasn't quick, he was a lovely passer, especially with his left foot, and rarely did he squander possession. He was adept at shielding the ball, too, and while not a ball-winner in the accepted sense, he tackled forcefully enough, occasionally showing flashes of the family spirit. One criticism was that he rarely got forward and that when he did his finishing was poor, but he was giving enough in other areas for that to be overlooked.

Without making extravagant claims for the promising 20-year-old, pundits began to praise his unobtrusive but consistent contribution to United's recovery from a slow start. But after he was sidelined by a hamstring strain in November, the side began to take off in his absence and he never regained his place, though the Championship statuette he received at season's end was rich consolation.

That autumn the Fergusons spoke of Darren's need to look elsewhere and when Wolves bid £500,000 in January 1994 he headed for Molineux. Mystifyingly, his progess in the Black Country proved disappointingly fitful but he made a fresh beginning with Wrexham, whom he served admirably for more than half a decade before following his father into management, leading Peterborough to promotion from League Two in 2007/08.

DARREN FERGUSON

BORN: Glasgow, 9 February 1972.
HONOURS: League Championship 92/3.
OTHER CLUBS: Wolverhampton Wanderers 93/4-98/9 (117, 4); Cosenza, Italy, and Sparta Rotterdam, Holland, both on loan 98/9; Wrexham 99/00-06/07 (297, 24).
MANAGER: Peterborough United (07-).

GAMES	22 (8)
GOALS	0

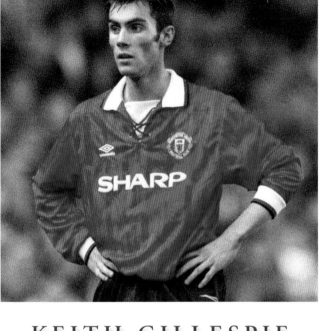

DION DUBLIN

1992/93 → 1993/94

After a desperate shortage of goals in the second half of 1991/92 cost United the League Championship, Alex Ferguson acted decisively. First he tried to sign Alan Shearer from Southampton, but lost out to Blackburn; then he switched his attention to Dion Dublin, the shaven-headed six-footer who had been at the sharp end of Cambridge United's long-ball success story. The Abbeymen had conducted the sale of their leading scorer by video, circulating a tape of his goals to all top clubs. Alex had been impressed by the variety of the 23-year-old Midlander's strikes and came up with the requisite £1.1 million.

Clearly Dion was not a typical Old Trafford signing, lacking the finesse of most expensive acquisitions, but his size and physical presence offered a different attacking option. He responded by scoring a late winner at Southampton in his first full game, only to fall victim to cruel fortune in his third. A tackle from Crystal Palace's Eric Young, later exonerated from blame by all concerned, left him with a fractured leg and horribly damaged ligaments. Less resilient characters might never have played again, but he fought back in time to take a seat on the substitutes' bench that spring. However, subsequent opportunities proved few and in September 1994 he joined Coventry for £2 million, a deal which satisfied all the participants. Dion left Old Trafford with his all-round game improved immeasurably, the Sky Blues had obtained an effective spearhead and United had doubled their money. His subsequent rise to England status was a resounding triumph for brave perseverance.

KEITH GILLESPIE

1992/93 → 1994/95

When Keith Gillespie ghosted unstoppably past two Newcastle defenders before netting thrillingly from 16 yards at Old Trafford in October 1994, he made an indelible impression on visiting manager Kevin Keegan. So much so that come January, when Alex Ferguson enquired about the availability of Andy Cole, Kevin agreed to sell – providing Keith joined the Geordies as a £1 million component in the £7 million deal. Alex was reluctant to part with his richly promising rookie but so keen was he on Cole, and with Andrei Kanchelskis then blocking the 19-year-old flankman's path to the senior side, he accepted Newcastle's terms.

Had Ferguson known of the Ukrainian's growing determination to depart, maybe his decision would have been different. Whatever, while the Reds' new striker blew hot and cold, Gillespie's breathtaking skills established him quickly as a favourite on the Tyne.

Glancing back at his early development, that was hardly surprising. Wingers have an extra cross to bear at Old Trafford, especially if, like Keith, they are slim and dark and hail from Ulster. But his head was not for turning, either by meaningless comparisons or the natural ebullience of youth. Quick and confident enough to take players on at need, he knew when a safe pass was the more sensible option, and the accuracy of his centres was improving at the time of his transfer. Keith survived fitness problems and relegation after joining Blackburn, and later returned to the Premiership with Sheffield United. Good luck to him and, it must be said, well done to Kevin Keegan.

DION DUBLIN
BORN: Leicester, 22 April 1969.
HONOURS: League Championship 92/3. 4 England caps (98).
OTHER CLUBS: Cambridge United 88/9-91/2 (156, 52); Coventry City 94/5-98/9 (145, 61); Aston Villa 98/9-03/04 (155, 48); Millwall on loan 01/02 (5, 2); Leicester City 04/05-05/06 (58, 5); Celtic 05/06 (11, 1); Norwich City 06/07-07/08 (70, 12).

GAMES	6 (11)
GOALS	3

KEITH ROBERT GILLESPIE
BORN: Larne, Northern Ireland, 18 February 1975.
HONOURS: 81 Northern Ireland caps (94-).
OTHER CLUBS: Wigan Athletic on loan 93/4 (8, 4); Newcastle United 94/5-98/9 (113, 11); Blackburn Rovers 98/9-02/03 (113, 5); Wigan Athletic on loan 00/01 (13, 4); Leicester City 03/04-04/05 (42, 2); Sheffield United 05/06- (96, 4).

GAMES	7 (7)
GOALS	2

MICHAEL APPLETON

1996/97

A sturdy, industrious midfielder who could tackle and pass with equal facility. Michael's problem was that the Red Devils were so richly blessed in his department, and he became Preston's record signing in a £500,000 deal before injury scuppered his promising career.

MICHAEL ANTONY APPLETON
BORN: Salford, Lancashire,
4 December 1975.
OTHER CLUBS: Lincoln City on loan 95/6 (4, 0); Grimsby Town on loan 96/7 (10, 3); Preston North End 97/8-00/01 (115, 12); West Bromwich Albion 00/01-01/02 (33, 0).

GAMES 1 (1)
GOALS 0

PAT McGIBBON

1995/96

Central defender who was sent off during his only senior appearance for United in the mortifying League Cup reverse against York City at Old Trafford in 1995. Pat, a £100,000 signing from Portadown, later joined Wigan for £250,000.

PATRICK COLM McGIBBON
BORN: Lurgan, Northern Ireland,
6 September 1973.
HONOURS: 7 Northern Ireland caps (95-00).
OTHER CLUBS: Portadown, Northern Ireland; Swansea City on loan 96/7 (1, 0); Wigan Athletic 96/7-01/02 (173, 11); Scunthorpe United on loan 01/02 (6, 0); Tranmere Rovers 02/03 (4, 0).

GAMES 1
GOALS 0

COLIN McKEE

1993/94

A pacy front-runner who was prominent during United's 1992 FA Youth Cup triumph. However, he never made a successful transition to the senior ranks, leaving a few months after his sole appearance, against Coventry in May 1994.

COLIN McKEE
BORN: Glasgow 22 August 1973.
OTHER CLUBS: Bury on loan 92/3 (2, 0); Kilmarnock 94/5-97/8 (76, 11); Falkirk 98/9 (4, 0).

GAMES 1
GOALS 0

JOHN O'KANE

1994/95 → 1996/97

A polished full-back who could also operate in midfield, John was an ever-present in the triumphant FA Youth Cup campaign of 1992. Skilful and composed, he was expected to progress as a Red but perhaps lacked the requisite dynamism.

JOHN ANDREW O'KANE
BORN: Nottingham, 15 November 1974.
OTHER CLUBS: Bury on loan 96/7 (13, 3); Bradford City on loan 97/8 (7, 0); Everton 97/8-98/9 (14, 0); Burnley on loan 98/9 (8, 0); Bolton Wanderers 99/00-00/01 (38, 2); Blackpool 01/02-02/03 (52, 4).

GAMES 5 (2)
GOALS 0

WILLIAM PRUNIER

1995/96

A footballing centre-half, composed and comfortable in possession, William shone in his first outing as a Red Devil in a victory over QPR, but struggled in his second, a heavy defeat by Spurs, and rejected the offer of a further trial.

WILLIAM PRUNIER
BORN: Montreuil, France, 14 August 1967.
HONOURS: 1 France cap (92).
OTHER CLUBS: Auxerre 84/5-92/3 (221, 20); Marseille 93/4 (35, 4); Bordeaux 94/5 (20, 0), all France; FC Copenhagen, Denmark, 96; Montpellier, France, 96/7; Napoli, Italy, 97/8; Courtrai, Belgium, 98/9; Toulouse, France, 99/00-03/04.

GAMES 2
GOALS 0

GRAEME TOMLINSON

1994/95

A shattered leg while on loan at Luton effectively scuppered the Old Trafford career of the rookie marksman who had cost an initial £100,000 when signed from Bradford City. Thereafter he never regained top form and left in 1998.

GRAEME MURDOCH TOMLINSON
BORN: Watford, Hertfordshire,
10 December 1975.
OTHER CLUBS: Bradford City 93/4 (17, 6); Luton Town on loan 95/6 (7, 0); Bournemouth on loan 97/8 (8, 1); Millwall on loan 97/8 (3, 1); Macclesfield Town 98/9-99/00 (46, 6); Exeter City 00/01-01/02 (56, 6).

GAMES 0 (2)
GOALS 0

PAUL INCE
. . . .
1989/90 → 1994/95

The void was gaping, the situation potentially desperate. Manchester United had suffered debilitating disappointment on the last lap of the 1991/92 title race and as they regrouped for what many saw as a make-or-break new campaign for Alex Ferguson's expensively assembled team, one question gave rise to grave concern.

The years were finally catching up with Bryan Robson, no longer the unquenchably dynamic force of seasons past, so to whom would the Red Devils turn for midfield motivation? Who would drive them, lift them, inspire them by mammoth personal example? Cometh the hour, cometh Paul Ince.

He was, of course, the obvious candidate, having improved steadily over his three seasons at the club, but now came a crossroads. Some reckoned he would remain in that heavily populated category of value-for-money competitors destined to fall marginally short of the top class. Others had faith that he could step up to join the select band who can seize a game and mould it, make the difference between winning and losing by sustained excellence and application – and they were right.

Throughout 1992/93 Paul asserted himself majestically to become the new hub of the side, compiling a sequence of colossal performances as United won the League at last. Shuttling ceaselessly between penalty areas, he exuded energy and enterprise, sometimes scything into tackles like a runaway motor-mower, though more often winning possession crisply and neatly. He carried the ball with skill and purpose, too, and his right-footed distribution was invariably sensible, occasionally incisive.

As a bonus, he obliged with a few goals, hitherto a shortfall in his game, including an emphatic low 25-yarder with his weaker left foot in the Manchester derby at Old Trafford and an overhead kick at Loftus Road that would not have shamed Denis Law. Most welcome of all, though, and one which summed up Paul's surging, irrepressible presence, was the late clincher at Crystal Palace as the Reds closed in on the title. Bursting unstoppably on to a pass from Eric Cantona, he hustled past a defender, bore down on the 'keeper and netted with a fierce cross-shot.

That summer Paul was elevated, albeit temporarily, to the exalted rank of England captain, underlining the wisdom of Ferguson's gamble in taking the immature and rebellious but immensely promising 21-year-old from West Ham in September 1989. It had been a messy transfer, with the player posing for the press in a red shirt long before the deal was completed, and one complicated by a mystery pelvic injury which resulted in a pay-as-he-played agreement up to the reported fee of £1.7 million.

At the time, Ince seemed to be nursing a grievance against the world, a legacy of an unsettled childhood, and United set to work on his attitude as well as his football. During a first season in which he demonstrated his all-round ability by filling in as an emergency full-back, he proved his basic pedigree; thereafter, gradually, he enhanced every aspect of his play as he helped to compile a glittering collection of trophies.

A combination of marriage, fatherhood and sound advice speeded up the maturing process; moaning at referees decreased, snarls became less frequent than smiles and, while an underlying narkiness would always remain, the temper was on a tighter rein.

Throughout the double-winning term of 1993/94 and much of the ultimately disappointing 1994/95 campaign Paul continued to exert a towering influence, though following his part in the Cantona affair at Selhurst Park in January '95 his effectiveness decreased. Thereafter certain tensions surfaced within the club and that summer, to the dismay of many but not all United-lovers, the self-styled 'Guv'nor' was sold to Internazionale of Milan for a reported £7 million.

Though his play lacked the perception of Roy Keane's, Paul was not far from being the complete modern midfielder, and there was understandable anxiety about how he would be missed. Ferguson's answer was to pair Keane with Nicky Butt and to win everything, while there were no medals for the 'Guv', either in Milan, or later at Liverpool, Middlesbrough or Wolves. So the final verdict on Paul Ince? A magnificent player, yes. Indispensable, by no means.

However, years passed and, to the surprise of most observers, there followed a fabulously promising start to his managerial career, throwing up the intriguing if distant possibility that one day he just might be calling the shots at Old Trafford after all.

PAUL EMERSON CARLYLE INCE

BORN: Ilford, Essex, 21 October 1967.

HONOURS: European Cup Winners' Cup 90/1. League Championship 92/3, 93/4. FA Cup 89/90, 93/4. League Cup 91/2. 53 England caps (92-00).

OTHER CLUBS: West Ham United 86/7-89/90 (72, 7); Internazionale, Italy, 95/6-96/7 (54, 9); Liverpool 97/8-98/9 (65, 14); Middlesbrough 99/00-01/02 (93, 7); Wolverhampton Wanderers 02/03-05/06 (115, 10); Swindon Town 06/07 (3, 0); Macclesfield Town 06/07 (1, 0).

MANAGER: Macclesfield Town (06-07); Milton Keynes Dons (07-).

GAMES 276 (5)
GOALS 29

ANDREI KANCHELSKIS

1990/91 → 1994/95

Of the three heroes whose departures ruffled the summertime calm of Old Trafford in 1995, the one most sorely missed, and by a considerable distance, was Andrei Kanchelskis. The gaps left by Messrs Ince and Hughes were filled with relative ease, the first directly, the second by a tactical variation. But while David Beckham offered his own special delights in Andrei's right-flank slot, and even though the 'double double' was secured, United were immeasurably the poorer for losing the options afforded by the flying Ukrainian's extreme pace.

Kanchelskis was a refreshing footballer. Ironically for a fellow who failed ultimately to find happiness at a succession of clubs, he played the game with a smile never far from his face and, when the ball was at his feet, it was a fair bet that the fans were enjoying themselves, too. Whether devastating defenders with searing straight-line speed or beguiling them on jinking, shoulder-shrugging runs, he was an entertainer and a match-winner.

During 1993/94 there was no more potent weapon in the Premiership for transforming defence, suddenly and explosively, into penetrating attack. In that most riveting of campaigns, United were blessed with a trio of brilliant but contrasting flankmen, each of whom captivated crowds in their turn. So what a telling tribute it was to Andrei that, with due respect to Ryan Giggs and Lee Sharpe, he was the most consistently productive of the three.

When the 22-year-old outside-right arrived as a £1 million signing from Donetsk in May 1991, it was a clear case of 'Andrei Who?' Though he was a Soviet international, he was little known outside his native land, but before long the Old Trafford regulars had taken him to their hearts. When he was on form, they thrilled to his free-running style, his close skills and his rasping shot, while applauding his willingness to forage. Equally important to a young man making his way in an alien environment while worrying about events in his strife-torn homeland, they warmed to him as a personality, appreciating the boyishly wholesome air and the perky optimism which suffused his play.

Nevertheless, Andrei was not the finished article as a player, either in 1991/92, when he missed only a few senior games, or in the subsequent title-winning term, when his outings were limited by Sharpe's return from injury and illness. Though his potential was never in doubt, he lacked awareness of passing options, too often pounding forward naively as though fitted with blinkers, and his crossing quality was variable.

However, he became frustrated when left out of the side and there was speculation that he would move in June 1993. The manager, though, was loth to lose such a gem and persuaded Andrei that, with patience, there was a bountiful future for him at Old Trafford. Sure enough, the next term another enforced absence for the unlucky Sharpe presented Kanchelskis with an extended opportunity and he shone as never before. Now his game had matured, he slotted smoothly into the team pattern and United never looked more incisive than when he was in full cry.

Examples of Andrei's verve clamour for description, none more so than an incandescent piece of individualism in the FA Cup semi-final replay against Oldham, when he cut inside from the right, danced across the face of the Latics' defence, then swivelled to dispatch the sweetest of 20-yard curlers just inside the far post with his unfavoured left foot. More typical were any number of grass-singeing dashes from deep inside his own half which climaxed invariably with low, crisply struck shots.

Yet the Reds' squad was extensive and, still haunted by doubts and with top Continental clubs dangling untold riches before him, the popular winger spoke once more of departing in 1994. The threat evaporated for a time but a season later – one in which he had contributed 15 goals, including a rampaging hat-trick against Manchester City – he declared that his differences with Ferguson were irreconcilable. He was upset over tactical omissions from the side and dogged by nagging fitness problems, but the suspicion lingered that money came into it somewhere.

Whatever the whole truth, there was no way any club could hang on to such an unhappy player and he was sold, oh so reluctantly, to Everton for £5.5 million. Even that acrimonious exit could not mar the memory of his achievements as a Red, but how frustrating it remained for United fans that Kanchelskis' prime years were being spent elsewhere. As it turned out, though, Andrei's exploits on Merseyside, in Italy and in Scotland were to prove less than wholly satisfying.

ANDREI ANTANASOVICH KANCHELSKIS

BORN:	Kirovograd, Ukraine, 23 January 1969.
HONOURS:	League Championship 92/3, 93/4. FA Cup 93/4. League Cup 91/2. 23 USSR and CIS caps (89-92); 36 Russia caps (93-98).
OTHER CLUBS:	Dynamo Kiev 88-89 (22, 1); Shakhtyor Donetsk 90-91 (21, 3), both USSR; Everton 95/6-96/7 (52, 20); Fiorentina, Italy, 96/7-97/8 (26, 2); Glasgow Rangers 98/9-01/02 (71, 11); Manchester City on loan 00/01 (10, 0); Southampton 02/03 (1, 0); Al-Hilal, Saudi Arabia, 02/03; Saturn Ramenskoye 04/05; Kryila Sovetov 05/06-06/07, both Russia.

GAMES	132 (29)
GOALS	36

LEE SHARPE

1988/89 → 1995/96

The relative decline of Lee Sharpe and his departure from an Old Trafford stage which he had illuminated with a rare talent for more than half a decade was frustratingly premature. By the time he joined Leeds for £4.5 million in August 1996 he seemed little more than a squad player, a shadow of his former vibrant self and no longer a likely match-winner, despite his involvement in all but eight matches of the 1995/96 double-winning campaign.

Yet still he was only 25, quick and skilful, bright and brave. He worked hard during games and was unselfish to a fault; his temperament was even and he was vastly experienced for such a young man.

A fair combination. In fact, one veteran monitor of the Old Trafford scene, a perceptive and frequently astringent observer not given to fulsome praise, reckoned that Lee possessed the raw materials to become the finest left winger the club had ever had. Alex Ferguson, too, had waxed lyrical, especially about the Sharpe contribution to the 1992/93 Championship triumph, pointing out that, while Lee netted only once, he supplied no fewer than 18 'assists' between his November return from a career-threatening bout of meningitis and season's end.

Indeed, it was the rare quality of the England international's final ball that marked him out as special, particularly when he was forced to deliver under pressure. Lee demonstrated a priceless knack of bending his crosses with perfect weight, teasing defenders to distraction, delighting his own front-men with his accuracy.

Glorious examples on the road to that first title included the raking dispatch that set up Andrei Kanchelskis to score at Loftus Road in January, the exquisite centre that met Eric Cantona's forehead for an equaliser at Maine Road two months later, three Boxing Day presents to his strikers at Hillsborough . . . the point is made.

On his day Sharpe could produce a devastating finish, too. Consider his League Cup Highbury hat-trick in November 1990, comprising a 25-yard scorcher, a neat glancing header and a precisely angled shot; or, more spectacular still, the long-range volley out of the blue that stunned Everton at Goodison in October 1993.

However, life was not all hip-wiggling goal celebrations after Lee's £200,000 purchase from Torquay, a deal struck at Plainmoor one night in May 1988 after Alex Ferguson, fearful of being spotted by rival scouts, had reportedly disguised himself in a balaclava to watch his quarry in action.

Apart from facing the sternest imaginable competition for a place from Giggs, Kanchelskis and then a new wave of brilliant youngsters, Lee was plagued by injury and illness. There was a hernia operation, protracted groin problems and, most serious of all, that horrifying 1992 encounter with meningitis. His resilience in recovering from each setback seemed remarkable but, in the long term, maybe they left their mark.

Also, if we are searching for reasons for Lee's loss of impetus, he might not have been helped by occasional role switches made by his manager in the team's broader interests. Admittedly he had looked typically unflustered at left-back – notably when an injury crisis pitched him into top-flight action shortly after his arrival from Torquay – but, emphatically, he was not a natural defender.

More simply, though, Lee was, and remains, a refreshingly easy-going fellow who enjoyed the privileged life of a handsome young star to the full. Whether he retained the necessary raw hunger for success in such tempting circumstances, or whether a modicum of complacency crept in, can only be the subject of conjecture.

Back in 1991, still only 19, he was voted young player of the year and won his first full cap, and as the century ended he ought to have been enjoying his prime. But at Elland Road he found a club in a difficult stage of transition and his early form, while not disastrous, was hardly convincing either.

Thereafter he lost the whole of 1997/98 to injury, then slipped out of the first-team picture. A new start beckoned with ambitious Bradford City, but another succession of injuries laid him low and it became regrettably evident that Lee Sharpe was never going to meet the lofty expectations created during the vivid highlights of his Old Trafford sojourn. There was life after football, though, and the erstwhile United dreamboat proved a resounding hit on the TV show *Celebrity Love Island*.

LEE STUART SHARPE

BORN: Halesowen, Birmingham, 27 May 1971.
HONOURS: European Cup Winners' Cup 90/1. League Championship 92/3, 93/4, 95/6. FA Cup 93/4. League Cup 91/2. 8 England caps (91-93).
OTHER CLUBS: Torquay United 87/8 (14, 3); Leeds United 96/7-98/9 (30, 5); Sampdoria, Italy, on loan 98/9 (3, 0); Bradford City 98/9-01/02 (56, 4); Portsmouth on loan 00/01 (17, 0); Exeter City 02/03 (4, 1).

GAMES **213 (50)**
GOALS 36

GARY PALLISTER

1989/90 → 1997/98

Bargain was not the word which sprang to mind in the weeks immediately following Manchester United's £2.3 million purchase of 24-year-old Gary Pallister from Middlesbrough in August 1989. The coltish 6ft 4in centre-half oozed anxiety, shouldered the blame for several goals and left many Old Trafford loyalists fearing that Alex Ferguson had made a towering blunder.

However, the manager was to claim handsome vindication for a bold piece of business carried out under mounting pressure to improve his team. Indeed, five years on Gary was at least the equal of any British stopper – many within the game put him in a class of his own – and in terms of the fees mooted in the 1990s to secure players in key positions, yes, most certainly he could be considered a bargain.

In fact, Reds fans needed only moderate patience to discover that Pally was less white elephant than mammoth asset. That same term he steadied himself to play an increasingly commanding role as United won the FA Cup, and was made supporters' player of the year for his pains. Two years later he received even more meaningful approbation, that of his peers, in the shape of the PFA players' player award; and come 1993 he laid persuasive claim to a regular England place while being spoken of as a possible future United skipper.

At that point it was pleasing to reflect that the club had turned to Gary only when Liverpool pipped them for the signature of Glenn Hysen. With every respect to the imposing Swede, that was one race which, in retrospect, the Mancunians were delighted to lose.

Indeed, Pally became a truly majestic, all-round central defender; and he was still near the height of his powers in 1997/98, when it appeared possible that he might serve United – sore back permitting – until the turn of the century. In the air he was well-nigh impregnable, his massive presence subduing attackers psychologically as well as physically; on the ground he controlled the ball deftly with either foot, passed it accurately and intelligently, and was capable of carrying it past opponents in the imperious manner of a latter-day Alan Hansen.

Crucially, too, he was blessed with a startling turn of speed for such a big fellow, leaving only an occasional tendency to lose concentration as an area for concern. He worked hard to eradicate that flaw though, and instances of dozing off on the field became rare, an advance due partly, no doubt, to some well-judged metaphorical boots up the behind from manager and team-mates. True, there remained anxious moments of apparent casualness, but such was Gary's assurance that the fans' palpitations were seldom justified.

Clearly, Pally's progress owed most to his own natural ability, but the club deserved credit for ensuring that he made the most of it. On arrival he was altogether too slender, unable to punch his weight and lacking in stamina, but specialist training wrought a gradual transformation into a bull-necked colossus who remained as strong at the final whistle as at the first. Gary's outlook, too, needed toughening, but there can be few men more adept at inbuing single-mindedness and 'devil' than the Reds' boss.

The result was self-evident, as Wimbledon's renowned warrior John Fashanu found out in an FA Cup clash at Selhurst Park in February 1994. Fash ran out breathing fire, an intimidating prospect before which many a so-called hard-man has faltered. But Pally met the challenge implacably, refused to be unsettled and reduced the Dons' destroyer to helpless anonymity.

Despite the efficiency of Messrs Johnsen and Berg during 1997/98, United's rearguard never seemed quite right when Gary was sidelined for a worrying spell by a recurrence of the back injury which cost him his England place for Euro '96.

He was the only player to have shared in all nine of the major triumphs during the Ferguson reign to that point, and it did not seem fanciful to suggest that still he had not finished. But the signing of Jaap Stam alerted Bryan Robson to a possible scoop and Pally completed a £2 million return to Middlesbrough in the summer of 1998. The Dutchman's excellence dispelled fears that United had dropped a costly clanger and one of the most accomplished defenders in Old Trafford history went on to play an influential, if injury-plagued part in consolidating 'Boro's Premiership future.

	GARY ANDREW PALLISTER
BORN:	Ramsgate, Kent, 30 June 1965.
HONOURS:	European Cup Winners' Cup 90/1. League Championship 92/3, 93/4, 95/6, 96/7. FA Cup 89/90, 93/4, 95/6. League Cup 91/2. 22 England caps (88-96). PFA Footballer of the Year 92.
OTHER CLUBS:	Middlesbrough 85/6-89/90 (156, 5); Darlington on loan 85/6 (7, 0); Middlesbrough 98/9-00/01 (55, 1).

GAMES **433 (4)**
GOALS **15**

PETER SCHMEICHEL

1991/92 → 1998/99

As the living embodiment of United's superiority – and widely perceived arrogance – for the better part of a decade, Peter Schmeichel was never the most popular person in English football.

His combination of excellence and self-assurance, coupled with his ranting at anyone within earshot at moments of stress, made him despised by fans all over the country and even alienated many of his fellow professionals. That is the inescapable conclusion from the players' decision to vote for David James as the best 'keeper in the Premiership during 1995/96, then David Seaman in 1996/97 and Nigel Martyn in both 1997/98 and 1998/99. Quite simply, with the giant Dane's monumental input to United's modern success outstripping that of any single colleague, and with every respect to the aforementioned trio, there must have been an element of 'I'm not supporting that bad-tempered so-and-so' when the votes were cast.

In reality, surely, Schmeichel's frequent near-omnipotence was more than enough to confirm his stature as one of the all-time goalkeeping greats, let alone merely the pick of one English season.

Consider: in spring '96 as United clawed themselves back into a title race which had seemed dead, the lion's share of the bouquets went to Eric Cantona, yet Peter's saves earned at least as many points as the Frenchman's goals. His contribution was encapsulated in microcosm at St James' Park in March when once, twice, three times he denied Les Ferdinand when it seemed the England striker was certain to score. Without those priceless interventions, Eric's dramatic volley would have been no more than a consolation, rather than the dagger to Newcastle's heart it turned out to be.

Not that Peter had it all his own way as a Red Devil following his £750,000 transfer from Brondby in August 1991. He had to survive an uncertain start while he adjusted to the greater incidence of crosses in British football and, like any net-minder, he knew his share of palsied moments and feeble fumbles. But, in general, Peter flourished on the grand scale.

Some individual saves will never be forgotten – for instance, the Banks-like plunging scoop to keep out Rene Wagner's downward header in Vienna in December 1996 – but it was to be his astonishing expertise in one-on-one confrontations which was to become his trademark. As a lone attacker bears down on any goalkeeper, there is an analogy to be drawn with a predator approaching its prey. But somehow, when the 'keeper was Schmeichel, it was the forward who took on the role of likely victim. Quick off his line for such a big fellow, the Dane offered precious little goal to aim at and frequently saved the apparently unsaveable with a spreadeagled parry.

In addition, Peter was a formidable launchpad for attacks, hurling the ball instantly and accurately to beyond half-way. Occasionally, too, if the Reds were trailing late on, he would charge upfield in search of a goal, his only success being the header against Rotor Volgograd in September 1995 which preserved, albeit temporarily, the club's unbeaten home record in Europe.

Clearly, such an accomplished performer with more than a century of international caps to his credit might have been expected to rejoice in widespread affection as did, say, David Seaman. But in Peter's case, a few little, er, eccentricities, got in the way. Though his seemingly hysterical bombast at the first hint of a problem – nothing was ever his fault – did little for his public image, he declared there was no malice involved, that it was merely his method of self-motivation. This explanation was accepted readily by his oft-abused team-mates, who were inspired by his reassuring presence and welcomed his elevation to the captaincy for most of 1997/98 following Roy Keane's injury. However, nothing could gainsay the fact that his tantrums could strike an offensive note, appearing especially inappropriate when they coincided with a run of indifferent personal displays, for example towards the end of 1993/94.

After that, though, Peter regained his pedestal, his customary authority dented only marginally by fleeting aberrations of form, most notably in the middle of 1998/99. It was during this clanger-strewn lean spell, when he was troubled by back problems, that he announced his intention to quit United at season's end, explaining that he no longer felt able to cope with the intense demands of the English game. It was a perception he was to revise in 2001 when he made a surprise Premiership comeback with Aston Villa, and later he astonished many of his old fans even further by enlisting with Manchester City.

Meanwhile back in early '99, after a mid-term holiday, he returned to his best, but would not change his mind about leaving. In Keane's absence, Peter led United to European Cup glory, even contributing to the equaliser in the final against Bayern with his late sortie into attack, and there could be no more fitting climax to his imperious reign. Has there been a better goalkeeper in the world than big Schmeichel during the modern era? In the view of this humble layman, the answer is an emphatic 'no'.

PETER BOLESLAW SCHMEICHEL

BORN: Gladsaxe, Denmark, 18 November 1963.

HONOURS: European Cup 98/9. League Championship 92/3, 93/4, 95/6, 96/7, 98/9. FA Cup 93/4, 95/6, 98/9. League Cup 91/2. 129 Denmark caps (87-01).

OTHER CLUBS: Gladsaxe-Hero, Hvidovre, Brondby, all Denmark; Sporting Lisbon, Portugal, 99/00-00/01 (50, 0); Aston Villa 01/02 (29, 1); Manchester City 02/03 (29, 0).

GAMES	398
GOALS	1

BEN THORNLEY

1993/94 → 1997/98

It was right to remember Ben Thornley amid the euphoria that engulfed Manchester United during the honour-strewn 1990s. A thrustful young winger with tantalising skills and a startling change of pace who had helped to lift the FA Youth Cup in 1991/92, he made his senior debut as a substitute at West Ham in February 1994. Thereafter he hit top form on the reserves' left flank and six weeks on, as his 19th birthday approached, a major breakthrough seemed possible.

With Ryan Giggs out of sorts and Lee Sharpe injured, Ben came under serious consideration for United's FA Cup semi-final against Oldham. But four days before that Wembley date, his world caved in. A tackle by Blackburn's Nicky Marker in a reserve game left Ben with a chronic knee injury and his footballing future in jeopardy. He spent much of 1994/95 in an excruciating limbo of mental and physical anguish, eventually returning to action and gaining experience in loan spells the following term.

By 1996/97 he was back in senior contention, displaying commendable craft and crossing ability during sporadic outings as Giggs' deputy, but lacking the pace to be truly penetrative. Several hefty bids for his services were rejected but in the summer of 1998 he moved to Huddersfield, later enlisting with Aberdeen. Unfortunately Ben did not become established at Pittodrie or elsewhere, but he deserved vast credit for courage in the face of adversity.

BENJAMIN LINDSAY THORNLEY
BORN: Bury, Lancashire, 21 April 1975.
OTHER CLUBS: Stockport County on loan 95/6 (10, 0); Huddersfield Town on loan 95/6 (12, 2); Huddersfield Town 98/9-00/01 (99, 5); Aberdeen 01/02-02/03 (30, 3); Blackpool 02/03 (12, 0); Bury 03/04 (5, 0).

GAMES **6 (8)**
GOALS 0

KEVIN PILKINGTON

1994/95 → 1997/98

Kevin Pilkington was a competent young goalkeeper for whom it was difficult not to feel a smidgin of sympathy. Following his installation as understudy to Peter Schmeichel during 1994/95, the plucky youngster attempted to grow up – in a footballing sense – in the mighty one's all-encompassing shadow, and it was not easy.

After excelling on his senior debut as the Dane's substitute in a home victory over Crystal Palace in November 1994, Kevin knew some trying moments between the Manchester United posts. For instance, he was on duty for the 3–0 League Cup humiliation by York City in September 1995 and although he did not deserve particular blame, he was targeted by whingers who sighed: 'If only Peter'd been here . . .'

In fact, Pilkington was a promising all-rounder but he failed to do himself justice in most of his senior appearances. Accordingly United sought more experienced men, first Tony Coton and then Raimond van der Gouw, to serve as second string while the blond rookie was loaned to other clubs. He did well in spells with Rochdale and Rotherham and extended his horizons further at Celtic in the spring of 1998. However, on his return it was decided that Kevin was not good enough to become Schmeichel's long-term successor and he was freed, going on eventually to thrive as skipper of Mansfield.

KEVIN WILLIAM PILKINGTON
BORN: Hitchin, Hertfordshire, 8 March 1974.
OTHER CLUBS: Rochdale on loan 95/6 (6, 0); Rotherham United on loan 96/7 (17, 0); Port Vale 98/9-99/00 (23, 0); Mansfield Town 00/01-04/05 (167, 0); Notts County 05/06- (116, 0).

GAMES **6 (2)**
GOALS 0

CHRIS CASPER

1994/95 → 1996/97

When Chris Casper was locking up the centre of defence for United's 1992 FA Youth Cup winners, he was rated as likely to succeed as most of his talented team-mates. But given Alex Ferguson's understandable caution over that key position, the tall, dark Lancastrian found progress frustratingly slow.

At first his road was blocked by Steve Bruce and Gary Pallister, a formidable barrier indeed, yet even after Steve's departure, Chris found himself in a queue behind the likes of David May, Ronny Johnsen and Henning Berg. Beyond that, his confidence could hardly have been boosted by the arrival of Dutch star Jaap Stam and the encouraging start made at Premiership level by young Wesley Brown.

Admittedly there was a handful of senior opportunities during a 1996/97 injury crisis and the England youth international, the son of former Burnley hero Frank Casper, stepped into the breach calmly and efficiently enough.

However, though there were no particular howlers and Chris maintained his reputation as a stylish, footballing centre-half, there remained question-marks over his authority and ruthlessness. Season 1997/98 brought a successful loan spell with Swindon and a new two-year contract, but with the certainty of ferocious ongoing competition for a place, he opted for a £300,000 switch to Reading, where his progress was cruelly curtailed by injury. In 2005, aged 30, he became the League's youngest manager with Bury.

SIMON DAVIES

1994/95 → 1996/97

English-born Welsh international flankman Simon Davies was more of a jinker than a flier. On his day he could produce a beguiling stepover and purvey a dummy with bewildering persuasion, yet his pace was unremarkable and he did little to suggest that he would make the leap from Central League stalwart to Premiership regular with Manchester United.

As a lanky left-sided teenager, Simon displayed much skilful promise during the successful FA Youth Cup campaign of 1991/92, then consolidated in the reserves. The next step came with League Cup and European outings during 1994/95, the highlight being his goal against Galatasaray at Old Trafford. Showing commendable composure, Simon chested down a cross from Gary Neville before unleashing an emphatic ten-yard cross-shot to start the Reds on their way to a 4–0 victory.

Though that senior opportunity had been due largely to the rules then restricting the number of foreigners to be used in European competition, Simon had done enough to earn several appearances at League level. Understandably in view of the murderous competition for wing and midfield berths at Old Trafford, he could not cement a place and became unsettled. A transfer request was granted but a move never materialised and he signed a new contract in 1996. However, in summer '97 United accepted a £150,000 offer and Simon joined Luton Town.

CHRISTOPHER MARTIN CASPER		
BORN: Burnley, Lancashire, 28 April 1975.		
OTHER CLUBS: Bournemouth on loan 95/6 (16, 1); Swindon Town on loan 97/8 (9, 1); Reading 98/9-99/00 (47, 0).	GAMES	4 (3)
MANAGER: Bury (05-08).	GOALS	0

SIMON ITHEL DAVIES		
BORN: Middlewich, Cheshire, 23 April 1974.		
HONOURS: 1 Wales cap (96).		
OTHER CLUBS: Exeter City on loan 93/4 (6, 1); Huddersfield Town on loan 96/7 (3, 0); Luton Town 97/8-98/9 (22, 1); Macclesfield Town 98/9-99/00 (48, 3);	GAMES	10 (10)
Rochdale 00/01 (12, 1).	GOALS	1

ERIC CANTONA

1992/93 → 1996/97

Manchester United had been waiting a long time for such a man; since the early 1970s, in fact, when a certain Irishman's progress down a sad and slippery slope became, in sporting terms, distressingly irreversible. Back then, a little boy was playing in the Provence hills where he was raised, unaware of the aching need that was to grow steadily at Old Trafford, not knowing that to him would fall the glorious destiny of meeting that need.

The Red Devils required a genius, no less, one who could supply the final frisson of inspiration and style that would transform a collection of fine players into champions. In November 1992, United found their messiah in Eric Cantona.

As Alex Ferguson has admitted, his purchase of the tempestuous but supremely brilliant Frenchman owed plenty to sheer good luck. The unexpected deal, which had most Leeds fans groping for the sackcloth and ashes, sprang from no more than a casual inquiry by the Reds' boss. Old Trafford's latest title challenge had been endangered by a goal drought and reinforcements were being sought when – *pouf!* – the Gallic charmer, whose late contribution had helped Leeds land the 1991/92 Championship at United's expense, simply fell into Fergie's lap.

The reason for the Yorkshiremen's readiness to sell – and for a mere £1.2 million – has never been explained satisfactorily, but really it doesn't matter. The fact was that the Reds had signed one of the world's most gifted footballers. Now, could they use him to best advantage? Many critics dismissed him as an unwarranted luxury whose flicks and tricks were an attractive but impractical adornment; others reckoned his propensity for falling foul of authority would see him sink without trace. All of them were wrong.

Eric strutted proudly on to the Old Trafford stage, and before long his flair and imagination had given United an extra dimension, a decisive edge which resulted in an exhilarating title triumph in 1992/93 followed by the hallowed League and FA Cup double a year later.

There might even have been a third successive title, but for Cantona's eight-month ban after attacking a lout who had goaded him at Selhurst Park in January 1995. After that, as personal oblivion beckoned, he confounded his detractors to emerge impressively rehabilitated from a period of self-examination. The upshot was yet another Championship, with Eric's goals winning match after match as Newcastle's vast lead was steadily overhauled. All that remains to mention of 1995/96 is that United appointed their Frenchman as captain and they won the FA Cup, courtesy of a late and lordly winner from . . . Eric Cantona.

Notwithstanding his darker side, which tainted his talent occasionally and resulted in disruptive suspensions, his football was unique. Often he seemed to saunter disdainfully while others strained every muscle, but suddenly he would find space where there had been none. Then Eric the innovator would reveal the perfection of his touch with passes of the sweetest subtlety, orchestrating incisive attacks with a distinctive swagger. Yet despite such delicacy, the Cantona cocktail contained strength and athleticism, too, frequently enabling him to brush defenders aside with an imperious shrug.

For all that, it was Eric's goals which provoked the purest wonder. Whether he wielded the rapier (his chips were particularly exquisite) or the bludgeon (long-range bombshells a speciality), the result was the same – utter beauty. Naturally he was feted with awards, notably by his fellow players in 1994 and, more controversially, by the football writers two years later when his rebirth as well as his ability was being honoured.

After that, after everything, what was left for United's turbulent talisman, who had entered his 31st year just two weeks on from the double double? The early months of 1996/97 saw his form falter for the first time, but a melancholy autumn gave way to a more fruitful spring as a renewed quest for glory gathered momentum. However, his wan contribution to the European Cup semi-final prompted suggestions that the end of a magnificent reign was nigh, and so it proved. Just a week after leading the Reds to a fourth Premiership crown in half a decade, he announced his retirement.

Not for him a slow descent into mediocrity; he left as he had arrived, dramatically and on his own terms. Given the nature of the man, the decision to depart at the top was a correct one. The multitudes who lionised him, and his young colleagues in whose development he played such a mammoth part, were left to bid a graceful farewell and cherish the profusion of deathless memories this unique player left behind him.

Back in 1992, Eric Cantona was described as an uncontrollable free spirit, a capricious bird of passage who would never linger. In the four and a half years that followed he became the single most influential footballer in the English game. *Touché!*

ERIC DANIEL PIERRE CANTONA

BORN: Paris, 24 May 1966.

HONOURS: League Championship 92/3, 93/4, 95/6, 96/7. FA Cup 93/4, 95/6. 45 France caps (87-95).
PFA Footballer of the Year 94; FWA Footballer of the Year 96.

OTHER CLUBS: Auxerre 83/4-85/6 (13, 2); Martigues 85/6 (0, 0); Auxerre 86/7-87/8 (68, 21); Marseille 88/9 (22, 5); Bordeaux on loan 88/9 (11, 6); Montpellier 89/90 (33, 10); Marseille 90/1 (18, 8); Nimes 91/2 (17, 2), all France; Leeds United 91/2-92/3 (28, 9).

GAMES	184 (1)
GOALS	82

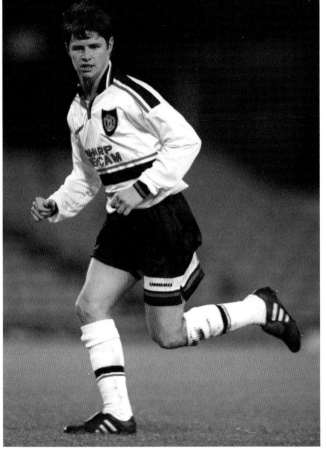

TERRY COOKE

1995/96 → 1996/97

Not many youngsters, no matter how talented, find themselves compared to Diego Maradona on their debut, but it happened to Terry Cooke. To be fair to the journalist with the ultra-fertile imagination, he was referring to just one fleeting moment of inspiration – and it was a bit special.

It happened like this at home to Bolton in September 1995: operating in his favoured attacking position near the right touchline, Terry delivered a sweet, first-time backheel to Paul Scholes, took the instant return in his stride and delivered a perfect cross for Ryan Giggs to score. Of course, it set an awesome standard for the pacy, industrious but rather lightweight little Midlander to maintain and further opportunities proved to be limited, even before a serious knee injury cost him most of the 1997/98 season.

Thus in April 1999, after a perky loan stint, Terry was sold to Manchester City for £600,000 down with a possible £400,000 to follow, and he starred in the Blues' successful promotion campaign before falling out of favour.

TERENCE JOHN COOKE
BORN: Marston Green, Warwickshire, 5 August 1976.
OTHER CLUBS: Sunderland on loan 95/6 (6, 0); Birmingham City on loan 96/7 (4, 0); Wrexham on loan 98/9 (10, 0); Manchester City 98/9-99/00 (34, 7); Wigan Athletic on loan 99/00 (10, 1); Sheffield Wednesday on loan 00/01 (17, 1); Grimsby Town 01/02-02/03 (28, 1); Sheffield Wednesday 03/04 (23, 2); Colorado Rapids, USA, 04-.

GAMES	2 (6)
GOALS	1

PHILIP MULRYNE

1997/98 → 1998/99

When Philip Mulryne scored a fine hat-trick against Birmingham City in one of United's friendly preambles to the 1998/99 campaign, it begged an obvious question. Was the skilful, tenacious right-sided midfielder of sufficient quality to make the Old Trafford grade?

Particularly with widespread speculation at that time about the future of David Beckham in the light of his World Cup trauma, the matter had immediate relevance. However, the England star buckled down to work, Philip receded to the outer fringes of Alex Ferguson's sizeable squad and when Norwich City placed a £500,000 offer on the table in March, it was accepted.

There were those close to the club who regretted the departure of the Belfast-born 21-year-old, who had won full international honours before making his senior debut for United in a League Cup tie at Ipswich in October 1997. They believed that, if he was given time to build up his stamina, Philip was capable of demonstrating his worth. He was afforded the opportunity to prove them correct, or otherwise, at Carrow Road, where he made a commendably impressive start only to have his early impetus jolted by a broken leg.

PHILIP PATRICK MULRYNE
BORN: Belfast, 1 January 1978.
HONOURS: 27 Northern Ireland caps (97-).
OTHER CLUBS: Norwich City 98/9-04/05 (161, 18); Cardiff City 05/06 (4, 0); Leyton Orient 06/07 (2, 0).

GAMES	4
GOALS	0

MICHAEL CLEGG

1996/97 → 2001/02

The most meaningful compliment that can be played to Michael Clegg is that whenever the determined and efficient right-back was plunged into senior action as a Red Devil, he didn't look out of his depth.

But sadly for the calm Mancunian, his limited first-team exploits over five campaigns never translated into solid progress towards a regular squad berth, and his choice became stark: either settle for life in the reserves or move on. Duly, in February 2002, he accepted a free transfer to Oldham Athletic, and it seemed certain that he would thrive at the lower level.

Even in the frenzied atmosphere of an FA Cup encounter with Wimbledon at Old Trafford in January 1997, he had been utterly self-possessed, turning in a cool, competent performance that would not have shamed a veteran. He had passed sensibly, overlapped enterprisingly, made crucial tackles and faced up to the Dons' formidable aerial threat with courage and sound judgement.

Clegg took the eye again in March 1998 when he rose from the bench to enter the European Cup quarter-final fray at home to Monaco. Quick and combative, he stormed forward convincingly and came close to scoring with one fierce drive. In the end, though, he needed a change, and it was a major surprise that he was not more successful at Boundary Park.

MICHAEL JAIME CLEGG
BORN: Tameside, Manchester, 3 July 1977.
OTHER CLUBS: Ipswich Town on loan 99/00 (3, 0); Wigan Athletic on loan 99/00 (6, 0); Oldham Athletic 01/02-03/04 (46, 0).

GAMES **15 (9)**
GOALS **0**

JOHN CURTIS

1997/98 → 1999/2000

John Curtis faced an extra opponent every time he ran on to the pitch as a Red Devil. Having been tipped constantly for stardom since he entered his teens and having captained England at a succession of junior levels, the athletic utility defender was saddled with massive expectations beneath which many a lad would have been crushed.

For a long time, it seemed that John could handle it. An archetypal old head on young shoulders and a born leader, he radiated composure, determination and a certain brand of cool certainty that characterises winners. Of course, he could play a bit, too. The Curtis method was to read the game intelligently, spot danger early and deal with it decisively, an approach buttressed by a splendid all-round technique.

In his mid teens John seemed a natural centre-half, but when he failed to grow beyond 5ft 9ins he switched to full-back, where he made an impressive impact in sporadic senior appearances during 1997/98. A chasing by Arsenal's Marc Overmars showed that there was still a distance to travel, but there was no disgrace in struggling against a world-class player and John learned from the experience.

However, a relentless diet of reserve team football sapped the confidence of the England 'B' and under-21 international and, after impressing on loan with Barnsley, he accepted a £2.25 million switch to Blackburn in May 2000. At Ewood he flourished, helping Rovers rise to the Premiership, but then surprised many admirers by returning to a lower level.

JOHN CHARLES KEYWORTH CURTIS
BORN: Nuneaton, Warwickshire, 3 September 1978.
OTHER CLUBS: Barnsley on loan 99/00 (28, 2); Blackburn Rovers 00/01-02/03 (61, 0); Sheffield United on loan 02/03 (12, 0); Leicester City 03/04 (15, 0); Portsmouth 03/04-04/05 (7, 0); Preston North End on loan 04/05 (12, 0); Nottingham Forest 04/05-06/07 (79, 0); Queen's Park Rangers 07/08 (4, 0).

GAMES **9 (10)**
GOALS **0**

JORDI CRUYFF

1996/97 → 1999/2000

There is no dressing up the bald fact that Jordi Cruyff was not an unqualified success with Manchester United. True, he was unfortunate with injuries but, even when fully fit, the tall, slender Dutchman failed to convince, partly because there was something about him which conveyed a distinct, if misleading, impression of languor. Even in the tumult of Premiership combat, Jordi could exude an incongruous serenity, like some preoccupied young aristocrat heading for drinks on the terrace. In fact, under that blond thatch and graceful demeanour, there existed a footballer alive with immense possibilities. Fiery he was not, but he could play.

His blessings were many, but most important were the silky technique and sharp intelligence which befitted the son of Johan Cruyff, Europe's premier soccer talent of the 1970s. It was a pleasure to watch Jordi when he received the ball in a wide position and pondered a cross into a crowded penalty box. Only seldom would he hit and hope; instead he would attempt to thread a pass to a specific colleague. Of course, he risked tame anti-climax, for the odds were against him when confronted by a forest of opponents, yet it was a mark of his quality that he attempted the harder but potentially more rewarding option.

For lengthy spells Jordi could seem anonymous, appearing to drift on the action's outer edge, but then suddenly he would dispatch a lovely raking pass, unleash an unexpected shot or jink away from an unwary marker. He boasted deceptive pace without having to strain for it, could finish forcefully and his aerial prowess was not inconsiderable. An abrasively physical cutting edge was not on offer, and neither was heart-on-sleeve passion, but there was a measure of beauty in his football.

Jordi developed under his father's management at Barcelona, leaving the Nou Camp for Old Trafford in an £800,000 deal soon after the 22-year-old had performed promisingly for Holland during Euro '96. To Alex Ferguson he offered a classy option as central striker or wide midfielder and, due partly to United's injury situation, he started the League campaign.

To the surprise of some pundits, who had thought him lightweight, he fared pretty well and was in the team more often than not until the late autumn of 1996. Thereafter, though, the injuries piled up and sometimes he looked a Red without much devil. Still, he re-emerged as a useful squad member in October 1998, playing some of the most effective football of his Old Trafford tenure before being loaned to Celta Vigo in January 1999.

Later that year, after making his fourth consecutive Charity Shield appearance, he revealed new-found urgency and earned lavish praise from his manager after rising from the bench to equalise at home to Wimbledon. Understandably, though, Jordi had become sick of life on the periphery and he joined Alaves in June 2000.

JORDI CRUYFF
BORN: Amsterdam, Holland, 9 February 1974.
HONOURS: League Championship 96/7. 9 Holland caps (96).
OTHER CLUBS: Barcelona 94/5-95/6 (41, 11); Celta Vigo on loan 98/9 (8, 2); Alaves 00/01-02/03 (94, 7); Espanyol 03/04 (30, 3); all Spain; Metalurh Donetsk, Ukraine.

GAMES 26 (32)
GOALS 8

KAREL POBORSKY

· ·

1996/97 → 1997/98

One delicious moment of outrageous invention during Euro '96 saddled Karel Poborsky with a burden of expectation under which he laboured anxiously throughout a disappointing Old Trafford tenure. Indeed, that steeply flighted chip which settled the Czech Republic's quarter-final clash with Portugal took on a poignant once-in-a-lifetime aspect as its diminutive author struggled, manfully but sometimes painfully, to come to terms with Premiership life.

Karel was the fleet-footed right-flanker for whom Alex Ferguson had been scouring the world since Andrei Kanchelskis had decamped to Everton and his signing that summer, for £3.5 million from Slavia Prague, was seen as a coup. As a prime factor in both his country's progress to the European final and Slavia's to a UEFA Cup semi-final, the scampering Czech had been feted for his cocktail of industry, tenacity and sparkling skill, and had been courted by Liverpool as well as leading Continental clubs. With his distinctive gaunt features and flowing locks, Karel was portrayed as the latest addition to United's roster of high-profile characters. All that remained was for the newcomer to perform.

He started perkily enough and cut a dash in several early games, most upliftingly at Elland Road in September when he tortured his hosts mercilessly and received what is possibly a unique tribute for a Red Devil. After waltzing through the home defence to

set up goals for Nicky Butt and Eric Cantona, and netting brilliantly himself, he was cheered from the pitch by Leeds supporters!

After that, it seemed that Karel was on the right track, that his verve and imagination would be given full rein, but somehow the 'Czech Express' began to splutter. The potentially destructive distribution became depressingly errant, the darting incursions reduced to fitful wanderings and, despite plenty of encouragement from the stands, Karel's confidence evaporated almost visibly.

Some sympathy was in order. Not speaking English, it could hardly have been easy to adjust to everyday life in a strange land, let alone cope with the searching demands of the Premiership. To his credit, he continued to work hard and, in fairness, he managed some reasonable performances. Of course, a settled sequence in the side would have helped, though that was always an unlikely luxury given his form.

Karel's discomfort ended in December 1997 when he swapped a regular seat on the Reds' bench for a place in the Portuguese sun, joining Benfica for a reported £2 million. Apparently relieved of pressure, he shone both in Lisbon and subsequently back in his homeland, finding true consistency and going on to accumulate more than a century of caps, a Czech record.

What a shame that Old Trafford never witnessed Karel in his pomp. He had once said: 'I want United's fans to remember Poborsky.' So they will, but not quite in the manner he intended.

KAREL POBORSKY

BORN: Jindinchuv-Hradec, Czechoslovakia, 30 March 1972.

HONOURS: League Championship 96/7. 118 Czech Republic caps (94-06).

OTHER CLUBS: Ceske Budejovice 91/2-93/4 (82, 15); Viktoria Zizkov 94/5 (27, 10); Slavia Prague 95/6 (26, 11), all Czech Republic; Benfica, Portugal, 97/8-00/01 (61, 11); Lazio, Italy, 00/01-01/02 (47, 5); Sparta Prague 02/03-04/05 (87, 26); Ceske Budejovice 05/06-06/07 (26, 10), both Czech Republic.

GAMES **28 (20)**

GOALS 6

RYAN GIGGS

1990/91 →

The undimmable brilliance of Ryan Giggs is reflected in his status as one of the most decorated footballers on the planet. There has always been about the dashing Welshman an indefinable spark which marks him out as extraordinary, even among the ever-changing kaleidoscope of stars who flash constantly across the Old Trafford firmament. But if that priceless ability to scintillate, if not quite on demand then not very far from it, has made him widely revered, there is another dimension to the Giggs phenomenon which is equally remarkable, namely his astonishing longevity.

Ryan was illuminating the top flight of English football some 19 months before the advent of Eric Cantona, and he was still there, his desire burning as brightly as ever, alongside Tevez, Nani and the rest of the Reds' new generation more than 17 seasons later. Small wonder, then, that in May 2008 he achieved what many had believed to be impossible given the mountainous demands of the modern game – the outstripping of Bobby Charlton as the man who has made more appearances for United than anyone else in their 129-year history.

From the moment Giggs exploded into the public consciousness, there was no doubt about either his quality or his hunger to succeed. As this writer put it at the time: 'The eyes are cold, the expression deadpan. The slim body hovers over the ball, swaying mesmerically. One enchanting step-over follows another and he is gone, more elusive than a mayfly, as uncatchable as a shadow. Yet again, Ryan Giggs is running free, flowing through a defence as smoothly, as cleanly, as water ripples over the stones on a river bed. In a flash, the sheer beauty of the moment is overtaken by high drama as he changes direction, wriggles like some frenzied eel past several unavailing challenges and draws back his left boot. The ball is struck, the net swishes; the stadium erupts and the day is made for all who prize the extraordinary in sport. The Welsh prodigy plays for Manchester United but he belongs to the world and on occasion, in rapt appreciation of his unique talent, even the fans of his victims have been moved to applaud.'

After being snatched from Manchester City – he had been enrolled in the Blues' School of Excellence, only to sign schoolboy forms with United on his 14th birthday – Ryan made meteoric progress at Old Trafford, tasting senior action as a 17-year-old in March 1991 before emerging coruscatingly during the subsequent season.

The combination of attributes which set him apart read uncommonly like a blueprint for soccer perfection. The total mastery over the ball and the startling acceleration, the exquisite balance and the deceptive strength, they melded together to irresistible effect. There was courage and industry, too, and crucially, his head was not for turning by any amount of adulation. The native nervelessness which enhanced his efforts on the pitch was mirrored by an appealing, level demeanour off it; indeed, had he been any other way, then Alex Ferguson's strenuous efforts to protect him from media predators must have proved fruitless.

Yet for all the gilded glory that began rapidly to accumulate, was Giggs capable of assuming the mantle of true, lasting greatness? Come the dawn of the new millennium, the only reasonable answer was in the affirmative as a purple patch of form announced the onset of his prime. Certainly his running with and without the ball was more destructive than ever, he appeared increasingly aware of passing options, and his crossing became more frequently devastating than dreadful. In summary, he was terrifying his opponents, who knew that if he was on song then, quite simply, they couldn't stop him.

The improvement came as a relief to supporters perturbed by earlier fluctuations of confidence, debilitating injuries and a burgeoning public profile. Ever alert to danger signs, Alex Ferguson reacted with firm understanding, offering periodic rests, extra coaching and sound advice. The results were plain to see in 1995/96 when a re-galvanised, fully fit Ryan played the best all-round football of his life to that date. The impetus was maintained over subsequent terms as he attained gratifying consistency, habitually terrorising some of the world's most accomplished defenders.

For a long time Ryan was best deployed on his natural left flank, offering balance to the team as he tormented victims on the touchline while adding periodic spice by cutting inside like some high-velocity sidewinder. But as he matured as an all-rounder, he proved he could be deadly as an auxiliary front-man, or hugely influential as a wily, string-pulling play-maker in central midfield.

Wherever he has played, he has worked like a demon, and the unforgettable memories have piled up: the sublime run and goal at Loftus Road in early '94 that was Giggs in microcosm; the near-post howitzer that jolted Juventus at Old Trafford in October '97; and, most compelling of all given its context of unhinging the tightest defence of modern times, the bewitching dribble and thunderous drive which evicted Arsenal from the 1999 FA Cup near the end of a spellbindingly dramatic semi-final replay.

There were very occasional losses of form, notably early in 2003, when he attracted a moronic barrage of jeers at Old Trafford. However, then came a sensational slalom to undo Juventus at the Stadio Delle Alpi, and soon he had confounded the puerile critics by a sustained resurgence.

By 2007/08, in which he cemented the League title at Wigan with a smooth-as-molasses clipped finish, the grandeur of his game was barely diminished by the passing of years. Ryan Giggs was still creating havoc, albeit in a more measured manner than in his pomp. His take on the future? Ten Premiership gongs and two European crowns . . . but still counting!

RYAN JOSEPH GIGGS
BORN: Cardiff, 29 November 1973.
HONOURS: European Cup 98/9, 07/08. League Championship 92/3, 93/4, 95/6, 96/7, 98/9, 99/00, 00/01, 02/03, 06/07, 07/08. FA Cup 93/4, 95/6, 98/9, 03/04. League Cup 91/2, 05/06. 64 Wales caps (91-07).

GAMES 669 (90)
GOALS 144

GARY NEVILLE

1992/93 →

Say what you like about Gary Neville – and his countless critics often do, usually but not always from outside the club circle – but the day he strides out on to Sir Matt Busby Way, puts Salford at his back and rides off into the Stretford sunset for the last time, then Manchester United will be so much the poorer. The invariably voluble, sometimes tediously strident Bury-born defender is the Red Devils' Captain Steadfast, an Old Trafford soldier with United in his bones. His passion, his work ethic and his downright bloody-minded commitment to the cause combine with courage, resilience and rather more footballing ability than his detractors usually allow, to form the sort of durable, trustworthy package most Premiership managers would kill for. Not for nothing did Sir Alex Ferguson choose the older Neville brother as the man to replace the redoubtable Roy Keane as his skipper.

Gary's trademark obsession with United dates back to his short-trouser days, when his father started taking him to Old Trafford. The boy was a natural sportsman, who signed as a 16-year-old trainee Red in July 1991, soon forged a promising central defensive partnership with Chris Casper at junior level and captained United's victorious FA Youth Cup side in spring '92. That September marked his senior debut, then came a lull, but a major breakthrough was imminent.

Injuries to Paul Parker and David May in autumn '94 offered an opening at right-back which Gary seized, impressing with his composure, intelligent reading of the game and unfussy tackling. He excelled at smuggling the ball away from danger, unobtrusively but effectively, and he was above average in the air for a full-back. He showed commendable initiative as a speedy overlapper, too, and there was the attacking bonus of his long throw.

That term the slim rookie enjoyed two settled first team spells and although his learning curve proved not so much steep as well-nigh vertical, his aptitude was underlined dramatically in the summer when he was elevated to the England team, having made just 17 Premiership starts. Predictably enough, the extraordinarily calm youngster was not fazed by finding himself so unexpectedly on the international stage. Whether operating at full-back or on the right of a back three, he did well enough to nudge towards the status of England regular. But then, perhaps inevitably there occurred a momentary blip in Gary's runaway success story.

During periods of 1995/96 his customary consistency was less pronounced and there were moments when his habitually fierce concentration appeared to slip. In striving to remedy the situation, perhaps he tried too hard, and the point came when the manager decided that Gary needed a rest. Ironically, the man to benefit was his younger brother Phil, who denied Neville Snr a start in the FA Cup Final against Liverpool. That said, Gary missed only seven League appearances during United's second double-winning campaign and returned resiliently to feature in Euro '96.

Over subsequent seasons he played the best football of his life to that point on the right flank of the Reds' rearguard – his well-oiled link with his chum, David Beckham, proving particularly effective – though periodically his boss would lament the fact that Gary lacked the physical stature (at 5ft 10ins) to operate dominantly in the middle. In all other respects, particularly his ability to order a back four and to cover for team-mates under pressure, Alex Ferguson insisted that he was a natural for the job.

However, trends in football change and, with height perhaps not such an issue in the modern game, Neville was deployed at centre-back for lengthy spells during several injury crises, partnering the likes of Jaap Stam, Wes Brown and Laurent Blanc and emerging from the repeated examinations with his reputation notably enhanced. For example, his speed and anticipation has reduced no less an adversary than Michael Owen to virtual impotence, and he shone in the demanding role in both 2000/01 and 2001/02. Still, when there is a full squad from which to choose, Gary is viewed principally as a right-back of formidable quality, the type who tends to provoke attention only when he blunders, and that is not a common occurrence. True, fans have become accustomed to the occasional horrifically off-beam pass, then there was the mortifying 'mugging' by Shaun Goater in the Manchester derby debacle at Maine Road in November 2002, when Neville dwelt on the ball inadvisably. That cost United a goal and the full-back his place, albeit briefly.

Taking the broader view, however, Gary has been enduringly impressive. Maybe his heart-on-sleeve fervour for United has been difficult for Liverpool fans to stomach, and there was a childish head-butting incident with Manchester City's Steve McManaman; certainly, too, he has riled neutral observers by one or two peevish outbursts as the England players' 'shop steward', though if such interventions were misguided, at least they were born out of loyalty, one of his principal attributes.

More relevant has been his solidity as a defensive bulwark, and his perceptible improvement in the delivery of crosses – not before time, some might say. Tangible recognition has come in the shape of his selection by his professional peers as the best right-back in the Premiership on six occasions, overwhelming acclaim by any standard.

Injury has been his bane in recent seasons – he did not play for more than a year from mid-March 2007, giving rise to fears that his career might be in jeopardy – though he was fit enough to hold aloft the Premiership trophy two months later, and as he did so it seemed that he might explode with pride. He was Gary Neville, victorious captain of Manchester United, a man fulfilled.

GARY ALEXANDER NEVILLE
BORN: Bury, Lancashire, 18 February 1975.
HONOURS: European Cup 98/9. League Championship 95/6, 96/7, 98/9, 99/00, 00/01, 02/03, 06/07. FA Cup 95/6, 98/9, 03/04. League Cup 05/06. 85 England caps (95-).

| GAMES | 514 (27) |
| GOALS | 7 |

RONNY JOHNSEN

1996/97 → 2001/02

Ronny Johnsen was one of the most underrated of all Manchester United footballers. A bargain buy who helped to retain the Championship in his first season at Old Trafford, and who then excelled as the Red Devils lifted the unique treble in 1998/99, the Norwegian international centre-half surely would have doubled his appearance tally but for a savage sequence of injuries which threatened to wreck his career.

How telling it was that after every absence, Sir Alex Ferguson welcomed Ronny back to first-team duty no matter how frenetic the competition for places from established campaigners and promising youngsters alike.

It was easy to see why: the man who was recruited as a comparative unknown for a mere £1.5 million from Besiktas of Turkey in July 1996 was quick and decisive, sure-footed and sharp-eyed, and commendably consistent, thus being admirably equipped to negate any manner of opponent. Speed merchants, battering rams, subtle tricksters, they were all countered with implacable efficiency, yet somehow he was never hailed as a star by the media. No matter. To his manager, his team-mates and fans who have studied him closely, Johnsen remained a rare gem.

In fact, his enduring all-round excellence should have surprised no one because Ronny was virtually a one-man football team. Though primarily a central defender, the slim but muscular six-footer could also operate to the Red Devils' lofty standards in midfield, and he filled in at full-back, while there was yet another dimension to his adaptability. As recently as 1994 he was employed regularly as a striker, the position in which he began his soccer career, in Norway's first division. Indeed, it was a fair bet that such a gifted natural athlete could have acquitted himself soundly even if pressed into emergency duty between the posts.

Those supporters who wondered 'Ronny who?' when he arrived as a prospective replacement for the recently departed Steve Bruce were soon to be reassured. Johnsen was seen at his best frequently during his first term as a Red, notably at Stamford Bridge in February 1997, coping with more composure than most Premiership defenders when confronted with Chelsea's Gianfranco Zola. After scoring an early goal, the brilliant Italian threatened to run amok during a one-sided first half. But Ronny tracked his elusive quarry faithfully, eventually wearing him down, and United duly regained a foothold in the game. Another emphatic example of the Johnsen class came in the home victory over Aston Villa the following December, when he earned man-of-the-match accolades for his well-ordered dominance of Stan Collymore and Savo Milosovic.

In addition, he delivered some of his most persuasive displays as an energetic midfielder during that same season. Back in familiar Turkish territory in October he completed a sternly efficient marking job on Fenerbahce's key man, the Nigerian Jay-Jay Okocha, then excelled as a rock-steady holding player at home to Porto. Similarly he was outstanding when Juventus were overcome at Old Trafford.

For all his aforementioned solidity, Ronny was no slouch with the ball at his feet, either. Though not especially creative, his distribution was invariably sensible, his control was assured and it was not unknown for him to leave an opponent for dead through sheer sleight of foot. Scoring goals was not his prime concern, but after failing to hit the target during his first campaign, he became more of a threat, especially in the air from set pieces, thanks to the splendid timing and often remarkable height of his leaps.

Unfortunately, after contributing royally to the 1998/99 silverware-fest, he succumbed to knee problems which put him out of contention for virtually the whole of the subsequent season, not returning until the win at Southampton with which United clinched the 1999/2000 League crown. Thus, having played in all three legs of the treble, Ronny became possibly the first man to appear in four consecutive games in which major trophies were secured.

A sprightly start to 2000/01 spawned optimism that he still had a future as rather more than a quiz question; cue another breakdown and a career-determining knee operation. That went well and he was shining once more by the following autumn, only to be afflicted yet again, this time being sidelined until February 2002.

Then, with the Red Devils eying further glory on both the domestic and European fronts, the endlessly resilient Ronny slotted in seamlessly alongside Laurent Blanc, for a while performing with all his old poise and resolution as he attempted to earn a new contract. Sadly, but understandably in view of his serial difficulties, it was not forthcoming and he departed to see out his declining Premiership days with Aston Villa and Newcastle.

JEAN RONNY JOHNSEN

BORN: Sandefjord, Norway, 10 June 1969.

HONOURS: European Cup 98/9. League Championship 96/7, 98/9, 00/01. FA Cup 98/9. 61 Norway caps (91-04).

OTHER CLUBS: Tonsberg 91-92; Lyn Oslo 92-93 (31, 7); Lillestrom 94-95 (23, 4), all Norway; Besiktas, Turkey, 95/6 (22, 1); Aston Villa 02/03-03/04 (49, 1); Newcastle United 04/05 (3, 0).

GAMES 131 (19)
GOALS 9

DAVID MAY

1994/95 → 2002/03

The broadest grin at the Riverside on 5 May 1996 belonged to David May, and no one had more heartfelt reason for celebration than the affable blond centre-half. It was the day Manchester United clinched their third Championship in four years and David had headed the opening goal in a 3–0 victory over Middlesbrough, then gone on to play a blinder as Bryan Robson's men had briefly threatened to stage a party-pooping revival.

Beyond that, the man signed as a possible long-term successor to Steve Bruce could feel that he had finally arrived as a Red Devil, having survived some torrid times since his £1.2 million acquisition from Blackburn in the summer of 1994.

When the deal was announced, his capture from United's local rivals was hailed as a coup by the fans. Not only had Rovers been outstripped in the recent title race, but now one of their most promising youngsters had been lured to Old Trafford. Soon, however, that sunny scenario was to take on a gloomy aspect. David took time to adapt to the Reds' slick passing style and cruel jibes began emanating from the direction of Ewood Park. Then, when the squarely-built six-footer proved woefully sluggish during a run in his unfavoured role of right-back – notably in the European Cup debacle in Gothenburg, where he was substituted after being tormented by Jesper Blomqvist – he became the butt of many so-called United supporters, too.

Sadly, just when he needed to play to restore his confidence, David was sidelined by a hernia, not returning to action until the spring of 1995, ironically about the time his former club was relieving his new employers of their Premiership crown.

It was a situation demanding enormous courage and determination, and the former Rover displayed both in abundance. Overcoming further fitness problems in the course of 1995/96, he offered competent cover when Gary Pallister suffered a midwinter injury and attained new heights when called up again in March. Indeed, so dominant was David during the run-in to the League and FA Cup double that Steve Bruce, no less, could not gain a Wembley place.

Infectiously enthusiastic, a doughty aerial battler and a first-rate tackler whose shrewd reading of the game compensated for a lack of outright pace, he had learned to cope with every United game being a high-pressure affair and there could be no doubting his worthiness to wear the red shirt.

Thereafter David excelled as the title was retained in 1996/97, but a combination of further debilitating injuries and heightened competition raised uncertainty about his Old Trafford future. Even so, he performed nobly when called upon during the final month of the momentous treble-winning campaign, notably in the Wembley eclipse of Newcastle's Shearer and Ferguson.

Four days later his 'Last Night of the Proms' show in Barcelona, orchestrating the celebrations even though he didn't play in the European Cup Final, further endeared him to fans. After that, sadly, David's injury curse returned with a vengeance, repeatedly preventing him from stepping in when central defensive rivals suffered mishaps. However, his experience and calming presence proved useful to United's rookie reserves in 2002/03, his farewell season at the club.

DAVID MAY
BORN: Oldham, Lancashire, 26 June 1970.
HONOURS: League Championship 95/6, 96/7. FA Cup 95/6, 98/9.
OTHER CLUBS: Blackburn Rovers 88/9-93/4 (123, 3); Huddersfield Town on loan 99/00 (1, 0); Burnley 03/04 (35, 4).

GAMES 98 (20)
GOALS 8

HENNING BERG

1997/98 → 2000/01

The lack of a work permit cost Manchester United a cool £5 million and the services of Henning Berg for a decade. During the late 1980s, the blond Norwegian defender arrived at Old Trafford for a trial and Alex Ferguson liked what he saw. But that crucial piece of paper was not forthcoming and the promising teenager departed to continue his fledgling career in his native land. Ten years on, the Red Devils' boss finally got his man, but not before Henning had been a key component in the Blackburn side which had denied United the title in 1994/95.

In fact, Alex had made further protracted attempts to complete the signing during 1996/97, a deal reportedly falling through because of strained relations between Ewood Park and Old Trafford. However, the player was desperate to join the club he had supported since boyhood and when he got his wish in August 1997 it signalled the temporary end of United's worldwide quest for a centre-half. Though Messrs Pallister, Johnsen and May were already *in situ*, the manager was determined that his plans would never again be undermined by an injury crisis in such a key area.

Duly Henning settled seamlessly into the side. Icily composed, immensely strong and an assured distributor, he read the play so shrewdly that he seemed to stroll through the most tumultuous sequences of action. At times that term he excelled, particularly under heavy fire away to Juventus and in the siege at Monaco, but at others he appeared ponderous against pace and, handicapped by a niggling hernia problem, gradually he slipped down the pecking order.

Come 1998/99, Stam, Johnsen, Gary Neville, May and Brown comprised a daunting quintet of rivals and by autumn speculation about Berg's future was mounting. But when given an extended first-team run in the New Year, Henning responded magnificently and at the San Siro in March the Norwegian truly captured the hearts and minds of United fans with his coolly polished display against Ronaldo and company. A series of implacable tackles on some of the world's most talented forwards was a colossal factor in the Reds' triumph, while one acrobatic scooped clearance from the head of Ivan Zamorano offered vivid evidence of his athleticism and powers of improvisation.

That April Henning fell prey to further injury, but come early 1999/2000 he was back in the side, only to be ousted soon by newcomer Mikael Silvestre. At that point his prospects seemed bleak, but when the Frenchman lost form in the spring, back bounced Berg, as composed and competent as ever.

It proved but a temporary reprieve, though, and a loan stint back at Blackburn was followed by a £1.75 million transfer in December 2000. Happily Henning thrived once more at Ewood, helping to earn promotion to the Premiership, then skippering Rovers to League Cup glory.

HENNING BERG
BORN: Eidswell, Norway, 1 September 1969.
HONOURS: League Championship 98/9, 99/00. 100 Norway caps (92-04).
OTHER CLUBS: KFUM Oslo, Valerengen, Lillestrom, all Norway; Blackburn Rovers 92/3-97/8 (159, 4) and 00/01-02/03 (91, 3); Glasgow Rangers 03/04 (21, 0).

GAMES **81 (22)**
GOALS 3

NICKY BUTT

1992/93 → 2003/04

Nicky Butt was not blessed with the breathtaking flair of a Beckham, the sweet skills of a Scholes or the studied composure of the brothers Neville. But while those fellow graduates from the Old Trafford academy of soccer excellence attracted a deafening chorus of approval from some of the game's shrewdest judges, United's red-haired midfield buzz-bomb was not exactly lacking in eminent admirers himself.

When Bryan Robson departed for Middlesbrough in 1994, he picked out Nicky as the rookie Red Devil most assuredly bound for the top, while Kevin Keegan, who had managed the combative Mancunian at England under-21 level, predicted a long-term international future. More extravagantly still, no less a personage than the incomparable Pele described Butt as one of the best players in the 2002 World Cup Finals after his sturdily efficient contribution to Sven-Goran Eriksson's generally disappointing team.

It was a remarkable assessment and it might have spurred Nicky to new heights. Instead, disappointingly, the opposite happened. Faced in subsequent seasons by new competition for a club place from the likes of Djemba-Djemba, Kleberson, Fletcher and a re-invented Phil Neville – and with the peerless Keane and Scholes operating on an altogether more celestial plane – Butt receded inexorably to the periphery.

How could that happen? Surely the lavish praise of the Brazilian icon had not turned his notably phlegmatic head? That seems unlikely, but it's a fact that Nicky, whose game had been based on doing the simple things inordinately well, began to introduce unnecessary embellishments, dwelling on the ball, attempting more ambitious passes – and it didn't suit him.

At the outset of his career, the midfielder's most enthusiastic advocate had been Alex Ferguson. After the uncomplicated, hard-working youngster muscled his way to the fringe of the senior reckoning in 1992, the United boss appeared to feel a particular affinity with him, perhaps perceiving in the boy a mirror image of his own passionate desire to succeed.

In the summer of 1995, Ferguson was to demonstrate his faith in unequivocal manner, parting with Paul Ince and paying Nicky the mammoth compliment of not replacing the England star with an expensive new recruit. Indeed, he went further, declaring that he had pondered the wisdom of buying Paul Gascoigne but decided it would not be fair on Old Trafford's crop of youthful talent – particularly Butt, whom he asserted could be held back no longer.

Those who questioned the manager's judgement needed only to re-examine one of United's darkest footballing hours for evidence to back Ferguson's viewpoint. Not many plus points emerged from the Reds' annihilation by Barcelona in November 1994, but certainly the performance of Nicky Butt was one. On that sorry Nou Camp night, he was a study in unshakeable resolution and controlled fire, standing tall as the walls caved in around him and taking responsibility like a veteran.

Thereafter there was ample opportunity to appreciate the midfielder's admirable qualities. A hyperactive ground-coverer with a biting tackle and no mean ability in the air, he was unselfish, endlessly persistent and his sinewy strength made him devilishly difficult to dispossess. His toughness, though not in doubt, tended to be of the calmly uncompromising rather than malicious variety and, unlike some dispensers of hard knocks, he could take them without complaint. As a distributor, Nicky was at his most effective when he kept it simple, which he did most of the time when he was at his best, winning the ball and giving it sensibly, with just the very occasional cute delivery thrown into the mix.

He was never a prolific goal-scorer, though several of his strikes remain vivid in the memory, namely a flying header from David Beckham's exquisitely driven cross in the 1996 Charity Shield drubbing of Newcastle, a savage 20-yarder which won a tight encounter with Leeds at Old Trafford in November 1998, and a dramatic scissors-kick at West Ham in March 2002.

Crucially in the mega-competitive environment of the modern game, his self-belief appeared to be total, he could not be intimidated and his disregard for reputations was comprehensive. Indeed, whether whipping the ball from the foot of an illustrious opponent or directing Monsieur Cantona where to pass (!) the spikily formidable Butt gave every appearance of being nerveless.

As a proven high-quality performer, he would have been a first-team regular at almost any other club in the early 2000s, but United's stellar midfield collection frequently relegated him to the bench. Still, he played 41 times in 2000/01, a campaign during which he contributed the best football of his life, and he appeared content.

But come 2003/04, when he was an England regular but an increasingly marginal figure at Old Trafford, his situation became too bleak to accept, and in July he joined Newcastle United for £2.75 million. Since then, during what might have been his prime, Nicky Butt has sometimes stuttered a tad forlornly, his career ebbing apparently towards an inappropriately low-key end.

NICHOLAS BUTT
BORN: Manchester, 21 January 1975.
HONOURS: European Cup 98/9. League Championship 95/6, 96/7. 98/9, 99/00, 00/01, 02/03. FA Cup 95/6, 03/04. 39 England caps (97-).
OTHER CLUBS: Newcastle United 04/05- (84, 5); Birmingham City on loan 05/06 (24, 3).

GAMES **307 (80)**
GOALS **26**

PAUL SCHOLES

1994/95 →

Paul Scholes is an unobtrusive master of the midfield art, a national footballing treasure for more than a decade, and – begging Ryan Giggs' pardon – the most consistently effective, enchantingly creative attacker of the Ferguson years. The self-effacing, semi-reclusive Salfordian, who has to be practically prised from the United dressing room for post-match interviews when he is desperate to disappear without ceremony in the direction of home and family, becomes almost painfully embarrassed when informed of his exalted status within the game. However, he's had to get used it it, having earned universal acclaim from the most illustrious of his peers. Such lordly contemporaries as Zidane, Vieira and Davids have all lionised him as England's finest, while Europe's leading coaches and managers have added their own heartfelt homage.

By turns subtle and explosive, Paul Scholes is a virtuoso passer with no superior at one-touch football, and a serial scorer of breathtaking goals. He offers imagination, precision and an incessant flow of intelligence way beyond the scope of virtually all his fellow labourers in the Premiership vineyard. Crucially, too, he is no occasional maestro. He applies his sublime gifts on a regular basis, almost matter-of-factly, revealing the unfussy practicality of the true craftsman, getting on with the job while disdaining the extravagant posturing which plagues top-level sport in the 21st century.

No one has captured the chunky redhead's essence more unerringly than that most eminent of wordsmiths, James Lawton of *The Independent*, who in drawing parallels with David Beckham and Liverpool's intermittently splendid but distinctly fitful Steven Gerrard, observed that Scholes was 'a stake aimed at the heart of celebrity football.' Amen to that. Yet another of Paul's fervent admirers was his one-time England boss, Kevin Keegan, who quipped after the United man's head-hand-and-foot hat-trick against Poland at Wembley in 1999 that 'the little fellow deserves a knighthood.'

Sir Paul Scholes? At first glance, he more closely resembles a refugee from the pages of *Just William*. With his scamp's face and wirily boyish build, he lacks only a scruffy school cap and a catapult protruding from a torn blazer pocket to complete an irresistible picture. But place a ball at his feet and a United shirt on his back, and our scallywag is transformed into a soccer thoroughbred, the most perceptive talent of an Old Trafford generation.

For many years he was chronically underrated in the media, but there has never been the remotest doubt about his quality in the mind of the Red Devils' manager, who once affectionately dubbed him a 'bloody little nuisance' for putting so much pressure on the selection process by his sustained excellence. Paul possesses an innate knack of drifting unnoticed into space, even when closely marked in the heart of enemy territory, a capacity which yielded bountiful dividends during the 1995/96 League and FA Cup double-winning campaign. Despite making only 18 senior starts that term, he returned 14 goals to finish as the club's second-highest scorer, behind Eric Cantona. Telling testimony to the pedigree of Scholes the marksman is offered by the sheer variety of his finishing repertoire. Both delicate, eye-of-the-needle placements and savage, long-range howitzers are upliftingly within his compass – mention must be made of two wondrous volleys, the perfect hit from Beckham's corner at Bradford in March 2000 and the awesome looper at Villa Park two days before Christmas 2006 – although clinical clips and nondescript nudges tend to be equally productive. His aerial work is outstanding, too, his timing and courage compensating amply for lack of inches.

No defects? Only one. Although the value of his natural aggression cannot be overstated, he is not a tidy tackler. Indeed, some Scholes challenges have been horribly misjudged and his build-up of needless indiscretions has led to costly suspensions, notably the one which caused him to miss the 1999 European Cup Final. Down the years there has been some debate about his optimum position. He excelled as a rookie front-man, performed sumptuously in 'the hole' behind the main striker and even did selfless work wide on the left, but undoubtedly he is at his scintillating best as the chief orchestrator in central midfield. When Cantona reigned supreme, Paul had to be patient, often occupying the bench when his exceptional ability screamed out for inclusion. But that stage was over by the turn of the century, when he had emerged as a leading light for club and country, both teams lacking a certain constructive dimension in his absence.

His effectiveness was impaired, through no fault of his own, during 2001/02 when the arrival of Juan Veron precipitated the selection of a five-man midfield, but he was shining more lustrously than ever as the title was regained in 2002/03, his *piece de resistance* a gorgeous springtime hat-trick at Newcastle, part of a 20-goal haul in all competitions. For England he suffered for his adaptability, and it's hard to believe that Sven-Goran Eriksson's ill-conceived midfield fiddling, which saw Paul shunted periodically to the left flank, did not heavily influence his decision to depart the international scene in 2004, when he was still, by a distance, his country's premier creative force. There followed a worrying interlude in 2005/06 when fears mounted that an eye problem might end his career, but he returned with renewed vigour and inspiration to star, and to garner his seventh title medal, a season later.

Come 2007/08, knee trouble laid him low for several months, but he remained a compelling contributor from whom United's young midfield bucks had plenty to learn, his classic 25-yard rasper at home to Barcelona providing a luminous highlight on the road to European fulfilment and yet more domestic glory. By that stage only Bobby Charlton, Ryan Giggs and Bill Foulkes had played more games for Manchester United. What fitting company for the great Paul Scholes.

PAUL SCHOLES
BORN: Salford, Lancashire, 16 November 1974.
HONOURS: European Cup 07/08. League Championship 95/6, 96/7, 98/9, 99/00, 00/01, 02/03, 06/07, 07/08. FA Cup 95/6, 98/9, 03/04. 66 England caps (97-04).

GAMES **474 (96)**
GOALS **139**

PHIL NEVILLE

1994/95 → 2004/05

Phil Neville spent a decade in the first-team reckoning with one of the world's premier clubs, averaging around 30 starts per season and excelling in several positions, garnering eight major honours and collecting more than half a century of international caps along the way. Yet still there were those who ridiculed him, refuted his obvious talent and sought to make him a scapegoat when matters went awry. From this quarter, however, such bilious observers are dismissed as malicious, envious or, the majority of them, just plain daft.

Admittedly, it is true that for all his attainments, Neville the younger never quite scaled the dizzy heights predicted for him as a teenager. Probably he suffered from being exceedingly versatile, performing splendidly in both full-back positions and as a midfield enforcer, which rendered him supremely useful to his manager while maybe decreasing his chances of nailing an individual niche.

Phil could be forgiven had he been flummoxed by two mighty jolts which disrupted the runaway success story of his early career – and the fact that he wasn't speaks volumes for his resolution. First he fell victim to glandular fever; then, while struggling to regain prime form in the wake of that debilitating affliction, he was a last-minute omission from the England party for France '98.

Thus a draining physical ailment was followed by a crushing psychological blow, and the leaps-and-bounds progress which had characterised Phil's rise was not maintained during the first half of 1998/99. What a tribute to him, then, that he bounced back to play his part in the springtime treble triumph, and continued to thrive as an integral member of the squad thereafter.

At this point, a glance back at Phil's pedigree is in order. By the time the Reds took their burgeoning title challenge to Newcastle in March 1996, he had already provided ample evidence to suggest that he was an exceptional defender. In addition to his impeccable all-round accomplishments, he exuded colossal composure, way beyond the norm for a boy of 19. Yet if there did exist any flaw in Phil's cool, surely it would be revealed by a remorselessly searching test on Tyneside.

How calmly he faced his black-and-white-striped inquisitors. In the first half, as Newcastle went for a quick kill, he defended sensibly, occasionally brilliantly, against the likes of Asprilla and Beardsley at their most voracious. Then, shortly after the interval, he set up the only goal of the game. Sprinting down the left flank, Phil exchanged passes with Andy Cole before dinking a tantalising cross for Eric Cantona to supply the *coup de grace* with a far-post volley.

A heady business, indeed, yet no one who had followed Phil's sporting development would have been surprised. Since childhood he had excelled at ball games, even having to decide whether his future lay with the Reds or as a batsman with Lancashire CCC. Having chosen to follow Gary into football, he emulated his big brother's absolute dedication and rose smoothly through the junior ranks.

A senior breakthrough arrived in 1994/95, a term which ended upliftingly for Phil when he captained United to victory in the FA Youth Cup, and he found himself in the first team for most of the euphoric double-winning campaign which ensued. A natural right-footer, he combined pace with intelligence, easy ball control with deceptive strength; his tackling was neat, he offered reliable cover to colleagues and he possessed a finely honed attacking instinct.

Twelve days after the FA Cup Final defeat of Liverpool, Phil's career gathered further prodigious momentum when he was capped by England, but all too soon he was faced by deteriorating health. There followed that courageous fightback, after which competition for places became hotter than ever, but Phil remained steady, even during the ludicrous vilification which followed his concession of the penalty which precipitated England's elimination from Euro 2000.

Most frequently he operated, with commendable consistency, on the left flank of the rearguard, though perhaps in another era, unhindered by Gary's presence, he might have played hundreds of games on the right. Sometimes, more eye-catchingly, he was deployed in central midfield, his ruthless steamrollering of Patrick Vieira in the season-turning triumph over Arsenal in December 2002 and his stumbling waltz into the Rangers box to score at Ibrox in October 2003 offering two deathless memories of his prowess in that role.

Indeed, there were some calls for Phil to be anointed as the long-term successor to Roy Keane as ball-winner in chief, but they were not heeded and by the end of 2004/05, the 28-year-old was so sick of life on the margins, his feelings possibly chafed still further by the use of striker Alan Smith in centre-field, that he accepted a £3.5 million move to Everton.

Somehow it grated to see Phil Neville in a blue shirt, but his fervent desire for regular first-team football was entirely understandable and his rapid emergence as a key figure, and skipper, at Goodison came as no surprise.

PHILIP JOHN NEVILLE
BORN: Bury, Lancashire, 21 January 1977.
HONOURS: League Championship 95/6, 96/7, 98/9, 99/00, 00/01, 02/03. FA Cup 95/6, 98/9.
59 England caps (96-).
OTHER CLUBS: Everton 05/06- (106, 3).

GAMES 301 (85)
GOALS 8

ANDY COLE

1994/95 → 2001/02

The advent of Dwight Yorke in August 1998 might have shattered the aspirations of Andy Cole, whose remarkable strike rate of approximately a goal every two starts in his three and a half seasons as a Red Devil had failed to earn the acceptance, much less the affection, which he might have considered his due. But instead of shrinking at the prospect of further high-class competition – remember he had Messrs Solskjaer and Sheringham to contend with already – the much-maligned Midlander struck up a joyful professional and personal empathy with the irrepressible Tobagan. The result was a deluge of goals for both men and the transformation of a widely held, if rather unkind, image of Andy.

Now the so-called morose misfit was perceived anew as a gleeful executioner, a top performer at peace with himself and his world. Grins became more commonplace than glowers, as if some obscure chip was being shed from the Cole shoulder, and the swashbuckling pair cut swathes through bewildered defences with their lightning interplay and untrackable dummies as they spearheaded United's progress towards an unprecedented treble.

Come 1999/2000, his technique ever more refined, Andy contributed a new series of nerveless masterpieces, notably the bicycle kick at home to Leicester and the scintillating swivel, sprint and dink that sunk Leeds at Elland Road. Thereafter that sumptuous form continued into the new century as he became for a time the top-scoring Englishman in the history of European competition, and that despite the waning of his friend's fortunes.

In truth, Andy had done more than enough back in pre-Yorke 1997/98 to repudiate his doubters. He netted 25 times, he was runner-up to Dennis Bergkamp as the players' player of the year and he gave the lie to accusations that he couldn't produce in crucial matches, witness fabulous examples of individual opportunism at Liverpool, Chelsea and Blackburn. Finally he demoralised Everton at Old Trafford with a chip so sublime that, had it emanated from the hallowed boot of Eric Cantona, it would have been hailed as a stroke of genius.

Yet while statistics proved that Cole was no flop, one circumstance which no amount of number-crunching could disguise was that, in his early days as a Red, he had made supporters weep with his profligacy, cutting a poignantly abject figure as chance after chance had gone begging. That image was most vivid at West Ham in the final League game of 1994/95, when United lost the title for the want of one goal and Andy squandered a succession of late openings. Unjust or not, it seemed that some supporters would never forgive him for that. His apologists could assert, with justification, that until 1997/98 he had never enjoyed a lengthy settled sequence without injuries or illness. Fully fit at last, they could add, he proved himself comprehensively.

And indeed, whereas earlier it had been reasonable to ask whether Andy lacked the skill and composure to capitalise on an acceptable percentage of the openings which his own searing pace and predatory instinct helped to fashion, the question became ever less valid. Unquestionably, he could do it.

In retrospect it seems almost surreal to recall how, following his shock arrival in January 1995 in exchange for £6 million and Keith Gillespie, he became something of an aunt sally, the chemistry between crowd and footballer somehow lacking something even in times of triumph.

How gratifying to record, then, how Cole matured into a splendid all-round forward, even apart from his goals; one whose speed and variety of movement off the ball created confusion which was exploited gloriously by colleagues; one who became as much a maker as a taker of chances. All along he worked assiduously, never hiding from responsibility even at his lowest ebb as a whipping boy. For that alone, he deserved enormous respect.

In the end, Andy was chronically unlucky to be edged out, while still in his prime, by world-class newcomer Ruud van Nistelrooy. True, the manager's decision was spot-on, but equally the 30-year-old Englishman's frustration at the prospect of continued bench-warming in the run-up to a World Cup had to be appreciated.

The upshot, in December 2001, was an £8 million move to Blackburn, where he lost no time in completing his set of domestic gongs by grabbing the goal which clinched the League Cup.

Happily, despite his exit, it is not too late for United fans everywhere to cherish the memory of Andy Cole. After his fabulously adroit title-clincher against Spurs in May '99 had laid the ghost of Upton Park, and two more terms of shining achievement had followed, it was the very least he deserved.

ANDREW ALEXANDER COLE

BORN: Nottingham, 15 October 1971.

HONOURS: European Cup 98/9. League Championship 95/6, 96/7, 98/9. FA Cup 95/6, 98/9.
15 England caps (95-01).

OTHER CLUBS: Arsenal 90/1 (1, 0); Fulham on loan 91/2 (13, 3); Bristol City 91/2-92/3 (41, 20);
Newcastle United 92/3-94/5 (70, 55); Blackburn Rovers 01/02-03/04 (83, 27);
Fulham 04/05 (31, 12); Manchester City 05/06 (22, 9); Portsmouth 06/07 (18, 3);
Birmingham City on loan 06/07 (5, 1); Sunderland 07/08 (7, 0);
Burnley on loan 07/08 (13, 6).

GAMES: 231 (44)
GOALS: 121

OLE GUNNAR SOLSKJAER

1996/97 → 2006/07

Ole Gunnar Solskjaer is one of the most beloved Red Devils of the Ferguson era – and not just because his jewel of a volley unfurled a mushroom-cloud of emotion into the Catalonian sky one mild spring evening in 1999.

There is something about the personable Norwegian, an aura born from a mixture of deathless derring-do in the shirt of Manchester United and a certain indefinable quality which maybe comes down to sheer, everyday wholesomeness, that has earned him the undying affection of the Old Trafford faithful.

Yet Solskjaer's immediate success after arriving in July 1996 had been a revelation even to his manager, who had viewed him as a £1.5 million investment for the future. That theory was shattered, comprehensively and gleefully, when pre-season training began. One moment smiling cherubically on the touchline, the next Ole was fizzing between startled defenders like some demonic firecracker and embarrassing Peter Schmeichel with the power and accuracy of his shooting. Duly he was introduced to the Premiership fray as a substitute during the visit of Blackburn in August. Soon the bank holiday crowd was transfixed as the effervescent newcomer administered a dose of pure adrenaline to the hitherto sluggish home attack. A darting, twisting, high-velocity wraith, he nonplussed Rovers' defence with his constant movement, got in six attempts on goal and equalised from one of them. Ole had arrived, and he was to be involved in most of United's matches during the remainder of a hectic campaign.

The son of a champion wrestler, the wand-like Solskjaer bore scant resemblance to an archetypal grappler, though he inherited his father's supple strength and natural balance. He was blessed, too, with searing acceleration, a knack of turning and shooting in one blur of action, and assured ball skills. Ole was quick-witted, so that when the ball was played into a crowded box, he tended to be the first to react, whipping decisively away from his markers; and he would make run after run into unexpected areas. All that, and ideal temperament to boot, made Solskjaer a rare bargain, and in his first term as a Red he attained a chemistry with the fans which others must have envied. His boyish looks and endearing enthusiasm had much to do with that, but his goals – 18 in only 33 starts – were the crucial factor.

At season's end, the 24-year-old must have been barely able to credit his meteoric rise, and his second campaign, inevitably laden with higher expectations, proved more difficult. But then came four more years of high achievment to establish Ole as an all-time Old Trafford favourite. During that period, throughout which he never complained about his status as perennial substitute, he was repeatedly offered more money to play regularly elsewhere, but each time he smiled that engaging smile, proclaimed his loyalty to the Reds, and watched his collection of medals continue to grow. Come 2001/02, above the tumultuous acclaim which greeted that term's string of unforgettable goals by the arch opportunist, another sound became distinctly audible; not quite as obvious, perhaps, but joyously and insistently resonant for all that. It was the unmistakable report of an exploding myth.

Prior to that bountiful campaign, he had been saddled with the reputation of the world's greatest substitute, a substantial compliment in itself but carrying with it the unspoken rider that, somehow, for all his match-winning exploits, there was something lacking in the Solskjaer game. Some pundits had even declared that the arrival of Ruud van Nistelrooy would finally fracture Ole's renowned patience, that having won everything as a Red Devil he would opt for a guaranteed start elsewhere rather than join a never-ending battle with Cole, Yorke and the Dutchman to become United's first choice. How wrong could they be? Cole was transferred, Yorke was marginalised and Solskjaer overcame Sir Alex Ferguson's initial inclination to field a lone striker by forging a fabulous dual spearhead with van Nistelrooy. True, devastating cameo contributions would remain a lethal aspect of his job description, but now, at last, Ole began match after match – and he scored more freely than ever before.

Thus this study in gleeful audacity, this quicksilver elf who made the transformation from virtual unknown to the apple of Old Trafford's eye in the space of one exhilarating campaign, had catapulted himself into a new dimension. Already immortal in United terms for his European Cup Final winner against Bayern Munich, and his four goals in 11 minutes at Nottingham Forest earlier in 1998/99, now he had proved the doubters wrong. Incontrovertibly, he was as effective from the first whistle as he was when summoned to perform one of his trademark late rescues.

Yet there was still another Solskjaer revelation in the offing. In 2002/03 he unseated David Beckham on the right of midfield, proving pacier than the troubled England skipper and almost equally adept at delivering sumptuous crosses. But even as he began to flourish in his new role, Ole was struck down by agonising knee problems which seemed likely to finish him, and he was sidelined for the best part of three seasons. Written off in many quarters, he refused to admit defeat and in 2006/07, with the Reds engulfed by an injury crisis, he effected a prodigious renaissance, scoring 11 goals and collecting his sixth title medal.

Finally, that August, he retired as a player, but departure was unthinkable. Thus he started work as a coach and, in a wildly popular move, Manchester United nominated Ole Gunnar Solskjaer to walk in the gilded footsteps of Sir Bobby Charlton as an ambassador for the club he had served so nobly, through joy and occasional near-despair, for more than a decade.

OLE GUNNAR SOLSKJAER
BORN: Kristiansund, Norway, 26 February 1973
HONOURS: European Cup 98/9. League Championship 96/7, 98/9, 99/00, 00/01, 02/03, 06/07. FA Cup 98/9, 03/04. 67 Norway caps (95-07).
OTHER CLUBS: FK Clausenengen 89/90-94/5; Molde 95/6, both Norway.

GAMES 216 (150)
GOALS 126

TEDDY SHERINGHAM

1997/98 → 2000/01

Technically accomplished, immensely experienced, an England regular, respected by his peers . . . Teddy Sheringham was all these things when he joined Manchester United from Tottenham Hotspur in a surprise £3.5 million deal in the summer of 1997. Yet by the end of his first season as a Red Devil he had been dropped by club and country and could be fairly described as a considerable disappointment.

End of story? Not quite. After recovering from a knee operation in February 1999, Teddy shone on occasional outings, culminating in his man-of-the-match Wembley display against Newcastle, when he rose from the bench to score one goal and create another. Then, for a golden encore, he tucked away the life-giving European Cup Final equaliser against Bayern Munich.

Yet even his exploits on the treble road proved merely the prelude to the full flowering of Teddy Sheringham in 2000/01. Instead of filling the back-up role envisaged for him by dismissive pundits, the cerebral (in a football sense) 34-year-old hit the form of his life, flourishing once more on the international stage while finishing yet another title campaign as United's leading scorer and the double Footballer of the Year. Some of his goals, notably the divine chip which kicked off his hat-trick at home to Southampton in October, were masterpieces of touch, precision and intelligence, attributes which infused his entire game.

In all fairness, the task facing the tall, inventive, but rather ponderous marksman on arrival at Old Trafford was a supremely unenviable one. No matter how strenuously he or Alex Ferguson chose to deflect attention from the circumstance, Teddy was bought to fill the vacuum left by the sudden retirement of Eric Cantona. Not surprisingly, it proved beyond him, as it would have proved beyond most men. He had his moments of achievement in that first term, indeed he gave a handful of splendid performances, but overall his influence was peripheral.

After an anonymous beginning, however, he settled into the United system, more as a deep-lying linkman than a front-runner, and began to show the attributes for which he was renowned. Terrific in the air, a beautiful controller and passer of the ball and a subtle prompter whose wit and composure brought colleagues into the game, Sheringham began to have a positive influence on a winning team. On the debit side at that juncture, he was not the sprightliest of movers, his finishing seemed horribly unreliable and his impact was inconsistent, but there were grounds for hope.

These redoubled when he gave two of his most productive displays: at home to Juventus in October he timed his run to perfection to equalise with a towering header from a Ryan Giggs cross, then returned the compliment by laying on United's third for the Welshman; at Arsenal in November he netted twice, with a firm header after slipping his marker and with a first-time left-footer on the turn from 20 yards.

But it was one exquisite moment against Feyenoord in Holland which, for this onlooker, gave rise to real hope that Teddy might prove an acceptable replacement for Cantona. Taking a short ball from Giggs on the edge of the centre-circle, he looked up and took out three defenders with a sumptuous dispatch to Denis Irwin, who was breaking down the left. Sheer wonder, but sadly it was not to prove typical over the difficult months that lay ahead. While the Reds were purring in mid-term, the Sheringham input was fine, but when the team's fluency evaporated ominously after Christmas, and seasoned campaigners such as he might have been expected to lead by example, he became ever more lacklustre.

Come 1998/99 his prospects deteriorated as newcomer Dwight Yorke gelled spectacularly with Andy Cole, while Ole Solskjaer returned to form. To make matters worse Teddy fell victim to injury and was confirmed in a scapegoat role by many fans, who saw him as a liability. But an enterprising autumn display in Munich offered a telling reminder of his capabilities, then came the fairytale spring revival and, ultimately, that celestial Indian summer.

In consequence he was offered a contract for 2001/02 but opted for a return to Tottenham secure in the knowledge that the epitaph to his Manchester sojourn would be of the hallowed variety. Once blamed, ludicrously it's true, for a trophyless season, Teddy Sheringham had survived and prospered. Thus when he left Old Trafford it was as a genuine hero, but even that wasn't the end of the story as this supreme professional continued to shine as a potent Premiership force into his forties.

EDWARD PAUL SHERINGHAM
BORN: Highams Park, London, 2 April 1966.
HONOURS: European Cup 98/9. League Championship 98/9, 99/00, 00/01. FA Cup 98/9.
51 England caps (93-02). PFA Footballer of the Year 01. FWA Footballer of the Year 01.
OTHER CLUBS: Millwall 83/4-90/1 (220, 93); Aldershot on loan 84/5 (5, 0); Nottingham Forest 91/2-92/3 (42, 14); Tottenham Hotspur 92/3-96/7 (166, 76) and 01/02-02/03 (70, 22); Portsmouth 03/04 (32, 8); West Ham United 04/05-06/07 (76, 28); Colchester United 07/08 (19, 3).

GAMES 102 (51)
GOALS 46

DENIS IRWIN

1990/91 → 2001/02

The young bucks clamoured incessantly for his place, but Old Man Irwin, he just kept rolling along, all the while accumulating medals with the same relentless efficiency and metronomic consistency which characterised his football. Renowned as the quiet man of Old Trafford, Denis was genuinely unassuming, even unobtrusive; but let no one doubt that those gentle qualities concealed a core of tempered steel and a fierce ambition which burned brightly to the last.

When his Premiership peers voted the Irishman the League's best left-back in the spring of 1994 – an accolade they repeated in 1999 – they were merely confirming a belief that had been growing steadily in Manchester for several seasons. Indeed, after United had lifted the Championship in 1992/93, Alex Ferguson described Denis as one of the finest flank defenders in the world. No voice was raised in argument then – and the silence in the success-laden years that followed was deafening.

No player was more reliable as the Reds yomped to League and FA Cup doubles in 1993/94 and 1995/96 and the treble in 1998/99, and if the public plaudits rained inevitably on the heads of Cantona *et al*, that never bothered the amiable Irwin, whose £650,000 capture from Oldham Athletic in June 1990 was to prove an absolute steal.

By the time United faced the Latics in two FA Cup semi-final clashes that year, they had already been tracking the progress of the 24-year-old right-back who had revived his career at Boundary Park after being released by Leeds in 1986. His calm and class on both occasions made up Ferguson's mind, and Denis was wearing the Reds' number-two shirt as the new campaign got under way. In typically unspectacular fashion, he used that term to bed himself in: at the back, he impressed with his pace, precise passing and resourceful reading of the game, while his ability to deliver wickedly curving crosses, low-trajectory missiles that bent around defenders and lured 'keepers from their lines, became a potent offensive weapon.

Then 1991/92 brought change and a challenge to which the Eire international responded magnificently. The manager's decision to deploy new arrival Paul Parker at right-back saw Denis switch flanks, and initially he looked a little out of place. But though naturally right-sided, he was blessed with splendid touch in both feet and soon he settled seamlessly at number three. Thereafter, while remaining solid in defence, he blossomed as an attacking force. His incisive overlaps became a joy to behold and, as his confidence mushroomed, his knack of hitting the ball cleanly brought rich rewards.

That season Denis netted four times and in the next he went one better, with no strike more welcome than his low 20-yarder which claimed the points in a tight April confrontation at Coventry. Come 1993/94 the all-round Irwin game reached new heights, his rearguard duties being discharged with the usual unshowy excellence, while two of his efforts at the other end would have done credit to any star in the Old Trafford constellation. At Anfield in January, Denis curled the sweetest free-kick imaginable past Liverpool's wall; next, at Selhurst Park against Wimbledon in the FA Cup, he exchanged passes cleverly with Paul Ince before conjuring his way past two opponents with Giggs-like élan, then applying the most clinical of finishes.

If United's largely unsung hero had a weakness, it was in the air (he stood only 5ft 8in), though even when he couldn't win the ball outright, usually he managed to distract the opposition with a well-timed leap. In any case, to dwell on such a marginal flaw is to be over-fussy. In general, he was a mature defensive anchor of enduring value, as a generation of frustrated young challengers for his shirt – all of whom soaked up priceless wisdom from the veteran – would testify eloquently.

Irwin's stature was enhanced still further in the autumn of 1997 when he succeeded Teddy Sheringham as penalty taker and again in the following spring when he stood in for Peter Schmeichel as skipper. During 2000/01 he became only the sixth man to pass the 500-game milestone for the club, then changed his mind about departure to enjoy yet another season of top-level competition, understandably no longer as a first-team regular.

Finally, in his 37th year, when he stepped aside to begin a characteristically efficient spell for Wolves, there was a cacophony of tributes ringing in his ears. We'll finish with one of the most telling, from his former Oldham boss Joe Royle, who said: 'Denis Irwin has been the best full-back in British football for at least a decade.' That said it all.

JOSEPH DENIS IRWIN

BORN: Cork, Republic of Ireland, 31 October 1965.

HONOURS: European Cup 98/9. European Cup Winners' Cup 90/1.
League Championship 92/3, 93/4, 95/6, 96/7, 98/9, 99/00, 00/01. FA Cup 93/4, 95/6. League Cup 91/2.
56 Republic of Ireland caps (90-99).

OTHER CLUBS: Leeds United 83/4-85/6 (72, 1); Oldham Athletic 86/7-89/90 (167, 4); Wolverhampton Wanderers 02/03-03/04 (75, 2).

GAMES	511 (18)
GOALS	33

ROY KEANE

· ·

1993/94 → 2005/06

Roy Keane was Manchester United's most influential footballer of his day, bar none. Booed like a pantomime villain on grounds up and down the land and possessed by a rage to win that matched Sir Alex Ferguson's, he remained for more than a decade the player most coveted by opposing managers, the man who made his team play in difficult times.

Never was this more apparent than in Turin in April 1999, with the Reds two adrift after 11 minutes and facing Champions League oblivion. Then, when the need was most dire, the ferociously driven Irishman transformed the contest by a sustained act of sheer will. He headed an unstoppable goal which sent visible tremors through Juventus and, more crucially still, dictated play with an implacable authority which rapidly established psychological supremacy.

It was typical of the man. One moment scrapping like a yard-dog, the next passing like a master, he was both a physical colossus who breathed confidence into team-mates, and a creative fixer with a hand in every phase of play. That night, as became the norm after his recovery from a career-threatening knee injury which sidelined him for most of 1997/98, he was the heartbeat of Alex Ferguson's pulsating side, brimming with commitment, his concentration never faltering for a split second.

The infamous, self-destructive clash with his international boss in the run-up to the 2002 World Cup notwithstanding, Keane proved himself the natural choice to succeed Eric Cantona as club skipper, becoming ever more forthright as he grew into the job and dispensing barbed homilies with devastating clarity – witness his scathing reference to the prawn-sandwich brigade of executive-box fans, his barely controlled post-match fury after various defeats and the final tumultuous rant against under-achieving colleagues which was the prelude to his unceremonious leave-taking to join Celtic in November 2005.

Yet for all that passion, and despite the bookings which cost him his place in the 1999 European Cup Final, he demonstrated that, except in rare instances such as his inexcusable foul on Manchester City's Alfie Haaland in April 2001, he could achieve the fine balancing act on the pitch between vigour and excess.

After becoming a Red Devil for a British transfer record of £3.75 million in July 1993, the Eire midfielder completed a highly satisfactory first term, taking the eye with his lung-bursting box-to-box surges while helping to secure the League and FA Cup double. In 1994/95 he seemed to plateau a little, overshadowed perhaps by fellow dreadnought Paul Ince, and it was 1995/96 before he was revealed in all his glory as the Reds' midfield anvil, sometimes building, frequently destroying, invariably controlling. Then, revelling in the extra responsibility entailed by the departure of the England star, he reached new heights of consistent excellence, a standard he maintained, and embellished mightily, in subsequent seasons.

Indeed, after a 12-year United career, it could hardly be clearer why Ferguson had pursued the former boxer, Gaelic footballer, sprinter and marathon runner since he had first surfaced at Nottingham Forest. Yet back in '93, after clocking in at Old Trafford, the sought-after 21-year-old was confronted by a few early home truths. They were imparted on that most revealing of arenas, the practice pitch, where his general sharpness and aspects of his technique were found wanting. To his credit, Roy worked prodigiously to improve and reacted to the challenge with disarming self-deprecation, declaring: 'I just run around a lot.' True, limitless stamina allied to pace and aggression was important to his input, but any objective observer would go on to speak of far, far more natural ability than he would mention himself.

Much later in his United career, Keane was written off periodically, notably after a hip operation in 2002. But though his body creaked ever more alarmingly, and he had become more a screener of the rearguard than a rampaging attacker, on each occasion he would snap back to volcanic form, never more compellingly than in early 2005, when in quick succession he humbled Liverpool's Steven Gerrard and Patrick Vieira of Arsenal, the two pretenders to his title of the Premiership's most dynamic midielder.

When, as a teenager, he wrote to most top English clubs asking for a trial, he didn't bother with United because he didn't think he was good enough. As it turned out, the price of a stamp could have saved the Red Devils a fortune. Understandably, when club and player sat down to contract talks a few years on, he was more sure of his value.

As for the multitude of fans who roared his name ceaselessly and with such reverence, they never entertained the merest sliver of doubt about their talisman's worth, even when his demons of frustration, given voice partly by his own waning powers, were tormenting him grievously in the weeks before his stormy exit.

Indeed, when he excoriated some of his young team-mates so mercilessly on MUTV for their perceived complacency, he was, broadly speaking, echoing supporter opinion, and he was hailed in many quarters as the conscience of the club. After that, no manager could have allowed him to stay. But even at that late hour Roy Keane was still burning to win, still contemptuous of those whose fervour did not equal his own; still, until he walked out the door, unquestionably Manchester United's main man.

ROY MAURICE KEANE

BORN: Cork, Republic of Ireland, 10 August 1971.
HONOURS: League Championship 93/4, 95/6, 96/7, 98/9, 99/00, 00/01, 02/03. FA Cup 93/4, 95/6, 98/9, 03/04.
67 Republic of Ireland caps (91-05). FWA Footballer of the Year 00. PFA Footballer of the Year 00.
OTHER CLUBS: Nottingham Forest 90/1-92/3 (114, 22); Celtic 05/06 (10, 1).
MANAGER: Sunderland (06-).

GAMES	458 (22)
GOALS	51

DAVID BECKHAM

1992/93 → 2002/03

David Beckham's distressing descent into relative mediocrity with Real Madrid, his Spanish title medal of 2007 notwithstanding, should never be allowed to obscure his earlier majestic contribution to the Manchester United cause. Though he excited ever more passionately conflicting emotions as his celebrity spiralled, inflaming his fans and detractors alike, there could be no doubt that he was special. Not because of his untold wealth, or the extravagant trappings of his fame, or the widespread obsession with the trivia of a lifestyle divorced from everyday reality. He was special because he created moments of wonder on a football field, flashes of beauty that remained vivid in the memory long after a match, or a season, was over. He was not the perfect player, yet there were occasions on which he could lift sporting endeavour to truly rarefied heights. That cannot be said of many performers in the modern game and so, despite the oceans of tediously irrelevant media fluff which so often suffocated the original cause of his prominence, Beckham the footballer deserved to be cherished.

There was strength of character to be admired, too. In a previous edition of this book, reference was made to David's need to curb his temperamental excesses, no matter how understandable they might be for a boy scrutinised so relentlessly by the public eye. That was written before his infamous indiscretion against Argentina during France '98, an incident which catapulted the slim Londoner and his family into a nightmare of moronic and astonishingly venomous vilification. He might have quailed and retreated, but he battled on, his form somewhat muted at first but improving dramatically until he had earned the respect of all right-minded observers. In time he was elevated to the England captaincy, maturing rapidly and effecting a seismic turnaround in his public perception, particularly following his inspirational performance and typically sensational late free-kick against Greece which secured World Cup qualification in 2002.

David's progress was of the storybook variety after he left home, practically in West Ham's backyard, to join United as a skinny but delectably skilful 16-year-old in July 1991. Within ten months he had helped to win the FA Youth Cup, then made his senior debut in September 1992. There followed two years in the reserves, learning his trade while adding physical strength to his bountiful natural gifts, which he paraded impressively against Galatasaray in December 1994. That night his coolly taken goal and all-round expertise served notice of what might be expected of young David Beckham. Duly in 1995/96 he began to deliver. Deployed on the right in the void created by the departure of Andrei Kanchelskis, he made an exhilarating contribution to United's second League and FA Cup double. But it was in 1996/97 that the words Beckham and star began to be used in meaningful conjunction. A scintillating Charity Shield show against Newcastle was followed by his celebrated long-distance miracle against Wimbledon. In the weeks thereafter, though United spluttered, the 21-year-old shone so brightly that he was picked for England.

What set him apart from his peers? There was the power and dexterity with which he struck a football, whether curling it unstoppably towards goal or arrowing it to a colleague, a golden knack that saw him dubbed the world's finest crosser and premier free-kick specialist; then there was the panoramic vision of his passing, its astonishing accuracy over vast distances, and an invaluable facility for disguising the direction of delivery. Add to that an undimmed eagerness to learn, a commendable work rate and the combination of zest and initiative which characterised his entire game, and the picture of a head-turning entertainer took on increasingly sharp focus. But even such a near-comprehensive catalogue of qualities did not tell the entire tale. There was one more characteristic, far from evident from his conversation, that rounded off the Beckham phenomenon. David was not an arrogant boy – far from it – but there was an arrogance in his play, a certain sureness which proclaimed, even on a poor day, that here was a man who could change the course of events.

His best position? Some said only central midfield offered maximum scope to his immense gifts, but he never produced a body of evidence to support the theory. Most sound judges maintained that he was most effective wide on the right, where he became the Reds' principal goal-maker, not matching Kanchelskis for speed – indeed, rarely taking the ball past a marker – but outstripping the Ukrainian for soccer intelligence. However, even as one memorable campaign followed another with the Beckham work-ethic never faltering, a certain inconsistency became apparent in his game as his life was engulfed increasingly by the media madness which he did nothing to defuse. Not surprisingly, Alex Ferguson, a football man to his core, saw Beckham-mania as a crazy distraction, and gradually a terminal rift grew between them, coming to a head in 2002/03 when the manager was justified in sometimes selecting Ole Gunnar Solskjaer ahead of the icon on merit.

At the end of that term United upset some supporters and earned the approbation of others by accepting a £25 million bid from Real Madrid. Thereafter the most marketable footballer of all time met the Spaniards' need for global brand domination, but not for supremacy on the field. During his first three years at the Bernabeu, there were no championships. Then again, those seasons yielded no titles back at Old Trafford, either. Whether United and David Beckham would have tasted further serial glory had they remained together remains a matter for impassioned debate.

DAVID ROBERT JOSEPH BECKHAM

BORN: Leytonstone, London, 2 May 1975

HONOURS: European Cup 98/9. League Championship 95/6, 96/7, 98/9, 99/00, 00/01, 02/03. FA Cup 95/6, 98/9. 100 England caps (96–).

OTHER CLUBS: Preston North End on loan 94/5 (5, 2); Real Madrid, Spain, 03/04-06/07 (63, 7); LA Galaxy, USA, 07/08- (13, 3).

GAMES 356 (39)

GOALS 85

JAAP STAM

1998/99 → 2001/02

To stunned Manchester United fans, when news broke of Jaap Stam's £16.5 million sale to Lazio in August 2001 the shock was as profound as it was shattering. How could Sir Alex Ferguson part willingly with the iron gladiator at the heart of his treble-winning rearguard, the colossal centrepiece of three successive title triumphs, an Old Trafford cult idol twice voted Europe's top defender?

Then, as now, there was an element of mystery about the Dutchman's dramatic departure, but on reflection a thread of logic began to materialise. Jaap's form had deteriorated following a lengthy injury lay-off, albeit not drastically; the Italians' offer was handsome in a year when the club had made a £50 million transfer outlay; and there was the manager's assertion that Stam was not the natural teacher he craved to educate comparative rookies such as Wes Brown and Mikael Silvestre in the advanced defensive arts.

But what, exactly, had United lost? Well, some stoppers are endowed with Herculean physical strength and overwhelming presence, others take to the field armed with prodigious mental toughness, while yet more are blessed with speed, intelligence and an assured technique. However, those who did battle with Jaap Stam – he of the Goliath-like frame topped with that sternly chiselled, imperious glare – faced a rare and daunting combination of all those attributes. That is why, certainly during most of the first two of his three full seasons as a Red Devil, it was hard to imagine a more complete defender anywhere in the world.

In the view of Johan Cruyff, his fellow Dutchman merited that accolade already when PSV Eindhoven asked Manchester United £15 million for their man-mountain in the spring of 1998. Eventually, thanks in part to the player's determination to join the club he had supported as a boy and his absence of greed during financial deliberations, a deal was struck for £10.75 million, still enough to make him the costliest defender on the planet.

Thereafter, having taken his place on that unenviable pedestal, Jaap became a natural target for media snipers who dwelt mercilessly on a handful of errors during Holland's progress to the World Cup semi-finals. Then followed further ill-judged ridicule as he strove to adjust to the hectic pace of the English game.

Naturally, there were teething troubles, particularly growing accustomed to the Reds' offside tactics while not operating in a settled central defensive partnership. However neither Stam, nor those who appreciated the massive extent of his ability, allowed their heads to drop; faced with adversity, he merely rolled his sleeves a little higher and concentrated all the harder. The situation echoed initial criticism of Gary Pallister and the cheap, vacuous 'donkey' treatment once meted out to Tony Adams and, sure enough, the Dutchman prevailed in similar triumphant manner to the two Englishmen.

Before long he struck a vein of consistent form that had his erstwhile detractors queueing to lavish praise. It was easy to see why: Jaap's vast strength made it virtually impossible to muscle him out of any challenge, he was deceptively quick and nimble for such a big man and he was a decisive timer of tackles, usually attempting to place his body between opponent and ball and then turning away in possession, rather than committing himself by diving in rashly. He read the game with immense perception, he could control instantly a ball plummeting from the sky, and he could pass with calm accuracy. In addition, if he made a mistake he was not outwardly upset by it, just getting on with the job with a minimum of fuss.

During the momentous spring of 1999, Stam exerted a towering influence as United achieved their treble, and he was never mightier than in the tumultuous semi-final clashes with Arsenal and Juventus, emerging as a quiet leader, a performer to be trusted implicitly. Duly he was voted the outstanding defender of that Champions League campaign and Premiership managers nominated him as the player they coveted above all others.

Though 1999/2000 brought occasional moments of vulnerability as he sought to build understandings with newcomers Mark Bosnich and Mikael Silvestre, Jaap remained the benchmark by which all other stoppers were judged, and his stature was emphasised by his appointment as deputy skipper to Roy Keane.

Achilles damage caused a protracted absence during 2000/01 and a few slips ensued, but a new long-term contract was signed and his Old Trafford future did not appear in the remotest doubt.

Then came that abrupt exit and subsequent suspension in Italy over alleged use of a banned steroid, an offence he denied strenuously. As to the wisdom of parting with Jaap Stam, history will be the only judge that matters.

JAKOB STAM

BORN:	Kampen, Holland, 17 July 1972.
HONOURS:	European Cup 98/9. League Championship 98/9, 99/00, 00/01. FA Cup 98/9. 67 Holland caps (96-04).
OTHER CLUBS:	FC Zwolle 92/3 (32, 1); Cambour Leeuwarden 93/4-94/5 (66, 3); Willem II 95/6 (19, 1); PSV Eindhoven 95/6-97/8 (81, 11), all Holland; Lazio, Italy, 01/02-03/04 (38, 1); AC Milan, Italy, 04/05-05/06 (34, 1); Ajax, Holland, 05/06-07/08 (31, 1).

GAMES	**125 (2)**
GOALS	1

DWIGHT YORKE

1998/99 → 2001/02

After scaling the giddiest peaks of club football as a Red Devil, sparkling rapturously on the path to treble glory in 1998/99, Dwight Yorke plumbed infuriating depths of under-achievement as he failed to maintain his early impact. But despite the inevitable frustration at the stagnation of an incandescent talent, it would be a curmudgeonly United fan, indeed, who would not glance back and rejoice at the enchanting derring-do of the effervescent Tobagan.

With the utmost respect to Dwight's Villa Park achievements, it's fair to say that there was hardly communal rejoicing among the Old Trafford legions when Alex Ferguson paid a club record £12.6 million to sign the striker in August 1998. The Reds had been linked with a succession of international stars – the likes of Gabriel Batistuta and Patrick Kluivert – and Yorke's name would not have appeared on many laymen's lists of top transfer targets. Indeed, when the tiresomely protracted negotiations culminated in the Villa favourite becoming the sixth most expensive footballer in history, there was widespread condemnation of the deal. The sanity of the game in general, and the Reds' boss in particular, was called into question.

Oh, we of little faith! During 1998/99 the fee looked less exorbitant with each of Dwight's 29 goals as the newcomer illuminated the United attack with a capacity for the unexpected which had been largely lacking since the departure of Eric Cantona. Yorke emerged as Old Trafford's laughing cavalier, his infectious zest embellishing his bountiful ability with a feelgood factor and an all-too-rare sense of enjoyment which was refreshingly welcome in the pressurised, stress-laden world of top-level football.

Throughout most of that epoch-making campaign, Dwight exuded impudence without arrogance. Clever, unorthodox and endlessly audacious, he augmented his lavish skills with industry, courage and resilience. Apart from his exceptional strike rate, he impressed as an all-rounder who could drop deep to telling effect, a legacy from a midfield stint during his Villa days. With his subtle movement and assured control, he offered an ever-present passing option, while his potent partnership with Andy Cole was rightly eulogised. Their high-speed choreography, their bewildering cocktail of dummies, step-overs and some of the slickest one-two passing combinations ever seen at Old Trafford, gave the attack a pulsating and much-needed new dimension.

But while the chemistry between Dwight and Andy made them the manager's first-choice combination, the Tobagan demonstrated that he could thrive alongside Ole Gunnar Solskjaer and Teddy Sheringham as well, while link-ups with Ryan Giggs and Paul Scholes meant he had been half of no less than five frontline duos before the end of September.

Variety was a feature, too, of the Yorke goal catalogue. Fierce drives and adroit volleys were supplemented by subtle dinks and routine tap-ins while, though not outstandingly powerful in the air, he displayed a priceless knack of sneaking unnoticed between defenders. But if one goal summed up the appeal of Dwight Yorke it was the second of his brace at Chelsea in the FA Cup quarter-final replay. After a typical piece of persistence by Cole, the ball ran loose some 25 yards out in the inside-right channel. There seemed little immediate danger to Ed de Goey's goal but Dwight delivered an instant chip with the outside of his right foot which sent the ball arcing unerringly over the stranded 'keeper to nestle in the far corner of the net. Sheer, unadulterated brilliance.

Perhaps inevitably after enjoying such a buoyant start, Yorke suffered a late springtime hiccup to his form, when the goals ceased to flow and his touch seemed suddenly uncertain. Happily he was back on song for the climax of a tumultuous campaign in which he had exceeded virtually all expectations except, presumably, those of the man who mattered most.

There followed, though, more prolonged blips in subsequent seasons, even though he plundered 20 Premiership goals on the way to the 1999/2000 title and contributed a superb hat-trick to the 6-1 home thrashing of Arsenal as a third successive League crown hove into sight.

Lurid tales about his private life became common currency in the tabloids and, all too often, he was a travesty of his former self on the pitch. Reasons advanced included nagging injuries, disruptive international calls and the unexpectedly masterful climax of Sheringham's career, which cost him his place in the side for much of 2000/01.

Whatever, that old Yorke brio never fully returned and in the summer of 2002 he was sold to Blackburn for £2 million, linking up once more with his old chum, Cole. Despite everything, though, Dwight deserves to be remembered in Manchester with gratitude, affection and, most appropriately, downright glee. After all, his United ratio of better than one strike for every two starts was exceptional; and, almost as important, he scored his goals for fun.

DWIGHT EVERSLEY YORKE
BORN: Canaan, Tobago, 3 November 1971
HONOURS: European Cup 98/9. League Championship 98/9, 99/00, 00/01. FA Cup 98/9.
58 Trinidad and Tobago caps (89-).
OTHER CLUBS: Aston Villa 89/90-98/9 (231, 75); Blackburn Rovers 02/03-04/05 (60, 12);
Birmingham City 04/05 (13, 2); Sydney, Australia, 05/06 (22, 7);
Sunderland 06/07- (52, 6).

GAMES **120 (32)**
GOALS **66**

JESPER BLOMQVIST

1998/99

Alex Ferguson believed that lack of high-quality left-flank cover for Ryan Giggs cost the Red Devils dearly when the Welshman was injured in the spring of 1998 – and so, that summer, he bought Jesper Blomqvist.

When he paid Parma £4.4 million for the one-time whizz-kid of Swedish football, Ferguson was acquiring a player he had coveted for several years, perhaps since an uncomfortable evening in Gothenburg in November 1994, when Jesper had tortured the out-of-position David May and reduced United's Champions League dreams to tatters.

Now, after several failed attempts to sign him, the Old Trafford boss was getting a more mature, experienced performer with four Swedish title medals to his credit, even if he had not made the impact expected of him in Italy.

Initially Blomqvist expressed reservations about the move, not wanting to languish in the shadow of a star, but reached agreement after hearing that the option of playing Ryan in the centre was under active consideration. As it turned out through a variety of circumstances, the newcomer received plenty of opportunities and there were instances when, if hardly a like-for-like replacement, he earned his corn as a credible alternative to Giggs.

After an understandably tentative start, Jesper grew in confidence and revealed flair and guile aplenty during the autumn, as well as a willingness to tackle back, albeit clumsily on occasion. At Southampton and in Brondby he demonstrated the capacity to beat defenders before dispatching delightfully perceptive passes, but it was in the return match with the Danes that he enjoyed his most outstanding moment, embarking on a run from his own half past three opponents before freeing David Beckham to set up a goal for Dwight Yorke.

However, it was not always thus. Sometimes he lacked penetration, proving indecisive when in menacing positions, notably at Middlesbrough in May 1999. His critics reckoned that he cut inside too much, yet without the goal sense to justify it. Still, none could question his effort and there was the mitigating factor of a niggling long-term foot problem which limited his effectiveness in the European Cup Final.

The best of Blomqvist, it was hoped, lay ahead, but a knee injury suffered in a late-summer Hong Kong friendly was the start of a nightmare for the affable Swede. A succession of operations, setbacks and false dawns followed, but despite brave and protracted efforts to return he was never to play another senior game for United.

Instead in November 2001, two and a half years on from scaling the summit of European football, Jesper was freed for a fresh start at Everton. All who recognised his vast potential, and grieved at his cruel misfortune, wished him the best of luck. Alas, he was released at season's end, his career in terminal decline.

LARS JESPER BLOMQVIST

BORN:	Tavelsjo, Sweden, 5 February 1974.
HONOURS:	European Cup 98/9. League Championship 98/9. 30 Sweden caps (94-02).
OTHER CLUBS:	Tavelsjo IK, Sweden; UMEA, Sweden; IFK Gothenburg, Sweden, 92/3-96/7 (71, 18); AC Milan, Italy, 96/7 (20, 1); Parma, Italy, 97/8 (28, 1); Everton 01/02 (15, 1); Charlton Athletic 02/03 (3, 0); Djurgarden, Sweden, 03/04.

GAMES	29 (9)
GOALS	1

RONNIE WALLWORK

1997/98 → 2001/02

'He will be a first-team player. He is a great reader of the game, a fine passer and tough mentally.' For Ronnie Wallwork these were comforting words at nightmare's end, particularly as they came from Sir Alex Ferguson.

The bad dream in question was the young central defender's life ban imposed after an alleged attack on a Belgian referee towards the end of 1998/99, while on loan with Royal Antwerp. The draconian sentence was rescinded on appeal, but only after several months of torment, and Ronnie's characteristic single-mindedness was illustrated graphically by his convincing performance as a midfield holding player when rising from the Anfield bench to replace Nicky Butt in September 1999 – just six days before the hearing that would determine his future.

Yet for all his power and competence that day, it was at the heart of the back four rather than just in front of it that the muscular Mancunian tended to thrive. Not the tallest but hugely determined, endlessly industrious and deceptively skilful, Ronnie was a boyhood United fan who arrived at the club when he was ten.

However, though he picked up a title medal in 2000/01, increasingly fierce competition prevented the ultimate fulfilment of the Ferguson prophecy, and he was released in 2002, 'the best Bosman signing available' according to the Old Trafford boss. Initially under the guidance of Bryan Robson, he did well for West Bromwich Albion without quite justifying all that early optimism.

RONALD WALLWORK
BORN: Manchester, 10 September 1977.
HONOURS: League Championship 00/01.
OTHER CLUBS: Carlisle United on loan 97/8 (10, 1); Stockport County on loan 97/8 (7, 0); Royal Antwerp, Belgium, on loan 98/9; West Bromwich Albion 02/03-06/07 (93, 2); Bradford City on loan 03/04 (7, 4); Barnsley on loan 06/07 (2, 0); Huddersfield Town on loan 07/08 (16, 3); Sheffield Wednesday 07/08- (7, 0).

GAMES **10 (18)**
GOALS **0**

DANNY HIGGINBOTHAM

1997/98 → 1999/2000

The standing ovation accorded to Danny Higginbotham when a sharp attack of cramp removed him from the action shortly before the end of his home Premiership debut against Leicester City in November 1999 was tumultuous even by Old Trafford standards.

It was a fitting reward for a practically foot-perfect performance which underscored the huge potential of the tall, self-possessed left-back. Indeed, his composure was in evidence in the opening minute when his first touch produced a concerted handball appeal, but the referee waved play on and Danny remained utterly unfazed.

The young Mancunian was firm, neat and sensible in his defensive duties, but it was his ability to control and then use the ball creatively – perhaps a legacy of his schoolboy days as a winger – which commanded the eye.

Danny excelled during a lengthy loan spell with Royal Antwerp in 1998/99, and it was a pity when his Belgian sojourn ended with a ban after he became involved, along with Ronnie Wallwork, in an altercation with a referee. Still, with that controversy behind him, his United future seemed bright.

However, the progress of newcomer Mikael Silvestre obstructed his path to a regular berth, and when Derby County offered a hefty £2 million to sign the 21-year-old in July 2000, the Reds accepted and Danny Higginbotham was gone.

DANIEL JOHN HIGGINBOTHAM
BORN: Manchester 29 December 1978.
OTHER CLUBS: Royal Antwerp, Belgium, on loan 98/9; Derby County 00/01-02/03 (86, 3); Southampton 02/03-05/06 (94, 4); Stoke City 06/07-07/08 (45, 7); Sunderland 07/08- (21, 3).

GAMES **4 (3)**
GOALS **0**

WES BROWN

1997/98 →

Wesley Brown was once described by his manager as the best natural defender in the country, a view endorsed by that most clear-headed of Manchester soccer sages, the late John Doherty. Some observers might ridicule the notion, but it is the vehement contention here that, but for a grisly succession of potentially career-shattering injuries, the agreeably unassuming Longsight-born stopper, who has matured so impressively in the face of serial adversity, would have justified comprehensively the confidence of those eminent judges. As it turned out, he hasn't done so badly anyway, and he still has power to add.

Unlike so many young men who have been long on talent but short on nerve, Brown has never been afraid to play for Manchester United. Indeed, of the myriad attributes screaming for attention in the footballing make-up of the stylish six-footer, it is his utter imperturbability that is the most compelling. No matter how colossal the occasion, how frenetic the hype or how daunting the challenge, he remains a monument to self-possession.

True, down the years there has been a handful of high-profile errors which have attracted disproportionate flak, but they have tended to happen when he has been rusty from one of his lengthy absences. When he has been able to establish momentum, and hone his powers of concentration through an uninterrupted run in the team, he has been a study in calm, unobtrusive efficiency.

Nature equipped Wes supremely well to excel as a centre-half in the modern game. Quick and awesomely athletic, endowed with a slender but whippily resilient frame, he is formidable in the air, a limpet-like marker, a dexterous tackler and generally assured in possession of the ball. He tidies up unfussily, without apparent strain, often appearing to sense danger before materialising instinctively in the ideal position to snuff it out. This is a priceless asset which, given better fortune with his fitness than he has enjoyed hitherto, could yet lead to Laurent Blanc-type longevity. Unusually for a central defender, he has excelled as a full-back, too, deputising effectively for Gary Neville throughout 2007/08 and steadily improving as an overlapper, though the quality of his crossing remains variable.

There have been other flaws, though not many. For instance, his communication with fellow defenders has been shaky on occasions, although it has improved, and still he must beware of having his pocket picked, as it was so embarrassingly by Michael Ricketts in the unexpected home defeat by Bolton in October 2002. But such aberrations have been rare and overall he has been a shining vindication of the perspicacity of Doherty, who predicted correctly that he would win an England cap before he was 21.

Wesley Brown was discovered by former United winger Harry McShane playing under-12 football in the early 1990s, then rose meteorically through the Reds' junior ranks before enjoying one of the most confident senior debuts ever witnessed at Old Trafford. The lithe 19-year-old was called on as a substitute for David May against Leeds in May 1998, and he shone against such assertive operators as Jimmy Floyd Hasselbaink and Harry Kewell. In front of 55,000 fans and a massive TV audience he was ready to put his foot on the ball, pass it with distinction and even go past opponents with a sway of his hips and a burst of acceleration which belied his relaxed style.

Come 1998/99 and Wes was ready for a settled first-team run, and he didn't disappoint. Momentarily, perhaps, he appeared a tad too casual for some observers, but that was an illusion caused by his easy, loose-limbed gait, and mistakes were few. At that juncture he played mostly at right-back but clearly his ideal position was in the centre, where Alex Ferguson predicted he would enjoy a fruitful future. Understandably, though, the United boss was wary of overtaxing his prodigy in his first full season in the squad, preferring the experienced May when injuries caused a vacancy alongside Jaap Stam as the Premiership scrap reached a crescendo. Also, it should be noted that when Wes won his first England cap after only 12 League starts, a record, in all honesty he did not appear ready for the international stage. Thus it was recognised that continued grooming was necessary, but that process was cruelly interrupted by knee damage sustained during preparation for 1999/2000. He went under the surgeon's knife and missed the whole season.

Displaying admirable stoicism and immense strength of character, Brown recovered in time for 2000/01 and astonished even his manager by his majestic form during the first two-thirds of that title-winning term, earning a deserved England recall along the way. For the Reds, given a longer run than expected because of injury to Stam, he excelled alongside Gary Neville before his consistency faltered in the spring, entirely understandable in a young man returning from such a major setback. Despite that late blip, Wes was selected for the PFA team of the season and at the outset of 2001/02 his horizons seemed unclouded. However, he didn't quite regain his former consistency, then suffered lengthy absences through mishaps to knee and ankle, but even worse was in store. Another hideous injury cost him the first part of 2003/04, and at the time of writing he is believed to be the only professional to recover after rupturing cruciate ligaments in both knees, plus damaging the medial in one of the joints, and breaking an ankle.

Wesley's resilience, both mental and physical, has been astonishing, and in the spring of 2008 he was playing as beautifully, as economically, as effectively as ever, making more appearances than any of his team-mates in that climactically fulfilling campaign. Given luck – and he would be the last to take that circumstance for granted – a 'Golden Brown' Indian summer remained a delicious prospect.

WESLEY MICHAEL BROWN
BORN: Manchester, 16 March 1979.
HONOURS: European Cup 07/08. League Championship 98/9, 00/01, 02/03, 06/07, 07/08. FA Cup 03/04. League Cup 05/06. 16 England caps (99-).

GAMES **271 (34)**
GOALS 3

MASSIMO TAIBI

1999/2000

He was big, he was oozing with self-belief and if he made a mistake he tended to look elsewhere to place the blame. But that was not what the headline-writer had in mind when he penned 'United hail new Schmeichel' following Massimo Taibi's debut against Liverpool.

That morning at Anfield in August 1999, the 6ft 3in Italian – signed for £4.5 million from Venezia because Mark Bosnich was afflicted by injury and indifferent form – made a succession of brilliant saves and the visitors departed with three hard-won points. Apart from one horrible blunder, when he failed to catch a cross and allowed Sami Hyypia to head into an empty net, it had been a triumphant entry and instant stardom seemed to beckon.

In fact, misery was in store. After an uneventful encounter with Wimbledon, Massimo dropped a colossal clanger at home to Southampton, allowing a soft shot from Matt Le Tissier to squirm embarrassingly through his grasp and earning further tabloid attention as 'The blind Venetian'. Still worse was to come at Stamford Bridge where he conceded five, starting with a carbon copy of his Merseyside bloomer, this time letting in Gus Poyet after only 28 seconds. It couldn't go on. Soon Taibi was dispatched to Reggina on loan for the rest of the season, explaining as he went that he had been unused to the bombardment of crosses which is part of the English game and vowing that he would return to prove his critics wrong. Alas for Massimo, they are still waiting.

MASSIMO TAIBI
BORN: Palermo, Italy, 18 February 1970.
OTHER CLUBS: Licata, Trentino, AC Milan (twice),
Como Calcio, Piacenza,
Venezia, Reggina,
Atalanta, Torino, all Italy.

GAMES 4
GOALS 0

JONATHAN GREENING

1998/99 → 2000/01

At Bootham Crescent, Jonathan Greening was viewed as exceptional, a boy wonder; at Old Trafford, he was merely one of many starlets striving for a berth in the big time. For a while the former Minsterman appeared on course for long-term graduation but eventually, and understandably, frustration at being stuck behind David Beckham and company induced his departure.

Sir Alex Ferguson entertained lofty hopes for Jonathan, who arrived in Manchester in March 1998, York City banking a reported £350,000 with more to come depending on his progress. It was a significant investment for a teenager with only five League starts to his name.

Thereafter, despite being granted only a handful of senior outings and never quite seizing the day, the tall, willowy striker cum wide midfielder did enough to suggest that the basics of a Premiership footballer were in place. Though there were rough edges to be honed – notably a tendency to dwell too long in possession – long-striding Jonathan revealed commendable pace, deft control, a bewildering body-swerve and a fierce shot.

The England under-21 international was willing to graft, too – witness his determined chasing and dispossessing of David Ginola after Nicky Butt had been beaten at White Hart Lane in December 1998 – and he made a promising start under former United coach Steve McClaren at Middlesbrough, where he moved for £2 million in August 2001.

JONATHAN GREENING
BORN: Scarborough, Yorkshire, 2 January 1978.
OTHER CLUBS: York City 96/7-97/8 (25, 2); Middlesbrough 01/02-03/04 (99, 4);
West Bromwich Albion 04/05- (160, 5).

GAMES 13 (14)
GOALS 0

MARK WILSON

1998/99 → 1999/2000

An eminent Old Trafford insider predicted at the outset of 1999/2000 that Mark Wilson would consolidate his place in the senior squad by season's end. It didn't happen for the tall England under-21 midfielder, a combination of serious injury and overwhelmingly formidable competition for places closing the door, and instead he joined Middlesbrough for £1.5 million in August 2001.

Mark was an assured, all-purpose performer whose game boasted a natural authority. Snappily combative in the tackle, he tracked back and tidied up efficiently, while being eager to embark on enterprising forward runs. A neat passer who was comfortable on the ball, he packed a powerful shot, too, as he demonstrated with a sizzling strike in the Eric Cantona testimonial match.

Alex Ferguson proved his confidence in 'Willo' by blooding him at senior level as a substitute away to Brondby in October 1998, the teenaged Humbersider responding with composed competence. Thereafter he did well on the 1999 summer tour of Australia and the Far East, and earned a trip to Rio for the Club World Championship. But he suffered a ruptured Achilles during the following summer and on recovery, desperate for first-team football, Mark accepted that working under ex-United coach Steve McClaren at the Riverside was a sensible and appealing option. He never made a sustained Premiership impact, though, but later thrived in the USA.

MARK ANTONY WILSON
BORN: Scunthorpe, Humberside, 9 February 1979.
OTHER CLUBS: Wrexham on loan 97/8 (13, 4); Middlesbrough 01/02-04/05 (16, 0);
Stoke City on loan 02/03 (4, 0); Swansea City on loan 03/04 (12, 2); Sheffield
Wednesday on loan 03/04 (3, 0); Doncaster Rovers on loan 04/05 (3, 0);
Livingston on loan 04/05 (5, 0); Dallas Burn, USA, 05-.

GAMES 6 (4)
GOALS 0

QUINTON FORTUNE

1999/2000 → 2004/05

There was an indefinable spark about Quinton Fortune, a hunger to succeed which emanated, perhaps, from his humble origins in a poor, crime-riddled township. He exuded cheerful determination, he would run until he dropped, he was quick, strong and tolerably skilful, and his versatility was a boon in the age of frequent squad rotation. But for all those admirable attributes, the most feted of all South African footballers never stepped up from useful deputy to major player on the Old Trafford stage.

Why? Despite his name he was, in fact, woefully unfortunate, invariably suffering injury whenever he might have been on the verge of improving his status, such as in 2003/04 and 2004/05. But also there was a question-mark about his overall quality and awareness, particularly in defensive situations, which was never quite erased.

Still, Quinton proved immensely useful in all left-sided positions from back to front, and occasionally in his favoured role as a central midfielder, following his £1.5 million purchase from Atletico Madrid in August 1999. He scored on his first Premiership start, at home to Bradford City, then bolstered his confidence with two smart finishes against South Melbourne, after which his huge grin lit up the Maracana.

Once described by Terry Venables, who took him to Tottenham as a 14-year-old, as 'the finest schoolboy player in Africa', Quinton was a popular fellow who gave his all as a Red Devil and deserved better luck. Sadly he didn't get it, being dogged by new fitness woes following his switch to Bolton in the summer of 2006.

QUINTON FORTUNE
BORN: Cape Town, South Africa, 21 May 1977.
HONOURS: 47 South Africa caps (96-05).
OTHER CLUBS: Mallorca, Spain, 95/6 (8, 1);
Atletico Madrid, Spain, 95/6-98/9 (7, 0);
Bolton Wanderers 06/07 (6, 0).

GAMES	88 (38)
GOALS	11

MICHAEL STEWART

2000/01 → 2002/03

When Michael Stewart signed a four-year contract in 2002, it seemed he had a buoyant future at Old Trafford, but such was the furious heat of competition that the promising youngster could not progress and returned to his home city of Edinburgh to seek his footballing fortune.

There was a reassuring simplicity about Michael's game. A red-haired Scottish midfielder, endowed with all the fire and combativeness which that combination traditionally entails, he was the embodiment of the pass-and-move ethos. He operated efficiently, unflashily, economically, though there was energy to burn when distance needed to be covered and challenges needed to be made.

Initially he had been targeted by a bevy of top clubs on both sides of the border, and when the choice narrowed down to Glasgow Rangers or Manchester United, he opted for Old Trafford. That was in 1997, after which Michael earned lavish plaudits for a loan interlude with Royal Antwerp in 1999/2000, then won the Red Devils' reserve of the year award for 2000/01. That term, too, he made his senior entrance, being granted a clutch of League outings after United had sealed the Championship with five weeks to spare.

With the title race being much tighter in 2001/02, Michael's opportunities were fewer, but he continued to make strides, skippering the reserves to their league crown and earning a full Scotland call-up. But then came loans, a loss of impetus and a free transfer to Hibernian in 2005.

MICHAEL JAMES STEWART
BORN: Edinburgh, 26 February 1981.
HONOURS: 3 Scotland caps (02-).
OTHER CLUBS: Royal Antwerp, Belgium, on loan 99/00;
Nottingham Forest on loan 03/04 (13, 0); Heart of
Midlothian on loan 04/05 (17, 0); Hibernian 05/06-
06/07 (54, 2); Heart of Midlothian 07/08- (28, 3).

GAMES	7 (7)
GOALS	0

MIKAEL SILVESTRE

1999/2000 →

Old Trafford has never embraced Mikael Silvestre with the passionate, full-blooded fervour it reserves for it's 'A-list' of beloved sons; there is something in his cool, almost insouciant air which precludes that degree of intimacy.

Yet the pacy, polished Frenchman can be content with his medal-laden stint as a Red Devil. By any rational judgement, he has done enough to earn the trust and respect of fans initially perturbed by what they saw as undue casualness in moments of high peril. Most would admit now, surely, that such a hastily conceived perception was misguided, and acknowledge that when Silvestre is at his injury-free best, his place among the Premiership's most effective defenders is not in question.

However, it would be idle to contend that his pathway to acceptance has been unremittingly smooth. Mikael started on the glorious high of his accomplished contribution to a victory at Anfield, then descended dramatically to the point of vilification as it became apparent that his learning curve was steep, before rising steadily once more as he adjusted to the rigorous standards demanded by Manchester United.

Mikael had become available for transfer from Internazionale in September 1999 because he was unhappy with his deployment as a wing-back and soon Liverpool and United were locked in a battle for his signature. At first, the French connection appeared to make Gerard Houllier favourite to prevail, but an assurance from Alex Ferguson that Silvestre would be given opportunities in his favoured central role paved the way for a £4 million move to Manchester. Ironically, just days later, Mikael made his Premiership entry at Anfield as a left-back. Enraged Kopites booed his every touch, but he wasn't fazed, taking the eye with his athleticism, authority and control.

Clearly the newcomer was an immensely accomplished all-round footballer, as powerful in the air as he was composed on the deck, but soon that characteristic calm was causing palpitations in stands and dugout alike. Several times he was caught in possession by nippy opponents – one instance cost United a home victory over Southampton – and his concentration was questioned.

Thereafter he was granted his wish of moving to the heart of the rearguard alongside Jaap Stam, but while his passing, tackling and, above all, his speed earned plaudits, there were some disturbingly shaky moments. Occasionally these were the result of a heavy bias towards his left foot, which offered welcome balance to the defence but, once or twice, limited his options when under pressure. In fairness to Mikael, a model professional and engagingly eager to learn, he needed time to adjust to the English game, and it didn't help that the Reds' goalkeeping situation was volatile throughout much of his debut campaign.

Ferguson, who believed the Frenchman's pace was priceless, persisted with him and, for the most part, the positive outweighed the negative. At times he was omitted from the side, but always with the intention of a comeback, and as 1999/2000 reached its climax, the shaven-headed six-footer was making steady progress.

This continued in 2000/01 and 2001/02 when he emerged as one of the club's most improved performers, though it was at left-back that he shone the brightest. Given a settled sequence in the side, Mikael's confidence burgeoned and he became noted for his explosive bursts down the touchline, a welcome addition to United's attacking armoury which allowed for Ryan Giggs to drift inside with more freedom.

Indeed, when Silvestre mounted a head of steam he looked practically unstoppable, driving at opponents and unnerving them with high-velocity sidesteps before crossing. His delivery could be sumptuous and Ruud van Nistelrooy and company benefited from silver service at times, even if a tad more quality control would have been welcome. Similarly, his general distribution could verge on the majestic, especially with long-distance left-to-right dispatches, though still the occasional sloppy pass crept in.

Meanwhile, while still appearing deceptively casual in possession, Mikael refined his defensive technique to a point where he was rarely caught unawares or out of position. Painful experience, and no doubt a few interesting chats with his manager, were paying dividends.

Still, though, Mikael was not in his pomp. He reached that in his preferred central slot in 2002/03, forming a terrific partnership with Rio Ferdinand as United regained the Premiership crown, and he maintained it throughout most of the next two campaigns. During this purple patch he became a potentially lethal force in opposition penalty areas, too, his sweetest contribution being the two emphatic headers which sank Liverpool at Old Trafford in September 2004.

However, Silvestre remained prone to the occasional aberration and his long-term prospects suffered a double blow with the arrival of centre-half Nemanja Vidic and left-back Patrice Evra during the January 2006 transfer window. There followed inevitable rumours of a move abroad, but the Frenchman opted to stay and fight for his place, and despite breaking a foot and dislocating a shoulder he qualified for his fourth championship gong in 2006/07.

A serious knee injury in September 2007 sidelined him for most of that campaign, but the resilient 30-year-old, who had already demonstrated repeatedly that he was not to be intimidated by the arrival of starry new recruits, remained commendably adamant that another sustained comeback was not beyond him. Duly he returned to full fitness but it seemed likely that he would enlist with Laurent Blanc at Bordeaux in the summer of 2008.

MIKAEL SAMY SILVESTRE

BORN: Chambray-Les-Tours, France, 9 August 1977.

HONOURS: League Championship 99/00, 00/01, 02/03, 06/07, 07/08. FA Cup 03/04.
League Cup 05/06. 40 France caps (01).

OTHER CLUBS: Rennes, France, 95/6-97/8 (49, 0); Internazionale, Italy, 98/9 (18, 1).

GAMES	326 (35)
GOALS	10

RAIMOND VAN DER GOUW

1996/97 → 2001/02

During the first half of 1999/2000, with Manchester United striving to adjust to life without Peter Schmeichel, the safest pair of hands at Old Trafford belonged to Raimond van der Gouw.

In contrast to Mark Bosnich and Massimo Taibi, both of whom proved fitfully errant, the tall, lithe Dutchman gave several short sequences of solid displays interspersed with a couple of stunning ones, notably in the landmark triumph at Highbury and the home win against Valencia.

Each time, though, Raimond would give way, thus occasioning considerable frustration to United fans intolerant of the newcomers' uncertainty and mightily impressed by the consistent, unflashy competence of the man who had spent three seasons as steady understudy to the giant Dane, no doubt learning plenty in the process.

Perhaps, had van der Gouw not been closer to his fortieth birthday than his thirtieth – he is the oldest man to play first-team football for the Red Devils since the war – he might have prevailed. As it was, he stepped up again when Bosnich was omitted in March, performing splendidly against Liverpool at Old Trafford before dropping an uncharacteristic clanger in Bordeaux, then slipping quietly back to the bench.

When the club had sought a goalkeeping number-two in the summer of 1996, they were not looking for an ambitious young buck who would be straining to supplant Schmeichel as premier custodian. What they required was an experienced deputy whose reassuring presence would mean that any enforced absence by Peter need not be viewed as an unmitigated calamity. For such a purpose, Raimond proved ideal.

His first-team opportunities were limited throughout most of 1996/97, though he did enough on his rare outings to confirm his all-round competence and cool temperament. True, he could not equal the immense physical presence of Schmeichel but that was hardly surprising and, crucially, when he was really needed, Raimond was not found wanting.

Stepping into the breach when Peter was unfit for the first leg of the European Cup semi-final confrontation with Borussia Dortmund, van der Gouw excelled, making several fine saves before being beaten once, by a deflected shot. It was only his fourth senior outing for United but he had played 17 times in European competition for his previous club, Vitesse Arnhem, and it showed. A season later, in similar circumstances, he shone again, making three blinding stops at home to Monaco in the quarter-final.

Apparently unswervingly content in his supporting role, even after young Roy Carroll arrived as chief deputy to Fabien Barthez, fitness fanatic Raimond had proved his worth many times over by the time of his departure to join West Ham United in the summer of 2002. What a pity that he wasn't just a few years younger when Schmeichel left Old Trafford.

RAIMOND VAN DER GOUW	
BORN:	Oldenzaal, Holland, 24 March 1963.
HONOURS:	League Championship 99/00, 00/01.
OTHER CLUBS:	Go Ahead Eagles 85/6-87/8; Vitesse Arnhem 88/9-95/6, both Holland.

GAMES	48 (12)
GOALS	0

MARK BOSNICH

$1989/90 \rightarrow 1990/91 \ \& \ 1999/2000$

It would be wonderful to report that Mark Bosnich slotted seamlessly into the Manchester United defence during his one-season bid to become the Reds' long-term goalkeeper, and that Peter Schmeichel was barely missed. If only it were true.

Not that the massively self-assured Australian was a flop, exactly, after arriving from Aston Villa to commence his second spell at Old Trafford in July 1999. After all, he did pocket a title medal, and certainly it was fair to accentuate the positive regarding his rollercoaster progress as the near-omnipotent Dane's successor, because there was plenty of it.

For example, his exceptional display at the Bernabeu kept the Reds in contention in their European Cup quarter-final with Real Madrid, and United would not have lifted the Inter-Continental Cup in Tokyo but for his succession of fabulous saves which thwarted Palmeiras. Similarly, he performed superbly in the white heat of Elland Road, a major factor in a crucial victory.

Undoubtedly Mark proved himself a magnificent shot-stopper, arguably the most acrobatic and sharp-witted in the English game that term. He was faultlessly courageous when diving at feet; he presented a formidable barrier in one-on-one situations, and he was endlessly determined.

However, there was a flip side. For all his confidence, Bosnich did not dominate his box. When crosses came in there was every chance of an ineffectual flap, such as the one which gifted a goal to Paul Ince at Middlesbrough in April 2000,

and colleagues appeared uncertain of his intentions. Though there were mitigating factors, such as the need to bed in the new central defensive partnership of Stam and Silvestre, it was unusual for table-toppers to concede more goals than the five teams below them. Yet that was the case in the spring of 2000, and a considerable portion of the responsibility rested with the goalkeeper.

In addition, despite his protestations to the contrary, Mark's kicking was abysmal at times, his feeble dispatches frequently placing United under instant and unnecessary pressure. True, he was handicapped by an early-season hamstring injury, but even when he was fit his kicking was woefully inconsistent.

Bosnich, who served United briefly as a teenager during the Ron Atkinson era before work-permit problems forced him to move, returned on a free transfer under the Bosman ruling, but failed to impress in his early outings.

Then, amid widely voiced doubts about his attitude, came his injury, the signing of Massimo Taibi and a string of fine displays from the solid Raimond van der Gouw. Suddenly Mark appeared to be third in the pecking order, and a gutsy recovery from that unenviable position was to be applauded.

However, the ebullient six-footer's relationship with the manager deteriorated alarmingly – Bosnich later ascribed the rift to his own right-wing political views, although that seemed a lame excuse – and Fabien Barthez arrived for 2000/01.

Duly, after much acrimony, the Australian's contract was cancelled in the following January and he joined Chelsea. Sadly, any hope of reviving his career at Stamford Bridge disappeared when he was banned for nine months after failing a drugs test.

MARK JOHN BOSNICH
BORN: Fairfield, Australia, 13 January 1972.
HONOURS: League Championship 99/00. 22 Australia caps (89-97).
OTHER CLUBS: Croatia Sydney, Australia; Aston Villa 91/2-98/9 (179, 0); Chelsea 01/02 (5, 0).

GAMES 38
GOALS 0

FABIEN BARTHEZ

2000/01 → 2002/03

Bold, bald Barthez, brilliant but bizarre. Flamboyant, erratic, blazingly eccentric . . . mere words pale into insignificance beside the remarkable reality, but some might add 'infuriating' to this particular lexicon, together with a few choice expletives. Whatever, he was a born entertainer utterly dedicated to winning, an instinctive and passionate performer whose cocktail of tumultuous talent and volatile character pushed him to the ragged edge of his capabilities, frequently shredding the emotions of Manchester United fans in the process.

Yet for all the hair-raising excursions, audacious dribbles, wicked wind-ups and occasional calamitous clangers which made Liverpool's maverick from earlier days, the endlessly idiosyncratic Bruce Grobbelaar, seem like a veritable monument to convention in comparison, it must be stressed that Fabien was a world-class goalkeeper who arrived at Old Trafford in the summer of 2000 with nothing to prove.

Here was a man who had contributed mightily to winning the World Cup, the European International Championship, the European Cup and three French titles in his time, yet still he was consumed by ambition. Thus it was hardly surprising that Sir Alex Ferguson should identify him as a logical candidate to succeed Peter Schmeichel.

Unfortunately, when the Dane departed in 1999, the Frenchman was not ready for a move to Old Trafford, so Mark Bosnich was handed a gilded opportunity, which he failed to seize. But one year on Fabien judged that the moment had arrived to cross the English Channel and duly the Red Devils paid £7.8 million to secure his vastly accomplished but vividly individual services.

Like Schmeichel before him, Barthez needed a few matches to become accustomed to the physical intensity of the Premiership, but then he embarked upon a fabulous personal contribution to United's latest runaway title triumph. Many was the game in 2000/01 which they won at a canter ultimately, but in which they were deeply indebted to a handful of spellbinding saves from the astonishingly athletic shot-stopper.

As to Fabien's famous foibles, he seemed to live a charmed life throughout that campaign. The supporters were enchanted by his assured touch on the ball as he trifled with opponents as a matador might toy with a bull, and they were thrilled by the odd close scrape provided there was always a happy ending.

Certainly his all-round ability was a wonder to behold. Though not tall for a modern 'keeper, he was rarely found wanting in the air; he specialised in reflex close-range blocks which prevented seemingly certain goals; he radiated confidence among his defenders in a manner reminiscent of Schmeichel, and his distribution, particularly with his left foot, was even deadlier than the Dane's. Indeed, Barthez could play a through-pass as penetrating as any play-maker, and every time he took possession he looked to attack.

In addition, his decision-making was instant, he was unfailingly courageous and he seemed to thrive on pressure, an expression of rapt, almost manic pleasure flickering across those distinctive features at moments which other men might describe as stressful.

However, his critics declared that he was an accident waiting to happen, and they were crowing in the autumn of 2001 when a series of Barthez blunders in key contests cost United dearly. Most excruciating were two headlong rushes from his line which presented Deportivo with goals at Old Trafford and a pair of late schoolboy errors which enabled Thierry Henry to secure three points for Arsenal at Highbury.

At that troubled juncture there were calls for Sir Alex to axe the increasingly unpredictable Frenchman, and only the Reds boss knows how many more mistakes it would have taken for that to happen. But all the while the indefatigable Fabien continued to make wonderful saves, Fergie kept the faith and by mid-December the normal impeccable service was resumed.

As it turned out, though, Barthez was living on borrowed time. Though still performing minor miracles in February 2003 – he was United's most impressive performer by a street at Bolton that month – his star tumbled dramatically. After several moments of uncertainty in subsequent outings, he was beaten at his near post by Ronaldo early in the titanic clash with Real Madrid at Old Trafford in April, and was never selected again. In mitigation, he had been left fearfully exposed by his defenders and his axing appeared unduly harsh. In October 2003 he was loaned to Marseille, with whom he proved his enduring quality, but still was released by the Reds at season's end.

As fiercely independent as his chum, Eric Cantona, and used to being lionised in his native land – when he adorned the cover of the magazine *Paris Match*, he attracted more sales than for any issues except those covering the deaths of Princess Diana and President Mitterand – Fabien could not have been an easy personality to manage, but few fans would disagree that, despite the occasional trauma, he was worth the Ferguson effort.

Comparisons are odious, they say, but irresistible, too, especially where 'keepers are concerned. So let's ask the big question: did Fabien Barthez match Peter Schmeichel when that great man was in his pomp? The answer, surely, must come in the negative, though at times he was close; and that in itself is one gigantic compliment.

FABIEN ALAIN BARTHEZ

BORN: Lavelanet, France, 28 June 1971.

HONOURS: League Championship 00/01, 02/03. 86 France caps (94-06).

OTHER CLUBS: Toulouse 91/2 (26, 0); Marseille 92/3-94/5 (106, 0); Monaco 95/6-99/00 (143, 0); Marseille 03/04-05/06 (74, 0), all France.

GAMES	139
GOALS	0

LUKE CHADWICK

1999/2000 → 2002/03

It said plenty about Luke Chadwick that, when his game was flowing freely, some of the world's top players were happy to present him with the ball and let him get on with it.

Running at defenders was Luke's speciality and, on song, the spindly dasher could turn a match with one sinuous excursion, unhinging opponents with his speed off the mark, assured balance and twinkling footwork.

Though naturally right-sided, the tall, rather gawky flankman could operate tellingly on the left, too, and while it was hardly realistic to compare him to the glorious Giggs, there were occasions when the Welshman's unavoidable absence was rendered a tad less painful to United fans by the Chadwick verve.

Ironically in view of the perennial struggle for supremacy between the Red Devils and Arsenal, Luke's immense potential was once viewed with more pleasure at Highbury than at Old Trafford. However, having been affiliated to the Gunners at 14, he moved up to Manchester, where his talents developed apace.

Though he had still not progressed beyond reserve level, in August 1999 Luke earned England under-21 recognition, displaying typical flair and scoring on his debut. Two months later he made his senior Reds entrance against Aston Villa in the League Cup, and then came the first of two spells on loan to Royal Antwerp.

Chadwick flourished in Belgium, once again netting on debut and emerging as a local cult hero as he helped to gain promotion from the Second Division. Accordingly the Royals welcomed him back for another temporary stay in August 2000, but he was recalled in October and his United career gathered momentum.

After sparkling at Derby on his first full Premiership outing, Luke left the pitch to an ovation from the travelling Reds supporters, Sir Alex Ferguson's avuncular arm around his shoulders. In January a mazy run and subtle turn set up Teddy Sheringham's late FA Cup winner at Fulham and then came a coolly taken goal at Bradford followed by a crucial strike at Leeds.

That April, so fearless was his enterprise that he startled a posse of world-class defenders when called on in the dying minutes of a lost cause against Bayern Munich at Old Trafford, and at season's end his manager spoke of Chadwick's peripheral but important contribution in glowing terms: 'He's been a revelation and he offers us options. The boy has a chance.'

Come 2001/02 Luke excelled at home to Everton and scintillated at Sunderland, lacerating massed defences with his pace and chicanery, and creating goals in each match. But, all the while, he seemed a little lightweight, lacking in both composure and confidence for the Premiership fray and, for all his natural ability, few observers expected him to overcome Old Trafford's stellar competition for a regular senior berth.

So it proved, and Luke Chadwick slipped away to ply his tricky trade at a slightly less rarefied level.

LUKE HARRY CHADWICK

BORN: Cambridge, 18 November 1980.

HONOURS: League Championship 00/01.

OTHER CLUBS: Royal Antwerp, Belgium, on loan 99/00 and 00/01; Reading on loan 02/03 (15, 1); Burnley on loan 03/04 (36, 5); West Ham United 04/05 (32, 1); Stoke City 05/06-06/07 (51, 5); Norwich City 06/07- (17, 2).

GAMES	18 (21)
GOALS	2

ROY CARROLL

2001/02 → 2004/05

Roy Carroll made a fair fist of minding the Manchester United net, first as a steady deputy to Fabien Barthez and then during a seesawing toe-to-toe battle with Tim Howard for possession of the jersey, but he failed to convince Sir Alex Ferguson that he was the consistent, top-quality custodian needed for the long haul.

Most of the time the undemonstrative Ulsterman exuded an air of reassuring solidity as he sought to command his area. Agile, brave and alert, he left his line decisively, he worked hard to improve his positioning and his distribution was composed and precise. In the end, though, despite occasional heroics, there were too many high-profile bloomers and United signed Edward van der Sar, freeing Roy to join West Ham in June 2005.

With so much attention riveted on the extravagantly expensive arrivals of van Nistelrooy and Veron, it was hardly surprising that there was only the merest gleam of Old Trafford limelight to spare for the man who took the Red Devils' spending in the summer of 2001 to some £50 million. Still, the £2.5 million purchase of Carroll from Wigan Athletic was deemed a preliminary success as the Northern Ireland international settled in competently as understudy to Barthez.

Despite being beaten by the first shot he faced – from Darius Vassell – when given his Premiership debut at Villa Park, the blameless newcomer was unfazed, going on to complete a workmanlike performance. Then when Fabien was axed for the last three games of 2002/03 with the League title still at stake, Roy stepped up and justified Ferguson's faith in him, only to be faced with a mammoth new challenge in the form of Tim Howard.

At first the American dominated, but when his form dipped and Roy was recalled in the spring, the Irishman responded with heartening resilience. Indeed, but for his serial brilliance in the FA Cup semi-final against Arsenal, including a reflex tip-over from a point-blank Kolo Toure header, it is unlikely that the Reds would have made it to the Millennium Stadium.

Though Tim was reinstated, somewhat controversially, for the final, Sir Alex showed his sentimental side by bringing on Roy as a late and deserving substitute in the easy victory over Millwall.

And so to 2004/05, which was to prove decisive for Carroll's Old Trafford ambitions as he found himself frequently exchanging the number-one slot with his rival. A blinding near-post parry from United old-boy Karel Poborsky against Sparta in Prague showcased his talent but grotesque errors at home to Lyon and AC Milan counted heavily against him.

Then there was the slapstick sequence when he fumbled a steepling chip from Tottenham's Pedro Mendes over his line at Old Trafford, only to scoop it clear and be reprieved by a linesman's astonishing misjudgement.

All that remained was an FA Cup Final start against Arsenal, and Roy Carroll was on his way.

ROY ERIC CARROLL

BORN: Enniskillen, Northern Ireland, 30 September 1977.
HONOURS: League Championship 02/03. FA Cup 03/04. 19 Northern Ireland caps (97-).
OTHER CLUBS: Hull City 95/6-96/7 (46, 0); Wigan Athletic 97/8-00/01 (135, 0); West Ham United 05/06-06/07 (31, 0); Glasgow Rangers 07/08 (0, 0); Derby County 07/08- (14, 0).

GAMES	68 (4)
GOALS	0

JOHN O'SHEA

1999/2000 →

Even in the most comprehensively talented Manchester United squad assembled in half a century, nestling unassumingly among a constellation of star performers coveted and idolised the world over, John O'Shea has a lustre that is all his own.

It would be fatuous, indeed, to contend that the engagingly amiable young Irishman – in his own modest words, a normal person doing an extraordinary job – possesses more than the merest fraction of the natural gifts paraded so luxuriantly at Old Trafford on a regular basis by the stellar likes of Ronaldo or Rooney, Tevez or Anderson, Giggs or Scholes.

Nor is he a towering back-line bulwark in the stirring mould of the warrior Vidic, or a heart-on-sleeve trumpeter of the United gospel in the mode of captain Neville, and if he was transferred – not a likely scenario – his fee would never match, or remotely approach, the astronomical figure commanded by Ferdinand.

Yet while he would be unlikely to start, say, a European Cup Final if all his team-mates were fit, there are sound reasons, both professional and personal, why his stock remains so enduringly high with his manager, his fellow Red Devils and the supporters who have monitored his development since he made his senior entrance during the dying embers of the last millennium.

Beyond the circumstance that O'Shea is an extremely competent all-round footballer with rather more flair than some pundits allow, his versatility knows virtually no bounds. He has served – and excelled – in his initial position of centre-half, in both full-back slots and in central midfield; he has thrown his energy into the role of emergency striker, and when Edwin van der Sar was injured at White Hart Lane in February 2007, he pulled on the green jersey and wore it with distinction, even dashing from his penalty box to foil fellow Republic of Ireland international Robbie Keane in a frantic one-on-one confrontation.

It is hardly surprising, then, that John is popular with the fans, a status enhanced by his invariably cheerful demeanour on the pitch. While top-level football in the 21st century appears such a grim business for so many of its excessively privileged participants, the tall, dark, clean-cut Munsterman exudes an easy-going, wholesome aura as refreshing as it is uncommon.

His full Premiership debut coincided with a shock home defeat by West Ham in December 2001, arguably the nadir of United's troubled campaign to that point, but O'Shea offered at least one reason for the Reds to rejoice on that dismal afternoon. Despite stepping into a team temporarily shorn of confidence, the rookie central defender positively shone, oozing class and composure aplenty.

One early incident summed up the 20-year-old's *sang froid* perfectly. Placed under pressure by an uncharacteristically chancy Phil Neville dispatch, he put his foot on the ball, executed an audacious drag-back and passed immaculately out of danger. That spoke volumes for an unflappable temperament and considerable ability, and soon it became apparent that he possessed a Laurent Blanc-style knack of timing his challenges sweetly and making intelligent interceptions; that he was endowed with vision and technique to carry the ball forward with confidence, and that while he was no hare, he was no tortoise, either.

After two seasons as a fringe contributor, he became established in 2002/03, often impressing as an overlapping full-back and occasionally dazzling with exquisitely delicate skill. At home to Juventus there was a Cruyff turn which left the bullish Edgar Davids sprawling, and no less a personage than Luis Figo was nutmegged when Real Madrid were the visitors. But the *piece de resistance* was an outrageous manoeuvre which bemused Newcastle's Nolberto Solano and Aaron Hughes on the left touchline before John cut in to crash a rasping drive against the crossbar, from which Ryan Giggs netted during a swingeing 6-2 victory at St James' Park.

Though he topped United's appearance chart in 2003/04 his consistency was variable – there were too many sloppy passes and lapses of concentration – and he was in and out of the side over the next two terms. Still, at Highbury in February 2005, operating as a midfield substitute, he delivered what many followers cherish as the supreme pinnacle of the O'Shea career to date when, accepting a typically incisive delivery from Paul Scholes, he pirouetted to beat Arsenal 'keeper Manuel Almunia with the daintiest of chips using his unfavoured left foot. Setting the seal on a 4-2 triumph, it was in the Cantona class, both in conception and execution.

As Gabriel Heinze appeared, wrongly as it turned out, to be entrenched in the left-back slot, there was talk that John might depart Old Trafford, but his magnificent form as a holding player alongside Giggs in central midfield during the spring of 2006 offered fresh evidence of his versatility.

Come the following campaign, an O'Shea exit became unthinkable as he was Johnny-on-the-spot with two priceless tap-ins, first cementing a late and largely larcenous win at Anfield, then starting the rousing comeback at Goodison Park which accelerated United's successful title surge.

There remained demanding observers who reckoned he needed a tad more nastiness about his game, but John O'Shea stayed true to his nature, confirmed his status as one of Sir Alex Ferguson's key assets, and continued to rejoice in roughly equal measures of affection and respect.

JOHN FRANCIS O'SHEA
BORN: Waterford, Republic of Ireland, 30 April 1981.
HONOURS: League Championship 02/03, 06/07, 07/08. FA Cup 03/04. League Cup 05/06.
44 Republic of Ireland caps (01-).
OTHER CLUBS: Bournemouth on loan 99/00 (10, 1); Royal Antwerp, Belgium, on loan 00/01.

GAMES 215 (73)
GOALS 12

MICHAEL TWISS

1997/98 – 1999/2000

Tall, strong and a crisp user of the ball, the midfielder cum defender made an impact at youth level but, after being pitched into FA Cup action at Barnsley in 1998, he was called up only once more before being freed to join Port Vale.

MICHAEL JOHN TWISS
BORN: Salford, Lancashire, 26 December 1977.
OTHER CLUBS: Sheffield United on loan 98/9 (12, 1); Port Vale 00/1 (18, 3); Morecambe 07/08- (36, 6).

GAMES **1 (1)**
GOALS **0**

ALEX NOTMAN

1998/99

A feisty little front-man whose stamina and courage were matched by his neat ball control. However, after enjoying only 20 minutes of senior football as a Red, the Scotland under-21 international joined Norwich for £250,000 in November 2000.

ALEXANDER McKEACHIE NOTMAN
BORN: Edinburgh, 10 December 1979.
OTHER CLUBS: Aberdeen on loan 98/9 (2, 0); Sheffield United on loan 99/00 (10, 3); Norwich City 00/01-03/04 (54, 1).

GAMES **0 (1)**
GOALS **0**

RICHARD WELLENS

1999/2000

A promising midfielder brimming with confidence and determination, Richard was assured in possession and a sharp tackler. But consistency in the reserves earned only a fleeting senior opportunity and he was transferred to Blackpool in March 2000.

RICHARD PAUL WELLENS
BORN: Manchester, 26 March 1980.
OTHER CLUBS: Blackpool 99/00-04/05 (188, 16); Oldham Athletic 05/06-06/07 (87, 8); Doncaster Rovers 07/08- (45, 6).

GAMES **0 (1)**
GOALS **0**

ERIK NEVLAND

1997/98 → 1998/99

Already a full international when he was recruited from Viking Stavanger, the dashing marksman showed promise for United reserves, but failed to fashion an Old Trafford niche and returned to his homeland, where he flourished once more.

ERIK NEVLAND
BORN: Stavanger, Norway, 10 November 1977.
HONOURS: 3 Norway caps.
OTHER CLUBS: Viking Stavanger 95/6-96/7; IFK Gothenburg on loan 98/9; Viking Stavanger 99/00-04/05; Groningen 04/05-07/08; all Norway; Fulham 07/08- (8, 2).

GAMES **2 (3)**
GOALS **1**

NICK CULKIN

1999/2000

'Keeper Nick saw only ten seconds of senior service and touched the ball once, a free-kick to clear his lines after coming on as a late, late substitute for the injured Raimond van der Gouw in a tense League victory at Highbury. A series of fruitful loan spells followed.

NICHOLAS JAMES CULKIN
BORN: York, 6 July 1978.
OTHER CLUBS: Hull City on loan 99/00 (4, 0); Bristol Rovers on loan 00/01 (45, 0); Livingston on loan 01/02 (21, 0); Queen's Park Rangers 02/03-03/04 (22, 0).

GAMES **0 (1)**
GOALS **0**

DAVID HEALY

1999/2000 → 2000/01

Much was expected of the quick, skilful marksman after he netted twice on debut for Northern Ireland, having not made a full appearance for the Reds. However, David failed to consolidate, and joined Preston for £1.5 million in December 2000. Later he became his country's record goal-scorer.

DAVID JONATHAN HEALY
BORN: Downpatrick, Northern Ireland, 5 August 1979.
HONOURS: 64 Northern Ireland caps (00-).
OTHER CLUBS: Port Vale on loan 99/00 (16, 3); Preston North End 00/01-04/05 (139, 44); Norwich City on loan 02/03 (13, 2); Leeds United 04/05-06/07 (111, 29); Fulham 07/08- (30, 4).

GAMES **0 (3)**
GOALS **0**

PAUL RACHUBKA

1999/2000 → 2000/01

After making his senior entrance at the Maracana in the Club World Championship, goalkeeper Paul kept a clean sheet on his sole League outing, but didn't progress with United and was sold to Charlton for £200,000 in May 2002.

PAUL STEPHEN RACHUBKA
BORN: San Luis Obispo, California, USA, 21 May 1981.
OTHER CLUBS: Royal Antwerp, Belgium, on loan 01/02; Oldham Athletic on loan 01/02 (16, 0); Huddersfield Town on loan 03/04 (13, 0); Milton Keynes Dons on loan 04/05 (4, 0); Northampton Town on loan 04/05 (10, 0); Huddersfield Town 04/05-06/07 (76, 0); Peterborough United on loan 06/07 (4, 0); Blackpool 06/07- (54, 0).

GAMES **1 (2)**
GOALS **0**

ANDY GORAM

2000/01

The vastly experienced veteran 'keeper was recruited from Motherwell when United's ranks were thinned by injuries towards the end of 2000/01. Though a trifle portlier than in his international prime, the genial Scot held the fort adequately.

ANDREW LEWIS GORAM
BORN: Bury, Lancashire, 13 April 1964.
HONOURS: 43 Scotland caps (85-98).
OTHER CLUBS: Oldham Athletic 81/2-97/8 (195, 0); Hibernian 87/8-90/1 (138, 1); Glasgow Rangers 91/2-97/8 (184, 0); Notts County 98/9 (1, 0); Sheffield United 98/9 (7, 0); Motherwell 98/9-00/01 (57, 0); Coventry City 01/02 (7, 0); Oldham Athletic 01/02 (4, 0); Queen Of The South 02/03 (19, 0); Elgin City 03/04 (5, 0).

GAMES	2
GOALS	0

DANNY WEBBER

2000/01 → 2002/03

England under-20 international Danny is a pacy, effervescent striker who top-scored for the reserves during 2001/02. Surprisingly to some observers, he was allowed to join Watford after a loan stint, then later he showed lively form for Sheffield United in the Premiership.

DANIEL VAUGHN WEBBER
BORN: Manchester, 28 December 1981.
OTHER CLUBS: Port Vale on loan 01/02 (4, 0); Watford on loan 01/02-02/03 (17, 4); Watford 03/04-04/05 (55, 17); Sheffield United 04/05- (78, 19).

GAMES	1 (2)
GOALS	0

BOJAN DJORDJIC

2000/01 → 2001/02

Clever in possession and enterprising at dead-ball situations, the left-sided Sweden under-21 midfielder emphasised his potential with a beautifully chipped goal against Celtic in Tom Boyd's testimonial game. But he couldn't make the next step, either with United or Rangers.

BOJAN DJORDJIC
BORN: Belgrade, Yugoslavia, 6 February 1982.
OTHER CLUBS: Bromma Pojkarna, Sweden, 98/9; Sheffield Wednesday on loan 01/02 (5, 0); AGF Aarhus, Denmark, on loan 02/03; Red Star Belgrade on loan 03/04; Glasgow Rangers 04/05 (4, 0); Plymouth Argyle 05/06-06/07 (39, 4); AIK, Sweden, 07/08-.

GAMES	1 (1)
GOALS	0

LEE ROCHE

2001/02 → 2002/03

Having garnered priceless experience during a season with Wrexham, the industrious overlapping full-back made his United entrance in the League Cup at Highbury. Lee was prominent as the Reds' reserves topped their table in 2001/02, but an Old Trafford breakthrough never came.

LEE PAUL ROCHE
BORN: Bolton, 28 October 1980.
OTHER CLUBS: Wrexham on loan 00/01 (41, 0); Burnley 03/04-04/05 (54, 2); Wrexham 05/06-06/07 (86, 1).

GAMES	2 (1)
GOALS	0

DANIEL NARDIELLO

2001/02 → 2003/04

The son of Donato Nardiello, a Welsh international winger of the 1970s, Daniel is a bustling front-runner, adept at retaining possession and passing intelligently. He made little impact with United, but fared better for Barnsley.

DANIEL ANTONY NARDIELLO
BORN: Coventry, 22 October 1982.
HONOURS: 3 Wales caps (07-).
OTHER CLUBS: Swansea City on loan 03/04 (4, 0); Barnsley on loan 03/04-04/05 (44, 14); Barnsley 05/06-06/07 (64, 14); Queen's Park Rangers 07/08- (8, 0); Barnsley on loan 07/08 (11, 1).

GAMES	1 (3)
GOALS	0

JIMMY DAVIS

2001/02

Equally at home at centre-forward or on the right flank, Jimmy was a potent raider who rose through United's junior teams alongside Danny Webber. He helped the reserves top their League table in 2001/02 and earned England under-20 honours, but then lost his life in a car crash.

JAMES ROGER WILLIAM DAVIS
BORN: Bromsgrove, Worcestershire, 6 February 1982.
OTHER CLUBS: Swindon Town on loan 02/03 (13, 2).
DIED: Oxfordshire, 9 August 2003.

GAMES	1
GOALS	0

RUUD VAN NISTELROOY

2001/02 → 2005/06

Ruud van Nistelrooy was Manchester United's modern-day marksman supreme, a ruthless opportunist so revered at Old Trafford that Sir Alex Ferguson once mooted the possibility of a statue to the prolific Dutchman, who plundered 150 goals while making a mere 200 starts for the club. Ironically, an estrangement between manager and centre-forward in the spring of 2006 resulted in Ruud's £11 million departure to Real Madrid, thus putting paid to any permanent memorial to match the Stretford End's bronze likeness of the iconic Denis Law, the last Red Devil to supply goals in such prodigious quantities.

Whether or not Sir Alex's monumental musings were to be taken seriously, there can be no doubt that van Nistelrooy was a scoring phenomenon to rank with the finest in living memory – and surely not the least of his achievements during his first season in Manchester was in influencing a certain sexagenarian to jettison thoughts of slippers and fireside in favour of a few more campaigns at United's helm.

During that 2001/02 term the dynamic newcomer's achievements were remarkable. On the rebound from a year on the sidelines nursing the career-threatening knee injury which scuppered his move to Old Trafford in 2000, Ruud plundered 36 goals in 49 games, five of which he began on the bench. There was no talk of needing time to settle in a foreign land following his £19 million switch from PSV Eindhoven, no moaning about being deployed frequently in the thankless role of lone frontman. He merely got on with his job, making history along the way as he became the first United man to find the net in ten successive games.

Crucially, there was never the slightest doubt about character or discipline, or whether his heart might be elsewhere. Ruud emerged as a model professional, yet behind his paragon-of-virtue image, there lurked a further truth, arguably the key one. The man was obsessed with scoring goals, his ferocity of purpose almost frightening, and reportedly he was a sore-headed grouch after any match in which he failed to register. That overweening hunger was vividly apparent in his constant willingness to work, always straining for an extra yard whether probing opponents with off-the-ball runs or defending doggedly from the front, and it was satisfied through a catalogue of attributes which was pretty well comprehensive.

Van Nistelrooy brought to his game a compelling fusion of finesse, power and pace. One moment he seemed to be ambling, apparently at a loose end, but the next he had exploded unstoppably from the shoulder of an unwary marker, bearing down on goal like some super-canine greyhound with a grudge. As for his finishing, it was awesome whether he employed force or delicacy, and he excelled at both, with right foot and left, from virtually any angle. At his peak his concentration was complete, his combination of positioning and execution a source of pure wonder.

Yet while goals were the Dutchman's *raison d'etre*, there was far more to admire about his game. For instance, he was capable of dazzlingly deft footwork somehow unexpected in a strapping centre-forward, and that, accompanied by the strength of a bull buffalo, enabled him to retain possession, apparently for as long as he liked. Then there was the vision and accuracy of his passing, his aerial menace and, at least until his unhappy final months as a Red, an eagerness to join in team play not always to be found in specialist scorers.

Astonishingly, some people underrated him. After a fleeting lean period early in 2002/03, Sam Allardyce opined that Ruud had been rumbled by Premiership defenders. Come the spring he had given the sceptical Bolton boss 44 reasons to believe, and pocketed a title medal to boot.

For those with a yen to wallow in vintage van Nistelrooy moments, that unforgettable campaign offered plenty of prime samples. There was the dance along the byline in Basle before curling home from a seemingly impossible angle; the exquisite outside-of-the-boot finish after a sumptuous dragback and swivel at home to West Ham in the FA Cup; the untypical but exhilarating dash from halfway which spreadeagled the Fulham defence at Old Trafford before a disguised early shot left 'keeper Maik Taylor mesmerised; the duping of Sol Campbell and the skinning of Martin Keown on the way to a devastating stiletto thrust at Highbury as the Championship advantage changed hands.

Thereafter the man who sprang to worldwide attention under Bobby Robson at PSV rarely stopped scoring, via spectacular volleys, rasping drives, adroit tap-ins, clinical placements, soaring headers . . . the van Nistelrooy catalogue embraced the lot, although amazingly he managed only one goal for United from outside the box.

On the minimal debit side, in some quarters he was vilified as a diver, but though he was known to spiral theatrically on occasions, he was no worse than most of his contemporaries; in particular, Arsenal's attempts to condemn him were contemptibly hypocritical.

At Old Trafford he was adored and it was a shame that his exit should be soured by drawn-out conflict with the man who had initially shown so much faith in him. But even though he cut a forlorn figure at the end, Ruud van Nistelrooy goes down in United history as a genuine hero. His footballing epitaph? Close, Ruud, but no statue . . .

RUTGERUS JOHANNES MARTINUS VAN NISTELROOY

BORN:	Oss, Holland, 1 July 1976.
HONOURS:	League Championship 02/03. FA Cup 03/04. 59 Holland caps (98-). PFA Footballer of the Year 02.
OTHER CLUBS:	Den Bosch 93/4-96/7 (69, 17), Heerenveen 97/8 (31, 13), PSV Eindhoven 98/9-00/01 (67, 62), all Holland; Real Madrid 06/07- (62, 41).

GAMES	200 (19)
GOALS	150

JUAN SEBASTIAN VERON

2001/02 → 2002/03

No one who cherishes all that is beautiful in sport would dispute that Juan Sebastian Veron was among the half-dozen most gifted manipulators of a football on the planet. A sublimely enchanting entertainer, the sweet-passing Argentinian artist was an imperious showman, too, his best work dusted richly with panache, perception and a due measure of arrogance. With his feathery touch, uncanny accuracy and outrageous audacity, he could transform any contest with a single shaft of sudden, incandescent brilliance. So why, having spent only two terms at Old Trafford, and after becoming the first player from his country to collect an English title medal, was he branded a £28 million misfit, even by fans who desired nothing more than to lionise him as their latest idol?

The principal problem facing Sir Alex Ferguson was how to accommodate this exotic talent in a midfield already bursting with inspirational performers. Veron's preferred role was in the centre, where Roy Keane was incomparable and Paul Scholes was ideally suited, and while the newcomer gave his most persuasive performances from that base, he was horribly inconsistent. He was tried on both right and left flanks, but too often he looked uneasy and was of less assistance to his defenders than either David Beckham or Ryan Giggs. At one point he was even pushed forward to the shoulder of lone front-man Ruud van Nistelrooy, but in that advanced position he was denied the space in which to play; he seemed lost, even confused, and consequently failed to exercise a telling influence.

The next question, then, must be why did the Reds pay Lazio a fortune in the summer of 2001 to make the 26-year-old play-maker the fifth most costly footballer of all time? The answer speaks volumes for the all-consuming ambition of the man who bought Eric Cantona for much the same reason. Despite the playing riches already at his disposal, Sir Alex craved a creator to provide a final touch of fantasy, to add the extra fractions he believed necessary to lift his majestic team to new levels of excellence, to furnish unmatchable moments that no coach could counter.

Encouragingly soon after the transfer, which was delayed initially by passport problems, 'The Little Witch' was casting his magical spell for the Red Devils. The son of Juan Ramon, who faced United for Estudiantes in the 1968 World Club Championship, he was tall and strong, elegant and composed, a flamboyant ball juggler who would have adorned any circus and, most important of all, a distributor divine.

With either foot, Veron could spear sudden destructive passes which could flummox any rearguard, his range comprehensive, his angles astonishing, his inventiveness, imagination and precision a sheer joy. In addition there was dead-ball expertise to rival Beckham's and, if his fabulous one-two interchange with Roy Keane before netting savagely at home to Everton in his first English autumn was any yardstick, then he would be contributing his share of goals, too.

Duly Veron capped a rousing contribution to a stunning comeback from three goals down at White Hart Lane with the venomous strike which put United in front, and after he was voted Premiership player of the month for September 2001, the shaven-headed South American appeared on course to become the Reds' new talisman.

However, come a crucial series of big matches in November and December, Veron was found wanting. His input in horrible defeats by Liverpool, Arsenal and Chelsea was ominously negligible; he was guilty of sloppy passing and inadequate covering when possession was surrendered; his body language did not speak of a warrior whose heart was in the battle; pundits declared that his presence unbalanced the side.

There were mitigating factors. In Argentina and Italy he had grown used to a type of game far more deliberate than the notoriously frenetic Premiership; he must have been distracted by anxieties about his family in his strife-wracked homeland; he suffered from niggling injuries, notably to an Achilles tendon; and his lack of a settled position can hardly have helped.

For the remainder of that season, and throughout the next, his form continued to fluctuate wildly. Broadly speaking, he could be sensational in Europe – his quickfire exchange with Beckham followed by a delectable outside-of-the-right-foot clip over the Olympiakos 'keeper at Old Trafford in October 2002 was unforgettable – but in the Premiership, all too frequently, he was almost wantonly wasteful of hard-won possession and clearly not suited temperamentally to defensive responsibilities.

Not surprisingly given his fee, sometimes it seemed that Ferguson was striving to accommodate the Argentine at any price, but even during the title-winning term few fans would have wept if 'The Little Witch' had mounted his broomstick and flown away forever.

Come August 2003, with the player dismayed by constant criticism, the sad and sorry Seba saga was concluded by a £15 million transfer to Chelsea. United were left to tot up a staggering £13 million loss and reflect on a disruptive gamble that hadn't come off, while an elated Claudio Ranieri spoke glowingly of 'the best midfielder in the world.' However, the Chelsea boss was not laughing for long . . .

JUAN SEBASTIAN VERON

BORN: Buenos Aires, Argentina, 9 March 1975.

HONOURS: League Championship 02/03. 60 Argentina caps (96-03).

OTHER CLUBS: Estudiantes 93/4-95/6 (60, 7); Boca Juniors 95/6 (17, 4), both Argentina; Sampdoria 96/7-97/8 (61, 7), Parma 98/9 (26, 1), Lazio 99/00- 00/01 (53, 11), all Italy; Chelsea 03/04 (7, 1); Internazionale, Italy, on loan 04/05-05/06 (49, 3); Estudiantes on loan 06/07 (30, 2).

GAMES **75 (7)**

GOALS **11**

LAURENT BLANC

2001/02 → 2002/03

Much-maligned Laurent Blanc was the finest footballing centre-half Manchester United ever had, bar none. True, that is not the same as being the most effective pure stopper, and few neutral observers would accord that particular accolade to the stately Frenchman.

However, far from being the weak link lambasted so mercilessly by hysterical critics who cited his lack of pace, he was an imperious defender throughout most of his first campaign at Old Trafford, the only pity being that Sir Alex Ferguson did not acquire his serenely majestic services a few seasons earlier.

Laurent was signed on a free transfer from Internazionale of Milan in September 2001 and strolled nonchalantly into the yawning gulf in the Red Devils' rearguard left by the recent shock departure of Jaap Stam – and there was the rub.

The mountainous yet pacy Dutchman was a folk-hero who exuded muscular authority, a craggy symbol of warrior-like strength, while his 35-year-old replacement projected a vividly contrasting image. With his unhurried air, drooping socks and slightly quizzical, almost lugubrious expression, Laurent might have been an absent-minded professor and, sure enough, the manager required him to conduct a season-long seminar for such richly promising but inexperienced colleagues as Wes Brown and Mikael Silvestre.

Naturally, Blanc needed time to settle into the English game, which was far more frenetic than anything he had encountered before in his long and fabulously illustrious career. Even in his youth he had never been quick and now at the veteran stage he seemed positively ponderous, looking particularly vulnerable on the turn against nippy Premiership predators.

Laurent was an easy target for those seeking scapegoats for a succession of dreadful results in the autumn of 2001, but much of the personal flak was unwarranted and gradually – for all but the blind and the prejudiced – there emerged the picture of a master craftsman.

As assured on the ball as befitted a man who first sprang to fame as a deep-lying attacker, and nervelessly composed in everything he did, Laurent read the action with unrivalled perception, breaking up countless raids with exquisitely timed interventions. Once in possession he was not disposed to waste it, invariably rolling a precise pass to a team-mate's feet.

Yet all that unadulterated class should not obscure altogether the Frenchman's more commonplace attributes. For example, he was magnificent in the air, witness his leading by the nose of the formidable Duncan Ferguson throughout his United debut at home to Everton, and he did not earn 97 French caps without being able to tackle.

Having been persuaded by Sir Alex Ferguson to stay for a second year instead of laying aside his boots as originally planned, the increasingly deliberate veteran enjoyed fewer outings in 2002/03, inevitably enough following the arrival of Rio Ferdinand, but still he collected a deserved title medal before retiring in the spring.

Perceptions of Laurent Blanc will always differ radically among United fans, but here is one layman who regrets that Sir Alex failed in three earlier attempts to sign this most stylish and visionary of central defenders. Better late than never, though.

LAUREN ROBERT BLANC
BORN: Ales, France, 19 November 1965.
HONOURS: League Championship 02/03. 97 France caps (89-00).
OTHER CLUBS: Montpellier, France, 83/4-90/1 (243, 76); Napoli, Italy, 91/2 (31, 6); Nimes, France, 92/3 (29, 1); St Etienne, France, 93/4-94/5 (70, 18); Auxerre, France, 95/6 (23, 2); Barcelona, Spain, 96/7 (28, 1); Marseille, France, 97/8-98/9 (63, 13); Internazionale, Italy, 99/00-00/01 (67, 6).
MANAGER: Bordeaux, France (07-).

GAMES 71 (4)
GOALS 4

DIEGO FORLAN

2001/02 → 2004/05

Diego Forlan was an unusual hero in that he was engulfed in heartfelt, often uproarious affection by the majority of Old Trafford regulars without ever assembling an exceptional body of work.

True, he did have his triumphs, none more satisfying than the brace that claimed victory so dramatically at Anfield in December 2002. Then there were two beautifully dispatched winners against Chelsea in League Cup and Premiership soon afterwards and a handful of other strikes both crucial and spectacular.

But beyond his goals – when they eventually arrived! – the amiable Uruguayan was embraced for himself; for his warm, open personality and the dignity, resolution and good humour with which he greeted the ridicule which descended on his head during what must have been a mortifyingly embarrassing interlude following his £7.5 million purchase from the Argentinian club, Independiente, in January 2002.

In fairness, it should be stressed that cameo appearances as a substitute heavily outnumbered his starts as he went goalless in 23 Premiership games, and with Messrs van Nistelrooy and Solskjaer more than making up for his shortfall, many fans made due allowances for a young stranger struggling manfully to come to terms with life, culture and football in an alien hemisphere.

All the while the blond newcomer was a study in perpetual motion, running willingly off the ball and shooting from practically anywhere with either foot. The trouble was he kept missing, and though Diego remained outwardly cheerful, his long-term prospects took on a melancholic hue.

Eventually he registered with a penalty against Maccabi Haifa, but it was not until he met a Mikael Silvestre cross with a flashing header into the Aston Villa net to equalise at Old Trafford in October that the curse was truly lifted and the place went wild.

The mayhem was redoubled in the next match when he unleashed a late howitzer to sink Southampton, but even that was nothing to the celebrations which greeted his pair at Liverpool, the first courtesy of a bizarre fumble by the Merseysiders' 'keeper Jerzy Dudek, the second a scorching drive.

After that, Diego would always be beloved of Alex Ferguson's Red and White Army, but still there was a perception among unsentimental observers that, for all his pace, eagerness and ability to deliver the occasional stunning strike, he did not possess sufficient all-round quality to warrant a long-term future with United.

That view seemed a trifle uncharitable in the autumn of 2003 when he was outscoring even van Nistelrooy, hitting the target seven times in nine outings, including a sensational twisting volley at home to Rangers in the European Cup.

But the momentum wavered, Alan Smith was recruited and Wayne Rooney lined up, and suddenly Forlan was wanted no more. Duly in August 2004 he joined Villarreal for a meagre £1.5 million, and some pundits predicted a rapid decline into obscurity. Far from it.

That term he netted 25 times for the Spaniards, thus sharing the European Golden Boot award with Thierry Henry and, perhaps relishing the sun on his back, finally proved his pedigree. Meanwhile back in Manchester, his former admirers rejoiced for him with a resounding chorus: 'He comes from Uruguay, he made the Scousers cry!'

CORAZO DIEGO FORLAN
BORN: Montevideo, Uruguay, 19 May 1979.
HONOURS: League Championship 02/03. 45 Uruguay caps (02-).
OTHER CLUBS: Penarol, Uruguay; Independiente, Argentina, 98/9-01/02 (77, 36); Villarreal, Spain, 04/05-06/07 (106, 54); Atletico Madrid, Spain, 07/08- (36, 16).

GAMES	37 (61)
GOALS	17

RIO FERDINAND

2 0 0 2 / 0 3 →

ew, if any, Manchester United footballers have polarised opinion more radically, or caused more passionate debate on their perceived merits and faults, than Rio Ferdinand. He has been variously dubbed the best defender in the world, the Old Trafford club's finest in living memory and the most cultured of his generation, but some acerbic observers have maintained that such extravagant bouquets have been a trifle over the top.

While allowing that the lanky, loose-limbed Londoner has touched impressive new heights of consistency, even played the best football of his life, since forming a settled partnership with the indomitable Serb Nemanja Vidic, they claim there have been too many instances of sloppy defensive discipline and sketchy concentration since his £30 million arrival from Leeds United in the summer of 2002 for Ferdinand to be rated above the likes of, say, Bill Foulkes or Steve Bruce, Gary Pallister or Jaap Stam.

In truth, that is a view which might not be rooted solely in the England regular's performances on the pitch, there being a school of thought which reviles Rio, rightly or wrongly, as a convenient high-profile symbol of the excesses which disfigure the top-level game in the 21st century.

However, this is not the place for an examination of the periodically controversial Ferdinand's wider persona; rather it is an honest attempt to arrive at a fair and balanced view of the richly gifted centre-half who, at the time of writing, had retained for six years the tag of United's most expensive acquisition.

The opinion here is that while some of plaudits showered on his head have been overblown, as he approached his thirties there was no more accomplished stopper in the Premier League than Rio, and there was encouraging evidence of a new-found solidity about his work at the back, which was beginning finally to match his undeniably sumptuous ability with the ball at his feet.

Before shattering the Old Trafford transfer record, Ferdinand was already the world's most expensive defender following his £18 million switch from West Ham to Leeds in 2000, but having become a Red Devil he found himself under the media microscope as never before – and it proved, at times, to be a traumatically unforgiving experience. At the time the Arsenal boss, Arsene Wenger, offered the helpful observation that the player was over-priced by £10 million, and there were other respected judges – and these were motivated neither by mischief nor envy – who concurred. But United made their move immediately after the 2002 World Cup finals in Japan and Korea, during which Ferdinand had performed magnificently, thus hiking his fee skywards.

What had the Red Devils got for their gigantic outlay? Although they won the League title in his first term, and a succession of niggling injuries offered mitigating circumstances, his form was worryingly variable. At his best he was fabulous, a lean, powerful, beautifully balanced athlete, seemingly untouchable in his authority and his effortless elegance. He could read the play assuredly, and when danger threatened he was quick and imperturbable. He was ravishingly smooth in possession of the ball, boasting the quick-footed skills and measured distribution of a play-making midfielder. There was everything to admire and nothing not to like.

But it wasn't always like that. There were dark days, too, when he appeared not to possess a true understanding that his first job was to prevent the other side from scoring. For all the pretty passes and majestic forward runs, where was the basic they-shall-not-pass instinct of a natural defender? He might switch off and allow an opponent to drift behind him; he might dawdle and dither and have his pocket picked in areas of high peril; he might be out-muscled by a determined centre-forward like Jimmy Floyd Hasselbaink; he might even appear a tad insipid, unable to focus as if his life depended on it, as all great centre-halves have to do.

Given his awesome potential, all this was overwhelmingly frustrating, particularly as there were lengthy sequences when Rio did live up to practically all the hyperbole. For instance, it was agonising for United fans when his superlative form in the first half of 2003/04 was halted by an eight-month ban for missing a routine drugs test. Few believed there was anything sinister in his failure to provide the requisite samples, but his explanation that he was pre-occupied by the prospect of moving house was greeted with widespread derision and little sympathy.

Come 2007/08, though, having established a mighty and formidably efficient partnership with Vidic, it seemed that Rio Ferdinand's prodigious all-round talent might be on the verge of full bloom at last. It appeared that he was maturing as a personality, and many pundits backed him to ascend to the captaincy of his country. Certainly he was more popular than previously, the residue of various episodes such as the drugs fiasco and an unsavoury wage dispute having gradually receded in the face of sustained excellence in protecting United's net.

In more recent times, too, he has begun to contribute a modicum of goals on his own account, none more rapturously received than the late headed winner against Liverpool at Old Trafford in January 2006, although it was run close by the clincher at home to the same opponents ten months later, when he controlled an awkwardly dropping ball with his right foot, swerved into space like some wing wizard and dispatched a sweet left-footer into the far top corner of Jose Reina's net.

Such deathless moments inspire a certain degree of affection, but if Rio Ferdinand, for all his glorious ability, is one day to bow out of Old Trafford as a United hero of the very front rank, he needs to consolidate for several seasons on the improved defensive reliability he exhibited in 2007/08.

RIO GAVIN FERDINAND

BORN:	Peckham, London, 7 November 1978.
HONOURS:	European Cup 07/08. League Championship 02/03, 06/07, 07/08.
	League Cup 05/06. 66 England caps (97-).
OTHER CLUBS:	West Ham United 95/6-00/01 (127, 2); Bournemouth on loan 96/7 (10, 1);
	Leeds United 00/01-01/02 (54, 2).

GAMES	**263 (4)**
GOALS	7

TIM HOWARD

2003/04 → 2005/06

Despite his expensive blunder against Jose Mourinho's Porto which cost United a Champions League quarter-finals place, Tim Howard enjoyed a fabulous debut campaign as a Red Devil, rocketing from comparative obscurity in the USA's Major League Soccer to earn the goalkeeping berth in the 2003/04 team of the season selected by his Premiership peers.

However, the meteoric progress of the imposing American stalled frustratingly during the following term as he performed inconsistently while battling for his place with Roy Carroll. Then he was jolted further, first by the arrival of the experienced, formidably excellent Edwin van der Sar in the summer of 2005, next by the emergence of Ben Foster and Tomasz Kuszczak as longer-term rivals. Come 2006 Howard was loaned to Everton and, suddenly, his hitherto dazzling Old Trafford prospects were all but extinguished.

With all due respect for Tim's achievements as a rookie custodian across the Atlantic, when he arrived at Old Trafford in July 2003 for a fee of £1.35 million, rising to £1.8 million with add-ons, there was barely a fan in the country who had heard of him.

Even Sir Alex Ferguson was a trifle hazy about the credentials of his 6ft 3in acquisition, but Howard had been scouted comprehensively by goalkeeping coach Tony Coton, who assured his manager: 'Once you see Tim in action there will be no more questions.'

Sure enough, the personable newcomer lost no time in justifying Coton's confidence. As he had been signed to compete for a place with Carroll following the departure of Fabien Barthez, most observers expected him to consolidate gradually, but his superb pre-season form demanded instant recognition.

Throughout that first autumn and winter in Manchester, Tim exuded an authoritative presence which bred composure among his fellow defenders, and he reinforced that calm aura by exceptional agility, unquestionable courage, impressive powers of concentration and adroit handling which presumably owed plenty to his lifelong brilliance at basketball.

Though afflicted by Tourette's Syndrome, a neurological complaint which can produce uncontrollable muscular tics and involuntary emotional outbursts, he made nonsense of predictions that the condition might affect his work, never revealing a hint of a problem.

He touched his spectacular best against Rangers at Ibrox in October, thrilled United's travelling contingent with a quartet of sensational saves at Bolton in January, then practically defied belief with a reflex parry to deny Joey Barton at home to Manchester City in the FA Cup in February.

But March brought the Porto blip, when his spill from a free-kick allowed Costinha to equalise at the death, and thereafter he never seemed quite as reliable again. The lapses were ascribed to inevitable fatigue, as he had played a full US season at the time of his arrival, but more fumbles followed during 2004/05, when his rotation with Carroll was dictated by both men's periodic fallibility, and his stock declined.

However, Tim bounced back to excel for Everton during 2006/07, and it was clear that a Premiership future was well within his compass. But it would not be spent at Old Trafford.

	TIMOTHY MATTHEW HOWARD			
BORN:	North Brunswick, USA, 6 March 1979.			
HONOURS:	FA Cup 03/04. 27 USA caps (02-).		GAMES	76 (1)
OTHER CLUBS:	New York/New Jersey MetroStars, USA, 98-03 (85, 0); Everton 06/07- (72, 0).		GOALS	0

ERIC DJEMBA-DJEMBA

2003/04 → 2004/05

If the ultimate failure of Eric Djemba-Djemba at Old Trafford was disappointing for all United fans in the wake of the Cameroon international's auspicious start, it was particularly devastating for those numerous unlucky youngsters who had opted to sport his name on their new shirts. Such a dismal outcome was barely imaginable at the Millennium in August 2003, a month after the stocky holding midfielder had been signed from the French club Nantes for a fee of £3.5 million, scheduled to rise to £4.2 million.

Though it was always accepted by sane observers that there was never going to be a ready-made replacement for Roy Keane, when Eric rose from the bench in the Community Shield clash with Arsenal, he offered instant grounds for optimism that Sir Alex Ferguson had recruited a reliable performer who could be expected to improve.

Abrasively combative but intelligent, too, the newcomer passed sensibly and displayed impressive stamina as he shuttled between penalty boxes, appearing to relish the responsibility of confronting Patrick Vieira and company. However, as Djemba-Djemba strove to settle, his season was fragmented by onerous international duties and a serious illness to his mother which necessitated a prolonged absence from Manchester. Thus his United career was disrupted at its outset and when he became available again he appeared humdrum in the extreme, his distribution woefully loose, his concentration poor, his overall impact inadequate.

Inevitably Eric was shipped out, to Aston Villa for a mere £1.35 million in January 2005, his initial promise seeming like a poignant mirage, his sad legacy a legion of abandoned shirts . . .

ERIC DANIEL DJEMBA-DJEMBA
BORN: Douala, Cameroon, 4 May 1981.
HONOURS: 20 Cameroon caps (02-).
OTHER CLUBS: Nantes, France, 01/02-02/03 (42, 1); Aston Villa 04/05-06/07 (11, 0); Burnley on loan 06/07 (15, 0); Sports Club, Qatar, 07/08-.

GAMES 27 (12)
GOALS 2

JOSE KLEBERSON

2003/04 → 2004/05

There can be no disguising the bald truth that Jose Kleberson was an Old Trafford flop; but, hand on heart, who could have predicted it? After all, he was young (24), gifted and Brazilian; and, if prospective purchasers needed any further convincing of the lithe midfielder's worth, he had been ever-present in Luiz Felipe Scolari's exhilarating side during the South Americans' triumphant 2002 World Cup campaign.

True, there was a certain regret among many of the Red Devils' disciples that Kleberson's more flamboyantly talented countryman, Ronaldinho, had not been secured instead, but still the £5.5 million capture from Paranaense was hailed by most fans as a coup in August 2003.

Sadly the man recruited to replace the disappointing Juan Sebastian Veron was to flounder even more desperately than his Argentinian predecessor in the furiously physical maelstrom that is the English Premiership, his progress hindered by a succession of debilitating injuries.

Deployed variously in central midfield, on the right flank and in the 'hole', the slim, elegant Kleberson proved an astute one- and two-touch footballer, imaginative when given the time, and he packed a powerful right-foot shot. There were instances of sheer quality when he delicately constructed goals for Scholes, Giggs and van Nistelrooy, with all of whom he could mesh delightfully on occasion. But far too frequently the Brazilian, who found it difficult to settle in England with his young family, looked off the pace, even forlorn, his presence increasingly desultory and anaemic. Eventually his £2.5 million move to Besiktas in August 2005 came as a relief for all concerned.

JOSE PEREIRA KLEBERSON
BORN: Urai, Brazil, 19 June 1979.
HONOURS: 27 Brazil caps (02-).
OTHER CLUBS: Nichika, PSTC, both Brazil; Atletico Paranaense, Brazil, 99-03 (100, 12); Besiktas, Turkey, 05/06-07/8 (42, 3); Flamengo, Brazil, 07/08-.

GAMES 24 (6)
GOALS 2

KIERAN RICHARDSON

2002/03 → 2006/07

For all his cocksure swagger and his range of opulent skills, Kieran Richardson never quite convinced as a Manchester United player. There was always a certain brittleness to his contribution, a feeling that no matter how dazzling he appeared when the ball was dancing to his tune, frustration was never very far away.

In fairness, his chances to impress were limited. Even when he did enjoy a sequence of more than two or three senior starts at a time, as he did in 2005/06, it was an infuriating fact of life for the brash young south Londoner that he would be cast aside to accommodate Ryan Giggs or some other luminary when the gala occasions beckoned.

Undeniably Richardson was laden with natural ability and it found its most persuasive expression as he skipped and scurried on the left flank of midfield, gulling defenders with a combination of deft footwork and a devastating change of pace.

He was no mean performer in a central role, either, as he demonstrated vividly during a loan spell with Bryan Robson's West Bromwich Albion in the spring of 2005. The Baggies appeared to be certainties for the drop when Kieran arrived, but a dozen games later they were saved melodramatically on the season's last day, and the United man was chaired from the pitch a hero. Though it wasn't enough to net him a regular berth at Old Trafford, it did secure a surprise full England call-up and he responded brilliantly with two beautifully taken goals on his debut against the USA in Chicago.

Richardson, who had been on West Ham's books as a boy, made his senior entrance during 2002/03, the term in which he scored in the first leg of the FA Youth Cup Final triumph over Middlesbrough. There followed sporadic first-team opportunities over the next few campaigns, and he revealed glimpses of breathtaking potential.

He was an entertaining runner with the ball and he carried a potent shot – a bullet of a 20-yarder at Debrecen in August 2005 was a fine example – but the fans never took to him. He was inclined to be irritatingly flashy, appearing at times to be consumed by his own cleverness, and there was a tendency to commit the cardinal footballing sin of conceding possession unnecessarily.

However, during 2005/06 there were gratifying signs of increased maturity, and he didn't disgrace himself when deployed as an emergency left-back during an injury crisis, but still he received stick from the stands at Old Trafford. Indeed, he was booed spitefully when he came on as a substitute during the home massacre of Roma in April 2007, when even his most vehement detractors might have been in a benevolent mood, and he accepted that a change of club was inevitable.

Accordingly, in the summer of 2007 Kieran Richardson was sold for £5.5 million to Sunderland, where Roy Keane accepted the challenge of nurturing a tantalising talent towards fulfilment.

KIERAN EDWARD RICHARDSON
BORN: Greenwich, London, 21 November 1984.
HONOURS: League Championship 06/07. League Cup 05/06. 8 England caps (05-).
OTHER CLUBS: West Bromwich Albion on loan 04/05 (12, 3); Sunderland 07/08- (17, 3).

GAMES 44 (37)
GOALS 11

PHIL BARDSLEY

2003/04 → 2007/08

There was a time, when he was compiling a run of eight straight first-team outings in the autumn of 2005, that Phil Bardsley looked to be the natural successor to Gary Neville as Manchester United's right-back.

But there were two factors militating against the flinty young Salfordian's long-term elevation. Though Neville was past 30 he showed not the slightest inclination to step aside for a new man, and in little Danny Simpson there was emerging a daunting challenge from a sparky competitor some 18 months Bardsley's junior.

Even so, Phil's case was not a flimsy one. In many ways he mirrored Neville, there being a certain hungry air about his play, a steely resolve and a mental resilience perhaps honed during a period of struggle on loan at Royal Antwerp. He was disciplined and firm in his work at the back, he overlapped ebulliently and he was versatile enough to switch flanks at need.

There was a particularly impressive display at home to Benfica in September 2005 when he delivered a string of menacing crosses, and he was one of United's few successes in a disappointing team effort in the goalless home draw with Lille the following month.

But then Neville's return from injury closed the door, and a succession of competent loan stints preceded a £2 million move to Sunderland in January 2008. Roy Keane might just have returned to the Old Trafford coalface to unearth a gem.

PHILIP ANTHONY BARDSLEY
BORN: Salford, Lancashire, 28 June 1985.
OTHER CLUBS: Royal Antwerp, Belgium, on loan 03/04; Burnley on loan 05/06 (6, 0); Glasgow Rangers on loan 06/07 (5, 1); Aston Villa on loan 06/07 (13, 0); Sheffield United on loan 07/08 (16, 0); Sunderland 07/08- (11, 0).

GAMES 10 (8)
GOALS 0

DAVID JONES

2004/05 → 2006/07

When David Jones skippered Manchester United to FA Youth Cup glory in 2003, he was seen as a genuine contender to reach for the sky as a Red Devil.

An all-purpose central midfielder, play-maker and enforcer rolled into one, he looked comfortable on the ball, passed perceptively, especially with his left foot, and he didn't shrink from a physical challenge. Crucially, too, he was a mature individual blessed with a commendably level temperament.

Yet despite those positives, underlined by his rise to England under-21 status, so fierce was the Old Trafford competition that David was unable to earn a run in the side, let alone a regular berth. Thus, after productive loan spells at Preston and the Dutch club Nijmegen, he was sold to Derby County for £1.1 million midway through 2006/07.

For those who had monitored his rise through United's junior ranks with increasing optimism, when Roy Keane was headed for the exit door and Paul Scholes was unfit during 2005/06 it was frustrating to witness Alan Smith and John O'Shea being played out of position in centre-field while the promising Jones toiled elsewhere.

Eventually, of course, Sir Alex Ferguson had to make a quality judgement on the rookie whom he had described as his team's best player during his first senior start in United's goalless FA Cup draw at home to Exeter City in January 2004.

Clearly, while admiring the dynamic young Lancastrian, the manager felt he was not quite good enough. As David Jones seeks to prove Sir Alex wrong at Pride Park, his progress will be fascinating.

DAVID FRANK LLWYD JONES
BORN: Southport, Lancashire, 4 November 1984.
OTHER CLUBS: Preston North End on loan 05/06 (24, 3); NEC Nijmegen, Holland, on loan 05/06; Derby County 06/07- (42, 7).

GAMES 3 (1)
GOALS 0

DAVID BELLION

. . . .

2003/04 → 2004/05

If it was easy to see why Manchester United took a £2 million gamble on signing David Bellion from Sunderland in July 2003, all too soon it became blindingly obvious why it wasn't going to pay off.

The tall, slender Frenchman could run like the wind and there was barely a defender in the land who could hope to catch him once he had hit his scorching stride. But although coaches stress *ad nauseam* that pace is of paramount importance in the modern game, it has to be augmented by other attributes, particularly footballing awareness, and it was in this crucial area that David proved seriously lacking.

Though there were rare shafts of brilliance, such as the sudden dart, slick sidestep and emphatic finish after taking a pass from Ryan Giggs at home to Spurs in March 2004, too often the young frontman-cum-winger squandered the advantage of his searing speed by sprinting thoughtlessly into traffic.

Similarly, while he could pass perceptively – witness the pinpoint dispatch to set up Liam Miller's strike at Crewe in October 2004 – Bellion's distribution was often as sloppy as his first touch was unreliable. In fairness, however, it should be stressed that he was not the world's worst finisher, his record of eight goals being eminently respectable given his shortage of starts.

Towards the end of his Old Trafford tenure David began to take verbal flak from fans frustrated by his inability to make the most of his potential, and he appeared increasingly nervy. Thus it seemed a timely decision to make a fresh start in his homeland in 2005.

DAVID BELLION
BORN: Sevres, France, 27 November 1982.
OTHER CLUBS: Cannes, France; Sunderland 01/02-02/03 (20, 1); West Ham United on loan 05/06 (8, 0); Nice, France, 05/06-06/07 (45, 13); Bordeaux, France, 07/08-.

GAMES **15 (25)**
GOALS **8**

CHRIS EAGLES

. . . .

2003/04 →

How long can a player be classified as promising without making a definitive breakthrough? It's a question which has haunted the Manchester United career of Chris Eagles, but at the time of writing there had been no conclusive answer.

A slender, skilful, right-sided attacking midfielder, comfortable in both wide and central roles, he earned rave reviews as United won the FA Youth Cup in 2003, and soon there followed a senior debut when he rose from the bench in a League Cup encounter at Elland Road to torment Leeds' experienced full-back Ian Harte. But for all his pace, verve and confidence, Chris was deemed too lightweight for regular exposure at the top level and he embarked on two years of successful loan travels.

On his return a transfer seemed possible, but when the squad was weakened by injuries he was sent on to replace Ole Gunnar Solskjaer soon after United had battled back from two goals down to lead 3-2 at Goodison as the title race reached a crescendo in April 2007. He might have frozen when Wayne Rooney sent the ball into space behind the Toffees' back line, and his legs did momentarily buckle, perhaps with excitement, as he raced on to the clever delivery – but then he steadied himself like a veteran and coolly bent home the clinching goal.

It was an ecstatic moment, but with Ronaldo and company holding sway so compellingly in 2007/08, it was difficult to discern a settled Old Trafford future for the talented 22-year-old.

CHRISTOPHER MARK EAGLES
BORN: Hemel Hempstead, Hertfordshire, 19 November 1985.
OTHER CLUBS: Watford on loan 04/05 (13, 1); Sheffield Wednesday on loan 05/06 (25, 3); Watford on loan 05/06 (17, 3); NEC Nijmegen, Holland, on loan 06/07.

GAMES **7 (10)**
GOALS **1**

LIAM MILLER

2004/05 → 2005/06

Liam Miller never came up to scratch as a Red Devil, but the unassuming Republic of Ireland international midfielder could hardly be blamed for failing to meet the idiotically inflated expectations with which he was saddled following his £2.4 million arrival from Celtic in the summer of 2004.

Partly because he hailed from the same city, Cork, as Roy Keane, the diminutive newcomer was touted in some quarters as a convenient long-term replacement for United's incomparable captain. It proved to be a risible proposition.

In fact, Miller was nothing like Keane as a player. True, he was immensely skilful and a neat passer, but any vestige of similarity ended there. Indeed, by the time he had bedded in at Old Trafford it was difficult to comprehend such judgements as that passed by Henrik Larsson during their time together at Celtic, to the effect that Liam was the world's best midfielder for his age.

Certainly his impact in his handful of appearances for United was flimsy. Usually operating on the right, he appeared passive as the action raged around him. No one could fault him for effort but, barring the occasional clever touch, there was little to suggest that he was not simply overawed by the size of his new club.

An encouraging loan spell with Leeds followed, and it was a tad ironic that Liam's new mentor, as he strove to prove himself in English football following his free transfer to Sunderland in August 2006, was none other than Roy Keane.

JONATHAN SPECTOR

2004/05

Once in a while, at every club, there arises a young footballer who impresses home fans and neutral observers mightily but who, in perplexingly short order, finds himself surplus to the manager's requirements. Such was the Old Trafford experience of Jonathan Spector.

Having been recruited as a teenager from Chicago Sockers, the stylish American utility defender made rapid progress, earning the Jimmy Murphy Award for the reserves' player of the year in 2003/04 and promotion to the senior squad for the following term. Though naturally a right-sided centre-half, he slotted in smoothly at left-back, exhibiting strength, athleticism and ball skill aplenty. But the most eye-catching of the Spector attributes was an apparent maturity remarkable in one of such tender years. When the Reds' rearguard came under fire, he countered with reassuring composure, intelligent positioning and an instinct for protecting pressurised team-mates which augured promisingly for the future.

Trusted by Sir Alex Ferguson for the vital Champions League qualifier at home to Dinamo Bucharest in August 2004, Jonathan was not found wanting and he followed up with a man-of-the-match effort against Everton. Though he stepped aside when more experienced men returned to duty, he had laid down a telling marker and rose quickly to full international status. Come 2005/06 Spector did well on a season-long loan to Charlton, but after returning from the Valley the talented 20-year-old was sold for £500,000 to West Ham. Admittedly, competition for a permanent berth in United's back line was brisk, but many observers maintained that a potentially outstanding performer had been allowed to slip away.

WILLIAM PETER MILLER
BORN: Cork, Republic of Ireland, 13 February 1981.
HONOURS: 16 Republic of Ireland caps (04-).
OTHER CLUBS: Celtic 99/00-03/04 (26, 2); Aarhus, Denmark, on loan 01/02; Leeds United on loan 05/06 (28, 1); Sunderland 06/07- (54, 3).

GAMES	11 (11)
GOALS	2

JONATHAN MICHAEL PAUL SPECTOR
BORN: Arlington Heights, Illinois, USA, 1 March 1986.
HONOURS: 9 USA caps (04-).
OTHER CLUBS: Chicago Sockers, USA; Charlton Athletic on loan 05/06 (20, 0); West Ham United 06/07- (51, 1).

GAMES	4 (4)
GOALS	0

CRISTIANO RONALDO

2003/04 →

Cristiano Ronaldo might be the most thrilling entertainer in the world game but his nauseatingly tiresome procrastination about a possible move to Real Madrid in the summer of 2008 produced a significant mood swing against him among many of his erstwhile admirers. They were dismayed that his astonishing achievement in scoring 42 goals as United lifted both European and domestic crowns should be tainted by perceived disloyalty within days of the celebrations reaching full swing. As the outcome of the unseemly brouhaha was not known as this book went to press, there is no intention to further press the controversy here. Instead, mercifully, the focus will remain on his football.

And so to the Great Debate, which gathered pace from the sunlit Old Trafford afternoon in August 2003 when he lacerated Bolton's defenders so bewitchingly with his provocative repertoire of strutting stepovers that they barely knew which way there were facing. Was Ronaldo a unique thoroughbred, or a narcissistic show pony whose brain didn't always keep pace with his feet? Argument raged passionately for several seasons, with the central accusation laid at the door of the flamboyant young Portuguese being that, for all the ostentatious alchemy, there wasn't enough end-product.

End-product? In 2006/07 he scored 23 goals and Manchester United regained the Premiership crown; in 2007/08, usually starting as a right winger but also operating on the left and often roaming through the middle, staggeringly he almost doubled his tally as the two big prizes were annexed. Clearly he had made the journey from infuriatingly flashy appendage to the potent centrepiece of the Red Devils' attack, thus forcing detractors to give ground.

Still, though, not everyone has been enraptured by Ronaldo. There remain thoughtful and unbiased observers of the Old Trafford scene who maintain that true greatness will elude him until he stamps his authority regularly on the grandest occasions. They cite his wan contributions during debilitating defeats in the second leg of the 2007 European Cup semi-final in Milan, and in the FA Cup Final against Chelsea two weeks later, but that seems more than a tad harsh. After all, no player in history has sparkled in every game and the young man from Madeira has been electrifying in plenty of encounters of colossal import. Indeed, he was hardly ineffectual in the 2008 Champions League Final, in which he nodded his goal with exquisite precision.

Cristiano Ronaldo was transformed from a mere blip on United's scouting radar to a high-priority transfer target in the summer of 2003, when the 18-year-old prodigy, who was equally devastating on either flank and when using either foot, terrorised the Red Devils' rearguard in a Lisbon friendly. With Liverpool holding a watching brief, United signed him from Porto for £12.24 million, roughly double what any rival was prepared to pay, but the merest fraction of his market value half a decade later when Real Madrid coveted him so desperately.

Tall, coltishly slender and still to grow into his full strength, Cristiano was clearly a work in progress, but as Bolton and a succession of other Premiership opponents were to discover in his first English campaign, he was a truly original talent who mesmerised markers with his impudent, sometimes even insolent footwork, then left them panting with his scorching acceleration.

True, his serial fripperies could be infuriating, not least to United fans who expected an intelligent pass at the end of a coruscating run, or to Ruud van Nistelrooy, who appeared to be less than consistently enamoured by the newcomer's decision-making, but clearly he was special and he capped his first term in Manchester with a headed goal in the FA Cup Final triumph over Millwall.

The attainment of professional maturity was not to be instant, but over the next couple of campaigns Ronaldo began to assimilate the reality that tricks and eye-popping dexterity meant nothing without tangible benefit to his side. His physical development continued apace, too, so that he was big enough and strong enough to pose a telling aerial threat, as well as soak up and shrug off most of the violence to which he was subjected almost routinely.

As for jibes about diving, it would be idle to deny that there were occasions early in his career when he appeared to go to ground too easily. However, as his lightning manoeuvres induced so many opponents to deliberate no further than whether to grasp his shirt or lash at his legs, he deserved a certain amount of understanding. In more recent times, almost invariably he has opted not to tumble, preferring to punish the miscreants by creating or scoring a goal.

The summer of 2006 brought a watershed in Ronaldo's affairs when he was embroiled in controversy and vilified for allegedly trying to get Wayne Rooney sent off during the World Cup. There were fears that he might depart Old Trafford, but he showed startling steeliness by staying and, over the following two terms, producing the finest form of his life. At last he had cottoned on that the posturing from which he could not wholly desist was acceptable only if leavened with deadly purpose. Now the more he was taunted the more he scintillated, and duly he became a gilded talisman in 2007/08, his output including a handful of trademark dead-ball rockets, a thunderous header in Rome and an amazing sidefooted flick at home to Aston Villa. Now, no less qualified a judge than his revered countryman, Luis Figo, was saying: 'He can do things with a football which make me touch my head and wonder how on earth such things could be possible.'

The view here is that of all the men to be compared to George Best, Cristiano Ronaldo is the most compelling. Okay, it's still a daft comparison . . . but not half so daft as it was.

CRISTIANO RONALDO DOS SANTOS AVEIRO	
BORN:	Funchal, Madeira, 5 February 1985.
HONOURS:	European Cup 07/08. League Championship 06/07, 07/08.
	FA Cup 03/04. League Cup 05/06. 53 Portugal caps (03-).
	FWA Footballer of the Year 07, 08. PFA Footballer of the Year 07, 08.
OTHER CLUBS:	Sporting Lisbon, Portugal, 02/03 (25, 3).

GAMES **196 (43)**
GOALS 92

ALAN SMITH

2004/05 → 2006/07

Alan Smith enjoyed not one scintilla of luck during an all-too-brief Old Trafford career which began with the former Leeds firebrand threatening to make fools of pundits who declared he did not possess sufficient quality for Manchester United, and ended with a definitive verdict on his potential rendered impossible by an horrendous injury.

However, without being uncharitable towards a selfless warrior who always played with every last scrap of his ability and his heart, even before he had snapped his left leg and mangled his ankle as he fell awkwardly when blocking a shot by Liverpool's John Arne Riise at Anfield in February 2006, there were reservations about his efficacy at the very top level.

Unquestionably he was a formidable asset for any manager to summon from the bench to graft in attack or midfield, to bring a rousingly bold and fierce spirit to the fray when more subtle talents were waning. But as a regular starter and consistent goal-scorer, he left a little bit to be desired.

As Leeds were forced to sell their prize playing assets in a vain bid to ward off financial meltdown, Smith remained for a time as a lonely figurehead, a passionately loyal symbol of the Yorkshiremen's expiring identity as a major power. So when a £7 million move to Manchester was mooted in May 2004, his Elland Road admirers could scarcely credit that he would switch allegiance to their loathed traditional rivals across the Pennines.

But having demonstrated amply his genuine affection for Leeds, he revealed practicality, ambition and courage by enlisting as a Red Devil, and he experienced no difficulty in settling in the camp of the old enemy. Alan hit the ground at high velocity, earning immediate acceptance from his new supporters with his dynamic commitment at a time when some of his colleagues were looking uncharacteristically pallid.

Certainly, during the early autumn Smith was United's outstanding performer. An old-fashioned, rumbustious barger of a centre-forward boasting few frills but bristling with aggressive intent, he hurled himself into every challenge, held the ball up skilfully and drew fouls from his rattled markers. And, best of all, he scored goals, spectacular goals.

There was a wickedly dipping volley on debut in the Community Shield against Arsenal, a lashed last-minute point-rescuer at Blackburn and a muscularly majestic header at home to Middlesbrough, but the pick of them was the winner against Norwich in his first Old Trafford outing in a red shirt. Ryan Giggs headed into the box and Smith stunned the ball on his chest before swivelling to dispatch a looping left-foot cross-shot which stirred memories of Mark Hughes. More typical was a near-Herculean effort at Fulham in December when he lost possession in the Cottagers' area, then won it back ferociously before rampaging through two tackles to net from an acute angle.

But just as Alan had appeared to have created a sustainable momentum, it was shattered by an ankle injury which sidelined him for six weeks and, with Wayne Rooney, Ruud van Nistelrooy and Louis Saha all in contention for striking berths, he was never quite the same irresistible force as a front-man again.

Neither was he an unqualified success when switched to midfield at a time when Sir Alex Ferguson was seeking a long-term successor to the virtually irreplaceable Roy Keane. Smith might have been able to emulate the Irishman in terms of muscle, industry and enthusiasm, even self-belief, but he lacked the vision, awareness and passing skills, the all-embracing nous of the departing captain, and those were attributes which could not be learned.

Of course, he tried with every fibre of his being and there were several titanic displays, notably in the 1-0 home victory over Chelsea in November 2005 which interrupted momentarily the Londoners' procession towards another title. But, in general, while he was a fearsome competitor in any midfield rough-and-tumble, as a prospective pivot of the side he was out of his depth.

That reality was beginning to sink in by the time he suffered his sickening accident against Liverpool, a misfortune which would have broken some footballers but which Alan greeted calmly, even philosophically, later recalling how he lay on the Anfield turf 'with my left leg pointing one way and my ankle pointing to Hong Kong.'

Thereafter he mounted a heroic comeback, slaving to regain fitness and returning ahead of schedule, only to find that he had rushed back too soon. Other clubs sought his services on loan, but he was determined to give himself the best possible chance at Old Trafford and in his second reappearance, in the spring of 2007, he was far more convincing. His highlight was an exquisitely steered volley which capped a sweeping team move in the 7-1 annihilation of Roma, but his input meant more than that, his indefatigable attitude offering his comrades an almost spiritual lift as they closed in on the Premiership crown.

Re-establishing himself fully proved beyond him, but Alan Smith had given it everything and when he joined Newcastle for £6 million during the following summer, he departed with immense honour and a bottomless well of respect.

ALAN SMITH			
BORN:	Rothwell, Yorkshire, 28 October 1980.		
HONOURS:	League Championship 06/07. 19 England caps (01-).	GAMES	61 (32)
OTHER CLUBS:	Leeds United 98/9-03/04 (172, 38); Newcastle United 07/08- (33, 0).	GOALS	12

GABRIEL HEINZE

2004/05 → 2006/07

It was a crying shame that Gabriel Heinze departed Old Trafford with jibes of 'traitor' ringing in his ears, but that's how it was in the late summer of 2007.

To fans who had lionised the swashbuckling, sometimes ruthlessly rugged Argentinian international defender as an authentic hero following his £6.9 million arrival from Paris St Germain three seasons earlier, it was barely credible that now he wanted to join Liverpool.

No doubt he was mortified at having fallen behind the Frenchman, Patrice Evra, in the battle for the Red Devils' left-back berth, and, heaven knows, there might have been a financial implication in his unbending resolve to head for the exit. Certainly his transfer record before joining United, encompassing relatively brief spells at four major clubs in four different countries, hardly suggested enduring stability. But still . . . Anfield?

Was there no appreciation for the sensibilities of the supporters, the people who had paid his wages and with whom he had appeared to have struck up such a warm rapport?

Thanks to a clause in his contract (which had two years to run), inserted with remarkable prescience by Manchester United, he was unable to join one of their main Premiership rivals, eventually opting for Real Madrid, who paid a reported £8.4 million to acquire him, although cynics suggested it might not be too long before he found his way to Merseyside.

But whatever labyrinthine machinations might have been involved in the unscheduled sale of one of the world's most accomplished back-line performers, there was never any doubting that Gabriel Heinze was his own man.

Soon after Sir Alex Ferguson had secured his signature in June 2004 it emerged that he would miss the first few weeks of his first English campaign due to a last-minute call-up to represent Argentina in the Olympics.

There were plenty of persuasive voices from Old Trafford, including one with a strident Glaswegian accent, urging him to turn his back on his country in the interests of his new club. But Gabriel stood firm, eventually fetching up in Manchester the proud possessor of a gold medal, leaving the United boss infuriated by an absence prolonged by World Cup qualifiers.

In his pique Ferguson intimated that Heinze's decision might even cost him his future at the club, but it wasn't long before the newcomer with the bulldozer build had cemented his berth on the left flank of the Reds' rearguard. He scored with an airborne sidefooted volley on his debut at Bolton and soon, with his unquenchable zest, bone-shaking tackles and express-train charges down the left touchline, he was being described as a South American version of Stuart Pearce.

Heinze was terrific in the air, too – often Argentina employed him at centre-half – and he was a shrewd anticipator of danger, although occasionally his enthusiasm for getting forward left gaps for opposition attackers to exploit. As a man-marker he was tenacious, if occasionally a tad impetuous, and the majority of his ball-work was smooth and assured.

Perhaps not since the days of big Jim Holton had a United defender of the rough-hewn variety earned such instant approbation from the Old Trafford crowd. He played the game with a smile, his initial lack of English didn't prevent him from roaring advice in the heat of battle and, in the words of commentator Tony Gale, in every challenge he gave it the kitchen sink.

Of such endearing stuff are cult heroes made, and it wasn't only the fans who warmed to Gabriel, who at the end of 2004/05 was voted United's player of the season by his team-mates and compared to his eminent countryman, the World Cup-winning skipper Daniel Pasarella, by a delighted Sir Alex.

Sadly, a cruel reversal of fortune was imminent. Shortly after netting with a pair of headers against Hungarian champions Debrecen in a Champions League qualifier in August 2005, he suffered a ruptured cruciate knee ligament when falling awkwardly during a goalless encounter with Villarreal in Spain, then missed the remainder of the season.

Come the following summer he pronounced himself fit enough to play in the World Cup finals but, after pledging his future to United when courted by Real Madrid and speaking of his loyalty to Ferguson for standing by him during his lay-off, he broke down again, and was absent for the start of 2006/07.

That enabled the improving Evra to stake his claim at left-back, and when Heinze did return in mid-September, the old razor-sharp edge appeared to be missing, prompting thoughts that he might have stretched himself prematurely on international duty.

As the season wore on he continued to be less formidable, more fallible, than during his first triumphant term as a Red Devil, but still he was expected to bounce back to his best and it seemed unthinkable that he was about to abandon the United cause.

Then news broke of his desire to make the sacrilegious journey west along the M62 and Gabriel Heinze, once so beloved of the Old Trafford legions, was dislodged from his pedestal and cast into outer darkness. If he ever returns, particularly if he is wearing a Liver Bird on his chest, his welcome will be passionate, indeed.

GABRIEL IVAN HEINZE

BORN: Crespo, Argentina, 19 April 1978.
HONOURS: League Championship 06/07. 43 Argentina caps (03-).
OTHER CLUBS: Newell's Old Boys, Argentina, 96/7 (8, 0); Sporting Lisbon, Portugal, 98/9 (5, 1); Valladolid, Spain, 99/00-00/01 (54, 1); Paris St Germain, France, 01/02-03/04 (99, 4); Real Madrid 07/08- (20, 1).

GAMES 75 (8)
GOALS 4

LOUIS SAHA

· ·

2003/04 →

Louis Saha is like some sleek and mettlesome but tantalisingly fragile thoroughbred racehorse. In the four and a half seasons since his tediously acrimonious and drawn out £12.8 million transfer from Fulham, he has treated Manchester United to enough moments of shimmering virtuosity to emphasise the boundless range of his potential. But there is a snag. Serial injuries have limited his impact so drastically that many frustrated observers, patience long exhausted and hair in shreds, would applaud his removal and replacement by a centre-forward who would, at least, be available to take the field on something approaching a regular basis.

It must represent a dilemma of immense proportions for his manager. Imagine disposing of an indisputably gifted marksman, someone who can transform half-chances into unforgettable goals, a rare performer who might limp away from Old Trafford only for his brilliance to light up the sky above the stadium of a rival club. It hardly bears thinking about.

Even presuming that he is retained, there remains a *Catch-22* element to the optimum handling of Saha. Whenever possible he has been nursed because of his propensity to lose fitness, but plenty of time on the pitch is needed to massage his sometimes suspect self-belief. It is for coming up with the correct answer to such conundrums that soccer bosses earn their money.

Yet in case anyone doubts the extraordinary prowess of the lithe and pacy Parisian, or wonders why Sir Alex Ferguson expended so much time, energy and hard cash on his capture in January 2004, a flick through DVD replays of his exploits in a United shirt would be apposite. They reveal extravagant skill allied to superlative athleticism and, mostly, calm assurance under pressure.

Frequently there is a stunningly deft take from a long-distance delivery followed by a mesmerising movement to lose a marker and a breathtakingly emphatic finish. Into this category fall goals at Charlton in August 2006, in Benfica's Stadium of Light a month later and in an FA Cup replay at Reading in February 2007, an especially memorable example. Twisting to take a raking punt from Rio Ferdinand on his chest even as it dropped over his shoulder, the Frenchman wrong-footed two defenders before netting with a sudden, savage cross-shot with his favourite left foot from such a narrow angle that a successful strike seemed barely credible.

Then there was the dynamic charge through the centre of Fulham's defence, capped by a fulminating drive – a sequence accompanied by cries of 'Judas' from the Craven Cottage stands, coming as it did only a month after he left the west Londoners – and the unerringly threaded sidefoot from the edge of the box at home to Chelsea in November 2006, both typical offerings from an enviably rich repertoire.

Most sumptuous of all, though, showcasing predatory instinct and devastating touch, came at Wigan the previous month, when he stretched with his right foot to control a scooped cross from Wayne Rooney, then swivelled adroitly to dispatch a venomous volley with his left. It was outrageous in its opulence, destructive in its impact, a statement of staggering capability which explained more eloquently than a million words why Ferguson retained faith in Louis Saha.

The relationship between player and club had begun with sweet promise as he rattled in seven goals while making only ten starts in the late winter and spring of 2004, mostly in tandem with the prodigiously prolific Ruud van Nistelrooy. But his 2004/05 contribution was minimal because of injury, and after he returned to fitness nearly halfway through the subsequent campaign, following an eight-month lay-off, Louis might have moved on but for differences which arose between the Dutchman and Sir Alex. As it was he regained impetus with a slew of League Cup goals, including one in the final victory over Wigan.

Then came a potent early input into the 2006/07 title triumph and hopes for his ultimate fulfilment burgeoned. Indeed, in mid-December the former Newcastle loanee was the Red Devils' leading scorer with a dozen goals in all competitions before, with sickening inevitability, injury took its toll and he found the net only once more after Christmas.

Rooney was joined by Carlos Tevez for 2007/08, but even with such world-class operators available, a player of the Saha type was demonstrably necessary. He offered something different, being the only frontline striker at the club with the outright speed to run in behind defences and the only one to offer a telling aerial threat at the far post, though it must be admitted that Cristiano Ronaldo addressed those deficits rather usefully from his starting position on the wing! In addition Louis' fluid and perceptive movement, his neat chest control and his ability to shield the ball made him an ideal target man, and he was clever enough in possession to link perceptively with his quicksilver colleagues.

Sometimes, when his confidence sagged, he might infuriate with interludes of ineffectiveness bordering on the inept, but fundamentally there was never any doubting the quality of Louis Saha. When he was there, that is . . .

LOUIS SAHA

BORN: Paris, 8 August 1978.
HONOURS: League Championship 06/07, 07/08. League Cup 05/06. 18 France caps (04-).
OTHER CLUBS: Metz, France, 97/8-99/00 (47, 5); Newcastle United on loan 98/9 (11, 1); Fulham 00/01-03/04 (117, 53).

GAMES 76 (48)
GOALS 42

EDWIN VAN DER SAR

2005/06 →

Edwin van der Sar was the tenth goalkeeper to taste first-team action for Manchester United following the departure of Peter Schmeichel, and without being disrespectful to his nine predecessors, the 6ft 5in Dutchman offered a rather more reassuring security blanket to team-mates and supporters than any of them. And why wouldn't he? Of the others, only Fabien Barthez could boast similar status in the game, or could point to comparable experience, and for all his undeniable entertainment value it's fair to say that stability was hardly the eccentric Frenchman's long suit.

If we suspend disbelief for a moment, and imagine the pair taking the stage as a comedy duo, then surely van der Sar would play the straight man to Barthez's flamboyant clown. Translating that to a football setting, and allowing that the duo's talent levels are roughly equal, there seems little doubt which would be the logical choice for a trophy-hunting manager. Indeed, when Schmeichel did step aside following the treble-winning euphoria of 1999, it was to Edwin that Alex Ferguson's thoughts initially turned as an ideal replacement. Unfortunately the timing wasn't right, the lanky custodian having not long joined Juventus from Ajax of Amsterdam, with whom he had collected multiple honours, including a European Cup winner's medal, over the past decade.

Even when van der Sar was deposed by the £32 million man Gianluigi Buffon, who thus became the world's most expensive 'keeper, circumstances dictated the United manager did not launch a bid, as Barthez had just pocketed a title medal at the end of his first Old Trafford campaign. So Edwin joined Fulham, newly promoted to the Premiership, and served them ably for four years during which the Red Devils tired of the erratic Fabien, then gave Roy Carroll and Tim Howard prolonged opportunities. Finally in June 2005, neither of those rivals having been judged to pass muster, Manchester United handed over £2 million to sign the fellow they had wanted six seasons earlier. At the time the deal attracted a degree of criticism because the first major recruit of the Malcolm Glazer era was not far short of his 35th birthday; but he was naturally lean, still as athletic as most players a decade younger, and still consumed by an insatiable desire for success.

Van der Sar, not as mountainous a figure as Schmeichel despite being an inch taller but still a commandingly authoritative presence between the posts, began impressively with five straight clean sheets. Though nothing loth to rollick a team-mate at need, in general he was unflappable, breeding confidence among the men in front of him, and he brought to his work a keen intelligence. Invariably his positioning was impeccable and his distribution, both by throw and by kick, was accurate and perceptive, the occasional opportunistic route-one delivery into the path of a rampaging Ruud van Nistelrooy or Wayne Rooney proving especially eye-catching. There was a crisp certainty about all his footwork, a crucial part of the goalkeeper's craft since the law-change forbidding the picking up of back-passes, a compliment which could not always be paid to Monsieur Barthez.

True, there would be isolated moments when he appeared to be on a different wavelength to Rio Ferdinand – for instance, when the centre-half's sidefooted dispatch rolled beyond him for an embarrassing own-goal at Portsmouth during a momentary falter on the 2006/07 championship run-in. During that same spring, too, there was a fleeting spell following an injury absence when his characteristic sureness of touch seemed to desert him, and a couple of ill-directed parries cost goals. Indeed, mystifyingly, for a man normally so reliable at claiming crosses, there came an occasional game when he appeared to be operating in a personal fog.

In general, though, there was, and remains, precious little to complain about and a great deal to praise. Indeed, Dirk Kuyt of Liverpool, admittedly a fellow Dutchman, avers that Edwin is the best 'keeper in the world, and there has been a catalogue of stupendous saves to support the viewpoint.

A handful which remain vivid here include the point-blank blocking of a Tim Cahill header on Edwin's League debut for United at Goodison, a fearless block at the feet of Frank Lampard to facilitate a desperately needed home victory over Chelsea in November 2005 and two flying efforts to keep Sporting Lisbon at bay in Portugal in September 2007. Then, of incalculable value though hardly as spectacular, there was the kneeing to safety of Darius Vassell's late penalty at the City of Manchester Stadium in May 2007, a stop which virtually clinched that year's Premiership crown; and finally, impossible to forget, in the rain-sodden tumult of a melodramatic Moscow night there came the inspired plunge to repel Nicolas Anelka's spot-kick, thus claiming the Reds' third European crown.

Midway through 2007/08 Edwin van der Sar agreed a new deal which should keep him at Old Trafford until June 2009. By then he will be approaching his 40th year, but it does not require too huge a leap of the imagination to envisage that, even then, the playing days of Holland's most capped footballer may still have a distance to run.

	EDWIN VAN DER SAR		
BORN:	Voorhout, Holland, 29 October 1970.		
HONOURS:	European Cup 07/08. League Championship 06/07, 07/08. League Cup 05/06.		
	123 Holland caps (95-).		
OTHER CLUBS:	Ajax, Holland, 90/1-97/8 (192, 1); Juventus, Italy, 98/9-00/01 (100, 0);	GAMES	142
	Fulham 01/02-04/05 (127, 0).	GOALS	0

DARREN FLETCHER

2002/03 →

It's hardly a recipe for superstardom, but Darren Fletcher is rarely less than quietly, unobtrusively effective whenever he gets a chance to employ his workaday mix of serial graft and periodic craft in the Manchester United midfield. The leggy, spare-framed Scottish international is an intelligent, composed, lung-searingly energetic performer whose passing can be inventive and penetrative when he finds his range, and whose tackling and covering are rigorously conscientious. True, on a lacklustre day he can appear stiffly predictable, but even then he can never be faulted for his effort and perseverance, and it's also a fact that there are contests on which he emblazons his mark indelibly, playing like a man possessed.

Just ask Arsenal, whose 4-0 FA Cup evisceration by United in February 2008 was due in no small measure to the insatiable hunger exhibited by Darren as he charged at high velocity, and with a relentless purpose and bite which verged on the ferocious, to every corner of the Old Trafford pitch. Indeed, so blazing was his contribution to an embarrassingly one-sided confrontation between the two bitter rivals that it wouldn't have been surprising had he left a trail of scorched grass in his wake.

Regrettably, though, like plenty of fine and underrated Red Devils before him, he falls victim to a fitfully vociferous minority among the Old Trafford 'faithful' when events are not unfolding serenely for their team. These carpers, gorged on the more spectacular exploits of Fletcher's high-profile colleagues, and loth to excoriate their gilded favourites at any cost, are ever-ready to lacerate the honest journeyman with their imbecilic ridicule.

In such a climate, it is not the least of the young man's attributes that he handles the flak so maturely. Happily he enjoys the enthusiastic support of Sir Alex Ferguson, who is adamant that eventually the fans will learn to appreciate the unshowy merits of a fellow Scot who had already captained their country in his early twenties.

Darren enlisted at Old Trafford as an 11-year-old and was only an administrative oversight away from becoming United's youngest ever senior player at the age of 16 years and 74 days. But after being picked to face Aston Villa in May 2000, it emerged that he was still on schoolboy forms and thus forbidden from making a professional entrance.

Shortly afterwards his momentum was halted temporarily by a broken foot and other injuries which delayed his big-time debut until March 2003, when he performed confidently, even exuberantly, at home to FC Basel. In subsequent seasons he became a regular squad member, demonstrating lucidly that he possessed the talent and the temperament to deserve his continued elevation.

Although his 'engine' never splutters and his eagerness doesn't wane, Fletcher is more of an endurance runner than a sprinter, and thus lacks the outright pace to go past nippy opponents. Therefore he has looked more at home in central midfield, his preferred and most effective position, than on the right flank, where sometimes he has been deployed out of necessity.

Darren, who brings yet another dimension to the United squad by his competence and willingness when asked to put in a shift as an emergency right-back, offers only a negligible goal threat, though there have been several gems. The looping header at Old Trafford in November 2005, which proved that Jose Mourinho's hitherto unbeaten Chelsea were not invincible after all, was particularly satisfying, while the Charlton Athletic defenders unhinged by the multiple swerves which preceded his drilled near-post finish at the Valley in August 2006 are not likely to recall the experience without a shudder.

One of Fletcher's most impressive all-round displays to date came at home to AC Milan in April 2007 when he contributed tirelessly to a rousing victory, yet as he measured his prospects for the following campaign, he could be excused if he blanched at the prospect of unrelenting competition for a place from Messrs Scholes, Hargreaves, Carrick and Anderson.

But Darren Fletcher is made of stern stuff, and he opted to stay and fight when one of his former international managers, Alex McLeish, sought to take him to Birmingham City. Never mind the idiotic barrackers, that was terrific news for Manchester United.

DARREN BARR FLETCHER
BORN: Edinburgh, 1 February 1984.
HONOURS: League Championship 06/07, 07/08. FA Cup 03/04. 34 Scotland caps (03-).

GAMES 126 (46)
GOALS 9

RICARDO

2002/03

Ricardo made his debut for Spain only a week before arriving at Old Trafford for £1.5 million from Valladolid, but did little to suggest he was a goalkeeper of international class. On his rare outings he looked distinctly erratic, his frisky presence hardly calculated to engender confidence among his fellow defenders.

RICARDO FELIPE LOPEZ
BORN: Madrid, Spain, 31 December 1971.
HONOURS: 1 Spain cap.
OTHER CLUBS: Atletico Madrid, Spain, 96/7 (1, 0); Valladolid, Spain, 99/00-01/02 (53, 0); Racing Santander, Spain, on loan 03/04 (34, 0); Osasuna, Spain, 05/06-.

GAMES **3 (2)**
GOALS **0**

DANNY PUGH

2002/03 → 2003/04

A neat left-sided midfielder or full-back, Danny suffered the trauma of missing a clutch of scoring chances in a televised League Cup tie with Burnley, but put it behind him with consistent form for the reserves. A perceptive passer endowed with pace and stamina, he deserves to succeed elsewhere.

DANIEL ADAM PUGH
BORN: Manchester, 19 October 1982.
OTHER CLUBS: Leeds United 04/05-05/06 (50, 5); Preston North End 06/07-07/08 (52, 4); Stoke City 07/08- (30, 0).

GAMES **3 (4)**
GOALS **0**

MADS TIMM

2002/03

A skilful young attacker for whom an exciting career was once predicted, Mads looked utterly out of his depth when brought on as a substitute in Israel against Maccabi Haifa. His undoubted potential never flowered in Manchester and he returned to his homeland sadly unfulfilled.

MADS TIMM
BORN: Odense, Denmark, 31 October 1984.
OTHER CLUBS: Odense, Denmark; Viking Stavanger, Norway, on loan 03/04 (4, 1); Lyn Oslo, Norway, on loan 05/06 (1, 0); Walsall on loan 05/06 (9, 1); Odense, Denmark, 06/07-.

GAMES **0 (1)**
GOALS **0**

MARK LYNCH

2002/03

A pacy, industriously efficient and versatile defender whose preferred role was full-back, Mark had the misfortune to nod an own goal against Deportivo in his sole senior appearance for the Reds. He showed his maturity by not becoming rattled, going on to turn in an accomplished all-round display.

MARK JOHN LYNCH
BORN: Manchester, 2 September 1981.
OTHER CLUBS: St Johnstone on loan 01/02 (20, 0); Sunderland 04/05 (11, 0); Hull City 05/06 (16, 0); Yeovil Town 06/07-07/08 (31, 0); Rotherham United 08/09-.

GAMES **1**
GOALS **0**

EDDIE JOHNSON

2003/04

There was something tantalisingly reminiscent of Mark Hughes about teenage marksman Eddie Johnson, a combination of skill, strength and intelligence which engendered genuine optimism that he might be first-team material. It never happened at Old Trafford, but he found a productive midfield niche with Bradford City.

EDWARD WILLIAM JOHNSON
BORN: Chester, Cheshire, 20 September 1984.
OTHER CLUBS: Royal Antwerp, Belgium, on loan 03/04; Coventry City on loan 04/05 (26, 5); Crewe Alexandra on loan 05/06 (22, 5); Bradford City 06/07- (64, 7).

GAMES **0 (1)**
GOALS **0**

SYLVAN EBANKS-BLAKE

2004/05 → 2005/06

A speedy, muscular and aggressive marksman who stretched defences with his enthusiastic running and scored plenty of goals at junior levels, Sylvan formed a productive partnership for United reserves with the more subtle Giuseppe Rossi, but was never offered the chance to make a lasting impact at senior level.

SYLVAN AUGUSTUS EBANKS-BLAKE
BORN: Cambridge, 29 March 1986.
OTHER CLUBS: Royal Antwerp, Belgium, on loan 05/06; Plymouth Argyle 06/07-07/08 (66, 21); Wolverhampton Wanderers 07/08- (20, 12).

GAMES **1 (1)**
GOALS **1**

PAUL TIERNEY

2003/04

Having progressed promisingly through United's junior ranks, solid central defender Paul Tierney experienced a torrid first-team baptism against West Bromwich Albion's big Danny Dichio in December 2003. Thereafter competition proved too hot at Old Trafford, and he has travelled extensively in search of a niche.

PAUL THOMAS TIERNEY
BORN: Salford, Lancashire, 15 September 1982.
OTHER CLUBS: Crewe Alexandra on loan 02/03 (17, 1); Colchester United on loan 03/04 (2, 0); Bradford City on loan 04/05 (16, 0); Livingston 05/06 (31, 0); Blackpool 06/07- (10, 0); Stockport County on loan 07/08 (16, 0).

GAMES **1**
GOALS **0**

DARRON GIBSON

2005/06 →

A midfielder both polished and powerful, Ulsterman Darron was an under-16 international for the country of his birth, but then transferred his allegiance to the Republic, for whom he has earned senior honours. For all his ability, it is difficult to see him overcoming the frenetic competition for midfield berths at Old Trafford.

DARRON THOMAS DANIEL GIBSON
BORN: Londonderry, Northern Ireland, 25 October 1987.
HONOURS: 2 Republic of Ireland caps (07-).
OTHER CLUBS: Royal Antwerp, Belgium, on loan 06/07; Wolverhampton Wanderers on loan 07/08 (21, 1).

GAMES **0 (1)**
GOALS **0**

RITCHIE JONES

2005/06 →

Joined United on his ninth birthday, eventually switching from centre-forward to become a solid midfielder, combining box-to-box energy with clever touches on the ball. He was seen at his best in the League Cup against Crewe in 2006 when he won the ball, then crossed beautifully for Ole Gunnar Solskjaer to score.

RICHARD GLYNN JONES
BORN: Manchester, 26 September 1986.
OTHER CLUBS: Royal Antwerp, Belgium, on loan 05/06; Colchester United on loan 06/07 (6, 0); Barnsley on loan 06/07 (4, 0); Yeovil Town on loan 07/08 (9, 0).

GAMES **3 (2)**
GOALS **0**

ADAM ECKERSLEY

2005/06

Full-back Adam Eckersley left United for Port Vale in 2007 after 13 years affiliation to the Old Trafford club. A natural defender – tenacious as a marker and a fearsomely enthusiastic tackler – he also offered quality on the ball, being a tidy passer and a crisp striker of free-kicks. Senior opportunities, though, were lacking.

ADAM JAMES ECKERSLEY
BORN: Manchester, 7 September 1985.
OTHER CLUBS: Royal Antwerp, Belgium, on loan 05/06; Brondby, Denmark, on loan 06/07; Barnsley on loan 06/07 (6, 0); Port Vale 07/08- (18, 1).

GAMES	1
GOALS	0

LEE MARTIN

2005/06 →

United pipped several leading rivals to sign energetic winger Lee Martin from Wimbledon as a 16-year-old in 2003, and his lively form during a series of loan spells indicates that he may yet make the grade. He offers pace, skill and industry aplenty, he is willing to take the knocks and he scored with a cracking 35-yarder on United's 2007 Asian tour.

LEE ROBERT MARTIN
BORN: Taunton, Somerset, 9 February 1987.
OTHER CLUBS: Royal Antwerp, Belgium, on loan 05/06; Glasgow Rangers on loan 06/07 (7, 0); Stoke City on loan 06/07 (13, 1); Plymouth Argyle on loan 07/08 (12, 2); Sheffield United on loan 07/08 (6, 0).

GAMES	2
GOALS	0

PHIL MARSH

2006/07

Phil Marsh survived a serious car accident in January 2004 and deserves immense credit for fighting to rebuild his career. Capable of playing at the front or the back, he tasted senior action as a striker in the League Cup encounter with Crewe in 2006, but failed to make his mark and moved on.

PHILIP MARSH
BORN: St Helens, Lancashire, 15 November 1986.
OTHER CLUBS: Blackpool 07/08.

GAMES	1
GOALS	0

KIERAN LEE

2006/07

Kieran enjoyed a euphoric senior debut when he rose from the bench to score a brilliant extra-time winner from the edge of the box at Crewe in the League Cup in 2006. Capable of playing at full-back or in midfield, he is a dashing overlapper, accomplished passer and sturdy tackler who shows a mature awareness of team needs.

KIERAN CHRISTOPHER LEE
BORN: Stalybridge, Tameside, 22 June 1988.
OTHER CLUBS: Queen's Park Rangers on loan 07/08 (7, 0); Oldham Athletic 08/09-.

GAMES	1 (2)
GOALS	1

MICHAEL BARNES

2006/07 →

Red-haired Lancastrian Michael Barnes is a potential crowd-pleaser, a quick and skilful winger capable of bewitching his markers through sleight of either foot. At reserve level he has proved devastating whether cutting inside or flitting down the touchline, but the next step up represents an enormous challenge.

MICHAEL BARNES
BORN: Chorley, Lancashire, 24 June 1988.
OTHER CLUBS: Chesterfield on loan 07/08 (3, 0); Shrewsbury Town on loan 07/08 (2, 0).

GAMES	0 (1)
GOALS	0

DONG FANGZHUO

2006/07 →

Chinese international marksman Dong has not found the transition easy from football in his homeland to the English top level since his £500,000 (plus add-ons) move in 2004. His form improved after ending a long scoring drought for the reserves, but he has looked overawed on his rare senior outings.

DONG FANGZHUO
BORN: Liaoning, China, 23 January 1985.
HONOURS: 13 China caps (04-).
OTHER CLUBS: Dalian Saidelong, China, 01-02 (14, 20); Dalian Shide, China, (8, 0); Royal Antwerp, Belgium, on loan 03/04-06/07 (70, 34).

GAMES	2 (1)
GOALS	0

FRAIZER CAMPBELL

2007/08 →

An England under-21 livewire striker brimming with confidence, Fraizer made his senior entrance late in the Manchester derby defeat at Eastlands in August 2007 but had little scope to parade his undoubted talents. When given an extended first-team run on loan at Hull, he delivered goals and hope for the future, helping the Tigers to reach the top tier.

FRAIZER CAMPBELL
BORN: Huddersfield, Yorkshire, 13 September 1987.
OTHER CLUBS: Hull City on loan 07/08 (34, 15).

GAMES	0 (2)
GOALS	0

RYAN SHAWCROSS

2006/07 →

A goal-scoring Gordon McQueen-type centre-half who joined Stoke for an initial £1 million, Ryan disappointed Sir Alex Ferguson by accepting the move but understandably sought first-team football. Big and hard but still far from polished, he contributed seven strikes as the Potters rose to the Premier League in 2007/08.

RYAN JAMES SHAWCROSS
BORN: Chester, Cheshire, 4 October 1987.
OTHER CLUBS: Royal Antwerp, Belgium, on loan 06/07; Stoke City 07/08- (41, 7).

GAMES	0 (2)
GOALS	0

DAVID GRAY

2006/07 →

A classy and intelligent foraging right-back who is versatile enough to fill most positions, the level-headed Scot cost United a reported £50,000 when they signed him in 2004 as a 16-year-old from Hearts. A knee injury set him back in 2007, but he has recovered to become a regular in the reserves and may yet rise higher at Old Trafford.

DAVID GRAY
BORN: Edinburgh, 4 May 1988.
OTHER CLUBS: Royal Antwerp, Belgium, on loan 06/07 (1, 0); Crewe Alexandra on loan 07/08 (1, 0).

GAMES	1
GOALS	0

WAYNE ROONEY

2004/05 →

Wayne Rooney is a gift from the gods, an otherwise ordinary boy blessed with footballing ability on a breathtaking scale. He is endowed with the talent to consume an opposition single-handed, the self-belief to inflict himself on any situation, the blazing virtuosity to light up the skies. He gives his team the chance of winning every game in which he plays, his ungovernable brilliance often inspiring victories that would be impossible without him.

Indeed, such is his extraordinary scope, Rooney can lift a team to the heavens or he can carry it on his shoulders – he has done both for Manchester United often enough – and about his best work there is a glorious certainty. It's not arrogance exactly, although undeniably there is a dash of that, but more an essential recognition deep within himself that he operates on a different plane from almost all his competitors. According to some of the young Duncan Edwards' closest friends, it was an impression conveyed, without a hint of conceit, by the peerless Busby Babe as he stood on the threshold of the prime he would never live to embrace.

For the former Evertonian, whose father bought him a Toffees shirt on the day he was born, the future could hardly have glittered more alluringly as he kicked off his fifth campaign as a Red Devil in August 2008, still more than two months short of his 23rd birthday. He was one of the least dispensable components of arguably the most talented squad assembled in England since Matt Busby first invested so passionately in youth more than half a century earlier, and there seemed no reason why he shouldn't achieve his stated desire of remaining at Old Trafford for the rest of his career.

The perfect player has never been born, but even when it is placed under the most intense scrutiny, it is not easy to discern a flaw in the footballing make-up of Wayne Rooney. The basic physical requirements – speed, strength, agility, balance – are all there, along with unlimited supplies of courage and resilience. No one in the modern game is endowed with more acute football intelligence, the instinct for doing the right thing at the right time, whether it be passing, shooting, dribbling, running into space. His empathy with the ball is total, the way he controls it, caresses it, distributes it, propels it towards goal with savage power or infinite delicacy, using right foot or left. He is awesomely potent either as a front-man or a deeper-lying prompter, and such is his willingness to chase back and fight for possession when it is lost, it is reasonable to suppose he would even make an exceptional defender, too.

Yet there is a chink in the Merseysider's armour and it concerns his temperament. To say that he is combustible is putting it mildly; maybe volcanic is a better word. Indeed, when Wayne is peeved he gives a passable impression of a walking tinderbox. For referees or opponents subjected to his profane eruptions, when his face contorts and he spits venom, the heat must be searing. From the safety of the stands, the perception of steam from the boiling testosterone venting from his ears is irresistible. On such occasions he can be a silly boy, and the fear of dismissal and consequent suspension hangs over him, but no one with United in their heart – not the manager, the other players, the fans – would want to remove Wayne's 'devil'. That cyclonic tendency is part of what gives him his edge and as long as he controls it most of the time, as did earlier greats such as Denis Law and Roy Keane, it will be deemed acceptable.

United had monitored the meteoric progress of the Croxteth-born prodigy even before, while still only 16, he riveted the attention of the wider world with a wonder goal for Everton against Arsenal in October 2002, prompting Arsene Wenger to describe him as the most talented young Englishman he'd ever seen.

Nearly two years later when the chance to sign him arose, Sir Alex Ferguson did not hesitate, even at a cost of £27 million. As the Reds' boss put it: 'We had to have him. The fee was nothing. The fans would have burned down Old Trafford if we'd missed him.'

His debut, at home to Fenerbahce in September 2004, could hardly have been more seismic in its impact as he delivered a sublime hat-trick, every goal a crisply-struck masterpiece from outside the box. Since then there have been so many unforgettable hits, far too many to chronicle here, but space must be made for the steepling long-range chip and lashed volley which evicted Middlesbrough from the FA Cup at Old Trafford in January 2005, the swerving thunderbolt which transformed a dreary home display against Newcastle three months later, and the silken chip which eluded Pompey custodian David James in front of the Stretford End, sealing another FA Cup victory in January 2007.

Exactly where he will stand eventually in the pantheon of Old Trafford immortals will be determined only when he has attained maturity, but that a place will be reserved for him already seems inevitable. A wise man of vast experience and not prone to exaggeration, John Giles, has even ventured to compare him with Pele and Maradona, while conceding that to attain true greatness he must maintain his standard over a full career. Does Wayne Rooney carry that final dimension of genius within him? Don't bet against it.

WAYNE MARK ROONEY	
BORN:	Croxteth, Liverpool, 24 October 1985.
HONOURS:	European Cup 07/08. League Championship 06/07, 07/08. League Cup 05/06. 42 England caps (03-).
OTHER CLUBS:	Everton 02/03-03/04 (67, 15).

GAMES	171 (18)
GOALS	77

PATRICE EVRA

2005/06 →

There is much to admire about Patrice Evra. The vim and bravado of the French swashbuckler's attacking play from left-back, certainly, but also the indomitable fighting spirit that set him on the path to Old Trafford redemption after an ignominious start to life as a Red Devil.

Few men have suffered a more painful United introduction than Evra, who was hooked off halfway through a Manchester derby defeat, having been given a fearful chasing by the feisty City winger Trevor Sinclair only four days after his £5.5 million arrival from Monaco in January 2006.

On that miserable day at Eastlands, it seemed inconceivable that the disorientated newcomer would go on to win a three-way battle for a regular place with the formidable Gabriel Heinze, already a fans' favourite, and the experienced Mikael Silvestre, but so it was to prove.

Patrice used the remainder of that term to bed in, aided by the Argentinian's absence through injury, but still finished the campaign with the jibes of critics ringing in his ears. He was dismissed by many as a full-back who couldn't tackle and a winger masquerading as a defender, a flashy operator on the ball but a fellow who could not be trusted to fulfil his primary obligation at the back.

At this point Evra might have crumbled, and later he admitted that he became depressed, briefly even questioning his own worth. But the man who had gone through a tough upbringing as one of more than 20 siblings, first in Senegal and then in France from the age of six, and who had escaped from a life of potential hardship by forging a professional football career so successfully that he had skippered Monaco to the European Cup Final only a year earlier, was not going to be beaten easily.

Thus he spent the summer of 2006 building up his strength to cope with the physically demanding English game, and come the next season he was bristling with energetic intent and seemingly more organised. He bit into tackles where previously he might have held back, proving adept at insinuating himself between opponent and ball, and he scuttled forward at high velocity in a manner mildly reminiscent of the widely admired Brazilian Roberto Carlos.

Now, while Heinze didn't look as sharp as before his long injury lay-off, Evra was a revelation, entertaining thrillingly with his rampaging overlaps and frequently audacious touches on the ball. Backheels, nutmegs, bicycle kicks, they were all part of his repertoire, and he approached everything at full tilt. Sometimes there was a tendency to overdo the clever stuff in tight areas, but such was his remarkable speed of recovery if he did surrender possession or lose position, those occasional lapses were rarely punished.

Having been so thoroughly rehabilitated that he was picked by his fellow professionals in the Premiership team of season 2006/07 – alongside seven Old Trafford comrades, including the entire defence – the French international began 2007/08 in characteristically effervescent vein, combining sweetly with Cristiano Ronaldo to set up Ryan Giggs' goal against Chelsea in the Community Shield.

His acute darting run inside Bacary Sagna to receive a Louis Saha dispatch before sending in Ronaldo to net at the Emirates in November 2007 showcased his zestful attacking enterprise to perfection, and Sir Alex Ferguson, pilloried initially for buying a duffer, was entitled to feel supremely satisfied that the real Patrice Evra had stood up.

At the end of his first day with Manchester United, the engagingly open-hearted newcomer reportedly turned to skipper Gary Neville and asked where he could find the nearest church to the Carrington training ground, because he wanted to thank God for his move to Old Trafford. Perhaps when he located his place of worship, he added a little prayer that he would taste glory with the Red Devils; or maybe, in view of his lifelong experience of striving effectively to triumph over adversity, he subscribed to the old adage that God helps those who help themselves.

PATRICE EVRA
BORN: Dakar, Senegal, 15 May 1981.
HONOURS: European Cup 07/08. League Championship 06/07, 07/08. League Cup 05/06.
9 France caps (04-).
OTHER CLUBS: Marsala, Italy, 98/9 (24, 3); Monza, Italy, 99/00 (3, 0); Nice, France, 00/01-01/02 (39, 1); Monaco, France, 02/03-05/06 (120, 1).

GAMES	85 (13)
GOALS	2

NEMANJA VIDIC

2005/06 →

If they had heard of him at all, Nemanja Vidic was an obscure, shadowy figure from the unknown depths of Eastern Europe to most Manchester United fans when he was signed from Spartak Moscow for £7.2 million in January 2006. Yet by year's end the rugged Serb was being clasped to the collective bosom of Old Trafford as a talisman, a much-loved gladiator, a sainted amalgam of Jaap Stam and Steve Bruce with a generous dash of Big Jim Holton thrown in for good measure.

The fans glory in his willingness to put his body on the line, the absolute lack of fancy-dan posturing. A former coach ventured that: 'He plays like he wants to kill someone.' Sir Alex Ferguson declared: 'He's the best central defender in the Premiership.' If the first statement seems a tad extreme, the second is mightily difficult to refute.

For all his fearsome combativeness on the field – illustrated so decisively by his subduing of Chelsea's formidable Didier Drogba in the 2008 Champions League Final – Vidic is careful to keep the importance of football in perspective, an attitude born of his upbringing in the strife-torn former Yugoslavia, where he made his first major impact in the professional game with Red Star Belgrade. Though still in his early twenties, he captained Red Star to their domestic league and cup double in 2004, then spent a season with Spartak Moscow during which he was courted keenly by both United and Liverpool. A fee was agreed with the Red Devils on Christmas Day 2005, but Malcolm Glazer's biggest footballing purchase to that point made a tentative start to Premiership life as he strove to settle in the West.

It didn't help that he had been out of training for weeks following an interlude in the Russian season, and he appeared over-anxious to impress. His abrasive qualities were readily apparent and his courage was unquestionable, but in his eagerness to win the ball he was conceding too many free-kicks in dangerous areas. Sometimes, too, his positioning was awry and there was the occasional lapse of concentration. Ferguson, though, never entertained a doubt about his quality, and when he was given an extended opportunity during the absence through injury of Wes Brown in the spring, it became increasingly apparent that United had struck gold.

Now Nemanja emerged as the virtual *Identikit* of the ideal centre-half. A clattering tackler and formidably ferocious aerial battler, he was quick and he read the unfolding action intelligently. In addition, although he wasn't afraid to dispatch the ball to Row Z and beyond when the threat to United's goal was acute, he could pass precisely, too, joining in seamlessly with flowing team interchanges.

Arguably the Serb's coming of age as an Old Trafford hero coincided with Arsenal's visit in April 2006. That Sunday afternoon he set the Reds on the way to a 2-0 victory when he won possession from Robin van Persie and started the move which climaxed with Wayne Rooney opening the scoring.

Come 2006/07 and Vidic was getting on the scoresheet himself, opening his account with a murderous eight-yard header at Wigan. Indeed, his presence at corners has given United a much-needed extra attacking dimension, especially when there is no big man among the forwards, and while he doesn't always win the ball, he is a constant menace.

As that triumphant term progressed, Nemanja's broad forehead propelled unstoppable bullets into the nets of Portsmouth, Benfica and Tottenham, and when he broke a collar-bone at home to Blackburn in March the prospect of a prolonged absence was greeted with dismay. However, the steely stopper was back within a month, helping to seal the Premiership crown and sharing in European and FA Cup disappointments, then his magnificent form in 2007/08 confirmed his burgeoning status as one of the finest defenders in the world.

In September his winning goal at Goodison Park offered a template for the perfect near-post routine, when he brushed aside Everton's Joseph Yobo and Tony Hibbert as if they didn't exist to meet Nani's corner and net with a thunderous header. It was a combination of utter fearlessness, exquisite timing and impeccable technique reminiscent of Steve Bruce, and it prompted his manager to set him a target of five to ten strikes for the campaign. That proved fanciful, but still he threatened mayhem every time he stormed forward, his bullish cavortings distracting opponents' attention and creating space for the likes of Messrs Rooney, Ronaldo and Tevez.

Meanwhile at the other end of the pitch, the real business end as far as Vidic is concerned, his partnership with Rio Ferdinand continues to develop majestically. Indeed, it is arguable that it has taken the doughty Serb to bring the very best out of the more elegant Englishman in terms of relentless game-after-game consistency. For that alone he deserves every bit of adulation that comes his way.

As for his doting, chanting legion of Old Trafford admirers, no doubt they will go on asking, to the tune of a popular ditty, the same searching question: 'What's that coming over the hill? Is it Nemanja? Is it Nemanja?' For the continued security of the United rearguard, any answer but an enthusiastic affirmative would be, well, monstrous.

NEMANJA VIDIC

BORN:	Subotica, Serbia, 21 October 1981.
HONOURS:	European Cup 07/08. League Championship 06/07, 07/08. League Cup 05/06. 26 Serbia and Montenegro caps (02-).
OTHER CLUBS:	Subotica, Serbia, 00/01 (27, 6); Red Star Belgrade, Serbia, 01/02-03/04 (68, 12); Spartak Moscow 04-05 (39, 4).

GAMES **94 (4)**
GOALS **5**

MICHAEL CARRICK

2006/07 →

If a footballer's worth depended entirely on his ability to pass the ball, accurately and imaginatively and with perfect weight over long distances and short, retaining composure while other players mill frenetically in all directions, then Michael Carrick would be priceless.

Of course, there is more to the game than that, and sometimes it has been asserted that the engagingly unassuming north-easterner's delicious distribution is not enough, on its own, to earn him a place in the Manchester United side.

Heaven knows, in 2008 there was enough central midfield competition at Old Trafford, from the likes of the magnificent but ageing Paul Scholes, the dynamically industrious Owen Hargreaves, the sublimely promising Anderson and even the eternally dutiful Darren Fletcher, to make all but those with iron self-belief quail inwardly before drifting meekly out of contention. After all, plenty of other talented internationals of contrasting styles and personalities – the likes of Veron, Kleberson, and Djemba-Djemba – had tried and failed in recent times to stamp their authority in an area which was graced so long, and so effectively, by Roy Keane.

So what of Carrick? The feeling here is that he deserves more generous credit than he has received for his part in winning a brace of Premier League titles and the European crown in his first two terms at Old Trafford, that in an unobtrusive manner he contributes much of value beyond his lovely passing to the speed merchants around him, and that if a squad the size of Sir Alex Ferguson's cannot accommodate such an unusually gifted individual, then there is something wrong with the game.

Think back to his two seasons with Tottenham Hotspur, who paid £2.75 million to enlist him from West Ham in 2004, then sold him to the Red Devils for a cool 500 per-cent profit in the summer of 2006, the initial fee of £14 million reportedly rising to a staggering £18.6 million depending on appearances and achievements.

Long-time Spurs fans maintained that Carrick could unloose killer dispatches, using either foot, with greater facility than anyone since Glenn Hoddle, and his manager at White Hart Lane, Martin Jol, was desperate to keep him after he had excelled in front of the back line as the north Londoners spent most of 2005/06 in the Premiership's top four. As the Dutchman declared plaintively at the time: 'I didn't want to lose Michael. Nearly every one of our attacks started with him.'

After missing United's curtain-raiser through injury, the costly newcomer bedded in steadily rather than spectacularly at Old Trafford. Tall, with a slight stoop and a deceptively languid gait, Michael did not cut a flamboyant or a forceful figure, his demeanour on the pitch reflecting his modest character. But before long the beauty of his passing was speaking eloquently enough.

As United confounded many critics by winning the Championship, Carrick slotted in productively alongside Scholes, both complementing and learning from the inspirational little general. Capable of taking out entire defences as he speared unerringly precise deliveries through dense thickets of opponents, he displayed exquisite visionary qualities, but in addition he proved to be far more effective defensively than some detractors allowed.

Though Michael is not a shirker in the tackle, as no midfield holding player can afford to be, he does not customarily win the ball by dint of furious physical challenge; rather he specialises in canny interceptions, the product of the same acute football intelligence that is the launchpad for so many attacks, his method reminiscent of Ray Wilkins some quarter of a century earlier. Invariably, too, if Gary Neville or Wes Brown surges down the right flank, Michael will be the one to drop back and cover, not necessarily a service to attract lavish praise from press-box and stands, but crucial nevertheless and deeply appreciated by his team-mates.

The argument against him goes that he doesn't assert himself sufficiently, that he doesn't mould a game to his will as might be expected of such a costly capture, and that he doesn't score enough goals. In truth, that last point is supremely irrelevant if he fashions enough bullets for Rooney, Ronaldo, Tevez and company to fire, and he did chip in with half a dozen hits in 2006/07, including a marvellously adroit clip and a pulverising long-distance drive in the 7-1 demolition of Roma.

In 2007/08 Carrick was less prolific, not registering until his too-late strike in the demoralising anti-climactic home defeat by Manchester City in February, but still his creative juices flowed. Indeed, while Ronaldo was engulfed with adulation following his January hat-trick against Newcastle at Old Trafford, it was the Wallsend man who had been a prime architect of the Magpies' 6-0 mauling. Perhaps inevitably, given the combination of the Red Devils' midfield riches, Carrick's north-eastern origins and the circumstance that Kevin Keegan was seeking an influential play-maker, rumours began to circulate in the spring that Michael might be tempted to join the latest revolution on the Tyne. For Manchester United, that would have been a chronic pity and duly Sir Alex moved smartly to secure him on a new long-term contract.

Those who had maintained that he would wither and decline when faced with such potent rivals as Hargreaves and company had been proved wrong. Instead Carrick had grown in stature as his second Old Trafford campaign had worn on, showing himself to be a play-maker of rare and original quality. Though he tends to lie deeper than Paul Scholes, in many ways he is the veteran red head's natural long-term heir, and he ought to be cherished.

MICHAEL CARRICK

BORN: Wallsend, Northumberland, 28 July 1981.

HONOURS: European Cup 07/08. League Championship 06/07, 07/08. 14 England caps (01-).

OTHER CLUBS: West Ham United 99/00-04/05 (136, 6); Swindon Town on loan 99/00 (6, 2); Birmingham City on loan 99/00 (2, 0); Tottenham Hotspur 04/05–05/06 (64, 2).

GAMES	87 (14)
GOALS	8

GIUSEPPE ROSSI

2004/05 → 2005/06

Rarely has the regret been quite so profound when a young footballer has been allowed to leave Old Trafford as in the case of Giuseppe Rossi.

The diminutive Italian-American is a natural goal-scorer, oozing with flair and intelligence, seemingly a thoroughbred in the making, and he was only 20 when Manchester United sold him to the Spanish club Villarreal for £6.7 million in the summer of 2007.

In fairness, Sir Alex Ferguson was loth to part with a player of such sumptuous potential, but Rossi was desperate for regular first-team football, which could not be guaranteed had he remained a Red Devil.

He arrived in Manchester as a 16-year-old, already labelled as one of Europe's most promising teenagers following a series of sensational performances at youth level for Parma.

Immediately Giuseppe impressed seasoned judges with his subtle skills, incisive brain, mature temperament and, above all, a rare knack for scoring goals of every description.

Soon he formed a productive partnership with the more direct Sylvan Ebanks-Blake for the reserves, and when he was offered a Premiership debut at Sunderland in October 2005 he responded by netting with a sharply drilled left-footer.

Thereafter Rossi riveted the eye with his class on virtually every outing and it was clear that he had outgrown the stiffs. However, a loan stint at troubled Newcastle proved unproductive before he shone for Parma and joined Villarreal.

There was one chink of light for disappointed United fans – a clause which gives the Reds an option to buy him back if he moves on again. Watch this space.

GIUSEPPE ROSSI
BORN: Clifton, New Jersey, USA, 1 February 1987.
OTHER CLUBS: Newcastle United on loan 06/07
(11, 0); Parma, Italy, on loan 06/07 (19, 9);
Villarreal, Spain, 07/08- (27,11).

GAMES	6 (8)
GOALS	4

HENRIK LARSSON

2006/07

Sheer class. That's what Henrik Larsson brought to Manchester United's Premiership title party in 2007, and if he left before the bauble was handed over, no one should underestimate the part he played in its capture.

The venerable Swede, who had enjoyed a stellar career with Celtic and set up Barcelona's 2006 European Cup Final victory over Arsenal, joined United on a ten-week loan agreement from Helsingborg in January 2007, stressing that he would return home on schedule because of family commitments.

At 35, could he score goals in England? As his former Parkhead boss Martin O'Neill was quick to declare, he could score goals in any league he chose.

Yet it was not mere marksmanship that rendered his contribution priceless. After starting with a wondrously slick finish against Aston Villa in the FA Cup – a velvet first touch set up an almost casual dispatch with a precisely angled instep – he netted only twice more, but he passed on a world of experience to Louis Saha and particularly Wayne Rooney, with whom he struck up a spellbinding instant understanding.

The unselfish Larsson's intelligence and instinctive movement off the ball were a joy to behold, as was the lithe athleticism of an ultimate professional who had looked after himself impeccably.

Sir Alex Ferguson, who had tried unavailingly to sign Henrik in his prime, offered him the chance to stay beyond March, and he must have been sorely tempted. But he was true to his word and departed, leaving nothing but glorious memories behind.

HENRIK EDWARD LARSSON
BORN: Helsingborg, Sweden, 20 September 1971.
HONOURS: 93 Sweden caps (93-).
OTHER CLUBS: Helsingborg, Sweden, 91/2-92/3 (56, 50);
Feyenoord, Holland, 93/4-96/7 (101, 26);
Celtic 97/8-03/4 (221, 173); Barcelona, Spain,
04/05-05/06 (29, 10); Helsingborg 06/07-.

GAMES	10 (3)
GOALS	3

GERARD PIQUE

2004/05 → 2007/08

Without wishing to confer an undue burden of expectation on an amiable young fellow in a ferociously competitive business, it is difficult not to wax lyrical about Gerard Pique. In truth, it is not easy to identify a flaw in the footballing make-up of the tall, elegant Catalonian central defender. Certainly it is understandable why Barcelona were virtually apoplectic in 2004 when Manchester United pipped Arsenal in the race to whisk him away from the Nou Camp, and why they were delighted at the prospect of reclaiming him, even at a cost of £4 million in the summer of 2008.

On arrival at Old Trafford Pique was coltishly slender, but despite his easy-going, almost languid air, he proved capable of taking hard knocks and was ready to crunch into tackles. In addition, he was a composed reader of the game, smoothly accomplished on the ball and admirably capable in the air. But just as in the case of Gary Pallister 15 years earlier, Gerard needed building up physically, so after a handful of promising performances for United, and a starring role as the reserves lifted three trophies in 2005/06, he was loaned to Real Zaragoza for 2006/07.

So luxuriantly did he flourish back on native soil that he was courted by several Spanish clubs, but Pique returned to Manchester for 2007/08, by now a much more muscular specimen. He impressed hugely when given a handful of senior opportunities, chipping in with two smartly headed goals in European competition and demonstrating versatility by excelling at full-back. However, finding a way past the Vidic-Ferdinand combo was tough, and a return to his home city proved irresistible.

		GAMES	14 (9)
GERARD PIQUE BERNABEU		GOALS	2
BORN:	Barcelona, Spain, 2 February 1987.		
OTHER CLUBS:	Real Zaragoza on loan 06/07; Barcelona 08/09-, both Spain.		

TOMASZ KUSZCZAK

2006/07 →

Will Tomasz Kuszczak step up to become Manchester United's number-one goalkeeper when Edwin van der Sar finally lays aside his gloves? It wasn't an impossible proposition, but it did seem improbable as the 26-year-old Polish international completed his second season at Old Trafford in the spring of 2008.

On arrival in August 2006 – initially on loan from West Bromwich Albion, the move formalised by a £3 million transfer a year later – Sir Alex Ferguson declared that Kuszczak had been acquired as a genuine competitor for the Dutch veteran, but there has been little sense of the ambitious newcomer pushing van der Sar for his place. Indeed, Tomasz will have been closely monitoring the return to fitness of another contender, England cap Ben Foster, who missed most of 2007/08 with a serious knee injury.

The Pole experienced an eventful United debut against Arsenal at Old Trafford in September 2006, felling Emmanuel Adebayor to concede an early penalty, then plunging to his right to save Gilberto Silva's spot-kick, and later pulling off a terrific save from a Tomas Rosicky screamer.

During subsequent sporadic appearances he revealed himself to be an agile shot-stopper who was unfailingly brave at attackers' feet and generally, if not quite always, reliable when claiming crosses under pressure. Highlights have included several point-blank saves to preserve a clean sheet at Chelsea in May 2007 and a stupendous mid-air adjustment to tip away a deflected shot by Birmingham City's Gary McSheffrey at St Andrew's in the following September.

As for Tomasz Kuszczak's long-term future at United, the jury remained out at the time of writing.

		GAMES	25 (4)
TOMASZ KUSZCZAK		GOALS	0
BORN:	Krosno Odrzansia, Poland, 20 March 1982.		
HONOURS:	4 Poland caps (03-).		
OTHER CLUBS:	Uerdingen, Poland; Hertha Berlin, Germany; West Bromwich Albion 04/05-05/06 (31, 0).		

OWEN HARGREAVES

2007/08 →

It doesn't sound very glamorous, but no matter; Manchester United paid a fortune, and waited what seemed like an eternity, to make Owen Hargreaves their 'ratter', the player whose principal responsibility is to break up attacks, protect the Reds' back four and see to it that influential opponents have little time or space to parade their deadly wares.

Imagine if the Canadian-born England international with the deep Lancastrian roots had been remorselessly patrolling his withdrawn midfield beat when United met AC Milan in the Champions League semi-final of 2007. Would Kaka, the delectably subtle Brazilian predator, have enjoyed the freedom to tantalise Sir Alex Ferguson's men so destructively, first at Old Trafford and then during that grisly San Siro meltdown, had the sparky Hargreaves been gnawing at his heels?

Probably not, but be sure that Owen's absence that season did not indicate a lack of effort on Sir Alex Ferguson's part. The United boss had striven desperately to sign the sinewy, dynamic enforcer in the previous two transfer windows but his club, Bayern Munich, had remained obdurate, flatly refusing to sell, not relenting until £17 million changed hands in the summer of 2007.

Had United identified his worth before the 2006 World Cup finals they might have picked him up immeasurably cheaper. Hargreaves went into that tournament besieged by critics, even derided by some England fans as 'ordinary' and 'colourless', but he emerged from it with almost heroic stature, his country's top player as voted by supporters and professionals alike, a much-needed antidote to the ludicrously dubbed 'golden generation'. Thus his stock, and with it his transfer value, was enhanced astronomically.

However, the desire at Old Trafford to acquire the 26-year-old who had helped Bayern to lift the European Cup once and the German championship four times was all-consuming. He was seen as the ultimate team man – he is also a more-than-useful right-back at need – who would liberate the Red Devils' constellation of creative stars to express themselves and wreak havoc.

Initially hampered by a lengthy and worrying bout of tendinitis in his knees, Hargreaves made a stop-start beginning to life with United, but when he did get on to the pitch he was impressive, earning man-of-the-match accolades on his first three appearances, against Manchester City, Spurs and Sunderland.

Finally on display in a red shirt were all his vaunted attributes, the energetic hustling, the resilience, the tenacity, but also a sharp intelligence, a certain selflessness and a matchless determination to do the simple things so well that a platform would emerge on which his more elaborately gifted comrades could excel.

But while accepting that the undemonstrative Owen will figure only rarely in a game's headline moments, it's likely that he has even more to offer the United cause than was evident for most of 2007/08, when he made fewer starts than he would have liked, even taking his fitness problems into account.

For instance, he is a beautiful striker of the ball and there were few efforts on goal, though there were a couple of notable exceptions. At Fulham in March a deliciously curled free-kick ensured three points, then six weeks later an even more climactic replica saw Arsenal leave Manchester with their title aspirations in shreds. They were handy contributions by any estimation, though the tousle-headed midfielder's strike rate is hardly a priority, given the goal-power elsewhere in the team.

Rather more relevant was his buccaneering display on the right of midfield when Roma visited Old Trafford for the second leg of a European Cup quarter-final in April. It might be stretching a point to compare Hargreaves to Cristiano Ronaldo, who was resting on the bench that night ahead of future exertions, but the quiet man from Calgary made a more than passably fair fist of impersonating the multi-talented Portuguese.

There were several invigorating high-velocity scampers along the touchline, a succession of deliciously flighted crosses – from one of which Carlos Tevez hurled himself horizontal to nod the only goal of the contest – and the Englishman was denied a personal appearance on the scoresheet only by two examples of exceptionally diligent Roman defending.

Importantly, this unveiling of hitherto unsuspected Hargreaves flair did not signal any flighty departure from his customary abrasiveness, as one clattering challenge on David Pizarro illustrated graphically, shortly before the Italian departed ruefully from the fray. But it might have pointed the way towards the former Bayern ball-winner becoming a more complete player in the long term as he competes for his place with the likes of Anderson, Michael Carrick and Darren Fletcher. Meanwhile, as long as the Hargreaves fire burns brightly in the heat of battle, there will be few complaints.

OWEN LEE HARGREAVES
BORN: Calgary, Canada, 20 January 1981.
HONOURS: European Cup 07/08. League Championship 07/08. 41 England caps (01-).
OTHER CLUBS: Bayern Munich, Germany, 00/01-06/07 (145, 5).

GAMES 23 (11)
GOALS 2

JI-SUNG PARK

2005/06 →

Cynics who declared that Manchester United bought Ji-Sung Park principally as a marketing tool for their Far East tour in the summer of 2005 can still their tongues.

Though the livewire South Korean's £4 million arrival from Dutch club PSV Eindhoven that July did little harm on the commercial front, with sales of shirts bearing his name rocketing through the roof in the main Seoul outlet, it is a foul calumny on a dedicated and talented professional to imply he is not worth his presence at Old Trafford on purely footballing considerations.

Indeed, Sir Alex Ferguson has variously described the becomingly undemonstrative attacking midfielder as the best off-the-ball player at Old Trafford, and one of the most underrated United men of the modern era. Both assertions have much to commend them, and both have their roots in his quite phenomenal work rate and levels of energy.

Defenders can never dawdle when Park is around, as a countryman who should have known better, his close friend Young-Pyo Lee of Tottenham Hotspur, discovered to his cost at White Hart Lane in April 2006. The full-back dallied in possession and Ji pounced, robbing his chum and setting up Wayne Rooney for the goal which proved to be the difference between the two sides.

Such is his endurance that in his homeland he is nicknamed 'The Oxygen Tank', though all the attention paid to his remarkable industry, tenacity and pace should not obscure the slick ball skills and invaluable versatility – he is comfortable operating on either midfield flank or in the centre – which made him a national hero as he starred in South Korea's progress to the semi-finals of the 2002 World Cup and proved hugely instrumental in PSV reaching the last four of the European Cup three years later.

Shortly after that Sir Alex made his move and in his debut term, although he was not perceived as a first-team regular, Park made 45 appearances in all competitions. He became a crowd favourite, partly because of his ceaseless effort and obvious good nature, but also in tribute to his deftness in possession, the only apparent flaw being a lack of composure in front of goal which limited him to two successful strikes during that first campaign as a Red Devil.

Unfortunately two serious injuries – first to an ankle, then to a knee – kept him out for vast swathes of the title-winning season that followed, though he managed enough outings to qualify for a medal. He bounced back, vitality undiminished, halfway through 2007/08 and struck prime form immediately, confirming his enormous value to a squad habitually fighting on so many fronts.

Indeed, as that tumultuous term approached its dramatic double denouement at the JJB Stadium in Wigan and Moscow's Luzhniki stadium, Ji-Sung Park took his game to new heights of endeavour and consistency, earning a succession of starts on United's left flank ahead of such formidably gifted rivals as Ryan Giggs and Nani, thus laying down a telling marker for the years ahead.

After typically effervescent displays in both legs of the European Cup semi-final against Barcelona, and the subsequent crucially important title-clinching triumphs over West Ham and Wigan, Park was horribly unlucky to miss out on the big night against Chelsea in Russia, where he wasn't even accorded a place on the substitutes' bench. Before the game his manager had warned that such was the extent of United's squad, some excellent players were going to be disappointed, but few observers suspected that the faithful South Korean would be among them.

Finally, it is humbling to record one remark by this amiable man, delivered in puzzlement after sampling the English game: 'When a player makes a mistake in Asia, the spectators don't criticise it, and the other players encourage you to do better next time.' Sounds Utopian, but the link with Premier League football is not altogether clear . . .

JI-SUNG PARK		
BORN:	Seoul, South Korea, 25 February 1981.	
HONOURS:	League Championship 06/07, 07/08. League Cup 05/06. 65 South Korea caps (01-).	
OTHER CLUBS:	Kyoto Purple Sanga, South Korea, 00-02 (76, 11); PSV Eindhoven, Holland, 02/03-04/05 (64, 13).	

GAMES	53 (30)
GOALS	8

ANDERSON

. . . .

2007/08 →

Anderson Luis de Abreu Oliveira, only 19 years old and all the way from Brazil, proclaimed with endearingly wide-eyed wonder on his arrival at Old Trafford in the summer of 2007 that his £13 million move to Manchester United from Porto was 'a dream the size of the world'. Among his new fans during the season that followed, two observations cropped up repeatedly: firstly, that he was a surprise packet, because virtually nobody in England had heard of him; secondly, and far more importantly, that he was a box of footballing delights.

Despite the hefty fee, Sir Alex Ferguson had intended to be sparing in his initial use of the vivacious rookie who shared both a home-town and a spellbinding talent with the great Ronaldinho. However, an autumn injury to Paul Scholes changed United's midfield landscape, and the newcomer found himself pressed into increasingly regular duty.

Understandably enough, especially as he struggled to overcome a hamstring problem, he was tentative at first, and there were absurdly premature mutterings of discontent among critics who feared a transfer bloomer of Kleberson or Djemba-Djemba proportions. 'Wayward' and 'ineffectual' were two of the kinder adjectives employed following Anderson's debut at home to Sunderland in September, and he was rightly removed from the action at the interval.

There was precious little impact, either, during a subsequent handful of cameo appearances, though one sudden shoulder-dropping midfield thrust after rising from the bench against Roma at Old Trafford in October offered a broad nod in the direction of the sublime potential which was soon to emerge. More evidence of lurking excellence materialised later that month when Wigan were the Old Trafford guests, the Brazilian setting up a goal for Carlos Tevez with a superlatively weighted pass which sliced through the Latics' rearguard like a rapier through jelly.

Inexorably thereafter, as winter turned to spring, there became little room for reasonable doubt that, far from recruiting another expensive misfit, the United boss had enlisted a young footballer whose possibilities were virtually without limit – an extravagant notion, perhaps, but one which gained in substance as he shone in opposition to Arsenal's Cesc Fabregas and Steven Gerrard of Liverpool, lying deep to frustrate those most dangerous of adversaries.

Yet at first glance, Anderson hardly appeared an archetypal athlete, with his rolling gait and puppyish, almost cherubic aspect, an initial impression which has proved to be wholly false. In reality, he covers the ground at withering pace, tackles like a runaway rhino and resists attempts to take the ball from him with the insouciant power of an apprentice blacksmith who barely knows his own still-burgeoning strength.

When these physical attributes are placed alongside his intuitive flair and exquisite technical accomplishments, the picture of a truly exceptional prospect begins to take shape. Anderson passes a football with a combination of precision and audacity which can be breathtaking. His awareness of the bigger picture as it swirls around him is impressively acute, his repertoire encompassing all manner of high-quality dispatches. Sudden sweeping deliveries which change the direction of an attack in an instant are mixed intelligently with shorter-range deliveries, stabbed or stroked depending on circumstance, and, crucially, a high percentage of both reach their intended destinations. Then there is that facility which is impossible to learn, which has to be inborn, that priceless knack of drifting past opponents with ball at feet, somehow gulling them with the merest shimmy of shoulder or hip, a manoeuvre which Anderson in full flow pulls off as naturally as breathing.

All this is not to suggest that the effervescent tyro is the complete player, at least not yet. For instance, his emphatic finish in the penalty shoot-out against Chelsea in the Champions League Final notwithstanding, when he has found himself in a position to shoot during open play, usually his execution has been has been poor, even clumsy, as if he lacked confidence or technique. That's a laughable proposition in one so gifted and it is surely a flaw that will be eradicated as he becomes increasingly established.

Although he has never been a prolific scorer, back in his homeland Anderson is revered for one astonishing effort for Gremio which secured the Brazilian Second Division title. After his team had been reduced to seven players in a turbulently rumbustious encounter against promotion rivals Nautico, he carried the ball virtually the length of the pitch before netting a spectacular winner. Later in 2005/06, having been voted player of the tournament in the World Cup for under-17s, he joined Porto and help his new club to land the Portuguese league and cup double. In October 2006 his impetus was jolted by a fractured leg, but he returned after six months, just in time to play a significant part as Porto retained their title.

As the climax of his first English campaign approached, Anderson was emerging as a cult hero among the junior denizens of Old Trafford, but perhaps more telling was the interim verdict on his contribution by seasoned observers of the Premiership scene, soccer sages whose judgement has been shaped by a lifetime in the game. They have pronounced Anderson as potentially special, even by Manchester United's standards. The lad has a long way to go, a lot of work to do; but for the moment, he could hardly be offered a more compelling endorsement.

ANDERSON LUIS DE ABREU OLIVEIRA
BORN: Porte Alegre, Brazil, 13 April 1988.
HONOURS: European Cup 07/08. League Championship 07/08. 4 Brazil caps (07-).
OTHER CLUBS: Gremio, Brazil, 05 (5, 1); Porto, Portugal, 05/-06-06/07 (21, 3).

GAMES **25 (13)**
GOALS 0

CARLOS TEVEZ

2007/08 →

It requires no quantum leap of the imagination to picture Carlos Tevez with a cutlass between his teeth, swarming up the rigging of an old-time man-o'-war to close in deadly combat with some bloodthirsty buccaneer. Indeed, with his swarthy looks, dark flowing locks and a prominent neck scar which is the legacy of a childhood accident with scalding water – or could it be the livid souvenir of being strung up from Cap'n Jack's yard-arm? – he might have swaggered directly from the set of *Pirates Of The Caribbean*.

The point of this flight of fancy? Just that the big-hearted little Argentinian with a grin as wide as the Pampas is a footballing free spirit, a born swashbuckler who hurls himself into the professional game with all the infectious abandon with which he used to cut a swathe through his young friends as a boy on the mean streets of Fuerte Apache, the Buenos Aires slum where he grew up.

'Carlito' loves to play and he communicates his joy in doing so every time he appears on a pitch. His work rate, as he scuttles constantly to all attacking areas with or without the ball, as well as foraging deep in search of further involvement, is quite phenomenal, and it has endeared him to the Old Trafford fans, his team-mates and his manager.

Then there is the small matter of his ability, and that is unquestionably world class. His catalogue of ball skills is comprehensive and he bubbles with flair, but he doesn't flaunt these assets, being content to subjugate them to the team ethic. If he or a nearby colleague loses possession, then Tevez doesn't stop chasing until it has been recovered, never expecting anyone else to do his work for him. When he is closing in on a target, he is inescapable, a pugnacious, indomitable terrier who will harry and scrap as long as he has breath in his body. His constant movement, frequently of the explosive variety, makes him deucedly difficult to mark, too, and he is adept at spinning in behind defenders, leaving them for dead before they have time to react. Even if they do reach him in time for a challenge, such is his strength and determination that often they bounce off him ineffectually, like tennis balls off a Sherman tank.

Carlos Tevez, who has acknowledged that football removed him from a life of potential poverty and crime, sprang to prominence with his home-town club, Boca Juniors, in the early years of the new millennium, earning early and unhelpful comparisons with another former idol of La Bombonera, one Diego Maradona. After winning league titles with Boca and making his full international entrance at the age of 20, he joined Corinthians of Brazil in December 2004 for £8.9 million, a record deal between South American clubs. Showing immense strength of character to thrive in a land where Argentinians win few popularity contests, Carlos was named the top player in the competition as he inspired the Sao Paulo side to championship glory in 2005, then stunned his new admirers by joining West Ham in a controversial and deeply complicated transaction in 2006.

He remained at Upton Park for only one term, saving the Hammers from relegation with a winning goal at Old Trafford in the last match of the campaign, then joined the Red Devils in a loan deal of labyrinthine intricacy after seemingly interminable negotiations in August 2007. It was reported that the initial two-year arrangement, which involved payments to third parties, cost United some £10 million, and that the eventual outlay, when the club made good its intention of making the move permanent, would total somewhere between £20 million and £35 million.

To Old Trafford regulars, the whole tiresome, murky rigmarole mattered not a jot. All that concerned them was the quality of the new man, and that, they realised pretty well immediately, was exceptional. His play crackled with intensity, the colossal physical effort mirrored by an acute intelligence, and when he broke the deadlock at home to Chelsea in late September with a flying near-post header from an exquisite Ryan Giggs cross, he was confirmed as a favourite son.

Still, though, in the minds of some observers, there lurked the reservation that Carlos might be 'too similar to Wayne Rooney', as if such a state of affairs might not be altogether desirable. But any fears that the thoroughbred pair would fail to gel were dispelled comprehensively in October by serial examples of scintillating interplay. At Villa Park it was Tevez creating a goal for Rooney with a sweetly incisive delivery with the outside of his right foot, but the *piece de resistance* came at Old Trafford against Middlesbrough when the Argentinian dinked delicately to Wayne inside the visitors' crowded penalty box, then dashed through a gaggle of defenders to meet the Englishman's almost insolent backheel with the coolest of sidefooted conversions. It represented a sublime consummation of a still-improving partnership between two of the best footballers on the planet.

Carlos Tevez scored 19 goals in his first season with Manchester United, including the winner at Anfield in December, and several crucial late efforts, notably the adroit glancing header at Blackburn in April which salvaged a point, enabling the Reds to retain control of the title race. He looked as though he was having fun, like a man who could hardly believe his luck at escaping from a darker previous existence. He is a diamond in the rough . . . but how he sparkles.

CARLOS ALBERTO TEVEZ

BORN: Cuidadela, Buenos Aires, Argentina, 5 February 1984.
HONOURS: European Cup 07/08. League Championship 07/08. 37 Argentina caps (04-).
OTHER CLUBS: Boca Juniors, Argentina, 01/02-04/05 (75, 26); Corinthians, Brazil, 05 (29, 20);
West Ham United 06/07 (26, 7).

GAMES	39 (9)
GOALS	19

DANNY SIMPSON

2007/08 →

In this age of colossally expensive foreign imports it is anything but a *fait accompli*, but there would be a heartfelt groundswell of satisfaction among United's more traditionally inclined supporters if Danny Simpson bucked the trend to become a first-team regular.

The chirpy, bright-eyed little full-back from Eccles is a lifelong fan of the Red Devils, he has worked his way through the revamped Old Trafford academy system which he joined at the age of nine, and in his limited senior opportunities to date has done plenty to suggest that he might make the grade.

Certainly his loan stint at Sunderland in the spring of 2007, which earned him a Championship medal, indicated quality, as did his crisply decisive work on his Premiership entrance for the Reds, at home to Wigan in the following October. This climaxed with a high-speed scamper down the right touchline and a perfectly floated cross for Wayne Rooney to nod home.

There followed dashing cameos against Dynamo in Kiev and at home to Newcastle, both of which showcased his efficiency and industry, though there was the painful experience of being withdrawn at half-time at Old Trafford after he had struggled against Everton's tricky Steven Pienaar.

Simpson is versatile enough to operate on either defensive flank, he is a faultlessly diligent professional blessed with a level temperament, and he has a contract to 2010 in his pocket. Further development is needed but he has a chance.

DANIEL PETER SIMPSON
BORN: Eccles, Manchester, 4 January 1987.
OTHER CLUBS: Royal Antwerp, Belgium, on loan 06/07; Sunderland on loan 06/07 (14, 0); Ipswich Town on loan 07/08 (8, 0).

GAMES **4 (4)**
GOALS **0**

JONNY EVANS

2007/08 →

Like his fellow rookie stopper Gerard Pique, Jonny Evans is a thoroughbred on the rise. At the time of writing, the tall, almost willowy Ulsterman had enjoyed only three senior outings for Manchester United, but he had done enough under Roy Keane on loan at Sunderland, and in the green shirt of his country, to prompt seasoned observers to muse knowingly about his unlimited potential.

When exposed to the harsh reality of the Black Cats' promotion dogfight in the second half of 2006/07, many a callow hopeful might have wilted under the relentless pressure. But Evans thrived, relishing the rigorous test, and finishing the term clutching a hard-earned Championship medal.

It had been the same story the previous September when he had been pitched into the international caudron to make his full debut against Spain in a European Championship qualifier, and he emerged as one of the heroes of an unforgettable 3-2 victory.

That night, and in his subsequent sojourn at the Stadium of Light, Jonny showcased his unflappable temperament, incisive intelligence and smooth all-round technique. It was no surprise at season's end when Keane was eager to recruit him on a permanent basis.

He couldn't be blamed for asking, but the former United skipper could hardly have expected Sir Alex Ferguson to part with such a gem, albeit one of the uncut variety. However, Evans did return to Sunderland in January 2008 to gather more experience on loan, an arrangement that suited all parties.

JONATHAN GRANT EVANS
BORN: Belfast, 3 January 1988.
HONOURS: 10 Northern Ireland caps (06-).
OTHER CLUBS: Sunderland on loan 06/07 (18, 1) and 07/08 (15, 0).

GAMES **2 (1)**
GOALS **0**

BEN FOSTER

2007/08 →

Despite playing only one game in three years for Manchester United following his £1 million transfer to the Red Devils from Stoke City in the summer of 2005, Ben Foster has been tipped widely to become England's goalkeeper for the foreseeable future. It's been a curious and potentially disruptive scenario, but one which the tall, athletic Midlander has handled with commendable composure.

After leaving the Potters, for whom he never made a senior appearance, Foster was loaned immediately to Watford. He excelled as the Hornets rose to the top tier in 2005/06, then was the runaway winner of their player of the year poll as they fought valiantly but unsuccessfully to avoid relegation at the end of the next campaign.

So exceptional was his form that he was awarded a full England debut in February 2007, and many pundits expected him to challenge Edwin van der Sar's position as United's first-choice custodian during the following term. But that summer he underwent knee surgery and didn't return to action until the spring of 2008 when, with the Dutchman injured and Tomas Kuszczak suspended, he finally made his Premiership entrance for the Reds.

He seized his chance avidly, making two smart saves in a 1-0 victory at Derby, and impressing generally with his agility, assurance and astute distribution. Ben Foster has about him an imposing presence which bodes well for his long-term future between United's posts.

BENJAMIN ANTHONY FOSTER
BORN: Leamington Spa, Warwickshire, 3 April 1983.
HONOURS: 1 England cap (07).
OTHER CLUBS: Kidderminster Harriers on loan 04/05 (2, 0); Wrexham on loan 04/05 (17, 0); Watford on loan 04/05-05/06 (73, 0).

GAMES **1**
GOALS **0**

NANI

2007/08 →

The game had barely begun and there was no sense of impending drama as Nani received the ball near the left touchline. Even when he looked up and drifted inside, almost casually, beyond the reach of two half-hearted challengers, Mark Schwarzer in the Middlesbrough goal would not have been feeling especially threatened. But then, with an easy, comfortable grace, as if he was enjoying an untroubled kickabout with his mates in some dusty Lisbon backstreet, the young Portuguese flankman unleashed a sudden missile with his right foot, an arcing, spitting 30-yarder which left the Aussie custodian flailing almost comically at thin air as his net ballooned behind him.

A sequence of pure theatre was completed as United's recent £17 million acquisition catapulted head over heels in his trademark 'death leap' celebration, a potentially hazardous manoeuvre more suited to a circus ring than a football pitch, but which is all part of the rich and exotic mixture that is Nani.

All this should have come as no surprise to Old Trafford regulars on an October afternoon in 2007 which ended with a thumping 4-1 home victory, not if they had been present two months earlier when the audacious 20-year-old had conjured a similarly thunderous masterpiece. That one had sealed a distinctly streaky 1-0 win over Spurs which had provoked rather more relief than rapture in the stands and private boxes. But for Nani there was nothing but praise – and he deserved it.

Though he had been on United's radar for two years, Sir Alex Ferguson would have preferred to allow another season's experience with Sporting Lisbon before pouncing to secure him, but there were ominous signs of competition for his services so delay would have been perilous. Still, though, the United boss did not envisage extensive senior opportunities for the boy in his first term as a Red, but so swiftly did Nani settle that he confounded such conservative expectations. While clearly lower in the pecking order than Ryan Giggs, whose left-wing berth he is expected to inherit eventually, the newcomer demonstrated both a level temperament and exciting natural ability.

Capable, like Giggs, of filling any attacking berth, Nani is quick and delightfully balanced. He can dance past defenders on either side, he is a dazzling manipulator of the ball and he is tough enough to withstand the brutal attentions of unscrupulous markers. He carries a devastating goal threat, he can cross like a dream and he is ever willing to attempt the unexpected.

Naturally there is occasional evidence of rawness, of holding the ball too long, of squandering possession cheaply, but that dissolves to nothingness when set against his golden potential. The instinctive flick which freed Wayne Rooney to score at home to Roma in October 2007, the wondrous one-touch interplay with Ronaldo which culminated in Cristiano's opener against Portsmouth at Old Trafford the following January, the sustained wizardry that tormented Arsenal during their FA Cup horror show two weeks later – they all proclaim that, in terms of general awareness, he is more advanced than was his illustrious countryman at a comparable age.

The full flowering of Nani is awaited with rare anticipation.

LUIS CARLOS ALMEIDA DA CUNHA
BORN: Praia, Cape Verde Islands, 17 November 1986.
HONOURS: European Cup 07/08. League Championship 07/08. 7 Portugal caps (06-).
OTHER CLUBS: Sporting Lisbon, Portugal, 05/06-06/07 (58, 9).

| GAMES | 26 (15) |
| GOALS | 4 |

PLAYERS' STATISTICS

JANUARY 1946 → MAY 2008

Dates shown indicate first year of each season. Thus 64–66 means 1964/65 to 1966/67. A single entry means one season only, eg 2002 refers to 2002/03

Player	Season	League App	(Sub)	Gl	FA Cup App	(Sub)	Gl	League Cup App	(Sub)	Gl	Europe App	(Sub)	Gl	Others App	(Sub)	Gl	Total App	(Sub)	Gl
Albiston A	74–87	364	(15)	6	36	(0)	0	38	(2)	1	26	(1)	0	3	(0)	0	467	(18)	7
Allen R	50–52	75	(0)	0	5	(0)	0	0	(0)	0	0	(0)	0	0	(0)	0	80	(0)	0
Anderson	07–	16	(8)	0	2	(2)	0	1	(0)	0	6	(3)	0	0	(0)	0	25	(13)	0
Anderson J	47–48	33	(0)	1	6	(0)	1	0	(0)	0	0	(0)	0	1	(0)	0	40	(0)	2
Anderson T	72-73	13	(6)	2	0	(0)	0	0	(0)	0	0	(0)	0	0	(0)	0	13	(6)	2
Anderson V	87-90	50	(4)	2	7	(0)	1	6	(1)	1	1	(0)	0	0	(0)	0	64	(5)	4
Anderson W	63-66	7	(2)	0	2	(0)	0	0	(0)	0	1	(0)	0	0	(1)	0	10	(3)	0
Appleton M	1996	0	(0)	0	0	(0)	0	1	(1)	0	0	(0)	0	0	(0)	0	1	(1)	0
Aston J Snr	46–53	253	(0)	29	29	(0)	1	0	(0)	0	0	(0)	0	2	(0)	0	284	(0)	30
Aston J Jnr	64-71	139	(16)	25	5	(2)	1	12	(3)	0	8	(0)	1	2	(0)	0	166	(21)	27
Bailey G	78-86	294	(0)	0	31	(0)	0	28	(0)	0	20	(0)	0	2	(0)	0	375	(0)	0
Bainbridge W	1945	0	(0)	0	1	(0)	1	0	(0)	0	0	(0)	0	0	(0)	0	1	(0)	1
Baldwin T	1974	2	(0)	0	0	(0)	0	0	(0)	0	0	(0)	0	0	(0)	0	2	(0)	0
Ball J	47–49	22	(0)	0	1	(0)	0	0	(0)	0	0	(0)	0	0	(0)	0	23	(0)	0
Bardsley P	03–07	3	(5)	0	2	(1)	0	3	(1)	0	2	(1)	0	0	(0)	0	10	(8)	0
Barnes M	06–	0	(0)	0	0	(0)	0	0	(1)	0	0	(0)	0	0	(0)	0	0	(1)	0
Barnes P	85-86	19	(1)	2	0	(0)	0	5	(0)	2	0	(0)	0	0	(0)	0	24	(1)	4
Barthez F	00–02	92	(0)	0	4	(0)	0	4	(0)	0	37	(0)	0	2	(0)	0	139	(0)	0
Beardsley P	1982	0	(0)	0	0	(0)	0	1	(0)	0	0	(0)	0	0	(0)	0	1	(0)	0
Beardsmore R	88–91	30	(26)	4	4	(4)	0	3	(1)	0	2	(3)	0	0	(0)	0	39	(34)	4
Beckham D	92–02	237	(28)	62	22	(2)	6	10	(2)	1	79	(5)	15	8	(2)	1	356	(39)	85
Bellion D	03–04	5	(19)	4	2	(1)	0	5	(0)	2	2	(5)	2	1	(0)	0	15	(25)	8
Bent G	54–56	12	(0)	0	0	(0)	0	0	(0)	0	0	(0)	0	0	(0)	0	12	(0)	0
Berg H	97–00	49	(17)	2	7	(0)	0	3	(0)	0	19	(4)	1	3	(1)	0	81	(22)	3
Berry J	51–57	247	(0)	37	15	(0)	4	0	(0)	0	11	(0)	3	3	(0)	1	276	(0)	45
Best G	63–73	361	(0)	137	46	(0)	21	25	(0)	9	34	(0)	11	4	(0)	1	470	(0)	179
Bielby P	1973	2	(2)	0	0	(0)	0	0	(0)	0	0	(0)	0	0	(0)	0	2	(2)	0
Birch B	49–51	11	{0)	4	4	(0)	1	0	(0)	0	0	(0)	0	0	(0)	0	15	(0)	5
Birkett C	1950	9	(0)	2	4	(0)	0	0	(0)	0	0	(0)	0	0	(0)	0	13	(0)	2
Birtles G	80–81	57	(1)	11	4	(0)	1	2	(0)	0	0	(0)	0	0	(0)	0	63	(1)	12
Blackmore C	83–92	150	(36)	19	15	(6)	1	23	(2)	3	11	(0)	2	2	(0)	1	201	(44)	26
Blanc L	01–02	44	(4)	1	3	(0)	0	0	(0)	0	24	(0)	3	0	(0)	0	71	(4)	4
Blanchflower J	51–57	105	(0)	26	6	(0)	1	0	(0)	0	5	(0)	0	1	(0)	0	117	(0)	27
Blomqvist J	1998	20	(5)	1	3	(2)	0	0	(1)	0	6	(1)	0	0	(0)	0	29	(9)	1
Bogan T	49–50	29	(0)	7	4	(0)	0	0	(0)	0	0	(0)	0	0	(0)	0	33	(0)	7
Bond E	51–52	20	(0)	4	1	(0)	0	0	(0)	0	0	(0)	0	0	(0)	0	21	(0)	4
Bosnich M	89–90 & 1999	26	(0)	0	0	(0)	0	1	(0)	0	7	(0)	0	4	(0)	0	38	(0)	0
Bradley W	58–61	63	(0)	20	4	(0)	1	0	(0)	0	0	(0)	0	0	(0)	0	67	(0)	21
Bratt H	1960	0	(0)	0	0	(0)	0	1	(0)	0	0	(0)	0	0	(0)	0	1	(0)	0
Brazil A	84–85	18	(13)	8	0	(1)	0	4	(3)	3	2	(0)	1	0	(0)	0	24	(17)	12
Brazil D	88–89	0	(2)	0	0	(0)	0	0	(0)	0	0	(0)	0	0	(0)	0	0	(2)	0
Brennan S	57–69	291	(1)	3	36	(0)	3	4	(0)	0	24	(0)	0	3	(0)	0	358	(1)	6
Briggs R	60–61	9	(0)	0	2	(0)	0	0	(0)	0	0	(0)	0	0	(0)	0	11	(0)	0
Brown B	47–48	4	(0)	0	0	(0)	0	0	(0)	0	0	(0)	0	0	(0)	0	4	(0)	0
Brown W	97–	175	(23)	2	29	(2)	0	16	(2)	0	50	(7)	1	1	(0)	0	271	(34)	3
Bruce S	87–95	309	(0)	36	41	(0)	3	32	(2)	6	25	(1)	6	4	(0)	0	411	(3)	51
Buchan G	1973	0	(3)	0	0	(0)	0	0	(1)	0	0	(0)	0	0	(0)	0	0	(4)	0
Buchan M	71–82	376	(0)	4	39	(0)	0	30	(0)	0	10	(0)	0	1	(0)	0	456	(0)	4
Buckle T	46–49	20	(0)	6	4	(0)	1	0	(0)	0	0	(0)	0	0	(0)	0	24	(0)	7
Burke R	46–48	28	(0)	16	6	(0)	6	0	(0)	0	0	(0)	0	1	(0)	1	35	(0)	23
Burns F	67–71	111	(10)	6	11	(1)	0	10	(1)	1	10	(1)	0	1	(0)	0	143	(13)	7
Butt N	92–03	210	(60)	21	23	(6)	1	7	(1)	0	58	(13)	2	9	(0)	2	307	(80)	26

360

Player	Season	League App	(Sub)	Gl	FA Cup App	(Sub)	Gl	League Cup App	(Sub)	Gl	Europe App	(Sub)	Gl	Others App	(Sub)	Gl	Total App	(Sub)	Gl
Byrne R	51–57	245	(0)	17	18	(0)	2	0	(0)	0	14	(0)	0	3	(0)	1	280	(0)	20
Campbell F	07–	0	(1)	0	0	(0)	0	0	(1)	0	0	(0)	0	0	(0)	0	0	(2)	0
Cantona E	92–96	142	(1)	64	17	(0)	10	6	(0)	1	16	(0)	5	3	(0)	2	184	(1)	82
Cantwell N	60–66	123	(0)	6	14	(0)	2	0	(0)	0	7	(0)	0	2	(0)	0	146	(0)	8
Carey J	37–52	306	(0)	17	38	(0)	1	0	(0)	0	0	(0)	0	2	(0)	0	346	(0)	18
Carolan J	58–60	66	(0)	0	4	(0)	0	1	(0)	0	0	(0)	0	0	(0)	0	71	(0)	0
Carrick M	06–	53	(11)	5	10	(1)	1	0	(1)	0	23	(1)	2	1	(0)	0	87	(14)	8
Carroll R	01–04	46	(3)	0	7	(1)	0	5	(0)	0	10	(0)	0	0	(0)	0	68	(4)	0
Casper C	94–96	0	(2)	0	1	(0)	0	3	(0)	0	0	(1)	0	0	(0)	0	4	(3)	0
Cassidy L	47–51	4	(0)	0	0	(0)	0	0	(0)	0	0	(0)	0	0	(0)	0	4	(0)	0
Chadwick L	99–02	11	(14)	2	1	(2)	0	5	(0)	0	1	(5)	0	0	(0)	0	18	(21)	2
Charlton R	56–72	604	(2)	199	78	(0)	19	24	(0)	7	45	(0)	22	5	(0)	2	756	(2)	249
Chilton A	39–54	353	(0)	3	37	(0)	0	0	(0)	0	0	(0)	0	2	(0)	0	392	(0)	3
Chisnall P	61–63	35	(0)	8	8	(0)	1	0	(0)	0	4	(0)	1	0	(0)	0	47	(0)	10
Clark J	1976	0	(1)	0	0	(0)	0	0	(0)	0	0	(0)	0	0	(0)	0	0	(1)	0
Clayton G	1956	2	(0)	0	0	(0)	0	0	(0)	0	0	(0)	0	0	(0)	0	2	(0)	0
Clegg M	96–01	4	(5)	0	3	(1)	0	7	(1)	0	1	(2)	0	0	(0)	0	15	(9)	0
Clempson F	49–52	15	(0)	2	0	(0)	0	0	(0)	0	0	(0)	0	0	(0)	0	15	(0)	2
Cockburn H	45–54	243	(0)	4	32	(0)	0	0	(0)	0	0	(0)	0	0	(0)	0	275	(0)	4
Cole A	94–01	161	(34)	93	19	(2)	9	2	(0)	0	43	(7)	19	6	(1)	0	231	(44)	121
Collinson C	1946	7	(0)	0	0	(0)	0	0	(0)	0	0	(0)	0	0	(0)	0	7	(0)	0
Colman E	55–57	85	(0)	1	9	(0)	0	0	(0)	0	13	(0)	1	1	(0)	0	108	(0)	2
Connaughton J	1971	3	(0)	0	0	(0)	0	0	(0)	0	0	(0)	0	0	(0)	0	3	(0)	0
Connell T	1978	2	(0)	0	0	(0)	0	0	(0)	0	0	(0)	0	0	(0)	0	2	(0)	0
Connelly J	64–66	79	(1)	22	13	(0)	2	1	(0)	0	19	(0)	11	0	(0)	0	112	(1)	35
Cooke T	95–96	1	(3)	0	0	(0)	0	1	(2)	1	0	(1)	0	0	(0)	0	2	(6)	1
Cope R	56–60	93	(0)	2	10	(0)	0	1	(0)	0	2	(0)	0	0	(0)	0	106	(0)	2
Coppell S	74–82	320	(2)	54	36	(0)	4	25	(0)	9	11	(1)	3	1	(0)	0	393	(3)	70
Coyne P	1975	1	(1)	1	0	(0)	0	0	(0)	0	0	(0)	0	0	(0)	0	1	(1)	1
Crerand P	62–70	304	(0)	10	43	(0)	4	4	(0)	0	41	(0)	1	5	(0)	0	397	(0)	15
Crompton J	45–55	191	(0)	0	20	(0)	0	0	(0)	0	0	(0)	0	1	(0)	0	212	(0)	0
Crooks G	1983	6	(1)	2	0	(0)	0	0	(0)	0	0	(0)	0	0	(0)	0	6	(1)	2
Crowther S	57–58	13	(0)	0	5	(0)	0	0	(0)	0	2	(0)	0	0	(0)	0	20	(0)	0
Cruyff J	96–99	15	(19)	8	0	(1)	0	5	(0)	0	4	(7)	0	2	(5)	0	26	(32)	8
Culkin N	1999	0	(1)	0	0	(0)	0	0	(0)	0	0	(0)	0	0	(0)	0	0	(1)	0
Cunningham L	1982	3	(2)	1	0	(0)	0	0	(0)	0	0	(0)	0	0	(0)	0	3	(2)	1
Curtis J	97–99	4	(9)	0	0	(0)	0	5	(0)	0	0	(0)	0	0	(1)	0	9	(10)	0
Dale J	1947	2	(0)	0	0	(0)	0	0	(0)	0	0	(0)	0	0	(0)	0	2	(0)	0
Daly G	73–76	107	(4)	23	9	(1)	5	17	(0)	4	4	(0)	0	0	(0)	0	137	(5)	32
Davenport P	85–88	73	(19)	22	2	(2)	0	8	(2)	4	0	(0)	0	0	(0)	0	83	(23)	26
Davies A	81–83	6	(1)	0	2	(0)	0	0	(0)	0	0	(1)	1	0	(0)	0	8	(2)	1
Davies R	1974	0	(8)	0	0	(2)	0	0	(0)	0	0	(0)	0	0	(0)	0	0	(10)	0
Davies S	94–96	4	(7)	0	0	(0)	0	3	(2)	0	3	(1)	1	0	(0)	0	10	(10)	1
Davies W	1972	15	(1)	4	1	(0)	0	0	(0)	0	0	(0)	0	0	(0)	0	16	(1)	4
Davis J	2001	0	(0)	0	0	(0)	0	1	(0)	0	0	(0)	0	0	(0)	0	1	(0)	0
Dawson A	56–61	80	(0)	45	10	(0)	8	3	(0)	1	0	(0)	0	0	(0)	0	93	(0)	54
Delaney J	46–50	164	(0)	25	19	(0)	3	0	(0)	0	0	(0)	0	1	(0)	0	184	(0)	28
Dempsey M	83–85	1	(0)	0	0	(0)	0	0	(0)	0	0	(1)	0	0	(0)	0	1	(1)	0
Djemba-Djemba E	03–04	13	(7)	0	2	(1)	0	5	(0)	1	6	(3)	1	1	(1)	0	27	(12)	2
Djordjic B	00–01	0	(1)	0	0	(0)	0	1	(0)	0	0	(0)	0	0	(0)	0	1	(1)	0
Doherty J	52–57	25	(0)	7	1	(0)	0	0	(0)	0	0	(0)	0	0	(0)	0	26	(0)	7
Donaghy M	88–91	76	(13)	0	10	(0)	0	9	(5)	0	2	(3)	0	1	(0)	0	98	(21)	0
Donald I	1972	4	(0)	0	0	(0)	0	2	(0)	0	0	(0)	0	0	(0)	0	6	(0)	0
Dong Fangzhuo	06–	1	(0)	0	0	(0)	0	1	(0)	0	0	(1)	0	0	(0)	0	2	(1)	0
Downie J	48–52	110	(0)	35	5	(0)	1	0	(0)	0	0	(0)	0	1	(0)	1	116	(0)	37
Dublin D	92–93	4	(8)	2	1	(1)	0	1	(1)	1	0	(1)	0	0	(0)	0	6	(11)	3
Dunne A	60–72	414	(0)	2	54	(1)	0	21	(0)	0	40	(0)	0	5	(0)	0	534	(1)	2
Dunne P	64–65	45	(0)	0	7	(0)	0	1	(0)	0	13	(0)	0	1	(0)	0	67	(0)	0
Duxbury M	80–89	274	(25)	6	20	(5)	1	32	(2)	0	17	(1)	0	2	(0)	0	345	(33)	7

Player	Season	League			FA Cup			League Cup			Europe			Others			Total		
		App	(Sub)	Gl	App	(Sub)	Gl	App	(Sub)	Gl	App	(Sub)	Gl	App	(Sub)	Gl	App	(Sub)	Gl
Eagles C	03–	2	(4)	1	1	(0)	0	2	(4)	0	2	(1)	0	0	(1)	0	7	(10)	1
Ebanks-Blake S	04–05	0	(0)	0	0	(0)	0	1	(1)	1	0	(0)	0	0	(0)	0	1	(1)	1
Eckersley A	2005	0	(0)	0	0	(0)	0	1	(0)	0	0	(0)	0	0	(0)	0	1	(0)	0
Edwards D	52–57	151	(0)	20	12	(0)	1	0	(0)	0	12	(0)	0	2	(0)	0	177	(0)	21
Edwards P	69–72	52	(2)	0	10	(0)	0	4	(0)	1	0	(0)	0	0	(0)	0	66	(2)	1
Evans J	07–	0	(0)	0	0	(0)	0	0	(0)	0	1	(1)	0	0	(0)	0	2	(1)	0
Evra P	05–	62	(6)	1	7	(2)	0	1	(2)	0	14	(3)	1	1	(0)	0	85	(13)	2
Feehan S	1949	12	(0)	0	2	(0)	0	0	(0)	0	0	(0)	0	0	(0)	0	14	(0)	0
Ferdinand R	02–	183	(1)	6	20	(1)	0	9	(1)	0	49	(1)	1	2	(0)	0	263	(4)	7
Ferguson D	90–93	20	(7)	0	0	(0)	0	2	(1)	0	0	(0)	0	0	(0)	0	22	(8)	0
Fielding W	1946	6	(0)	0	1	(0)	0	0	(0)	0	0	(0)	0	0	(0)	0	7	(0)	0
Fitzpatrick J	64–72	111	(6)	8	11	(0)	1	12	(0)	1	7	(0)	0	0	(0)	0	141	(6)	10
Fletcher D	02–	79	(28)	7	11	(7)	2	10	(0)	0	26	(9)	0	0	(2)	0	126	(46)	9
Fletcher P	72–73	2	(5)	0	0	(0)	0	0	(0)	0	0	(0)	0	0	(0)	0	2	(5)	0
Foggon A	1976	0	(3)	0	0	(0)	0	0	(0)	0	0	(0)	0	0	(0)	0	0	(3)	0
Forlan D	01–04	23	(40)	10	2	(2)	1	4	(2)	3	8	(15)	3	0	(2)	0	37	(61)	17
Forsyth A	72–77	99	(2)	4	10	(0)	1	7	(0)	0	0	(1)	0	0	(0)	0	116	(3)	5
Fortune Q	99–04	53	(23)	6	8	(1)	1	8	(0)	0	16	(12)	2	3	(2)	2	88	(38)	11
Foster B	07–	1	(0)	0	0	(0)	0	0	(0)	0	0	(0)	0	0	(0)	0	1	(0)	0
Foulkes W	52–69	563	(3)	7	61	(0)	0	3	(0)	0	52	(0)	2	6	(0)	0	685	(3)	9
Garton W	84–88	39	(2)	0	3	(0)	0	5	(1)	0	0	(1)	0	0	(0)	0	47	(4)	0
Gaskell D	57–66	96	(0)	0	16	(0)	0	1	(0)	0	5	(0)	0	1	(1)	0	119	(1)	0
Gibson C	85–89	74	(5)	9	8	(1)	0	7	(0)	0	0	(0)	0	0	(0)	0	89	(6)	9
Gibson Darron	05–	0	(0)	0	0	(0)	0	0	(0)	0	0	(0)	0	0	(0)	0	0	(1)	0
Gibson Don	50–54	108	(0)	0	6	(0)	0	0	(0)	0	0	(0)	0	1	(0)	0	115	(0)	0
Gibson T	85–86	14	(9)	1	1	(1)	0	0	(2)	0	0	(0)	0	0	(0)	0	15	(12)	1
Gidman J	81–85	94	(1)	4	9	(0)	0	5	(0)	0	7	(2)	0	1	(1)	0	116	(4)	4
Giggs R	90–	469	(66)	101	55	(7)	10	25	(5)	7	107	(11)	25	13	(1)	1	669	(90)	144
Giles J	59–62	99	(0)	10	13	(0)	2	2	(0)	1	0	(0)	0	1	(0)	0	115	(0)	13
Gill A	86–88	5	(5)	1	2	(2)	1	0	(0)	0	0	(0)	0	0	(0)	0	7	(7)	2
Gillespie K	92–94	3	(6)	1	1	(1)	1	3	(0)	0	0	(0)	0	0	(0)	0	7	(7)	2
Givens D	1969	4	(4)	1	0	(0)	0	1	(0)	0	0	(0)	0	0	(0)	0	5	(4)	1
Goodwin F	54–59	95	(0)	7	8	(0)	1	0	(0)	0	3	(0)	0	1	(0)	0	107	(0)	8
Goram A	2000	2	(0)	0	0	(0)	0	0	(0)	0	0	(0)	0	0	(0)	0	2	(0)	0
Gowling A	67–71	64	(7)	18	6	(2)	2	7	(1)	1	0	(0)	0	0	(0)	0	77	(10)	21
Graham A	83–84	33	(4)	5	1	(0)	0	6	(0)	1	6	(1)	1	1	(0)	0	47	(5)	7
Graham D	87–88	1	(0)	0	0	(1)	1	0	(1)	0	0	(0)	0	0	(0)	0	1	(2)	1
Graham G	72–74	41	(2)	2	2	(0)	0	1	(0)	0	0	(0)	0	0	(0)	0	44	(2)	2
Gray D	06–	0	(0)	0	0	(0)	0	1	(0)	0	0	(0)	0	0	(0)	0	1	(0)	0
Greaves I	54–59	67	(0)	0	6	(0)	0	0	(0)	0	2	(0)	0	0	(0)	0	75	(0)	0
Greenhoff B	73–78	218	(3)	13	24	(0)	2	19	(0)	2	6	(0)	0	1	(0)	0	268	(3)	17
Greenhoff J	76–80	94	(3)	26	18	(1)	9	4	(0)	1	2	(0)	0	1	(0)	0	119	(4)	36
Greening J	98–00	4	(10)	0	0	(1)	0	6	(0)	0	2	(2)	0	1	(1)	0	13	(14)	0
Gregg H	57–66	210	(0)	0	24	(0)	0	2	(0)	0	11	(0)	0	0	(0)	0	247	(0)	0
Griffiths C	1973	7	(0)	0	0	(0)	0	0	(0)	0	0	(0)	0	0	(0)	0	7	(0)	0
Grimes A	77–82	62	(28)	10	5	(0)	1	6	(0)	0	4	(2)	0	0	(0)	0	77	(30)	11
Grimshaw A	1975	0	(1)	0	0	(0)	0	0	(1)	0	0	(0)	0	0	(0)	0	0	(2)	0
Hanlon J	38–48	64	(0)	20	6	(0)	2	0	(0)	0	0	(0)	0	0	(0)	0	70	(0)	22
Hargreaves O	07–	16	(7)	2	2	(1)	0	0	(0)	0	5	(3)	0	0	(0)	0	23	(11)	2
Harrop R	57–58	10	(0)	0	1	(0)	0	0	(0)	0	0	(0)	0	0	(0)	0	11	(0)	0
Hawksworth A	1956	1	(0)	0	0	(0)	0	0	(0)	0	0	(0)	0	0	(0)	0	1	(0)	0
Haydock F	60–62	6	(0)	0	0	(0)	0	0	(0)	0	0	(0)	0	0	(0)	0	6	(0)	0
Healy D	99–00	0	(1)	0	0	(0)	0	0	(2)	0	0	(0)	0	0	(0)	0	0	(3)	0
Heinze G	04–06	45	(7)	1	10	(0)	1	4	(0)	0	16	(1)	2	0	(0)	0	75	(8)	4
Herd D	61–67	201	(1)	114	35	(0)	15	1	(0)	1	25	(0)	14	2	(0)	1	264	(1)	145
Heron T	57–60	3	(0)	0	0	(0)	0	0	(0)	0	0	(0)	0	0	(0)	0	3	(0)	0
Higginbotham D	97–99	2	(2)	0	0	(0)	0	1	(0)	0	0	(1)	0	1	(0)	0	4	(3)	0
Higgins M	1985	6	(0)	0	2	(0)	0	0	(0)	0	0	(0)	0	0	(0)	0	8	(0)	0
Hill G	75–77	100	(1)	39	17	(0)	6	7	(0)	4	8	(0)	2	1	(0)	0	133	(1)	51

Player	Season	League App	(Sub)	Gl	FA Cup App	(Sub)	Gl	League Cup App	(Sub)	Gl	Europe App	(Sub)	Gl	Others App	(Sub)	Gl	Total App	(Sub)	Gl
Hogg G	83–87	82	(1)	1	8	(0)	0	7	(1)	0	10	(0)	0	1	(0)	0	108	(2)	1
Holton J	72–74	63	(0)	5	2	(0)	0	4	(0)	0	0	(0)	0	0	(0)	0	69	(0)	5
Houston S	73–79	204	(1)	13	22	(0)	1	16	(0)	2	6	(1)	0	0	(0)	0	248	(2)	16
Howard T	03–05	44	(1)	0	10	(0)	0	8	(0)	0	12	(0)	0	2	(0)	0	76	(1)	0
Hughes M 83–85 & 88–94		336	(9)	120	45	(1)	17	37	(1)	16	30	(3)	9	5	(0)	1	453	(14)	163
Hunter R	1958	1	(0)	0	0	(0)	0	0	(0)	0	0	(0)	0	0	(0)	0	1	(0)	0
Ince P	89–94	203	(3)	25	26	(1)	1	23	(1)	2	20	(0)	0	4	(0)	1	276	(5)	29
Irwin D	90–01	356	(12)	22	42	(1)	7	28	(3)	0	73	(2)	4	12	(0)	0	511	(18)	33
Jackson T	75–76	18	(1)	0	0	(0)	0	4	(0)	0	0	(0)	0	0	(0)	0	22	(1)	0
James S	68–74	129	(0)	4	12	(0)	0	17	(1)	0	2	(0)	0	0	(0)	0	160	(1)	4
Johnsen R	96–01	85	(14)	7	8	(2)	1	3	(0)	0	32	(3)	0	3	(0)	1	131	(19)	9
Johnson E	2003	0	(0)	0	0	(0)	0	0	(1)	0	0	(0)	0	0	(0)	0	0	(1)	0
Jones D	04–06	0	(0)	0	1	(0)	0	2	(1)	0	0	(0)	0	0	(0)	0	3	(1)	0
Jones M	50–57	103	(0)	1	7	(0)	0	0	(0)	0	10	(0)	0	1	(0)	0	121	(0)	1
Jones P	1957	1	(0)	0	0	(0)	0	0	(0)	0	0	(0)	0	0	(0)	0	1	(0)	0
Jones R	05–	0	(0)	0	1	(0)	0	2	(2)	0	0	(0)	0	0	(0)	0	3	(2)	0
Jordan J	77–80	109	(0)	37	11	(1)	2	4	(0)	2	1	(0)	0	0	(0)	0	125	(1)	41
Jovanovic N	79–80	20	(1)	4	1	(0)	0	2	(0)	0	2	(0)	0	0	(0)	0	25	(1)	4
Kanchelskis A	90–94	96	(27)	28	11	(1)	4	15	(1)	3	7	(0)	1	3	(0)	0	132	(29)	36
Keane R	93–05	309	(17)	33	44	(2)	2	12	(2)	0	81	(1)	14	12	(0)	2	458	(22)	51
Kelly J	1975	0	(1)	0	0	(0)	0	0	(0)	0	0	(0)	0	0	(0)	0	0	(1)	0
Kennedy P	1954	1	(0)	0	0	(0)	0	0	(0)	0	0	(0)	0	0	(0)	0	1	(0)	0
Kidd B	67–73	195	(8)	52	24	(1)	8	20	(0)	7	16	(0)	3	2	(0)	0	257	(9)	70
Kinsey A	1964	0	(0)	0	1	(0)	1	0	(0)	0	0	(0)	0	0	(0)	0	1	(0)	1
Kleberson J	03–04	16	(4)	2	1	(0)	0	4	(0)	0	3	(2)	0	0	(0)	0	24	(6)	2
Kopel F	67–68	8	(2)	0	1	(0)	0	0	(0)	0	1	(0)	0	0	(0)	0	10	(2)	0
Kuszczak T	06–	14	(1)	0	5	(1)	0	3	(0)	0	3	(2)	0	0	(0)	0	25	(4)	0
Lancaster J	1949	2	(0)	0	2	(0)	0	0	(0)	0	0	(0)	0	0	(0)	0	4	(0)	0
Larsson H	2006	5	(2)	1	3	(1)	1	0	(0)	0	2	(0)	1	0	(0)	0	10	(3)	3
Law D	62–72	305	(4)	171	44	(2)	34	11	(0)	3	33	(0)	28	5	(0)	1	398	(6)	237
Lawton N	59–62	36	(0)	6	7	(0)	0	1	(0)	0	0	(0)	0	0	(0)	0	44	(0)	6
Lee K	06–	1	(0)	0	0	(0)	0	0	(2)	1	0	(0)	0	0	(0)	0	1	(2)	1
Leighton J	88–90	73	(0)	0	14	(0)	0	7	(0)	0	0	(0)	0	0	(0)	0	94	(0)	0
Lewis E	52–55	20	(0)	9	4	(0)	2	0	(0)	0	0	(0)	0	0	(0)	0	24	(0)	11
Lowrie T	47–50	13	(0)	0	1	(0)	0	0	(0)	0	0	(0)	0	0	(0)	0	14	(0)	0
Lynch M	2002	0	(0)	0	0	(0)	0	0	(0)	0	1	(0)	0	0	(0)	0	1	(0)	0
Lynn S	47–49	13	(0)	0	0	(0)	0	0	(0)	0	0	(0)	0	0	(0)	0	13	(0)	0
Macari L	72–83	311	(18)	78	31	(3)	8	22	(5)	10	9	(1)	1	1	(0)	0	374	(27)	97
McCalliog J	73–74	31	(0)	7	1	(0)	0	5	(1)	0	0	(0)	0	0	(0)	0	37	(1)	7
McClair B	87–97	296	(59)	88	39	(6)	14	44	(1)	19	17	(6)	5	3	(0)	1	399	(72)	127
McCreery D	74–78	48	(38)	7	1	(6)	0	4	(4)	1	4	(3)	0	0	(1)	0	57	(52)	8
MacDougall E	1972	18	(0)	5	0	(0)	0	0	(0)	0	0	(0)	0	0	(0)	0	18	(0)	5
McFarlane N	1953	1	(0)	0	0	(0)	0	0	(0)	0	0	(0)	0	0	(0)	0	1	(0)	0
McGarvey S	80–82	13	(12)	3	0	(0)	0	0	(0)	0	0	(0)	0	0	(0)	0	13	(12)	3
McGibbon P	1995	0	(0)	0	0	(0)	0	1	(0)	0	0	(0)	0	0	(0)	0	1	(0)	0
McGlen W	46–51	110	(0)	2	12	(0)	0	0	(0)	0	0	(0)	0	0	(0)	0	122	(0)	2
McGrath C	76–80	12	(16)	1	0	(0)	0	0	(2)	0	3	(1)	0	0	(0)	0	15	(19)	1
McGrath P	82–88	159	(4)	12	15	(3)	2	13	(0)	2	4	(0)	0	1	(0)	0	192	(7)	16
McGuinness W	55–59	81	(0)	2	2	(0)	0	0	(0)	0	2	(0)	0	0	(0)	0	85	(0)	2
McIlroy S	71–81	320	(22)	57	35	(3)	6	25	(3)	6	10	(0)	2	1	(0)	0	391	(28)	71
McIlvenny E	1950	2	(0)	0	0	(0)	0	0	(0)	0	0	(0)	0	0	(0)	0	2	(0)	0
McKee C	1993	1	(0)	0	0	(0)	0	0	(0)	0	0	(0)	0	0	(0)	0	1	(0)	0
McMillan S	61–62	15	(0)	6	0	(0)	0	0	(0)	0	0	(0)	0	0	(0)	0	15	(0)	6
McNulty T	49–53	57	(0)	0	2	(0)	0	0	(0)	0	0	(0)	0	1	(0)	0	60	(0)	0
McQueen G	77–84	184	(0)	20	21	(0)	2	16	(0)	4	7	(0)	0	1	(0)	0	229	(0)	26
McShane H	50–53	56	(0)	8	1	(0)	0	0	(0)	0	0	(0)	0	0	(0)	0	57	(0)	8
Maiorana G	88–89	2	(5)	0	0	(0)	0	0	(1)	0	0	(0)	0	0	(0)	0	2	(6)	0
Marsh P	2006	0	(0)	0	0	(0)	0	1	(0)	0	0	(0)	0	0	(0)	0	1	(0)	0
Martin, Lee A	87–93	56	(17)	1	13	(1)	1	8	(2)	0	6	(6)	0	1	(0)	0	84	(26)	2

Player	Season	League App	(Sub)	Gl	FA Cup App	(Sub)	Gl	League Cup App	(Sub)	Gl	Europe App	(Sub)	Gl	Others App	(Sub)	Gl	Total App	(Sub)	Gl
Martin, Lee R	05–	0	(0)	0	0	(0)	0	2	(0)	0	0	(0)	0	0	(0)	0	2	(0)	0
Martin M	72–74	33	(7)	2	2	(0)	0	1	(0)	0	0	(0)	0	0	(0)	0	36	(7)	2
May D	94–02	68	(17)	6	6	(0)	0	9	(0)	1	13	(2)	1	2	(1)	0	98	(20)	8
Miller L	04–05	3	(6)	0	2	(2)	0	3	(0)	2	3	(3)	0	0	(0)	0	11	(11)	2
Milne R	88–89	19	(4)	3	7	(0)	0	0	(0)	0	0	(0)	0	0	(0)	0	26	(4)	3
Mitten C	46–49	142	(0)	50	19	(0)	11	0	(0)	0	0	(0)	0	1	(0)	0	162	(0)	61
Moir I	60–64	45	(0)	5	0	(0)	0	0	(0)	0	0	(0)	0	0	(0)	0	45	(0)	5
Moore G	1963	18	(0)	4	1	(0)	1	0	(0)	0	0	(0)	0	0	(0)	0	19	(0)	5
Moran K	78–87	228	(3)	21	18	(0)	1	24	(1)	2	13	(1)	0	1	(0)	0	284	(5)	24
Morgan W	68–74	236	(2)	25	27	(0)	4	24	(1)	3	4	(0)	1	2	(0)	1	293	(3)	34
Morgans K	57–60	17	(0)	0	2	(0)	0	0	(0)	0	4	(0)	0	0	(0)	0	23	(0)	0
Morris J	46–48	83	(0)	32	9	(0)	3	0	(0)	0	0	(0)	0	1	(0)	0	93	(0)	35
Moses R	81–87	143	(7)	7	11	(0)	1	22	(2)	4	12	(1)	0	0	(1)	0	188	(11)	12
Muhren A	82–84	65	(5)	13	8	(0)	1	11	(0)	1	8	(0)	3	1	(0)	0	93	(5)	18
Mulryne P	97–98	1	(0)	0	0	(0)	0	3	(0)	0	0	(0)	0	0	(0)	0	4	(0)	0
Nani	07–	16	(10)	3	2	(0)	1	1	(0)	0	7	(4)	0	0	(1)	0	26	(15)	4
Nardiello D	01–03	0	(0)	0	0	(0)	0	1	(2)	0	0	(1)	0	0	(0)	0	1	(3)	0
Neville G	92–	349	(15)	5	41	(3)	0	16	(1)	0	100	(7)	2	8	(1)	0	514	(27)	7
Neville P	94–04	210	(53)	5	25	(6)	1	16	(1)	0	43	(22)	2	7	(3)	0	301	(85)	8
Nevland E	97–98	0	(1)	0	2	(0)	0	0	(2)	1	0	(0)	0	0	(0)	0	2	(3)	1
Nicholl J	74–81	188	(9)	3	22	(4)	1	14	(0)	1	10	(0)	1	1	(0)	0	235	(13)	6
Nicholson J	60–62	58	(0)	5	7	(0)	1	3	(0)	0	0	(0)	0	0	(0)	0	68	(0)	6
Noble R	65–66	31	(0)	0	2	(0)	0	0	(0)	0	0	(0)	0	0	(0)	0	33	(0)	0
Notman A	1998	0	(0)	0	0	(0)	0	0	(1)	0	0	(0)	0	0	(0)	0	0	(1)	0
O'Brien L	86–88	16	(15)	2	0	(2)	0	1	(2)	0	0	(0)	0	0	(0)	0	17	(19)	2
O'Kane J	94–96	1	(1)	0	1	(0)	0	2	(1)	0	1	(0)	0	0	(0)	0	5	(2)	0
Olive L	1952	2	(0)	0	0	(0)	0	0	(0)	0	0	(0)	0	0	(0)	0	2	(0)	0
Olsen J	84–88	119	(20)	21	13	(3)	2	10	(3)	1	6	(1)	0	1	(0)	0	149	(27)	24
O'Neil T	70–72	54	(0)	0	7	(0)	0	7	(0)	0	0	(0)	0	0	(0)	0	68	(0)	0
O'Shea J	99–	138	(53)	9	15	(5)	1	18	(1)	1	42	(13)	1	2	(1)	0	215	(73)	12
Pallister G	89–97	314	(3)	12	38	(0)	2	36	(0)	0	39	(1)	1	6	(0)	0	433	(4)	15
Park JS	05–	39	(21)	7	7	(2)	0	3	(0)	1	4	(7)	0	0	(0)	0	53	(30)	8
Parker P	91–95	100	(5)	1	14	(1)	1	15	(0)	0	7	(3)	0	1	(0)	0	137	(9)	2
Paterson S	76–79	3	(3)	0	0	(0)	0	2	(0)	0	0	(2)	0	0	(0)	0	5	(5)	0
Pears S	1984	4	(0)	0	1	(0)	0	0	(0)	0	0	(0)	0	0	(0)	0	5	(0)	0
Pearson M	57–62	68	(0)	12	7	(0)	1	3	(0)	1	2	(0)	0	0	(0)	0	80	(0)	14
Pearson Stan	37–53	315	(0)	128	30	(0)	21	0	(0)	0	0	(0)	0	1	(0)	0	346	(0)	149
Pearson Stuart	74–78	138	(1)	55	22	(0)	5	12	(0)	5	6	(0)	1	1	(0)	0	179	(1)	66
Pegg D	52–57	127	(0)	24	9	(0)	0	0	(0)	0	12	(0)	4	2	(0)	0	150	(0)	28
Pegg K	1947	2	(0)	0	0	(0)	0	0	(0)	0	0	(0)	0	0	(0)	0	2	(0)	0
Phelan M	89–93	88	(14)	2	10	(0)	1	14	(2)	0	14	(3)	0	1	(0)	0	127	(19)	3
Pilkington K	94–97	4	(2)	0	1	(0)	0	1	(0)	0	0	(0)	0	0	(0)	0	6	(2)	0
Pinner M	1960	4	(0)	0	0	(0)	0	0	(0)	0	0	(0)	0	0	(0)	0	4	(0)	0
Pique G	04–07	6	(6)	0	3	(0)	0	2	(2)	0	3	(1)	2	0	(0)	0	14	(9)	2
Poborsky K	96–97	18	(14)	5	2	(0)	0	3	(0)	1	5	(5)	0	0	(1)	0	28	(20)	6
Prunier W	1995	2	(0)	0	0	(0)	0	0	(0)	0	0	(0)	0	0	(0)	0	2	(0)	0
Pugh D	02–03	0	(1)	0	0	(1)	0	2	(0)	0	1	(2)	0	0	(0)	0	3	(4)	0
Quixall A	58–63	165	(0)	50	14	(0)	4	1	(0)	2	3	(0)	0	1	(0)	0	184	(0)	56
Rachubka P	99–00	1	(0)	0	0	(0)	0	0	(1)	0	0	(0)	0	0	(1)	0	1	(2)	0
Redman W	50–53	36	(0)	0	2	(0)	0	0	(0)	0	0	(0)	0	0	(0)	0	38	(0)	0
Ricardo	2002	0	(1)	0	0	(0)	0	0	(0)	0	3	(1)	0	0	(0)	0	3	(2)	0
Richardson K	02–06	20	(21)	2	8	(2)	4	11	(2)	3	5	(11)	2	0	(1)	0	44	(37)	11
Rimmer J	67–72	34	(0)	0	3	(0)	0	6	(0)	0	2	(1)	0	0	(0)	0	45	(1)	0
Ritchie A	77–80	26	(7)	13	3	(1)	0	3	(2)	0	0	(0)	0	0	(0)	0	32	(10)	13
Roach J	1945	0	(0)	0	2	(0)	0	0	(0)	0	0	(0)	0	0	(0)	0	2	(0)	0
Robins M	88–91	19	(29)	11	4	(4)	3	0	(7)	2	4	(2)	1	0	(1)	0	27	(43)	17
Robson B	81–93	326	(20)	74	33	(2)	10	50	(1)	5	26	(1)	8	2	(1)	2	437	(25)	99
Roche L	01–02	0	(1)	0	0	(0)	0	1	(0)	0	1	(0)	0	0	(0)	0	2	(1)	0
Roche P	74–81	46	(0)	0	4	(0)	0	3	(0)	0	0	(0)	0	0	(0)	0	53	(0)	0

Player	Season	League App	(Sub)	Gl	FA Cup App	(Sub)	Gl	League Cup App	(Sub)	Gl	Europe App	(Sub)	Gl	Others App	(Sub)	Gl	Total App	(Sub)	Gl
Rogers M	1977	1	(0)	0	0	(0)	0	0	(0)	0	0	(0)	0	0	(0)	0	1	(0)	0
Ronaldo C	03–	126	(37)	66	21	(3)	12	8	(0)	2	40	(3)	11	1	(0)	0	196	(43)	92
Rooney W	04–	116	(11)	53	16	(4)	10	5	(2)	2	33	(1)	12	1	(0)	0	171	(18)	77
Rossi G	04–05	1	(4)	1	2	(0)	2	3	(2)	1	0	(2)	0	0	(0)	0	6	(8)	4
Rowley J	37–54	380	(0)	182	42	(0)	26	0	(0)	0	0	(0)	0	2	(0)	3	424	(0)	211
Ryan J	65–69	21	(3)	4	1	(0)	0	0	(0)	0	2	(0)	0	0	(0)	0	24	(3)	4
Sadler D	63–73	266	(6)	22	22	(1)	1	22	(0)	1	16	(0)	3	2	(0)	0	328	(7)	27
Saha L	03–	52	(34)	28	6	(4)	3	9	(0)	7	9	(10)	4	0	(0)	0	76	(48)	42
Sartori C	68–71	26	(13)	4	9	(0)	1	3	(2)	0	2	(0)	1	0	(1)	0	40	(16)	6
Scanlon A	54–60	115	(0)	34	6	(0)	1	3	(0)	0	3	(0)	0	0	(0)	0	127	(0)	35
Schmeichel P	91–98	292	(0)	0	41	(0)	0	17	(0)	0	42	(0)	1	6	(0)	0	398	(0)	1
Scholes P	94–	328	(67)	96	27	(12)	12	11	(5)	8	98	(12)	23	10	(0)	0	474	(96)	139
Scott J	52–55	3	(0)	0	0	(0)	0	0	(0)	0	0	(0)	0	0	(0)	0	3	(0)	0
Sealey L	89–90 & 1993	33	(0)	0	4	(1)	0	9	(0)	0	8	(0)	0	1	(0)	0	55	(1)	0
Setters M	59–64	159	(0)	12	25	(0)	1	2	(0)	0	7	(0)	1	1	(0)	0	194	(0)	14
Sharpe L	88–95	160	(33)	21	22	(7)	3	15	(8)	9	15	(2)	3	1	(0)	0	213	(50)	36
Shawcross R	2006	0	(0)	0	0	(0)	0	0	(2)	0	0	(0)	0	0	(0)	0	0	(2)	0
Sheringham E	97–00	73	(31)	31	4	(5)	5	1	(0)	1	20	(11)	9	4	(4)	0	102	(51)	46
Sidebottom A	72–74	16	(0)	0	2	(0)	0	2	(0)	0	0	(0)	0	0	(0)	0	20	(0)	0
Silvestre M	99–	224	(24)	6	19	(2)	1	13	(1)	0	60	(7)	2	8	(0)	1	326	(35)	10
Simpson D	07–	1	(2)	0	0	(1)	0	1	(0)	0	2	(1)	0	0	(0)	0	4	(4)	0
Sivebaek J	85–86	29	(2)	1	2	(0)	0	1	(0)	0	0	(0)	0	0	(0)	0	32	(2)	1
Sloan T	78–80	4	(7)	0	0	(0)	0	0	(1)	0	0	(0)	0	0	(0)	0	4	(8)	0
Smith A	04–06	43	(18)	7	2	(6)	0	4	(2)	1	11	(6)	3	1	(0)	1	61	(32)	12
Smith J	37–45	37	(0)	14	5	(0)	1	0	(0)	0	0	(0)	0	0	(0)	0	42	(0)	15
Solskjaer O	96–06	151	(84)	91	15	(15)	8	8	(3)	7	36	(45)	20	6	(3)	0	216	(150)	126
Spector J	2004	2	(1)	0	1	(0)	0	0	(1)	0	1	(1)	0	0	(1)	0	4	(4)	0
Stam J	98–01	79	(0)	1	7	(1)	0	0	(0)	0	32	(0)	0	7	(1)	0	125	(2)	1
Stapleton F	81–86	204	(19)	60	21	(0)	7	26	(1)	6	14	(1)	5	2	(0)	0	267	(21)	78
Stepney A	66–77	433	(0)	2	44	(0)	0	35	(0)	0	23	(0)	0	4	(0)	0	539	(0)	2
Stewart M	00–02	5	(2)	0	0	(1)	0	2	(2)	0	0	(2)	0	0	(0)	0	7	(7)	0
Stiles N	60–70	311	(0)	17	38	(0)	0	7	(0)	0	36	(0)	2	3	(0)	0	395	(0)	19
Storey-Moore I	71–73	39	(0)	11	0	(0)	0	4	(0)	1	0	(0)	0	0	(0)	0	43	(0)	12
Strachan G	84–88	155	(5)	33	22	(0)	2	12	(1)	1	6	(0)	2	0	(0)	0	195	(6)	38
Taibi M	1999	4	(0)	0	0	(0)	0	0	(0)	0	0	(0)	0	0	(0)	0	4	(0)	0
Taylor E	57–58	22	(0)	2	6	(0)	1	0	(0)	0	2	(0)	1	0	(0)	0	30	(0)	4
Taylor T	52–57	166	(0)	112	9	(0)	5	0	(0)	0	14	(0)	11	2	(0)	3	191	(0)	131
Tevez C	07–	31	(3)	14	2	(0)	1	0	(0)	0	6	(6)	4	0	(0)	0	39	(9)	19
Thomas M	78–80	90	(0)	11	13	(0)	2	5	(0)	2	2	(0)	0	0	(0)	0	110	(0)	15
Thornley B	93–97	1	(8)	0	2	(0)	0	3	(0)	0	0	(0)	0	0	(0)	0	6	(8)	0
Tierney P	2003	0	(0)	0	0	(0)	0	1	(0)	0	0	(0)	0	0	(0)	0	1	(0)	0
Timm M	2002	0	(0)	0	0	(0)	0	0	(0)	0	0	(1)	0	0	(0)	0	0	(1)	0
Tomlinson G	1994	0	(0)	0	0	(0)	0	0	(2)	0	0	(0)	0	0	(0)	0	0	(2)	0
Tranter W	1963	1	(0)	0	0	(0)	0	0	(0)	0	0	(0)	0	0	(0)	0	1	(0)	0
Turner C	85–87	64	(0)	0	8	(0)	0	7	(0)	0	0	(0)	0	0	(0)	0	79	(0)	0
Twiss M	97–99	0	(0)	0	0	(1)	0	1	(0)	0	0	(0)	0	0	(0)	0	1	(1)	0
Ure I	69–70	47	(0)	1	8	(0)	0	10	(0)	0	0	(0)	0	0	(0)	0	65	(0)	1
Van der Gouw R	96–01	26	(11)	0	1	(0)	0	8	(1)	0	11	(0)	0	2	(0)	0	48	(12)	0
Van der Sar E	05–	99	(0)	0	9	(0)	0	3	(0)	0	30	(0)	0	1	(0)	0	142	(0)	0
Van Nistelrooy R	01–05	137	(13)	95	11	(3)	14	5	(1)	2	45	(2)	38	2	(0)	1	200	(19)	150
Veron J	01–02	45	(6)	7	2	(0)	0	4	(1)	0	24	(0)	4	0	(0)	0	75	(7)	11
Vidic N	05–	66	(2)	4	10	(0)	0	0	(2)	0	17	(0)	1	1	(0)	0	94	(4)	5
Viollet D	52–61	259	(0)	159	18	(0)	5	2	(0)	1	12	(0)	13	2	(0)	1	293	(0)	179
Waldron C	1976	3	(0)	0	0	(0)	0	1	(0)	0	0	(0)	0	0	(0)	0	4	(0)	0
Walker D	1962	1	(0)	0	0	(0)	0	0	(0)	0	0	(0)	0	0	(0)	0	1	(0)	0
Wallace D	89–92	36	(11)	6	7	(2)	2	4	(3)	3	5	(2)	0	1	(0)	0	53	(18)	11
Wallwork R	97–01	4	(15)	0	1	(1)	0	4	(1)	0	0	(1)	0	1	(0)	0	10	(18)	0
Walsh G	86–94	49	(1)	0	0	(0)	0	7	(0)	0	6	(0)	0	0	(0)	0	62	(1)	0
Walton Joe	45–47	21	(0)	0	2	(0)	0	0	(0)	0	0	(0)	0	0	(0)	0	23	(0)	0

Player	Season	League			FA Cup			League Cup			Europe			Others			Total		
		App	(Sub)	Gl	App	(Sub)	Gl	App	(Sub)	Gl	App	(Sub)	Gl	App	(Sub)	Gl	App	(Sub)	Gl
Walton John	1951	2	(0)	0	0	(0)	0	0	(0)	0	0	(0)	0	0	(0)	0	2	(0)	0
Warner J	38–49	105	(0)	1	13	(0)	1	0	(0)	0	0	(0)	0	1	(0)	0	119	(0)	2
Watson W	70–72	11	(0)	0	0	(0)	0	3	(0)	0	0	(0)	0	0	(0)	0	14	(0)	0
Wealands J	82–83	7	(0)	0	0	(0)	0	1	(0)	0	0	(0)	0	0	(0)	0	8	(0)	0
Webb N	89–92	70	(5)	8	9	(0)	1	14	(0)	1	11	(0)	1	1	(0)	0	105	(5)	11
Webber D	00–02	0	(0)	0	0	(0)	0	1	(1)	0	0	(1)	0	0	(0)	0	1	(2)	0
Webster C	53–58	65	(0)	26	9	(0)	4	0	(0)	0	5	(0)	1	0	(0)	0	79	(0)	31
Wellens R	1999	0	(0)	0	0	(0)	0	0	(1)	0	0	(0)	0	0	(0)	0	0	(1)	0
Whalley B	35–46	33	(0)	0	6	(0)	0	0	(0)	0	0	(0)	0	0	(0)	0	39	(0)	0
Whelan A	1980	0	(1)	0	0	(0)	0	0	(0)	0	0	(0)	0	0	(0)	0	0	(1)	0
Whelan W	54–57	79	(0)	43	6	(0)	4	0	(0)	0	11	(0)	5	2	(0)	0	98	(0)	52
Whitefoot J	49–55	93	(0)	0	2	(0)	0	0	(0)	0	0	(0)	0	0	(0)	0	95	(0)	0
Whitehurst W	1955	1	(0)	0	0	(0)	0	0	(0)	0	0	(0)	0	0	(0)	0	1	(0)	0
Whiteside N	81–88	193	(13)	47	24	(0)	10	26	(3)	9	11	(2)	1	2	(0)	0	256	(18)	67
Whitworth N	1990	1	(0)	0	0	(0)	0	0	(0)	0	0	(0)	0	0	(0)	0	1	(0)	0
Wilkins R	79–83	158	(2)	7	10	(0)	1	14	(1)	1	8	(0)	1	1	(0)	0	191	(3)	10
Wilkinson I	1991	0	(0)	0	0	(0)	0	1	(0)	0	0	(0)	0	0	(0)	0	1	(0)	0
Wilson D	1988	0	(4)	0	0	(2)	0	0	(0)	0	0	(0)	0	0	(0)	0	0	(6)	0
Wilson M	98–99	1	(2)	0	0	(0)	0	2	(0)	0	2	(2)	0	1	(0)	0	6	(4)	0
Wood N	85–86	2	(1)	0	0	(0)	0	0	(1)	0	0	(0)	0	0	(0)	0	2	(2)	0
Wood R	49–58	178	(0)	0	15	(0)	0	0	(0)	0	12	(0)	0	3	(0)	0	208	(0)	0
Worrall H	46–47	6	(0)	0	0	(0)	0	0	(0)	0	0	(0)	0	0	(0)	0	6	(0)	0
Wratten P	1990	0	(2)	0	0	(0)	0	0	(0)	0	0	(0)	0	0	(0)	0	0	(2)	0
Wrigglesworth W	36–46	30	(0)	8	7	(0)	2	0	(0)	0	0	(0)	0	0	(0)	0	37	(0)	10
Yorke D	98–01	80	(16)	48	6	(5)	3	3	(0)	2	28	(8)	11	3	(3)	2	120	(32)	66
Young A	70–75	69	(14)	1	5	(0)	0	5	(4)	0	0	(0)	0	0	(0)	0	79	(18)	1

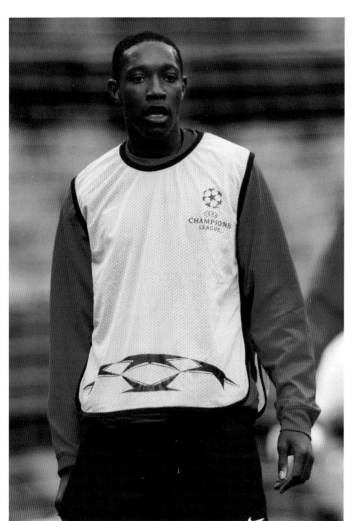

Left: Danny Welbeck, United's thrillingly gifted young striker who will be striving to make his mark at senior level in 2008/09.

Facing page: Skipper Ryan Giggs confirmed the Red Devils' tenth Premier League title on the last day of the 2007/08 Championship race with a silky finish at Wigan. Thereafter United joy was unconfined.

Overleaf: Messrs Ronaldo and Scholes both made telling contributions to the unforgettable Champions League triumph over Chelsea in Moscow, but the hero at the death was Edwin van der Sar.